ALSO BY RICHARD L. BUSHMAN

King and People in Provincial Massachusetts
(1985)

Joseph Smith and the Beginnings of Mormonism
(1984)

From Puritan to Yankee:
Character and Social Order in Connecticut,
1690–1765
(1967)

EDITOR

Uprooted Americans:
Essays to Honor Oscar Handlin
(1979)

The Great Awakening:
Documents on the Revival of Religion,
1740–1745
(1970)

THE REFINEMENT OF AMERICA
Persons, Houses, Cities

The Refinement of America

Persons, Houses, Cities

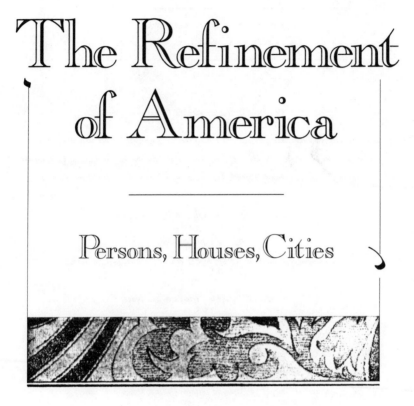

Richard L. Bushman

ALFRED A. KNOPF

New York

1 9 9 2

Library of Congress Cataloging-in-Publication Data

Bushman, Richard L.
The refinement of America: persons, houses, cities / by Richard L. Bushman
p.   cm.
Includes bibliographical references and index.
ISBN 0-394-55010-2
1. United States—Social life and customs—Colonial period, ca. 1600–1775.   2. United States—Social life and customs—1775–1865.   3. Middle classes—United States—History.
4. Architecture, Domestic—United States—History.   5. House furnishings—United States—History.   6. Material culture—United States.   I. Title.
E162.B986   1992
973—dc20   91-23075
CIP

*For the Curators of
America's History Museums*

Contents

Acknowledgments

THIS book would never have been written if I had not taken a position in the History Department at the University of Delaware. Teaching in Delaware's graduate programs, offered in association with the Winterthur and Hagley museums, started me to thinking about material culture. More particularly, I benefited from knowing the doctoral candidates in the History of American Civilization Program who were pursuing the meaning of objects in their own work. I learned from them, and their interest made my discoveries seem worthwhile. I think of this book as part of a joint effort with them.

The faculty in these programs created an atmosphere congenial to the investigation of house furnishings, landscapes, and costumes, the materials that historians frequently neglect. David Hounshell, Kenneth Ames, Scott Swank, Damie Stillman, Wayne Craven, Bernard Herman, David Allmendinger, James Curtis, John Bernstein, and Brian Greenberg were all involved in studies of their own that influenced and sustained my work. George Basalla was an extraordinarily generous and stimulating fellow worker and a good friend. At the Winterthur Museum, Neville Thompson guided me to library materials, and McSherry Fowble gave me access to the museum's splendid collection of prints.

As the project began to take form, Norman Fiering made crucial suggestions as to its form, and then in a stroke of good fortune I called Brooke Hindle for suggestions about fellowship aid for study at the National Museum of American History. He and Gary Kulik submitted my name in nomination for a Regents Fellowship, which afforded me a pleasant and educative year in Washington. At the museum Susan Myers and Rodris Roth served as warmhearted and well-informed hosts and guides to the collections. I also greatly appreciated the help of Anne Golovin, Anne Serio, Barbara Smith, and Claudia Kidwell. Roger Kennedy presided over the museum with unmatched intellectual and entrepreneurial energy.

Besides the time at the Smithsonian, I used a year under a National Endowment for the Humanities Research Fellowship to begin preliminary work on the subject, and also enjoyed a year's leave at the University of Delaware's Center for Advanced Study under the university's generous support program for senior scholars.

Numerous individuals assisted in the task of assembling illustrations, and I am especially indebted to the extra efforts of Mary Ison at the Library of Congress, Constance Cooper at the Historical Society of Delaware, William Hosley and Elizabeth Kornhauser at the Wadsworth Atheneum, and Theresa Piercy at Old Sturbridge Village.

I first wrote on this subject in response to an invitation from Jack Greene and J. R. Pole to discuss culture in British America as part of a conference at St. Catherine's College, Oxford, in 1981. Since that time a number of scholars helped shape my thinking. A chance comment by Mark Girouard during a visit to the University of Delaware was influential unbeknownst to him. Serious readings followed by strenuous, penetrating criticism came from Richard D. Brown, David Hall, and Dell Upton. I am grateful for their assistance and friendship.

Jane Garrett at Alfred A. Knopf recognized the possibilities in this topic when it was still a brief outline and encouraged me for nearly a decade. Claudia Bushman read every word and improved virtually every sentence. The topic is really hers. She first became interested in domestic life as one of the pioneers of women's history. I was drawn to the subject because of what she told me. We have worked together from beginning to end. The most happy outcome of the book for me is our growing scholarly collaboration.

Finally, two sources of information on refinement are unnamed in the notes. They are my mother, Dorothy Lyman Bushman, and my grandmother, Hildegarde Sophia Schoenfeld Lyman, who taught me what refinement can mean in everyday life.

RICHARD L. BUSHMAN
New York
May 1991

Introduction

E. MCCLUNG FLEMING planted the seed for this book many years ago. A teacher in the Winterthur Program in Early American Culture, Fleming made a casual observation about the collections related to early American domestic life in the Henry Francis du Pont Winterthur Museum. Fleming noted that the volume of materials in the museum enlarged enormously for the years after 1690. Du Pont had assiduously collected seventeenth-century interior furnishings, but the number of beds, chairs, candlesticks, and tables from the earlier period was much, much smaller than for the years after 1690, far smaller than could be accounted for by the size of the population. Perhaps Mr. du Pont collected more after 1690 because he favored beautiful objects, but that too raised a question. Many more beautiful things in ceramic, silver, and wood have survived from the eighteenth century, as if America's aesthetic sensibilities were suddenly awakened in those years. What brought about the change?

Later, when I took a position at the University of Delaware and began teaching in the Winterthur Program, I saw the truth of Fleming's observation for myself. Not only were there more fine furnishings worthy of a connoisseur's interest, but, looking beyond the museum, I saw that the houses displaying the furnishings changed. They grew larger, more embellished, more intricately planned. There had been a only handful of what could be called mansions in the American colonies before 1690. After that date, and still more after 1720, two- and three-story mansions sprang up from New Hampshire to the Carolinas. Virtually all of the colonial mansions we visit today were constructed after 1720. These houses were different as well as bigger than before. They were adorned and beautified, as most houses were not in the seventeenth century, and the rooms were arranged differently. The people in these houses seemed to follow a different pattern of living than before. For the first time Americans lived in style.

This book is my effort to understand the meaning of those houses and their furnishings. Ultimately I concluded that the houses were in truth but outward signs of what the inhabitants hoped would be an inward grace. They wished to transform themselves along with their environments. To explain the houses I have been compelled to explain the people as well, and more particularly the ideal of a cultivated and refined inward life which I believe the houses were meant to express and support. The interplay between the personal ideal and the material world interests me profoundly, and the pages that follow were written in the hope of showing how ideals interacting with materials changed the American environment and reshaped American culture.

The refinement of America began around 1690. Refinement originated in an aspiration that had been revitalized in the Renaissance and spread first to the European courts and then to the upper middle classes. The ideal was encompassed in words like "genteel," "civil," and "urbane" and first was the property of courtiers. Located on the margins of European society, England was among the last to embrace civility, but by the early seventeenth century the English court pursued it in all its forms. After the Restoration of 1660, the English upper middle class, the equivalent of America's greatest merchants and planters, did the same. The urban middle classes started to build stylish town houses in provincial cities like Bristol, and the minor rural gentry began remodeling their manor houses or built new ones according to the current fashion. Not long after, mansions began to appear in the colonies, and from then on the refining process in the two countries went on together. The changes in America were a variant of changes occurring in all the British provinces at roughly the same time. With the houses went new modes of speech, dress, body carriage, and manners that gave an entirely new cast to the conduct and appearance of the American gentry. Altogether these changes created what the eighteenth century called polite society.

Small tokens of gentility can be found scattered through all of American society in the eighteenth century, like pottery sherds in an excavated house lot. Estate inventories of many middling people show a teacup, a silver spoon, knives and forks, and a book or two among the household possessions. Over the course of the century, probably a majority of the population adopted some of the amenities associated with genteel living. But it would be an error to conclude that by the Revolution most Americans were genteel. Gentility flecked lives without coloring them. Gentility was the proper style of the gentry alone in the eighteenth century, as earlier it belonged to courtiers. "The gentlemen of the place," as documents commonly called them, were the ones who took it upon themselves to refine their manners, their appearances, and their houses. By the Revolution, it was incumbent upon all gentlemen broadly defined—the great merchants and planters, the clergy and professionals, the officers of courts and government—to live by the genteel code. Lesser people might look on with envy, awe, or hatred, they might imitate and borrow, but they were onlookers, thought to be presumptuous if they assumed the manners or showed the possessions of a gentleman.

Not until the end of the eighteenth century and the beginning of the nineteenth did the middle class—smaller merchants and professionals, ordinary well-off farmers, successful artisans, schoolteachers, minor government officials, clerks, shopkeepers, industrial entrepreneurs, and managers—come to believe that they should live a genteel life. Most such people lacked the means to erect mansions, send their children to academies, and dress in silk and fine woolens, but less expensive substitutes could be found. A small, reasonably priced house could contain a parlor and be painted on the outside. The government could be persuaded to provide free public schools. Entrepreneurs and mechanics devised methods for manufacturing inexpensive, printed fabrics to adorn the daughters of aspiring farmers. With the help of enterprising industrialists, middling people found ways to assemble the requisite accoutrements of what might be called vernacular gentility. At the same time, parents assumed the burden of instructing their children in the arts of please and thank you, clean hands and posture, and perhaps of imparting a rudimentary appreciation of beauty. By the middle of the nineteenth century, vernacular gentility had become the possession of the American middle class. All who aspired to simple respectability had to embody the marks of the genteel style in their persons and their houses.

This book narrates the story of these changes in American society beginning around 1690 and continuing until gentility was thoroughly entrenched in the middle classes in the middle of the nineteenth century. The book focuses on the material world that was created to sustain genteel life, and that is why the book is dedicated to the curators of America's history museums. Beginning with McClung Fleming, a teacher in a museum, I have relied on museum scholars for the information and judgments on which the book is based. The dedication is meant to express my appreciation and respect.

I cannot claim to have learned the methods of curatorial scholarship with its emphasis on vast quantities of highly specific and exact knowledge. Perhaps I come closest to the curatorial style in the organization of the book. Curators often divide their subject matter according to the materials of which objects are made or their mode of manufacture; there are curators of glass, metals, wood or furniture, fabrics, and paper or prints. In the spirit of curatorial scholarship, I have organized this work according to the nature of the objects—persons, houses, and cities—rather than by broad analytical themes.

But the themes are significant, and the chief historical reason for studying these materials. One of these themes, introduced in Part One, is the idea of performance. Gentility heightened self-consciousness, not in any deep philosophical sense, but in the common meaning of becoming aware of how one looked in the eyes of others. Self-aware performance came about naturally as a result of adopting genteel standards of behavior to elevate human life. People were instructed in a hundred details of how to dress, hold their bodies, and converse, all for the purpose of becoming more pleasing. While improved taste and sensibility led to a more satisfying life for its own sake, gentility always aimed to form brilliant and harmonious societies where people came together to perform for one another. In the meetings of these societies, people were aware of watching and being watched. In Chesterfield's telling phrase, the aim of genteel discipline was to shine in the best company. Genteel society created beautiful stage sets on which people performed in public view.

The harsh side of this impulse to perform was the license it gave to criticism. Performers are in the spotlight, to be either praised or scorned. They please the company or suffer its disdain. While outwardly harmonious and kindly, genteel society was inwardly judgmental and censorious. After the ball, participants gave person-by-person critiques of the dancers. Who was well dressed, who danced poorly, whose manners were a scandal, who was the greatest beauty? The same was true for the refreshments and the decoration of the rooms. All that went into the grand performance was subject to criticism. The same spirit prevailed from day to day between entertainments. One's house, its yard, one's carriage, dress, and posture were perpetually on display. To be caught in the kitchen, not fully dressed, unready for examination, greatly embarrassed a lady.

One of the powerful impulses released by gentility is what I have called its beautification campaign. Everything from houses to barns to village streets was to be made beautiful; every scene was to be turned into a picture. That beneficent undertaking had the unfortunate side effect of turning its promoters into critics who identified the ugly as the first step in creating the beautiful. Under their gaze, life became a continuous performance, perpetually subject to criticism. Everyone and virtually everything could be brought to judgment before the bar of refinement and beauty. Not only was criticism directed outward to others, but people had to watch themselves through the eyes of others. They had to perform for themselves and suffer from their own self-criticism. Performance was unrelenting.[1]

The habit of criticism necessarily deepened cultural and social divisions, a second notable theme introduced in Part One. Refinement created a standard for exclusion as well as a mode of association. One of the great pleasures of genteel life was to enjoy the company of refined persons, but the presence of vulgar persons marred that pleasure. The rude had to be excluded for the refined to achieve the elevated condition that was their desire. As people strove to discipline themselves and their children in the modes of genteel conduct, they divided themselves from all who refused to embrace the new principles. Dirty hands, slovenly clothes, ungainly speech marked off the coarse and rude from the refined and polite.

In eighteenth-century society, gentility was the visible expression of gentry status, the most sharply defined social class in the colonies. Everyone at the time recognized the existence of ladies and gentlemen, set off from the middling and lower sorts by their wealth, education, and authority in government. Gentility simply gave expression to a universally acknowledged division, and actually had the comforting effect of reinforcing the established social order.

In Part Two, "Respectability: 1790–1850," cultural classification takes on a different meaning. In the nineteenth century, a dilute gentility associated with respectability spread widely through the middle levels of American society. The line that once divided gentry from the rest of society now dropped to a lower level and separated the middle class from workers and marginal people. The enlargement of the genteel realm gave the middle class the exhilarating sensation of ascent and a heightened respectability, but made the separation of the lower orders more demeaning than ever. The vulgar masses were not merely excluded from gentry society, they were pushed to the cultural margins and denied a claim to simple respectability.

Surprisingly, that marginalization, while painful, did not intensify class consciousness among the lower orders as much as might be expected. The spread of gentility confused rather than clarified the issue of class. For one thing, what did gentility mean when common clerks and small-town farmers lived in houses with parlors, read books, and tried to be mannerly? Were they also ladies and gentlemen? The debasement of those words to include virtually everyone in the audience at a circus suggests the distortions of former emblems of class. The situation was still more confusing when ordinary working people joined the throng and when they moved into houses with parlors.

Gentility concentrated among the wealthy, of course, and was nearly absent among the most abjectly poor, but that did not eliminate perplexity in the vast middle. The division between rude and refined only roughly corresponded to wealth, education, family, work, or any other measure of social class. Genteel culture became an independent variable, cutting across society, and leading, I argue, to the confusion about class that has long been characteristic of American society. Gentility offered the hope that anyone, however poor or however undignified their work, could become middle-class by disciplining themselves and adopting a few outward forms of genteel living. Under those circumstances how could working-class consciousness harden into a distinct culture or the upper class become a fixed elite?

The question of class blends with another issue in Part Two. How could Americans reconcile their commitment to aristocratic gentility with their devotion to republican equality? At the very period when the nation broke with England and embraced republican government, gentility was extending its reach deeper and deeper into the American middle class. The promoters of gentility acknowledged its aristocratic origins, and recognized the incongruity of aristocratic gentility spreading in egalitarian America. They frequently observed that refinement was most fully realized in European palaces and mansions. And yet the genteel handbooks urged people to conform their lives to the patterns of the best society, meaning always society elsewhere and ultimately in aristocratic Europe, even while Americans were intent on creating an egalitarian culture and society consistent with republican government.

The contradiction was not only logical but existential. Middle-class adoption of an aristocratic culture led to innumerable discomforts and discontinuities in the experience of everyday life. A culture formed for a wealthy, leisured, and governing class was not easily assimilated by people whose very existence depended on hard work and parsimonious habits. The jokes about shuttered parlors told the tale. What was the purpose of a room filled with the family's most expensive and beautiful possessions that was rarely used and that made the family uncomfortable? Why was it installed in the first place? Doubtless in reality parlors were used for many purposes, but the caricatures of the forbidding parlor highlighted an important fact. Parlors were made for genteel performance, in imitation of aristocratic drawing rooms. They were tokens of the family's covenant with gentility, their claim on the dignity of a higher level of existence, when actually they spent most of their lives in hard work. Their ordinary everyday lives did not easily conform to parlor standards. A farmer coming from the barnyard with dirty boots had to transform himself before entering this sacred room in his own house. We have become so accustomed to such rudimentary transformations that we may forget the alienation and discomfort that gentility initially caused. Because it was formed for an aristocratic leisured class, gentility was out of place in republican, middle-class America, ill suited to the lives of the people who so fervently adopted it.

Finally, I am interested in how this strangely alien culture blended with other cultural values in the first half of the nineteenth century. In a sense gentility was engaged in a struggle with other cultural systems, since it was frequently at odds with them on fundamental issues. Gentility was worldly not godly, it was hierarchical not egalitarian, and it favored leisure and consumption over work and thrift. These values ran at cross-purposes with religion, republicanism, and the work ethic, powerful complexes of values subscribed to by the same people who wanted to become genteel. But instead of leading to competition for dominance, as might be expected, in most instances the result of the interplay was mutual exchange and compromise.

Chapters 8, 9, and 10 are devoted to the interaction of gentility with domesticity and religion, two instances where the exchanges went both ways. Gentility exercised a powerful influence on religion; in certain circles good taste became virtually a principle of Christian morality. Gentility also took over more and more of the house and yard, attempting to refine all the domestic activities in those spaces and setting the tone of respectable home life. But gentility in turn came under the influence of domesticity and religion. They reduced gentility's high-toned aura and gave aristocratic refinement a homely cast. Middle-class respectability was a composite of these values, each one modifying the other. The refined Christian home with its parlors, books, and well-mannered children combined the highest forms of piety and gentility under the superintendence of a tasteful, devout, and well-read mother.

Perhaps the most interesting of these interactions, and one that receives less attention in this book than it deserves, is the relationship of refinement and capitalism. At first glance, capitalism and the work ethic seem like direct contradictions of refinement. Capitalism rested on an ethic of disciplined work and self-denial in the effort to maximize production and reinvestment. To flourish in a capitalist economy one had to husband resources for investment and devote oneself doggedly to productive effort. Success in a capitalist world depended on engraining thrift and industry into the habits of the heart.

Gentility was the polar opposite of both. Books on gentility depicted a world of leisure and consumption where the inhabitants engaged in conversation, dancing, and cards, where they surrounded themselves with fanciful, costly, and decorative objects that were useless for purposes of production. Refined persons were never shown at work or taught to save. They met for balls and talk, walked in gardens, and drank tea, spending but never getting. Capitalism and gentility should have been enemies.

But they were not. Capitalism and gentility were allies in forming the modern economy. Now we can see that a capitalist economy requires both frantic getting and energetic spending. The populace must work hard to produce and then just as conscientiously consume what it has made. How were people to learn both to work and save and to spend and enjoy? We are perfectly accustomed to both, but how did this self-contradictory combination come about in the first place? What turned producers into consumers? As late as the seventeenth century the main responsibility for consumption of all but basic necessaries rested with the gentry, while toil was left to the middling and lower orders of society. They were positively enjoined not to purchase luxuries or make the disastrous mistake of living beyond their means. For capitalism to thrive, the broad base of the population had to learn to consume as well as to work, even when work and saving, not leisure and consumption, marked the sure road to success. In effect the population had to be taught to live like gentlemen and ladies even when the productive mechanisms of society instructed them to work like slaves.

The irresistible lure of gentility made a powerful contribution to this transformation. People justified the purchase of luxury items as a means of raising themselves to a higher plane. Parlors became a necessity for achieving respectability and so were installed in house after house. Refinement offered a set of countervailing values to offset the injunctions against luxury, so that capitalism and gentility came to reinforce one another. Ironically the allure of a noncapitalist, even an anti-capitalist culture, was a major force in setting the industrial machinery in motion.

Gentility's involvement in the material environment suited it more than other cultural systems for making the change. The genteel life depended on the creation of proper environments, made up from mansions, pictures, silver spoons, teacups, and mahogany tables. Gentility did not suggest new activities for people; it elevated old ones. Singing, cardplaying, eating and drinking, conversing went on in every tavern. All that distinguished genteel drawing rooms was the manner of the people and the style of the objects that surrounded them. To elevate life to a higher level of beauty and grace required support from a beautiful environment. Wine sipped from a crystal wineglass had a different meaning than rum gulped down from a redware mug. Talk before a fireplace with a decorated chimney breast in a plastered and painted room with high ceilings differed from conversation before the gaping maw of a kitchen fireplace in a dark, low room with exposed beams overhead. A polished environment was as much the essence of gentility as polished manners.

As gentility spread to the middle classes in the nineteenth century, the need for refined objects created an unprecedented mass market for hundreds of individual items. People wanted carpets, mahogany furniture, tableware, fine fabrics, brooms, candlesticks, buckles and buttons, hats, books, and on and on. They formed a market that brought into existence a vast manufacturing and distribution system spread across the nation. So closely intertwined were economic growth and the expansion of gentility that it becomes impossible to determine which was cause and which effect. Capitalism certainly did not create gentility, but with equal certainty gentility was promoted and spread by an army of industrialists, artisans, merchants, and shopkeepers, whose livings came to depend on the enlarging market for genteel goods.[2]

Ironically, gentility did its part not by appealing to modern liberal and capitalist values but by drawing on the aristocratic past. In recent years, we have focused on republicanism and capitalism as the overarching forces molding development in the first half of the nineteenth century. We are inclined to seek ultimate explanations of change in democracy, industrialization, or the market, since they seem to define the future toward which America was headed. But in the refining process, Americans were preoccupied with an aristocratic past at the same time as they were rushing into a democratic and capitalistic future. The prescriptions for refined living that motivated so much consumption descended from the Renaissance courts to the colonial gentry and thence to the American middle class. Nineteenth-century etiquette books, among the foremost guides to gentility, contained rules written for courtiers centuries earlier. At a time when the Revolution had ended the principles of monarchy and aristocracy and the forces of capitalist enterprise were leading Americans into industrialization, Americans modeled their lives after the aristocrats of a society that was supposedly repudiated at the founding of the nation. The spread of gentility speaks for the enduring allure of royal palaces and great country estates, for the enticing mystery of nobility and gentry, for the enchantment of those seemingly charmed and exalted lives, for enthrallment with their grace of movement, speech, and costume. The hold of the old regime on the imaginations of Americans cannot be overlooked in explaining the spread of refinement and the creation of a mass market.

There were indeed practical benefits to be gained from refinement. Gentility bestowed concrete social power on its practitioners. It was a resource for impressing and influencing powerful people, frequently a prerequisite for inspiring trust. All who sought worldly advancement were tempted to use refinement as a bargaining chip in social negotiations. Moreover, it afforded a convenient identity and a definition of position in the confusing fluidity of democratic society. But at the center of refinement's great power, the reason it could serve these other functions, was this imagined vision of a noble life once enjoyed by the aristocracy of the Old World. The refinement of America involved the capture of aristocratic culture for use in republican society. Refinement held out the hope of elevation from ordinary existence into an exalted society of superior beings. That promise and hope, rooted in the memory of a forbidden old regime, gave gentility its strength.

How that strength worked to refine America and what refinement wrought in personality, society, and the material world is the story told in the pages that follow.

Gentility

1700 - 1790

CHAPTER I

The Gentrification of Rural Delaware

IN THE SPRING of 1772, William Corbit began work on a new house in Cantwell's Bridge, Delaware, a little village twenty miles south of Wilmington made up of fourteen households strung along a low bluff overlooking Appoquinimink Creek. The Corbits were well known in the area by the time William started construction. For three generations, the family had prospered on the fertile land surrounding Cantwell's Bridge, growing the soft, white wheat for which the area was renowned and involving themselves in the east-west trade across the peninsula between Chesapeake Bay and the Delaware River.

William did not inherit one of the farms worked by his father and grandfather. Two older brothers were given the land, while William was sent to Philadelphia to learn tanning from his cousin. He returned in 1767 at age twenty-two to set up his own tanyard near the creek. Within six years, by virtue of the family name and his own enterprise, he married well twice, first to the daughter of an eminent local farmer and then in 1773 while the house was under construction to a Wilmington woman who came to the marriage with an estate of £700 in her own name.[1]

The house, completed in 1774, was a magnificent structure, a square block two stories high with four rooms and a hall on each floor. The kitchen was in the basement, and under the roof were three additional bedrooms and a square hall. The house was extraordinary for Cantwell's Bridge and for the entire region, notable for its size and even more for its elaborate decoration. The projecting chimney breasts in downstairs parlor and upstairs drawing room are impressive even today. Upstairs, fluted pilasters framed the drawing-room chimneypiece, and a broken pediment surmounted the overmantel frame. Pediments crowned the matching doors at each side of the fireplace.

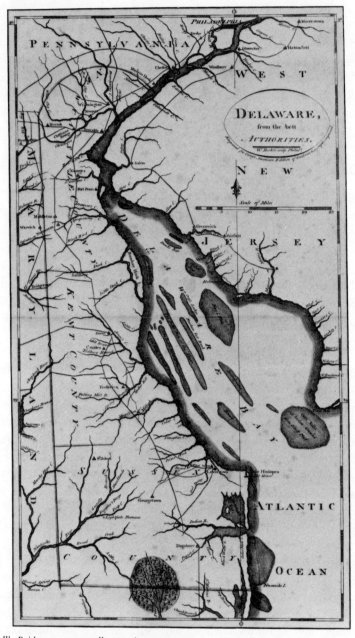

Cantwell's Bridge was too small to merit an appearance on W. Barker's map. The village was located at the juncture of Drawyer's Creek and "Apoquinimy" Creek near the point where the Delaware River widens to become Delaware Bay. Water was the main transportation route to Philadelphia from Cantwell's Bridge. The road from New Castle in the north to Lewes in the south served the inland towns, including Dover, the capital, located in the middle of the state.

Corbit spent considerable money on the decoration of the house, going well beyond the rudimentary expense of raising the building. Among the basics, the cost of laying 89,250 bricks and all of the cellar came to £78; on the luxury side, the carpentry bill for the 935 feet of purely decorative cornice inside and out came to more than £102. The broad staircase that descends from the second floor into the entrance hall cost another £35, and paint and painting, entirely absent from most houses, amounted to more than £45.[2] Somewhere, perhaps in Philadelphia, where he apprenticed, or perhaps from the master carpenter who installed the interiors, William Corbit perceived that a village tanner in Cantwell's Bridge should have a residence that matched the grandeur of Philadelphia's great town houses.[3]

Corbit's elegant house in Cantwell's Bridge was extraordinary, but not unprecedented. David Wilson, Corbit's brother-in-law and a village merchant, had started construction on a house next to the Corbit site two or three years earlier. The Wilson house, though only one room deep rather than two, had the same five-bay façade, a pedimented doorway, a grand stairway in the entry, and two formal downstairs rooms. Another, similar house across Appoquinimink Creek was erected about the same time. Scores of contemporary two-story brick mansions in northern Delaware still exist or can be located in the records. William Corbit's was the largest and most embellished of this group of fine houses, but it did not stand alone.[4]

New-style houses, most properly called mansions, were built all up and down the coast in eighteenth-century America. Elegant town houses first appeared in the major cities and second-level ports. A little later merchants and major government officials built country houses a few miles outside the largest cities. At the same time, beginning about 1725, the great southern planters and the large landholders in the middle and northern colonies raised large houses on their rural estates. After 1750, prosperous yeomen and tradesmen in rural villages like Cantwell's Bridge joined in, usually with somewhat more modest versions of the mansion. The colonies had prospered in the eighteenth century—the per capita wealth in the century before 1770 increased by 50 to 100 percent—and much of this new wealth was spent on houses.[5] By the eve of the Revolution, the men who counted themselves among "the gentlemen of the place," as the Corbits' prominence and long residence in Cantwell's Bridge qualified them to do, felt obligated to construct worthy residences. Hundreds of these mansions still stand as evidence of the aspirations of the eighteenth-century colonial gentry.

A comparison of William Corbit's house with one built seventy years earlier and occupied by Corbit's maternal grandfather, William Brinton, illustrates the extent of the change. The Brintons had migrated from Staffordshire to Pennsylvania in 1684 and established themselves in Birmingham and Concord townships just north of the Delaware boundary. Although prosperous in comparison with their neighbors, for twenty years the Brintons lived in a small frame house, twenty-one by twenty-five feet. In 1704, their son built a much larger, two-story stone house, twenty-two by forty feet, one of a handful of structures of these proportions and pretensions scattered two or three to a township through Pennsylvania.

Architecturally, the Corbit and Brinton houses each stood at the peak of rural society, and yet the differences are more remarkable than the similarities. The absence of decoration in the Brinton house is immediately evident. The windows and door, while roughly symmetrical, are simple incised rectangles with no framing embellishments. The batten door, though quite grand for its day, consists of three thicknesses of boards nailed together

William Corbit had this house built at about the time of his second marriage.

William Brinton, William Corbit's maternal grandfather and a member of the second generation of Brintons in America, built and lived in this house, which was twenty-two by forty feet and known as "William Brinton's Great House."

without paneling. In both the hall and the parlor, the fireplace surrounds are molded but lack mantels, and the paneling on the fireplace walls lacks any design beyond the molded crease at the joints of the vertical boards. Narrow boxed stairs fitted against the sides of the chimney stacks twist upward from both hall and parlor with no space for balusters or rails, and are nothing like Corbit's broad staircase flowing down into the front hall with turned balusters and a rail that swirls to its conclusion at the bottom. The builder of the Brinton house achieved his effects simply and inexpensively, although there are touches here and there indicating a wish to adorn the barebones structure. The low ceilings, the exposed structural members in the ceilings and in the corners of the walls, and the absence of paint testify that at the

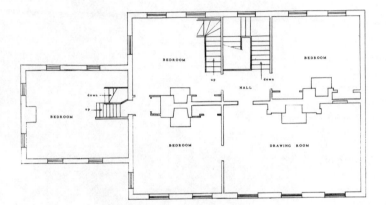

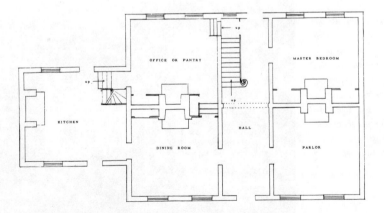

William Corbit's house conformed to the classic Georgian plan of four rooms on a floor divided by a stair passage from front to back.

beginning of the century the Brintons were satisfied with a much different environment than the one their grandson made for himself in Cantwell's Bridge seventy years later.[6]

No listing of architectural details does justice to the contrasting experience in entering the two houses. Seventeenth-century houses feel low, closed, shadowy; the decoration is invariably simple and severe. The eighteenth-century houses, even those in the middle range, because of their larger windows and higher ceilings, seem open and light. Signs of polish and

Located on the second floor at the head of the stairs, the long room was designed as space for formal entertainments. The inventory of William Corbit shows a bed in this room, suggesting how practical necessity sometimes overcame original intent in pretentious country houses.

Built for a prosperous storekeeper-farmer, David Wilson, the Wilson-Warner house exemplified the high cultural ambitions of prosperous families in small villages after the middle of the eighteenth century. Wilson was a friend of William Corbit, whose house can be seen on the adjoining lot.

elegance are everywhere. Even when furnished sparingly, the mansion houses create an aura of grandeur and grace.

Why were hundreds of new mansion houses built in every American colony between 1700 and the Revolution? Was the elegance of the Corbit house a simple consequence of greater prosperity or the desire to follow the latest fashion? The houses themselves suggest that something beyond prosperity and pride was involved. In moving from a seventeenth-century dwelling to an eighteenth-century mansion we move into another world. The houses create a new environment. Besides standing for more and better, the construction of the great houses implies a transition of culture. And what of the owners? Before undertaking his massive project at such vast expense, Corbit must have envisioned significant improvement for himself. Did he too pass through a transition? Do the houses suggest a change in person to match the change in architecture?

THE RIDGELYS OF DOVER

TWENTY-FIVE MILES south of Cantwell's Bridge in Dover, Delaware, the Ridgely family, contemporaries of the Corbits, conducted an extensive correspondence during the initial period of mansion building in Delaware, and their letters afford a glimpse into life in the great houses. The Ridgelys were of more distinguished origin than the Corbits, but of lesser wealth; the fine house that the Ridgelys built twenty years earlier than William Corbit's house was much less pretentious. But the families were alike in thinking of themselves as among the gentry of their respective places and seem to have shared a common culture.

Much of the Ridgely correspondence passed between parents at home and their children away at school. The earliest preserved exchange involved Charles Greenberry Ridgely, who began his classical studies at the Philadelphia Academy in the fall of 1751. Charles was thirteen when he sailed eighty miles up the Delaware River to enroll with James Dove, the headmaster of the academy. Nicholas Ridgely, the boy's father, wrote young Charles in October soon after he had arrived; a regular correspondence continued for a little over three years, until the winter of 1755, when Nicholas died in his sixty-first year.

The letters immediately dispel any thought that Delaware's provincial gentry were culturally isolated, or that they had degenerated into rustic boors. Though living in a remote county in the provinces of America, the Ridgelys knew the requirements of the Anglo-American genteel style. At one time or another Nicholas sent Charles a wig box, six linen caps, three ruffled shirts, the boy's copy of *The Young Man's Companion*, and authorized purchase of *The Spectator.* Nicholas reluctantly agreed to excuse Charles from dancing lessons, although Nicholas believed that dancing "adds to the accomplishment of Behaviour and Carriage and Qualifies a person for Polite company." Nicholas insisted on Charles's learning French, which he did, although Latin was the center of his study.[7]

For his part, Charles purchased items for the Ridgelys which could not be obtained in Kent County. Charles saw the family's Philadelphia shoe-maker about a pair of red damask shoes for his mother, and later received a request for twenty yards of "the best black Callimanco of a Shining Clear black" for her and sister Ruthy, and another ten yards of "Scarlet Cal-limanco" for sister Polly. When Nicholas needed a new wig, he entrusted Charles with the purchase, instructing him to ask Mr. Dove and Mr. Biddle about the best shop. The wig was to be long, "full and big in the caul or head," and "as light a gray as you can gett for that price, and as full of hair and good." To help Charles gauge the right size, Nicholas enclosed a thread "which measures round from my forehead to my pole." Partly through Charles's dealings with Philadelphia tradesmen and shopkeepers, the Ridge-lys imported fashionable elements of genteel culture into Kent County from distant England.[8]

The influence of that culture went deeper than clothes or wigs. For someone reading the letters now, the strongest impression is of Charles's precocious manners. He wrote his first surviving letter at age fourteen, probably with the aid of his schoolmaster, and the last in the series when he was not yet seventeen. Always Charles presented himself with a polished deference that now seems comically incongruous in one so young. He began each letter with the address "Honored Sir" and ended with a closing like "I am, Honoured Sir, your ever Dutiful & loving son, Chas. Green[berr]y Ridgely." The language in between, with few exceptions, sustained the elevated tone. Charles adorned simple requests with elaborate rhetorical phrases. In June 1753 he asked for a few shillings to rebind books damaged when the shallop coming up from Dover overset, along with money for a tunic and some new volumes. All of which, he wrote his father, he hoped "you will be pleased to give me, and thereby acting according to your wonted Kindness, which has hitherto, and always will exact my most grate-ful Returns of Duty and Love, which I hope will always make a shining Figure in my Character."[9]

These words reflected the obligation that a gift from any powerful person in society imposed on a recipient. In promising grateful returns of duty and love to his father, Charles echoed the language of all the king's subjects to their royal master and every client to his patron. Charles had absorbed the ethic so completely that he could shape the relationship in a few sentences. The father's pride and love and the son's reciprocal affection and respect

shine through every letter, but always under the discipline of heavily stylized manners. Even in the intimacy of a private correspondence, and presumably in the Ridgely home itself, the son related to the father within a
structure of expression as strictly laid out as a formal garden.[10]

Like the houses, the letters pose some questions: What culture sustained
them and gave them meaning? What values enforced the discipline of that
language? Beyond the language, why the father's careful attention to clothing, books, and schooling? What ideal did he wish his son to realize? Likely,
the life in the letters and the life implied by the houses' architectural
elegance were related; the conduct Nicholas Ridgely expected of his son was
the behavior intended for the mansions. And so the questions of the houses
and the questions of the letters may be joined into one: What culture
produced Charles Ridgely?

Charles's elegant manner resulted from three generations of aspiration.
His great-grandfather Henry Ridgely, a migrant from Devonshire, England,
in 1659, purchased 6,000 acres in Anne Arundel County, Maryland, near
what became Annapolis. Henry rose high in Maryland society, serving as
justice of the peace, member of the Assembly, and major and colonel in the
militia. But he could not read, a sign that, however rich, he was not a
complete gentleman as his grandson and great-grandson understood the
term. The first Henry's son, Henry Jr., married Katherine Greenberry, the
daughter of an even more distinguished neighboring planter. Nicholas
Greenberry was President of the Council and acting governor of the province in 1693. Nicholas Ridgely was the second son born to Katherine and
Henry Jr. in 1694.

Nicholas's father left him 547 acres in Maryland, but the estate was not
large enough to keep him there. After his first wife died, Nicholas in 1723
married Ann Gordon, the daughter of a New Castle, Delaware, merchant,
Robert French, and the widow of James Gordon. By 1735 he had formed
connections in Kent County, forty miles to the south of New Castle, serving
as foreman of the grand jury in that year. After Ann died, Nicholas married
again in 1736, and settled in 1738 near Dover with his new wife, Mary Vining
of Salem, New Jersey. After renting for a decade, the Ridgelys purchased a
plantation a mile west of Dover in 1748. They built a brick house and called
their land Eden Hill. By then the government of the lower counties had
shown every sign of respect for Nicholas Ridgely. In 1738 he was appointed
justice of the Court of Common Pleas and in 1746 a judge of the Superior
Court. This immediate rise to power doubtless had something to do with the
learning, the bearing, the appearance, and the manners of the parents, to all
of which Charles was heir when he left for the Philadelphia Academy in
1751.[11]

Charles would not have learned his manners from the larger society in which he was reared. Nicholas Ridgely did not choose Kent County for the advanced culture of its inhabitants. The construction of mansions for the leading families and a host of other cultural improvements came over the county around midcentury, but the major changes still lay ahead when the Ridgelys arrived. Kent County was only partially developed in 1735 and was much less wealthy than Anne Arundel County, Maryland, where Nicholas grew up. In 1742 Kent's population was estimated to be 5,000 persons in a county that measured thirty-one miles along Delaware Bay and at Dover extended nineteen miles inland from the bay to the Maryland border. Settlement was comparatively recent as well. The Duke of York did not begin to grant tracts of land in the area until after 1670. When the inhabitants petitioned for a separate county in 1680, they estimated 100 tithable inhabitants, suggesting a total population of perhaps 500.[12] Far from nurturing gentility, Kent County in the early eighteenth century was just beginning to show a few meager signs of civilization.

Initial settlement in the county formed along the edges of the Delaware River, but after an inland highway was laid out in a large arc from New Castle in the north to Lewes in the south, the most rapid growth occurred on either side of the road. By 1694 the settlers agreed that Dover, the county seat, should be laid out astride the king's highway, a little under ten miles inland from the river. In the eighteenth century, the densest settlement occurred on the rich soils on either side of the road. Growth was most rapid along the Kent County stretches of the highway. To the south in Sussex County the forests were slower to go down. When George Whitefield traveled from Lewes in Sussex to Dover in Kent in 1739 on his way to Philadelphia, he rode twenty-seven miles through the woods on the first day. But once beyond Dover, he said, "we rode as pleasantly and with as much Ease as though we were riding through Hide Park."[13]

To the west of this central core of settlement lay the pine forests on the sandy land near the Maryland border; to the east were the marshes along the bay. In both forest and marshes the population was thinner and less civilized. Well after the Ridgelys were entrenched in the county, life at the margins of Kent County remained primitive. The Reverend Charles Inglis, the Anglican missionary assigned to Dover in 1758, occasionally visited the people who inhabited "the large Forests which lie between us and Maryland, and the vast Marshes that stretch along the River Delaware." He found them "in a deploreable state of Ignorance. Few of them can read, and they scarce ever hear a Sermon." Most claimed no church.[14]

Civilized life began in the center of the county at Dover in the third decade of the century. Sufficient population had collected by 1717 to sustain a town, at least a tiny one. The Provincial Assembly had purchased two hundred acres in 1694 and presented it to Kent County. A courthouse was built on the property in 1697. In 1717 the Assembly of the lower counties (which had separated from Pennsylvania's Assembly in 1704) laid out streets in Dover in the expectation that individuals would purchase lots and build houses on them. The commissioners did not want the haphazard, spontaneous growth that occurred in towns that sprang up at Newark in New Castle County to the north or at Elkton in Cecil County, Maryland, to the west. Newark and Elkton grew up at crossroads, without forethought, developing on their own from wide places in the road to unsymmetrical collections of dwellings and shops. Dover followed the tradition of Philadelphia, where a plan preceded settlement. The commissioners laid out the streets at right

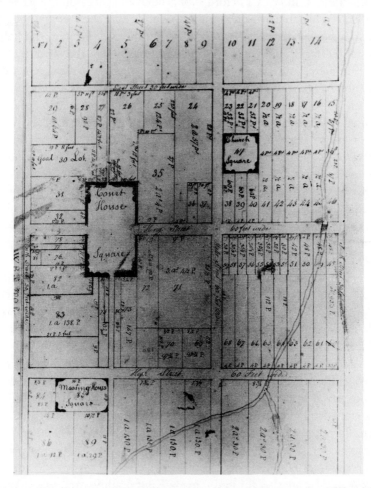

Dover was laid out in rectangular square blocks with a "Court House Square" and "Church Square" as civic centers. Narrow lots for shopkeepers lined King Street between "Court House Square" and the landing on St. Jones Creek to the south. The plan modestly emulated the ideal of a balanced and orderly city.

angles, oriented to the cardinal points of the compass. At the center, Court House Square provided a setting for the structure where the quarterly courts met. The commissioners planned other squares for the meetinghouse and the church. By 1711, the first Church of England missionary, Thomas Crawford, had completed a small wooden building with glazed windows and pews, doubtless the inspiration for Church Square, and in 1733 the Anglicans started construction of a brick building.

But these meager signs of civic aspiration were slow to bear fruit. After Thomas Crawford left in 1711, the Society for the Propagation of the Gospel refused to replace him. For twenty years, the population was deemed too thin and scattered. In 1733 Crawford's long-delayed successor, the Reverend George Frazer, began a brick church in Dover despite the fact that the town was only "a small village of about 15 or 16 families." Even with the help of the substantial farm families in the surrounding region, the small building was not completed nine years later. In the 1730s there was little demand for lots. Eventually the commissioners of the town plot all died, leaving no one authorized to sell property in town before the Assembly got around to appointing successors.[15]

The promise of improvement arrived with the other genteel families who came to Dover about the same time as Nicholas Ridgely. He was not the only notable individual to recognize the advantages of Kent's relatively inexpensive land. Other younger sons of third-generation gentry were interested because they suffered from a peculiarly American kind of land shortage: well-off planters lacked sufficient property to provide for all their children. Many seventeenth-century founders, like the first Henry Ridgely, had obtained large quantities of low-cost wilderness land. Even down to the third generation, sizable estates, like Nicholas's 547 acres, could be dealt out to all the sons, with an added share to the eldest. Nicholas's inheritance could have afforded him a comfortable existence in Maryland, but the life plans of the American gentry required more than that. A single plantation of 547 acres, while more than sufficient for an individual farmer, fell short of the expectations of a man like Nicholas, who thought not just of himself but of his children down through the generations. Estates for future Ridgelys had to be carved from new land, and for that purpose his Maryland inheritance was inadequate. Men like Nicholas looked to the west, of course, but also to underpopulated pockets along the seaboard like Kent County, where large tracts could be obtained for relatively low cost. The rising price of wheat on the international market and Kent's water access to Philadelphia, the best American market for grain, made Kent doubly attractive.[16] Within the two decades after 1738, the date of Nicholas Ridgely's arrival in Kent, the number of gentry families probably more than doubled.

Gentlemen had settled in the county earlier. The Rodneys were residents before 1700. Nicholas Loockerman, third-generation American through a Dutch family that lived first in New York and then in Maryland, moved to Kent in 1723. But in the 1730s settlement quickened. Samuel Chew moved from Anne Arundel County in 1738, the same year the Ridgelys arrived. He erected his mansion on Berry's Range, and was appointed chief justice for the lower counties in 1741. Samuel Dickinson, father of John, came in 1741. Others of comparable standing were building their brick mansions in the same years. As a rough measure, the county probate records from 1726 to 1750 list three decedents who were termed gentleman. From 1751 to 1775, fifteen decedents were so titled. In the earlier period, three individuals were called merchants, people who in some cases lived at a comparable level. In the later period, there were eight.[17] The increase in notables cannot be accounted for by population growth, which rose from an estimated 5,000 people in 1742 to 9,000 in 1776, a much slower rate than the fivefold increase in gentlemen in the probate records.[18] An ever larger number of genteel establishments dotted the landscape in the central settled core of the county from 1735 on, a refining and perhaps unsettling influence.

The society of other mansion people supported the discipline behind Charles Ridgely's manners and made the construction of a mansion worth the cost. A great house had to be more meaningful than an individual endeavor, more than an expression of isolated vanity. The presence of other genteel families in Kent made house construction a social act. In the company of others who shared genteel values, the possessors of houses, costumes, and manners created a modest polite society. Membership in that society gave an immediate point to the effort and expense of living a genteel life.

GENTRY MATERIAL CULTURE

THE new county gentry brought a distinctive manner of life to Kent, and their houses made the differences visible. Most eighteenth-century Kent farmers built their houses of hewn logs clad in clapboards. The ordinary house probably had one room and an attic. The new gentry invariably raised their houses to two stories plus attic and built them of brick. Doubling the height in itself increased the visibility of the new houses on the landscape, and the color made them stand out even more. Rarely was the usual eighteenth-century house painted. Only the best houses had whitewashed interiors. Weather-beaten to a gray-brown and huddled among a motley assemblage of similarly dulled outbuildings, the predominant log house blended with trees and fields. The red brick, two-story house by contrast stood out against the land. With outbuildings to the rear, the house faced the road directly, with large, glazed windows on the front, at least four of them and sometimes as many as nine. Samuel Dickinson even considered planting hedgerows to replace the rail fences and having a flower garden before the door instead of the usual hardened dirt pad and stack of firewood.[19]

The interiors of the houses bespoke a new way of life as well. The traditional hall-and-parlor plan of the standard farmhouse gave way to the central hall of the new Georgian style. That hall introduced a different manner of entertainment. Visitors did not enter immediately into the family's round of work and relaxation as they had in the traditional hall with its entrance directly from the outside. In the new plan, the central hall isolated visitors from the activities of the house. Visitors paused before admission into the rooms to the side, while the everyday life of the family was hidden to the rear and upstairs. The house embodied the same stylized formality as Charles's letters to Nicholas. The hall seemed to require formal address to an "Honored Sir" and an application for admission. Both guests and hosts were to present a better, more disciplined self when they met.[20]

Over forty-three of these eighteenth-century brick houses still stand in Kent County. Some twenty-five were constructed before 1776. Of this number, just three brick houses remain from the period before 1740. Then a rash of building took place. Within two years after 1740, Samuel Dickinson, Nicholas Loockerman, and Samuel Chew all put up large houses, some of the finest of the century. In the next twenty-five years, at least another twenty-two houses were built which still stand today, and doubtless there were others now gone. All the houses were located in the central area, no more than eleven miles from Dover either north or south and in a strip five to ten miles wide from east to west, forming a concentrated block of brick structures. William Corbit's house, constructed just over the Kent County boundary in New Castle County, was a northward extension in the same fertile region.

Not all of the houses included the fashionable Georgian central hall; about half incorporated versions of the traditional hall and parlor, though modified to introduce a measure of formality and separation. Nor were all the houses residences of new gentry. Older, less distinguished families followed the lead of the auspicious newcomers. But the new houses were of brick, with similar two-story symmetrical Georgian exteriors that everywhere up and down the seaboard expressed the growing genteel style.[21]

Nicholas Ridgely, after taking a decade to accumulate properties for a plantation, built his Eden Hill house in 1749, a mile west of Dover. The three-bay house had the door to the side of the two first-floor windows, not the full Georgian spread of the Dickinsons or Chews. The long hall at Eden Hill, ordinarily a central hall, went along the side of two downstairs rooms, with a stairway at the far end. On the other side of the hall, doors opened into smaller rooms which were part of an older house on the property when the Ridgelys purchased it. While not as splendid in external appearance, the plan at Eden Hill formed the same formal interior structure as the classical Georgian houses of the neighboring gentry and enabled the Ridgelys to entertain with the same degree of propriety.

When Nicholas Ridgely died in 1755, his personal estate did not elevate him to the rank of gentleman in the probate papers of Kent County. Two men who were accorded that honor and died in the same decade had much larger estates. Nicholas's personal estate in 1755 was £648; Charles Hillyard's was £1,020, and Nathaniel Luff's was £1,102. Still, by comparison with most of his neighbors, Nicholas was a wealthy man. His personal estate ranked second among the nineteen men and one woman whose probate inventories from 1755 survive. The median personal estate in that year was valued between £75 and £86, and the low was £8.

Nicholas's belongings can be used to illustrate the life of an average country gentleman at midcentury. Reconstructing the interior of Eden Hill from the inventory, one is struck by the absence of luxury and splendor.[22] The spare interior permitted only a modestly comfortable life. The surfaces were hard and bare. No carpets lay on the floor, no curtains hung at the windows, no padding or upholstery cushioned the chairs; everywhere one saw and felt bare wood, with no fabrics or cushions to soften the surfaces. The wooden floors and furniture were surrounded by plain plaster walls. The only adornments to break the flat plane of the walls were looking glasses in two of the rooms. The only softness occurred at the beds, where sheets smoothed the soft surface of the mattress and pillowcases covered the pillows. Like all colonials, the Ridgelys invested heavily in bedding and

In 1749 Nicholas Ridgely constructed the larger block of the house to the left, joining it to an older house already on the property at Eden Hill.

furniture. The mattress and bedstead in the master bedroom were valued at £6, and there were beds worth £5 and £4 10*s.* elsewhere in the house.

Some ragged edges in the household heighten the impression of plainness. Caesar Rodney and Stephen Paradee, who took the probate inventory, noted among the best china in the parlor "4 Cups and 3 Saucers, old and broken" and brought down the value accordingly. A set of "5 China plates" had "some broken" among them. Of the three "China bowls," one was broken. The books, decanters, two tables, and tin punch bowl were labeled "old," and not in the sense of well-preserved antiques, but as shabby pieces that had lost their value. Instead of carrying the broken items to a back room for repair or dumping them in a pit to gladden the heart of a latter-day archaeologist, the Ridgelys left these wounded pieces in the best parlor among the fine items used to entertain guests.

By modern standards, Nicholas did not indulge in great personal display. Rodney and Paradee noted only two suits among his personal apparel, plus some old ones. Nicholas would have worn the same clothes day after day. He would have changed his shirt and his stockings, as he had nine of the first and eleven pairs of the latter. These aspects of a gentleman's costume had to be spotless even if the suit was commonplace and perhaps rumpled. Nicholas also owned a silver watch worth £5 (his two suits were worth only £9) and a riding chair valued at £8. Cutting a proper figure at the Kent County courts may have depended more on accoutrements such as these than on the variety and splendor of one's suits.

The inventory offers clues about the Ridgelys' values by indicating which activities merited finer furnishings. Of the three tables in the parlor—an old mahogany valued at 25*s.,* an old walnut at 12*s.,* and a tea table, probably a small table, at 40*s.*—the last was of greater worth than the other two combined. The valuable tea table draws attention to the other items in the parlor associated with it, eighteen cups and thirteen saucers in the parlor. Some of these dishes were broken, but that fact suggests frequent use. One set of six cups and saucers had no broken items among them and, judging by its value, was the best set. With the tea and its attendant rituals can be associated the twelve wineglasses, none of them broken, nine tumblers, three decanters, three china bowls, and a tin punch bowl.

These items project the picture of tea, wine, and punch being served in the parlor to groups of six or eight. The Ridgelys had the equipment to entertain, and the presence of eight chairs suggests the number of guests ordinarily expected. Each of these chairs was valued at 16*s.,* more than half the worth of the mahogany table. The investment measures the importance of the rituals surrounding tea, wine, and punch in the Ridgely parlor. Besides presenting an exterior face to passersby, the brick house brought people together, warmed them with tea or liquor, and facilitated exchange.

In the parlor there were also twelve china plates and twelve china dishes, and upstairs were two damask tablecloths and twenty-four napkins, the napkins alone worth as much as the twelve china plates (30*s.*). The company, drinking wine, could move from the parlor to the front room to dine, where a better walnut table stood with six chairs. Rodney and Paradee listed forty-three ounces of silver worth £13 in all, and probably most of these items were hollowware for dining. The Ridgelys' residence was organized to entertain guests, an important undertaking for all who aspired to gentility.

Entertainment received more material support than any other activity within the house. The parents' bedroom had the best bed, an old dressing table, an old chest of drawers, a looking glass, six chairs, and no more. The other sleeping spaces were similarly spare. Six beds, only three of them of value, were placed in five rooms which also contained an occasional looking glass and chest and an armchair. Nicholas had an old desk worth 25*s.* and two red leather trunks in his office.

The genteel style in this provincial household did not require polish in every aspect of life. Instead certain times and particular objects made the difference. The house itself, standing as a monument for all to see, was the starting place. Beyond that, entertainment merited careful attention. The arrival of guests in the hall, their seating in the parlor, the tea, the punch, the dinner, had all to be managed properly. And judging from Charles's correspondence with his father, the speech on these occasions had to be rightly formed, with due deference to all who merited honor. Good sense and learning in speech, and probably grace and wit, earned respect for the speakers. A later Ridgely, Charles's second wife, could not abide affectation in her children, but she thought it important that they learn to enter a room properly.²³

The Ridgely house and the others like it, with their teacups, mahogany tables, punch bowls, and looking glasses, along with the rituals and the conversations implied by those objects, formed Charles Ridgely's aspirations before he left for Philadelphia in 1751. The objects and the rooms created a setting for the growth of personality as much as for vain display. What Nicholas hoped for in his son was better expressed in Charles's letters than in his ruffled shirts. The culmination of the genteel lifestyle was the genteel person, disciplined, deferential, spirited, polite, knowledgeable, forceful, graceful. The long list of desired traits, when integrated into a single character, created a magnetism and power that was the ideal of the age.

Nathaniel Luff, a physician who was reared in Kent County and who later practiced there, sensed the force of the genteel personality in his teachers and models. Luff was apprenticed to a learned and competent English-trained doctor in Philadelphia in the 1770s. "Yet I early discovered," Luff commented in his reminiscences, "that there was something wanting (like a

*In the first enthusiasm
of restoring the
Corbit-Sharpe house to its
eighteenth-century condition,
the furnishings in the stair
hall conformed to the ideal of
Colonial Revival decoration.*

*The room-by-room inventory
of William Corbit's estate
showed that decoration in the
stair hall was much simpler
than first envisioned. The
rural gentry lived in a much
plainer style than their city
equivalents.*

polish) to make [the doctor] shine in the learned world, and without which, the best finished furniture or finest marble will lose half its lustre, which, when added, decorates and greatly ornaments it." Luff found this polish in Charles Ridgely.[24]

OLD AND NEW GENTRY

NOT all of the brick-house inhabitants mastered the genteel style as completely as Charles Ridgely, but their houses and furnishings all expressed an aspiration, and perhaps a troubling one. Whether or not their children could speak with the polish of young Charles, the owners of the houses made vast expenditures for buildings and possessions almost entirely unknown in the county earlier, betokening a wish to live in the Ridgely style. Where before there had been only weather-beaten cabins and small two-story frame houses, now large brick and frame mansions set a standard for gentry living largely foreign to the area before 1730. How was the coming of the new manner received? Did the arrival of the Chews, Dickinsons, and Ridgelys disturb the older county leaders, perhaps because of a rivalry for position or merely resentment because of the expensive new houses needed to keep up? We wonder if the coming of the gentlemen offended the older population, creating a cultural gulf between the old and the new people.[25]

A handful of eminent families had led Kent County from the beginning, among whom the Rodneys were preeminent. The most famous of the clan, Caesar Rodney, a signer of the Declaration of Independence, was the third generation of Rodneys in Delaware. His grandfather William (who spelled his name Rodeney) was descended from an English gentry family and rose to modest prominence in America. Rodney took a leading part in Delaware's separation from the Pennsylvania Assembly in 1704 and served as the Speaker of the House when the lower counties first met in their own Assembly. His sons carried on, one as a member of the Assembly, another as sheriff of Kent County. The father of Caesar, also a Caesar, born in 1707, married Elizabeth Crawford, the daughter of the onetime Anglican missionary in Dover, Thomas Crawford, and took his own place in Kent County politics. By 1728, when Caesar Jr. was born, the Rodneys were well entrenched as the leading county family.[26]

From 1727 to 1729 Caesar Rodney, Sr., kept a diary which helps us to measure the impact of the genteel immigrants. Rodney's candid account of his daily round illuminates the simple pleasures of country life before gentility imposed its restraints, and raises the question of how the old-style gentry adjusted to the pretensions and self-discipline of the new. Considering Charles Ridgely's education, Rodney's failure to attend any school at all until age thirteen is especially striking. He went then for a few months and then again for four months two years later. He read the Bible and wrote a little. At age nineteen he studied navigation and astronomy. He was not averse to books; at age twenty he was reading from Sir Walter Raleigh. But the normal pattern of his culture did not require him to attend school.[27]

Nor was he required to devote himself to a frantic schedule of hard labor. He seems to have been quite content with a leisurely mixture of work and play. Each morning after breakfast he sat and smoked his pipe. When worn out from his labor or a demanding evening of fiddling and dancing, he stopped to nap at midday, even in the busy June barley harvest season, which was accompanied by nightly dances. After helping his future father-in-law on June 12, that "night we had fidling and Danceing and was very Merry till Mid Night then I came home and three or four more with me—." The merriment went on for four successive nights after the day's work, usually until about midnight. On June 15, Rodney abbreviated his diary report by recording the "Usual ceremony" again at night, and later in another entry referred once more to the "old Seremony of fidling and Danceing" as if the play were a ritual as well as a reward to the workers.[28]

The reward could not be overlooked. Apparently no payment passed between owner and the workers at harvest other than the merry time and the drink. To prepare for his own harvest, Rodney went about collecting rum; when he had eleven gallons he was still looking for more. Rodney himself labored in the field of his father-in-law, and also worked alongside his friend Daniel Needham, one of the largest taxpayers in the county. They joined in the harvest labor out of a sense of communal obligation, and the fellowship of the drink sustained the neighborly fraternity. No sense of shame in working at a tedious job hindered Rodney's participation. He worked at whatever task came his way. On another occasion, he "Went to White Washing My house." Nor was his harvest labor a matter of obligation to a future father-in-law. During the second half of June, Rodney harvested for three neighbors besides himself and Crawford. He relied on them in turn for help, though on one occasion he went to his field expecting workers and reported disconsolately that he would have to go again because "the People Did Not Com." What made them come at all was not wages but neighborly obligation and the pleasures of fraternization. When they reaped his wheat in early July, the "Cheef of my work," he reported, "wass to Play on the fiddle," as if the workers liked music as they reaped.

Harvesting was a cooperative communal effort among local landowners with no official accounting of debts and credits. Doubtless there was an informal sense of what was due one another, but it was the evening's fun that recruited and sustained labor. In the camaraderie of drink, dancing, fiddling, and even fighting, the workers assured each other of their fraternal commitments. Without that, the fear of inequities and exploitation would have arisen. Wherever there was business or work, fraternal association had its part. In August, when "the Carpenders wass a Laying the barn florr," Rodney "went and Smokt a Pipe with them." When he bought a small store of goods in Philadelphia to resell from his house, he offered a prize of seven yards of fabric to the winner of a shooting contest. After the winner was decided, "we plaid at Quites and Cards the Rest of the Day—at night we had fidling and Dancing." Rodney recorded a half dozen purchases on the same day.[29]

How would this carefree fiddler who played all the way down St. Jones Creek in a shallop on the way to Philadelphia react to the tea parties, the wineglasses, and formal dinners of the brick houses? Rodney's entertainments were the ceremonies of the harvest or an informal moment such as when at Thomas Crawford's "We Got to fidling Dancing and Drinking of Punch tell 10 o'clock." At Hart's one night he had to send for his fiddle at home and then "Plaid awhile and Danced." A good time for him was an evening not long before his marriage when he and his friend Sturges went to "a grape vine. Meet 3 young women. Stay till midnight," or "went to take a walk whare we met with Sum young People. We Staid plaing till Midnight."[30]

Would this Caesar feel ill at ease amid the fine talk and manners of the Ridgely gatherings? Apparently not. Rodney was in his thirties when Nicholas Ridgely settled in Kent County, and he appears to have assimilated the new style without difficulty. By 1743 Rodney's son Caesar, then just fifteen, was in Philadelphia studying Latin. Caesar Sr. wrote from Kent, "Dear Child be Diligent at your Books and make what progress you posably can in Learning while you have an opportunity." Save for the spelling, the words could have been written by Nicholas Ridgely to his son Charles. Nicholas and Caesar Sr. grew close enough for Nicholas to be made the guardian of Caesar Jr. The father died in 1745 when Caesar Jr. was just seventeen, and Nicholas Ridgely saw to the continuation of the boy's education. Along with his classical education, young Caesar learned dancing and fencing as befitted a gentleman.[31] He absorbed the genteel ideals as effortlessly as did young Charles. Although Caesar never married, his house at Poplar Grove, a three-bay, two-story brick structure, contained the elegant furnishings expected of a gentleman. In the parlor when he died in 1784 were ten mahogany chairs with horsehair bottoms, two of them with arms, a pair of mirrors with gilt frames, two mahogany tables, a walnut table with tea board, four Venetian crimson nankeen curtains, fancy andirons with fluted brass pillars, along with the tea service and other ceramics that went with the furniture. The bedroom, his apparel, his carriage were all those of a gentleman.[32] In 1767 Caesar thought it entirely appropriate to commission William Tod of Philadelphia to paint the Rodney coat of arms on his chariot.[33]

Rodney seems to have exemplified the proper personal qualities as well. Thomas Rodney, his younger brother, said of Caesar after his death that "he was remarkably genteel and elegant in his person, dress and manners, had a pleasant and noble disposition, and a greate fund of wit and humour of the pleasing kind, so that his conversation was always lively and engaging. His understanding was bright and strong and conducted by wisdom."[34] However distant from his own father's personal style, Caesar cultivated the genteel virtues and prized them. Without offspring himself, he gave instructions in his will that his nephew Caesar "be educated as liberally in classical learning, Natural and Moral Philosophy and every other Branch of literature that has a tendency to improve the Understanding and polish the Manners as may reasonably be in America."[35]

Rather than resist gentility, the Rodneys adopted it as rightfully their own, the proper style for a family descended from English gentry and accustomed to leadership in Kent County society. Far from competing with the Ridgelys, the Rodneys formed an alliance, an active alliance in politics, in which they joined in the same coalition by 1755, and an implicit cultural alliance.[36] Among others of the same class, the reception was equally cordial. The large number of brick houses built after 1740 implies that many people of means accepted the new standards just as warmly. The informal, open habits of an earlier time apparently evolved without resistance to more urbane ways.

The Corbits, like the Rodneys, were among the older settlers who were well established on the land when the new style swept over them. The first Daniel Corbit lived in lower New Castle County as early as 1717 and purchased one farm of 250 acres in 1723 and a still larger farm a few years later. His 1756 estate inventory reveals him as a prosperous man with eighteen chairs in his house, eighteen forks and eleven knives, and fifty-three pounds of pewter, but none of the marks of real elegance. When he died he had just one suit of clothes, which he left to his son Daniel. His daughters married sons of local farm families. Daniel satisfied the Brintons when he asked for their daughter's hand in marriage—as a mark of their goodwill they gave her £300 in trust. But Daniel's estate when he died was worth just £260. These were middling gentry, leaders in their local spheres, prosperous but not extravagantly wealthy.[37]

Daniel's son William was apparently the first of his family to recognize the significance of the brick houses and to see that the Corbits must join the ranks of the mansion people. Why he chose to make such an extravagant statement and how he managed to avoid the exaggerations and imbalances of others who strove for grandeur too suddenly cannot now be known. What seems clear is that he wished to embrace the genteel style, as befitted one who stood at the summit of his little society, and thus to identify with all the others across the landscape who thought of themselves as "the gentlemen of the place."

His decision benefited his offspring when they reached the age to marry. Leaving behind the farm families of lower New Castle County, his children moved easily into a higher society. One son married the daughter of a man who was later elected governor. Another, who wrote poetry in imitation of Sir Walter Scott, married the daughter of a judge. Sarah Corbit, William's daughter, married Presley Spruance, later United States senator. The others married into well-to-do families of local leaders. William's prosperity helped to make them eligible, but without the manner and style of the great house, the children would have lacked the polish to enter the circles where such partners were found.[38] Whether or not he was aware of it at the time, in breaking ground for his mansion in 1772, William Corbit laid the foundation for his family's entry into polite society.

PLAIN PEOPLE

WHILE putting the Corbit children in touch with promising prospective mates, their father's house inevitably cut them off from neighbors in Cantwell's Bridge who still lived in two-room log dwellings. In Kent County, as everywhere else, the mansions divided society. Houses represented a system of personal culture, as well as wealth and taste, giving the mansions the power to set apart some of the population as refined, polite, and learned, leaving the rest to be vulgar, coarse, and ignorant. Those lines were less clearly drawn earlier in the century. Caesar Sr. at twenty was clearly destined for higher offices and greater wealth than most of his neighbors, yet he found his fun in dancing and drinking with the harvesters and took pleasure in a pipe with the carpenters. Would the son, after his classical training in Philadelphia, have taken that pipe as naturally as the father? Would not the son's dress, his speech, his education, and his manners have inhibited him and the carpenters both? The power of the genteel ideal lay in its transformation of personality; it lifted properly reared persons to a higher plane. At the same time, gentility implicitly diminished the rest, creating differences which were difficult to forget. The tensions between polite and vulgar may rarely have risen to the surface, but they were ever present.

The nature of the tensions is suggested by the gentry's characterizations of the masses of people who, though nearly invisible in private correspondence, existed all around the brick houses. The descriptive terms that the gentry unconsciously used combined a primitive social classification scheme with sharply pointed moral judgments. On one side of the formulation, ordinary people appeared crude and debauched, a lower order of life as well as of wealth. The Anglican missionaries coming from England under sponsorship of the Society for the Propagation of the Gospel complained particularly of swearing and drunkenness as signs of generally loose character. Charles Inglis, perhaps the most cultivated of all the missionaries before the Revolution, wrote home in dismay of Kent County election practices during the selection of representatives and sheriffs.

> To ingratiate themselves with the people, candidates for these offices appointed places, where they invited the Inhabitants to treat them with Liquor, provided for that purpose. These meetings, which were held once a week for near 2 months before Election Day, the first of Octr., were attended with the most pernicious consequences. The People's morals were entirely debauched at them, for he was best liked who gave the most liberal treat. By this means they became Scenes of the grossest debauchery and Vice.

Inglis claimed that by preaching near the treating places he drew people away and the "Riots dwindled," but then Anglican missionaries had made similar claims for the past half century without visible effect.[39]

Others besides the high-toned newcomers saw Kent County society in that debauched light. Nathaniel Luff, who grew up in Dover in the 1760s and 1770s, remembered that "card-playing, billiards, horse-racing, cock-fighting, dogs, boys, was a general round of diurnal revolutions," and in retrospect it all amounted to a "remarkable depravity in the Dover youths." In retrospect the drunkenness seemed especially heavy. He painfully recalled that "on a certain occasion in harvest time, liquor being dealth out freely, I was made drunk."[40]

Luff's reference to harvest drunkenness suggests that the behavior that he and Inglis thought reprehensible was the continuation of the older culture which Caesar Rodney, Sr., casually recorded in his diary. He had then given the harvest parties the friendly aspect of neighborly good times and had enjoyed the rum and the dancing as heartily as anyone. He doubtless attended the election treats and sponsored many of them himself. What Inglis considered to be coarse behavior in the 1760s was the common culture of gentry and commoner alike in the 1720s.

At other times, the gentry saw the people in a more favorable light. Words like "industrious," "laborious," "sober," "sensible," and "pious" were used then. Charles Ridgely used these terms in a letter to Charles Inglis, who became Ridgely's close friend and brother-in-law during Inglis's Dover years. After Inglis accepted a pulpit in New York, Ridgely wrote to him expressing opinions on the policies of the Society for the Propagation of the Gospel in Kent. In 1767 Ridgely opposed the effort to separate the church members at Duck Creek in northern Kent from Dover and to attach them to the Appoquinimink Mission. The purported reason for the change was Duck Creek's lack of wealthy church supporters. The "neighborhood is not sufficiently polite nor the income large enough for a gentleman," Inglis said. Ridgely bridled at that. Surely some young cleric would be content to labor among a simple people. Is there not, he asked, "one single Clergyman to be met with so unprovided but £150 a year might tempt him to pass some, or even all his days among a parcel of impolite, yet honest and worthy men?"[41] Ridgely could not promise the young missionary refined company. But there was another kind of ordinary person, one who was honorable and upright if more plain, and certainly honest and worthy. Such persons were the good ordinary people of the county.

The drunken and debauched people on one side and the sober, industrious, and honest people on the other were the two images of commoners in the minds of the gentry in midcentury Kent County. In one sense, they were the reverse of one another, the good and the bad. In another sense, they were the same. Both characterizations placed the common people below the upper level on which Ridgely and Inglis stood. The language which differentiated people assumed a clear difference between polite and impolite, between gentlemen and the merely honest and worthy. And there was no question which was superior. Of course a clergyman would prefer a neighborhood that was "sufficiently polite." Only someone of lesser means could content himself with the income and the company of plain men. The assumption underlying the social description was of hierarchical levels, with wealth and manners placing one person above another.

That assumption was fixed in nearly every expression of gentility. Even among the gentry elite, one person deferred to another. Charles acknowledged his father's superior position, and fine gradations of respect were observed in every drawing room. But the great leap came with the passage from genteel to common. The houses, the clothing, the rituals, and the personal radiance of the genteel formed a cultural and social gulf in Kent County. In their imaginations, Charles Ridgely, Charles Inglis, and Nathaniel Luff divided society into the polite and the plain. The gentry were genteel and all others, whatever their virtues and vices, were of another order. The sense of diminished sensibility and lower moral worth may account for the absence of ordinary people from the correspondence. Ordinary people were so lacking in moral presence and force, it was assumed, that they were not significant individual presences and were worth writing about only as a class.

The imagined boundary, however, was always under assault. The imprecision of its definition necessarily made it vulnerable. One could never specify exactly what accumulation of virtues, possessions, and honors made one polite. A decanter of wine, a mirror, a parlor, a dancing lesson, a gesture, even a spoon, radiated its own degree of gentility. By acquiring a part, a person enjoyed some benefits of the whole. Thus it was that even in 1755 among the inventories of ordinary people of modest estates can be found looking glasses, punch bowls, and tea services. They were still more common in 1774. (See table, page 229.) Besides looking on admiringly or resentfully, the honest and worthy common people brought a few tokens of gentility into their own lives.

Most ordinary families could never afford a brick house or an academy education or dancing lessons. But small genteel possessions appeared with remarkable frequency in the inventories, and the desire for intangibles like a little classical learning and a touch of polite manners made people strive for improvements. Many times their very eagerness betrayed them. Nathaniel Luff said that in the 1760s the hunger for the proper education enabled incompetent schoolmasters to swindle people in Kent. "A few men anxious for the promotion of their children, were excessively gulled by tutors." The parents being themselves "unacquainted with the learned languages and sciences, prompted by ambition, and secured by wealth, they were willing to go to great lengths; but, for want of proper knowledge, they expended their money to little purpose and established habits that were unsubstantial and hard to eradicate."[42] The construction of an academy building in the 1770s in Dover may say very little for the educational level of the town, but it surely meant people wanted proper schooling for their children. Parents were willing to pay for instruction even when they were incapable of evaluating what they got for their money.

This earnest effort of unlearned parents to provide their children with more than the parents had enjoyed themselves, though halting and misguided at times, worked to great effect in the long run. The students may have learned very little Latin, and teacups in the hall of a weatherboarded cabin may not have bestowed anything like real gentility, but the striving of thousands of people in time amounted to a great movement. These exertions gradually enabled the excluded class, the honest and worthy, to encroach upon, invade, and finally appropriate many of the honors and privileges of the genteel.

As the century wore on, the evidence of gentility increased in modest households. Education became more available, and polite manners spread downward and outward. Rather than remaining the exclusive preserve of the gentry, the pleasures and refinements of genteel living were appropriated by people on a level below. The life that at midcentury was conceived as proper only for the gentry became, in less than a century, the standard of respectable living for the entire middle class. Conceived originally as fundamentally hierarchical and deferential, the genteel style, as borrowed and adapted, enabled people of lesser rank to elevate themselves and thus, ironically, to blur and dilute social distinctions. Already in Kent County at midcentury the urge to adopt the dignities of the mansion people can be detected in the modest possessions of those who still dwelt in log cabins.

The line that gentility drew through society would never be erased. When common people built two-story houses, a new standard for residences emerged to distinguish people at the very top. But the purchase of looking glasses and tea services suggests that gentility also motivated people to cross the line rather than passively observe its limitations, to strive for elevation rather than resent subordination. The ordinary people of Kent were not content to be left behind and below. As rapidly as distinctions were drawn between refined and vulgar, people strove to overcome the invidious comparison, and to secure, if they could, a foothold in the ranks of polite society.

CHAPTER II

The Courtesy-Book World

MANSION houses like those in Kent County went up in every American colony in the eighteenth century. Where new gentry families did not introduce the genteel styles, as the Ridgelys, Chews, and Dickinsons did in Kent, the old families learned about fashionable architecture in other ways—from observing the houses going up in port cities, from visits to England, from design books, or from migrant builders. In every region, the gentry erected dwellings with spaces and furnishings to stage the occasions of genteel life; they learned appropriate conduct and taught it to their children; they dressed, ate, and carried themselves to suit the part. As they learned manners, the aspiring gentry, in some ways rough and awkward, in other respects elegant and imposing, formed themselves into a polite society.

The adoption of gentility could not be accomplished without effort. The colonials had to attend to every aspect of life to achieve even a pale facsimile of English gentility. Manners had to be studied and formed with great diligence. Ideally, a courtier learned his manners at court by observing refined people. But even noble youths received outside instruction in conduct along with all the other lessons appropriate to their station. And if young princes had to be molded and formed, how much more a Charles Ridgely or a Caesar Rodney, even to achieve a much lower level of civility? Great effort and discipline went into the making of a son who could write a letter like young Charles. Especially for the first generations reared to politeness, life became an artifice, self-consciously shaped and regulated. Lord Chesterfield, the foremost teacher of fine manners in the eighteenth century, considered a polite person a work of art; he found exquisite pleasure in instructing his son in genteel conduct. In one of the famous letters, Chesterfield remarked to young Philip, "I wish to God that you had as much pleasure in following my advice, as I have in giving it to you!"[1]

COURTESY BOOKS

INSTRUCTION for youth found its way into print as courtesy books, a vast literature in Western civilization going back to classical times. In their modern form, courtesy manuals were imported into the colonies beginning in the early eighteenth century. In fact, their appearance in colonial libraries and bookshops helps to track the spread of polite society in America. The courtesy books, of course, represent only a tiny fraction of the instruction in polite behavior that mainly went on in private houses under the eyes of parents and tutors who had no manuals to work from; but like the mansions, the books signal the arrival of the genteel code.

Eleazar Moody, a Boston schoolmaster, published one of the earliest American courtesy manuals, *The School of Good Manners,* in 1715, marking the presence of fashionable gentility in Puritan New England at that date. His work was a peculiar combination of the religious and the secular. Moody divided his book into two parts. One taught children to practice the virtues that we associate with a proper Puritan upbringing: devout prayer, obedience to parents, pure thoughts, and seeking to know God. These pages admonished children to "let thy Recreation be Lawful, Brief and Seldom," and to "let thy Meditations be of Death, Judgment and Eternity."[2]

The other half of the book contained another set of rules altogether. This half admonished children to "Gnaw not bones at the table, but clean them with thy knife," and "At play make not thy Cloathes, Hands or Face dirty or nasty, nor sit upon the ground." This section said almost nothing of God or divine punishment. For its sanctions, the manners part of the book called on another kind of authority. The author told his young readers, "Children, these are the Chief of those Rules of Behavior, the observation *whereof* will deliver you from the disgraceful titles of sordid and clownish, and intail upon the mention of you, the honour of genteel and well bred children." This author had another kind of punishment in mind than the conventional Christian doom of clergymen such as Michael Wigglesworth. "There is scarce a sadder sight, than a clownish and unmannerly Child. Avoid therefore with greatest diligence so vile an Ignominy."[3] Sordid and clownish were the hell of the manners book, as well-bred and genteel were its heaven.

A more notable conduct manual never made its way into print in an American edition. George Washington copied his "Rules of Civility and Decent Behaviour In Company and Conversation" from an English courtesy book of the previous century, *Youth's Behaviour, or Decency in Conversation among Men.* Washington's 110 numbered rules included such directions as "In the Presence of Others Sing not to yourself with a humming Noise, nor Drum with your Fingers or Feet," and practical helps for behaving in the presence of superiors: "In Company of those of Higher Quality than yourself Speak not ti[ll] you are ask'd a Question then Stand upright put of your Hat and Answer in few words."[4]

Washington also had practical training in the social graces from his older brother Lawrence Washington, who introduced the sixteen-year-old George at Belvoir, the mansion next to Lawrence's Mount Vernon. At Belvoir, Washington met young George William Fairfax, a recently elected burgess and the well-bred and English-educated son of Colonel William Fairfax. That same year, George William married Sarah Cary, whose charm and beauty enthralled Washington. He prepared to make a favorable impression during his visit to Belvoir by packing nine shirts, seven waistcoats, and four neckcloths. In these years he learned to play whist and loo, the fashionable card games of the Chesapeake gentry, and about the same time probably attended dancing school. The "Rules of Civility" had practical application as Washington made his entry into the society of the great Virginia houses.[5]

Judging from their prevalence, books of manners must have served a useful purpose in colonial America. Washington's industry in copying his 110 rules indicates how much civility meant to him. Moody's book went through thirteen printings in the eighteenth century, in places like Portland, Maine, and Windsor, Connecticut, as well as Boston and New London. This popularity leaves little doubt that people wanted instruction in genteel conduct. And yet neither book was originally intended for use in the fresh, growing, mobile society of America. Both were copies of much older books prepared for entirely different settings. Moody borrowed the manners portion of his volume from a book printed in London in 1595 under the title *A.B.C. or, the first schoole of good manners,* and reprinted in various editions throughout the century, including another London edition of 1685 called *The school of good manners.* The 1595 English version was itself a translation of a French book, *L'A, B, C, ou instruction pour les pettis enfans. Après laquelle s'ensuit La Civilité Puérile . . .* published in 1564. By the time Moody printed his book, the contents were 150 years old and had passed from Paris to London to Boston.[6]

Washington took his maxims from a manual translated in 1640 by Francis Hawkins as *Youth's Behavior, or Decency in Conversation among Men,* which in turn was a set of rules compiled by French Jesuits in 1595 at the College of La Flèche mainly from an Italian book, *Il Galateo* by Giovanni della Casa, archbishop of Benevento, first published in 1558.[7] Washington's rules were nearly two hundred years old and had an Italian, French, and English ancestry.

These books speak for the enduring connection of New World culture with Europe and for the surprising adaptability of centuries-old values to life carried on under vastly different social circumstances from those where the books originated. Through the books' rules, the cultural practices of an aristocratic European society, quite removed from anything known on these shores, flowed into Britain's raw and unfinished American colonies. In the drawing rooms and parlors which the colonials constructed for themselves on the edge of the North American wilderness, Americans in Boston and on the Potomac lived by rules written for Italian noblemen and French princes. To all appearances, the readers of the books wanted instruction in the arts of genteel living, and the aristocratic pedigrees of the courtesy books, if anything, only enhanced their value in the eyes of the colonists.

Through the books, the colonists actually tied into a still older genre of instruction. Washington's and Moody's books were late manifestations of a tradition that reached back beyond the sixteenth century to the royal courts of antiquity. One source of this tradition was the mirrors for princes, manuals written by counselors and tutors of the king's sons to prepare them for the monarchy and life at court. These books were the ancestors of the many advice manuals for rulers that proliferated in Medieval and Renaissance Europe. A late descendant of the mirrors was the New England election sermon preached to members of the Great and General Court when they first gathered to elect the colony's officers. The mirrors and the election sermons considered all the virtues required to govern and admonished rulers to incorporate them in their practice. Manners, when they were discussed (as they generally were not in seventeenth-century New England), were only one theme among many. The mirrors covered a wide range of subjects from religion and ethics to politics, history, military strategy, and medicine and varied in form from sober treatises to poems and stories to amuse and instruct. But frequently the mirrors advocated fine bearing and sweetness of manners as sources of regal influence over the people and so became instruction in polite behavior.[8]

The manuals for princes exercised a broad influence over society as a whole because the courtiers surrounding the king wished to adopt kingly virtues for themselves. The aristocracy, especially those close to the monarch, took a great interest in the literature prepared for princes. James I of England, while still king of Scotland, wrote *Basilikon Doron* for his son, but after James became king of England, the book was published and widely read. This wider circle that grew up around virtually all the books for princes constituted a new audience, and recognizing the need, experts wrote guidebooks directly for the gentlemen who would serve the king at court. Baldassare Castiglione addressed *The Book of the Courtier* to his fellow courtiers who wished to make themselves desirable and useful servants of the prince. In volumes for courtiers, in contrast to the earlier mirrors, manners were preeminent. Well before Castiglione emphasized gracefulness of person, other books included specifications for speech, bearing, and personal beauty. *Secretum Secretorum,* an English mirror of 1445, one of many such books by that name, listed among the counselors' qualifications "courtly, faire spekyng, of swete tonge . . . sped in eloquence," and "of good manners and complexion, softe, meke and tretable."[9] Such instructions were not aimed only at the king's immediate counselors. Virtually everyone at court was required to practice courtesy in their behavior. Civility books like those from which Moody and Washington borrowed were often written for pages, sons of noblemen sent to court to be trained and educated. These rules, though written for the understanding of children, were simplified versions of the instructions to courtiers. Everyone at court, from the king down to the pages, was expected to comply with rules to refine and beautify court life.[10]

This ideal of personal conduct as it descended to the medieval courts drew heavily on classical principles of urbanity, another source of courtesy-book culture. The Greeks and Romans prized the polish, charm, and elegance of urban life as contrasted with the boorish coarseness of rusticity, and made that life the subject of literature. Horace, Ovid, and Cicero among the Romans explicated the principles of urbanity most eloquently, and Cicero, primarily in his *De Officiis,* conveyed classical notions of a perfect statesman and an ideal court to medieval emperors. The rulers of the Holy Roman Empire, who conceived of themselves as heirs to ancient Rome, sought to adorn their courts with the grace of classical urbanity and to instill similar virtues in their nobles. Under the influence of imperial courtiers, the nobility added courtliness to the warrior virtues and the idealization of romantic love to form the chivalric code.[11]

As royal courts grew in power in the late Middle Ages, the courtly ideal came to full flower. Courtliness flourished because of the heightened attention to classical texts in which urbanity was propounded, and, more important, because courtliness was a necessity of life at court. A noble who desired a place there had to heed the instructions of the guidebooks, for the changing structure of power in the emergent nation-state required him to seek the benefits of royal favor. At one time, the strength of the nobility had come from their armies and their success in battle. As kings suppressed independent armies and conducted wars themselves, the European aristocracy of necessity gravitated to the royal courts, where power was henceforth won and lost. There the practice of the courtly virtues became as essential to success as valor in battle had once been. Stephen Jaeger, writing about the origins of courtliness in the medieval courts, has commented on the interplay of manners and power and the constant need to offer a polished performance:

[At court] the two main complicating factors are policy and competition for favor. These two make of speech and action something quite different from what they are in everyday life. Words, gestures, intonation, and facial expression all bear meaning, express policy—no act or gesture is random. . . . Conduct becomes so highly structured that life approaches art: the courtier is himself a work of art, his appearance a portrait, his experience a narrative.

Courtliness achieved its most complete realization in that world.[12]

Driven by the new dynamics of state power, one after another European monarch created glorious courts known for patronage of the arts, elaborate ceremony, the brilliance of the assembled company, and gracious and refined manners. To survive under the new order, rugged warlords had to transform themselves. Castiglione's *Book of the Courtier* was the most successful of a long line of manuals and treatises designed to instruct the European aristocracy in the virtues that would win favor from the monarch and contribute to the glory of the court. The religious zeal and military virtues of the chivalric code gradually gave way to the pacific and secular qualities of grace and ease as warriors made themselves over into courtiers.[13]

Renaissance court culture as it spread took on distinctive colorations, suitable to national predispositions. In England native productions like Sir Thomas Elyot's *The Boke Named the Governour* (1531) or a century later Richard Brathwait's *The English Gentleman* (1641) devoted themselves to the sober moral virtues of a responsible ruler rather than to the more decorative qualities of Castiglione's courtier. Still, the refinements of the French, Italian, and Spanish courts exercised a broad influence even in England. All of the continental classics of the sixteenth century were published in English translations; besides *The Book of the Courtier*, Erasmus's *De Civilitate Morum Puerilium* (1526), Giovanni della Casa's *Il Galateo* (1558), and Stefano Guazzo's *Civile Conversation* (c. 1570) were available in English before the end of the sixteenth century. Adapted, bowdlerized, and plagiarized, they came to print in many more forms. Della Casa's *Il Galateo* found its way to George Washington through Hawkins's *Youth's Behaviour, or Decency in Conversation among Men*. Sir Philip Sidney, the beau ideal of late-sixteenth-century England, studied Castiglione religiously and then became the model for portions of Edmund Spenser's *Faerie Queene*.

By the time Charles I organized a High Renaissance court in the 1620s, the courtly ideal was firmly entrenched in England. He adopted the ceremonial rituals, art patronage, and refined conduct that Francis I of France and other European monarchs had embraced earlier. From the time of Charles I onward, the English press continuously produced instructional books on the arts of genteel living, and *The Book of the Courtier* and *Il Galateo* achieved the standing of classics. Dr. Johnson complimented Addison and Steele's *Tatler* and *Spectator* when he said that these papers gained an influence with the English public comparable to that of Castiglione and della Casa. By the end of the seventeenth century, French courtesy books, translated into English, were nearly as widely used in Britain as in France. The nobility universally set standards of polite conduct for themselves, and lesser persons demanded civility of aristocratic superiors as a condition of respect.[14]

As time went by, the courtly ideal extended beyond the court. By the end of the seventeenth century, the upper echelons of the English middle class were absorbing and adapting courtliness under the name of gentility. This extension of court manners and ideals led to Moody's publication of *The School of Good Manners* and Washington's attention to Hawkins's *Youth's Behaviour.* Scores of similar manuals were published for country gentlemen, merchants, professionals in provincial towns, and many others with no access to the court. *The Tatler* and *The Spectator* carried instructions in genteel conduct to a very broad audience, and later novelists did the same. While Robert Carter's sons studied Latin in the 1770s in Virginia, his daughters read *The Spectator.* Samuel Richardson's *Sir Charles Grandison* (1753–54), a voluminous handbook on the personal conduct of an ideal gentleman and of an equally ideal lady, Harriet Byron, reached a vast audience. The glacially moving plot was sustained over an interminable length by interest in observing the behavior of these two in reaction to various forms of vulgarity and rudeness. Americans understood that they were being instructed as they read Richardson's novels. In the 1780s, when *Pamela* and *Clarissa* were in print in American editions along with *Sir Charles Grandison,* Nancy Shippen, a young Philadelphia matron, noted in her diary: "In the Evening alone reading Clarissa H. I like it very much, her character is fine and her letters are full of sentiment—I must adopt some of her excellent rules."[15]

Lord Chesterfield's letters, containing page after page of rules for genteel living, held the same interest. Though intended only for his son, the letters were an immediate sensation when published in 1774. There were five editions within the year, and eleven editions before 1800. American publishers brought out eighteen versions of Chesterfield's letters before 1800, if we count all the adaptations. A host of readers, who would never see life as Chesterfield lived it, wished to glean what they could for themselves as they attempted to make small courts of their own in drawing rooms and parlors.[16]

Although the English middle class altered and adapted the courtly ideal, gentility never lost the marks of its origin in the royal courts. Civility and urbanity were coming to a climax at the Versailles court of Louis XIV in the same years when the English middle class bought manners books that incorporated essentially the same code of conduct. The link between English parlors and the court of the Sun King seems tenuous, but the books attest to the reality of this unlikely connection.[17] The circumstances differed so much that middle-class interest in courtesy-book rules seems beyond reason. At the court of Versailles, the royal presence brought the exquisite sensibilities of refined behavior to the highest pitch. No effort was spared to enhance the king's glory and to beautify his environment. His very presence demanded perfection of manners and gave a point to the necessary self-discipline. Back in their parlors, middle-class people had to subject themselves to the discipline of genteel conduct without the compelling presence of a monarch and with only the vaguest idea of court life. But a faint light from the court still shone in their rooms. Genteel behavior always reflected the belief that somewhere a glorious circle existed where life was lived at its highest and best, where fashions were set, where true gentility was achieved, where perfect harmony, grace, and beauty could be found. Occasionally a representative of that realm in the person of a titled lord or a habitué of the best European circles appeared in the narratives of middle-class life, and those persons exercised great authority over the muddling efforts of lesser people to refine existence.

Chesterfield's court experience increased the value of his *Letters* for the middle class. Even a pious critic who wished to discredit Chesterfield on this account betrayed his fascination with the writer's mastery of the courtly style.

The manners, the honours, the splendor of courtly life had charms irresistible in his eye; here he moved most gracefully, as in his proper sphere; in an element in which he might seem to have been born and bred, and to have past all his days. Here he presides as the genius of the place, and holds out a court-garment composed of all the insinuation, the art, the address, the versatility, the respect, the condescension, the complacency, the sweetness, the ineffable graces, the elegancies and proprieties of polish and splendor necessary to be put on, and worn by all such who aspire to be favourites and ministers.[18]

Successors to Chesterfield who were known to have shone "in the best companies," as he did, exercised irresistible influence over middling aspirants to gentility. Even in the absence of such emissaries, the authority emanating from a distant place gave meaning and resolve to provincial attempts to achieve refinement. The exact location of those exalted circles was not always given; nor was the adoption of manners or fashions simply imitation of a certain group in a known place. A much more generalized sense of a higher life moved the followers of gentility. Without knowing where precisely, they believed in a superior life somewhere and aspired to emulate that existence. In this belief in a higher life of beauty, grace, and ease, we can detect, much modified and distorted by its passage across the years and through society, a memory of the royal courts in which gentility had its origins.

CONDUCT

FROM the seventeenth century on, conduct books were ordinarily written for people who would never see the court and yet who wished to take their manners from court life. The books seem to span a huge gulf between London high life and provincial parlors in remote places, but the books' popularity suggests that the gulf was somehow bridged. The authors assumed that the court ought to be a model for the conduct of all well-bred people, and many readers appear to have acted on that principle. By the eighteenth century, the authors did not always have in mind the actual royal court, but rather "people of fashion" in London or Paris. Nor did readers slavishly follow every rule in the manners books. Like all readers, the provincial gentry must have read selectively and adopted those portions that suited their circumstances. Many never read such books at all, learning from parents or teachers.

All these qualifications must be kept in mind, but courtesy books remain the essential guides to the principles of genteel behavior in the eighteenth century because they codified the ideals of polite society. Taken together, the courtesy books created an imaginary world, much as poetry or novels do, with plots, themes, characterizations, and myths. To understand the lives of the American gentry, at least in their parlors and formal rooms, we must make an effort to recover life in this courtesy-book world. Although a listing of the rules in Washington's "Rules of Civility" seems at first glance sterile, we can recover from that one book alone some of the basic themes of this life. Three stand out: respect for rank, bodily restraint, and regard for feelings.

Of the three, respect for rank now seems most exaggerated and unsuited to egalitarian society in the American colonies. Seventeenth-century courtesy books, especially those from France, reached an extreme in observations of deference to people of superior rank. Antoine de Courtin's *Rules of Civility*, though translated into English in 1671 and reprinted again in the eighteenth century, went well beyond the requirements of English courtesy. In Courtin's world every person, every place, and even many individual objects were ordered by rank, and every act was to be performed with these rankings in mind. Every room had a head and a foot, the location farthest from the door being the place of highest rank; in a bedroom, the bed was the place of honor. When walking into a bedroom, the person of highest honor was to be given the "upper hand," as it was called, closest to the bed. Places on sidewalks and seats in carriages were ranked, the back and right seat being uppermost in a carriage. As Courtin instructed, civility could not be practiced without reference to "1. Our own Age and Condition; 2. The Quality of the Person with whom we converse; 3. The Time; and 4. The Place of our Conversation." These conditions required attention to a hundred niceties of behavior. Chairs had their ranks: armchairs, backchairs, and stools in descending order, and the superior person was to occupy the superior chair. At the door of a great person, an inferior was not to knock, but only to scratch. Letters were to be written on paper graduated in size according to the rank of the recipient: bigger paper for bigger people. The space between the greeting, "My Lord, or Sir," and the beginning of the body of the letter was also to reflect the person's position: "the greater the Person, the greater the Blank."[19]

Courtin confessed that some people went too far even for his taste. "Some have been so *refin'd* in Foreign parts, that they will neither be cover'd nor sit with their backs turn'd toward the Picture of an eminent Person." The English editor of *Rules of Civility* occasionally noted where Courtin's own injunctions were to be disregarded. Punctilious observation of formal courtesy generally relaxed in the eighteenth century as people came to value ease and grace above rigorous correctness. But respect for rank still remained prominent in the protocols of proper conduct in England and America. Courtin offered a general proposition that continued to govern the gentry's conception of society: "All humane Conversation is either betwixt Equal and Equal, Inferiour and Superiour, or Superiour and Inferiour." One could not hope to conduct himself or herself properly on entering a room without immediately assigning a rank to every person there.

Although the rules that Washington copied from Hawkins's courtesy book contained none of Courtin's extreme prescriptions, rank figured in a large number of them. When walking with a superior, for example, he was to be given the right-hand place, and the inferior was to follow him as a woman was led at a dance. "Stop not till he does and be not the first that turns, and when you do turn let it be with your face towards him." Position was of considerable importance. "Walk not with him Cheek by Joul but Somewhat behind him; but yet in Such a Manner that he may easily Speak to you." Washington's book included rules about who got the best bedroom, about taking off and putting on hats, about how and when to speak, and who started first at a meal. The general principle was "Let thy ceremonies in Courtesie be proper to the Dignity of his place with whom thou conversest for it is absurd to act the same with a Clown and a Prince."[20]

We can never know how consistently anyone in the colonies followed these innumerable rules, but we would err in thinking that American egalitarianism would not tolerate such obsequities. Our adoption of republican government at the Revolution has partially obliterated the memories of our earlier commitment to monarchy and to a hierarchical society. America before the Revolution was less egalitarian in principle than it was in fact. Americans believed the creation was ordered by ranks that were to be respected and maintained. Certainly this was true for gentry families like the Ridgelys. We can see in young Charles's deferential letters to his parents one locus of hierarchy that existed in the colonies. Eleazar Moody's *School of Good Manners* indicates the way the Ridgely children might have behaved at home in the spirit of the respect shown in the letters. The Ridgelys may well have adopted Moody's injunction to "never speak to thy Parents without some Title of Respect, *viz.* Sir, Madam, &c according to their Quality." The Ridgely children might also have followed another directive: "never sit in the Presence of thy Parents without bidding, tho' no Stranger be present," and possibly even "If thou passest by thy Parents, at any Place where thou seest them, when either by themselves or with Company, Bow towards them."[21] Whatever the exact details of behavior, the children were surely taught forms of respect like these.

Beyond the family, the hierarchical ordering of people manifested itself in many settings. New Englanders in the seventeenth century assigned meetinghouse seats according to the worshippers' standing in town society, along with other marks of usefulness, and people objected if they believed they had been misplaced. Ministers in a procession to greet the royal governor in Massachusetts argued over their positions in the line. Entering Harvard students were ranked according to the social position of their parents. In eighteenth-century colleges, as Melvin Yazawa has pointed out, students were subjected to protocols nearly as demanding as those of Courtin. Freshmen, the lowest members of college society (servants were scarcely recognized as members at all), were forbidden to wear academic gowns or to walk with canes. They were to doff their hats in the front dooryard of the president's or a professor's house, and when the president approached, hats were to be removed at ten rods. Hats went off at eight rods for professors, and five rods for tutors. Holders of the B.A. degree were to be greeted as "sir," and graduates with an M.A. were to be called "Mr." Lines in academic processions were formed by rank, as was the seating in meetings. All this seemed perfectly appropriate to members of the gentry in training, suggesting that the courtesy-book rules about regard for rank conformed to the spirit of colonial society rather than contradicting it.[22]

Besides making us forget the importance of rank before the Revolution, our republican perspective may mislead us in interpreting its significance in colonial society. We think of a hierarchy as a ladder to be climbed, the higher the better, and we assume that everyone else thinks the same. Aspiration could certainly be found in colonial drawing rooms, and the royal courts that preceded them seethed with ambition and intrigues for power. But a central purpose of the courtesy books was to restrain ambition and to cloak aspiration in modesty.

Chesterfield told his son that ambition and avarice ruled at court. Consequently, courts "are the seats of politeness and good-breeding; were they not so they would be the seats of slaughter and desolation. Those who now . . . embrace, would affront and stab each other if manners did not interpose."[23] Restraints had to be strong precisely because ambition was so powerful. The courtesy books never encouraged readers to aspire to higher places; instead, the authors continually urged readers to give way to superiors, to remain firmly within one's rank, to make no effort to claim more than was one's due. Whereas we might expect our aspiring colonial subjects to purchase the finest clothes, the most elaborate furniture, the most pretentious houses they could afford, quite the opposite was required of them by the code of the courtesy books—the principle of respect for rank required readers to clothe and house themselves in the style most suitable to their positions in society. To do otherwise was a breach of taste and an affront to genteel principles. A truly refined person understood his precise position in society and regulated his conduct according to the proprieties of that rank.

The second aspect of courtesy-book behavior, bodily restraint, has been discussed at length in Norbert Elias's *History of Manners*. Following the manuals through the centuries, Elias charted what he called a rising threshold of embarrassment. The earliest books forbade certain public forms of bodily activity, such as passing wind, but still discussed them openly. In later courtesy books, the subject could not even be mentioned. It surprises us today to read John Locke's observations on how to regulate bowel movements in his *Some Thoughts Concerning Education* (1693), citing his own experience as evidence. A hundred years later, it would embarrass readers to find bowel movements mentioned in courtesy books at all; the subject had been transferred to medical manuals.[24]

So the threshold continued to rise from the sixteenth to the nineteenth century. Thomas Rodney wrote to his brother Caesar Rodney, Jr., in 1795 that after his, Thomas's, daughter Lavinia had a baby, he paid her a visit: "Sat a While but did not go up to see her As it appears to Me too Vulgar and Indecent to go Into Even the room of a daughter So Early after her delivery." Washington deleted most embarrassing references when he copied his rules, and exceeded the bounds of modern propriety only in rule 13: "If you See any filth or thick Spittle[,] put your foot Dexteriously upon it[;] if it be upon the Cloths of your Companions, Put it off privately, and if it be upon your own Cloths return Thanks to him who puts it off."[25]

The overall aim of the courtesy books seems to be a redefinition of the body in two ways: to create an immaculate body for purposes of polite conversation and to isolate one body from another, especially at the mouth. The books include many little rules for keeping the body clean and immaculate: "Keep your Nails clean and Short, also your Hands and Teeth Clean yet without Shewing any great Concern for them." In the same vein clothes were not to be "foul, unript or Dusty" and to be "Brush'd every day at least." Children were told to keep out of the dirt. By the same token, hands and fingers were to be kept out of food. Formerly people had dipped their bread into the sauce and picked up meat from the platter with their fingers. The introduction of forks in the late seventeenth century as an aspect of the general adoption of gentility was in reality part of the effort to keep the body immaculate. Grease on the clothes, an inevitable result of eating with fingers without napkins, became a mark of lower-class rudeness. Besides keeping the body and clothes free of grease and dirt, there were to be no reminders of the existence of base parts of the body. The rule "When in Company, put not your Hands to any Part of the Body, not usually Discovered," suggests not only sexual modesty but a sense that some bodily functions had to be hidden and never brought to mind in polite conversation. In company the body was to be presented and conceived of as immaculate, devoid of every form of filth and baseness.[26]

Despite these efforts to cleanse the body, polite people were never to presume to make bodily contact with others for fear of polluting them within the shells of their immaculate bodies. Once a spoon had gone into one's mouth, it was not to be used to ladle food out of the common dish. Even this remote contact of one mouth with another through a spoon, food in the dish, and another spoon offended polite people.[27] Perhaps for this reason, rank and bodily restraint converged at one singular point in the seventeenth century. A form of privilege at the court was to enjoy familiar intimacies with the monarch or the noble whom one attended. The closer one drew to a body, with the shields of clothing and formal setting removed, the higher the privilege. The great person showed his favor by inviting a guest or a lesser person into the bedroom. An elaborate etiquette of greeting was worked out in the most formal households for meeting and welcoming a person through the long line of reception rooms into the bedchamber or closet. The closer one approached to the innermost sanctuary, the greater the honor shown. Thus, at Versailles, to be present when the king rose and dressed, or undressed and retired, was a high honor afforded only to those Louis XIV wished to favor. Every morning and every evening, in the ceremonies of the levée and the couchée, nobles stood about while Louis dressed or undressed, and even remained as he sat upon the *chaise percée*. Louis disciplined himself to pass through this ritual night after night, even if he intended to sleep elsewhere, simply because his attendants expected the favor. Whereas a refined person ordinarily concealed and controlled his body, bodily familiarity of a great one was taken as an honor by those granted this intimacy in the seventeenth century.[28]

That practice fell away in the eighteenth century, leaving only remnants of earlier court life in the habits of a more bourgeois polite society. For a time noble levees still began with a select few in the great man's dressing room, and grand ladies might still entertain in their bedrooms while their maids did their toilets, not necessarily as a prelude to an amorous encounter, but to show favor to their closest friends. Those occasions were to disappear, but faint manifestations of the general principle of honor through intimacy held on. One of Washington's rules enjoined people "in Speaking to men of Quality do not lean nor Look them full in the Face, nor approach too near them[;] at lest Keep a full Pace from them." Putting face by face or body by body hinted of assuming a presumptuous degree of intimacy and thus honor. In the same spirit, among the grandest company on the most formal occasions, women wore dresses with the lowest necklines, showing more of themselves to a company of notables who merited the honor than they revealed to ordinary people on the street.[29]

The third principle of the courtesy books, regard for feelings, resembled in spirit the second, bodily restraint. Both assumed that polite society consisted of sensitive beings who might suffer irritation and offense if treated wrongly. Delicate sensibilities would draw back in revulsion at a mouth agape in a yawn or upon contact with a spoon that someone else had touched. Those same delicate sensibilities would take offense at emotional abuse, if a person's self-regard were in any way damaged. In Washington's "Rules," as in virtually every courtesy book, cautions about feelings outnumbered all the others. Rule number one summed up the intent of many: "Every Action done in Company, ought to be with Some Sign of Respect, to those that are Present." High rank was never to be an excuse for hurting someone. The rules required genteel people to avoid any feeling of degradation associated with a lower rank, just as the principles of hierarchy were meant to honor those of higher rank. In the courtesy-book world, respect was due to inferiors as well as superiors. The true gentleman, rather than shunning or scoffing at inferiors, showed affability and condescension to all who were below him.[30]

The rules conceived of people as within a protective shell never to be invaded. The admonition to "Jog not the Table or Desk on which Another reads or writes, lean not upon any one," relates closely to the shell around the immaculate body. Just as one was not to speak so closely as to bedew another with spittle, so it was wrong to read another's books or writings without permission or to be curious about private affairs or to approach people engaged in private conversation.[31]

But neither respect for rank nor regard for privacy encompasses the majority of the rules. They extended to include any behavior that might hurt another's self-esteem. One was not to appear glad at another's misfortunes, though an enemy; neither was one to make biting jests, appear happy when another was in pain, or stare at marks or blemishes. Scores of rules provided help for scores of potential unkindnesses. One was to "Speak not injurious Words neither in Jest nor Earnest[;] Scoff at none although they give Occasion." Polite people were to soften every stroke that might wound another. Ideally all were cheerful, sweet, modest, and cautious never to give offense. Among the polite, all gentle spirits might thrive and radiate in an atmosphere of kindness and respect.[32]

In *Some Thoughts Concerning Education,* a courtesy book with wide circulation in the colonies, John Locke put respect and sensitivity at the heart of courtesy. He downplayed the trivial rules put upon children by maids and governesses. "If by a little negligence in this part, the Boy should not put off his Hat, nor make Leggs very gracefully, a Dancing-master will cure that Defect, and wipe off all that plainness of Nature, which the A-la-mode People call Clownishness." What mattered was the inner spirit of civility, *"Respect and good Will* to all People," which if properly cultivated would always find the right way to express itself. Training a son, a parent was primarily to "be sure to keep up in him the Principles of good Nature and Kindness." The word Locke used for this quality was "well-bred." This breeding had nothing to do with one's ancestry but was virtually a synonym for civility. The deep inner principle of good breeding in relation to others was "that general Good will and Regard for all People, which makes any one have a care not to shew, in his Carriage, any contempt, disrespect, or neglect of them; but to express, according to the Fashion and Way of that Country, a respect and value for them, according to their Rank and Condition." With that instilled in a child, "the Ornaments of Conversation, and the out-side of fashionable Manners," Locke promised, "will come in their due time."[33]

Locke's long discourse on breeding helps us to understand the implicit aims of the courtesy-book writers. A young man, he said, was to avoid any form of contemptuous behavior. He must avoid "a Natural *Roughness* which makes a Man uncomplaisant to others, so that he has no deference for their inclinations, tempers, or conditions." It was the "sure badge of a Clown not to mind what pleases or displeases those he is with." The key words were "please" and "displease." The well-bred young man tried to please his hearers. He was not to contradict people in conversation or to be censorious. Even mild raillery, though common in polite company, should be avoided, for "by a small mistake or any wrong turn" it may turn into a taunt. Some pointed comment might sting its target, and "one angry body discomposes the whole Company, and the harmony ceases upon any such jarring." Civility should put everyone at his ease. Clownish behavior, besides appearing awkward, disrupted the smooth flow of talk and feeling.

In these passages, Locke gives us an idea of the ultimate social purpose of civility. Good breeding, Locke said in summary, "has no other use or end, but to make People easie and satisfied in their conversation with us." He envisioned a world of people susceptible to irritation and offense who wished for ideal ease and harmony. Pleasure came from enjoying a society of harmonious and easy intercourse. A primary aim of education was to produce a person able to put people at ease. "He that knows how to make those he converses with easie without debasing himself to low and servile flattery, has found the true art of living in the World, and being both welcome and valued every where."

For Locke, simple regard for feelings was not enough. To be truly pleasing, one must discover "the most acceptable, and agreeable way of expressing that Disposition." Regard for feelings made one civil; elegance in expression made one *"Well-fashion'd,"* by which Locke meant "that decency and gracefulness of Looks, Voice, Words, Motions, Gestures, and of all the whole outward Demeanour, which takes in Company, and makes those with whom we may converse, easie and well pleased." The eighteenth-century word for this quality was "complaisance," the ability to please. Chesterfield used the word often, hoping to see such graces emerge in his son. Chesterfield marked the key passages in Locke's book and recommended them to young Philip. In 1748 he wrote that he was sending "the famous Mr. Locke's book upon education; in which you will find the stress he lays upon the Graces, which he calls (and very truly) good-breeding."

Locke believed that complaisance and the graces that pleased were more important in a tutor than his learning. The only way to learn grace and make it habitual, natural, and easy was by observation; so the tutor had to be above all "well bred, understand the Ways of Carriage, and Measures of Civility in all the Variety of Persons, Times and Places" in order to instruct the pupil by example. In the real world, learning would be useless without breeding. "Breeding is that, which sets a Gloss upon all his other good qualities, and renders them useful to him, in procuring him the Esteem and Good Will of all that he comes near." Locke went so far as to say that other abilities counted against a person unless wrapped in these preeminent qualities of civility. "There cannot be a good quality in him which want of Breeding will not warp, and disfigure to his Disadvantage. Nay, Vertue and Parts . . . are not enough to procure a Man a good Reception." One's good qualities simply could not shine unless polished. "No body contents himself with rough Diamonds. . . . When they are polish'd, and set, then they give a lustre."

The influence of the cultivated and urbane person in the drawing rooms of England was so great that Locke, the Whig publicist and anything but a courtier, could imagine no personal quality that would advance a person in the world without civility. "Good qualities are the Substantial Riches of the

Mind, but 'tis good Breeding sets them off: And he that will be acceptable, must give Beauty as well as Strength to his Actions. Solidity or even Usefulness, is not enough: A graceful Way and Fashion, in every thing, is that which gives the Ornament and Liking." Although Locke's book crossed an ocean to reach the colonies and was read in circumstances far different from those in which it was written, the book told the American gentry that rustic integrity and simple virtue alone would not qualify them to fulfill their appointed roles in society.[34]

SOCIETY

WHILE striving to cultivate the genteel virtues in individual persons, the courtesy-book authors always wrote with a whole society in mind. Locke's thoughts about education referred to relationships among people, not to self-centered perfections; the self-discipline of a well-bred person was preparation ultimately for elevated exchanges among people of like breeding. The courtesy books projected a society as well as a person and can be read as blueprints for an ideal world.[35]

But it was a strangely desiccated world, notable as much for what it omitted as for what it included. The rules and descriptions made no mention of work, family, business, or politics. Servants were generally invisible. In Washington's "Rules," "Artificers and Persons of Low Degree" were mentioned only to be told how to act around "Lords, or Others of high Degree," and not in any ordinary part of their lives. The rule to "let your Discourse with Men of Business be Short and Comprehensive" instructed readers to dispatch practical affairs quickly and return to more important matters.[36] The books' highly specialized world of conversation and social intercourse took place at balls and assemblies or formal dinners, during strolls in gardens or along city streets, while riding in carriages, and perhaps most commonly in drawing rooms. All else was banished. Life in the courtesy books was confined almost entirely to the times and places of formal entertainment.

This existence seems nearly irrelevant to the hardworking American gentry with their deep involvement in farming, trade, and family. Gentility should have been dismissed as the frivolous pastime of the European aristocracy. Yet Americans faithfully copied, republished, and read courtesy books. More important, they built houses with spaces where the life of the courtesy-book world could be carried forward. William Corbit, the tanner, was not a perfect gentleman, but he subjected himself to a vast expense to provide places where polite life could be conducted. The Ridgelys' parlor contained broken teacups along with the better tea service and dinnerware, but the furnishings enabled the family to entertain in keeping with the genteel values they embraced. Judging by their houses and furnishings, the American gentry, despite the long hours they spent in tanyards, cornfields, or countinghouses, took pains to claim a place for themselves in the courtesy-book world.

For many of them, personal diaries became chronicles of entertainment. Of all the events that occurred in the day, dining at so-and-so's or an assembly or ball, or tea and conversation, the occasions of formal entertainment were most religiously noted; social events structured genteel diaries, as weather and the exchange of work and goods did the journals of farmers. That emphasis was true for socialites like Nancy Shippen and Jacob Hiltzheimer in Philadelphia as well as for men of affairs like George Washington and John Adams. Formal social gatherings climaxed days of preparation; on more than one occasion Nancy Shippen recorded that she spent the whole day getting ready for the assembly. Afterward, a grand ball provided material for conversation for days.[37]

As gentility spread in the American provinces, so did grand entertainments, but rather strictly along geographical lines. Balls and assemblies, tea parties and formal dinners were features of life in town and on great plantations, not in the countryside, not even among farmers of some standing. Matthew Patten, a prosperous New Hampshire farmer and frequent representative in the colonial Assembly from Bedford, kept a diary for thirty years through the third quarter of the eighteenth century without mentioning a single event that could be called formal entertainment. Ann Moore Ridgely, second wife of Charles and well connected with distinguished Philadelphia families, noted few social occasions at her Eden Hill house or in nearby Dover. She wrote humorously to her son Charles in 1785 that "Dover will be improv'd in fashionable and polite entertainment before your return I make no doubt: Your Brother is now at a Tea Party—it is the second, you know, that has been here lately and I suppose they will be kept up"; but she mentions very few others. Meanwhile her daughters were whirling from one event to another during visits to the city.[38]

Braintree, Massachusetts, and York, Pennsylvania, as local centers for their districts, had social events but only irregularly. The Duke de La Rochefoucauld-Liancourt observed during his visit to the United States after the Revolution that "it is generally understood that these kinds of dissipation belong only to the towns, and particularly to large cities." Charleston, Boston, New York, and Philadelphia, the great regional metropolises, were noted for the gaiety and energy of their social events from at least the late 1720s. The Chesapeake plantation mansions were also the scenes of frequent dances and formal dinners. William Byrd described dinners at his house and balls at the governor's palace even earlier than the

1720s. In the 1770s Philip Vickers Fithian discovered a steady round of dinners, dances, and balls at the houses neighboring on Nomini Hall.[39]

Away from these expected loci of gay social life, activities on a smaller scale were recorded in lesser colonial capitals and secondary towns like Portsmouth, New Hampshire; Fayetteville, North Carolina; Providence, Rhode Island; Litchfield, Connecticut; Reading, Pennsylvania; Chestertown, Maryland; and Alexandria, Virginia, by the Revolution or shortly afterward. At little village crossroads like Cantwell's Bridge and still farther into the countryside, much less gaiety was to be found.[40]

The infrequency of formal entertainments in the country did not mean that they had no effect on country people. Ann Ridgely, like John and Abigail Adams, was conscious of the society in town when she only participated vicariously through her children. Rural gentry could not have been entirely oblivious or they would not have built backcountry mansions designed for formal entertainments or purchased the proper accoutrements. The decoration in William Corbit's Cantwell's Bridge house is noted for its similarity to that in Samuel Powel's elegant Philadelphia mansion; the rooms in both houses were of comparable design and proportions, although the uses were entirely different. Powel and his wife were among Philadelphia's most extravagant hosts; their house seems to have been organized primarily for entertainment. Corbit's entertainments were far fewer. Yet he spent a small fortune to erect a house with a ballroom and two formal parlors capable of holding dances and fine dinners. We can only conclude that the extent of genteel influence was far wider than the loci of actual high-style entertainments, and that the rural gentry embraced the culture before they were capable of practicing it.[41]

Given the centrality of formal entertainments in the courtesy-book world, what can we learn about genteel culture from these events? They were the characteristic activity of manners-book society in that people from their pages were depicted almost exclusively at entertainments, as if fine manners suited them only for that. That being so, we should expect to discover the inner spirit of genteel society at such occasions. At assemblies and tea parties people would make their bravest effort to live by the rules and to create a society that realized courtesy-book ideals. In the books, rules were only words, usually written long ago and far away; the entertainments were staged for real eighteenth-century colonials in their houses, taverns, and assembly rooms. The descriptions of entertainments tell us about genteel life as it was actually lived.

We note at once that polite entertainments were exclusive in comparison with the openness of entertainment in the world before (and below) gentility. The great entertainments of the medieval world had been essentially public events. Large castle halls accommodated the lord's entire household at dinner, along with the guests and passersby who were seated at long tables ordered by rank. Villagers celebrated holidays in the outdoors where all could participate. Races, shooting contests, morris dances were open to all.

Traditional entertainments did not travel well to the New World, bound as they were to the customs of a place or the largesse of a local noble, but some of this spirit of public festivals came to the colonies in the seventeenth century. The colonists invented open public entertainments of their own. Election days, military training days, and later Pope's Day were boisterous public occasions. In New England, Harvard commencement attracted everyone looking for a good time, not just the graduates and alumni. In Virginia's less structured communities, funerals turned into drinking parties for the neighbors, so much so that dying men began to request that immoderate drinking be forbidden. At one funeral five gallons of wine, three gallons of brandy, a steer, and three sheep were consumed. No one was excluded from these events because of class. At a tavern party after a ship launching, John Adams met "a wild Rable of both sexes, and all Ages, in the lower Room, singing, dancing, fiddling, drinking flip and Toddy, and drams." Though violence and drunkenness might be censured, traditional entertainments included people from all levels of society and tolerated coarse behavior by rude peasants along with the refined conduct of gentle ladies should they choose to attend.[42]

Private gatherings for social purposes had also been open. In 1697 the Reverend Teakle, of Accomac County, Virginia, complained in court that while he was away from his house Elizabeth Parker and Samuel Doe and wife paid Teakle's daughter Margaret a visit. In the course of the day they decided to have music and sent for a slave fiddler. When one James Fairfax

The etching captures the open, flowing quality of traditional village festivities, as contrasted with the exclusive, formal nature of genteel entertainments.

came to fetch the slave, they invited Fairfax to stay and dance. Margaret "made a feast" for the company, and the dancing went on from Saturday night until eleven Sunday morning, during which time Jane Hall and James Addison joined the party. Like many other traditional parties, this one sprang up spontaneously, enveloping whoever was present. Caesar Rodney, Sr., certainly welcomed anyone to the harvest dances after each day's mowing, and more than once he had to send for his fiddle for a spur-of-the-moment dance.[43] The organizers showed no concern that the presence of the wrong people would mar the occasion.

The opposite was true for polite entertainments. Invitations for tea parties ensured that only designated guests would attend. Little Peggy Livingston, Nancy Shippen's five-year-old daughter, invited twenty little misses "by card" to a tea party at the Philadelphia house of her grandparents. Many such invitation cards to eighteenth-century teas have survived two centuries, some indication of their value to recipients. In the evenings Peggy's mother sometimes served tea and played chess with visitors who happened by, but these guests came from a small circle of intimate friends. She would not have welcomed any neighbor who elected to drop in. Otto Louis, one of Nancy Shippen's beaux, walked by her house and saw company in the front parlor. The young Frenchman paused to peer in and later drew a sketch of what he saw, but he did not go to the door. Though he longed to see Nancy and was a frequent and welcome visitor at the Shippen house, Louis did not presume to call unexpectedly and invade the circle of invited guests. The elaborate ritual of calling and being called on, the reception or nonacceptance of callers preoccupied the gentry by the end of the eighteenth century. Nabby Adams, after her marriage to Colonel William Smith, refused to call on Lady Temple, a social superior in Philadelphia, because Sir John Temple had not yet received Colonel Smith; Nabby worried about how to greet Lady Temple when they met in company. The invisible lines defining inclusion and exclusion could be the cause of great anguish in the higher reaches of society.[44]

Dancing masters organized assemblies in the larger cities in the 1720s and 1730s, and at midcentury groups of private citizens sponsored still more ambitious gatherings. Philadelphia had an assembly in operation by 1749, New York by 1745, Boston by 1744, and lesser cities like Cambridge, Massachusetts, and Alexandria, Virginia, in the 1760s. Assemblies were formed to bring together larger groups than could assemble in single houses. In Philadelphia the assembly initially met in a house and store owned by Alexander Hamilton, and was so large as to require shifts: one group of eighty gathered on one evening and another of the same size two weeks later. People danced, played cards, talked, and enjoyed refreshments.

Though the membership encompassed a larger group than any one individual's circle of friends, the assemblies were self-consciously and resolutely exclusive. Admission was by ticket, for which one paid a price. In the first Philadelphia season, a ticket was 40*s.*; the next year the price went up to £3. The cost in itself excluded many, and judging by the complaints of the "mechanics," some who could afford to pay had been left out. The tickets to concerts by the St. Cecilia Society in Charleston were also intended to exclude the unrefined.[45] The managers of the concerts defined the city's elite population by issuing tickets to a certain group of gentlemen, who in turn invited ladies. The assemblies enabled the chosen group to recognize one another and to come together to enjoy pleasures attainable only in a select and genteel company.[46] Exclusivity implied a desire to create an artificial social environment, one that could not exist without consciously denying admission to coarse and vulgar people.

The creation of a beautiful setting was the second characteristic of formal entertainments. After a few early Philadelphia assemblies met in what seems to have been Mr. Hamilton's warehouse, there was a growing interest in the construction of spaces in taverns and of special assembly halls more worthy of the events, in imitation of the assembly rooms in English provincial cities. In private houses, where most of the entertainments took place, beautification was an essential principle. A large percentage of the fine goods that have survived from the years after 1690 adorned the rituals of formal entertainment. Cards could be played on any surface, just as a plain table could support a container of tea. Yet beautifully carved and finished tables of expensive materials were constructed specifically for those purposes. Other activities must have taken place on and around those tables, but tea and cards have provided the names, implying that those were the central activities which the cost and beauty of the tables were meant to honor.

Beyond the furniture, craftsmen shaped and decorated an endless array of forms in ceramics, glass, pewter, and silver to facilitate formal entertainment: elaborate tea equipage, plates, tumblers, punch bowls, tureens, wine coolers, knives and forks, sauceboats, dining tables, armchairs and side chairs, and on and on. Craftsmen like Wedgwood dreamed up new materials, such as his famous creamware, to achieve the most refined effects. Costly silver was fashioned into tea caddies and teaspoons. Forms were invented for each function associated with entertainment: special silver trays for cake, large silver tubs to cool wine and hold wineglasses, spoons specifically designated for dessert. Purchasers and makers alike believed that the accoutrements of formal entertainment merited the finest craftsmanship and materials to make beautiful settings for teas and dinners.[47]

Beautification was essential because the activities of polite entertainment were not in themselves distinctive. Everything that went on in Nancy Shippen's parlor or the Philadelphia assembly—eating, drinking, cards,

Much of the labor and skill of eighteenth-century craftsmen went into the creation of attractive environments intended primarily for entertainment. Scores of beautiful objects in silver, pewter, ceramic, wood, and fabric contributed to the exaltation of the activities in the rooms.

music, dancing, conversation, flirtation—had long been pictured by genre painters at peasant fairs and in the humblest roadside taverns. Simple laborers and broad-bottomed burghers sat on stools and benches pulled up to plank tables to drink, talk, eat, and play cards, or to rise and dance while a fiddler in a rough country costume made music. Only tea drinking began as an exclusively elite practice, and that was rapidly adopted by ordinary people.

The similarities of high and low entertainments sometimes put polite society in a contradictory position. The government, for example, outlawed cardplaying in taverns in order to control the excesses that sometimes went on there, while polite companies passionately enjoyed whist and loo in their own houses. Cards played on a mahogany table by the light of candles in silver holders, the genteel must have believed, was different from cards in the greasy hands of a day laborer in a dark tavern with a mug of beer at his elbow. The beautiful objects, along with clothes and manners, transformed cardplaying, as they did eating, drinking, and dancing, into an activity performed with "the utmost decency and decorum." The beautiful environment helped to change ordinary forms of vulgar entertainment into cultivated expressions of enlightenment and civilization.[48]

Exclusivity and the beautified environment contributed to a third characteristic of formal entertainments, their theatricality. The great balls were elaborately staged performances, with guests serving as both performers and audience. People did not attend such events to relax, but to present their most beautiful, gracious, and pleasing selves. The guests were performers on the stage that the host provided for the pleasure and delight of the guests.

Philadelphia entertainments reached a pinnacle at the ball of the French minister M. Luzerne on the occasion of the birthday of the Dauphin. Luzerne erected on the grounds next to his house a special dancing building, sixty feet wide on the street side, with painted and festooned pillars and a profusion of banners and pictures. Benjamin Rush said:

> the scene almost exceeded description. The numerous lights distributed through the garden, the splendor of the room we were approaching, the size of the company which was already collected, and which consisted of about seven hundred persons, the brilliancy and variety of their dresses, and the band of music, which had just begun to play, had together an effect which resembled enchantment.

A young lady in the party said her mind was "carried beyond and out of itself." At another French party given in New York while the federal govern-

The rural people in this scene were doing virtually everything that transpired at genteel entertainments—dancing, listening to music, eating, drinking, talking, flirting. Gentility transformed the ambience rather than the content of entertainments.

Tavern life seemed degrading to the elite, yet they played cards and drank in their own parlors. Elegant tables, finely finished chairs, and the attire and postures of the players transformed the meaning of these activities.

ment resided there, an entire wall in the refreshment room "was covered with shelves, filled with cakes, oranges, apples, wines of all sorts, ice creams, etc., and highly lighted up." Guests ordered anything they wanted.[49]

Very few could approach the splendor of these grand fetes. When a New York girl, Sally McKean, wrote home about President Washington's first levee in Philadelphia, she said, "You never could have had such a drawing-room; it was brilliant beyond any thing you can imagine," suggesting that other hostesses envied and would wish to emulate the brilliance achieved in exalted places. Philip Fithian described the setting of a plantation ball in Virginia in 1773. "The room looked luminous and splendid," he noted afterward, "four very large candles burning on the table where we supped; three others in different parts of the Room; a gay, sociable Assembly, and four well instructed waiters!" Not having learned to dance during his Presbyterian upbringing in New Jersey, Fithian thought the total effect of well-trained dancers in the ballroom as splendid as a staged performance.

> There were several Minuets danced with great ease and propriety; after which the whole company joined in country-dances, and it was indeed beautiful to admiration, to see such a number of young persons, set off by dress to the best advantage, moving easily, to the sound of well performed Music, and with perfect regularity, tho' apparently in the utmost disorder.

Ingenious hosts created beautiful effects by using confectionery sculpture as a table centerpiece, candles shining from tables or walls, a menu of special delicacies, an array of gleaming silver, the grandeur of a room's architecture, or the beauty and distinction of the guests. Of differing degrees of cost and complexity, these enabled the host to achieve some measure of "brilliance."[50]

At large events such as the assemblies, a manager staged the performance and scheduled the happenings, a certain order of dances, for example, creating a well-regulated ball. As part of the regulation, the highest-ranking figure present was accorded the right of presiding. The king had that honor at court, and a dancing manual published early in the seventeenth century in English said that, lacking the monarch himself, "at all regulated Balls a King and Queen are chosen," and "it is they who according to rule begin the dancing." Americans apparently did not follow that practice, but they did recognize colonial political authority at their entertainments. At the first Philadelphia assembly the governor selected one of the ladies and opened the dance. Samuel Sewall, an enemy of balls, persuaded the governor of Massachusetts not to attend an early ball in Boston, although the governor believed that propriety required him to preside. In the new government under the Constitution, the managers of a ball, wishing to observe the proprieties, gave Washington a role so monarchical in character that Jefferson's republican sensibilities were offended. He reported that President and Mrs. Washington sat on a sofa at the head of the room, raised several steps. Each gentleman, before he began to dance, led his partner to the foot of the sofa and made a low obeisance to the President and his lady. After each dance, the gentleman brought his partner back again to the foot of the sofa for new obeisances before retiring to chairs.[51]

Regulation by rank was part of the overall performance staged by the host; at the same time, each guest staged his or her individual performance. As the party went on, each guest thought of his role, his audience, and the impressions he was making. Guests had to be conscious of individual appearances, just as the host thought of the adornment of the entertainment rooms. Invited to a large party at the house of the Philadelphia Powels, Nancy Shippen said she

> spent great part of the day in making preparation—I wish'd to look well. Sett off about six oclock—my glass told me I look'd well—was dressed in pink with a gause peticoat—an Elegant french Hat on, with five white plumes nodding different ways—a bouquet of natural flowers—and a white satin muff.

On another occasion, Nancy could not consider attending a grand ball in honor of Washington because her hairdresser had arrived too late to do her hair properly. Although she would be caught up in the flow of talk and laughter at these events, she knew she would be watched and must look her best. Her brother Tommy, writing after getting a report on Nancy's social life, spoke of the double mind that characterized polite people at their gatherings. "I should have liked very much to see Papa attract the admiration of the Ballroom by his graceful minuet, and not less to observe you with your handsome partners setting an example worthy of imitation."[52]

The pleasures of the dance might well be exceeded by the pleasures of being watched and admired, a stance that moral critics derided. One English critic re-created the post-ball reflections of a young woman. Are you, he asked, "never chagrined about some punctilio of precedency, or elated on account of the extraordinary notice that was taken of you? especially if it was your happy lot to open the *Ball*, or to lead up the first country-dance with the most honourable personage in the room?" The self-consciousness of the performance could detract from the desired graciousness.[53]

The entertainment as performance in turn evoked critical reviews. Diarists and letter writers reported on balls and evening diversions as if they were producing a theatrical review, evaluating the performance and the performers. Benjamin Rush's description of the fete at M. Luzerne's was in reality an enthusiastic review. Reporters could be less charitable. George Washington, frequently a host himself, attended a ball organized by the merchants of Alexandria in the 1760s. Though not entirely disdainful, Washington looked over the arrangements with a critical eye and made a diary entry. He noted that "pockethandkerchiefs served the purposes of Table Cloths and Napkins," and refreshment consisted largely of tea and coffee that could not be distinguished from sweetened hot water, along with a "great plenty of Bread and Butter." He concluded with amused disdain that "I shall therefore distinguish this Ball by the Stile and title of the Bread and Butter Ball." Alexandria was not notably backward in its social development, but Nicholas Cresswell, a decade later, observed of a ball there that it "looks more like a Bacchanalian dance than one in a polite assembly." One way or the other, participants commonly evaluated the social occasions they attended, as when Josiah Quincy briefly noted, "Dined with Roger Smith Esq.—good deal of company—elegant table;—one cloth removed, a handsome dessert, good wines, and much festivity."[54]

Critics felt no compunctions about judging the people at social occasions with candid, often harsh remarks. The good-hearted Nancy Shippen, after reporting that "the most delightful company has just left me, I never spent a more lively Evening," launched into sharp characterizations of each member of the "delightful company." It was one thing to observe that "Miss Moore is vastly agreeable, and very sprightly, Mrs. H. Moore is an Elegant Woman, but rather haughty in her manners," but quite another to go on with "Miss s. Shippen is pretty in the face but badly Made, and appears to have a fund of good humor. Miss Molly Shippen is very ugly and very formal in her manners, but very good natur'd."[55]

While evenhanded in praise and blame, the young hostess seems less than charitable in her judgments. The conventions of social comment required candor. Philip Fithian, who felt out of place in the gay world of the Chesapeake and who scarcely considered himself a connoisseur of fashionable people, fell into the same practice. Though ordinarily favorable in his judgments, he was capable of recording that the daughters of Captain Middleton seemed "aukward in their Behaviour, and dull, and saturnine in their Disposition." Abigail Adams, a very sensible woman, continually appraised the women she encountered in the fashionable world and ranked them. She patriotically concluded that English beauties failed to outshine American women, proving the point with descriptions of the Duchess of Devonshire as "masculine in appearance" and Lady Salisbury as having a bad complexion, whereas Mrs. Bingham of Philadelphia was "the finest woman I ever saw." The passing of such judgments brought Adams great pleasure. She wrote John on the eve of his visit to a young woman that she wanted "her character drawn by your pen." "I know you are a critical observer, and your judgment of people generally plases me." From the frequency of the critiques, it would seem that the "judgment of people" generally pleased everyone in polite society.[56]

Small wonder, then, that every detail of behavior had to be carefully practiced. Any false move could come under the scrutiny of a critical eye. A French book reprinted frequently in America told the young woman for whom it was written, "wherever you are, imagine that you are observed, and that your Behaviour is attentively scanned by the rest of the Company all the while, and this will oblige you to observe yourself, and to be constantly on your Guard."[57] Chesterfield explained to his son why a young man must learn to enter a room without embarrassment, the simplest act of the young performer. Anyone unprepared might appear ridiculous "to the last degree."

> An awkward country fellow, when he comes into company better than himself, is exceedingly disconcerted. He knows not what to do with his hands or his hat, but either puts one of them in his pocket, and dangles the other by his side; or perhaps twirls his hat on his fingers, or fumbles with the button. If spoken to, he is in a much worse situation, he answers with the utmost difficulty, and nearly stammers.

What humiliation, to look like a rustic, fumbling with a button. How necessary to play the gentleman "who is acquainted with life, enters a room with gracefulness and a modest assurance, addresses even persons he does not know, in an easy and natural manner, and without the least embarrassment." One might take great pleasure in exhibiting an easy assurance and even more from shining on a public stage, but one also exposed oneself, if unready, to the withering blast of public scorn.[58]

These dangerous currents ran below the surface of formal entertainments in polite society, but the moving spirit at the events themselves was the pursuit of ease, the last of the qualities to be noted. Ease meant the free flow of good spirits in talk, laughter, and dance, without the emotional turbulence of offense being given or taken. A traveler who attended a Virginia wedding of a Beverly and a Johnson commented that after a full day of dancing and eating, dancing began again. "We were all extremely happy in each other's company, the ladies being perfectly free and easy and at the same time elegant in their manners." Ease implied a measure of friendly intimacy and openness within the framework of proper manners. Ease did not grow out of uninhibited informality, but depended on the discipline of all members of the company, their strict regard for the feelings of others, and their careful observance of proprieties. Beginning with that discipline, the well-bred person grew into complaisance, the ability to please, from which came the general ease and harmony possible in select companies. The great virtue of Philadelphia women compared with Bostonians, Nabby Adams thought, was "that they are more easy in their manners, and discover a greater desire to render themselves acceptable." That complaisance and the ease of the whole company equaled good breeding. The major achievement of the huge dance in Philadelphia at M. Luzerne's with seven hundred present, Benjamin Rush thought, was "the harmony of the evening." "The whole assembly behaved to each other as if they had been members of the same family." The word Rush chose to describe the experience was "joy."[59]

VIRTUE

SUCH scenes comprised what was called the gay world, the beau monde, or the fashionable world. The gay world was the world of formal entertainment where select groups of refined and polished people came together in beautiful settings to please one another with their grace and charm in an attempt to achieve the happiness of perfect ease. Though limited to towns and the great plantations, the influence of that sphere reached far beyond the rooms of formal entertainments. Young Mary Ridgely, raised in Dover, wrote to her brother after a season in Philadelphia with the Cadwaladers to tell him that "I know it is my duty to go home but really I had rather live here on bread and water than give up the society I enjoy here." Ann Ridgely insisted that her daughter Mary return to the dull routines of rural life in Kent County. Like others of the country gentry, Ann knew her life went on outside that radiant circle, and she betrayed a characteristic ambivalence. She stated emphatically that she preferred country life for herself and her children. "I think such a life as the fashionable World now leads would be very far from a pleasing one to me, and if I was worth ten thousand a year, I am very sure I should prefer a Country education for my children." Still she wished to save her children from the coarseness and torpidity of a rustic life.

> Do not think, from this, that I would chuse my daughters mere joans or my Sons clowns; I could not endure such a thought. I would desire both to be truly polite, and thoroughly instructed in every branch of education that could render them genteel, agreeable, sensible, and every way elegantly accomplish'd.

Alexander Graydon, a dashing Philadelphia beau, noticed at once the difference in gentry manners in rural York. He was well received by a leading citizen, but "with that formal, theoretical kind of politeness, which distinguishes the manners of those who constitute the *better sort*, in small secluded towns." Ann wished to erase those telltale signs of rusticity in her children and still to avoid fashionable affectation, which she despised. "I cannot suppose it impossible to have them thus polish'd," she wrote, "without being divested of the sweet, innocent, engaging simplicity and industry of the peasant, despising extravagance, affectation, and frippery of all kinds."[60]

Ann Ridgely found life in the world of fashion lacking and spoke for simpler, truer virtues. The authors of manners books themselves never claimed that their rules constituted a complete guide to life. Courtin, spokesman for high French fashion in the seventeenth century, recommended in his introduction two books on the Christian virtues as companion volumes to his treatise on civility. Only when built on a solid foundation, he explained, could civility "be a real Ornament." "Whereas without the concomitancy of Vertue, it is nothing else but a Phantasm, or Masquerade." Chesterfield presumed his student "already instructed in the principles of religion, and necessity of moral virtues; (for without these he must be most unhappy)."[61]

Guidance in the virtues could be drawn from the handbooks on piety and moral conduct that proliferated along with manners books in the seventeenth and eighteenth centuries. The many moralistic guidebooks published in England were naturally imported into America and republished in American editions. *The Friendly Instructor* went through nine editions after publication in Philadelphia in 1745; Moody's *School of Good Manners* had its more puritanical section and a long list of rules about piety and morality. The most popular of these books was *The Whole Duty of Man*, attributed to Richard Allestree, a seventeenth-century royalist clergyman and later Regius Professor of Divinity at Oxford. The book went through nearly a hundred English editions in as many years. *The Whole Duty of Man* was among the most common books in the libraries of southern colonial gentlemen in the eighteenth century and was well known in the North. The manners-book authors assumed that the existence of these books, along with the routine preachments of the Christian clergy, would complete the education of an ideal gentleman or lady.[62]

The moral guidebooks taught a different lesson than the manners books. *The Whole Duty of Man* enjoined submission to God and continual acts of piety and charity and could easily have been divided into sermons. Complaisance, shining in the best company, and the danger of ridicule had no place there. The book came out of the Christian tradition, not classical urbanity or Renaissance civility, and its world did not exist in parlors or assembly rooms. The people on its pages lived in families, dealt with one another in business and on farms, went to taverns for homely entertainments, prepared for the church sacraments, and looked inward at their hearts for signs of pride, love, and submission. Apparel was to hide nakedness, fence the cold, and indicate rank and gender, not to make an impression. Exclusivity, beautiful environments, and theatrical entertainments were not mentioned, although one could imagine the author finding pride and extravagance in such affairs. The guidebooks for gentility and those for morality and piety stood apart from one another, not contradicting so much as never meeting.[63]

The disparities did not prevent the eighteenth-century gentry from blending them into a single system for living. People known to live in the courtesy-book world owned and read *The Whole Duty of Man.* The two ethics lived side by side, the reader resolving the disparities; sometimes, as in *The School of Good Manners,* the books were bound together in a single volume.

But if melded in actual lives, the contradictions in the two systems remained and with significant implications. The presence of such tensions within genteel minds opened the fashionable world to criticism from within. The values that brought gay dissipations to judgment were held by ladies and gentlemen of fashion themselves. Moralists could indict gentility by its own standards. Ann Ridgely's desire that, along with a polite education, her children should not lose "the sweet, innocent, engaging simplicity and industry of the peasant, despising extravagance, affectation, and frippery of all kinds" was more than the yearning of a motherly heart. The sense of two sides to life, neither to be neglected, each with dangers and drawbacks, was characteristic of eighteenth-century gentility everywhere, the unavoidable consequence of two incompatible traditions blending in individual lives.

From the beginning, satires, mockeries, and indictments of civility warned of the dangers of court life in books written to prepare people to shine at court. Even courtiers knew that fashion quickly degenerated into outward show and vain glitter. In the end, the quest of the courtesy-book world was to separate the false from the true, to purge hypocrisy and vanity, to embrace the best qualities in Christian morality and Renaissance civility, and so to create refined and worthy hearts and minds.[64]

CHAPTER III

Bodies and Minds

THE word "gentility" derives from the French *gentil*, which entered English usage twice, first in the thirteenth century, when it turned into the English "gentle," and again in the late sixteenth century, when *gentil* kept more of its French pronunciation and became "genteel." This second migration occurred when Renaissance courtesy books were being translated into English and the word was useful to sum up the new style. Frequency of favorable usage seems to have peaked in the eighteenth century, at the time of the broad effort of the English middle class to assimilate courtly ideals and civility. By then it was enmeshed in a complex web of meaning involving kindred terms like "polite," "polished," "refined," "tasteful," "well-bred," "urbane," "civil," "fashionable," "gay," "beau monde," words that highlighted one or another facet of gentility.[1]

By the eighteenth century, "genteel" was used to describe a host of objects, situations, persons, and habits. There were genteel wigs, genteel saddles, genteel speech and letters. Martha Washington ordered a genteel nightgown from a genteel shop in London. Genteel persons with genteel educations practiced genteel professions. Strangers in taverns or boardinghouses were able to evaluate the gentility of the other guests, or of the host, the food, the furnishings. There were genteel schools and genteel towns. The word had vast scope and energy.[2]

In addition to its reach, "genteel" was powerful in the sense of commanding value. Not until the nineteenth century did the word take on a negative cast. In 1766, when a new innkeeper advertised her intention to keep "a very genteel plentiful house," she was promoting its virtues and appealing to the best people to patronize her establishment. She could charge more for genteel rooms and fare, and the same was true for all genteel objects. A genteel salver was of greater worth than a plain, neat tray; a genteel house on a genteel street commanded a higher price than a plain house. By the same token, genteel people were more highly valued than plain people and elicited better treatment from innkeepers and shopkeepers. At an inn in New Castle, Delaware, in 1744, Dr. Alexander Hamilton noted with amusement that a fellow traveler who came to breakfast "in a greasy jacket and breeches and a dirty worsted cap" got "scraps of cold veal for breakfast," rather than the better food served to other guests.[3] Gentility bestowed social power.

What did all this mean? The extensive use and social power of the word "genteel" leads us to surmise that it occupied a central position in a far-reaching cultural system, but the precise definition of gentility is elusive. The gathering of a wide variety of objects, actions, and people under the single head of gentility implies that all of the nouns modified by the adjective "genteel" had something in common. But the exact nature of that quality, like the essences of many culturally influential words, is difficult to define.

All that can be said for certain is that genteel things and actions were associated with genteel people. Close association with polite society was likely to invest objects or practices with an aura of gentility. But that answer begs the question, for what made polite people genteel in the first place, giving them the power to make other things genteel? If a wig acquired genteel qualities when genteel people wore it, what other than the wig made people genteel? Their clothes, their posture, their speech perhaps, but what in each of these was genteel? The extensive use of the word and its verifiable social power is evidence of its cultural importance, but how are we to understand gentility's basic nature?

If gentility is difficult to grasp abstractly, perhaps it can be understood concretely, beginning with the actions and qualities of specific individuals who were reputedly genteel. One such person was Alexander Graydon, a young Philadelphian who gained a reputation as a dashing man-about-town while training as a lawyer. Sent to York, Pennsylvania, in 1773 for practical experience, he encountered at his boardinghouse a fellow attorney. "He was an Irishman," Graydon wrote in his memoirs, "a man of middle age—the extent of whose attainments was certainly nothing more, than in a coarse, vulgar hand, to draw a declaration; and in equally vulgar arithmetic, to sum up the interest due upon a bond. His figure was as awkward as can well be imagined, and his elocution exactly corresponded with it." Though the description began disparagingly, Graydon actually admired the man. "Justice, however, requires it should be added, that his want of brilliant qualities, was compensated by an adequate portion of common sense, by unblemished integrity, and liberality in his dealings with the poor."

With such honorable qualities, why did Graydon not immediately recognize the Irishman's virtues? Why did he begin the description disparagingly? Graydon had to defend the Irishman because the man lacked genteel qualities: he wrote in a coarse, vulgar hand; his arithmetic was vulgar; his figure was awkward and his speech the same. Graydon's sharp eye noted one specific deficiency after another which together comprised vulgarity, a failing for which only a number of sterling virtues could compensate. Gentility required that handwriting, speech, and posture all be properly composed, and the Irishman's lacks in each of these details disqualified him as a genteel person.[4]

Graydon's comments imply that the genteel person was a set of aspects, almost a checklist of desirable traits and abilities. There seems to be no other way to recapture gentility than to assemble these diverse and at times confusing aspects and attempt to see how they came together in a unified whole. The courtesy books resorted to the same mode of analysis when they reduced their lessons to a set of maxims, as in Washington's "Rules of Civility" or Chesterfield's letters to his son. The acquisition of gentility required attention to a hundred details of conduct which the well-trained eye instantly observed and which courtesy-book writers summed up in their rules. A French courtesy book for young women, republished in America, informed readers that "there are Rules for all our Actions, even down to *Sleeping with a good Grace.* Life is a continual Series of Operations, both of Body and Mind, which ought to be regulated and performed with utmost Care."[5] In instructing neophytes, the courtesy books set out the rules for body and mind, and we can seek to delineate gentility by the same method, examining the specifics of the genteelly regulated body and the gentle mind.

REGULATED BODIES

AMONG the aims of the courtesy books, as we have seen, was the creation of an immaculate body through cleansing and isolation. Alexander Hamilton's inn mate at New Castle in 1744 bore the certain mark of vulgarity in the grease on his jacket. The man failed to keep himself clean and paid the price in loss of respect. Recipe books, which began to circulate in the colonies in the eighteenth century, provided formulas for removing grease spots from clothes. Washstands, a new furniture form, appeared in Thomas Chippendale's *Gentleman and Cabinet-Maker's Director* (1754), implying that washing the body merited a unique and elaborate furniture form. While washstands of this quality do not appear in American inventories, beautiful dressing tables do. These last emerged in late-seventeenth-century England as the upper middle class embraced gentility. Along with special shaving furniture, which was the male equipment for accomplishing one's toilet, the dressing table speaks for a heightened attention to the cleanliness, the adornment, and the fashionable manipulation of the immaculate body.[6]

All of the cleanliness exercises were part of a larger campaign to regulate the body. Clean hands and greaseless clothes were aspects of bringing the body to perfection through careful discipline. Regulation of the mouth received particular attention. In the matter of yawning, for example, the books advised learners to "Speak not in your Yawning, but put Your handkercheif or Hand before your face and turn aside." The rules forbade people from talking with their mouths full, stuffing so much into the mouth that the jowls bulged out, rinsing their mouths in the presence of others, spitting into the fire, walking with the mouth open, or breathing loudly. In every way the mouth had to be kept under firm control. "Do not Puff up the Cheeks, Loll not out the tongue rub the Hands, or beard, thrust out the lips, or bite them or keep the Lips too open or too Close."[7]

The mouth seemed to be associated with the base parts of the body and would have been concealed if speaking and eating had not made accessibility necessary. Short of hiding the mouth altogether, strict regulation had to bring it under perfect control. Rule after rule in Washington's book told the young man to keep his mouth closed, not to let his tongue hang out or jaw go slack. The look of a sagging mouth gave one the visage of an ignorant peasant. The firm, composed mouth, so indelibly associated with Washington, was the facial posture of a gentleman, a model for the treatment of the genteel person's entire body.

Chesterfield said that the limits on bodily actions were innumerable. "It would be endless to particularise all the instances in which a well-bred man shews his politeness in good company, such as not yawning, singing, whistling, warming his breech at the fire, lounging, putting his legs upon the chairs and the like, familiarities every man's good sense must condemn, and good-breeding abhor." Chesterfield objected to laughter, partly again because of the open mouth. He thought frequent, loud laughter the mark of a "weak mind" and a "low education." Wit "may create a smile, but as loud laughter shews, that a man has not the command of himself, every one, who would wish to appear sensible, must abhor it."[8] Failure to regulate the body left one looking clownish and ridiculous.[9]

To achieve artistic control of one's physical being, a primary rule was to remain erect, to keep the line from the base of the spine through the neck to the back of the head as straight as possible. To add to the upright posture, the chin was held up. While sitting for portraits, people turned their heads and even inclined them but without allowing their chins to fall. Shoulders were kept down and back with the chest and abdomen protruding. Hips were held back behind the line of the chest; when observed from the side, the body formed a slight S curve, from shoulders down the spine to the hips. As students of posture have observed, the genteel stance resembled the positions of formal ballet. Ballet received its first impetus from Louis XIV, himself a devoted dancer who received his sobriquet the "Sun King" from a role he danced in a court ballet. At the time, the dancers were aristocratic members of the court, and dancers assumed the ideal body positions of all who aspired to grace of movement.[10]

Colonial portraits, especially before 1760, almost invariably display this upright posture. If the colonial gentry did not always hold the ideal pose, we can still believe that they assumed it for formal occasions. At their entertainments, on occasions of state, and in the presence of superiors who required respect, genteel people stood and sat with their backs and heads straight, their chins up, and their shoulders down and back, much as they appear in their portraits. "The proper Posture of one that sits," one courtesy book said, "is to have that Part of his Body from the Waste upwards, upright, tho' free and moveable, and the lower Part firm, close to his Seat, and motionless, without crossing his Legs; for this is the respectful Behaviour which Civility exacts from an inferiour, in the presence of his Superiour." Portraitists obligingly placed their clients in genteel poses, just as they clothed sitters in fashionable dress. Nancy Shippen's mother wrote to ask whether she was learning to hold her head and shoulders properly along with how to enter and leave a room. The charge for teaching all of this fell upon the dancing masters, whose influence grew year by year, judging from the ubiquity of itinerant instructors. By the time of the Revolution even rural gentry families like the Ridgelys took dancing instruction.[11]

Fashionable clothing helped genteel people to hold their bodies in place. Men's coats pulled the shoulders down and back into the prescribed postures, and under their suit coats, men wore snug waistcoats. Before midcentury, the waistcoat, which reached from the shoulders nearly to the knees, ordinarily hung unbuttoned at the top with some lacy shirtfront showing. After midcentury, the waistcoat was invariably buttoned at the waist, and the name waistcoat, rather than vest, suggests that this place on the coat had special significance. An unbuttoned front would have been exceedingly informal, an affront to a visitor. Beyond that, the buttoned coat held the lower back in its proper position, serving for men something of the same function as stays did for women. The frame of bone stays, fastened tightly around women's midriffs, held them in the proper erect position, and their dresses usually fit as tightly at the waist as the waistcoats did.[12]

Erect posture was essential, but sometimes it was overdone. Urban gentlemen smiled at overly correct country people for holding themselves too stiffly. Ease of bearing was as important to the gentleman as ease of the company was to a brilliant entertainment. The bent elbow, the hand on the hip, the feet at an angle, and the open relaxed hand with palm up signified the sitter's ease. In the last half of the eighteenth century, the desire for ease grew stronger. Striking portraits exist of elegant women leaning against pillows or on the upholstered arms of sofas; John Singleton Copley painted

Mrs. Thomas Gage resting her head upon her hand. Copley portrayed John Hancock at his desk with his legs crossed, a posture which would have been highly informal and unsuitable a century earlier. In this later period, Matthew Pratt depicted himself leaning forward with his elbows on a table and arms crossed. The genteel thought it the height of elegance to relax their formal standards and move into these easy poses.[13]

But body regulation was not to be entirely relaxed. The recognized modes of vulgar dress and deportment had to be avoided. A coatless man with a free-flowing shirt and an unbuttoned vest would be instantly identified as a tradesman or laborer, never a gentleman. The flowing shirt or smock freed the arms to reach, lift, and swing, as was necessary for the work of commoners but unnecessary and unsuitable for gentry. A gentleman would no more appear with his vest unbuttoned than he would laugh aloud with mouth wide open. Copley pictured Paul Revere with his shirt loose on his body, his vest open, with no coat to confine his shoulders, and so stripped him of all pretensions to gentility, at least for the purpose of the picture. A British musician was shocked when a group of German farmers attended a performance in Lancaster, Pennsylvania. "At our first concert, three clownish-looking fellows came into the room, and, after sitting a few minutes, (the weather being warm, not to say hot) very composedly took off their coats: they were in the usual summer dress of farmer's servants in this part of the country; that is to say, without either stockins or breeches, a loose pair of trowsers being the only succedaneum. As we fixed our admission at a dollar each, (here seven shillings and six pence,) we expect this circumstance would be sufficient to exclude such characters."[14]

Posture was important because slumped shoulders and a hung head denoted a servility that was out of keeping with a gentleman's dignity and honor.[15] The genteel person, who might appear sometimes in shirt sleeves, could never allow himself to be seen in degrading postures. Nor was he to "loll," which implied relaxing the upright stance by leaning far back, putting up one's legs, lying down in public, curling up, or leaning far out of a window and resting on the sill. Chesterfield distinguished between vulgar slovenliness and self-indulgent lolling on the one hand and genteel ease on the other. He observed to his son that "you may also know a well-bred person by his manner of sitting. Ashamed and confused, the awkward man sits in his chair stiff and bolt upright, whereas the man of fashion, is easy in every position; instead of lolling or lounging as he sits, he leans with elegance, and by varying his attitudes, shews that he has been used to good company." The easy poses of the later eighteenth century, while a departure from the erect formality of earlier times, still required the straight back line, permitting one to lean to one side or the other, but not to loll.[16]

The posture of the body comprised only a portion of the protocol of body

A member of one of Maryland's wealthiest families, Richard Bennett Lloyd, here pictured in 1771 at age twenty-one, combined perfect ease with disciplined erectness. Two years later he purchased a commission in the Coldstream Guards, married a woman from the Isle of Wight, and subsequently moved to France before returning to America in 1780.

William Hall, the son of David Hall, Benjamin Franklin's partner in the printing business. Shown here in 1766, the young man has the right posture and correct clothing but lacks the polish of Richard Lloyd. The rising provincial gentry always stood in danger of falling short of genteel standards, risking the scorn of more practiced ladies and gentlemen.

regulation; proper motion was the other part. We can confidently speak of the erect stance because of the portraits; we can only read about the motions. For these, we must turn to written instructions on how to remove a hat, to bow, to walk, and above all to dance, the most severe test of body mastery. Social dances were far more elaborate then than now, approaching the complexity of theatrical dancing, and yet they had to be carried off with grace and ease, making the services of a dancing master a necessity for young ladies and gentlemen. To get the full picture of the genteel body, we must picture the people in the portraits walking, dancing, and gesturing with the same practiced ease as they stand or sit in the paintings.

The lengthy descriptions of the movement of great men and women suggest the hypnotic power of simple physical presence. Richard Rush remembered watching for Washington to open a session of Congress in Philadelphia in 1794 or 1795. An immense crowd gathered at Chestnut and Sixth to await his white carriage attended by liveried servants and drawn by four bay horses.

> Washington got out of his carriage, and slowly crossing the pavement, ascended the steps of the edifice, upon the upper platform of which he paused, and turning half round, looked in the direction of a carriage which had followed the lead of his own. Thus he stood for a minute, distinctly seen by every body. He stood in all his civic dignity and moral grandeur, erect, serene, majestic. His costume was a full suit of black velvet; his hair, in itself blanched by time, powdered to a snowy whiteness, a dress sword at his side, and his hat held in his hand. Thus he stood in silence; and what moments those were! Throughout the dense crowd a profound stillness reigned. Not a word was heard, not a breath. Palpitations took the place of sounds. It was a feeling infinitely beyond that which vents itself in shouts. Every heart was full. In vain would any tongue have spoken. All were gazing, in mute unutterable admiration. Every eye was riveted on that form—the greatest, purest, most exalted of mortals. It might have seemed as if he stood in that position to gratify the assembled thousands with a full view of the father of their country. Not so. He had paused for his secretary, then, I believe, Mr. Dandridge or Colonel Lear, who got out of the other carriage, a chariot, decorated like his own. The secretary, ascending the steps, handed him a paper—probably a copy of the speech he was to deliver—when both entered the building. Then it was, and not until then, that the crowd sent up huzzas, loud, long, earnest, enthusiastic.[17]

Much contributed to the power of that hushed moment on the steps: Washington's history, his authority, the beauty of the carriage, his dress. But the slow walk across the pavement, the dignified ascent of the stairs, the pause and half turn, and his serene, majestic bearing were part of the moment's magic. His presence stopped every sound until the spell broke and cheers burst forth.

On the other hand, the expectation of perfect grace was so high that any momentary lapse was noted. Senator William Maclay, ever the close observer, recorded an instance at Washington's house when he read a statement to a delegation from Congress.

> The President took his reply out of his coat-pocket. He had his spectacles in his jacket-pocket, having his hat in his left hand and the paper in the right. He had too many objects for his hands. He shifted his hat between his forearm and the left side of his breast. But taking the spectacles from the case embarrassed him. He got rid of this small distress by laying the spectacle-case on the chimney-piece. Colonel Humphreys stood on his right, Mr. Lear on his left. Having adjusted his spectacles, which was not very easy, considering the engagements of his hands, he read his reply with tolerable exactness and without emotion. I thought he should have received us with his spectacles on, which would have saved the making of some uncouth motions. Yet, on the whole, he did nearly as well as anybody could have done the same motions. Could the laws of etiquette have permitted him to have been disencumbered of his hat, it would have relieved him much.[18]

Reflecting on the occasion, Maclay considered how the awkward interplay of body and objects might have been eased. Above all, he did not want Washington to make "uncouth motions." Judging from the length and detail of the diary entry, the artistic management of a regulated body in the drama of everyday gentility meant as much to Maclay as the affairs of state.

DRESS

THE genteel presence created by bearing and graceful motion was further enhanced by clothing; dress signaled rank and character as surely as posture did. The meaning of the feel, the color, the cut, and the expense of clothing was clear enough to have been earlier codified in law. Sumptuary legislation, which detailed acceptable apparel as related to rank, was first enacted in England in the thirteenth century. The laws went through many revisions and varied efforts at enforcement before extraneous concerns about prerogative power led to repeal in 1604. Under the 1510 statute, the basic sixteenth-century legislation, only lords were permitted to wear gold or silver cloth or bone lace, and only knights blue or red velvet. Later statutes restricted silk, even in small patches, to men of adequate wealth. People lower in the social scale had to limit the cost of the materials in their clothing and the amount of fabric in a given garment. The legislation partly aimed to inhibit foreign imports and to protect English textile producers, but the main purpose was to stabilize the outward signs of rank and to stop extravagance among people who would suffer from dressing beyond their means. The legislation suggests how materials and colors bore well-defined social meaning from an early date.[19]

The genteel culture of the eighteenth century inherited and partially incorporated this code of meaning. Scarlet had traditionally signified royalty and grandeur in Western Europe, and bright rich colors, especially when worked into elaborate designs, continued to mark people of high birth and wealth. Indian cottons and especially chintz, which became immensely popular at the end of the seventeenth century, appealed to the English upper classes because of the vivid designs that could be painted or printed on them. Wool could also be impressed with color, but it held the hues less well under repeated washings. The chintzes brought the luxury of vivid color and elaborate design to the public in a more practical form and at less expense. Bright colors instantly marked a person of rank and fashion. Poorer people wore the dull, natural browns, greens, and off-whites of homespun clothing colored with vegetable dyes which blended with the hues of the natural world.[20]

Color, however, was not essential for gentility in the eighteenth century. Many portraits of American gentry present the sitters in browns, grays, and, later in the century, black. The gentry did not invariably dress in brilliant colors, although the plums and cocoa tans of their clothes were richer, stronger hues than the poor could manage with their vegetable dyes. Color was more firmly associated with rank than with gentility, and rank and gentility were not synonymous. Very wealthy Americans or those few with titles do appear in bright colors or elaborately patterned fabrics in their portraits, but the middling great planter or merchant and wife, who would certainly claim gentility, contented themselves with conservative hues. A person of gentility had to understand his or her exact position in the social order and never overstep it. A bright silk suit on an ordinary Boston merchant would have been a breach of good taste and decidedly ungenteel. The wearer of the plain brown suit was no less genteel for his lack of color. The principle of gentility almost required that the use of bright colors should be more restrained in the clothing of the American gentry, who, by English standards, were only upper-middle-class.[21]

American gentry also wore few ornaments. Brocade trim, lace, and gold and silver buttons and buckles were a part of aristocratic dress and unsuitable for lower ranks. But the American gentry did add small brilliant touches of adornment. Good buckles were necessary, and buttons were apparently an obsession. Eighteenth-century storekeepers stocked buttons by the thousands; large bags of them turn up in their inventories. But brocade trim rarely appeared in portraits, and buttons did not usually glitter. The principle of restraint operated in these details too.[22]

The genteel, however, were required to wear clean, fine linen at throat and wrists. Every male and female portrait shows fine white fabric at these points, and usually lace at the sleeve ends. Although Nicholas Ridgely had only two suits when he died, he had nine fine holland shirts. When George Washington visited Belvoir as a young man, he packed nine white shirts and white stockings. The genteel image required fine white fabric where skin met suit or dress, revealing that the immaculate body was covered by a film of white cloth.[23]

Aristocratic dress was traditionally characterized by smoothness. The fabrics regulated by sumptuary legislation were the smoothest available, silk satins and velvets. Restrictions on other fabrics were described by cost and amount, but silk fabrics were forbidden outright to the lower classes, as if finish, aside from price, set the fabric apart. People at the lower end of the scale wore rough homespun and coarse osnaburgs and fustians, establishing in effect a textural polarity between rough and smooth. This distinction in early sumptuary legislation entered wholly into the genteel aesthetic of dress in the eighteenth century. Fabric was ranged along a spectrum of increasing value and prestige according to the degree of smoothness. Stockings were priced according to their smoothness, as were women's straw hats. In the eighteenth century the English gentry took up the plaited straw hats of country women for informal wear, but chose imported leghorn plaiting, noted for its fineness, thus giving a genteel straw a distinguishing finish. Similarly, silk fabrics were preeminent for a woman's finest dresses, and velvet or superfine wool for a man's suit.[24]

Claudia Kidwell and Margaret Christman observe that virtually all the fabrics "used by the poorer sort shared a common quality of coarseness": osnaburg (a coarse linen), fustian (a mixture of cotton and linen), and linsey-woolsey, made of linen and wool, were all coarse. Plain cottons and wools of the poorer sort were also heavier and coarser than the chintzes and superfine wools of the polite. There were other important differences too, Kidwell and Christman say: "The floral patterns and chintzes on the one hand were arrayed against a mass of striped and checked and 'speckl'd' fabrics; the pure white linens versus the uncertain colors of country cloth; the rich red from expensive cochineal standing out against the neutral colors produced by most vegetable dyes." But most notable was "the very obvious difference in texture, the smooth as opposed to the rough."[25]

The expense and effort of spinning fine yarns and weaving smooth fabric raised the price of silks and velvets. But the price does not account for the inherent value of smoothness that made it worth the trouble and expense. The etymology of the word "coarse" suggests that the physical quality was linked to broader cultural values. It is thought that "coarse" derived from "course," meaning plain and ordinary, and came in time to mean rude or vulgar. The feel of coarse cloth was associated with the lower ranks of society and with rude personal traits. Meanings and feelings radiating from a debased social position and vulgar personal characteristics infused the sensory experience of the fabric through the word "coarse." By the same token, "polished" and "polite" linked smooth fabric with well-finished personal qualities. The application of the same words to materials and to persons suggests that fabrics became metaphors for personality. In paying higher prices for smooth fabrics, the gentry wished to reflect in their clothing the personal qualities they sought in their conduct.

As articulated by Edmund Burke, smooth and flowing surfaces went beyond clothing and personality to a much more general aesthetic. As a young man trying to distinguish the qualities of beauty, he identified smoothness as an essential trait of all beautiful things.

> The next property constantly observable in such objects is *Smoothness.* A quality so essential to beauty, that I do not now recollect any thing beautiful that is not smooth. In trees and flowers, smooth leaves are beautiful; smooth slopes of earth in gardens; smooth streams in the landscape; smooth coats of birds and beasts in animal beauties; in fine women, smooth skins; and in several sorts of ornamental furniture, smooth and polished surfaces. A very considerable part of the effect of beauty is owing to this quality; indeed the most considerable. For take any beautiful object, and give it a broken and rugged surface, and however well formed it may be in other respects, it pleases no longer. Whereas let it want ever so many of the other constituents, if it wants not this, it becomes more pleasing than almost all others without it. This seems to me so evident, that I am a good deal surprised, that none who have handled the subject have made any mention of the quality of smoothness in the enumeration of those that go to the forming of beauty. For indeed any ruggedness, any sudden projection, any sharp angle, is in the highest degree contrary to that idea.[26]

Burke may be unique among eighteenth-century observers in articulating the place of smoothness in beauty. But his assertion was based on observation; many desirable objects within genteel culture were smooth. Besides fabrics, ceramics ranged along a smooth-rough continuum from the finest porcelains to crude earthenwares. Burke enunciated an aesthetic principle that craftsmen of all kinds, without conscious collusion, had already incorporated into their products. Combined with shapes characterized by gradual variation, something smooth, like the shape and feel of a bird or a woman's neck, became irresistibly beautiful, as if an innate quality automatically called forth the pleasing sensation of beauty.[27]

Despite these ingrained distinctions, a visitor walking up High Street in Philadelphia in the middle of the eighteenth century might not always have been able to distinguish commoners from genteel people of fashion. Plain people doubtless fell heir to clothing once worn by ladies and gentlemen, and the irresistible urge to emulate people in power moved lesser men and women to wear cheaper or shabbier versions of fashionable dress. Pictures of High Street show street traders in knee breeches and waistcoats.

Yet it remained true in general that people carried the marks of their social position on their backs. If in individual cases people passed for something they were not, the polarities of polished and coarse were well understood by all. Trained by dancing masters to hold torsos and heads erect, the genteel did not amble or loll on a public street. Genteel clothing, with its

A mixed company mingled in the streets of Philadelphia in 1800. The dress of ladies and gentlemen set them apart, but people of middling standing who acquired genteel attire in one way or another took on some of the airs of the gentry.

color, rich adornment, smooth texture, and aristocratic cut and pattern, was easily distinguished from craftsmen's leather aprons over shirts with open vests, the smocks of farmers and drovers, the trousers of seamen and laborers, and the coarse jackets and petticoats of the serving girls.[28]

EATING

INSIDE Philadelphia houses, the physical activity of the inhabitants would also have informed a visitor of their degree of gentility, but such a visitor would not have found one class distinction common in Europe: the meals of rich and poor would not have differed as greatly as in England or on the Continent. In everyday fare, the menus of upper-class and lower-class people traditionally had been defined by one important difference—meat. Upper-class people ate meat regularly while peasants mostly ate grain, prepared in various ways as bread, gruel, or porridge. Vegetables in season garnished the cereals, as did occasional touches of meat and cheese.[29]

Plain farmers and the poor in America also subsisted primarily on cereals prepared as breads or as porridges, as the European peasantry long had done, but poor Americans ate much better than poor Englishmen. Sarah McMahon found meat in 65 to 80 percent of the estate inventories after the fall slaughtering period. She also discovered that wills called for meat in 70 to 90 percent of widows' dower provisions, an indication of the common view of a standard diet. In both instances, the percentages increased through the century. In 1728 the Boston News Letter summarized the diet of a respectable middle-class family as consisting typically of bread and milk for breakfast and supper, with pudding, bread, meat, roots, pickles, vinegar, salt, and cheese for dinner. Many farm families replicated that menu.[30]

More than menu, the visitor would have seen differences in presentation going from plain to genteel houses. If the food on a gentleman's table might not be entirely different from common food, the tables themselves in gentry and plebeian houses—the dishes, platters, drinking vessels, and flatware— would never be confused. The poor in the eighteenth century continued the primitive eating modes that were standard in seventeenth-century households, and these were a far cry from the manner of genteel dining. In the seventeenth century, many households lacked tables on which to place food as it came from the fireplace, and that condition was not unknown in some regions halfway through the eighteenth century. In Wethersfield, Connecticut, from 40 to 50 percent of the estate inventories showed no table before 1670, and as many as a quarter lacked a table as late as 1730. A third of the inventories in New Castle County, Delaware, in the 1750s listed no tables. Chairs were nearly as uncommon. Over 80 percent of the inventoried

Wethersfield households had chairs by the 1680s, but the average (mean) number was 2.6, meaning that many households had one or two.[31]

Planks laid on trestles for each meal, then dismantled to open up more space, can be hypothesized to account for this gap in furnishings. A visitor to the Western Reserve in 1811 saw a woman stick poles through the crevices in two of the cabin walls and rest a couple of oak planks on the poles to serve her guests breakfast. Or food might have been paced on a chest or left on the floor in front of the fireplace, especially in view of the fact that cooks at the fireplace ordinarily used the floor in place of a table. A Springfield, Massachusetts, man in 1650 said that he "took up my dinner and laid it on a little table made on the cradle head." There was little reason for tables of any kind when most of the diners lacked chairs. Stools and the long benches called forms appear no more frequently in the inventories. Probably people made do, sitting on chests, kegs, and other furniture not designed specifically for sitting. The visitors to the tableless Western Reserve cabin "sat down on the bed, for chairs or stools there were none." In tiny one-room houses, which were the norm for most people, family members may have carried their food outside in good weather and sat on the ground to eat. The orderly gathering of the family around a table, each with a place and a chair, would have been an exception for the poorest quarter of the population even in the early years of the eighteenth century.[32]

For the ordinary family, we should not think of the food being dished out onto plates for each eater. The inventories do not provide detailed information on individual eating utensils because the appraisers grouped plates and platters under woodenware and pewter. Individual wooden trenchers and pewter plates may be hidden under those words, but it would be wrong to assume that they were present. The individualization of eating arrangements for people at ordinary meals was still in process. In Europe spoons had not come into common use until the sixteenth century; before then people ate with their fingers from common pots. The recommended eating utensils for immigrants to New England in the early seventeenth century included spoons and bowls, but not plates.[33]

The simpler mode of eating was long in disappearing. The studies of Plymouth, Massachusetts, inventories from 1660 to 1760 list very few plates. Since more than half of the inventories in most places show no knives or forks even in the eighteenth century, plates, which served primarily as surfaces for cutting, were unneeded. Food that required no cutting—porridge, mush, or the various pottages—could be eaten as easily from bowls or dishes with spoons. Most commonly, then, people in poor households well into the eighteenth century probably ate their partially liquid meals from bowls with spoons, or perhaps in still more primitive ways.[34]

Alexander Hamilton, the Annapolis physician, was invited to a meal with the ferryman's family while crossing the Susquehanna River in Maryland in 1744. The ferry, Hamilton said, was

> kept by a little old man whom I found att vittles with his wife and family upon a homely dish of fish without any kind of sauce. They desired me to eat, but I told them I had no stomach. They had no cloth upon the table, and their mess was in a dirty, deep, wooden dish which they evacuated with their hands, cramming down skins, scales, and all. They used neither knife, fork, spoon, plate, or napkin because, I suppose, they had none to use.

Hamilton went on to comment that "I looked upon this as a picture of that primitive simplicity practiced by our forefathers long before the mechanic arts had supplyed them with instruments for the luxury and elegance of life," suggesting that in his experience, the ferryman's eating habits had an air of quaint antiquity. Scooping out a homely dish of fish by hand seemed rare in 1744, but it still occurred. Hamilton would have seen more of it if he had ventured farther from the main roads. In more settled areas, the poor likely ate their porridges and pottages from bowls with spoons.[35]

These conditions changed through the eighteenth century as tables and chairs increased in frequency. By the end of the century both items were nearly as common as beds in more settled areas. By the middle of the century irregular seating and eating from bowls with spoons and fingers remained mainly as an image at the lower end of the refinement spectrum to which genteel dining could be compared. Gentility regulated dining as it did the body, including the wish to keep the food clean, separated from dirt and fingers. The growing spirit of refinement placed people on chairs at tables, gave each individual utensils, and put the food on platters and in serving bowls. Bodies were placed before the food with knives and forks in hand separating the person from tactile contact with the food, and on chairs that encouraged people to sit upright in the proper erect posture. Genteel aesthetic principles thus took over the process of dining in its entirety, and refined and exalted it.

The advance of regulated and refined dining can be measured through the proliferation of the tools that made it possible: tables and chairs, knives and forks, and porcelain plates and serving dishes. Dining accoutrements were added one by one, usually beginning with chairs that lifted people from the floor and brought them to order around a table. Then rough plates of some kind, normally of pewter, were added and about the same time knives and forks, to separate bodies from the food. Smooth porcelain serving dishes and plates, with their fine polished surfaces, usually came last.

Differences in the rate of adoption varied sharply according to the sophistication of the region and proximity to international trade routes. Nearly 90 percent of the inhabitants of Wethersfield, Connecticut, one of the first towns settled in the Connecticut Valley and a prosperous minor trading center right on the river, had tables (88 percent) and chairs (90 percent) in their houses by the 1750s, only a few percentage points less than inventories with beds (91 percent). The average (mean) number of chairs was over ten and of tables two and a half. In the two northern Delaware counties, Kent and New Castle, and in Chester County, Pennsylvania, immediately north of New Castle, the figures were lower. In the middle decades of the eighteenth century, between 65 and 68 percent of inventories listed chairs, a figure probably more typical of settled rural areas of the coastal plain. By the 1790s the percentage of inventories with chairs and tables for this region had risen to 90 percent. Lewis Miller's sketches of rural Pennsylvania households gathered for meals at tables with each person on a chair represented the condition of middling and upper families between 1795 and 1810, a style of eating available to virtually everyone in the region by the end of the century. In more remote areas the figure would be lower.[36]

The assemblage of knives, forks, and plates, to go with individual chairs, became more common about the same time. Forks were used in Boston before the end of the seventeenth century, but were rare: only a gentleman's inventory listed a fork in 1721. Forks appeared much more commonly in the 1750s and 1760s. By that decade, between 32 and 57 percent of the decedents in the three-county region in Delaware and Pennsylvania had knife-and-fork sets in their estates. In Massachusetts, about half the inventories in 1774 showed knives and forks. In the Chesapeake the incidence of knives and forks was higher at midcentury and later, but probably a third of the population still lacked them. Bowls and spoons and fingers must have prevailed for many common people through most of the century.[37]

Because of the obscuring names earthenware, woodenware, and pewter, the frequency of plates is more difficult to measure, but evidence from archaeological excavations conducted by James Deetz suggests more common usage after 1760 in the Plymouth region. By the middle of the eighteenth century, about 43 percent of the inventories in Kent County listed fine ceramics of some sort (delftware, stoneware, or "china"), which most often would have included plates. In Massachusetts in 1774, a third of the inventories included ceramics and over half had tea equipment. A substantial population ate with knife and fork from finer ceramic plates, at least for formal dining. Another, larger group continued with pewter plates and trenchers.[38]

Altogether the evidence from Plymouth, Pennsylvania, Delaware, and the Chesapeake permits us to picture roughly half of the colonial population at midcentury eating from plates with knives and forks while sitting at tables.

A smaller group of this knife-and-fork population ate from some kind of refined earthenware like creamware which imitated the prized surfaces of imported porcelains. The rest of the knife-and-fork group ate from coarse earthenware, pewter, or wood. A tiny population dined on imported porcelains.

Among the half of the people who used knives and forks, some refined even their simple meals. The pewter and silver porringers that survive in such great numbers, 95 percent of them from after 1750, were made for porridges and mushes, the simplest of foods, as well as for the more genteel beverages of chocolate and coffee. Benjamin Franklin's wife believed that he deserved to eat his breakfast bread and milk with a silver spoon from a china bowl rather than from an earthen porringer. As the process of refinement spread through their lives, some people brought to every meal the silver and fine ceramic tablewares used to exalt the most formal dining.[39]

At the other end of the spectrum, a third to a half of the population ate with spoons or fingers, though likely sitting up at tables. They had no fine finishes on their tables or tablewares. They dressed in rough linens, linsey-woolseys, and leather. Their skin had likely been roughened by weather, fireplace heat, and work. They bent over their bowls unconcerned about posture or manners. Only on Sundays did they dignify their appearance with better suits of clothes or gowns, and then in simple blues or blacks. Under the beneficent influence of American plenitude, a common diet of simply prepared cereals and meat brought people together, but the modes of presenting food and the manner of eating it divided the polite classes of society from the vulgar and coarse.

By the end of the century, a large proportion of families had enough chairs, plates, knives, and forks to sit at a table with individual place settings.

GENTLE MINDS

IN 1744 Alexander Hamilton, the Edinburgh-trained physician living in Annapolis whom we have met before, prescribed a horseback journey for himself to improve his frail health. While riding north he met the ferryman at the Susquehanna who offered a meal of fish from a common pot, and later at New Castle in Delaware he encountered Morison, the would-be gentleman who was served veal scraps for breakfast because of his greasy jacket and dirty worsted cap. The episode with Morison, because it sheds additional light on the essentials of gentility and moves us beyond the body to the mind, is worth recounting in some detail.

At the inn, Morison tried without success to present himself as a gentleman. Hamilton saw at once that Morison was "a very rough spun, forward, clownish blade, much addicted to swearing, at the same time desirous to pass for a gentleman." When the landlady, seeing his shabby clothes and observing his "heavy, forward, clownish air and behaviour," presented him with veal scraps for breakfast, Morison flew into a rage. " 'Damn him,' " he swore, " 'if it wa'n't out of respect to the gentleman in company,' (meaning me) he would throw her cold scraps out at the window and break her table all to pieces should it cost him 100 pounds for damages." "Taking off his worsted night cap, he pulled a linnen one out of his pocket and clapping it upon his head, 'Now,' says he, 'I'm upon the borders of Pennsylvania and must look like a gentleman.' "

Morison believed that clothes were responsible for his treatment. He also sensed that his conversation was lacking and to redeem himself "made a transition to politicks and damnd the late Sr. R[obert] W[alpole] for a rascall. We asked him his reasons for cursing Sr. R[obert], but he would give us no other but this, that he was certainly informed by some very good gentlemen, who understood the thing right well, that the said Sr. R[obert] was a damnd rogue." Having made a pass at political conversation, Morison returned to his possessions.

> He told us that tho he seemed to be but a plain, homely fellow, yet he would have us know that he was able to afford better than many that went finer: he had good linnen in his bags, a pair of silver buckles, silver clasps, and gold sleeve buttons, two Holland shirts, and some neat night caps; and that his little woman att home drank tea twice a day; and he himself lived very well and expected to live better.

Others like Morison must have thought that a linen nightcap, silver buckles, holland shirts, and the drinking of tea, the physical accoutrements of gentility, would enable a person to pass for a gentleman. But of course none of these persuaded Hamilton. There was the "heavy, forward, clownish air and behaviour," the "naturall boorishness," and Morison's violent speech as well. Morison seemed to sense that his conversation lacked something and so turned to politics, where his ignorance only compounded his difficulties. But he was on the right track, for besides the regulation of the body and its adornment with fine linens and silver buckles, the mind needed polish. Gentility required a person to rise above boorishness and dullness, to display an abundant mind, especially in conversation, and to reveal a vivacious, sweet, and generous spirit. A parvenu could hire a tailor to dress his body and a dancing master to teach physical deportment. But to acquire the spiritual and mental traits of a well-bred gentleman required years of tutoring the intellect as well.

In its true and most refined form, gentility was meant to be a spiritual condition. A proper education, Locke said in *Some Thoughts Concerning Education,* formed the mind in its innermost core, and everything else about the person—manners, speech, dress—expressed the temper of the spirit. The pleasures the well-bred person gave to a company were the pleasures of knowing a refined being. "The Actions, which naturally flow from such a well-formed Mind, please us . . . as the genuine Marks of it; and being as it were natural Emanations from the Spirit and Disposition within." "This seems to me to be that Beauty, which shines through some Men's Actions," Locke went on, not tricks or flourishes or luxurious dress, but "little Expressions of Civility and Respect," which "seem not Artificial or Studied, but naturally to flow from a Sweetness of Mind, and a well turn'd Disposition." That quality, rare even among the well-bred, Morison lacked entirely. He could purchase linen and buckles without end and never come close to the essence of gentility. Probably few of the American gentry met Locke's high standards for good breeding, but many understood that houses, plates, knives and forks, posture, and polite speech were insufficient unless they became the outward signs of an inward grace.[40]

DELICACY, SENSIBILITY, AND TASTE

GENTILITY borrowed heavily from traditional Christianity for its inventory of personal virtues. In admonishing his student to "Let Chearfulness, Sweetness, and Modesty, be always blended in your Countenance and Air," the author of *The Lady's Preceptor* called on a common stock of Christian qualities. The popularity of *The Whole Duty of Man* among the American gentry shows how easily Christianity and gentility blended in the depiction of genteel character. The literature on the subject assumed that the true gentleman was a Christian—though his piety was regulated as closely as his body, to restrain, for example, the emotional excesses of evangelical religion. Instead, the gentleman embodied the Christian moral virtues of compassion, kindness, and humility. Good manners expressed a Christian regard for the happiness of others.[41]

At the same time, some genteel virtues went beyond the usual store of Christian qualities, and these were the ones most lacking in Morison. Three interrelated words sum up these peculiarly genteel qualities: "delicacy," "sensibility," and "taste." With them we come to the heart of genteel culture.

Delicacy was the eighteenth-century word for the rising "threshold of embarrassment" that Norbert Elias finds central to the civilizing process. The delicate person flushed with shame at the mere mention of the grosser bodily processes that civilization had driven from the conversation of polite people. Delicacy, in this vein, was aversion to every form of coarse behavior or thought, and even the suggestion of erotic passion. The strongest constraints were laid on young women. "One of the chiefest beauties in a female character," one conduct book insisted, "is that modest reserve, that retiring delicacy, which avoids the public eye, and is disconcerted even at the gaze of admiration."

Delicacy in the larger sense meant the capacity for fine discriminations and an appreciation for all that was refined and gentle. While suppressing the base, delicacy delighted in everything sweet and lovely. Delicacy caused the princess to suffer from the pea under the stack of mattresses. Delicacy required a sensitivity to human feelings, an exact discernment of the emotional effects of a word or an action, and a desire to protect people from every hurt. Delicacy forbade an individual to assert superiority or to degrade another. Delicacy detected the slightest shadow of blame or derogation and acted to lift that shadow from any across whom it fell. *A Father's Legacy* warned that wit, because it ridiculed its targets, "must be guarded with great discretion and good-nature, otherwise it will create you many enemies. It is perfectly consistent with softness and delicacy; yet they are seldom found united." Humor was "often a great enemy to delicacy" because it broke the first rule of gentility, complaisance, the wish to please. Delicate discriminations enabled the polite to put all company at ease.[42]

Sensibility, the second quality of the three, was interwoven with delicacy; a person with sensibility reacted strongly to experience and might be overcome with feeling. Sensible people wept easily at suffering or were carried away with compassion or gratitude. Delicacy, in the sense of fine discriminations, caused the sensitive spirit of the refined person to react powerfully. "There is a certain Delicacy of Passion," Hume wrote, "to which some People are subject, that makes them extremely sensible to all the Accidents of Life . . . And When a Person that has this Sensibility of Temper, meets with any Misfortune, his Sorrow or Resentment takes intire Possession of him."⁴³

Being overcome with feeling in consequence of delicate sensibilities was a pleasurable indulgence of the genteel life, all the more pleasurable because the surge of strong emotion attested to the possession of genteel virtues. Nancy Shippen, whose diary entries were a record of her considerable sorrows as well as the happiness of her life, candidly noted the pleasure she took in her sensibilities. "Sweet Sensibility! source of a thousand heaven born sensations, for the wealth of the Indies I wou'd not be without thee!—" Her mother-in-law cautioned Nancy to discipline her own daughter gently, "as she has so much sensibility that it would make her unhappy without complaining of it." Bad behavior must be curbed, but not sensibility, which was prized in a young spirit.

Feelings that arose from compassion for suffering or love for one's children were especially honored. In Susanna Rowson's *Charlotte Temple,* an old gentleman is outraged by the attempt of a worthless rake to court his daughter. After hearing of the old man's strong feelings, Charlotte's father comments that "the truly brave soul is tremblingly alive to the feelings of humanity," a perfect description of the combination of delicacy and sensibility that gentility prized. The old man goes on to say that "painful as these feelings are, I would not exchange them for that torpor which the stoic mistakes for philosophy. How many exquisite delights I should have passed

Charles Willson Peale's portrait of Julia Rush turns the qualities of taste and delicacy into a visual reality. The posture of body and face, her dress, the lute, the book, and the flower at her bosom testify to her refined qualities. Both her husband and her father, Richard Stockton, were signers of the Declaration of Independence.

by unnoticed but for these keen sensations, this quick sense of happiness or misery." We call this pursuit of emotion for the sheer pleasure of feeling sentimentalism. By the middle of the eighteenth century, sentimentalism had deeply ingrained itself into genteel culture, adding a rich emotionality to the cooler temperament of courtly civility.[44]

Taste and delicacy were interwoven just as delicacy and sensibility were, for delicacy aided in the detection of beauty. If delicacy of perception aroused strong feelings, it also made one aesthetically sensitive. Philip Fithian, the Robert Carter family tutor in the 1770s, in describing briefly the houses and gardens of Nomini Hall, said that "they discover a delicate and Just Tast."[45] The implication was that the owners had that fine appreciation of all the delicate touches required to create beautiful houses and gardens. In everyday discourse where the word had frequent usage, no effort was made to define taste, as perplexing a problem in that day as now, and yet good taste was always admired and it was a requisite of a refined personality. Such a person recognized beauty through the exercise of the powers of discrimination, and could unerringly evaluate the aesthetic qualities of a vase, an opera, a face, or a suit of clothes. More important still, such a person created beauty in all he or she possessed. The rooms, the furnishings, the exterior architecture, the gardens, and even the barns and fields of a genteel family exhibited a just taste, as those of the Carters did at Nomini Hall.

CONVERSATION

DELICACY and sensibility, although more closely tied to individual minds than taste, similarly interacted with society and the world beyond the person. All three virtues enhanced the most self-conscious and practiced art of eighteenth-century polite life, conversation. In conversation the most finely honed discriminatory powers and the delicately attuned sensibilities of the genteel spirit exhibited and confirmed themselves. The rules for conducting conversation were discussed at length in the courtesy books and exemplified in the dialogue of genteel novels like those of Samuel Richardson. Actual people, while they did not record complete conversations, did frequently comment on the conversational abilities of their associates, just as they judged the beauty of refined women. The Charleston newspaper, in extolling the virtues of Eliza Pinckney, said of her that "her understanding, aided by an uncommon strength of memory, had been so highly cultivated and improved by travel and extensive reading, and was so richly furnished, as well with scientific, as practical knowledge, that her talent for conversation was unrivalled."[46] Conversation was, in a sense, the culminating genteel art.

The ideal gentle mind was notable for vivacity, implying constant intellectual and emotional vitality. A vivacious mind, while composed and peaceful, also operated at a high pitch, displaying wit, repartee, knowledge, and lively emotional responses. A perfectly genteel person might hold back from conversation out of modesty, but would never lapse into torpor or dullness. One advice book cautioned a reader that "people of sense and discernment will never mistake . . . silence for dulness. One may take a share in conversation without uttering a syllable. The expression in the countenance shews it, and this never escapes an observing eye." Nancy Shippen disliked those days when she "felt dull and disagreeable, very low spirited and out of humor," for she knew that her vivacious spirit was a large part of her attractiveness. Dullness was painful as well as shameful.[47]

Peasants were torpid; the genteel were supposed to be gay, meaning high-spirited or vivacious. They sought amusement to keep their spirits high, and disliked dull times and boring people. The primary reason why people needed the arts, one person wrote, was "to awaken their Wit, and enliven their Taste." But among all activities, conversation offered the vivacious soul the most suitable field of play. In his essay on taste, Montesquieu commented that "esprit—wit and talent in their various connotations—enjoys exercising itself, as does curiosity." In conversation, genteel people exercised their sensibility, taste, vivacity, and their capacities for discernment and appreciation.[48]

The guides to genteel conduct spoke of conversation as "the Cement and Soul of Society," or as "the greatest commerce of our lives." Every courtesy book offered directions and rules, and a number made conversation the center of attention, as in *The Conversation of Gentlemen* (1738), Henry Fielding's *Essay on Conversation* (1743), or Jonathan Swift's satiric *Complete Collection of Genteel and Ingenious Conversations* (1738). Books catalogued figures of speech, maxims, rhymes, witticisms, and bons mots to aid those lacking ingenuity. The ultimate source book for genteel conduct, Castiglione's *Book of the Courtier*, praised the merits of good conversation and was itself written as a model of refined conversation among well-bred courtiers. Commonly courtesy books offered examples of sample conversations for learners who could pick up the rhythm and tone or memorize actual speeches for later use.[49]

Because conversation is ephemeral, the effect of these standards on the talk of the colonial gentry can only be inferred. There is little evidence of specialized books on conversation coming to America. *The Academy of Complements* was repeatedly imported from the late seventeenth century on, and the first of six eighteenth-century printings of *The American Jest Book* appeared in Philadelphia in 1789, and *The New Academy of Compliments* had two printings in the 1790s, but the more elaborate works on the subject were never reprinted here. Ideas about refined conversation, insofar as they were gleaned from books, had to be deduced from classic guidebooks such as Chesterfield's *Letters* or from novels. Samuel Richardson's *Clarissa, Pamela,* and *Sir Charles Grandison* together went through thirty or more American printings in addition to the copies imported from England. Richardson devoted page after page to conversation, not usually of the grave or learned kind, but raillery, compliments, flirtation, and wit.[50]

We cannot determine how much Americans learned from such books, but we know they valued conversation. A Boston paper in 1731, doubtless echoing London, declared that "to avoid conversation is to Act against the Intention of nature ... to live then as men we must confer with men; conversation must be one of the greatest pleasures of life." The recurrent references to the quality of conversation in the brief evaluations of people in letters and diaries suggest that some took the admonition seriously. An acquaintance was liked because "his conversation is interesting and agreable," or accepted for other good qualities despite the fact that he had "nothing to say of his own." Chastellux, a visiting French aristocrat, praised Elizabeth Willing Powel for "her taste for conversation, and the truly European use she knows how to make of her understanding and information." He thought her unusual among American women, but Philadelphia must have offered inducements for her to have learned to converse in the European mode. While not everyone acquired fluency, some had "the reputation of being witty and sharp," or made conversation which, as in the case of one young lady, was said to be "as pleasing as her figure."[51]

Polite conversation had various purposes, one being to show one's parts— that is, one's knowledge and opinions. At the beginning of the seventeenth century Henry Peacham recommended to young gentlemen the knowledge of antiquities, particularly statues, inscriptions, and coins. Peacham recognized that only the wealthy could afford such rarities, but to converse with the owners required some knowledge. "Sure I am that he that will travel must both heed them and understand them if he desire to be thought ingenious and to be welcome to the owners." Nor did vague familiarity suffice: "It is not enough for an ingenuous gentleman to behold these [rarities] with a vulgar eye, but he must be able to distinguish them and tell who and what they be." The Peacham principle applied to scores of other topics, politics, the arts, geography, animals, and gardens. The well-finished gentleman necessarily had to have some knowledge "to be thought ingenious and to be welcome" by well-informed people.[52]

So strong was the desire to show off that young people were tempted to trot out their information prematurely. Experienced men of the world had acquired knowledge of places, governments, people, and art, had formed their judgments, and so shone in conversation. A young man, entering into the world, risked humiliation in bringing up a subject which he understood imperfectly. Chesterfield advised his son not to take the initiative at first. "If you have parts, you will have opportunities enough of shewing them on every topic of conversation, and if you have none, it is better to expose yourself upon a subject of other people's than of your own." On the other hand, one could not simply hold back. One must prepare oneself by storing away knowledge. Chesterfield urged his son to read carefully, reviewing the material until it was mastered, to enable him to converse intelligently. Chesterfield scoffed at dimwits who read lightly and went into company without having brought the matter under control. Those with a command of general topics and some wit in discussing them won favor. The governor of Pennsylvania took an interest in Benjamin Franklin when he was only a printer's apprentice because of his ability to talk about books, a trait probably still uncommon in the colonies in the 1720s. But an inept performance subjected one to the silent scorn of the company.[53]

The need to sustain conversation as the cement of society played upon many aspects of genteel life. To begin with, conversation required subject matter, grist for its conversational mills, and grave subjects would not always do. Chesterfield told his son to cultivate small talk on trivial subjects. "By small-talk, I mean a good deal to say on unimportant matters; for example, foods, the flavour and growth of wines, and the chit-chat of the day." To overcome boredom at Versailles, it was said, the court talked with animation about the bleeding of the king or a cold of Mme de Maintenon. What a relief when an enterprising sea captain put a rhinoceros on display, which every-one, including the king and queen, went to see. The beast provided conver-sation for a week. The magic-lantern shows, peep shows, and models of distant places like Jerusalem or Rome that traveled through the colonies served the same purpose. An advertisement for John Bonnin's series of French scenes viewed through a "Philosophical Optical Machine" claimed that after a performance "instead of the common Chat, there is nothing scarce mentioned now, but the most entertaining Parts of Europe." After Mr. Bonnin exhibited scenes of New York City in 1748, the newspaper observed that ladies insisted on seeing the show.

> In short, there's nobody can set up the least face for politeness and conversation without having been with Mr. Bonnin; and embellishing their discourse with making judicious and elaborate observations and criticisms on this, that, and the other building, improvement, or dress.

The curiosities gave a double delight: the excitement of the first view and the pleasure of talking about them afterward.[54]

Polite people often assembled "conversation pieces" in their own houses. While the phrase is usually applied to paintings of domestic scenes, with the implication that viewers would react to the picture and talk about it among themselves, the term may be more generally applied to other objects used to start conversation. A well-planned garden, besides exhibiting the delicate and just taste of its owner, was a place and a subject for conversation. Philip Fithian recorded his pleasant walks with Mrs. Carter in the family garden, where they conversed about the plants. A vista from a house or a place with a view fixed a subject which might evoke questions and around which conversation might circle, as did books, prints, maps, and scientific instruments. One courtesy book was so specific as to instruct young men how to react when a jewel was brought into company for discussion. In England the virtuosi had whole cabinets of curiosities to which they might introduce their friends. The collection practice was less common in the colonies, but any picture on the wall, a vase on a shelf, a plant in the garden served the purpose. As refinement advanced in America, thoughtful hosts assembled various conversation pieces for the amusement of their guests.

The needs of conversation thus motivated sundry gentry activities—reading, collecting, and the planting of gardens or designing of landscapes. The objects afforded the guests as well as the hosts opportunities to show their taste, sensibility, and discernment. Judging mainly from letters and diary entries as we must, the proper reaction was a succinct, discerning judgment of the object, cleverly expressed. At its best the comment would show one's familiarity with other objects of the same kind, a comparison of one vase with another seen elsewhere, for example, or of Hudson Valley vistas with those of the Rhine. In a model conversation in a French courtesy book, an educated young woman observed of Descartes, "I like him well, because he is intelligible." No more was required than the sharp, clear point revealing her personal sensibility and judgment. She elaborated with another dictum: "I like him the better also, because he does not pretend to search too far into the Secrets of the Omnipotent." The conversation could then move on.[55]

This spirit pervades Josiah Quincy's diary entries during his coastal tour in 1774. After visiting Charleston he noted "there is a colossal statue of Mr Pitt at Charleston, much praised by many. The drapery was exquisitely well done; but to me the attitude, air, and expression of the piece was bad." He wrote in the same faintly imperious spirit in New York after the theater. "The actors make but an indifferent figure in tragedy,—a much better in comedy. Hallam has merit in every character he acts." The comments mixed perception, personal reactions, and judgment.[56] Quincy might well have delivered the same judgments in person. Morison attempted similar comments on Walpole in his conversation with Hamilton. He tried to deliver a quick judgment of Sir Robert's character, thinking it might pass for polite talk. Hamilton called his bluff, and Morison failed at the game for lack of a supporting comment. In more expert hands such comments, mixed with wit and pleasantry, would crackle around the circle for the amusement and edification of the company.

Conversation, where wit, vivacity, taste, and sensibility all might show themselves in full splendor, organized the acquisition of knowledge in polite society. Men of learning, clergymen, authors of books, statesmen, and doctors had other purposes in reading; the ordinary members of polite society read to talk. The admonition for young women in a standard courtesy book applied equally to men reading outside of their professional interests.

> For young Ladies when they have arrived to some knowledge by reading, afford great pleasure in their Conversation to others, and receive no less when they are alone by themselves; for Reading assisteth Conversation, and is absolutely necessary to make the Spirit acceptable and gratefull; for as in Reading they do gather and find, almost on all occasions, a fit subject for discourse, so by conversation they find a happy and easie method to deliver themselves with Ornament, and to joyn plenty to facility: And without this Education, Conversation is an intolerable Tyrant; for we cannot without torment intertain any Discourse with those Gentlewomen, who if they be of the Countrey, can administer no other Discourse unto you, but of their Ducks, or their Geese; or if they be of the City, can talk of nothing, unless it be of their Whisks, or their Gorgets, or those Attires that are most in Fashion.[57]

Reading raised a person's conversation above the boorish talk of rustics and the shallow obsession with fashion of city beaux and so-called fine ladies. Conversation gave a social point to books and to the study of paintings, scenery, horticulture, or anything beautiful or curious.

Conversational knowledge was acquired for social display and engagement. Familiarity with a wide range of materials enabled one to formulate a clever personal judgment for presentation in conversation so as to exhibit one's taste, sensibility, and discernment. In time cultural entrepreneurs recognized the market for the broad, shallow knowledge created by the needs of polite conversation, and organized museums, lyceums, libraries, and magazines. The participants may have noted only an object or two in a collection or heard only an hour's lecture on Egyptian culture, but that enabled them to show their capacity for illuminating judgments in the conversation that ensued, and added to the store of information on hand for polite talk.[58]

Personal relations also supplied conversational material. Richardson's novels and later Jane Austen's contain page after page of dialogue lacking any reference to books or art or even scenery. The talk might be flirtatious, gently mocking, sometimes full of gossipy comments on current romances, but in straying from books to people, polite conversation did not shed its gentility. Conversation remained an art form, characterized at its best by wit, grace, and ingenuity. The author of *The Academy of Complements*, in a book made up of 255 pages of graceful little speeches for every occasion written for the English aristocracy during the time of Charles I, noted that "it is eloquence which adornes our discourse; gives a grace and life to our actions." "Without this," he went on, "we resemble walking rocks, all our actions being dull and heavie." The popularity of the little volume in Boston bookstores at the end of the seventeenth century suggests that some members of the colonial gentry were striving to beautify their speech.[59]

The governing principle in this more lighthearted persiflage, as in every form of polite conversation, was, as Fielding put it, "the Art of pleasing, or contributing as much as possible to the Ease and Happiness of those with whom you converse." In the model conversation on Descartes in the French courtesy book, every proffered opinion was followed immediately by an expression of deference to the superior knowledge of the other. By the same token, ridicule and derogation were strictly forbidden. Raillery presented a problem because, while amusing to the company, it discomfited its target. Fielding said "the Raillery which is consistent with Good-Breeding, is a gentle Animadversion on some Foible; which while it raises a Laugh in the rest of the Company, doth not put the Person rallied out of Countenance, or expose him to Shame and Contempt." Another courtesy book, as we have seen, advised against any raillery; Fielding admitted it on condition that the jest "be so delicate, that the Object of it should be capable of joining in the Mirth it occasions." Running through Fielding's essay on conversation, and its injunctions against gossip and indecency as well as raillery, is an evident struggle between an older form of bawdy and derisive talk and the more recent demands of good breeding with its high-strung sensitivity to the ease of everyone in the company.[60]

Swift mocked the ungainly efforts of English polite society to speak stylishly when he offered a set of "polite Speeches which beautify Conversation," but his real intent was to improve social discourse.[61] He desired, along with all who wrote about good breeding, that taste, discernment, vivacity, and complaisance be evident in every word, just as beauty and taste were to shine through the details of one's personal appearance and every aspect of one's domestic setting. Conversation became an art, for which one read, collected objects, formulated opinions, practiced graceful phrases, and above all developed those delicate responses that enabled one to show constant regard for the feelings of all in the company.

LETTER WRITING

THE refinement of spoken words carried over into letter writing. Because "style is the dress of thoughts," Chesterfield told his son, writing told as much about a person as clothing. Ill-dressed thoughts had little chance of success. "If your style is homely, course, and vulgar, they will appear to as much disadvantage, and be as ill received as your person, though ever so well proportioned, would, if dressed in rags, dirt, and tatters." Letters became performances as did dancing and conversation, a means of judging a person's character and grace. When Benjamin Rush met his future wife Julia, she was a girl of seventeen, "engaging in her manners and correct in her conversation." But her letter made her irresistible. "I had seen a letter of her writing to Mrs. [Elizabeth Graeme] Ferguson which gave me a favorable idea of her taste and understanding. . . . From this moment I determined to offer her my hand."[62]

Letter writing emerged as an aristocratic art in sixteenth-century Italy, along with so much else later associated with gentility. The collections of Italian letters were, in turn, modeled on classical authors, notably Cicero, Pliny, and Seneca. By the seventeenth century the published letters of three modern authors had emerged to set the standard for later writers—the Spaniard Antonio de Guevara (1539–45), and the Frenchmen Jean Louis Guez de Balzac (1624) and Vincent Voiture (translated in 1655). These three men's letters were read and emulated in England for a century. By the middle of the eighteenth century scores of English letter collections were in print, and letters had been accepted as a minor literary form. Handbooks like *The Compleat Letter-Writer* gave examples of "Elegant Letters" for every occasion. People with no prospect of publication themselves were conscious as they wrote letters that they were undertaking small literary performances. Writing a letter resembled entering a room or engaging a polite company in conversation. The act had to be adorned with the proper gestures and carried off with aplomb and style.[63]

Abigail Adams, normally a candid and pungent correspondent like her husband, assumed a most self-conscious literary posture when she opened a correspondence with the formidable Mercy Otis Warren, already famous in 1773 for her literary achievements. The kind hospitality Adams had already received gave her the courage to write. "Thus imbolden'd I venture to stretch my pinions, and tho like the timorous Bird I fail in the attempt and tumble to the ground yet sure the Effort is laudable." Although she included a sixteen-line poem, perhaps of her own composition, in the letter, Adams still apologized that "I have so long neglected my pen that I am conscious I shall make but a poor figure."

Warren's diction was no less formal and self-conscious. In a passing comment on the recent hot weather she hoped that "as the gentle showers of the afternoon Extended to the River, as you kindly wishd, so I hope they shed there benign influence over the mountains and Valleys of Scadden," using a local name for the South Precinct of Braintree because of its poetic ring. The two proceeded on the same high level of eloquence to conduct the kind of exchange we can imagine going on in genteel conversation. Adams sent Warren a copy of Juliana Seymour's *On the Management and Education of Children*, asking that Warren "give me your Sentiments upon this Book." All the proper rhetorical flourishes adorned the request: "May the Natural Benevolence of your Heart, prompt you to assist a young and almost inexperienced Mother in this Arduous Business." In proper style Warren entered the demurral that her opinion of a book which "is Generally admired I think is of very Little Consequence." She despaired "of Reaching those more perfect plans Exhibited by superior Hands," and then went on to deliver her judgment as people of parts did in polite conversation. She observed that Seymour put generosity above truth among the virtues, while Warren believed "a careful Attention to fix a sacred regard to Veracity in the Bosom of Youth the surest Guard to Virtue." So the two women danced the genteel dance, offering opinions on books and politics, accompanied by deferrals to the other's superior judgment and protests of their own deficiencies, all couched in a high diction and formal syntax that sustained the exchange on a lofty plane.[64]

Later in their acquaintance, familiarity led Adams to moderate her prose to a more conversational tone. Six months after the first letter she asked for another reaction. "I send with this the I volume of Molière, and should be glad of your oppinion of them. I cannot be brought to like them, there seems to me to be a general Want of Spirit." That style was more typical. With other correspondents, her letters contained family news, expressions of love, political opinions, plans, feelings, all expressed in a more natural and candid tone, as in most collections of family letters. Whichever collection of genteel correspondence we pick up, the letters contain the usual business of life and friendship.[65]

But even in the most casual exchanges between close friends, the formal note returns, reminding us that the writers never completely forgot that their writings were a performance. Sally Fisher of Duck Creek Cross Roads in Kent County, Delaware, who was to become William Corbit's second wife in 1784, corresponded with Debby Norris in Philadelphia in the late years of the Revolution when the two were twenty-two and nineteen. The girls talked of parties, male admirers, prospective visits, and the expected family news, but then from time to time ascended into the elaborate sentences of high sensibility. Sally wrote after the death of an uncle that "I thought then as well as at many other times that nothing so exalts the human soul except the genuine flame of piety as the sweet emotions of humanity which affords a kind of pleasing pain and leaves serenity almost divine." For her part, Debby Norris, commenting a few months later on Sally's admired aunt, went into raptures: "How sweetly amiable and pleasing [is] sensibility, how beautifully does it gild and add lustre to other accomplishments; like the sun beam to the trembling dew drop!" Genuine affection and youthful energy radiate on every page of these letters. So does the inclination for literary affectations and pleasure in sententious eloquence.[66]

Informal letters of friendship among the colonial gentry proliferated in the eighteenth century. The letters served to enhance friendship and family ties to be sure, but as a secondary message, the letters presented a refined spirit in the act of revealing its sensibility, its vivacity, and its delicacy. These writers knew that they were practicing a genteel art, although they had no expectation of publication. The gracefully turned phrases, the high sentiments, the touches of wit were contrived to confirm the writers' sense of themselves as ladies and gentlemen of fashion.

HANDWRITING

BEYOND the words, the writing itself in polite correspondence shows evidence of instruction and pains; a good hand was necessary to grace a genteel correspondence. Alexander Graydon had noted in the uncouth Irish lawyer at York a coarse, vulgar handwriting and an equally vulgar arithmetic, and so judged him no gentleman. Polite people learned to form their letters as they learned to form their phrases and their sentiments. George Bickham, a famous London engraver and writing master of the seventeenth century, said a good hand will "give in Writing, what we admire in fine Gentlemen; an Easiness of Gesture, and disengag'd Air, which is imperceptibly caught from frequently conversing with the Polite and Well-bred." Chesterfield insisted that his son engage a writing master to improve the boy's handwriting, "which is indeed shamefully bad, and illiberal; it is neither the hand of a man of business, nor of a gentleman, but of a truant schoolboy." Chesterfield preferred "a genteel, legible, liberal hand." George Washington's "Rules of Civility" were as much an exercise in writing as instruction in polite conduct, and he copied them to improve his hand. Nancy Shippen's daughter learned penmanship from a steward on the Livingston estate who was "a very fine penman."[67]

The interest in refined handwriting began during the Italian Renaissance when Florentine humanists took their models from the scripts practiced in Charlemagne's empire. These stood in marked contrast to what they considered the barbaric "Gothic" scripts of their own time. The Caroline scripts received a wider currency when Pope Eugenius IV (1431–47) authorized a cursive style for documents issued by the Apostolic Chancery. The new writing, known as humanist, or chancery, or simply Italian, rapidly spread with Renaissance culture to other countries of Europe. Writing masters encoded Italian in copybooks, the first of which appeared in England in 1571 as *A Booke containing divers sortes of hands,* adapted by John Baildon from a French book by Jean de Beauchesne. In England the Italian hand met remnants of Gothic and a nearly illegible native writing called secretary. Through the seventeenth century both Gothic and Italian styles appeared in copybooks along with many variants and combinations, one appropriately called bastard Italian. In 1700 Gothic and secretary still crossed the pages of many public records; by the mid-eighteenth century anglicized versions of Italian had driven rivals from the field. This transition to a genteel script makes documents of the late eighteenth century much easier reading for modern eyes than those written a hundred years earlier.[68]

Handwriting copybooks were addressed to the scribes and clerks who carried the great burden of official and commercial correspondence but also to the "Gentlemen and Ladies and to the Young Masters and Misses." At first, Italian was the aristocratic hand; Queen Elizabeth and Charles I both took pride in their mastery of that script. In early Stuart England the writing master Martin Billingsley (1591–1622) taught a delicate Italian hand for ladies, a stronger Italian hand for cavaliers, and versions of Gothic for secretaries, lawyers, and ordinary people. As Italian gained ascendance in all realms, the distinctions became less marked; generally, narrower rather than broadly spaced uprights and a stronger slant marked genteel and feminine hands.

In 1748 Benjamin Franklin, who practiced penmanship as a youth while trying to emulate the style of the *Spectator* papers, pirated an edition of a well-known English manual for "Persons of Business" by George Fisher that included handwriting specimens. Franklin added the word "American" to the title to make it *The Instructor, or American Young Man's Best Companion* and inserted his own variant of a commercial version of Italian known as "Round Hand." He also included an "Italian Hand" with more flourishes than practical for commercial writing and with narrower spacing than Round Hand, presumably for the benefit of aspiring gentry. Washington's elegant hand was a form of Round Hand. Polite Americans did not necessarily respect these formal distinctions, but gracefully executed Italian writing was expected in some form from a gentleman or a lady. The invariably graceful signatures on the great political documents at the end of the eighteenth century, led off by John Hancock on the Declaration of Independence, testify to the attention the American gentry of that generation had devoted to penmanship.[69]

The gentry penman needed instruction to achieve this facility, and the craft of penmanship became an established vocation in England by the early seventeenth century. Not only the copybooks but actual writing masters arrived in America not long after settlement. Ordinary schoolmasters taught writing too, but in 1667 William Howard received permission to keep a "wrighting schoole" in Boston, and from then on specialists regularly augmented instruction from other sources. In the first two decades of the eighteenth century more than a dozen free-lance writing masters advertised instruction in Boston. In the 1730s and 1740s Peter Pelham, the famous mezzotint artist, regularly advertised his "Writing and Arithmetick School, near the Town House." In 1755, 216 pupils were enrolled in Boston's "South Writing School" and another 237 in the "North Writing School."

Outside of cities like Boston, scores of copybooks supplemented the instruction of people like the Livingston's steward who taught Peggy Shippen. Most such books came from England; there were twenty-one different

By 1776 all of the signers had learned the art of fine writing, one of the marks of a gentleman.

English copybooks in the library of a single Boston writing master, Abiah Holbrook of the South Writing School. George Fisher's *Young Man's Best Companion* came out in seventeen American editions over nearly a century. Not counting Franklin's American variant of Fisher in 1748, the first genuinely American copybook came from the press of Isaiah Thomas in Worcester in 1785. Often the books and the writing masters combined arithmetic with penmanship as Pelham did, which may account for Graydon's comment about the vulgar arithmetic of his York acquaintance. Not the addition and subtraction but the form of the numbers made the difference.[70]

The implications of polite letter writing lead to furniture. Nothing attests more eloquently to the significance of writing and correspondence in the eighteenth-century mentality than the appearance of a new furniture form to honor those activities—the desk. In the seventeenth century, papers had been kept in boxes, many of them well constructed and adorned. A slant lid on some boxes facilitated writing and made a kind of a desk that could be

One of the earliest settlers of New England, Roger Conant, sometimes called a gentleman in the records, wrote in the crabbed older style.

mounted on an open frame to bring it up to the right height. Near the end of the seventeenth century desks enjoyed a marvelous flowering. The simple joined boxes gave way to desks built onto chests of drawers and sometimes called bureau desks. Sometimes bookcases were mounted on top of these desks, the combined form rising six or seven feet from the floor. Inside the slant lid were drawers and openings of a size to hold folded papers. Desks were made of the best woods, mahogany, walnut, cherry, and maple, fitted with brass pulls, and adorned with pilasters, carved shells, and undulating fronts. The desks matched in workmanship any case pieces in the house and were often among the most costly.

Beyond any question, these forms were meant to honor the activities associated with them. As households adopted gentility in the eighteenth century, some aspects of life like cooking and washing disappeared into the back of the house. Writing, like dining, was not among the suppressed behaviors. The owners of desks wished to advertise their correspondence, to display their writing instruments, and to let it be known that they wrote and received letters. Desks placed in the formal front rooms of the house signified the presence of letter writers in the household. Commercial correspondence continued on desks of unpretentious pine mounted on simple open frames in shops and warehouses. Elegant residential desks spoke more for a genteel correspondence, written in a fine Italian hand, containing gracefully expressed sentiments, and written by women as well as by men.[71]

BEAUTIFICATION

WITH all of this before us, the composure of the body, the personal traits of delicacy, sensibility, and taste, and the genteel skills of conversing and writing, we can return to the question of gentility's basic nature. Does anything hold the diverse traits of so many activities and objects together? Do they have anything in common that approaches a definition? Perhaps of all the personal qualities, taste holds the most promise for shedding light on this puzzle. For one thing, "taste" was an active word, implying responsibilities. Taste required a person to change the world. A person who chose to live with ugliness and disorder could not claim to be tasteful. The word "taste" implicitly incorporated an elaborate cultural project. It implied a mission for the refined population to beautify the world, beginning with their own persons and radiating to all they possessed and influenced.

Though rarely articulated in America in the eighteenth century, the pursuit of this mission was in evidence everywhere. Whenever Washington's military and civic responsibilities permitted, he gave concentrated attention to the adornment of Mount Vernon—the house, the gardens, the room furnishings, and the table. As deeply engaged in public affairs and business as he was, he still devoted himself generously to the beautification of his environment. And Washington was not exceptional. Men of substance everywhere occupied themselves with the details of architecture, furniture design, and landscaping. The title of Thomas Chippendale's *Gentleman's and Cabinet-Maker's Director* implied that design was the province of gentlemen, not just craftsmen, and the American gentry took up the charge.

They did not act dutifully or out of self-sacrificing idealism. A grand house, properly laid out and decorated, anchored a person's standing in the community and even sustained political power. Gentility was interwoven with the totality of gentry culture. By the Revolution, those who lacked taste generally lacked power. A magnate who erected an expensive but hideous house lost strength. Power and the tasteful ideal were interrelated. Sir Charles Grandison's equipage was "perfectly in taste" because everything about that paragon of gentility had to be. Without taste he would have commanded little respect.[72]

In addition to the political support of beautification, intellectual backing came from distinguished intellectuals in England and on the Continent. Increasing use of the word "taste" in polite speech coincided with the appearance of a spate of treatises about aesthetics, a branch of philosophy that received renewed attention in the eighteenth century. In England, Joseph Addison, Francis Hutcheson, Sir Joshua Reynolds, David Hume, William Hogarth, Edmund Burke, and many lesser lights addressed the problem in the same years when the broad-based campaign to beautify houses, gardens, and persons was reaching a peak. In fact, the gentry's preoccupation with beauty may have prompted the efforts to define its nature. In an essay on taste in *The Spectator* in 1712, Addison commented that "as this Word arises very often in conversation, I shall endeavour to give some Account of it," and then proceeded to his discourse. On the other hand, the writers on beauty also wished to offer guidance and inspiration for the beautification campaign. One anonymous work on "the polite arts" stated explicitly the simple grounding of the project. "Taste has every where the same Rules. It wills, that we erase every thing that can give an unlovely impression, and that we offer all that can produce an agreeable one."[73] That was the imperative, inherent in genteel taste, that drove the beautification program.

Edmund Burke was one who sought to define the nature of beauty. His *Philosophical Enquiry into the Origin of Our Ideas of the Sublime and the Beautiful* influenced aesthetic philosophy both in England and on the Continent. The work is particularly helpful in understanding gentility because of the peculiar twist Burke gave to the meaning of beauty; he contrasted beauty not only to its polar opposite, ugliness, but to the sublime, which is exalted and aesthetic without being beautiful, and this distinction between the sublime and the beautiful serves to reveal more clearly the nature—and the limitations—of gentility.

Burke compiled a list of attributes that set beauty apart from ugliness. Smoothness, softness, and gently flowing curves are among the qualities that make an object beautiful rather than ugly. Sublimity, on the other hand, is distinguished from beauty by quite different traits. Sublimity is power and terror: great craggy peaks with their menacing shadows, sharp angles, and abrupt drops; ferocious storms at sea, with crashing waves and blasts of destructive wind. The exercise of power—the church at the judgment of a sinner, or civil government at an execution—arouses sublime emotions: dread, reverence, awe. Beauty is situated in a tranquil and peaceful region between ugliness and sublimity. The sublime and the beautiful, Burke observed, arise from different principles, "one being founded on pain, the other on pleasure."[74] Beauty pleases the human spirit rather than repulsing or terrifying it.

Gentility, being neither ugly nor sublime, belonged wholly to the beautiful. Gentility, whether in dress, personal manners, or architecture, was harmony, smoothness, polish, gradual rather than abrupt variation, the subduing of harsh emotions. Gentility beautified the world in Burke's sense. Eighteenth-century portraits, with their graceful and easy postures, fine clothes, and composed faces, present people who have overcome their baser impulses and learned to conceal the fearful secrets of their hearts. Painters consciously sought to make sitters neither ugly nor sublime, but smooth and beautiful.

Gentility beautified the persons of the sitters, then went on to beautify the environment, starting with the furnishing of formal rooms and extending outward into gardens and grounds. Outdoors, genteel nature was neither sublimely rugged nor ugly and coarse. While fashion might permit, say, a rough grotto on the grounds of a large estate, the predominant aim was to create a regulated landscape that repressed the sublime in favor of beauty's gentle curves and smooth surfaces. The aim of the polite arts, one theorist offered, was the imitation of "*beautiful* nature," neither the rugged, ominous nature of the sublime nor unkempt, disordered, ugly nature.[75] The harmony and beauty that genteel culture looked for in nature paralleled the ease and harmony in which genteel society took pleasure.

The aesthetic of the beautiful outlined in Burke's *Enquiry* was thus a philosophical expression of the spirit of gentility. At the same time, the *Enquiry* helps us to understand gentility's limitations. Gentility's devotion to beautiful nature put it at odds with both the ugly and the sublime. Horror and awe, emotions evoked by the sublime, were repressed in genteel natures, as were all things base and disturbing—the dissonant, the plebeian, the filthy.

All had to be concealed in the interest of beauty and harmony. But the attempt to control nature and society for the sake of a beautiful appearance necessarily made denial and repression essential traits of gentility. Even though in the service of a worthy purpose, the wish to conceal was, in the last analysis, shallow. Gentility hid what it could not countenance and denied whatever caused discomfort. That deficiency in candor and courage, however commendable the impulse behind it, was the flaw at the core of gentility, the reason why it proved at last to be weak and superficial.

CHAPTER IV

Houses and Gardens

WILLIAM CORBIT built his grand Georgian mansion in Cantwell's Bridge, Delaware, in 1772, just one lifetime after his grandfather constructed the Brinton house fifty miles to the north in 1704. The contrast of the two structures gives an idea of the transformation that came over American residential architecture in a relatively short span. One was elaborately decorated and sumptuous, the other plain, rudimentary, and frugal; one looks back to a traditional society, the other moves confidently into our present.

In style and posture, the two houses typify the changes occurring everywhere in the colonies. A match for the Corbit and Brinton pair can be found in every colony: saltbox simplicity in New England over against Isaac Royal's three-story fashionable town house in Medford, temporary two- and four-room houses for the Chesapeake gentry in the seventeenth century compared with Westover, Stratford, and Nomini Hall in the eighteenth century. The cost, the design, the size, the decor, the furnishings, the mood of gentry houses underwent a revolution from the seventeenth to the eighteenth century, compelling us to ask what the transformation means. Having examined courtesy books and genteel ideas of the body and mind, we turn now to the houses themselves.

RENAISSANCE HOUSES IN ENGLAND AND AMERICA

IF WE enlarge our field of vision to cross the Atlantic, we can see that the new houses were part of a broad transformation in upper-middle-class houses going forward in all of England's cultural provinces at about the same time. In the seventeenth century, Renaissance principles fundamentally reshaped English domestic architecture, beginning with royal and aristocratic residences, and after 1660 the houses of the gentry. The colonial houses were part of this widespread architectural movement.

The classical revival began in Italy and moved into England in the middle of the sixteenth century through design books, the ideas of Englishmen who traveled in Italy, and migrant artisans from the Continent who had absorbed Renaissance conceptions of building in their own countries. John Summerson has remarked that "taste in architecture reached London about 1615: taste, that is, in the exclusive, snobbish sense of the recognition of certain fixed values by certain people." Before then buildings had incorporated traditional ideas of construction, with decorative touches added by the master mason and carpenter under the overall direction of the client. After the classical revival reached England, chiefly through the work of Inigo Jones, the aristocracy adopted increasingly rigorous standards of aesthetic propriety based on classical models as interpreted by the Italian Palladio and then by the great English architects of the seventeenth century who expressed Renaissance classicism in a native idiom—notable among them, besides Jones, Roger Pratt and Christopher Wren.[1]

Renaissance taste only gradually gained dominance in England. To the end of the century and beyond, an eclectic style that incorporated touches of classical decoration without going over wholly to classical forms continued to shape many buildings. But riding the crest of England's general adoption of Renaissance culture, classical ideas steadily gained influence, not only among aristocratic builders of great country houses but also among the lesser gentry. As time went on, the nameless artisans who were responsible for the great bulk of housing construction achieved an ever surer command of the classical idiom. Moving through time and a number of social levels, Renaissance architectural principles were given idiosyncratic expression, without losing sight of common fundamentals.

Each region developed its own designs, employing regional materials, but all in the classical mode. In southeastern England a hip-roofed, central-passage brick house developed which later flourished in a colonial version along the James River in Virginia. Masons built two-and-a-half-story, double-pile houses with symmetrical fronts all over Kent and Sussex counties in the first decades of the eighteenth century. The first classically inspired town house in Bristol, England's second-largest city at the time, went up in 1700. Until then the town had been "medieval in character," according to one of its architectural historians, the buildings largely timber-framed. This one house was followed immediately by a host of brick structures in the classical taste arranged in residential squares and terraces. The lesser gentry in Ireland and Wales were likewise building Renaissance houses in large numbers in the same period. As the result of what amounted to a major building boom, virtually all of the gentry in England, Scotland, and Wales were housed in some version of a Renaissance house by 1740. John Harris has said that "the amount that was built [in England] between 1715 and 1745 has no equivalent in any other country." To facilitate the expansion, architects and artisans published a small library of guides to design and construction methods. Between 1724 and 1790, 275 new titles were published along with 170 editions of earlier books. Houses like William Corbit's were the American expression of this widespread movement.[2]

The changeover seems more dramatically revolutionary in the colonies because seventeenth-century gentry housing stock was so far below general English standards, and the contrast with later buildings therefore appears to be more stark. But English gentry houses before 1660, though larger and more comfortable, were equally traditional in design. In the eighteenth

Minster House was one of the scores of houses constructed for the middle class in southern England.

The Blounce façade was added in 1699 to give an older farmhouse a look in keeping with the latest style.

century all the British provinces, in England as well as America, underwent the change from nearly medieval modes of design, decor, and room arrangement to Renaissance style. The sharper contrast in the colonies points up the empire-wide transformation which the complex array of houses in England partly obscures.

Recognition of the broader transformation of residential architecture throughout the British provinces does not, however, explain the significance of the Corbit house for the residents of Cantwell's Bridge. To grasp the implications, we must look more closely at the mansions themselves and locate them within the matrix of the other houses in the village. No house stood alone, even in a dispersed countryside. Each one occupied a place among a group of houses, and the whole array of structures gave meaning to the individual dwellings. Corbit's house was one of a tiny number of mansions standing in an assemblage of much simpler houses. His house, besides looking much grander, implied a different pattern of life that is understood best when all are considered together.

THE SEVENTEENTH CENTURY

FROM the beginning of settlement in the seventeenth century, a tiny elite at the top of society found architectural devices, other than size, for setting off their houses. John Pynchon, the economic and political baron of the Springfield region in the Connecticut Valley, constructed a house in 1659 roughly on the plan of an English manor house. The house was remarkable in New England for being built of brick (only a dozen or so brick houses went up in the entire seventeenth century), but the more significant architectural feature was the porch tower. Throughout the century, a few eminent clergy, political leaders, and great merchants set their residences apart by placing two-story enclosed "porches" with gables on the fronts of their houses. (What were then called porches, we would call towers.) The dimensions of Pynchon's house, forty-two by twenty-one feet, were not exceptionally large for a gentleman's house, but the porch, along with the brick, was unusual. William Hosley, after closely studying Connecticut Valley architecture, estimated there were perhaps a dozen porched houses in the valley before 1680. Springfield had two, for example, one built for the minister in 1638 and Pynchon's in 1659.

The Connecticut Valley pattern held true throughout the colonies. Porches appeared elsewhere in New England, primarily in Boston, and also in the South. The most famous southern example of a porch, because it still stands, fronts Nathaniel Bacon's 1665 house in Surry County, Virginia. The main house at Clifts Plantation, Westmoreland County, also had a porch in

1675, though it was only a single-story frame house. Perhaps it was this feature that earned it the title of "manner house." Other porches likely adorned some of the seventeenth-century Chesapeake houses which have now rotted away.[3]

These few buildings aside, the rest of the colonial population lived in relatively homogeneous housing. Doubtless the differences appeared greater to them than to us, but the distinctions were far less marked than in the eighteenth century. The buildings that housed most of the people in the seventeenth century have now disappeared from the landscape. Architectural historians have redrawn the housing picture only by sifting through estate inventories to find those that list possessions room by room, by reconstructing building patterns from archaeological excavations, and by gleaning diverse clues scattered here and there in other sources. The picture that emerges up and down the coast from New England to the Carolinas is of one type of house for a third to a half or more of the common people: a one-room framed or log building. Above the single downstairs room was a room reached by a ladder or stairs; possibly on the back or side was a lean-to addition. The size of the single cell was remarkably uniform—around eighteen by twenty feet on the inside. Sometimes a partition broke this single room into two rooms.

Outside, unpainted riven weatherboards clad the frame of large timber pieces; inside, a large fireplace opening dominated one wall. In the typical case no decoration would enliven any of the other walls. Probably the nogging between the framing members, or the log walls, would be sheathed with clapboards; possibly the walls would be plastered and whitewashed.

Built for the leading figure in the upper Connecticut Valley in the mid-seventeenth century, the Colonel John Pynchon house combined a gabled porch with a central hall and brick construction to make it one of the most distinguished houses in New England at the time.

The windows were small openings, perhaps two feet by two feet, sometimes with glass panes, though as often as not there would be oilcloth or a sliding wood panel to cover the opening rather than glazing. One or two windows in the first-floor room along with the door provided all the natural light the room was to enjoy.[4] More colonial families in the seventeenth century lived in such dwellings than in any other kind of house.

In between the one-room houses of ordinary people and the porched houses of the great families were the two-rooms-to-a-floor, two-story houses which we most commonly associate with the colonial period. Some regional differences existed. In the South these houses commonly went up only a story and a half. In New England the kitchen and storage room were sometimes added on the back to create the saltbox profile. In the Chesapeake the kitchen was housed in a separate building. In both regions, the houses had hall rooms where work, eating, sleeping, and often cooking went on, and parlors, which were actually the best bedrooms and the location of the family's finest furniture. The rooms above, whether in a full story of half, were additional sleeping and storage spaces.[5]

This two-cell house obviously was an improvement over a single-cell dwelling: it could be twice as large. But the blend of the two house types makes it difficult to identify a sharp social division between the residents of one type of house and those of the other. For one thing, the size of the rooms

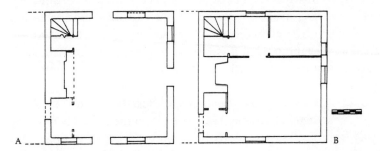

A   B

ABOVE. *In 1714 the Dilworth House in northern Delaware had a single room on the first floor (A) with a chamber above (B). The door opposite the fireplace and the second-floor subdivisions are later alterations. Many one-room houses had only a loft above the first floor.*

LEFT. *Throughout the seventeenth and eighteenth centuries most people lived in houses with one or two rooms on the first floor, like this late-eighteenth-century house in southeastern Pennsylvania.*

did not increase in the larger houses. Room dimensions in New England, for example, remained around eighteen by twenty feet even when the overall size of the house doubled. The large-house people did not seem to envision grander activities for themselves which required larger spaces and would warrant the more elaborate framing required to make bigger rooms. In the middle colonies, room sizes even shrank in larger houses. John Chad's house, built in the early years of the eighteenth century on the banks of the Brandywine in Chester County, Pennsylvania, measured twenty by thirty feet, but on both first and second floors partitions divided the space to make the rooms smaller than the customary eighteen by twenty, a reflection of ethnic preferences in the region. Chad, who inherited 500 acres and half of a corn mill from his father, a member of the Provincial Assembly, built a house larger than the ordinary single-cell house, providing more spaces, but not larger ones.[6]

There seems to have been no sense of shame or undue confinement associated with the one-room house. In such dwellings signs of finish or superior construction marked off better small houses from worse, suggesting that people of standing dwelt there. Living in a one-over-one, eighteen-by-twenty-foot house was not in itself demeaning. William Barns built an imposing brick structure a few miles east of John Chad on the Philadelphia–Nottingham road in the first decades of the eighteenth century. The overall dimensions were twenty by forty, but Barns lived in only half of the building. The main-floor hall and upstairs bedroom on the east were used as an inn for travelers. The family lived in the one-over-one pair of rooms to the west. Barns installed an elegant molded fireplace surround, paneled doors, and a number of decorative features which speak for his taste and aspiration, and yet he lived for thirty-one years in two rooms.[7]

The blending of the single- and double-cell houses seems to have been no different in New England. Among 144 houses from the period before 1725 still remaining from the Massachusetts Bay colony, 82 began as single-cell houses, all but a tiny handful of which were subsequently expanded. The purchasers or builders of the small houses presumably lived in them for some years and then added on. The single and double plans were not distinct species of housing, designed for entirely different levels of the social order; it was quite possible to move from one to the other. In 1655, John Whipple built a single-cell house in Ipswich, Massachusetts, and lived in it for twenty years or so, during which time he served as a deputy to the General Court. Sometime before 1683, his son Captain John Whipple, a prosperous merchant, added two rooms on the other side of the great fireplace to make a standard New England hall-parlor house.[8] The transition from small house to large represented a change in style and perhaps some improvement in wealth rather than a marked change in social position.

RIGHT: *The first floor of the Chad House of 1720 in Delaware County, Pennsylvania, was divided into two rooms and the second into two rooms and a hall.*

BELOW. *John Whipple was content with a single room on the ground floor when he built the original part of this house around 1655. His son added a parlor with a chamber above to complete the dwelling.*

In various important details the larger houses afforded more comfort or displayed signs of the occupant's wealth and dignity, without being ostentatiously different. The large houses were slightly better lit, but not greatly so. Window piercings remained small by later standards. The Buttolph-Williams house in Wethersfield, built in 1692, an elegant, generous house for its time and place, strikes the modern visitor as having blank front walls because there is only one, relatively small casement window opening into each room from the front rather than the two large sash windows customary in the eighteenth century. The absence of external decoration at the door and windows, along with the weathered, unpainted exterior, makes the house imposing but scarcely opulent. The occupants of these houses went far beyond the ordinary in applying lath and plaster to their walls, in chamfering beams, and in putting molded vertical sheathing on the fireplace walls, but the total effect is of extremely modest, if comely, decoration.[9]

Hall-parlor houses of this sort satisfied virtually all of the upper half of colonial society in the seventeenth century. Everywhere merchants and planters of means lived in four basic rooms no larger than twenty by twenty, two up and two down, with additional workrooms attached or set apart from

The Buttolph-Williams house. The original structure, built around 1693, was termed a "mansion house" in a 1698 inventory, but it more than quadrupled in value when it changed ownership again in 1711, suggesting major enlargements. Yet even a house of such pretensions still had tiny windows and a winding stair against the chimney, went unpainted, and kept the old hall-parlor plan of two rooms to a floor.

the houses. The sense of social place of the owners required no more. The lineaments of the social structure were doubtless as sharply perceived in the seventeenth century as later, but the material expressions were far less pronounced. Porches on housefronts, along with a small number of other architectural devices and expensive furnishings, distinguished the uppermost elite, but below that line the differentiations appeared externally as a smooth blend. The greatest visible break, between the one-room main-floor plan and the two-room, separated people less abruptly than we might imagine. People of wealth and recognized standing contented themselves with single-cell houses to the end of the seventeenth century and beyond.[10]

The similarities went beyond room size, poor lighting, and the low level of decoration. Both one- and two-cell houses, and also the porch-tower houses, embodied the same life plan in their architecture. All three houses had at their center a single room, the hall, where work, cooking, eating, sleeping, and talking went on. The name of the room was the same as for the great halls in lordly medieval houses where the master and his family dined with all the servants and underlings and where activities of many sorts went on. In structures high and low, this single room for a medley of activities lay at the heart of the house. The first colonists automatically built to the same plan, carrying over the pattern of living that concentrated activity in one room.

Certain changes in room arrangements that occurred after the medieval period also influenced seventeenth-century colonial housing. The main change, going back two centuries, was the containment of fire and smoke in a fireplace and chimney, which permitted a second floor to be installed above the great hall and partitioned for use as bedrooms. This separation of sleeping chambers from the hall, first for parents and then for others, was the most significant alteration in ordinary houses in the centuries before 1660. The construction of private bedrooms occurred in manor houses well before that date, and in the sixteenth and early seventeenth centuries, ambitious peasants erected houses with comparable private quarters called parlors.

The heavy expenditures for bedstead and bedding, so notable in seventeenth-century inventories, point to the interest in the furnishing of these sleeping parlors. The parlor bedroom and its furnishings represented the direction of ambition and improvement. The great advantage of the two-room house over the one-room was that it enabled a family to install private bedrooms, a parlor for parents and chambers above for other family members. Occupants of both one- and two-cell houses shared this sense of the desired line of improvement. The ambition of the one-room residents to add a parlor for private sleeping and the display of the family's best furniture was shown in New England by the large number of one-room houses that were enlarged to two. Though people in larger houses had achieved their goal, and the one-room people were still striving, everyone had the same pattern of living in mind.

THE EIGHTEENTH CENTURY

WHEN we move in our imaginations to the eighteenth century, we are inclined to fill the landscape with the gracious colonial mansions we loosely term Georgian. They are the houses that have survived two centuries of change, and their enduring beauty makes them the natural subject of innumerable picture books and the focus of attention for local historical society fund-raising. And yet we know that the bulk of the population could never have afforded such grandeur. Mansions obviously were homes for a wealthy elite. The houses of ordinary people in the eighteenth century differed little in basic plan from housing in the seventeenth century. The hall-parlor, double-cell house continued as the standard for the ordinary well-off farmer, and the single-cell, two-story or story-and-a-half house persisted in large numbers until 1800 and beyond for the bottom half of society.[11] Many even had porch-tower houses constructed.

We tend to obliterate the small houses from our imaginations, just as time has removed them from the landscape. But the records show them still standing in large numbers. The orphan's court records give us one cross section of housing stock. When the head of household died before making a will, the courts stepped in to protect the property of his minor heirs until they could take possession in their own right. Protection of the property required that virtually everything be listed along with its general condition. An analysis of the records from 1760 to 1830 in Kent County, Delaware, a prosperous agricultural region, shows that 67 percent of the described houses had less than 450 square feet on the ground floor, which, when the chimney stack is included, would be the size of the largest of the single-cell dwellings. Another 22 percent lived in houses from 450 to 600 square feet, space large enough for two rooms—though small ones—on the ground floor. Only 11 percent of the orphans' parents lived in larger dwellings—full hall-parlor houses. The information is recorded in such a way—by the political division called hundreds—that the marsh people along the river margins and the settlers on the sandy soils at the Maryland border are included with the more prosperous farmers in the central core, but since the central core was much more populous we must conclude that even there single-cell dwellings predominated at least until 1830.[12]

So it is that when we imagine the entire population of houses scattered across the eighteenth-century landscape, we must see many small frame or log houses rising a half story or a full story above the ground-floor room.

The mix of single-cell and double-cell plans varied from region to region. In the rich bottomlands along the Connecticut Valley there were far more two-story hall-parlor houses than in the hill towns east and west of the river. On the sandy soils of Sussex County, Delaware, just south of Kent, were many more single-cell houses than in the region around the Ridgelys' house near Dover. In Halifax County, in Virginia's poor southside, 80 percent of the houses in 1785 contained less than 400 square feet on the ground floor. We would expect many more larger houses north of the James. But amidst the variations, the main point is that the basic housing stock of the seventeenth century continued through the eighteenth century. Unpainted small houses, with tiny window openings and unfinished interiors, in a mix of single- and double-cell plans, were abundant everywhere in 1800 and in most areas predominated.[13]

The great eighteenth-century houses, like William Corbit's in Cantwell's Bridge, formed a layer above this continuing modest housing stock. While there were improvements in size, framing methods, ornament, and finish through all levels of housing during the eighteenth century, the dramatic

Lewis Miller noted that Michael Heinegac lived in York Township, four and a half miles from the town of York. Virtually all of Miller's pictures of houses outside of York in the first decade of the nineteenth century showed log houses, most one-room with a small window.

changes occurred at the top with the use of brick and painted clapboards, ornamented doorways and window openings, large sash windows distributed symmetrically across the façade, and broad open staircases and decorated chimney breasts. These grand houses stood out clearly from the traditional house forms, which still surrounded the mansions.

The first tiny group of the new mansions appeared in the late seventeenth century at the behest of merchants whose wealth gave them a claim to positions at the top of colonial society. These merchants were all recent immigrants who brought to the colonies firsthand experience with the stylish houses that the English middle class began to construct for itself after the restoration of Charles II in 1660. Going beyond the vernacular traditions of the English manor house that inspired Pynchon's porched dwelling, the provincial middle class in England began experimenting with simplified versions of continental and Renaissance houses. The new colonial builders had themselves seen what was happening in England and fashioned their houses in America along the same lines.

Peter Sergeant, who drew inspiration from Dutch house forms for his great house put up in Boston in 1679, was a London merchant before he came to Boston in 1667. Colonel John Foster moved to Boston from Buckinghamshire in 1675 and around 1688 erected a three-story brick house with Ionic pilasters that obviously drew on the Renaissance forms which Inigo Jones introduced to the English nobility earlier in the seventeenth century. The

Captain Archibald Macphaedris, a Scottish merchant who arrived from Britain in the early years of the eighteenth century, built this house in Portsmouth, New Hampshire, with the aid of an English-trained housewright. The house was far in advance of any in the town at the time.

great houses of Richard Whitpaine and Robert Turner, Jr., in Philadelphia, which greatly impressed contemporaries though their design is unknown, were constructed for wealthy merchants with recent English experience. Samuel Carpenter's hip-roofed brick house in Philadelphia built around 1687 was definitely in the Renaissance mold, and like all Philadelphians at that time, he was new to the colonies. The most influential house in the Chesapeake in the early eighteenth century, the Governor's Palace built in the style of Christopher Wren though likely not by his design, followed in the spirit of the capitol that was built at the behest of Governor Francis Nicholson, who made it his mission to bring to America the latest fashions in city planning. Apart from the palace, the prototype for private houses of the brick hip-roofed variety in Virginia was erected around 1715 by Edward Jacquelin, who migrated from Kent County, England, in 1704.[14] All of the early mansions were built for men whose English experience enabled them to transmit the new styles to the colonies.

After 1725, the native aristocracy began to build mansions on a still more elaborate scale. By then the best informed of the American elite could draw on examples like the Governor's Palace or learn about current English fashions from architectural design books and English-trained craftsmen. Though not recent immigrants, the mansion people continued to be the richest and most prominent members of colonial society. The owners of the finest houses to go up in Virginia from 1725 to 1750—Mann Page, Thomas Lee, William Byrd, Landon Carter, Robert Carter, John Randolph—were, as would be expected, the people who ran the provincial government and dominated the vestries of the church as well as controlling vast tracts of land and hundreds of slaves. Thomas Hancock, whose 1737–40 house on Beacon Hill exercised an influence in New England comparable to the Governor's Palace in Virginia, was a man of immense wealth.

Merchants in all the New England ports soon built tall town houses in various versions of fashionable Georgian design. Around the middle of the eighteenth century, the Connecticut Valley River Gods, the interlinked families who ran the government and the church, began erecting three-story, gambrel-roofed houses with overblown scroll-pediment doorways that must have appeared both immense and incredibly overdecorated compared with the flat-front, hall-parlor houses of their neighbors. Everywhere along the American coast in the eighteenth century, people of the greatest wealth and influence in city and country erected spacious, beautifully decorated Georgian houses in the general mode of William Corbit's house, many of them much more opulent.[15]

This new wave of mansion building was not reserved for the uppermost provincial elite, as was the case for the porch houses of the seventeenth century. The Georgian style spread widely among the colonial gentry as the porch design had never done. In Virginia few planters could raise a huge pile like Thomas Lee's Stratford or William Byrd's Westover or Mann Page's Rosewell. These vastly expensive undertakings strained the resources of the most affluent planters. But vernacular builders sensed the essence of the great houses and copied the fundamental elements for a much wider segment of well-off planters.

A few decorative features like sash windows carried over to the middle-range great house, but more important were two critical rooms: an entertaining room, usually called a parlor, and a stair passage. The entertaining room took the place of the old hall, and was sometimes called that instead of parlor, but it was adapted for more formal entertainment by removal of beds and other work furnishings in favor of better tables, chairs, and cupboards full of ceramics. The other crucial feature, the stair passage, usually in the center of the house, though sometimes to the side, contained a broad, open staircase with balusters that ascended to the second floor, even when it was but a half story under the roof. This open, decorated stairway became a primary mark of a fine house. Opposite the parlor on the other side of the stair passage, in the Virginia case, was the dining room, whose purposes were less definite than the name suggested, since inventories recorded beds and tools there along with tables and chairs. There were other work, storage, and sleeping spaces, but parlor and stair passage were the identifying rooms of the middle-range fine house.[16]

This house was built by a planter, Richard Taliaferro, whose daughter married George Wythe; the couple moved into the house soon after. The house follows the classic hip-roofed design common in Virginian and middle-class English mansions.

These modest houses took a slightly different form in New England. Only the grandest houses had stair passages that ran entirely through the center. Kevin Sweeney found forty-one houses in western Massachusetts with tall scroll-pediment doorways built by people who were not River Gods; only four of the forty-one are definitely known to have had central-hall plans. The other decorated houses retained the central chimney with the stairs close against it. But to achieve the proper effect, the entry was enlarged to make room for a dignified stairway with handrails, balusters, and a newel post. Instead of circling upward inside its case as in the seventeenth century, the open, front-entry stair rose to a landing, made a quarter turn, rose again to a second landing, and made another turn to reach the second floor. Though not as sweeping as a run of stairs in a stair passage, the New England version met the requirements of the lesser gentry.[17] These middling dwellings possessed the essential elements of mansions and permitted all planters with claims on gentry status to stage the rituals of polite society, without incurring excessive costs or indulging in inappropriate ostentation.

The Ridgely house at Eden Hill falls into this class of middling mansions. The house does not rank among the great houses of colonial America any more than the Ridgelys' modest estate had a place among the great American fortunes. Though distinguished in origin and eminent in Dover society, the Ridgelys were at best common gentry, bearing their part of the burdens of government and living their lives with a modicum of refinement. Most of the Kent County brick houses could claim to be nothing more than Eden Hill, and the families who occupied them were no more distinguished. They

Along with the parlor, the broad stair that rose in a straight line to a landing was a characteristic mark of the genteel house.

exemplify a large class of people with modest fortunes and strictly local dignity who nonetheless constructed houses with the requisite formal parlors and open stairways adorned with balusters and newel.

Although not ostentatious by later standards, these middling mansions reordered the relationship of houses and social class in the eighteenth century. The houses made it difficult for anyone with aspirations to social leadership to live in one of the modest, small houses that continued as the basic housing stock. A John Whipple in the seventeenth century satisfied himself with paneling a fireplace wall to dignify a one-over-one house. Until about 1730, a person of local note could remain in a single-cell house or expand to a simple hall-parlor plan without compromising his respectability. But as versions of the new Georgian mansion style went up on every side, local leaders could not disregard the new housing standards for long.

Besides building new houses, they redecorated older structures. Through the middle years of the eighteenth century older houses everywhere were added to and vigorously remodeled. In Chester County, for example, a one-and-a-half-story stone house, built in 1710 in West Marlboro Township, was added to in 1738 to create a center passage house called (inappropriately) Primitive Hall with two rooms on each side and wide stairs ascending in two flights to a second floor. The old structure was not abandoned, but it was transformed into something entirely different. Outside of New England, even in smaller houses, the remodeling usually resulted in a house with a stair passage and one room on each side.[18] In New England the upgraded stairs occupied enlarged front entries. Daniel Updike rebuilt the chimney of

Modest genteel houses in New England did not include a stair passage with enough room for a straight rise of stairs. The New England compromise was to open the stair, add balusters, and sometimes place a landing at the turns.

a house he inherited at Cocumscussocin, Rhode Island, to make room for a front-entry stairway with three runs and three turned balusters for each step; he then went on to panel the fireplace wall and case the summer beams in the ceiling of his entertainment room.[19]

The Philipse house in Westchester County, New York, went through a much more dramatic revision. In 1681 the first owner of the manor lands, Frederick Philipse, raised a two-story house with one room on each floor and was content to live in it although he was granted a baronial estate that stretched twenty-two miles along the east bank of the Hudson River. Between 1725 and 1730 a pair of rooms was added to the first structure to make a five-bay, central-passage Georgian house with large twelve-over-twelve windows and a modillion cornice. In 1745 the grandson, Frederick II, added a wing and redecorated the entire house. He constructed another passage of stairs with balusters of twisted mahogany instead of turned pine as in the first staircase. A molded plaster ceiling was installed in one parlor with engaged pilasters flanking the fireplace and a scroll-pediment chimneypiece.[20] By that time, a New York magnate like Frederick II was compelled to build to match his dignity.

People of much lesser standing also risked the appearance of eccentricity unless they brought their dwellings up to the new standard. Benjamin Mifflin of Delaware was shocked to find his own uncle living in "a Loansom Cottage a small Log House that serves for Kitchen, Parlour, Hall and Bed Chamber," with nothing to offer a guest but "rum, Water and Brown Sugar."[21]

Joseph Pennock built Primitive Hall in Chester County, Pennsylvania, as an addition to a one-and-a-half-story stone house dating from c. 1710. The new house was a compromise between the old style and the emerging new fashions. The front entrance has a batten door; the windows are large but not symmetrically placed; inside is a stair hall with a wide straight run of steps to a landing.

STAIRWAYS AND PARLORS

THE distinctive architectural features of the new mansions, stairway and parlor, are a little puzzling and require explanation. Why did gentry houses abandon encased stairs for the open, decorated stairs when one was far more practical than the other? The narrower stair winding up the chimney stack or rising unobtrusively in a corner of the room did offer less secure footing than broad straight stairs, but ease of ascent on broad stairs was more than counterbalanced by the additional space they occupied and the conduit the stairwell offered for warm air to escape from the first to the second floor.

RIGHT. *The stairs in the Governor's Palace at Williamsburg were of gubernatorial width.*

BELOW. *Encased stairs had the double advantage of occupying little space and keeping first-floor warmth from rising to the second story. What they lacked was the grace of a broad ascent to the floor above. In this eighteenth-century mansion, only the back stairs off the kitchen were still encased.*

Encased stairs at the back of the house remained in use for servants, who presumably would also require secure footing to carry food and bedding to the chambers above, if practicality alone was the main concern. Stairs from second to third floor were usually narrow and without decoration too. The symbolic and decorative force of the open stairway in the first-floor hall seem to be more significant than any practical benefits that wide stairs offered.

The purpose of the broad stairs does not immediately emerge from the documents. Peter Smith, speaking of Renaissance houses in Wales, says that stairways were their distinguishing feature. Earlier houses were "conceived first and the stair fitted in as an afterthought. In the final version of the centrally planned house the stair was envisaged from the beginning and the rest of the house was built around it." Though Smith calls this change "the most important architectural development of our period," he does not explain what it meant to the residents of the houses.[22]

We get some help from English aristocratic houses of a century earlier, in which stairs played a part in the ascent from a ground floor to the more formal apartments above, or from the great hall to more exclusive chambers up the stairs. In the two centuries preceding 1600, the master and his family withdrew from the hall, where all of the household dined, to more private and refined rooms for conversation away from the noise and vulgarity of the common dining room. Yet though he was not in the hall, the lord's presence had to be felt and the great stair marked the route of the ascent to his chamber. Up this path went footmen from the kitchen, through the hall, to the lord's private room. Along this parade route went distinguished visitors ascending to the finest rooms on the floor above.

After a visit to Holdenby in 1579, Lord Burghley complimented his host, Sir Christopher Hatton, on the stairs: "I found no one thing of greater grace than your stately ascent from your hall to your great chamber." In the famed prodigy houses of the Jacobean period, the stairs awaited the anticipated royal visit when majesty would ascend them. The idea was buried in the distant past by the eighteenth century, but still resonated. Isaac Ware, the eighteenth-century author of an important architectural guidebook, observed that in royal buildings stairs must be at least ten feet wide. Width apparently had to correspond with dignity, and perhaps that feeling hovered over the stairs in provincial houses. Ware also observed that a great house required decorated, broad stairs, for insignificant stairs implied that the chambers above were inferior. "The stair-case must present itself boldly and freely to the sight; otherwise all has a confused and poor aspect. It looks as if the house had no good upper floor." Stairs signified an ascent to grand rooms where guests were received with proper dignity.[23]

In the most elegant houses of the eighteenth century, people entertained on two floors, and stairs facilitated circulation among the spaces used for music, dancing, cards, and refreshments. The stairs in the Powel house in Philadelphia served that purpose, leading the way to the grand ballroom above the two ground-floor parlors. William Corbit's house copied the Powel house in placing its ballroom on the second floor as well, necessitating an impressive stairway to sustain refinement along all the passages through which guests might proceed. In less pretentious dwellings, the chambers above served primarily for sleeping and storage, making grand stairs less important. Yet even in smaller houses, the upstairs chambers held six or eight chairs, a tea table, and tea equipage fitted out for the entertainment of guests. The broad stairs with turned balusters and newel posts offered formal routes to these chambers. Enclosed narrow, winding stairs lay at the back of the house, set off from the paths of guests at formal entertainments. A host would have been embarrassed to lead his or her guests up a narrow, enclosed stairway entirely out of keeping with the dignity and refinement of the occasion.[24]

In these clues to the meaning of stairways, we can detect in the architecture of the new houses a new governing idea. The traditional house centered its plan on life in the hall, where virtually every activity went on, supplemented with a more dignified chamber to which the master and mistress of the house retired and where they located their finest possessions. The mansion houses of the eighteenth century, as the stairways suggest, embraced formal entertainment as their governing idea. Activities of every sort went on in the houses, and much besides entertainment happened even in the most formal rooms. But the stairway was to function as a parade route for guests, not only as a way from the first to the second floor. The stairs indicate that practical everyday functions gave way to relatively infrequent occurrences of primarily symbolic significance—the occasions of formal entertainment when gentility achieved its climactic expression.

The preeminence of the formal parlor in house plans of the period confirms the ruling idea of the mansions. These rooms received the most concentrated attention as well as the highest degree of decorative elaboration. The parlor cost more than any other room and all for uses with no economic purpose. The trend through the century was the removal of every practical function from this space—cooking, eating, work, and sleeping. The parlor might double as sitting room for the family, and other activities may have overflowed from the rest of the house, but the decoration, the design, and the furnishings defined the central purpose as a place for tea, a glass of wine, cards, sometimes dancing, and above all conversation.[25]

The house received guests, who entered through a sumptuously decorated doorway, passed through another splendid doorway into the parlor, or ascended the stairs to a chamber for tea and intimate conversation. The entries, the passages, the rooms were not designed for servants at their work, or for tradesmen, or neighboring farmers bartering for corn, or for children coming to play. The spaces and entries, in actual fact, doubtless served all kinds of people, but they were designed for the reception and entertainment of refined people. Fundamental conception as much as appearance set gentry houses apart from standard one- and two-cell houses. Eighteenth-century houses were not just larger or better decorated; they were built around a different idea.

Preparation for this transition began in the seventeenth century with the parental bedchamber. The contents of those older rooms suggest functions beyond sleeping quarters for the mother and father. Tables, chairs, best chests, and the bed itself, judging from the value of the items listed in the parlor inventories, were meant for display, and likely the heads of the household conducted their most important visitors into this room.[26] The very name of the room, parlor, suggests a purpose beyond sleeping. In the eighteenth century this label descended to the room given over entirely to talk and entertainment.[27]

In the seventeenth century, the old-style parlors defined the way to improve the house; a family added an additional cell to a one-cell house to have a private bedchamber for the parents in which they placed their valuable bed and bed frame. In the eighteenth century, in the new gentry houses, improvement led to new-style parlors, enhanced entertainment spaces with beds removed. When remodeling and making additions, people also enlarged the stairway or, in the biggest houses, built space for a ball-room—all to enhance the house as a place to entertain. Owners of the largest mansions kept adding bigger and more elegant rooms. In preparation for Governor Dinwiddie's arrival in 1751, the Virginia Assembly ordered a ball-room-and-supper-room wing longer than the original house built on to the Governor's Palace at Williamsburg. Thomas Hancock's Boston house was fifty-six feet by thirty-eight feet when it was completed in 1737, but sometime over the next fifty years a ballroom wing was added. John and Abigail Adams constructed a "Long Room" on their house at Braintree, and as soon as Andrew Craigie purchased his great house in Cambridge, he broke out a wall to build a hall for dining and entertaining. Among the lesser gentry, improvement took the form of removing beds from the parlor. Over the century, an increasing number of estate inventories record parlors devoid of beds, leaving the space to chairs, tea tables, and ceramics. The single most telling indicator of a household's commitment to genteel values was the presence of a parlor with no apparent function but to sustain visiting, conversation, and genteel rituals.[28]

Besides removal of extraneous functions, preparation of a parlor required extensive redecoration, or, as usually happened, the construction of a house with differently proportioned rooms and substantially altered surfaces. In New England, seventeenth-century rooms ranged from seventy-two to eighty-two inches in height; in the eighteenth century, room height rose to eighty-two to ninety inches, a foot or more higher on the average. Besides greater height, the eighteenth-century aesthetic called for smooth surfaces with elaborate applied decoration. Achieving this look on walls did not require major changes. Seventeenth-century houses at the upper end of the scale frequently had plastered, whitewashed walls, smooth from floor to ceiling, and fireplace walls sheathed with vertical boards. Only the crude structures in the bottom half of the housing stock left the nogging between the timber frames uncovered or sheathed it with clapboards like the exterior walls. The chief improvement in walls for gentry houses was the addition of baseboards and perhaps cornices where wall met ceiling and the installation of decorative paneling and chimney breasts on the fireplace walls. In remodeling jobs, the corner posts were boxed in; in new houses they were placed behind the wall line so as not to obtrude into the room.

Greater changes occurred in the ceilings. Beams and rafters and the flooring from the room above had formed the ceiling before, giving a rough top to the room even when everything above was whitewashed. To satisfy the new aesthetic, the beams had to be lathed and plastered to form a flat, smooth surface; in the finest houses, the resulting ceiling was then decorated. The end result was a finished and decorated box with no rough surfaces, except for the floor. The floor remained wide pine boards with little finish, until the end of the century, when owners of the most elegant houses placed carpets under the feet of guests, thus smoothing and decorating the final surface in the room.[29]

THE GEOMETRY OF USE

LIFE was different in these well-finished rooms. Besides the change from work to entertainment, a different geometry of use went into effect. The room not only looked different from the old hall and contained different furnishings; the loci of activity and the distribution of objects changed. In the seventeenth-century hall, rudimentary needs for heat and light focused use; in the eighteenth century, technological improvements facilitated another pattern entirely.

In the old traditional hall the inability of the gaping fire openings to heat the whole room pulled people toward the fire for warmth. So much heat went up the chimney that pitch at the ends of the logs froze. Cotton Mather and Samuel Sewall both recorded having ink freeze as they wrote at tables not far from the fire. Little seats were installed on the sidewalls right in the fireplaces as the best places to keep warm. Hardy as people may have grown when they lived year after year through bitter-cold winters in drafty houses, in the hall they moved toward the fire to warm themselves as they worked or talked.

On the other hand, when weather allowed, they moved to doors or windows for light; the very inefficiency of the fireplaces forbade large window openings through which cold air would seep, and thus the amount of natural light was reduced. The extant examples of seventeenth-century houses show a small number of window openings, most only a foot or two square. One-cell houses might have one or at most two such windows plus the door and fire for light. The corners of the room were cast into deep shadow most of the time, and none of the forms of artificial light satisfactorily dispelled the gloom. A little Betty lamp, made of a wick in a small vessel of oil, produced a dull, smoky light; candles were very expensive because tallow was costly, animals not undergoing the fattening process that they do today. Stories are told of families extinguishing the flame during long family prayers to save on candles. Daylight coming through windows or doors was by far the best light for reading, writing, or fine handwork. Activities in traditional houses clustered at fire or window according to the season.[30]

The genteel house greatly modified, if it did not entirely reverse, this clustering pattern—with the help of various technological advances. The fire and the window never lost their drawing power entirely, and through the nineteenth century pictures show people gathered at one or the other to work, read, or sit. But furnishings and the people in genteel rooms were much more dispersed. Indeed, pictures of country-house interiors in England in the eighteenth century often seem bare, with the people sitting and talking in the center of a nearly empty room. Open space seemed to please the owners. The preferred furnishing pattern in genteel parlors up through the early years of the nineteenth century was to push furniture back against the walls, leaving the center of the room open. Chair rails, one of the standard marks of a genteel room, were meant to protect walls from the furniture pressed against them. People much preferred tea and card tables with tilt tops; tilted and placed against the wall, the tables left maximum space in the center. When the need arose, tables and chairs were pulled into the center for use. The enlargement of the rooms plus the wider circulation patterns went hand in hand with improved technological changes in lighting and heating.[31]

Heating improvement was achieved by reducing the fireplace opening to a fraction of the former size. When cooking moved to the back of the house, there was no need for the huge cavity containing implements on cranes. In the new parlors, fireplaces measuring only two or three feet rather than two or three yards improved the draft and increased the heat output. By 1744, when Franklin wrote his treatise on stoves, he said "the large open fireplaces used in the days of our fathers" still persisted "generally in the country, and in kitchens," but that "most of these old-fashioned chimneys in towns and cities have been, of late years, reduced . . . by building jambs within them, narrowing the hearth, and making a low arch or breast."

The smaller fireplaces still had their defects, and the challenge of improving them attracted the interest of serious scientific minds. Benjamin Thompson, the Massachusetts man who won fame in Europe as a scientist and the title of Count Rumford in the Holy Roman Empire for his military exploits, wrote a treatise in 1796 devoted to fireplaces. He claimed to have doctored five hundred of them to improve the draft and heat efficiency. Franklin's solution was to insert an iron fireplace within the regular one and conduct the smoke around an air chamber before the hot air went up the chimney; the heated air from the chamber then passed into the room. His invention was an immediate success, and modifications and improvements continued to be made. Though still expensive by the end of the century, Franklin's stoves were widely used by those who could afford them, and in 1796 the American Philosophical Society offered a prize for improvements that would bring down the cost. Every possible device had to be attempted to fill the rooms with warmth so that the occupants could move about freely in the open space at the center.[32]

Larger windows and more of them improved lighting. The new gentry houses all had sash windows, hung so that at least one and usually two would slide up and down, replacing the smaller casement windows that swung open like a door. Though evidence is hard to find, some householders enlarged the windows when older houses were remodeled, and sash windows were installed. In 1710 Samuel Wentworth remodeled his Portsmouth house constructed in 1671 and installed double-hung sash windows. Wentworth was responding to the same impression as Thomas Bannister in Newport in 1705 when he recorded that "Sash windows are the newest Fashion." Large windows are a sure sign of an eighteenth-century house.[33]

Better candles helped with lighting at night. Wax candles produced a steadier flame than tallow, and after 1712, when the whale hunt in the North Atlantic began, spermaceti was used for the best candles. Though spermaceti candles were expensive, by 1775 the demand supported 150 whaling vessels in Newport alone. Eventually the combined demand from Europe and America depleted the whales in the North Atlantic, and the next generation of whalers had to carry the hunt to the South Pacific. For a guest to receive a wax or spermaceti candle to take to his or her chamber was a mark of honor. Philip Fithian was pleased when at Christmas in 1773 the Carters had "large clear and very elegant Spermaceti Candles sent into my Room."[34]

Though larger sash windows and wax and spermaceti candles added substantially to the cost of a house and living expenses, gentry families incurred the expense to light their rooms and facilitate the dispersal of activities away from the gathering points at fire and window. Better heating and more light gave gentry rooms an entirely different feel from the rooms of ordinary houses. One was high, smooth, bright, adorned, and open. In the smaller houses, rooms were more often shadowy, rough on floors and ceilings, plain and crowded. Beyond the change in sensation, people used space differently in the gentry houses. They opened the center for activities and moved about freely in keeping with the easy style that characterized gentility.

ABOVE. *The large kitchen fireplace was often the only fireplace in seventeenth-century houses and in later small dwellings.*

RIGHT. *In the eighteenth century, fireplace openings in formal rooms were much smaller in every dimension than the gaping maws of seventeenth-century cooking fireplaces. Small fireplaces minimized the loss of heat up the chimney and by warming the entire room enabled people to fill the space rather than cluster at the fire opening.*

The need for light in a mansion was more than practical. Light was an element in the brilliance of grand entertainments in parlors and drawing rooms. The number of candles measured the wealth of the host and the dignity of his guests. Though dim by modern standards, a dozen candles burning at night in a single room dazzled eyes accustomed to the usual tiny circle of light cast by one flame. Guests at grand parties commented on the lighting as they did on the food. To do honor to the lights, a number of new furniture forms like the gueridon and torchère were invented, and old forms like candelabra were worked in silver; a crystal chandelier was the peak of elegance and luxury. Silver candlesticks became required mansion furnishings, and mirrors to reflect and magnify the light hung in more parlors. All were part of genteel theatricality and performance. As William Thomas O'Dea writes in his study of lighting, none of this met a practical need. "The great enrichment and proliferation of light-holding devices that we have been examining were not the result of utilitarian pressures for better lighting, but of the evolution of a way of life whose chief objects were entertainment and display."

That need increasingly intensified the desire for better sources of light. At the end of the century, the quest for light resulted in the invention of improved lamps, the most notable by the Swiss Aimé Argand in 1784, and their dispersion to the wealthiest households. George Washington before his death in 1799 owned an Argand lamp. Light became a sensory metaphor for genteel society, rivaling polish and smoothness.[35]

This well-known painting illustrates the open, light air of genteel rooms where people could spread out rather than cluster at fireplace or window.

The purpose of the eighteenth-century gentry house was to transform life within its walls. The house hid the everyday vulgar activities of cooking and work in the back, in outbuildings, or in the cellar. In the front of the house were spacious rooms filled with light and warmth, where people stood or sat in conversation or at tea. They were not huddled at the fire reaching for the flame or drawn to the window in search of light, but moved graciously about through the space. Everywhere smooth surfaces, decorated with cornices, paneling, plasterwork, pediments, and carving beautified the environment. Broad stairways implied the existence of chambers above, where genteel living continued in more intimate settings. At night, when the occasion required, light from candlesticks and sconces sent brilliant gleams off polished surfaces throughout the room.

The rooms did not always glitter. Most of the time, the parlors, the stairways and passages, the candlesticks and tea tables watched over the ordinary routines of family life. People worked at their tasks, squabbled, suffered from illness, ate bread, sat silent. But during those long stretches the house was passive and latent, not acting according to its true nature. The rooms were meant for something different. They came to life only when refined people took the stage. When they gathered to talk and play, when well-bred bodies and minds had an occasion to perform, then people and environment harmonized. Then the decoration, the light, the smooth surfaces, the silver implements, the polished furniture served their true purposes, and the house fulfilled the measure of its creation.

GARDENS

RENAISSANCE houses came to America with gardens attached. Interest in gardens awakened along with the renewal of interest in classical architecture in fifteenth-century Italy. Led by Alberti, the humanists learned from descriptions of Roman villas how to attach gardens to the architecture of the house. Medieval gardens were conceived as outdoor rooms, enclosed spaces for meditation or love outside of the house. The humanists made the gardens extensions of house architecture, part of an overall plan, oriented to the plan of the house and vastly enlarging it. The great Italian garden architects reshaped the landscape around the house into terraces and vistas in which they placed long paths and planted beds in geometrical patterns, the square being most fundamental.

These were projects for kings and suitable mainly for palaces and the grandest houses; Henry VIII and Cardinal Wolsey attached large gardens to their palaces. But from their time on, people began to think of grand houses as appropriately surrounded by architectonic gardens. Charles I, patron of all the Renaissance arts in England, gave the fullest expression to architectural gardening with the help of the Norman engineer Salomon de Caus. By the early seventeenth century, gardening ideas were flowing into England. English travelers in Italy and France had learned to observe gardens, books on garden architecture were published in English, and it had become fashionable for English gentlemen to be connoisseurs of gardens as they were of architecture and furniture.[36]

A 1660 map of New York shows the geometrical lines of formal gardens reaching toward the Hudson River, precocious examples of colonial gardens—if the map is to be believed. But supposing the cartographer to have wished advanced signs of civilization into existence in the interests of promoting the city, his fictional depictions still indicate a belief in Dutch New York that occupants of the best houses should have gardens. The Dutch were not far ahead of the English in any case. Before the end of the century, a handful of Chesapeake planters, William Fitzhugh, Robert Beverly, Philip Ludwell, Robert "King" Carter, Dudley Digges, and William Byrd I began to take an interest in gardens. William Penn gave instructions for a garden

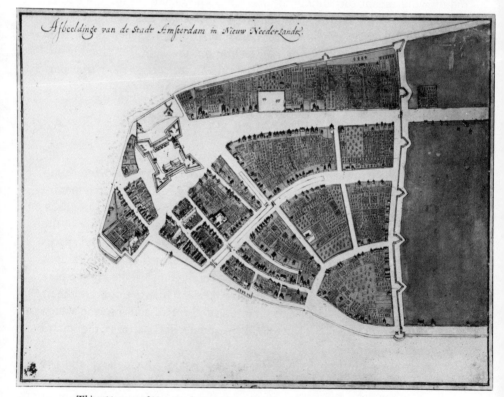

This 1660 map of New York shows formal gardens along the eastern edge of the town (at the top of the map).

at his Pennsbury Manor, and in 1698 Edward Shippen owned a house in Philadelphia with a flower garden and a summerhouse in the middle.

The grandest of the formal gardens was laid out at the College of William and Mary in 1694 with the help of a gardener from the royal residence at Hampton Court. The Reverend James Blair, a force behind the founding of the college, and Henry Compton, the bishop of London, who appointed Blair commissary, both had a deep interest in botanical gardens. The idea of gardening as a gentleman's diversion and a formal garden as the proper setting for a house was current almost as soon as the colonists decided to build grand mansions.[37]

When mansions began to rise in numbers after 1725, the installation of gardens became standard. Governor Alexander Spotswood led the way in Virginia by designing gardens for the Governor's Palace. William Byrd II helped the governor in the initial stages of the planning in 1712 and later visited many English gardens while also improving his father's gardens at Westover. John Bartram, the Philadelphia naturalist, wrote that after Byrd built his new mansion in the 1730s, he put in "new Gates, gravel Walks, hedges, and cedars finely twined and a little green house with two or three orange trees." Bartram thought Byrd had "the finest seat in Virginia," but there were gardens at Rosewell, Carter's Grove, Nomini Hall, Mount Airy, and elsewhere. New Englanders planted gardens nearly as conscientiously. While construction proceeded on his Boston mansion in 1735, Thomas Hancock contracted with a gardener to "layout the upper garden allys," "Trim the beds," "Gravel the Walks," and "Sodd the Terras," setting the pattern for other gentry mansions. In Pennsylvania after 1740, William Logan ordered hundreds of varieties of trees, shrubs, and flowers for Stenton, his country seat; John Penn hired a full-time gardener for Springettsbury at "Faire Mount" outside of Philadelphia; and Isaac Norris II was reordering the landscape at his Fairhill. By midcentury, John Laurens and Dr. Alexander Garden were searching the world for exotics for their gardens in South Carolina. From 1750 on, a garden was a requisite for every mansion.[38]

Most eighteenth-century American gardens were classic and formal. In their most extravagant expressions, as at the Governor's Palace in Williamsburg or the William Paca house in Annapolis, such gardens included terraces, parterres (geometric plantings in squares or rectangles), and paths of gravel or sand laid out in precisely straight lines among the parterres. An architectural feature such as a gazebo or summerhouse along with a small body of water added interest, and a wall or fence enclosed the whole. A smaller house might have a stretch of fenced grass, plantings, and straight walks.

Through the century, the revolution in English landscape design moderated the severe lines of the formal gardens, and the influence of the informal landscape moved to the colonies. After 1730 a group of English landscape architects emphasized a blend of the house with the natural landscape. In place of straight lines, the reform designers installed curved walks and roads, and rather than parterres and terraces, emphasized gentle slopes, broad open vistas, clumps of trees, and serpentine shorelines. Marks of this style can be detected in depictions of American gardens, and many show a mixture of influences, but in the eighteenth century informal and picturesque gardens remained subservient to the dominant influence of formal garden principles.[39]

Whatever the governing idea, all mansion gardens served similar purposes in the genteel pattern of living. A garden was an extension of the parlor, a place where polite people walked and conversed. In the bird's-eye views of English gardens, the artist usually populated the walks with strolling couples flirting or talking as they would in a drawing room. Nancy Shippen reported an agreeable afternoon with an acquaintance when "we chatted—sung—walk'd in the Garden." At night the gardens were illuminated to make them available for guests at evening entertainments. The formal finish on lawns, beds, and walks continued the polish and decor of the parade routes inside the house from door to parlor and up the stairways.

By the eighteenth century grand mansions in city or country commonly had large, terraced, formal gardens behind the house, like these at Carter's Grove near Williamsburg.

Nature had been smoothed and decorated as assiduously as walls and paneling inside the house.

Besides refining the environment for polite company, the plantings functioned just as pictures, ceramics, or books did—that is, as subjects for conversation. Philip Fithian recorded a pleasant interlude with Mrs. Carter in the Nomini Hall gardens when her knowledge of the plantings provided a topic for their talk. Fithian first strolled by himself, and then

> when I had gone round two or three Platts Mrs. Carter entered and walked towards me. I then immediately turn'd and met Her; I bowed—Remarked on the pleasantness of the Day—And began to ask her some questions upon a Row of small slips—To all which she made polite and full answers; As we walked along she would move the ground at the Root of some plant; or prop up with small sticks the bended *scions*—We took two whole turns through all the several Walks, and had such conversation as the *Place* and *Objects* naturally excited—And after Mrs. Carter had given some orders to the Gardiners (for there are two Negroes, Gardiners by Trade, who are constantly when the Weather will any how permit, working in it) we walked out into the *Area* viewed some Plumb-Trees, when we saw mr. Carter and Miss Prissy returning—We then repaired to the Slope before the front-Door where they dismounted—and we all went into the Dining Room.

There could be no better statement of the aim of all the objects in genteel houses than Fithian's comment that he and Mrs Carter engaged in "such conversation as the *Place* and *Objects* naturally excited." Garden plants worked as well as paintings or books to encourage conversation.

Serious gardeners delighted in gathering plants from the ends of the earth, doubtless for the pleasure of possessing rarities, but also for the conversation they stimulated. All of them loved to take guests for walks, discoursing on the treasures of the garden. A few became gardening virtuosi, with their cabinets of curiosities taking the form of a gardenful of exotics. John Custis in Williamsburg began exchanging plants with English botanists after 1717 and assembled scores of unusual specimens. During his quasi-scientific collecting efforts, he remained aware that plants facilitated conversation and correspondence with people of comparable interests in his class. He wrote in 1734 that "I am very proud it is in my power to gratify any curious gentleman in this [gardening] way . . ." His plants served the same purpose as the several "diverting prints to hang in the passage of my house," which he ordered from England in the same years. The prints entertained guests as plants did, providing suitable material for the conversation that was the commerce of genteel life.[40]

THE HOUSE AS PERFORMER

BESIDES providing a stage for genteel performances, the house with garden was itself a performer on its own stage. Houses and gardens, like individuals, were assessed in letters and diaries for their beauty and charm— that is, for their success in performing according to the standards of ideal genteel accomplishment. A visitor described a Philadelphia garden in 1800: "Mr. Pratts garden for beauty and elegance exceeds all I ever saw. . . . The beauty, Taste, and elegance which attends it, is perfectly indescribable—" Nearly the same words could be used for a person. A house could also be scorned and cause shame, as could awkward dancing at an assembly. Houses and gardens were on view and performing before critical audiences.[41]

By the eighteenth century, the meaning of gentry houses so far exceeded the practical functions they performed as sheltered warm places for sleeping, eating, and work that houses became a form of literature. The houses were stage sets for dramas, and like the characters themselves, could be envisioned within the frame of a story. Elevation from the realm of inconsequential background to the realm of literary significance made houses fit subjects for painting. Nothing deserved portraiture until it had a part in some societal myth, and placing a picture of a house within a frame was like putting a story within the covers of a book. The house entered the realm of society's art and literature.

Houses began to be portrayed in earnest in the Renaissance when architecture and gardening became aristocratic arts. Before then the palaces of kings had been portrayed in paint, just as royalty figured most prominently in stories. In the Renaissance, Italian magnates who were not royal built classical houses that also deserved portrayal in paint as part of the owners' myths about their own greatness and taste. That practice grew over the years until in the early eighteenth century virtually every great country house was depicted—in a bird's-eye view or as a simple landscape.

Though much less pretentious, American houses too began to appear in the background of the owners' portraits, occasionally qualifying as subjects of overmantel paintings in their own right, implying the house's role in the owner's story. The owners wished to present their houses for admiration and judgment alongside themselves, and polite society took an interest in viewing and evaluating houses as they enjoyed meeting and evaluating people.[42]

Visitors to great houses described them as if composing a picture, turning the scene into literature. Eliza Lucas Pinckney wrote at length of her visit to William Middleton's Crowfield on the Cooper River.

The house stands a mile from, but in sight of the road, and makes a very hansoume appearance; as you draw nearer new beauties discover themselves, first the fruitful Vine mantleing up the wall loading with delicious Clusters; next a spacious bason in the midst of a large green presents itself as you enter the gate that leads to the house, which is neatly finished; the rooms well contrived and elegantly furnished. From the back door is a spacious walk a thousand foot long; each side of which nearest the house is a grass plat enamiled in a Serpentine manner with flowers. Next to that on the right hand is what imediately struck my rural taste, a thicket of young tall live oaks where a variety of Airry Chorristers pour forth their melody; and my darling, the mocking bird, joyned in the artless Concert and inchanted me with his harmony.

Pinckney went on at what she called "an unreasonable length," describing house and garden by painting a scene, evoking a mood of pastoral harmony, and interweaving allusions with description. At the end she says, "Beyond this are the smiling fields dressed in Vivid green. Here Ceres and Pomona joyn hand in hand to crown the hospitable board." In a still more self-conscious effort to turn a house into literature, a friend who visited Alexander Garden's grounds at Otranto wrote a poem about his house and garden.[43] Doubtless, owners were pleased to see their houses elevated to the realm of art, for that gave meaning to the life within.

*A*PPEARANCES

HOW, then, would a mansion have looked in the eighteenth century? Few of the provincial gentry could afford the formal gardens that graced the largest mansions; they had to reduce grand plans for use on a smaller scale. But they certainly would have looked different from the plain houses left over from the previous century. Seventeenth-century houses a step above the simplest log cabins were, with very few exceptions, framed from timber and sheathed with weatherboards split from logs or with sawn clapboards. Whitewash commonly went on the inside of the house, but so far as can be told now, there is no evidence of exterior paint on the sheathing. At most, on the best houses at the end of the century, window and door frames and the facing under the roof might have been painted. Virtually all houses, with the exception of the few brick structures, must have been weatherbeaten brown-gray in color, blending into the background of greens and browns in fields and trees.

The adoption of brick for grand houses in the eighteenth century set the new mansions apart by color as well as by size and façade design. Red bricks clearly marked the houses of the gentry as they stood upright on the landscape. In New England brick was far less commonly used, even for the best houses, and color was achieved by painting. It is impossible now to tell when exterior paint became a requirement on frame houses, but after the middle of the eighteenth century it is likely that in cities and substantial towns, clapboards were painted. The few known examples suggest that house paints followed the hues common on New England churches—reds, browns, greens, and blues. The whites, when they occurred, were strongly tinted off pure white. Julius Sprat, who made his fortune in the China trade, commissioned a house in the "most elegant style" in Litchfield, Connecticut, in 1793 and ordered it to be painted white, but "white" could easily have meant pearl or a pale yellow in that year. On the other hand, the John Collins house, erected in Litchfield in 1782, was painted red and repainted white only in 1815. George Washington painted his house white in 1793, actually a repainting after many years, but added sand to simulate stone, changing the tint by so doing.

While the timing varied from region to region, it seems likely that all the best frame houses in prosperous regions such as the Connecticut Valley were painted by the first decade of the nineteenth century. A visitor to Litchfield in 1809 thought it was "one of the most beautiful towns in the world with houses that were large and elegant, neatly arranged and all painted." The previous half century had seen a coloration of the landscape as people with genteel aspirations painted their houses, setting them apart from the much larger number of ordinary log and frame houses still weathering to a brown-gray. A colored surface began a genteel house's performance.[44]

To continue the presentation of the brick or painted house, the owner arranged the immediate landscape to enhance the show. At Williamsburg the Governor's Palace stood at the end of a double avenue running from Duke of Gloucester Street to the house, so that it could be viewed from a distance by approaching guests. Eliza Lucas had noted that William Middleton's house on the Cooper River stood "a mile from, but in sight of the road, and makes a very hansoume appearance." Sometimes the approaching drive followed a rigorously straight line, sometimes a curved path as at Shirley Place, the country seat of Governor William Shirley of Massachusetts. But whether curved or straight, the idea was to place the house within sight from a distance and to mark a path, usually with poplars, along which the visitor approached. Eliza Caroline Burgwin Clitherall, daughter of John Burgwin, said of her father's house, the Hermitage, that while less handsome than some English estates she knew, "yet it was larger in the number of rooms, and had a more imposing aspect from the avenue to its approach." The route for polite company through the elegant doorway into the parlor or up the stairs actually began hundreds of yards away at the gate to the house.[45]

Few of the gentry could afford such an elaborate approach. Most had to content themselves with front yards. The Governor's Palace had both. The double avenue came to a wall before the house with a gate, and within the gate a path ran directly to the front door with grass or plantings on either side. Virtually every gentry house could adopt a courtyard, and since almost every bird's-eye view of English country houses around 1700 shows a formal courtyard before the house, the source of the front yard is easily identified. When they first appeared before colonial houses is less clear. An order to paint the fence of the Latin schoolmaster's house in Massachusetts in 1702 raises the possibility of a courtyard. A painted wooden fence, a brick wall, or later an iron fence marked the front boundary of the courtyard, and so the order to paint provides a clue.

Grand houses certainly had fenced courtyards by 1743, for two of them can be detected before the houses of Captain Nathaniel Cunningham and Peter Faneuil in William Burgis's drawing "A South East View of the Great Town of Boston," along with the parterres of the formal gardens. A fuller description of Faneuil's garden is available from five years earlier: "The deep courtyard, ornamented with flowers and shrubs, was divided into an upper and lower platform by a high glacis [artificial slope] surrounded by a richly wrought railing decorated with gilt balls." Few houses could boast terraces or wrought-iron fences topped with gilt balls. Ordinarily the owner planted grass, trees, and shrubs and contented himself with a picket fence.

Over the half century after 1750, this simple courtyard pattern took hold in New England at the same time as house surfaces were painted. In 1794 a traveler noted in Worcester that "most of the houses have a large court before them, full of lilacs and other shrubs, with a seat under them, and a paved walk up the middle." In the South, Burgwin's Hermitage and, in Philadelphia, Isaac Norris's Fairhill had fenced courtyards with planted lawn and shrubs. While pictures of town and country scenes around 1800 still show plenty of houses standing on bare land without planting or enclosure, every house of any pretension is surrounded by a yard of some kind and most with a fence, gate, and walk.[46]

A garden, including the front courtyard, created an artificially refined space from which the house itself could rise to greet its guests. At Carter's Grove on the James, where a formal garden below a terrace lawn was constructed around 1740, two feet of native soil was removed and replaced with humus. A three-acre site was enclosed by a fence, first with posts of rough-cut logs six inches to a foot in diameter and later with much smaller posts. Parterres and sand walkways with a central alley were laid out in the humus. At great expense and effort, Carter Burwell created a space made of natural objects but artistically transformed into a softer, more ordered nature.

With less effort and expense, owners of smaller houses aimed at a similar

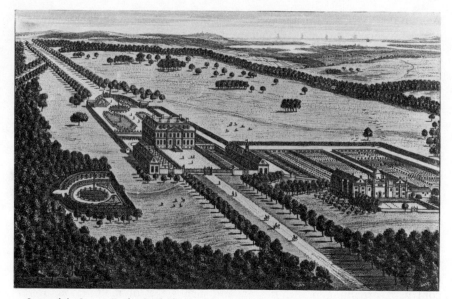

Stansted, in Sussex, England. The long approach drive lined with trees and the fenced courtyard immediately before the house reappeared in reduced form before the Governor's Palace in Williamsburg. Parts of this configuration were adapted for other American houses.

In restoring the approach to the Governor's Palace at the top of the picture, Colonial Williamsburg relied on archaeological evidence for the placement of trees to duplicate the eighteenth-century drive. The approach to the front and the formal gardens to the rear resemble the layout of English country estates of the same period.

effect with decorative fences, usually painted. Larger and smaller posts were often interspersed at regular intervals for a design to distinguish the fence, and thus the yard, from the rough field fences and the farmland on either side of the house. In later bird's-eye views, the painted house fence clearly delineates the yard around the house from the fields bounded by worm fences or post and rail. Within the yard, grass was mown to form a smooth surface edged by shrubs, trees, and sometimes flowers. The idea was not to deny the existence of rougher fields and pastures, but to distinguish the house as a place where roughness left off and refinement began.

By contrast, the one- and two-cell houses that made up the remainder of the housing array in the neighborhood made no effort to civilize their yards. Firewood was often stacked against the house in the front, and the house yard blended imperceptibly with the barnyard, often without a fence to separate the buildings. Mud, packed earth, weeds, and scraggly bushes surrounded the house haphazardly. Animals could approach the house as easily as people could. The gentry set off their mansions with courtyards to contain this world. They set the houses apart from animality and the coarse

This house, built for Elijah Boardman in New Milford, Connecticut, included, besides the stylish façade and Palladian window, an enclosed courtyard before the house.

realities of farm life by means of fences and lawns, in preparation for rooms so highly polished and decorated that mud, rough boots, and homespun clothing could never feel at home there. The genteel house turned its back on the barns, the animals, the farm laborers, addressing an audience of well-dressed, well-bred polite people whose posture and conversation harmonized with the refined spaces in the house. The houses were designed almost entirely to sustain the cultivated lives these favored few wished to lead.[47]

CHAPTER V

Cities and Churches

IN 1773 young Josiah Quincy from Boston arrived in Charleston, South Carolina, the first stop on a spring tour. After walking about the city on the first day of March, Quincy gave his impressions: "I can only say in general, that in grandeur, splendour of buildings, decorations, equipages, numbers, commerce, shipping, and indeed in almost every thing, it far surpasses all I ever saw, or ever expected to see in America." Over the next three weeks, Quincy offered appraisals of concerts, ladies, gentlemen's dress, churches, music, the food, everything in Charleston that might catch the eye of a self-conscious connoisseur of culture.

As he traveled north, he continued to comment on regional culture and to offer observations. Williamsburg in early April disappointed him. "I have just been taking a view of the whole town. It is inferior to my expectations. Nothing of the population of the north, or of the splendour and magnificence of the south." Philadelphia in May was more satisfying. "The streets of Philadelphia intersect each other at right angles; and it is probably the most regular, best laid out city in the world." Quincy framed the buildings and the forms of city life into pictures, permitting him to deliver judgment on the degree of splendor, simplicity, or decay. Cities, like people or houses, could be evaluated for their taste and beauty.[1]

Quincy's comments suggest that polite people were bringing cities within the domain of genteel culture in the eighteenth century. People of taste judged the energy of commerce, the layout of streets, the splendor of the public buildings, the beauty of private residences. Cities could be criticized because, by Quincy's time, certain principles of Renaissance city design had become embodied in American cities. When possible, genteel Americans introduced latter-day versions of Renaissance ideas into their cities as part of the overall beautification project. The city environment could be refined like the formal spaces in a house. These principles of design and adornment provided standards of judgment and the basis for Quincy's critique.

Beyond the aesthetics of the city, polite people wished to requisition spaces for their own purposes. They began the ordering of space for polite company with their own houses, with passages from entry to stairway to parlor, and extended the polish and decoration to the courtyard and garden. In these places polite people could converse, dine, and walk without an ugly environment marring the ease that afforded them such pleasure. But the city had to be refined as well. Where could polite people go for assemblies, for amusement, to shop or to walk? Where could they not go, especially the women among them, without compromising their dignity or offending delicate sensibilities? Polite people, with the help of the entrepreneurs and officials who served them, molded cities to suit their needs. Where refinement could not be achieved, the urban gentry mentally zoned the city into spaces for themselves and others for the vulgar public. In actuality and in conception, the refining process affected the appearance, the structure, and the use of eighteenth-century cities.

THE TRANSFORMATION OF CITY FORM

A NEW kind of city appeared in America near the end of the seventeenth century at about the same time as the new mansions began to go up. The differences in the cities were as strongly marked as the changes in residential architecture. In the earliest years of settlement, Boston and New York extended the haphazard street patterns of medieval cities to the New World. Boston's meandering street patterns resembled the medieval plans of English towns portrayed in John Speed's *Theatre of the Empire of Great Britaine,* published in 1611. Both English and American towns appear as tangles of twisting streets without conscious design.

In fact, neither English nor American towns were as planless as they appeared. English towns usually had open market spaces near the center and protective walls around the periphery. Boston had been carefully sited for the advantages of the harbor and the freshwater springs. Boston had no wall, but location on a peninsula gave it protection by water. The towns look planless because the streets did not follow straight lines. The town gave permission to individual developers to lay out streets on land where they intended to build, and the direction followed the builders' whims and the dictates of topography. No overall plan existed for the street pattern. New York's streets by 1660 were more orderly but bent to fit the shape of Manhattan Island without regard to rectangular blocks or long vistas. Residents disregarded precise boundaries, setting pigpens and privies in the streets beyond the bounds of individual lots. Smaller towns generally followed Boston and New York in letting topography and convenience govern the street plan. Most New England towns developed along a single street, others organized house lots into rough blocks, but neither showed concern for regularity or aesthetic effect.[2]

In these early years, a few more carefully planned cities sprang up in the colonies. The most notable example was New Haven, a town laid out with

English town plans traditionally focused on the defense perimeter and designation of a marketplace and a site for the church. Geometrical discipline in street layout played no part.

a central open square and a single ring of eight square blocks surrounding it. Neither the shoreline nor the natural undulations of the site interfered with a strict commitment to the geometry of the square. In another instance, on a much smaller scale, the houses within the palings of the original Plymouth Plantation were probably set out in straight lines.

These regular towns foreshadowed the standard plan for towns and cities in the latter half of the seventeenth century, when street patterns were laid out in advance in precisely straight lines. Charleston's streets, planned around 1672, while not surveyed to create perfectly rectangular blocks, followed straight lines. In 1682 Thomas Holme surveyed the site of Philadelphia on behalf of William Penn, creating the grid of streets which Josiah Quincy admired in 1773 as "the most regular, best laid out city in the world." In the 1680s and 1690s, Virginia planters who hoped, though in vain, to establish towns throughout the colony worked up more than a half dozen plans exhibiting geometrical regularity. By the end of the century, the regular geometric plan had entirely displaced the haphazard informality of the English medieval town except in New England. Outside of that one

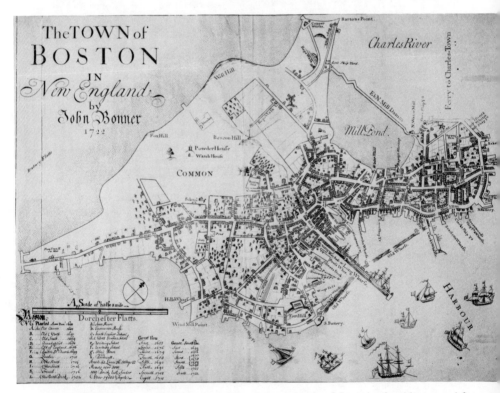

As in older English towns, Boston's streets followed the topography of the peninsula without regard for geometry. Water and a wall on the peninsula's narrow neck formed the town's defense perimeter.

region, every settlement with any aspiration began with a plan of straight streets forming regular geometrical blocks. Only the tiniest villages grew in the informal irregularity that had earlier sufficed for centers of commerce and government. In less than a hundred years a new conception of an ideal town had imposed itself on the people opening the American wilderness.[3]

Regular town plans developed from a medieval style enlarged and enriched by Renaissance humanists inspired by classical forms. Regular plans had existed for fortress cities and camps from the thirteenth century, and before that towns following Roman layouts were scattered across Europe. The bastide towns built along various European frontiers contained straight streets and right-angle blocks, often with open squares in the center. Renaissance humanists, led by Leon Battista Alberti (1404–72) and Antonio Averlino, called Filarete (c. 1400–69), produced fabulous plans for patterned fortress cities, most of them never built. Among the great artists, Leonardo, Michelangelo, Raphael, and Dürer all projected fortress-city plans. In the late sixteenth century, in the hands of architects including Palladio and his follower Vincenzo Scamozzi, the aesthetic qualities of the city came to the

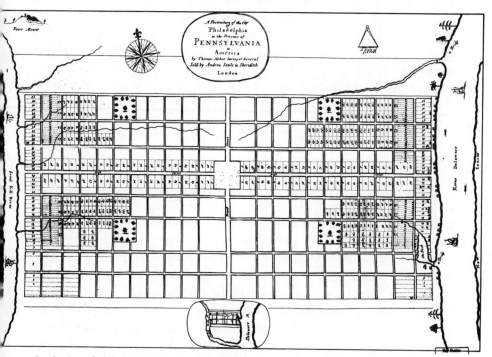

By the time of Philadelphia's founding, Renaissance notions of geometrical order were beginning to affect American city planning.

fore. Fortress walls became highly decorative and dropped away in some instances. City planning took on a new purpose: to glorify the ruler.[4]

In the sixteenth century, kings, popes, and great nobles began to sponsor projects to enhance the splendor of their capitals and to renovate urban areas near their residences. The form of the city became an expression of the glory of the court. In the second half of the sixteenth century, the popes launched a series of projects to open up streets and large piazzas in Rome, culminating in the efforts of Sixtus V between 1585 and 1590 to integrate individual improvements into a coherent plan. By then the absolutely straight street was appreciated, and Sixtus tried to create a number of long vistas leading to monuments or great public buildings. Henry IV of France, equally energetic and resolute, undertook a series of large civic improvements in the limited confines of crowded Paris in the first decade of the seventeenth century. He created the Pont Neuf, a bridge unlike any other in Paris because no buildings rose on it, and two large open squares, the Place Dauphine and the Place Royale. Later in the century Louis XIV laid out broad avenues in the town of Versailles as counterparts to his gardens, and at the promptings of Colbert, attempted to open boulevards and grand squares in Paris. As part of his Renaissance program in England, Charles I looked for ways to improve London, but, like Henry IV, he suffered from lack of space. Charles utilized the Earl of Bedford's desire to develop a portion of his city property to make a modest improvement; in return for royal permission to build, Charles required the earl to employ Inigo Jones as designer. The result was Covent Garden, Jones's version of Henry IV's residential square Place Royale. Charles's efforts to integrate Italian taste in other sections of the city met with limited success, but residential squares began to proliferate from this time forward until London led the world in that element of urban design.[5]

Significantly, the design of Covent Garden came from Jones under the king's sponsorship, not from the Earl of Bedford, who owned the property. Until the middle of the seventeenth century, urban design was the sport of kings, aided by scholars and artists like Jones. Only a monarch or a very great lord like Cardinal Richelieu commanded the means to form a town. But after 1660, like so much else in courtly culture, scaled-down imitations and adaptations of the kingly art became part of the culture of lesser gentry and the upper middle class. Besides cultivating a taste for grand city features in the manner of Josiah Quincy, the gentry gave thought to proper city design. Real opportunities for town planning occurred when fire struck in London in 1666, or a new section of Edinburgh opened in 1766, or a frontier area was settled in the New World. Like the managers in London and Edinburgh, William Penn and Thomas Holme, the Virginia town planners, and many others who wished to plant towns designed their towns in advance. By the end of the century, founders created orderly, and sometimes imposing, town plans. Francis Nicholson, governor of Maryland and Virginia and founder of both Annapolis and Williamsburg, aspired to elegant baroque designs. Others, like the moving spirits behind Wilmington, Delaware, wanted the satisfaction of straight streets with the houses in line with one another. But everywhere by the early eighteenth century (again, except New England), the founders of towns introduced Renaissance ideas about cities into the little urban places all over the colonies.[6]

THE ELEMENTS OF URBAN GRANDEUR

BY THE time this urban planning began, Renaissance ideas had passed through a century of adaptation and revision. Elements of Alberti and Palladio can be discerned in American town plans, but city-planning traditions changed under the influence of national preferences. The beauties of the straight street and the open square, both valued by the Italian theorists, carried over, but there were additions as well. Principles incorporated in actual cities shaped American thinking, and to understand what colonial planners hoped to achieve we must examine some of those cities, beginning with London.

London was too large and peculiar to provide a model for new towns in the colonies, but the very eccentricities of its development expose cultural purposes of cities that might otherwise be less evident. What we now think of as London was originally two separate cities, London and Westminster, that later joined to become the London we know. The two had different qualities and purposes, the one commercial, the other governmental, each jurisdiction independent of the other (as they are technically even today). These two elements comprised the grand city everywhere, but in most cities the two blended and overlapped, obscuring the qualities associated with each; in London we view them separately, enabling us to discern the cultural forces playing across city forms.

The commercial City, London proper, incorporated a port to receive and dispatch trade goods and an exchange where merchants conducted their business. Those two, port and exchange, were the heart of the City, embodied physically in the docks on the one hand and the Royal Exchange building on the other. The exchanges were usually courtyards with cloistered walks on the inside perimeter and shops opening into the court. The first exchange building appeared in Bologna in 1382–84, but the pattern was set by the Antwerp exchange, built by 1469. The London exchange, raised in 1566–70, was spacious and costly, leaving no question about the significance of the activities it sheltered.

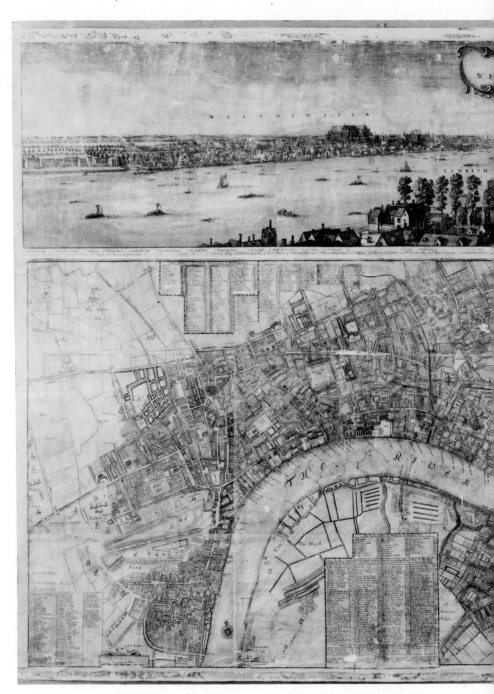

LONDON WESTMINSTER & SOUTHWARK

The importance of the port for London and for all major cities is evident from the across-the-water pictures that show harbors full of ships and lighters. For the artists and their patrons, viewing a city across the water through shipping traffic played up its grandeur. That was an uncontested evaluation. The nobility, while generally above trade, knew that kingdoms rested on commerce and did not disparage its importance. Josiah Quincy listed Charleston's commerce and shipping, along with its public buildings and equipages, among the city's grand features.[7]

To the west of the City, going up the Thames, Westminster contained the great public buildings at the heart of the governmental city. At the center of Westminster lay royal power with all the splendor that radiated from the throne. The palace and its ancillary buildings, such as the banqueting hall, were foremost, set in great gardens and more splendid than the houses of Parliament. The monarch's magnetic power commanded Westminster as the flow of trade ruled the commercial City. Some of the great houses along Pall Mall backed onto the royal gardens, where the king sometimes walked. At the back of the private gardens, platforms were built to make it possible to look over the wall. Guests in the great houses gathered on these "mounts," hoping to glimpse the monarch and his entourage strolling in the royal gardens. That activity was a metaphor for the royal magnetism that drew people to Westminster and to town houses lining residential squares. All the finest residences, including the residential squares of the seventeenth and eighteenth centuries that began with Covent Garden, were built to the west, drawn by the gravitational pull of the monarch.[8]

Westminster, then, was the site of the great public buildings, the royal palace, and the finest residences. London proper, the commercial City, was the place of the Royal Exchange, merchants' houses, and access to the nearby docks of the port. In theory, the artificial separation into two centers, in consequence of peculiar historical circumstances, clarifies the contrasting appearance and mood of the two elements, the one ceremonial, residential, and aristocratic, the other commercial, full of business, and middle-class.

In actuality, the separation in this divided city was not complete. Commerce came to Westminster, despite some aversion to its tainting presence. As Covent Garden became more and more of a marketplace, for example, the owners of the houses surrounding the plaza fled to other quarters; refined living and market stalls did not harmonize. But luxury shops were another matter, and they began to line the streets surrounding the residential squares. The houses facing the squares, at least initially, were occupied by great families, and the overall tone within the square was homogeneous. But shops occupied the side streets or those back a block, drawn by the trade of the wealthy residents on the squares. In Pall Mall, shops filled the buildings close to the elegant houses backing on the king's gardens. In Paris, the Duc

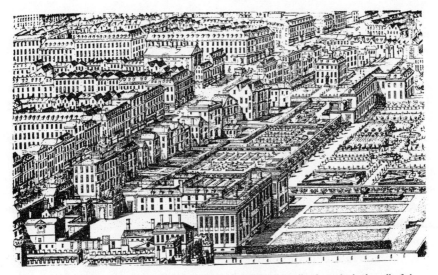

At the center are the gardens behind the residences lining Pall Mall. Along the back wall of the gardens can be seen platforms or "mounts" to which guests were conducted to peer over the wall at the company strolling in St. James's Park, the grounds of the palace.

Bloomsbury was one of many fashionable residential squares constructed in eighteenth-century London. Most were built in the West End.

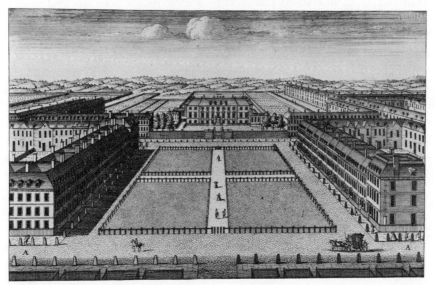

de Chartres developed Europe's finest shopping center in the gardens behind his own palace, and was the toast of the city for doing so. The Italian
theorist Alberti had suggested the placement of shops near aristocratic
residents, and in actual cities the commercial presence did not seem incongruous or drive away the best residents. Indeed, it became customary for
lines of shops to attach themselves to the best residential sections, injecting
a commercial strain into the most refined neighborhoods.[9]

By the same token, the commercial City had its ceremonial buildings and
great houses in the midst of its businesses. Besides the Royal Exchange, St.
Paul's in the heart of London seemed worthy of Sir Christopher Wren's
supreme architectural effort after the Great Fire. Wren's planned reconstruction of the City created ceremonial civic centers, placing the exchange
and the cathedral at focal points of broad avenues, achieving a baroque
grandeur far beyond the simple necessities of commerce. Tangled property
lines prohibited the adoption of Wren's ideas, but the actual legislation for
the rebuilding required four-story houses on the six principal streets of the
City, thus bringing into existence more splendid approaches to central civic
places—all in accord with Palladio's specifications. Though West Enders
scoffed at most of the City's private architectural efforts, and St. Paul's really
was anomalous in the City, the men of commerce nonetheless proved that
they desired great public buildings and ceremonial approaches in their own
city. In this they resembled the citizens of Amsterdam, the city in Europe
most purely dedicated to commerce, lacking palaces, a cathedral, and a
university. As if to compensate for the absences, the city erected a huge stone
town hall, 263 feet long, in the town square, "grander than any palace then
existing in Europe," Mark Girouard says, with a marble floor and so many
rooms that the upper half went unused. Huge maps of the heavens and the
earth were inscribed in the marble floor as tributes to navigation and world
commerce. The idea of a complete city demanded a ceremonial civic presence, and the great Burgersaal met the need.[10]

Like London and Amsterdam, most commercial cities balanced commerce and ceremony. A common city plan focused at two points: first the
docks and second a square set a few blocks back from the water's edge, the
one the exchange point between city and ships, the other the place where
church and governmental buildings formed a ceremonial center. A broad,
straight street carried traffic between waterfront and civic square. Often the
public buildings faced down the broad avenue toward the port, acknowledging its importance and welcoming visitors who came by sea. The configuration of wharves, avenue, and public buildings forming a T shape is readily
discerned on many town plans.[11]

COMMERCE AND CIVIC CEREMONY IN AMERICAN CITIES

THE elements of city design had solidified in English and European practice by the time American colonists began to lay out regular towns in the late seventeenth century. In some places, the double-sided nature of a grand city was fully realized; in others, one part predominated over the other, at least initially. But in the confusion of practical circumstances, the ideal of the balanced city, worthy of a connoisseur's praise, can still be seen struggling for expression.

Governor Francis Nicholson, whose fertile mind conceived two of the best-developed American cities, was one of those provincial administrators who practiced the kingly art of city planning. Nicholson, a military officer who traveled around the Mediterranean and across Europe before he became lieutenant governor of Virginia in 1689, was transferred to Maryland as royal governor in 1694. He immediately urged the Assembly to move the colony's capital from St. Mary's City, an obsolete location by that time, to Anne Arundel County farther up Chesapeake Bay.

Nicholson drew his plan for the new capital, Annapolis, at a site notable for its excellent harbor. Besides the inevitable waterfront port facilities, Nicholson provided for a government center several blocks up the hill in a circular space on a knoll. A block away in another circular opening he made room for a church. Nicholson introduced the two major elements of a grand city, the port and the ceremonial square, into his design at the beginning. His plan fell short in some respects. Ideally, a wide avenue carried people from the docks to the governmental center. In Annapolis the wide street led to the smaller church circle, and the street to the capitol required a dogleg turn. John Reps has pointed out the failure of the street lines to focus precisely on the center of each circle as required by standard Palladian planning. On the other hand, Nicholson planned a residential square, named Bloomsbury after its London counterpart, close to the governmental center and had ideas for a house of his own close by. Just as London's residential squares gravitated to Westminster, in Nicholson's Annapolis the center of power and the best residences clustered together. His plan embodied the aesthetic principles of a grand city—straight streets, plazas, and vistas—and the fundamental elements, a port and a ceremonial civic center with attendant grand residences. In time a line of shops extended from the circle to the harbor.[12]

Nicholson returned to Virginia as governor in 1698 and, using the occasion of a fire in the statehouse at Jamestown, proposed almost immediately a transfer of that province's capital to a new site at Middle Plantation, where once again he had occasion to plan a city. Middle Plantation was already the site of the newly founded William and Mary College, which Nicholson had helped to organize. Members of the college wanted the capital nearby, and one of the students supported the move in an address to an assembly of burgesses and Council members. The college lacked a good market, the student said, but even more "the conveniency of good company and conversation." He thought of a city in two dimensions, as a place of trade and as a civilizing influence. The meeting of the Council and burgesses, the address argued, brought together "the selectest and best company that is to be had within the Government," and their presence would prepare the students for real life. The orator spoke more generally of towns which were absent in Virginia. By joining together now they might "learn to improve our shipping and navigation, our trade and commerce, our minds and manners, and what no one man can do singly, by a friendly cohabitation and society to do jointly one with another." The student understood that cities had a double purpose, to improve trade and commerce and to refine minds, purposes roughly

Francis Nicholson's plan for Annapolis provided for a public circle, where the capitol was located, and a church circle. Nicholson also planned a Bloomsbury Square nearby for fashionable residences.

corresponding to the port and the assemblage of elite around the public buildings, the place of trade and the place of ceremonial elegance and elevated company.[13]

Williamsburg, as the town was designated in 1699 in the legislation to move the capital, was soon replete with public buildings: the college, which was already there; a capitol, begun in 1701; the Governor's Palace, started in 1706; Bruton Parish Church; and later a jail and hospital. Straight streets were laid out to form rectangular blocks. Except for the ever present line of shops and taverns between capitol and palace, Williamsburg in its entirety was a civic city replete with ceremonial buildings.

The great lack was the absence of a commercial center. But how could a town placed midway between two rivers on the ridge of a broad peninsula have a port? Not to be defeated by geography, Nicholson provided for, not one port, but two. Tributaries from the James and the York rivers, navigable at high tide, approached within a few miles of Williamsburg on each side of the peninsula. Nicholson located a port on each one and named the ports Queen Mary's Port in honor of the late queen and Princess Anne's Port in honor of Princess Anne of Denmark. Far from being desultory conveniences, the ports, as the names implied, were meant to be part of Williamsburg's rising glory. The two ports and the assemblage of public buildings in the town together made up the complete city.[14]

Lacking frontage on a large river or the sea, Williamsburg, in fact, could not keep in balance the two elements of a grand city and leaned ever more heavily toward the civic and ceremonial side. Elsewhere the tendency was usually the reverse. The commercial tended to overwhelm the governmental. Thomas Holme conceived of Philadelphia as Pennsylvania's capital and included in his plan both port and public square. He envisioned docks along the river, and back many blocks at the town's center a ten-acre public square, the site of public buildings, "as a Meeting-House, Assembly or State-House, Market-House, School-House, and several other Buildings for Publick Concerns." Between the two ran an extra-wide avenue in the classical fashion. All the proper elements were there at the beginning for a great city. But, unfortunately, the great public square came to nothing in the first century of growth. Stretching between two rivers, the original plat for Philadelphia was as large as London or Paris at the time, and the public square lay in the center. The city did not grow that far for more than a century. Churches and public buildings were erected on ordinary blocks of the plat, and the central public square remained deserted. The city and provincial government met in a small courthouse erected in the center of High Street.

Meanwhile the port grew vigorously in accord with Philadelphia's true nature, overwhelming all other urban elements. For fifty years, wharves spread along the waterfront, warehouses were erected, shops appeared, and a market house was built up the middle of the central avenue. Merchant residences clustered around the waterfront, enriching the mixture of heavy commercial activity and private dwellings. A half century after its founding Philadelphia was preeminently a commercial city with few amenities of a refined urban place.[15]

Many eighteenth-century towns besides Philadelphia tended to submerge the civic in the commercial. Founders invariably noted locations for docking, whether on river or sea, while often the center for market house, courthouse, and church received little attention. Spaces set aside for public purposes were often encroached on by houses and shops as the town developed. In Virginia in 1700 the General Assembly provided for land grants in the west with two-hundred-acre town sites "to be laid out in a geomitricall square." The geometrical shape indicated a rudimentary regard for Renaissance design principles, but within those boundaries the town could take many forms. William Byrd II, in advance of most of his contemporaries in urban sophistication, laid out two towns, Manakin in 1700 and Eden in 1737; both were built around central open squares leaving ample space for civic functions. If anything, the commercial side was downplayed. But elsewhere in Virginia, the emphasis was reversed. The act for the creation of Fredericksburg on the Rappahannock specified sites for "a church and church-yard, a market place . . . public key, and . . . publick landings," thus respecting the two sides of a balanced town. The plan showed an entire block for church and courthouse, in the right location, one street removed from the waterfront. But on a 1769 plat the special features were removed from this public block, and though public buildings did go up, other structures encroached on their space, denying them the preeminence they should have merited.

Other towns began with less civic space than Fredericksburg. Alexandria was a simple grid town on the waterfront. Market house, town hall, and churches were placed along the street with no special environment to set them off. The street names were the only remnant of the older idea of a center for governmental power. In Alexandria, streets going back from the river were named Duke, Prince, King, Queen, and Princess. The Chesapeake's little anonymous grid towns frequently used these names as if their nobility would imbue commercial streets with a touch of grandeur and civic ceremony.[16]

The subordination of civic to commercial seems inevitable in middle-class America, with its homegrown elite based on trade and agriculture and its lack of titled lords. Commercial London would be re-created in the colonies, it would seem, not Westminster. And yet the idea of a balanced city with ceremonial civic space to match its wharves and warehouses would not die. During the time when plain gridirons were laid out along the riverfront, a surprisingly large number of town founders were siting public buildings on the axes of the best streets or creating squares where courthouse, market house, church, and school were assembled. One would expect New Bern, North Carolina, to place its courthouse in an auspicious spot looking down two main streets of the town, since the Assembly met there and the governor erected a fabulous palace for himself. But Edenton, without being the capital, put its courthouse and jail in the center of a broad mall coming up from

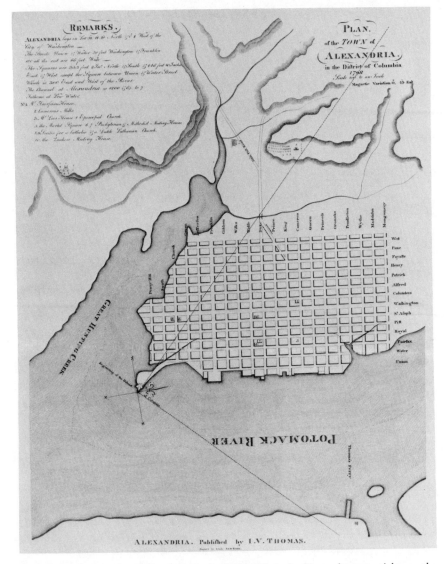

The Alexandria plat made no effort to feature its civic buildings. In this purely commercial town, the only traces of the civic element of a balanced city were the street names Duke, Prince, King, Queen, and Princess.

Albemarle Sound. Charlestown, Maryland, the colony's hope for a metropolis in the northern Chesapeake, laid out a courthouse square, a market square, and two additional public squares to match its extensive waterfront. Little Havre de Grace, which hoped to succeed to Charlestown's mantle

The Maryland Assembly created Charlestown in 1742 at the head of navigation on Chesapeake Bay. The county surveyor, John Vesey, laid out the plan to cover 200 acres. The rectangular grid and the squares for marketplace, courthouse, and meetinghouse show how widely diffused were ideas of a balanced and rectangular city by the middle of the eighteenth century.

when that city failed, crisscrossed its plat with two broad avenues and a square at the juncture, much like Philadelphia, part of whose wheat trade Havre de Grace hoped to steal. Dover, Delaware, the seat of Kent County, had a courthouse square on its plan and a church square a block away, a pair of spaces comparable to the two circles on Annapolis's pretentious plan. The aspiring city had two centers, one commercial, the other civil.[17]

Nor did commercialism strangle civic planning in larger towns. Philadelphia had disregarded the large public square in the middle of its original plan, but in the 1730s the Assembly made plans for a new statehouse on Chestnut Street between Fifth and Sixth. In 1732 they approved construction of a building 107 feet long for the Pennsylvania Assembly and Supreme Court and considered leveling the area around the building "in order that Walks may be laid out, and Trees Planted, to render the same more beautiful and commodious." Construction on the building dragged on until 1748 and it is not known if the walks were laid out then, but a vision of a public square directed the legislators through the century. By 1769 the remainder of the lots on the block had been purchased from private owners. In 1770 the Assembly enclosed the block with a brick wall seven feet high with a gate on Walnut Street behind the statehouse. Serious landscaping began in 1784

By 1800 the square behind the Pennsylvania statehouse in Philadelphia had been laid out as a park where citizens could stroll.

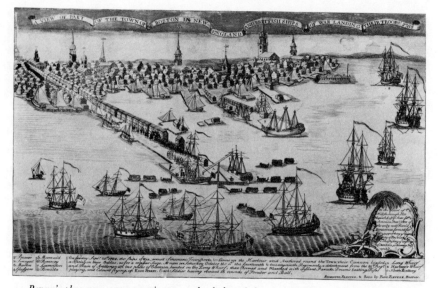

Revere's plan gave great prominence to the dock and the street leading to the statehouse, thus endowing Boston with the necessary civic and commercial elements arranged in the approved fashion, even though the city had originally been laid out on another plan.

The statehouse in Newport, known as the Old Colony House (1739–41), faced down a street to the docks. By the early nineteenth century, a small park and distinguished residences completed the complex of desired civic features.

under the direction of Samuel Vaughan, who laid out serpentine walks and planted a hundred elm trees. Reverend Manasseh Cutler, a visitor to the square soon after the landscaping, admired the garden and said "the public are indebted to the fertile fancy and taste of Mr. Sam'l Vaughan, Esqu, for the elegance of this plan." Although the statehouse was not ideally placed facing down a major avenue toward the port, by 1784 Philadelphia had a governmental center surrounded by walks, lawns, and trees to serve as the ceremonial focus of the city. In 1736 the building housed Mayor William Allen's feast for the citizens of the city, and from then on it was the natural gathering point on civic occasions.[18]

Virtually all the American capitals, and many county seats, centered governmental power in public squares by the end of the century. After 1657, Boston's town house faced the docks looking down Great Street from an open market square. In the eighteenth century the wharf at the end of the street was extended farther into the bay, and in 1711 a statehouse replaced the old town house on a street now called King. The total effect as shown in Paul Revere's view in 1768 approximated the classic vista up a straight avenue from docks to a civic square. In 1798 the General Court completed a new capital building on Beacon Hill overlooking a broad common, self-consciously creating a grand governmental center. Private developers soon lined the common and the streets on Beacon Hill with the city's finest residences, some on a residential square.

Like Boston's, Hartford's original plan had an open square a block from the river. The first statehouse was built in 1718, and in 1796 a new statehouse went up in the square, facing directly down State Street to the river, and landscaped with serpentine walks and an iron fence. In 1760 Providence began construction of the colony house on a long lot overlooking the harbor, as there was no natural site for the building. Providence had begun its existence with an informal street plan based on a main street running along the harbor. With no market square to start with, the colony house was sited back from the main street looking down to the docks. In 1772 the name of the street running in front of the state building was changed from Towne to King and other streets in the city received the names of William's, Prince, Constitution, and Hanover. In 1739 Newport merchants proposed construction of a wharf 2,011 feet long connecting directly with the street running to the new colony house, like Boston's Long Wharf. The entrepreneurs promoted the idea on the basis of the long vista, "the beauty and grandeur of which will appear the greatest perhaps in all New England."[19]

Ideas of urban grandeur had spread so widely by the end of the century that every state capital wanted its statehouse on an open square, facing the docks of the port if possible, and all the largest cities had to have imposing town halls in landscaped open spaces. All manner of ordinary merchants, speculators, and lesser public officials became town founders, laying out straight streets with the houses in line or providing for public centers. But there were still tiny places like West Chester, designated as the county seat of Chester County, Pennsylvania, in 1784, which failed to plan properly, much to the disgust of later historians. Suddenly transformed from a country crossroads to the center of government, the village could not manage the simplest elements of a geometrical plan for the town's two intersecting streets. The co-authors of a late-nineteenth-century history complained that "with that utter disregard of symmetry and lack of good taste which characterized the projectors of the plan and early buildings, neither of the streets crossed at right angles, and consequently none of the so-called squares was rectangular." It seemed to this pair that "an oblique policy, strongly redolent of barbarism, seemed to prevail among the primitive Cestrians, and its sinister influence was long perceptible." In West Chester, as in many New England towns and elsewhere, the improvement in the town plan was left to the nineteenth century, when a more enlightened citizenry tried to introduce principles of taste into the designs of once backward villages. Somewhat belatedly these reformers carried forward the impulse felt in the larger cities in the latter half of the eighteenth century, when, as *The Daily Advertiser* in New York put it in 1790, the urban gentry saw the townscape "every day growing into symmetry, elegance and beauty."[20]

RESORTS OF GENTILITY

TOGETHER, the great public buildings in an open square or on a broad avenue with accompanying fine residences and shops, plus the commercial port with shipping, docks, and warehouses, gave the eighteenth-century city its proper form. The two aspects made the city grand and elegant and won the approval of connoisseurs who visited and recorded their observations. But more was needed to sustain refined life in the city. The genteel population had to exercise its considerable influence to organize the city for genteel purposes. The desire for brilliant assemblages of the city's polite society required much larger spaces than the rooms in houses, and groups of gentlemen and entrepreneurs soon created such spaces as public extensions of the private genteel world.

In a few cities, leading citizens banded together to erect assembly rooms, like those built in English towns in the middle of the eighteenth century, where balls, dinners, and concerts for large groups of polite society could be held. The rooms in Salem, Massachusetts, built in 1766, contained "an elegant room 40 feet long, 30 feet wide and 18 feet high, with two handsome drawing-rooms adjoining and chambers over them and a neat musick-gallery on the west side." In 1782, after the conversion of this first assembly house into a meetinghouse, thirty leading citizens subscribed for a new set of rooms, larger than the first, designated for balls, concerts, lectures, and theatricals. The assembly house in Portsmouth, New Hampshire, constructed in 1750, was acclaimed by George Washington in 1789 as one of the best he had seen. The citizens of Annapolis erected dancing and card rooms on Duke of Gloucester Street in 1764, and Fredericksburg had similar rooms when the Virginia town was still very small.[21]

But these special structures for cultured events were less common in America than taverns with special rooms for assemblies. The dancing assemblies in New York met in Samuel Fraunces's Tavern and Edward Willet's Province Arms. In Alexandria, Virginia, it was the City Tavern. Frary Tavern in Deerfield, Massachusetts, raised in the 1760s, had a second-story ballroom with a musician's gallery at one end. By the end of the eighteenth century, in town after town certain taverns had come into the possession of polite society for the performances that its culture demanded.[22]

The use of tavern rooms for genteel events required changes in people's minds and in the taverns themselves. Seventeenth-century taverns were commonly scenes of disorder and brutish drunkenness rather than stages for polite entertainment. Inns were necessary, it was acknowledged in a Massachusetts statute of 1692, "for the Receipt, Relief and Lodging of Travellers and Strangers, and the Refreshment of Persons upon lawful Business," but had unfortunately degenerated into places for "lewd or idle people to spend or consume their money or time." The legislature limited the amount of time a person could spend in an inn and the amounts of liquor that could be purchased. In 1697–98 the Pennsylvania Assembly said, "As to Ordinaries, Wee are of the opinion that there are too many in the governmt, especiallie in Philadelphia, wch is one great cause of the growth of vice, & makes the same more difficult to be supprest & keept under." By 1744 there were over a hundred licensed public houses in Philadelphia and by midcentury thirty items of regulating legislation. John Adams lamented the profusion of taverns that were become "the eternal Haunt of loose disorderly People." "Young People are tempted to waste their Time and Money, and to acquire habits of Intemperance and Idleness that we often see reduce many of them to Beggary, and Vice." Taverns were the headquarters of the classic lower-class vices—cursing, fighting, lewdness, and drunkenness. How could so degraded a venue be transformed into a site for a brilliant, polite assembly?[23]

Taverns had always been ranked according to their respectability. When young Benjamin Franklin arrived in Philadelphia, he inquired about fit lodgings and was advised to stay at the Crooked Billet rather than the Sign of the Three Mariners. Tavern owners raised the tone of their establishments with high-quality food, cleanliness, and good service. But the best way to achieve distinction was to locate in a distinguished structure. In 1763 Samuel Fraunces purchased the Stephen De Lancey mansion at Broad and Pearl in New York for his Queen's Head tavern. Edward Willett bought another De Lancey mansion on Broadway for the Province Arms. William Munroe purchased a large square mansion on Lexington green in 1770. In Providence, Joshua Hacker converted his own mansion on Towne Street, the city's main street, into a hall where balls and parties were held. The height and size of the rooms in a mansion, the decoration, and the distinction of the former wealthy residents advertised the desire of the keeper for a genteel patronage, and in such a place polite people felt at home.[24]

In the latter half of the century, location also contributed to the ranking of taverns. Initially taverns clustered along the docks for the convenience of incoming mariners and travelers. Merchants gathered to do business near their warehouses and wharves. Philadelphia merchants who subscribed to purchase the London Coffee House in 1754 as a central exchange selected a building at Front and Market near the water. The elegant New York Tontine Coffee House of 1793 went up on the same site as the old Merchants Coffee House at the corner of Wall and Water, only a block from the East River docks. The energy of commerce held even pretentious taverns serving merchants close to the port well into the nineteenth century.[25]

At the same time, other forces pulled taverns away from the harbor. The most favored inns and taverns of mid-eighteenth-century Philadelphia, the Indian King, Clark's Inn, and the Conestoga Wagon, were farther up Market and Chestnut, three to five blocks from the water. In 1773 an extremely distinguished group of Philadelphians subscribed for the City Tavern to create a place for polite entertainment; they selected a site on Second Street between Walnut and Chestnut away from the hubbub of the docks. But in the same years areas still more notable for fine residences and great public buildings were crystallizing. The statehouse, particularly after the 1784 landscaping of the park behind the building, gave Chestnut Street that distinction in Philadelphia. In New York before midcentury the finest residences were grouped along Wall Street, where the city hall stood. By the end of the century, Broadway, with the governor's house at its foot, was attracting the best houses along with two elegant Anglican churches, Trinity and St. Paul's, and at the upper end the buildings of King's College, later Columbia. Washington lived on Broadway in 1790 when he was President.

Inevitably the best hostelries moved to Broadway. The De Lancey mansion that Edward Willett turned into the Province Arms was on Broadway, as was the elegant City Hotel, opened in 1796. After the city hall was erected near the park still farther up the street, John Jacob Astor could choose no better location for the Astor Hotel than a site on Broadway opposite the park. The combination of governmental buildings, grand residences, and the best shops, the same clustering as in Westminster, attracted upscale taverns and hotels, where polite society could gather for assemblies, concerts, and balls.[26]

To command that business, taverns created rooms worthy of the events and in fashionable locations. The finest taverns contained long rooms decorated like elegant parlors, though much larger. In the last quarter of the eighteenth century, the decor grew ever more elaborate. Establishments that once seemed elegant faded by comparison with newer places. The long room in Philadelphia's City Tavern was fifty feet long and probably thirty-five feet wide. When the tavern opened in 1773, John Adams thought it the most genteel tavern in the colonies. But in the 1790s Oeller's Hotel opened on Chestnut near the statehouse with a ballroom sixty feet square, and the City Tavern was doomed. In 1789, the City Tavern had advertised itself as "The Merchants' Coffee-House & Place of Exchange," indicating one kind of patron to whom it appealed, and on another line claimed to be a "Tavern and Hotel," the use of the French word implying a desire for fashionable patrons. Before then, the tavern had successfully combined the two identities. The City Tavern was located on Second Street, closer to the harbor than Oeller's, and accessible to merchants doing business; at the same time it was only a few blocks from some of the city's best residences. But in time it could not compete for both commercial business and genteel occasions.

Erected by the Tontine Association in 1792–93, the Tontine Coffee House stood at Wall and Water streets in the midst of New York's commercial section. Merchants conducted their business there, but it could not compete for formal social events which were attracted to the hotels and taverns on Broadway on the other side of the city near the civic buildings.

Located on more fashionable Chestnut Street near the center of government, Oeller's could better attract polite society. From the beginning, Oeller's adopted the title of hotel to set the tone, and created a mammoth assembly room "with a handsome music gallery at one end [and] papered after the French taste, with the Pantheon figures in compartments, imitating the same style as lately introduced in the most elegant houses in London." The City Tavern quickly lost out. New York's splendid Tontine Coffee House at Wall and Water attracted merchants on the exchange, but could not compete for genteel entertainments with the City Hotel across the island on more fashionable Broadway. The Golden Ball Inn in Providence, a large four-story building erected in 1784 on Benefit Street near the statehouse and a row of grand mansions, took the place of Hacker's Hall in an older house close to the waterfront.[27]

So there rose above the scores of taverns in the cities a tiny handful that polite society called their own. Erected in the polite end of town and housed in structures as pretentious as the patrons' own residences, this elite group of taverns created an additional genteel environment beyond the parlors and gardens of the great mansions. Besides balls and assemblies, the elite taverns hosted dinners for the leading political figures of the day and provided rooms for the meetings of government commissions and the Revolution's Committees of Safety. The Virginia legislature moved its rump session to the Raleigh Tavern after the governor's precipitate adjournment in 1774, and Delaware, lacking a statehouse at the time, ratified the Constitution in the Golden Fleece in Dover on the courthouse square. The power of government and the polish of high society came together in the best colonial taverns in that same exhilarating combination that made London's Westminster the center of the nation's social and political life.

And still polite society demanded more of the cities, demands that were only partially met. In Paris fashionable people had taken over especially pleasant places for walking. In 1597 an Italian, Raphael Salvety, laid out grounds for playing the game of pall-mall with a ball, mallets, and wickets. The avenue of trees lining the long playing course attracted strollers, and when a second course was opened along the Seine it became very popular for promenading. A few years later, in 1616, Marie de Médicis laid out the Cours la Reine in Paris, modeled after a similar walk in the Cascine Gardens outside of Florence, and soon a second, the Cours St.-Antoine, was laid out at the other end of the city. Over the next century and a half, the fashionable people of the city promenaded in their carriages on the Cours la Reine and then walked in the Tuileries.

Seeing the appeal of the promenade, Charles I laid out Pall Mall in London. When it became a street of fashionable shops instead, Charles II prepared the Mall in St. James's Park as an English equivalent of the

Tuileries. Only properly dressed and well-mannered people dared venture to join the strollers between the avenues of trees, but Moorfields to the north of the city offered benches and walks for lesser folk. Across Europe and in many British provincial cities, walks through gardens and avenues of trees became accepted amenities of urban life. The pleasure gardens of Vauxhall and Ranelagh in London, developed in the second quarter of the eighteenth century, extended the promenade, adding concerts and refreshments to the mingling, seeing, being seen, flirting, talking, and seeking amusement.[28]

Most American cities lacked polite walks. A British visitor to Philadelphia in the 1760s complained that "we have no plays or public diversions of any kind; not so much as a walk for the ladies, that there is no opportunity of seeing them but at church, or their own houses, or once a fortnight at the assembly." Mere city streets lacked the elegance of the promenades, where a lady could properly show herself and where the surroundings harmonized with the manners. The idea of a public walk was not unknown in the seventeenth century; it was said that the Commons in Boston was a place for walking. But it was too far out of town to be fashionable. Thomas Holme wrote that the open squares on his plan of Philadelphia were to be the city's Moorfields, Philadelphia's place for people to walk and play. The order for the Pennsylvania statehouse in 1734 called for walks in the grounds behind the building. Three New Yorkers leased land before the fort at the lower end of Broadway in 1733 to enclose and make a bowling green with "Walks therein, for the Beauty & Ornament of the Said Street," perhaps thinking of the success of Pall Mall in attracting fashionable strollers.[29]

These efforts met with only partial success until near the end of the century. Orders were continually issued to fence Bowling Green, and once in 1745 to lay turf there. Then after the Revolution, interest in walks grew, especially in New York. After the decay of the city during the war, Bowling Green was repaired just about the time the grounds behind Independence Hall in Philadelphia were landscaped. The old New York common, known as the Fields, was ordered fenced in 1785 and called a park. While living in New York as President, Washington enjoyed walking the Battery, which by then had become a park with trees lining the paths. In that last quarter of the century a host of minor versions of Vauxhall and Ranelagh, the London pleasure gardens, were attempted in New York City, meeting with some success. In 1791 Governor's Island just off the tip of Manhattan was planted with a thousand trees and gardens and walks were laid out. But in spite of all the available promenades, a visitor in 1807 said "neither the Park nor the Battery is very much resorted to by the fashionable citizens of New York, as they have become too common." The fashionable had another resort, he said. "The genteel lounge is in the Broadway, from eleven to three o'clock, during which time it is as much crowded as the Bond street of London: and the carriages, though not so numerous, are driven to and fro with as much velocity." These were the beginnings of genteel walks, substantial in New York City and much less elsewhere.³⁰

By such measures, a patchwork genteel world came to overlay the gruff irregularities of the actual city. Polite society marked the places peculiarly theirs, where they liked to go and where genteel activities took place. The mansions with their gardens for conversation and entertainments came first, then the assembly rooms and elite taverns where theatricals and concerts took place in the elegant environment of the long rooms. The right taverns were located on streets where public buildings elevated the atmosphere and where luxury shops catered to ladies and gentlemen. Here governmental power, polite society, and intellectual endeavor in the form of theaters or college buildings converged to create an atmosphere of cultivation, refinement, amusement, and public responsibility. Nearby were fenced parks with lines of trees for genteel promenading. Along these streets polite people happily walked or rode in their carriages, in their proper milieu and among people of their own kind.

Beyond these passages and locales lay the bulk of the actual city with tradesmen, laborers, seamen, industries, common shops, the docks, warehouses, the poor, criminals. Polite society could not entirely circumvent this common life. All of the streets of the city belonged to everyone. Scenes of the best districts show urchins, men with barrows, woodcutters, carters, and beggars mingling with grand ladies and fine gentlemen. There were no Tuileries where guards denied admission to shabbily dressed people. When the people of New York gathered to protest the Stamp Act, they came to the city hall on Wall Street, still in 1765 a street of fine residences. Protest marchers during the Revolutionary years came down Broadway from the Fields, marching past the elite Province Arms and Trinity Church. They burned an effigy of the royal governor on Bowling Green, a genteel promenade. In Philadelphia the mobs met in the yard of the statehouse square on Chestnut Street. The people claimed all of the streets as their own, and polite citizens who ventured into the city found themselves mingling with all kinds even in the genteel preserves.³¹

Gentlemen knew no limits within the city. Merchants walked the docks, brushed shoulders with seamen, ventured into any tavern they chose. Henry Drinker, a circumspect Quaker merchant, bathed in the Delaware River. Young blades ventured into common taverns for pleasure among the lowlifes. Alexander Graydon recorded with amusement his evenings begun in a cheap tavern with brash young companions, inflaming themselves with cheap liquor at the start of a night of dissipation. At "an obscure inn in Race street, dropping in about dark, we were led by a steep and narrow stair-case to a chamber in the third story, so lumbered with beds as scarcely to leave room for a table and one chair, the beds superseding the necessity of more. Here we poured down the fiery beverage; and valiant in the novel feeling of intoxication, sallied forth in quest of adventures." These wild flings were not out of character for dashing young gentlemen.[32]

Ladies were another matter. The British visitor in noting the absence of walks said Philadelphia lacked a place for ladies to show themselves. The true test of the gentility of a place was its suitability for ladies, the purest embodiment of genteel delicacy. Could they venture onto the streets? Ann Ridgely of Dover, Delaware, was shocked that her niece, Williamina Cadwalader, sent a Ridgely daughter and her brother onto the streets of Philadelphia with only a servant. "I am a plain Country woman," Ann Ridgely wrote, "and know little of modern politeness—possibly such conduct may be thought quite genteel, and proper, by the *fashionable people* of Philadelphia but I am very sure, it would, by the rustic Inhabitants of poor little Dover, have been thought not only rude, but unkind." That the young people went with the approval of the experienced Philadelphian suggests that city streets were not completely off-bounds for genteel ladies; a circa 1791–93 print shows a pair of respectable ladies alone on the sidewalk near the city hall

By the turn of the century, Baltimore contained all the proper elements for a genteel city. Barely discernible at the bottom, Calvert Street heads directly north from the Bason to terminate in the courthouse. Assembly rooms, pictured in the upper-right inset, were erected a few blocks away. In the nearby countryside, merchants and gentlemen built country houses and laid out formal gardens.

in New York. But Ann Ridgely's objection reveals that she thought the streets unfitting or dangerous. A servant could not shelter a young woman, since he was subject to her commands and perhaps lacking in courage. A gentleman must protect her dignity and physical well-being. A gentleman and a lady together created a genteel space about themselves that the vulgarity of the city could not penetrate. Together they might enter a tavern, a place a woman could never go alone, or walk on virtually any street.[33]

Toward the end of the century the standards of genteel delicacy rose ever higher, and polite society withdrew more and more from the coarseness of ordinary city life. Fashionable people objected to the muddy streets which ordinary men and women could not possibly avoid in the usual round of work. Philadelphia Anglicans complained that they could not attend services at Christ Church and St. Peter's because the streets were muddy. They obtained some relief by riding in carriages. The rapid increase in the number of carriages in the cities separated polite society from the streets, elevating feet in delicate shoes above the mud. In carriages, ladies and gentlemen traveled above the pavements, encased in decorated boxes that both advertised their position in society and formed a genteel space immediately about them. The owners adorned the carriages with coats of arms and elaborate colors and even upholstered the interior seats. A person moved from the confines of the house to the protection of the carriage without touching foot to ground, and emerged into the safety of another regulated environment. Ideally, there was no contact with vulgarity save the exchange of stares as the carriage passed by.[34]

Besides withdrawing into their carriages, the urban gentry gained control over the streets by improving the space in front of their houses. In scenes of Philadelphia and Brooklyn at the turn of the century, rows of trees at the curb line stand before some of the more pretentious houses. Trees had been associated with the promenades in Europe from their beginning in Antwerp and Paris, providing shade and a pleasing long straight vista comparable to the straight streets. In the grounds behind the Pennsylvania statehouse in Philadelphia, hundreds of trees were planted; the same was true at City Hall Park in New York. Trees lined the walks of the Boston Common. Lines of trees in gardens and cities defined the loci of genteel space. Gentlemen achieved some of the same effect on the walks before their own houses by planting trees. In smaller towns, fashionable people put in their own sidewalks when the local government did not act. In West Chester, Pennsylvania, in 1809, Dr. William Darlington installed a flagstone pavement before his house, and two neighbors put down bricks, more than a decade before the town government put in sidewalks elsewhere. A paved walk in a country town or a line of trees in the city marked a house where the owner wished

By 1800 the owners of fashionable houses on High Street (Market) in Philadelphia were beginning to plant trees along the sidewalk.

to extend the beauty and order of his residence and garden into the street, providing a walk between door and carriage that sustained the genteel ambience.[35]

CHURCHES

OUR understanding of eighteenth-century American cities owes much to the itinerant artists and mapmakers who offered prospects and maps to subscribers, recording in surprising detail the architecture and layout of the early towns. William Burgis came to New York from England in 1718 and published his "South East Prospect of the City of New York." Moving to Boston, he established himself at the Crown Coffee House and in 1722 prepared "A South East View of the Great Town of Boston in New England in America," which was engraved by John Harris in London and offered for sale in 1725 and again in 1743 by William Price, a Boston print dealer.

While accurate in many details, Burgis's "View" consciously exaggerates one aspect of the city—its churches. Twelve churches and meetinghouses appear in the 1722 scene and seventeen in 1743. In both views, the steeples and bell towers rise to an extravagant height above the low-lying city. The churches are identified by number, placing them among the significant public buildings that Bostonians apparently wished emphasized in depictions of their city.[36]

Forty years earlier the steeples would have been absent from the scene. The earlier churches had bell towers but not great spires. The spired church was an eighteenth-century addition to the urban skyline in America, appearing in full flower in the 1720s, at the same time as the great mansions began to dot the landscape. Seventeenth-century New England churches looked like large one-story houses; the Dedham church, built in 1638, was thirty-six by twenty feet, large for a house but still house size. Over the century churches grew larger in both height and floor size. One of the largest was the meetinghouse at Hingham, which still stands, two stories and seventy-three by fifty-five feet. These early churches were boxy; some were square and others close to square. Instead of placing the pulpit and altar at one end of the church and the main entrance at the other, with a long nave between, the pulpit stood against the longer wall, with doors opposite and also on the two shorter sidewalls. People entered from all sides and surrounded the preacher from left to right.

These meetinghouses were in the form of the Protestant auditory, built primarily for preaching rather than for celebrating the eucharist before an altar at the church's end. The early churches had no altars, only communion tables, placed usually under the pulpit. By the end of the seventeenth century, bell towers or watch turrets appeared on the large churches in New England: twenty of them are known. But these were squat structures, often more like cupolas placed in the middle of the roof. The Brattle Street Church in Boston, built in 1699, was the first meetinghouse with a spire. Though plain in decoration, the spired church was a portent, the equivalent of the Foster-Hutchinson mansion of 1691. Both prefigured changes to come later in the eighteenth century.[37]

The direction the changes would take was laid out clearly in the building erected for Christ Church parish in 1723 on Salem Street in Boston and now known as the Old North Church. William Price, the print seller, designed the building. He had been influenced by the churches that Christopher Wren erected in London following the Great Fire of 1666, most particularly St. James's, Piccadilly. Architectural historians speak of Christ Church as America's first Renaissance or Georgian church because of its extensive classical detailing. The spire above the tower rose 191 feet, higher by sixteen feet than the one that replaced it after a windstorm in 1807. The church had two rows of arched windows on the outside and on the inside classical fluted pillars, a raised pulpit with sounding board, square box pews, and paintings of cherubs on the chancel ceiling. The building was oriented the long way, with the entrance on the short wall to the west, and the altar in the apse at the opposite end.[38]

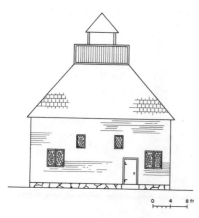

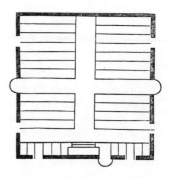

ABOVE AND RIGHT. *By midcentury, New England meetinghouses were beginning to assume a formal shape but still lacked the tower and steeple that were to come later.*

Brattle Street Church was the first Congregational meetinghouse to take on the demeanor of a church.

In traditional fashion, the main entrance of Old South was on the long side of the building, with the pulpit directly across the width. Yet, incongruously, an attached tower with a wooden spire rose 180 feet at one of the short ends of the building. Thus the building maintained the old Congregational forms while still meeting the challenge of the new Anglican churches.

The building's influence became apparent six years later, when the Third Church in Boston began construction of the Old South meetinghouse in 1729. Christ Church was Anglican and understandably responsive to English ecclesiastical style. Old South was Congregational and constructed when the growth of episcopacy in New England had precipitated a vitriolic pamphlet war over the proper form of church government. Yet Old South also had a tower and high spire, two rows of arched windows, and a high pulpit and sounding board. In all of these features, Old South foreshadowed the changes that would affect New England churches in every substantial town. Beginning in the 1730s, towers and spires became common features where they were unknown earlier. The familiar high-spired churches we associate with New England towns were an eighteenth-century development.

Inside eighteenth-century churches, the decoration of pews, pulpits, communion tables, doorways, and pillars became ever more elaborate. Country churches remained simple, but in cities and larger towns, Congregational meetinghouses rivaled Anglican churches. Old South did not follow the Old

North style in one important way: Old South retained the auditory arrangement of seating, with the pulpit on the long wall and an entrance opposite. In 1729, a longitudinal orientation, with entrance on one end and the communion table and pulpit at the other, looked too much like Rome. Yet by the end of the century a longitudinal orientation became commonplace in the meetinghouses of these latter-day Puritans. Gradually spires, decorated interiors, and eventually longitudinal orientation became the rule in the major towns, leaving the plain, boxlike auditories of the seventeenth century for worship in backward villages. Church buildings became self-consciously beautiful. *The New York Magazine* in 1795 said St. Paul's was "esteemed the most elegant in the city," having been "executed with a remarkable degree of taste."[39]

The Church of England took the lead in bringing about these changes. All major colonial cities had equivalents to Boston's Christ Church, a structure notable for its spire, its longitudinal orientation, and its internal decoration. In a single decade, the 1720s, the Church of England began to build in all American cities at once. The second Trinity Church in Newport, begun in 1725, closely followed the pattern of Christ Church in Boston, but was built

Christ Church, Philadelphia.

Modeled after London churches by Christopher Wren and James Gibbs, Philadelphia's Christ Church exemplified the aggressive construction of elaborate Anglican churches which overshadowed all other forms of church architecture in the colonies.

of wood. Christ Church in Philadelphia, begun in 1725 and perhaps the most ornate of all American Georgian churches, had a spire 196 feet tall. St. Philip's in Charleston, erected in 1727, was described by the Anglican clergy as "a Work of ... Magnitude Regularity Beauty and Solidity ... the greatest ornamt of this City." New York's Trinity Church, though strongly flavored with Gothic when completed in 1698, already raised a spire to the sky there. In the decade when mansions were first appearing in numbers, these Anglican churches brought the new church look to every region of the colonies and set the pattern for the city churches of all denominations for the rest of the century.[40]

This Anglican activity came when the Dissenting churches, especially in New England, were open to influence from England. While still devoted to the Calvinist doctrines and Congregational polity, New England suffered in 1700 from a sense of provincial inferiority. Instead of leading the Protestant Reformation as in 1630 and so the whole religious world, educated New Englanders knew they lived on the periphery of European culture. In every assertion of pride and love for their own country, they implicitly acknowledged that European capitals set the standard which New England must meet. Increase Mather himself sought a position in England in the 1690s, a startling admission of provincial doubt. Ambitious Harvard graduates left Boston to preach and travel in England before returning to pulpits nearer home. Benjamin Colman, who graduated in 1692, studied under tutor John Leverett, who encouraged the reading of Episcopal works as the best books to form the pupils' minds "in religious matters and preserve us from those narrow Principles that kept us at a Distance from the Church of England." Colman preached in England until 1699, when he returned to take the pulpit of the newly formed Brattle Street Church organized by Leverett and the broad-minded brothers William and Thomas Brattle. Colman was a perfect choice for the Brattle Street pulpit, which was considered by some as halfway between episcopacy and Congregationalism. A friend described his stature as "tall, and erect above the common Height; his Complection fair and delecate; his Aspect and Mien benign and graceful. ... And his neat and clean Manner of Dress, and genteel, complaisant Behaviour, Politeness and Elegance in Conversation, set off his Person to the best Advantage." He was cosmopolitan, tolerant, and polished, an admirer of Archbishop John Tillotson, the politest preacher of the time. When erected in Boston, the Brattle Street meetinghouse, while not fully in the Renaissance style, had a tall spire that revealed a willingness to embrace English ecclesiastical architecture.[41]

Other preachers in Boston were assuming a similar style. Thomas Prince, a Harvard graduate in 1707, left for London in 1709. It pleased him that his hosts there could not believe he was born in New England. "They wondered as much at my carriage & Deportment, as at the Fairness and accuracy of my Language." When he returned to Boston in 1717, Samuel Sewall failed to recognize Prince, "having a Wigg on and a Russet Coat." Five hundred people came to the dock to welcome him home. To his great pleasure, he was "embrac'd and Surrounded with Numbers of Friends, and many that seem'd to know Me at Once, tho' They never saw me before." Within forty-eight hours he was offered the pulpit at Hingham. A populace that loved this fair young man almost solely for his English experience and cosmopolitan style was surely open to many of the cultural currents of the homeland.[42]

The Church of England was thus well positioned in the early eighteenth century to influence ecclesiastical architecture. The Anglican clergy saw the buildings as part of a much broader campaign to recover the colonies for episcopacy. Church leaders wished to use their cultural advantage, including the superiority of their buildings, to bring down dissent in the colonies. The general desire of imperial authorities in the last quarter of the seventeenth century to regulate the American colonies culminated within the Church in the organization of the Society for Promoting Christian Knowledge in 1698 and the Society for the Propagation of the Gospel in Foreign Parts in 1701. Although organized with the Indians in mind, the activities of the SPG quickly focused on the establishment of Anglican missionaries among Quaker, Presbyterian, and Congregational populations in the middle colonies and New England. The society paid the salaries of ministers—329 of them between 1701 and the end of the Revolution—and financed church construction. Largely through the involvement of the SPG, Anglicans, before the Revolution, constructed 229 churches from Delaware to New-foundland in regions where the small numbers of Anglicans and their general poverty would otherwise have put decent buildings out of reach.

Anglican claims rested most heavily on scriptural support for a polity based on bishops and a line of authoritative ordinations going back to the first apostles. But their ecclesiastical arguments were enriched by the great learning of Anglican authors, the ceremonial appeal of the liturgy, and the beauty of the churches. Church architecture became an instrument of cultural conflict. Donald Friary, the authority on Anglican churches in the eighteenth century, has suggested that in New England, besides the usual reasons for spires, the "Anglicans appear to have given the steeple an additional function which was in fact primary. This was to act as an assertive symbol of the Anglican presence in the community." The two Christ Churches in Boston and Philadelphia summed up the power of the Anglican tradition as effectively as any book. Philadelphia's Christ Church, as the *Pennsylvania Packet* observed in 1772, "in point of elegance and taste, surpasses everything of the kind in America." John Tyler, a Connecticut Anglican, defended the custom of the Church of England in "expensively adorning their Houses of public worship" as showing the opposite of an "ungrateful, sordid narrowness of soul" that reduced houses of worship to a frugal meanness. People weary of "sordid narrowness" in worship and theology were enthralled by the Anglican churches.[43]

The aggressive proselytizing stance of the Anglicans and their success in winning converts rebuffed sympathetic New Englanders like Colman who wished to absorb Anglican culture without abandoning all their Puritan beliefs. A handful of others reacted differently. In 1722 Samuel Johnson, a minister in Stratford, Connecticut, announced his conversion. He was one of a number of Congregational ministers who converted to episcopacy, including the rector of Yale, Timothy Cutler. Johnson had fallen under the spell of the Anglican books that Jeremiah Dummer, a Harvard graduate living in England, had shipped to the infant college. In 1714 when he began reading in the library, Johnson felt that "the condition of learning (as well as everything else) was very low in these times indeed much lower than in the earlier times while those yet lived who had their education in England and first settled the country." Reading English poets as well as philosophers and divines "was like a flood of day to his low state of mind." Coupled with doubts about his own ordination, Johnson's reading prepared him to join Cutler in 1722.

This shocking conversion, along with the bellicose attacks of a few Anglican pamphleteers, upset even the most tolerant New England clergy. They understood Johnson's admiration of English learning and had been extending their hands to the Anglicans too, but they envisioned friendship, not defection. Colman objected as well to the "Course of angry Controversy" set off by "a Parcil of High-flyers." A nephew of Cotton Mather, Thomas Walter, a 1713 graduate of Harvard and reputed to be the most polished as well as the most brilliant young man in his class, flirted with Anglicanism in his college years, but after the Yale conversions, he returned to Congregationalism and wrote against the claims of the Church of England.[44]

The aversion to the Church of England's aggressive proselytizing might have turned the New England churches against every form of English ecclesiastical culture. Instead it had the opposite effect. While combating the Anglicans on one side, the Congregational clergy tried to upgrade the worship of their own people on the other, moved at least in part by a desire to counter the appeal of Anglican high culture. Old South's great brick tower and spire and its architecture modeled after Christ Church can be considered defensive measures, affirmations that the Congregational order could partake of ecclesiastical glory too.

In the very decade when they were trying to counteract the Yale conversions, Boston's ministers urged their congregations to upgrade church music by learning to sing by note. In 1715, John Tufts, a young ministerial candidate newly out of Harvard, published *An Introduction to the Singing of Psalm-Tunes, in a Plain and Easy Method,* largely derived from earlier English publications. He may have been influenced by the decision of Boston's King's Chapel parish to sponsor the publication of Tate and Brady's *New Version of the Psalms* in 1713. Over the next decade a number of ministers joined in, including Thomas Walter, now occupying a Roxbury pulpit. To their ears the practice of allowing each member of the congregation to sing as he or she pleased when the psalms were chanted sounded raucous and confusing. The books tried to teach people to hit the same note together and hold it for the same length of time. The city churches quickly adopted the new method, and singing schools and choirs became popular almost overnight.

The churches were less ready to install organs. Thomas Brattle, a wealthy merchant instrumental in the organization of the Brattle Street Church, purchased one for himself in 1711, and when he died two years later left it to the Brattle Street Church. This was too much of a departure even for this cosmopolitan assemblage, and they refused the instrument. Because organs were not mentioned in scripture, the old Puritan churches held back while Anglican churches installed organs as their resources allowed. Brattle's organ went to the Anglican congregation in King's Chapel, which soon hired an organist. Twenty-four Anglican churches owned organs before the Revolution, while Ezra Stiles said that no organ was installed in a Dissenting church in America until 1770.[45]

Anglicans do not deserve all the credit for the improvements in church decoration. They led the way to spires, elaborate internal decorations, and better music, but changes were in the air in the British ecclesiastical world, and even Dissenters in England were yielding to those influences. Isaac Watts, the Dissenting hymn writer, published his *Hymns and Spiritual Songs* in 1707; an edition appeared in Boston in 1720. Hymns were even more musical than psalms sung by note and more of a departure from the old way. In 1711, Benjamin Colman called Watts "a burning Light and Ornament of the Age," and in the coming decades his hymns became standards in many New England churches. By the same token, Dissenters could independently improve church architecture. They could look at Wren's London churches for themselves, without relying on Anglicans in the colonies for beautiful church models. The Old Brick meetinghouse in Boston, built in 1712 before the influence of Christ Church, conformed to the old style in its overall plan, but had box pews and a large, elaborate pulpit reached by spiral stairs. Powerful cultural forces apart from rivalry with the Church of England affected ecclesiastical architecture.[46]

Moved both by these influences and by Anglican competition, the refinement of urban churches moved ahead swiftly after 1700. Decoration of the inside of the meetinghouses often preceded changes on the outside.

Meetinghouses without steeples, built on the old auditory plan, with pulpit on the long wall and looking like houses, would sometimes have beautifully finished interiors. As with better houses, the ceilings were finished to hide the beams and rafters under the roof, and elaborate decorations were applied to doors and especially the pulpit. In the seventeenth century, some country churches went without pulpits, providing the preacher with a raised platform. In the eighteenth century, pulpits were lifted high above the congregation, and topped with sounding boards. Elegant stairs, some gracefully curved, provided a dignified ascent, comparable to the broad stairs of mansions. Fielded paneling, carving, and turned balusters adorned the pulpit assemblage. Pulpits which once had pillows were now frequently upholstered. Near the end of the century heavy drape hangings, often in red silk, were installed at the window behind. In some churches angels and seraphim were painted on the ceiling. Pews began to replace the long benches of the meetinghouses, first for dignitaries and then for everyone, usually with paneling and decorative touches that went far beyond the plainness of their seventeenth-century counterparts. Meetinghouses were painted, probably beginning in the late 1730s, just at the time when the great mansions were first

By the end of the eighteenth century, towers and steeples in the Anglican style were becoming standard for ambitious Presbyterian and Congregational churches and meetinghouses, as in the New Presbyterian Church in Newark, New Jersey. Orientation along the long axis of the building was also taking hold.

painted. By the end of the century many Boston meetinghouses had been beautified. They not only offered space for worship but pleased aesthetic sensibilities. Visiting the city in 1781, Abbé Robin commented that several of the churches were "finished with taste and elegance, especially those of the Presbyterians [Congregationalists] and the Church of England; their form is generally a long square, ornamented with a pulpit, and furnished with pews of similar fabrication throughout." He was equally impressed with their "grave and majestic" psalmody. Altogether, he thought, they provided lovely settings for elevated worship.[47]

All of these changes occurred roughly from 1720 on, in the same period when the great mansions were rising on the landscape, and when balls and assemblies were being organized in the long rooms of the best taverns. Moreover, the decorative style of both the churches and the mansions followed the Georgian mode. The paneling, the balusters, the pedimented doorways, the smoothed walls and ceilings, the cornices, and carving linked mansion and meetinghouse in a decorative continuum. Most spaces in the city, most houses, taverns, and shops, were rougher, darker, and plainer. Elaborate decorations were lavished only upon the great mansions, upon the assembly rooms and long rooms in the best taverns, and upon the churches.[48]

The Dissenting churches and the Church of England confronted each other most directly in New England, but the tie between mansion and church may have been even stronger in the South. Church construction rose sharply there after 1720 with a corresponding upgrading of design and decoration. Southern churches may appear simpler than their New England counterparts, for outside of the few cities, Anglican churches and chapels in the South did without towers and spires. But an increasing number after 1700—and all the principal churches—were built of brick, setting them off from the temporary wooden churches of the seventeenth century. Most were finished on the interior with cornices, paneled pulpits, and pulpit stairs with balusters, as in the best New England churches. And as with northern churches and meetinghouses, the interior appearance of southern churches closely resembled the decor of mansions. In fact, churches resembled mansions both outside and in, except for the steeples. Dell Upton, who has exhaustively analyzed Virginia churches, observes that "other than in churches, pilasters and pediments and similar modish decorations were found only in the homes of Virginia's wealthiest planters." Architecturally they were foreign to the bulk of the population, whose houses were made of wood, unpainted, roughly finished, and largely lacking in decoration. The interiors of the houses of worship "equated the universal values of the Church with the specific values of the gentry." What is true for Virginia was true everywhere. Because they were not constructed in the rough fashion of ordinary houses, churches and meetinghouses made themselves congenial to

polite society and elevated houses of worship far above the usual environments of ordinary people. In the inventory of city spaces, churches belonged
to the genteel. The Gothic churches had said that God was a king or a great
lord; the Georgian churches implied that God, as Upton says, was "the
greatest gentleman in the neighborhood."[49]

So churches joined the assemblage of urban places suitable for genteel
performances. Even sincere worshippers must have seen that they were on
display in a church, under the eyes of observers judging their personal
qualities. The Reverend Samuel Fayerweather, a visitor to Queen's Chapel
in Portsmouth in 1760, noted that the church held a "small but a Gay and
Shining Congregation in Respect to Dress and Appearance." Churchgoers
must look their best to please the watching eyes. Abbé Robin in Boston in
1781 wrote:

> Piety is not the only motive that brings the American ladies in crowds
> to the various places of worship. Deprived of all shows and public
> diversions whatever, the church is the grand theatre where they attend,
> to display their extravagance and finery. There they come dressed off
> in the finest silks, and overshadowed with a profusion of the most
> superb plumes.

Infants came to their christenings covered with blankets of richly woven
silks. The demands of genteel culture pursued adherents even into the
houses of God. Surprisingly, few in the congregation asked if the theatrical
quality of churchgoing endangered its deeper purpose, and if ordinary
people in humble dress could comfortably worship among fashionably attired people in a building adorned like a mansion.[50]

CHAPTER VI

Ambivalence

GENTEEL culture left traces everywhere on the American landscape in the eighteenth century. The desire for a refined existence resulted in beautified urban streets with fine houses, public buildings, assembly rooms, and tree-lined walks. In the countryside, genteel culture led to the construction of rural mansions set in geometrical gardens and fronted with fenced court-yards. Gentility fashioned dress, prescribed posture, furnished houses, and set tables. Above all, gentility created parlors, the most common and the most important site of refined living. A parlor emptied of beds and tools and ordained as a place for polite conversation was the single most telling mark of genteel aspiration. Though work, business, and play doubtless invaded real parlors in everyday life, and chipped saucers and sparse furnishing diminished the rooms' grandeur, a parlor signified that a family had sensed the attractions of genteel existence. Like Morison at the inn in New Castle, Delaware, they occasionally put on their best linen and good manners to claim places for themselves in polite society.

The parlor can easily be mistaken as a place for pecuniary display. We crudely surmise that people were proud of their wealth and wanted to show it off. Or, in another effort at a simple explanation, we note the similarities to English gentility and attribute the parlors to a provincial desire to copy the metropolis. Neither explanation of motive—display or imitation—does justice to the phenomenon. Then as now, display took many forms. Today books and paintings display wealth as walnut furniture did then, but the culture these objects represent is far more significant than their monetary worth. Objects in our time and theirs signify a commitment to a particular cultural style, not only to a crass urge to appear opulent. Reducing the meaning of objects to pecuniary exhibitionism obscures a large part of their message. In the same vein, the design of American doorframes, chairs, and ceramics can be traced to European sources, but their presence in American rooms did not mean that the provincials blindly imitated the metropolis, any more than concertgoers in Kansas blindly imitate concertgoers in New York City. Both colonial and English gentry embraced a cultural ideal that inspired the treatment of rooms and the conduct of lives. Devotion to the ideal had to precede emulation. The importance of the provincial parlor lay in the implied commitment of its occupants to refine their lives.

SOCIAL CLASS

THIS distinction must be kept in mind or the implications of gentility for the division of the population into social classes will be lost. The parlors meant more than that the owners were rich or in touch with English culture. The significance was deeper, and the implications for class comparisons more damaging. Brandishing possessions in the faces of the poor to demonstrate pecuniary superiority only signified a difference in wealth—a matter of simple, crass financial muscle. Creating parlors as a site for a refined life implied spiritual superiority. Parlor people claimed to live on a higher plane than the vulgar and coarse populace, to excel them in their inner beings. Pecuniary display was outward and by definition superficial; refinement was inward and profound.

The differences were not biologically innate. A book circulated in America entitled *The Polite Philosopher* did not attribute the superior ease and happiness of polite people to inherent ability. "It is Want of Attention, not Capacity, which leaves us so many Brutes," the author argued. Nonetheless, the failure to attend to the "Thousand little Civilities, Complacencies, and Endeavours to give others Pleasure," which made up politeness, left men "Brutes," living on a plane closer to the animals.[1] The parlor divided the world into levels of humanity: those who had disciplined body and spirit to flourish amidst beauty and ease and those too sluggish, too obtuse, or simply too unfortunate to have learned how.

This spiritual division was encoded in the words commonly used to describe people. "The better sort of People here live very well and Genteel," a visitor to Portsmouth, New Hampshire, observed in 1751. The writer knew his readers would understand who the "better sort" were and that far more than sheer wealth raised them above the rest of the population. At the other end of the spectrum, Charles Woodmason indicted his parishioners in the Carolina backcountry as "rude, ignorant—void of Manners, Education or Good Breeding—No genteel or Polite Person Among them." In Woodmason's mind the simple poverty of the country people did not make them repulsive; they suffered from a complete lack of refinement. Dismayed by their low level of civilization, George Washington considered the settlers of the Shenandoah Valley "a parcel of barbarians . . . an uncouth set of people."[2]

The line between cultivated and coarse did not correspond to any religious divisions, for salvation by every theology of the day could come to people on either side of the line. The boundary did not precisely divide the rich and poor, for there could be vulgar rich men and genteel poor, especially female poor. The coarse language of Admiral Montagu, who commanded the British navy in Boston Harbor and harassed American shipping, disgusted John Adams. Searching for the right insult, Adams said that "an American freeholder living in a log house twenty feet square, without a chimney in it, is a well bred man, a polite accomplished person, a fine gentleman, in comparison to this beast of prey."[3]

But if there were exceptions, gentility still established the ideal toward which wealth and power gravitated. The "best people," everywhere, as in Portsmouth, tended to live in the genteel fashion. In the overall, gentility deepened the division between rich and poor, adding a moral dimension to differences in wealth. Washington ranked himself morally above the uncouth barbarians of the Shenandoah Valley, assuming a superiority based not on his riches but on his refinement. Genteel dress, furnishings, manners, and speech implicitly passed judgment on the world and always in the gentry's favor.

How did ordinary people react to this unremitting trial of their moral worth? Large segments of the population were insulated from genteel scorn. Their very poverty erected a barrier against the judgments of the "better sort." The Susquehanna ferryman who offered Alexander Hamilton scaly fish to be scooped out by hand from a common pot appears to have suffered no embarrassment about his primitive mode of living. The ferryman knew he was no gentleman, had no hopes of becoming one, and felt no shame in the presence of a genteel guest. He acted as if he were oblivious to Hamilton's gentlemanly disdain. It is possible to imagine him living in another world preoccupied with its dangers and pleasures and indifferent to the haughty posturing of the great.

On the other hand, there is ample evidence that large numbers of common people engaged polite society more directly. For one thing, they purchased items associated with genteel living for use in their own households. What the objects meant must have differed widely. Some purchased silver spoons or teacups to escape degrading barbarism and to identify themselves with the respectable people of society. Morison, Hamilton's fellow traveler at New Castle, hoped his linen nightcap and silver buckles would redeem him in the eyes of the gentlemen at the inn. In his case, failure to win the respect of the landlady at breakfast threw him into an anguished rage. Gentility was a torturous thorn in his side. For others, gentility vaguely represented improvement and dignity. They naturally drew upon the inventory of genteel objects and manners to improve their lives or dignify occasions. Deborah Franklin surprised Benjamin with a silver spoon and a china bowl for his breakfast of bread and milk, justifying the extravagance by saying that her husband deserved what his neighbors had. She made the purchase out of vanity, not shame.[4]

Whether evoking outrage and envy or admiration and emulation, gentility was sometimes relevant to common people, not a matter left entirely to the wealthy who could afford its costly accoutrements. Rather substantial purchases by the very poorest people indicate their interest. Recent researchers, led by Lois Carr, Lorena Walsh, and Carole Shammas, have measured the extent to which genteel amenities entered colonial households after about 1720. No wealth category, as measured by the value of inventoried estates at the time of death, was totally exempt from genteel influences. In rural York County, Virginia, for example, only 3 to 8 percent of the poorest to middling decedents owned table forks between 1700 and 1709. By contrast, inventories taken between 1768 and 1777 show 21 percent of the poorest and 52 percent of the middling group with forks. About the same holds true for tea and tea services. At the beginning of the century there was virtually no sign of tea drinking in the rural areas of the county. Between 1768 and 1777, 29 percent of the poorest inventories and 57 percent of the middling group had some indication of tea in the household. In the highest categories, 83 to 85 percent of the inventories listed tea or tea services. In Massachusetts by 1774, 30.3 percent of the poorest group owned knives and forks and 42.4 percent tea equipment; for a more average group the corresponding figures were 50.4 percent for both knives and forks and tea equipment, and for the most affluent, 82.8 to 89.7 percent.

The same trend continued in towns, except that both tea and knives and forks were adopted sooner and turned up in a greater proportion of poor households. Whether we trace knives and forks and tea, or fine earthenware, glassware, and silver spoons, the general trend is the same. By the Revolution these little indicators of genteel living, seen only in the households of the uppermost elite in 1700, were touching people at every economic level.[5]

The material indicators of refinement, however, must not be given too much weight. The presence of a teacup in a household did not mean that the owner practiced all the genteel arts or even aspired to do so. Genteel material culture was infinitely divisible. One could possess a single sliver, enjoy its satisfactions, and go no further. No one at the time would have thought that ownership of a handkerchief or a silver buckle made ordinary people genteel, any more than Morison's bagful of good linen turned him into a gentleman. It was not necessary to transform one's entire life to drink tea from a delft cup or eat meat with a fork. Franklin admitted that the china bowl and silver spoon set his household on a path that eventually led to the purchase of much plate and other fine wares, but he did not become a gentleman the instant he consumed his bread and milk from a genteel vessel, and many went no further than a bowl and silver spoon.

The difference came when the desire for refinement spread through a person's life. The refined wished to refine all activities and beautify every personal environment. A common person might have a silver spoon and a teacup on a shelf or lying in a chest in a room that in every other respect was unpolished, with rough beams overhead, an encased stair winding up against a gaping cooking fireplace, with tools and casks and perhaps a bed occupying the corners of the room. While a source of pride, the spoon and cup did not signify a desire to transform a life.

But when the householder covered the beams of the room with a smooth ceiling, moved cooking and sleeping functions to another space, narrowed the fireplace and installed a mantel, when he placed a broad stair in a passage by itself and thought about decorating door and window frames and installing sash windows, then that person indicated a wish to transform his environment and presumably himself along with it.

After crossing that boundary, a person became alert for every little clue to proper behavior, every indication of current fashion among the informed and polite population. After the parlor one had to consider the dining room, then the garden and front yard, then behavior in taverns and at entertainments. Even the servants had to wear a genteel veneer. John Adams recommended a girl to serve partly because she was well-bred, on the assumption that a genteel household required a well-bred maid.[6] Gentility, for those who embraced that culture wholeheartedly, required the refinement of one part of life after another. A common person with a teacup had not made so encompassing a commitment.

The refining process went beyond the household to the public sphere. The ultimate test of one's position and culture was admission to the public activities of polite society. As we have seen, gentility did not introduce its own peculiar activities into the world of public entertainment. Instead it elevated the commonplace. Cards, dancing, eating, music, writing, conversing, plays all took on new meaning when carried out in refined environments and in polished forms to suit delicate and tasteful minds. Taverns were the rendezvous of the "Dreggs of the people," the scenes of rowdy parties, frequently resulting in drunkenness, gambling, and bloodshed, until the keepers installed long rooms and opened them to polite assemblies. Then once debased activities assumed an aura of brilliance and complaisance.[7] Theater and plays were associated with the raw pleasures of bullfighting and cockfighting until genteel advocates claimed the right kinds of plays had a

"Tendency to Polish the Manners and habits of Society, to disseminate the Social affections and to improve and refine the literary taste of our rising Republic." So construed, and housed in elegant halls adorned with the elaborate decor of fine mansions, playacting became an entertainment for the better sort.[8] This elevation of ordinary, even suspect activities into the regions of refinement was the characteristic project of genteel culture. The members of genteel society who joined in that broad undertaking were admitted to the public diversions of the polite.

By subjecting themselves and their environments to these changes, people like William Corbit crossed the line into polite society, the most significant boundary in eighteenth-century colonial culture. The men who constructed parlors for themselves, sent their sons to grammar school, and taught their daughters dancing were "the gentlemen of the place" and the possessors of gentility. Common people observed gentility, often with great interest; they even partook of it to some degree. But through the eighteenth century, it was not their culture. Gentility with all its material forms and preferred habits of conduct belonged to the gentry.

CRITICISM

ONCE refined, or pretending to refinement, people like Corbit looked with condescension, pity, or scorn on the vulgar common people existing on the other side of the spiritual divide. In a published letter, a man representing himself as a Philadelphia mechanic complained that he felt excluded from concerts and assemblies, although he was not formally forbidden entrance. "I do not say, that their regulations exclude Mechanicks; but then the distance that is always observed by those who move in the higher sphere, and the mortifications which I and my family must inevitably undergo, if we were with them, exclude us as much as if there was a solemn act of exclusion."[9] The formal rules mattered less to this unhappy writer than the invisible boundaries gentility had erected in society.

The exercise of such punitive social power would necessarily, one would think, generate opposition, and especially among the groups implicitly demeaned by the gentry's haughty airs. The exclusion of the vulgar from polite entertainments was itself enough to arouse animosity, as the letter from the Philadelphia mechanic suggests, and the practices of the assemblies only exemplified the widespread separation of social classes that was a plain fact of everyday life. The inevitable "mortifications" suffered by all who were considered coarse precipitated outbursts like the mechanic's letter or Morison's fuming at the New Castle inn. But surprisingly, the most virulent criticism of gentility arose not among the poor but among the educated elite themselves. Men and women of letters launched attacks on genteel life that could scarcely be exceeded in their venom by the anger of common mechanics and dirt farmers.

Criticism began in England in the early seventeenth century, almost as soon as gentility took root among the aristocracy.[10] In America the greatest impetus at first came from the reform clergy, both Puritan and Quaker, who saw in gentility worldly pride and competition for the affections of the people. Solomon Stoddard complained early in the eighteenth century that Harvard was only training its students to make bows in polite company. Quakers objected when singing, dancing, and music were taught in Philadelphia boarding schools in the 1720s. The Boston selectmen in 1716 refused a petition from Rivers Stanhope and Edward Enstone "to keep a School of Manners or Danceing in this Town," although the two went ahead anyway, confident of backing from the politically powerful Anglican faction. A letter to the Boston *Gazette* in 1732, on the eve of Peter Pelham's organization of six assemblies at his "Great Room," summed up Puritan reservations about the dangerous consequences of extravagance. Women would develop a taste for balls and impoverish their husbands with demands for gowns. Women so infected made terrible wives. "Woe be to the Men to whose Lot they fall: they will be a Moth in their Estates, and a Bane to their Happiness." And the depletion of estates was simply a palpable evidence of a more insidious sapping of moral strength. "In vain will our Ministers preach Charity, Moderation and Humility, to an Audience, whose thoughts are ingaged in Scenes of Splendour and Magnificence, and whose Time and Money are consumed in Dress and Dancing." The glories of the ball would win over the hearts of the people along with their treasures. The author sensed an omi-

The wife of a New York City merchant, Hannah Peck shows all the attributes of a refined lady, but does not display them with perfect ease and confidence. Durand's limitations as a painter are responsible in part, but the necessity of relying on second-rank artists typifies the middling gentry's difficulty in fully achieving refinement.

nous danger in assemblies "where a great part of the pleasure consists in being gaz'd at, and applauded, for the richness of their Cloaths, and the elegancy of this Fancy." Genteel delight in performance before a brilliant company, it was clear, drove out fear of God and laid the groundwork for innumerable vices. "This is laying a foundation for Pride, vain emulation Envy, and Prodigality." For all the same reasons, George Whitefield attacked the Charleston assemblies, and in Philadelphia the assemblies closed during the years when the city was under his sway. Chesterfield's apparent endorsement of loose sexual practices only confirmed long-held suspicions about gentility's enfeeblement of moral virtue.[11]

On the eve of the Revolution, a more sophisticated worldly criticism in the form of satires joined the clerical voices raised against gentility. These reverse guides to polite behavior made genteel society appear silly or vicious. John Trumbull's "The Progress of Dulness," for example, charted the course of a polite education that produced a fop rather than a gentleman. Trumbull, a writer bred to gentility, chose to satirize rather than glorify it. Born in 1750 the son of a Connecticut minister, Trumbull aspired to write poetry while still a child. He was so precocious that he passed the Yale entrance examination at age seven, and went on after graduation to tutor at Yale, practice law in Boston, and return to Connecticut to serve in the legislature and on the state's Superior Court. By lineage, temperament, and training he was a member of the colonial elite, and yet "The Progress of Dulness" after its publication in 1773 was widely read as an attack on genteel pretensions and on Yale.

Of the three characters whom Trumbull satirized, Tom Brainless, Dick Hairbrain, and Harriet Simper, Hairbrain is the fop. Trumbull made him the son of a wealthy farmer, a "Country-clown" who got rich "by villainy and cheats" and sent his son to college to make him a gentleman. Trumbull's criticism, while broadly farcical, went to the heart of an elemental genteel fear about appearing ridiculous in public. Since the ultimate aim of genteel self-discipline was to shine in the best company, the danger of a faulty performance haunted the members of polite society. Trumbull evokes that nightmare in Dick's first experience at college, where "bred in distant woods, the Clown Brings all his country-airs to town." Dick cannot bow properly, he mumbles his compliments out of fear, and cannot even walk as he should. By his "stiffen'd gait," his "awkward dress," a watch with a chain too large, clumsy shoes, a wrist ruffle five inches deep, and "with fifty odd affairs beside," he betrays "the foppishness of country-pride." Inevitably Hairbrain feels the sting of ridicule. His airs provoke "th' obstrep'rous laugh and scornful joke," the nightmare side of genteel dreams. All this was written without any sympathy for Hairbrain. Trumbull understood the anxiety of genteel novices, but showed no pity for the wounded vanities of would-be beaux.[12]

Hairbrain ultimately succeeded in polishing his appearance, but through empty contrivance rather than virtuous self-discipline. He relied on the tailor and the dancing master to create the right impression.

> Lo! from the seats, where (Fops to bless),
> Learn'd Artists fix the forms of dress.

From his tailor Hairbrain acquired a "laced suit glittring gay before," a ruffle, a rubied brooch, a coat with long tails, a modish hat, silk stockings, and "little toe-encircling shoes." The barber held curls in place with scented pomatum, spreading "a sprightly grace, o'er the dull eye and clumsy face." The dancing master taught gestures, trips, and bows, the final touches that lent the airs to "lure a Dutchess." These made Hairbrain what he was. Rather than forming himself into a gentleman, Hairbrain was the product of these tradesmen's arts, one of the "Mechanic Gentlemen," as Trumbull called them. To his appearance, Hairbrain added a turn for witty jests at the expense of religion, his counterfeit for true conversation.

> Loud noise for argument goes off,
> For mirth polite, the ribald's scoff.

And so, learning by rote, "like studious play'rs, the fop's infinity of airs," Hairbrain launched into the world, where he shone at card parties and balls.[13]

Men and women shared equally in the softening of American character, but women played a particular role, because of an assumed greater susceptibility to genteel vanities. The tutors in the genteel arts warned young ladies of their weaknesses. The author of *A Father's Legacy* told his young charge that "the natural vivacity, and perhaps the natural vanity of your sex, are

Satires of outlandish efforts to ape genteel behavior became a staple of eighteenth-century caricaturists.

very apt to lead you into a dissipated state of life, that deceives you, under the appearance of innocent pleasure." The characterization became a fixed part of an enduring female stereotype. On the positive side, women were more naturally delicate and sensitive and so more open to refining influences; on the negative, they suffered from an inclination to vanity and a delight in pleasure. They could not resist the allure of the ball, the elegant dress, the flatteries of male admirers. If less attracted to power, they were more drawn to superficial pleasures and fashion. Women drained their husbands' resources with insatiable desires for gowns, millinery, and carriages.[14]

Education was thought to be as much to blame for female weakness as innate character faults. John Trumbull's counterpart to Dick Hairbrain, Harriet Simper, was the victim of misguided training from age six, when a visitor reproached the little girl for her modesty.

> That old, unnatural trick of blushing;
> It marks one ungenteelly bred.

The same visitor told Harriet's mother to "dress her in the mode, to teach her how to make a figure." From then on, the young lady's doom was sealed as the older women in her life prescribed an education "gay in modern style and fashion." They taught Harriet to forgo

> Th' expressive glance, the air refin'd.
> The sweet vivacity of mind

that was her natural bent and made her instead "to dress and tinsel-show the slave." The aim seemed to be

> On follies fix their young desire,
> To trifles bid their souls aspire,
> Fill their gay heads with whims of fashion,
> And slight all other cultivation.

Totally absorbed in "ribbands, laces, patches, puffs, caps, jewels, ruffles, tippets, muffs," small wonder that Harriet became a coquette who flirted audaciously with her army of admirers and then cast each one off in turn.[15] Harriet's education committed her to the worship of superficial trivia and the practice of heartless vanities. Her instructors were the instruments of misguided genteel aspiration.

Trumbull did not mean to discredit all ladies and gentlemen with his Dick Hairbrain and Harriet Simper. At one point, he offered a glimpse of "the learn'd, the good, and the wise," in the background of Hairbrain's world, shunning the silly fop.

> What tho' the Fair, of higher mind,
> With brighter thought and sense refin'd,
> Whose fancy rose on nobler wing,
> Scorn'd the vain, gilt, gay, noisy thing![16]

The force of the satire grew from an implicit image of a virtuous person who despised everything Hairbrain stood for. But if intended for superficial gentility, the gentry's criticism of their own culture formed arguments that could be used more broadly. They cast doubt on all refinement by suggesting that it was mere hollow show, fashioned by barbers and tailors rather than by strenuous self-discipline. The implied moral superiority of a refined presence—the true source of genteel strength—could collapse into a formless pile of ruffles and little shoes. Gentlemen satirists like Trumbull, in attempting to purify their culture, created an instrument that could be used to subvert it. Gentility seemed to carry within itself the cultural seeds of its own destruction, a critique aimed at the foundations of its values.

The criticism grew in volume and force as the century went on, mounting in strength at the very time when the commitment to genteel culture became increasingly evident in the proliferation of country villas and elegant town houses, the construction of assembly rooms, and the formation of fashionable neighborhoods around great public buildings. During and after the Revolution, the standards of classical republicanism became directly applicable to gentry culture. Warnings about the debilitating effects of luxury brought into view the dark nether side of refinement. The assemblies of polite companies for cards and dances, common enough before the Revolution, were seen as threats to the state, especially in New England, where Puritan influence increased sensitivity to moral corruption. The organization of an assembly in Boston in 1785 aroused a storm of protest in the press, including a polemical drama condemning the gatherings, *Sans Souci, Alias Free and Easy: or an Evening's Peep into a Polite Circle,* possibly written by Mercy Otis Warren.[17]

Most of the characters in *Sans Souci* are guests at the Boston assembly, Young Pert, Little Pert, Madam Brilliant, Madam and Mr. Importance, and Doctor Gallant. They long to return to the "high bon ton" of pre-Revolutionary days and bemoan "the old musty rules of decency and decorum" now in place. One of their models is Lord Paxton, an especially obnoxious customs official driven out by Bostonians in 1766, but in the play recalled as the "essence of Chesterfield" and admired for his "Sans Souci air and address." An anonymous "Republican Heroine" who comes on the scene comments to another disturbed observer, "Mrs. W----n," on the rapid apostasy from republican principles. She did not expect Spartan simplicity, the heroine says, but she "did expect to find a cultivation of manners somewhat similar to their publick resolves." The observers fear extravagance: the cost of dress will break some families and high gambling stakes will be too much for others. The result will be, as Madam Importance explicitly states, the sifting of families so that only the richest and best qualified will survive. Assembly life will reintroduce nonrepublican rank. Doctor Gallant predicts that careful attention to etiquette will exalt the deserving.

> Professional characters must be supported with dignity—otherways, all distinctions will be lost in the levelling spirit of republicanism—therefore, if we expect to support taste and stile, we must keep up this parade, and by assuming an appearance above the commonality, we may stamp on our characters a *superiority* of rank.

In this vein Gallant wishes to bring the Tories into the assembly and erase distinctions based on sentiments toward the Revolution.[18]

Without any regard for subtlety, the play has the assemblies bringing aristocratic society back to life. The evil is sans souci, free and easy, the essence of the genteel style, that flowing grace and harmony sought after at all elegant entertainments. Ease was the polar opposite of the Spartan virtues suitable for a republic. The characters in the play complain of republican principles that "they are all calculated for rigid manners, and Cromwelian days." Little Pert yearns for "the free and easy air which so distinguishes the man of fashion, from the self-formal republican." Doctor Gallant, another of the monarchists, admires "the gracefulness of their dancing." "T----r," the doctor says of the current dancing master, "has a most happy faculty at teaching—like a limner, he *draws every grace of gentility, and blends ease and address in every feature.*" The playwright implicitly condemns that grace, for it results from a dangerously relaxed inner character. Mr. Importance has no affection for the ancient republicanism of Sparta and Rome "in the most rigid times." They practiced "principles of republicanism" of the uncivilized kind, harsh, austere, and Cromwellian.

> Now we soften them down in the school of politeness, and make them wear a more pleasing garb—the antient republican spirit is like the old principles of religion—staunch Calvinism—but now we have modernized them, and united them with the court stile of taste and fashion.

Tasteful and polite, yes, but the softening of character under the influence of genteel ease led to extravagance, gambling, aristocratic assertion, and, as suggested in one passage, voluptuousness. On its dark side, refinement enfeebled the republic, undermining the foundation of the state.[19]

RESOLUTIONS

THE contradiction between republicanism and fashionable living was most keenly felt in New England, where Spartan virtues harmonized with Calvinist religious restraints. But Calvinism was not the only seedbed for republican criticism of refinement. Royall Tyler's *The Contrast*, a dramatic condemnation of European gentility, was first performed in New York City in 1787, where it made a great hit. George Washington greatly admired the play, which contrasted the effete Billy Dimple, schooled in Chesterfield's polite arts, with Colonel Manly, the austere and sentimental Revolutionary patriot. Indictments of luxury appeared frequently in *The American Museum*, published by Mathew Carey in Philadelphia in 1787 as well.[20]

The contradiction between republican simplicity and genteel elegance was a general problem for many American men of letters trying to conceive a consistent American character. Their perplexity grew out of the very nature of gentility, beginning with its genealogy. Genteel culture had descended from the royal court, and was propagated through courtesy books and embodied in mansion parlors, miniature replicas of the court, designed for the entertainment of polite society. As Mr. Importance said of the assemblies and polite ways, these were the "court stile." John Adams had recognized the same genealogy when he associated balls, assemblages, cards, equipage, tea, and elegance of every kind with monarchy. The political and social power of the court had empowered gentility and given it the momentum that carried it deep into the ranks of the ordinary gentry throughout Anglo-America. With the adoption of republican government, the glories of court life became shameful and subversive, a seductive and debilitating influence rather than the grand exemplar. Refinement, the court, and European oppression were opposed to republican simplicity, virtue, and freedom. Where, then, was the moral base for American society when the highest personal ideal of the Old World, the refined lady and gentleman, was seen as insidiously aristocratic? What was the source of glory in America if gentility was corrupt?

Timothy Dwight, the Connecticut clergyman and poet, offered the plain farmers of his own parish in Fairfield as prototypes of a virtuous American citizenry, who, if not glorious, were inspiring. Dwight composed "Greenfield Hill" (published in 1794) with European splendor constantly in mind. He acknowledged the absence in Greenfield of elegant country houses "Eden'd round with gardens of enchantment, walks of state, and all the grandeur of superfluous wealth." But he depicted those as silly pomp and empty show, "fashion, frippery," in a world of "barbers, milliners, taylors, and mantua-makers, forming gods, their fellow-millions worship!" Their absence was no loss because splendor placed a crushing weight on the masses of people in Europe, where the glories of the great reduced everyone else to debilitating poverty.

> See the pale tradesman toil, the livelong day,
> To deck imperious lords, who never pay!

Thousands toiled to support one great lord, in a land "of wealth enormous, and enormous want." In Greenfield the practice of dividing property among all the sons, rather than giving all land to the eldest, created a common-wealth of small farmers, each one independent and "competent," and capable of supporting his family. In Europe primogeniture lifted the firstborn "into bloated pomp." In America

> Through the whole realm, behold convenient farms
> Fed by small herds, and gay with cultur'd charms.

The American farmer knew little elegance, but he did not suffer from a "griping landlord." Americans dressed in homespun of their own making, ate simple foods from their own lands, and filled their houses with "plenteous, and plain" furniture, "all form'd for use," not show. They exchanged pride for competence and comfort.[21]

Dwight did not mention gentility. He implicitly repudiated the genteel style with animadversions on balls, cards, tea, and Chesterfield. He detested social visiting that consisted of ladies stopping at thirty doors in a day to "drop the gilt card, and proudly roll away." People came to "swim through the drawing room, with studied air," deprecate their rivals, make pretty speeches,

> Or sit, in silent solitude, to spy
> Each little failing, with malignant eye.

All this Dwight despised. Refinement was another matter; he used the word frequently. American freedom in itself refined its people. "In other lands, the mass of men, scarce rais'd above the brutes, drags dull the horsemill round of sluggish life." That European kind of brutishness did not afflict free farmers. "Manners mild, and sweet, their peaceful sway widely extend. Refinement of the heart illumes the general mass." This kind of refinement had little of polish or ease in it. Dwight's "refinement of the heart" raised men and women above the brutes, but to make them kindly, cheerful, and modest, not polished.

> Refinement hence even humblest life improves;
> Not the loose fair, that form and frippery loves;
> But she, whose mansion is the gentle mind,
> In thought, and action, virtuously refin'd.

It was a pastoral refinement, suitable for America's middle landscape, not shiningly awesome, but simple and sweet. So refined, Dwight's populace of independent farmers gave America a moral foundation and a personal ideal, purged of European corruption.[22]

In Dwight's "Greenfield Hill," the cultural dilemma posed by courtly refinement in a republican society was resolved by promoting in its place another ideal type altogether. Dwight admitted his Greenfield neighbors lacked the suavity and glitter of the European nobility, but they more than made up for their homeliness with honest virtue and manly independence. Their simple goodness plus the absence of an oppressed underclass gave his portrait of Connecticut a wholesome appeal.

The question remaining after Dwight's evocation of a simple America was not the desirability of his agrarian society, but its reality. Did "Greenfield Hill" tell the truth about Connecticut? In his enthusiasm for his own conception, Dwight virtually eliminated every form of ruling class. He spoke of elected rulers but not militia officers, justices of the peace, wealthy merchants, large landholders, Yale graduates.

> Here every class (if classes those we call,
> Where one extended class embraces all,
> All mingling, as the rainbow's beauty blends,
> Unknown where every hue begins or ends)
> Each following each, with uninvidious strife,
> Wears every feature of improving life.

People were not actually separated into classes at all. Social distinctions faded into invisibility, and the refinements that the gentry had so assiduously implanted in their houses and lives through the eighteenth century were virtually erased from the scene. That was the society Dwight wished for; but could the Connecticut gentry blithely forgo the elegance they had struggled to achieve for the past century as his depiction implied they must?[23]

Of course they could not and did not. The multifaceted critiques of gentility did not impede in the slightest the pursuit of refinement. The critical language did provide a reservoir of invective for democratic politicians wishing to discredit their opponents. When Governor Christopher Gore visited Pittsfield, Massachusetts, in 1809, for example, the Pittsfield *Sun* likened his arrival to a royal procession. "Whether it was touched off exactly in the style of an English prince or noble, dashing down among his tenants, before an election, his Excellency from his long residence in England, is better qualified, than we are, to decide." But such slurs did not cause Gore to hesitate about building a magnificent house on his Waltham estate under the influence of the French architect Jacques Guillaume Legrand. An English visitor called it "the most elegant mansion in New England," built "and fitted up in patrician style."[24]

Although possibly the most elegant mansion of its day in New England, Gore Place was one of many. Mansions went up everywhere after 1790, including in Dwight's Connecticut. This was the era when the vocation of professional architect came into being, and one of the most noted, Asher Benjamin, began his career in the Connecticut Valley. Notable professional housewrights, the first builders to familiarize themselves with English building manuals, prospered in the valley towns. Their beautiful Federal mansions still grace the Connecticut landscape. A visitor to Hartford in 1808 said that in a few years "the stile of building has almost totally changed. The dwelling-houses, stores &c. erected of late, are generally in a stile of superior taste and elegance. The gothic and clumsy appearance which marked the buildings thirty years ago is entirely done away with." Dwight did not sketch any of these grand structures that were proliferating in Connecticut in the very years when he was sketching in his pastoral scenes. We know the appearance of the masters and mistresses of these houses from their portraits. Led by the prolific Ralph Earl, enough painters were active in Connecticut in the 1790s to form a recognizable Connecticut school. The painters portrayed their subjects in a somewhat subdued style, suitable for a provincial gentry, but still unmistakably in imitation of the European grand manner. The portraits leave no doubt that the Connecticut gentry aspired to gentility and refinement. In contrast to Dwight, Connecticut's Governor Treadwell in 1802 complained (with conventional hyperbole) of the distancing of the elite from common people: "The farmer is thrown into the shade; he feels that riches, as the world goes, give pre-eminence . . . with weary steps returning from the field, he sees with pain the powdered beau rolling in his carriage . . . and feels himself degraded."[25]

Elegant living along the Atlantic seaboard accelerated in the 1790s, just when criticism of luxury and refinement was in crescendo. Houses grew taller, staircases more elaborate (some of them hanging in suspended curves in the stair halls), wallpapers more richly painted. In Virginia the Assembly added house furnishings to the list of items subject to property taxes, indicating that legislators recognized the wealth going into interior decoration. The vision of a nation of independent farmers living in homely simplicity did not guide actual purchases, nor did the indictment of luxury inhibit the flowering of genteel culture anywhere.

Partly, the exaggerated condemnation of luxury helped resolve the contradiction. Extreme criticism protected the growth of gentility while seemingly attacking it. The satirists by the nature of their art caricatured reality; Dick Hairbrain and Harriet Simper were clearly unreal concoctions existing in some liminal state beyond the margins of actual Connecticut life. If every sensible person disapproved their egregious gestures and faults, ample space remained short of these limits in which true refinement could flourish. Trumbull himself let the shadows of worthy refinement cross his stage now and then, thereby acknowledging an acceptable form. He aimed to discredit the abuses of gentility, not genteel culture in its entirety. By the same token, Governor Treadwell's hyperbolic evocation of the "powdered beau rolling in his carriage" condemned all powdered beaux, but at the same time implicitly justified sedate and modest gentlemen who rolled in their carriages through the streets on legitimate business. The palaces in Dwight's Greenfield Hill made Connecticut mansions seem like the simple dwellings of honest farmers. The critics identified the evil in luxury and foppery and thereby justified the good that remained. By simply avoiding excess, a term impossible of precise definition, the provincial gentry cleared the way to construct costlier houses according to standards of ever more refined taste, thinking of themselves not as effete aristocrats but merely as republican gentlemen.

ANXIETY

THE most outspoken critics of refinement often showed the most ambivalence. John Adams, for one, sensed the dangers of luxury as strongly as any of the New England republicans, but at the same time he felt its seductive allure. During his courtship of Abigail Smith in the early 1760s, he contrasted the city and the country, Boston versus Abigail's home in Weymouth. "I mount this moment for that noisy, dirty Town of Boston," he wrote in 1763 as he was about to leave for the city, "where Parade, Pomp, Nonsense, Frippery, Folly, Foppery, Luxury, Politicks, and the soul-Confounding Wrangles of the Law will give me the Higher Relish for Spirit, Taste and Sense, at Weymouth, next Sunday." Boston elegance and fine manners mingled in his mind with its dirt, its politics, and its litigiousness. In a humorous catalogue of Abigail's faults written a year later, Adams blamed them on "the Effect of a Country Life and Education," which instead of teaching "the late Refinements of modern manners," common in the city,

brought a girl up to "a certain Modesty, sensibility, Bashfulness." He play-
fully reproached Abigail for unfamiliarity with cards, playing with "a very
uncourtly, and indifferent, Air," and urged her "to make a better Figure in
this elegant and necessary Accomplishment."

These Abigail could laugh away as a spoof of city follies, but then Adams
moved to more sensitive matters. "You very often hang your Head like a
Bulrush, and you sit with your legs crossed to the ruin of the figure." "A sixth
Imperfection is that of Walking, with the Toes bending inward. This Imperfection is commonly called Parrot-toed," and "the reverse of a bold and
noble Air." Adams wrote in a lighthearted vein, but his reproaches could be
taken seriously. He had noted flaws in her body deportment that fell short
of the genteel standard. Abigail laughed with him at the implied censure of
urban vices, but for the faults at the end of the list she promised to make
amends if possible. She understood that John wrote from a double mind that
was both critical of city urbanity and yet ashamed of rustic awkwardness.

He felt the strain even more acutely with regard to his children. He
congratulated his brother-in-law on the birth of a child with another half-
humorous lament that soon there "must be dancing Schools and Boarding
Schools and all that, or else, you know, we shall not give them polite
Educations, and they will better not have been born you know than not have
polite Educations." He closed by saying it was more important to have
children than to "make them gay and genteel," but despite the disclaimer the
requirements of polite education came to mind when he thought of a new
child to rear.[26]

The Revolution gave a new twist to his ambivalence about gentility.
Instead of pitting city against country, it was government men versus patriots. After 1774 especially, Adams identified elegance with the friends of
imperial government everywhere, while the patriots were the homely, rustic, and coarse party. "A Notion prevails among all Parties that it is politest
and genteelest to be on the Side of Administration, that the *better Sort*, the
Wiser Few, are on one Side; and that the Multitude, the Vulgar, the Herd, the
Rabble, the Mob only are on the other." Adams did not admire the ornamental tools of the crown, but he envied their riches and splendor. While he
labored arduously for small rewards, a rival lawyer in Newburyport with a
government appointment "built him an House, like the Palace of a Nobleman and lives in great Splendor." In Boston, a man throve only by taking
sides in politics, and mostly by engaging "on the Side of the Government,
the Administration and the Court." Adams felt that he was forced to choose
between riches, gentility, and dependence on one side and independence
and poverty on the other. He despised those who sold out to imperial power,
like the solicitor general, but in maintaining his independence, he knew he
must live a life of comparative penury, relying wholly on his own virtues.

"Let us take Warning and give it to our Children," he told Abigail after reviewing the solicitor general's ultimate downfall in 1776. "Whenever Vanity, and Gaiety, a Love of Pomp and Dress, Furniture, Equipage, Buildings, great Company, expensive Diversions, and elegant Entertainments get the better of the Principles and Judgments of Men or Women there is no knowing where they will stop, nor into what Evils, natural, moral, or political, they will lead us." He considered "Prodigality, in Furniture, Equipage, Apparell and Diet" the greatest sin prevailing among New Englanders as they entered the Revolution because it made them vulnerable to the blandishments of power. Adams shunned that path himself and wished to turn his children from it, but he believed himself doomed to a life of rustic simplicity. After considering the success of other lawyers compared to his own modest earnings, Adams pleaded with Abigail "for God Sake make your Children, *hardy, active* and *industrious,* for Strength, Activity and Industry will be their only Resource and Dependance." The moral superiority of these virtues was not the only reason for his impassioned endorsement; he believed they were the only recourse for people who refused to pander to official power.[27]

Despite these avowals, even at the height of republican enthusiasm during the Revolution, the Adams family could not forgo every form of refinement in favor of pure rural virtue. After describing the fortification of Dorchester Heights in March 1776, a triumph of American vigor, Abigail closed a letter to John with a request that he "purchase Lord Chesterfields Letters—I have lately heard them very highly spoken of." For his part, John at the Continental Congress lamented the lack of "Art and Address" in his New England colleagues. "Our N. England People are Aukward and bashful." "They want the exteriour and superficial Accomplishments of Gentlemen, upon which the World has foolishly set so high a Value." Delegates to the Congress "who have improved upon their Education by Travel, shine." New Englanders, having had little intercourse with strangers, "have not the faculty of shewing themselves to the best Advantage." Adams pledged himself, circumstances allowing, to "spend the Remainder of my days, in endeavouring to instruct my Countrymen in the Art of making the most of their Abilities and Virtues." Even in a revolutionary assembly, Adams recognized the advantage of those shining abilities that made a polished gentleman so winning.[28]

The test of Adams's republican mettle came in 1778 on his arrival in Paris, the capital of refinement. After four days, he wrote ecstatically to Abigail that "the Delights of France are innumerable. The Politeness, the Elegance, the Softness, the Delicacy, is extreme." He recognized the incongruity of his enthusiasm and yet could not temper his exuberance. "Stern and hauty Republican as I am, I cannot help loving these People, for their earnest Desire, and Assiduity to please." The grandeur of Paris overwhelmed him.

"The public Buildings and Gardens, the Paintings, Sculpture, Architecture, Musick, etc of these Cities have already filled many Volumes. The Richness, the Magnificence, and Splendor, is beyond all Description." It went beyond public buildings to private houses, "to Furniture, Equipage, Dress, and especially to Entertainments." Finally he pulled himself up short.

> But what is all this to me? I receive but little Pleasure in beholding all these Things, because I cannot but consider them as Bagatelles, introduced, by Time and Luxury in Exchange for the great Qualities and hardy manly Virtues of the human Heart. I cannot help suspecting that the more Elegance, the less Virtue in all Times and Countries.

He revealed his heart when he concluded by observing that "I fear that even my own dear Country wants the Power and Opportunity more than the Inclination, to be elegant, soft, and luxurious." Surely he spoke not only for his country but for himself.[29]

Adams insisted that, were the war at an end, "I should be happier, among the Rocks and shades of Pens hill: and would chearfully exchange, all the Elegance, Magnificence and sublimity of Europe, for the Simplicity of Braintree and Weymouth." The allure of Europe moved him to exhort his countrymen through Abigail "to avoid the Plague of Europe." "Luxury has as many and as bewitching Charms on your Side of the Ocean as on this—and Luxury, wherever she goes, effaces from human Nature the Image of the Divinity." Yet he himself felt again and again France's appeal. "This is a delicious Country. Every Thing that can sooth, charm and bewitch is here." Abigail warned him as she sent dispiriting news from America that "Luxery that bainfull poison has unstrung and enfeabled her sons. The soft penetrating plague has insinuated itself into the freeborn mind, blasting that noble ardor, that impatient Scorn of base subjection which formerly distinguished your Native Land." And still he could write that "I admire the Parisians prodigiously. They are the happiest People in the World." Indeed, he proclaimed, "their is such a Choice of elegant Entertainments in the theatric Way, of good Company and excellent Books, that nothing would be wanting to me in this Country, but my family and Peace to my Country, to make me, one of the happyest of Men."[30]

When it came to his children, Adams earnestly wished the best for them, grace and refinement included. His eldest son, John Quincy, accompanied Adams to Europe in 1778 and went from capital to capital with his father. In Amsterdam, Adams encouraged John Quincy to skate but to do it well, not merely with vigor but with "an Elegance of Motion." The Dutch skated with spirit and some with prodigious swiftness, "a few with a tolerably genteel Air, but none with that inimitable Grace and Beauty which I have seen some

Examples of, in other Countries, even in our own." "I would advise you, my Son, in Skaiting, Dancing and Riding, to be always attentive to this Grace." He was also to attend to his handwriting, "never to let a slovenly Word or Letter go from you." The shaping of the letters deserved his care along with the style. "There are not two prettier accomplishments than a handsome hand and Style," and John wanted his son's hand to be "manly and beautifull." For his own children, homely republicanism was not enough. Besides economy, industry, and hardihood, a good republican had to achieve the graceful embellishments of a polished gentleman.[31]

Adams stumbled over his own ambivalence in the case of his daughter's romance with Royall Tyler. From time to time, Abigail had asked John to allow his daughter Abigail, called Nabby, a few "fripperies" in the form of gauze, lace, and a few yards of ribbon to "appear when she goes from home a little like those of her own age." John made no protest at such trivial compromises with genteel taste, but he balked at Tyler. The scion of a distinguished Massachusetts family, Tyler graduated from Harvard in 1776 at age nineteen with such distinction that Yale immediately awarded him an honorary degree. By the time he moved to Braintree in 1782 to practice law, he had passed through a period of dissipation and was settling down to what became a distinguished career, culminating in appointment as chief justice of the Vermont Supreme Court. Abigail tried to make the best of the fact that Tyler had lost half of his considerable inheritance owing to "a sprightly fancy, a warm imagination and an agreable person." Besides the evidence of settling down to his Braintree practice, Abigail noted that she was not acquainted with "any young Gentleman whose attainments in literature are equal to his, who judges with greater accuracy or discovers a more delicate and refined taste."[32]

Adams exploded on receiving this news. Nabby was "not to be the Prize, I hope of any, even a reformed Rake." "A Youth who has been giddy enough to spend his Fortune or half his Fortune in Gaieties, is not the Youth for me, Let his Person, Family, Connections and Taste for Poetry be what they will. I am not looking out for a Poet, nor a Professor of belle Letters." Adams wanted the association ended at once. "I positively forbid any Connection between my Daughter and any Youth upon Earth, who does not totally eradicate every Taste for Gaiety and Expence. I never knew one who had it and indulged it, but what was made a Rascall by it, sooner or later." He softened his tone in a note to Nabby herself: "If I mistake not your Character it is not Gaiety and Superficial Accomplishments alone that will make you happy," but more solid virtues. His objections brought the courtship to a halt. Nabby herself had entertained suspicions that Tyler was at first "practicing upon Chesterfields plan," and the romance cooled. As the months went by, however, John's fury cooled too, and he finally wrote to Tyler and

Abigail giving permission if the young pair chose to go ahead. By then, however, mother and daughter had embarked for England and missed the letters.

In London, Nabby fell in love with Colonel William Smith, a "Gentleman of unblemished reputation." They married on June 12, 1786, but Adams's hopes for an honorable son-in-law were not to be realized. Thirteen years later while Tyler was rising at the Vermont bar, John wrote of Smith, "All the actions of my life and all the conduct of my children have not yet disgraced me as much as this man. His pay will not feed his dogs; and his dogs must be fed if his children starve. What a folly!" Adams's ambivalence about genteel corruptions palsied his judgment and led finally to family tragedy.[33]

In August 1776, a month after the Congress declared American independence, Adams served on a committee to prepare a great seal for the United States. Each committee member had his own idea for a representative picture. Adams proposed an engraving by Simon Gribelin of Hercules resting on his club between two emblematic women: "Virtue pointing to her rugged Mountain, on one Hand, and perswading him to ascend. Sloth, glancing at her flowery Paths of Pleasure, wantonly reclining on the Ground, displaying the Charms both of her Eloquence and Person to seduce him into Vice." For Adams that was the choice for America and for his own family. In Paris four years later the image came back to mind when he reported that "there is every Thing here that can inform the Understanding, or refine the Taste, and indeed one would think that could purify the Heart." Unfortunately, among all these delights "there is every thing here too, which can seduce, betray, deceive, deprave, corrupt and debauch it. Hercules marches here in full View of the Steeps of Virtue on one hand, and the flowery Paths of Pleasure on the other—and there are few who make the Choice of Hercules." Sorely tempted, drawn by the seductions of refined pleasures, Adams struggled to follow Hercules himself and proclaimed, "That my Children may follow his Example, is my earnest Prayer: but I sometimes tremble, when I hear the syren songs of sloth, least they should be captivated with her bewitching Charms and her soft, insinuating Musick."[34]

John Adams's anxiety over luxury did not prevent him from assembling a genteel establishment suitable to his dignified station. By remaining well on the safe side of French elegance Adams could indulge in refinements suitable for a republican gentleman. Abigail's request for an expensive carriage in the midst of the war did trouble the two of them enough that they referred to it in their correspondence as "The Machine" or "you know what." Yet it was purchased. While in England in 1787, they arranged for the purchase of the Vassall estate in Quincy, a few miles removed from their Braintree farmhouse. This bona fide mansion of seven bays and two stories with a third under the roof had a broad oak stairway and a fence and gate in front of a yard planted as a lawn. After their return to occupy the house in 1788, they planted flowers and Abigail saw to the erection of an additional wing and well-designed outbuildings with fanlights over the doors. They furnished the interior with upholstered Louis XV chairs and a sofa, and brought over a magnificent Vincennes wine cooler and two gueridons with fine inlay. Not the grandest establishment on the south shore by any means, the Adams's Quincy house still revealed the love of refinement and elegance that John struggled so manfully to hold in check.[35]

John Adams's history epitomizes the strains in American culture in the closing decades of the eighteenth century. Although drawn to the beauty and refinement of genteel culture, Americans saw danger lurking behind the polished surfaces. In his association of the Hercules image with French taste, Adams strung together a series of threatening words, "seduce, betray, deceive, deprave, corrupt and debauch." Abigail pictured luxury as a poison or a plague. The words all implied a loss of control, as if at some point a dam would break and all restraint be washed away.

The newspapers told stories of thrifty farmers who granted their wives permission to buy calico gowns and stoneware teacups and soon had to purchase silk and porcelain. As one of them said, "a man once engaged in this extravagant course of living, is seldom able to extricate himself in time, but is hurried on to the brink of ruin, reduces a helpless family to want and misery, and must at length sink under a weight of misfortunes." Most commonly the stories ended, if not in last-minute repentance, then in bankruptcy and poverty. In Adams's mind, indulgence led to dependence on power (as a source of wealth) and thus on to oppression and tyranny. Americans appreciated the lofty spiritual reaches of refined living and admired the beautification of the world that was gentility's great project. They simply had to establish firm limits to their indulgence. The satirical pictures of fops, rakes, and coquettes, of the splendors of Paris and later of great American cities, helped establish those limits, representing gentility gone berserk. By emulating, but by stopping short of the farthest reaches of refinement, Americans hoped to create a space in which citizens of a republic might safely enjoy the pleasures of genteel culture.[36]

Respectability

1790 - 1850

CHAPTER VII

Vernacular Gentility in Rural Delaware

CHARLES GREENBERRY RIDGELY, the thirteen-year-old Dover boy who wrote such polished letters to his father from the academy in Philadelphia in 1751, later studied medicine and returned to Dover to practice. For the convenience of his patients, he purchased a house on the courthouse square in Dover in 1767 and lived out his life there as physician, justice of the Court of Common Pleas, treasurer of Kent County, and moderate patriot in the Revolution, serving as chairman of the Kent County Committee of Correspondence. By two wives he fathered ten children, seven of whom lived to maturity. In 1785 he died and was buried in the family plot in the yard of Christ Church in Dover, where he had been a vestryman. At his death, his family and the Kent County citizenry honored him for his life of public service, his devotion to wife and children, and his high character. Like his father, Nicholas, before him, Charles was one of the local gentry who assumed responsibility for public affairs in Kent County as similar men did in every county and town in America in the eighteenth century.

People like Charles Ridgely were the first to be touched by the culture of refinement arriving from Europe in the late seventeenth century. They needed it to gain admission to polite society and, equally important, to have the proper manner to rule in society and the government. Among the gentry, personal deportment and public role went together as they had in the royal courts where civility first took root. A eulogy for Charles Ridgely noted that his powerful mind, his wide reading, "his strict integrity and honor, and his remarkable urbanity of manners, recommended him to his fellow citizens as a suitable candidate for a variety of public stations."[1] Manners were as much a part of the complete man as integrity and honor. Ridgely's large brick house standing prominently near the county courthouse on the public square, his bearing, his polished manners, all grew from his sense of himself as a county leader with broad responsibilities for the public well-being. In 1785, gentility was the face eminent people presented to the public who looked to them for leadership. Polite society was the society of public leaders—in the military, the government, the economy, and society.

Over the sixty or seventy years following Charles Ridgely's death, gentility spread to a much broader population. In keeping with the spirit of republican equality, people who lived their lives in a private sphere took possession of gentility. The beginnings of this diffusion could be noted in Kent County before Ridgely's death—in the appearance of knives and forks, teacups and saucers, looking glasses and clocks in middling households. That diffusion increased immeasurably in the first half of the nineteenth century as a middle class without pretensions to public office adopted a modest, vernacular gentility. These middling people practiced many forms of polite behavior, from carrying handkerchiefs to carpeting their floors. Like others who absorbed gentility, they thought of life as performance, with their deportment on the streets and the appearance of their houses and yards always under observation and judgment. But they felt little of the responsibility for the public good that Charles Ridgely naturally assumed as a duty and a right. The realm of the middling people was the family rather than town or county. Propriety, rather than the need for public dignity, sustained this simpler variant of gentility. The desired goal was respectability rather than eminence.

The diffusion of vernacular gentility into the homes of the middle class proceeded more quietly than did the arrival of gentry gentility in the eighteenth century. Earlier the appearance of the two-story brick mansions announced the presence of a new culture. In the nineteenth century, the number of modestly genteel houses grew steadily, and the frequency of walnut tables and mantel clocks increased every decade, but the continuity of genteel culture from one century to the next eliminated the need for new forms of material culture.

The dramatic observable consequences of vernacular gentility occurred away from the domestic sphere of Kent in the industrial economy, where the strikingly new structures resulting from spreading gentility were not house forms but factories, springing up to supply the vast new market for curtains, sheets, carpets, ceramics, and chairs. Industrialization cast only a faint shadow in Kent County, where an enlarged group of tradesmen built furniture and constructed carriages but no factories appeared.

The pertinent issue for Kent in the age of vernacular gentility was not industrialization, but class. What happened to the gentry as more and more people adopted the genteel style? In the eighteenth century, refinement sharply distinguished the gentry from the rest of society by fixing an easily observable spiritual division. The gentry, according to the ideal, possessed finer sensibilities, more delicate reactions, a more compelling taste for beauty. Lesser people were not simply poorer or less well educated; they stood lower on the scale of civilization, with less well-developed intellectual and emotional faculties.

What were the consequences of extending this genteel culture to a broader segment of the population? Did a spiritual kinship growing out of similar personal styles bring gentry and middling orders together—despite the differences in their public roles—collapsing social structure into a vast middle class with only a rude working class below it? Or, alternatively, did vernacular gentility deepen and complicate the social structure by marking a new line between the gentrified middle class and a rude and vulgar lower class, while the old gentry sustained their sense of distinct superiority? In other words, were three classes coming into being or were there still just two with the numbers of the genteel now exceedingly swollen? The Ridgelys and their fellow citizens in middle Delaware afford a glimpse of changes that went on as the refining process began to work among middling people.

THE RIDGELY FAMILY

IN 1838 *The Delaware Register and Farmers' Magazine,* a short-lived Dover publication, reprinted an essay on rural life that sounded a common lament. As much as it pleased the author to see the head of a happy family "occupying the patrimonial estate inherited from his ancestors," he regretfully noted that such scenes belonged to a time now past. "Most of the old and time honored families, who once adorned our society by their primitive manners, and friendly hospitality, have been broken up and scattered abroad. And their possessions have fallen into the hands of a few land jobbers; and they are let out to a migratory race, who changing their residence with every revolution of the seasons, form no attachment for their places of abode."

Although by then a commonplace of rural-decline literature, the observation implied that the leadership of the county was changing hands. The old families had moved away, died out, or faded, and new families, less stable and less respectable, were replacing them. The author gave no evidence for his impression, but the observation has been repeated in modern studies of American communities in the first half of the nineteenth century. The stable, hierarchical colonial order, anchored by a few leading families, gave way after the Revolution under the onslaught of new arrivals who derived their wealth from new sources of profit available in industrializing America. In Kent County, John Reed exemplified the parvenus. Reed moved to Dover in 1825, from Mispillion Hundred in the forest regions to the south, and purchased two corner lots on the public square, near the Ridgelys' house. He built a store on one lot and the Capital Hotel on the other, and operated several vessels plying the Delaware River out of nearby Leipsic. Within a few years he became the preeminent merchant in Dover.[2]

Although other examples could be cited, it would be an error to take the *Delaware Register* complaint too literally. The departure of some older families and the arrival of new leaders did not imply the demise of the colonial gentry. The Ridgely family, for one, held their position and throve in the changing economy, illustrating the continuing strength of older families even as new people found places in the public sphere. One of Charles's sons, another Nicholas (1762–1830), studied the law and inherited the farm at Eden Hill. He served in both houses of the Delaware legislature, was a delegate to the state Constitutional Convention in 1791–92, and held the offices of state's attorney and chancellor of Delaware. His younger brother Henry Moore Ridgely (1779–1847) studied law with Nicholas, and in 1800 moved into the Dover house inherited from his father. With his law practice established, Henry was elected to Congress in 1810 on the Federalist ticket and served until 1815. In 1827, he was appointed to serve two years of an unexpired term in the United States Senate, although as a Jackson supporter he failed of election in his own right when Adams men won control of the Delaware Assembly in 1829. In between the two periods of Washington service, Henry was elected to the state legislature, sat on the Levy Court, and served as register of wills and secretary of state. On the death of Nicholas, Henry refused an appointment to succeed his brother as chancellor. Although of all Charles's children only Henry had children who carried on the line, this branch of the family continued to flourish in succeeding generations. Descendants occupy the houses in Dover to this day and fill eminent positions in the state judiciary.[3] Amidst changes in the county's leadership, there were continuities like these.

Nicholas and Henry supported themselves, much as the previous Ridgelys before them had done, with a combination of farm income, professional fees, and salaries from public office. Nicholas managed Eden Hill, and Henry owned two Kent County farms. But they also made the best of new opportunities. Henry was a member of the canal company that in 1812 proposed to straighten the St. Jones River, Dover's access to the Delaware. He was chosen president of the Farmers' Bank when it was organized in 1807 and remained in that post until his death. In time a son and then a grandson succeeded him as president. Of the $5,464.47 in Henry's personal estate at his death, $2,300 was in forty-six shares of Farmers' Bank stock. Henry's son and namesake promoted the Delaware railroad project and became a director in 1852 when the company was organized.[4] The Ridgelys kept their places in society and government through vigorous enterprise, making the most of economic opportunities as they came along.

Nor did the Ridgelys lose command of the high ground in county culture. In 1803 Henry Moore Ridgely married Sally Banning, the daughter of a prominent Dover merchant, when she was just sixteen and fresh from boarding school in Philadelphia. There she had learned French, drawing and painting, and playing the piano. She bore the first of their children in 1804, and after that in steady succession fourteen others, the last in 1831. Not surprisingly, Sally Ridgely's health failed, and she died in 1837.

Eight of the Ridgely children survived to adulthood to carry on the family culture. All of them were well educated and literate. They were naturally taught the refinements that had characterized the family over four generations, and they all sustained that culture. Though they grew up in the relative simplicity of a country town, their careers were remarkably complex, illustrating the possibilities of their time. Yet they all maintained a natural polish and ease, sure of their breeding and nearly unaware of their gentility.

Charles George, the firstborn, excelled in his studies at the Dover Academy and at St. Mary's College in Baltimore. At age eighteen he received an appointment to West Point, and in 1826 he graduated fifth in a class of forty-one. He remained at the academy to instruct in French, until, for unknown reasons, his father insisted that Charles resign his commission and return to Dover. Charles had a serious drinking problem. In the succeeding years, he went from one kind of work to another—law, civil engineering, teaching, the episcopal ministry, and politics. Family hopes rose and fell as Charles appeared to have mastered his drinking habit and then stumbled again. In 1827, Chancellor Nicholas Ridgely wrote to one of Henry and Sally's daughters that Charles's "Conduct is so disreputable, so distracting to his Father and Mother, and fills them with such continued Vexation, Mortification, Pain and heart-rending Anguish, that I have, as to Myself, resolved to abandon him to his Course, and I shall suppress all Feeling in Relation to him."

A year later, in a letter to the same girl, Charles's mother rejoiced in the "complete reformation of your Brother, he is now every thing a fond Mother can wish, and is already filling in a great degree your Father's place in Society, tell your Aunt of it, I know she will rejoice with me in this great change—He is now an active member of a Temperance Society established in Dover, and goes in the day time without his crutches." The happiness was short-lived. Within a few months, his companions had dragged him back into his old habits.

Charles left Dover resolved to do better, but his father still refused to send him money, fearing it would go to dissipation. The family watched anxiously as Charles moved from place to place. Finally after a decade he settled in Georgetown, Delaware, where he practiced law and managed to win election to the state legislature as a Whig (the Ridgelys were otherwise Democrats). He died in 1844, never having fulfilled his early promise.[5]

Elizabeth, born in 1813, was an enchanting, romantic young lady. When she was barely fourteen she fell in love with a young man in Dover, suffered from deep melancholy when forbidden to marry him, and wrote a poem that seemed to hint of suicide. Whisked off to school in Philadelphia, she received unsolicited love letters, possibly from one of Charles's ne'er-do-well friends, written in a voice worthy of a Richardson novel. Uncle Nicholas wrote a stern letter, like a classic menacing patriarch from an eighteenth-century romance, forbidding her to give the slightest encouragement to the suitor, since he lacked the merit to attract "any Lady of Taste or Judgment." She dutifully sent the letters to her father, asking that they not be destroyed, but yielding to his judgment.

Back in Dover, still not twenty, she received plaintive letters from despairing suitors, who said their happiness rested entirely in her hands. In 1829, nearing her seventeenth birthday, she was converted to Methodism. A year later she fell ill, soon after contracted tuberculosis, and in 1833, only twenty, died of consumption.[6]

Elizabeth's younger brother Nicholas, born in 1820, was a serious, bookish child who transcribed verse and possibly wrote some. He took an interest in the Dover lyceum in his late teen years and delivered speeches there. His studies pointed him toward the law until the fall of 1839, when he became a Methodist convert. Under the influence of his religious convictions, Nicholas assumed responsibility for the Sunday schools in Dover, and decided, within two years, to enter the ministry.

Although the Episcopal Church in Dover had fallen on hard times, and Methodism dominated the religious scene in Kent County, Nicholas knew he exposed himself to disapproval in joining that sect. He wrote to his older sister Ann, "I am fearful that the step I have taken will not be approved by all of my Friends, but I rest satisfied with having acted conscientiously." Ann, who had married into the du Pont family, reassured him that Sophia du Pont, who Nicholas believed was critical of his decision, was "so gentle that she would never speak in other than high terms of any religious denomination." But the comment betrayed the fact that it required restraint to be tolerant of his choice. A friend believed he would find satisfaction in his calling but feared Methodist fervor would affect his sensibility. "I will freely tell you that I think your refinement of feeling will suffer more."

Nicholas received a circuit assignment in Caroline County, Maryland, and later a pulpit in Phoenixville, Pennsylvania, where he set up housekeeping with his wife. After a short time in Philadelphia, his health began to fail. His eyesight deteriorated, and he came down with pneumonia. He withdrew from the ministry and accepted a position as teller at the Farmers' Bank in Wilmington. Contracting tuberculosis like his sister Elizabeth, Nicholas died in 1849, age twenty-nine, and was buried in the yard of Christ Church in Dover alongside his Ridgely kinsmen.[7]

Others of the Ridgely children lived more stable and certainly longer lives. Ann (1815–98), who mothered the younger children while Sally Banning Ridgely was in poor health, married Charles I. du Pont, a textile manufacturer from Wilmington. They met when he was in Dover to serve in the state legislature. Although Charles was a widower with two children, it was a brilliant marriage. Nicholas wrote to congratulate Ann: "We have often and long heard of the kindness and affection, as well as the taste and intelligence of the family into which you have entered." He went on to say that "we flatter ourselves that with all her faults our sister has traits in her character which will ever win her friends." From Louviers, a du Pont family mansion, Ann continued to take a motherly interest in her brothers and sisters, buying a carpet for Nicholas's parsonage and sending Edward to school.

Henry (1817–1904), two years younger than Ann, studied medicine and practiced briefly in Dover before abandoning his profession to run the family farm at Eden Hill, raise peaches, preside over the Farmers' Bank, and bring the railroad to southern Delaware. Eugene (1822–94) devoted himself to another family farm, Linden, and Edward (1831–1900) studied law and practiced in Dover. Williamina (1827–59) married a prosperous farmer and politician.[8] These five pillars of the community, along with the intemperate Charles, Nicholas the Methodist preacher, and the romantic Elizabeth, played out many of the roles that rural Delaware opened to its most respectable families in the first half of the nineteenth century.

LETTERS, BOOKS, CITIES

WHAT remnants of the culture of their grandfather Charles Greenberry Ridgely did this assemblage of privileged children perpetuate in their own time? They certainly wore their refinement more lightly, showing fewer signs of self-conscious effort to be properly polite and polished. Their ease of manner displayed an unawareness of rank, with little apparent emphasis on the gestures of respect and deference that recognized hierarchical structure—at least according to their letters. When Nicholas Ridgely, the children's uncle, died in 1830, *The Delaware Register* cast him in the old style.

> During the whole of his long and active public life, although constantly thrown among gay and fashionable society, he adhered strictly to the manners and customs and fashions of his youth. In speaking, he used the old mode of pronunciation, without regard to Walker's Dictionary; and in writing, employed the same number of capital letters as were used in the days of Addison and Pope. The cut of his coat was the same for fifty years; and he constantly wore short breeches with kneebuckles and long fair-top boots to correspond.[9]

Nicholas, like all the old-school gentlemen, was spoken of with respect and regret, as if something valuable was passing, but never with the implication that the strict manners of the old days should be revived.

Laying aside the formal ways of their uncle, the Ridgely children spoke freely to one another and to their parents, letting nothing hinder the flow of feeling, news, and interest. They gave up much of the stylized speech that, while once undoubtedly elegant, had begun to sound artificial. Manners were more a part of their natures than of self-conscious policy. Still, without question, the principles of genteel conduct firmly governed this generation. In 1847 Henry wrote to Ann about their sixteen-year-old brother Edward, who had come to Wilmington for schooling, urging her to work on his posture. Henry's one brief comment on body deportment revealed that the Ridgelys noticed personal bearing, even when the precise deportment of the old school was losing importance.

Henry Moore Ridgely, father of the children, criticized women he met in Washington; he felt that he knew how a finished lady should appear. He wrote of Dolley Madison that "she received us pleasantly and with ease, and I confess I was pleased with her manner—I found her tho nothing remarkable for either beauty sprightliness or grace—she is large and fat, and

Charles I. du Pont and Ann Ridgely du Pont. The photographers of this distinguished couple followed the portrait painters' custom of including marks of the sitters' refinement in the pictures—here a book and a piano with music.

appears never to have possessed that delicacy of form and manners which man so much admires in the softer sex." Her sister, Mrs. Washington, was "quite a coarse looking woman." Ridgely still evaluated people, especially those high in public life, according to their conformity to genteel standards. Though little is made of manners and simple refinements in the letters, the Ridgelys automatically weighed these qualities.

Charles fell in love with a Philadelphia belle in 1829, claiming that he knew nothing of her fortune and considered her no great beauty. She won him by her mind and her manners. "Amid the whole circle of my acquaintance," he wrote Elizabeth, "I know of no one, more accomplished, or better educated. Her mind is indeed of the first order, and the delicacy of her feelings, her refinement, and her polish of manners, render her one of the most pleasant companions I ever met with, and if to this we add a singular and remarkable propriety of conduct, you can form some opinion of her." He apparently fell in love with her refinement.[10]

The Ridgelys continued to insist on well-written letters. Henry Moore Ridgely required young Charles George, when just eight, to write his father regularly, and in the letters to his son he included misspelled words which Charles was to locate. In one letter, Charles wrote about a writing master in Dover who offered fifteen lessons for five dollars. "I am afraid to make promises of great improvement, but I hope I shall write an excellent hand from his instruction." Henry was "very much pleased with his correspondence," and said that "if he wrote the letter without assistance, he has made great proficiency in writing and will soon, by attention and ease, write extremely well." His mother was largely responsible. She told her husband that Charles "is very fond of writing, and I make him write every day, I think he writes a very good hand for his age."

She herself felt embarrassed when she was unable to pen a letter properly. She apologized to Elizabeth for one hurried epistle: "It is seldom my dearest Child I have written so careless a letter do burn it at your Mothers' request." She was sensitive about the composition as well as the penmanship. When disturbances in the household broke into her thinking and confused her writing, she told Elizabeth to burn that letter too. Although the letters were passing among family members, the writers thought of the pages as presentations of themselves.[11]

While continuing the eighteenth-century devotion to fine penmanship and graceful expression, the deeper purpose of these nineteenth-century letters subtly shifted. The letters were less the instrument of polite society and more the exchanges of a circle of friends. Friendship and family love were present in the 1750s too, but the emphasis became much stronger sixty years later. Grandfather Charles Greenberry Ridgely had addressed his father as "Honored Sir." Young Charles George in 1812 wrote "My dear

Father," and closed "Your affectionate Son." Charles George opened one letter by saying, "Your last affectionate letter afforded me very great pleasure." That sentiment was as mannered in an eight-year-old as the starchier sentences of Charles Greenberry, but in the nineteenth century another kind of affectation seemed fitting for a young boy addressing his father.

Family members admonished one another to write letters as a duty, as if failure to correspond would weaken the ties. An aunt writing to Charles George pleaded for letters. "In vain my dearest George have I waited the arrival of every mail for very many weeks, anxiously expecting a letter from you, nor can I paint to you half my disappointment that this evening mail has brought no letter from you, for any of your Dover friends. I fear you are fast losing all the affection, I formerly, fondly, hoped you felt for me." Sally Ridgely told Elizabeth, ". . . do write one of your best letters to your Father—and I wish you would take pains and write to your Uncle Ridgely—it will afford both the former and the latter [pleasure] to receive a letter from you." Nicholas reprimanded Ann for neglecting to mention an aunt in recent letters. "Let me ask you if you do not think you have served Aunt [. . .] rather coldly. Of the two letters you have sent to us, her name is not so much as mentioned in either. She feels it too very sensibly." The absence of a name in a letter suggested an absence from mind and heart, an unwonted exclusion from the family circle.

A badly written letter, as much as being a disgrace, could be interpreted as a lack of affection. A friend of Nicholas apologized for a sloppy letter and explicitly tried to prevent such a reading. "You find this letter blotted and badly written it is not the result of carelessness but of the want of a convenient opportunity of writing—You must therefore excuse it, and not regard it as . . . a want of respect or affection." These little asides suggest that a letter, its handwriting and its contents, once meant to demonstrate propriety and polish, linking together a polite society across a distance, now carried messages of regard and love, creating an affectionate society of friends and family.[12]

The letters came to be written for much the same reasons as a half century earlier: Ridgely children were sent to school in Maryland and Pennsylvania, and family connections and friends were scattered across the region. These parochial gentry did not conduct an international correspondence as did the elite at the zenith of American society. On the other hand, the bounds of Dover and Kent County did not enclose their world either. They sent children to school in Baltimore, Wilmington, and Philadelphia. They visited and shopped in Philadelphia, and were likely to marry anywhere in the locus defined by their letters. Kinship, friendship, and urbanity maintained intimacy with people of their own class from Baltimore to Philadelphia.

The most important activity in their cultural region was schooling. If anything, education grew in importance in Ridgely family culture. Schooling was no more systematic than before; the children still moved from schools in Dover to Baltimore or Wilmington and thence to Philadelphia, apparently without the goal of getting a degree or completing a fixed course of study.

Henry, the son of Henry Moore Ridgely and Sally Banning, born in 1817, was the favorite of his Uncle Nicholas, the old-school gentleman who served as chancellor of the state. Nicholas was determined to give young Henry the best education and one more systematic than most. Henry spent time at Newark Academy in Newark, Delaware, when he was ten because Nicholas approved of "the Manners and Morals of the Place," then moved to Dwight's Gymnasium in New Haven, and in 1832 to St. Mary's College in Baltimore before entering the University of Pennsylvania, where he received his medical degree. His younger brother Edward studied in Dover, then St. Mary's College in Wilmington, where he received a degree, and then enrolled for one term in the Yale Law School in 1851. Considering that to be enough law school, he returned to Dover for private study and was admitted to the Delaware bar in 1853. These two, along with Charles George, who graduated from West Point, received the most systematic education. The other children studied here and there without completing degree programs.

But this pattern of education did not imply a casual interest in learning. Both parents urged the children to apply themselves closely to their studies. Writing from Washington, where he was serving in the House, Henry Moore Ridgely told young Charles, age nine, "Nothing affords me so much delight as to mark your improvement in useful knowledge and see you good and virtuous. This is the true source of happiness and honour." Goodness and learning came together in Henry's sentence, as if in his mind study was itself a moral precept. "If you avoid vice and folly," Henry enjoined Charles, "and devote your youth to the acquisition of learning and of wisdom, you will secure to yourself a source of future happiness and command the esteem and respect of all who know you."

The parents felt as strongly about their daughters' education. Elizabeth disliked the strict routine in the Philadelphia boarding school where her parents sent her after the thwarted Dover romance, but Sally Ridgely urged her daughter to stay on and devote herself to her studies. "Child you are in the first class, (how delighted I am at that) let your studies occupy your whole mind, and do be happy for your Mother's sake. You know the desire I feel to have you well educated, and all depends on your self." Charles, who had always been a model student, told Elizabeth that her future attractiveness as a woman depended on how well she stocked her mind in school.[13]

There was no mistaking the Ridgely expectation of studious habits in all of their children, but at the center they placed not a particular school or completion of a degree but books. Nicholas chose Newark Academy for young Henry not because of the instructors but because of the morals of the town. The children were placed in a variety of different schools, depending on factors extraneous to the curriculum itself—morals, or nearby relatives, or the daily routine. What mattered was the study of books, not instruction by a teacher. Henry did not comment on the quality of the instructors in any of his various schools until he was in medical school. Teachers primarily disciplined the students, holding them to their studies, rather than stimulating or enlightening the children.

When the parents finally permitted Elizabeth to return home, Sally warned her daughter the discipline would continue. "You will have to devote much of your time to study when you return home to improve your mind." Sally hoped that the influence of Charles, always the model student, would replace the discipline of the school. "Your Brother is so intelligent and very correct in his conduct—I hope my dear children will improve each other, and make me one of the happiest of Mother's." Charles's father encouraged him to read when he was very young. When Charles was eight, Henry could say he was "highly pleased that you read in Homer's Illiad every day and hope that you will continue to admire it more and more." "In truth no person of any taste can read it, but with delight."

Ann at twelve pleased her father with the report of reading Rollin's *History.* "Do my dear Ann," he told her, "read it attentively and understand and fix in your memory all you read." Henry had a vision of his children from an early age studying their books closely and storing away information. They were not to read casually. "If you are ever at a loss to understand any thing," he told eight-year-old Charles from Washington, "inquire of your mother and never rest till you do understand it." It was almost as if the little boy was to be allowed no childish play. Books were to displace everything else. "Love your books more than your play." "By attending to your books, you will soon acquire a habit of study which will be more delightful to you than all the frolics in which you can engage."[14]

On balance, there was more urgency than pleasure in these admonitions. Henry loved the *Iliad* and wanted Charles to enjoy it too. But the beauty of the poetry was not Henry's central theme. The keynote was struck in the statement "Now, my dear son, is the season, with you, for improvement." In Henry's mind, too much depended on Charles's studies for him to read for enjoyment. Learning would enable Charles to "command the esteem and respect of all who know you." Henry conceived of the world as ranking people according to their knowledge. "In proportion as you acquire knowledge and wisdom will be the respect that the world will show you." It seems incongruous in philistine and provincial America that such a conviction was so deeply engrained in a parent. But for Henry books elevated people and ignorance degraded them. He laid out the alternatives for Charles.

While other boys of your age waste their precious time in play and idleness, and very often in mischief, and grow up to be ignorant and worthless men, you, I trust, will take a different course, and by devoting a great portion of your time to study and to business and being obedient to your mother, obtain a plentiful stock of useful knowledge and information and become a worthy member of society.

A harsh division, but irrefutable: ignorance and worthlessness on one side, growing from play and idleness, and knowledge and worthiness on the other, coming from study, business, and obedience. The potent word "improvement" implied, on the one hand, the development of the self through acquisition of knowledge and, on the other, elevation through the ranks of society to respect and honor. As Sally told Elizabeth, "do not let all your acquaintances rise superior to you for the want of an education."

That preoccupation with improvement through books seemed to obsess many in the Ridgelys' circle. Benjamin Comegys, a Dover friend of young Nicholas, mourned the waste of twenty-one years, save for the last two, and pledged himself to read in every spare moment. Not just any books would do and certainly not those bewitching romances that stirred the blood but added nothing to the mind. A friend complimented young Sally Ridgely on the fact that her "taste for reading is not so depraved as that of the generality of the youthful part of our sex; other things than romances can entertain you." For a young woman poetry showed far better taste, since "there is no kind of writing that is better calculated to blend amusement with improvement than poetry." Amusement, yes, but improvement above all, and the right kinds of books were the key. Henry Moore Ridgely had nearly 600 titles in his library when he died in 1847, and all but two or three were definitely of the improving sort.[15]

CITY AND COUNTRY

THE Ridgelys emphasized study, books, and improvement knowing that their Dover was a country town and that the epitome of refinement could only be attained in cities. Acceptance of a cultural geography that placed their Dover house on the outskirts of civilization did not diminish their commitment to personal cultivation. Isolation may actually have intensified their aspirations. Sally Banning, Henry Moore Ridgely's future wife, spent her earliest years in Dover and nearby Camden, but after her father died and her mother remarried, she moved to Wilmington. Although Wilmington in 1800 with a population of around 4,500 fell short of metropolitan standards, it far overshadowed tiny Dover with under 700 inhabitants. Sally Ridgely never accustomed herself to the rustic isolation of Dover, and she perpetually complained to her husband and children that "Dover is as dull and uninteresting as usual." "Dover goes on the same dull round as ever, it affords no news." She apparently harped on the theme so frequently that her irritated husband offered to bring her home from a Wilmington visit if she would "condescend to return to so dull and trifling a place as this."

By dull, Sally may have meant lack of amusements. Her daughter Ann at age twelve echoed her mother's discontent, reporting to her sister that "you can not tell how dull Dover is their is not any balls or theater or Any other public Amusements." But more generally she referred to society, the circle of cultivated and vivid people whose company made life interesting, as compared with pedestrian common people with no sparkle of wit or learning. "This gloomy town affords no society," Sally told Henry when he was in Congress, "nor indeed any variety, it is always the same." She worried about the effect on her children. One reason for keeping Elizabeth in Philadelphia at school against her wishes was the lack of suitable friends in Dover. "The Society of Dover is so bad," Sally wrote her daughter, "there are scarcely any I should feel willing for you to associate with." "For my children's sake I do wish your Father would move from Dover, to some place where you would all meet with better Society."[16]

Though the frequency of the complaints speaks for Sally's sincerity, the dullness lament was partly a pose, for she said the same things about Wilmington. During a stay there, she wrote her husband that "this place in point of society is as stupid as Dover." He in turn more than once found Washington "dull and insipid." "No amusements—no society." Beyond the surface message of boredom and irritation, the dullness lament told the world that the speaker knew about genteel amusements and tolerated the tedium of rustic existence with impatience. A refined person could not embrace a simple country life without feeling a loss, and one should register one's sense of lack lest refined friends mistakenly believe that rustification had dulled one's sensibilities.

Young people in New Castle, Delaware, talked the same way about their town as Sally did of Dover. One referred patronizingly to "the dull, uninteresting Village which we inhabit"; another resident wrote sardonically to a friend that New Castle "is even more dull than usual, but I acknowledge that the possibility of that statement admits of a doubt." In accepting refinement's cultural geography, the inhabitants of country towns implicitly defined their own societies, and even their own lives, as backward and tedious in comparison with the city, but they assured one another of unreduced sensibility and taste by expressing impatience with their dull and uninteresting villages. After leaving Dover in 1828, Charles wrote to Elizabeth of his preference for Philadelphia:

I really find an immense difference between Philadelphia and Dover. In Philadelphia the Company which we so often meet, is so much superior to that which we only rarely find in Dover, and the amusements are so much more rational here than at home that really nothing could induce me to live in my native place. I need not describe it to you who are so well acquainted with it, but I sincerely regret that you should be compelled to make it your home. Without society save that of the family alone, you must indeed have become fatigued with the town.

Surely Charles did not intend to impress on Elizabeth the miseries of her existence; he was saying that you and I know better ways of living than the simple rustics of Dover.[17]

In actuality, the Ridgely children do not seem to have suffered by their upbringing in tedious Dover. The training given by their cultivated parents along with their schooling enabled them to enter the round of gay amusements in Wilmington or Philadelphia without hesitation. Charles George immediately received invitations to teas and dances when he moved from Dover to Philadelphia in 1828. He was chagrined at his first dance to have his partner, a Miss Elmaker, comment on his dancing. She took me, he complained, "for some unsophisticated child of the forest and congratulated me, upon my dancing stating that I was an apt scholar." He tartly replied "that I should certainly have been a very dull one, if after all my tuition I had not known my figures." He had to register with Miss Elmaker that he had not sprung from some rural backwater, a child of the forest, but had passed through dancing school, as was required of every well-bred young person. That was a rare instance; ordinarily the Ridgelys circulated with perfect ease among their cousins and friends in the city.[18]

They blended so readily because the family kept in close touch with Philadelphia taste and society. Sally's sister supervised the children while they were at school there, and could be relied on for help with purchases. Until midcentury the family continued to buy their best household furnishings and clothing in the city as they had done a hundred years earlier. As a Philadelphia friend who had just purchased a carpet for Sally observed, "there are many things requisite which it is utterly impossible to procure in Dover." Not only large items like the carriage Henry purchased when he and Sally married but small things, combs, collars, thimbles, rug fringe, bonnets, party dresses, all came from the city.

Purchases gave the children at school valuable experience in learning to buy. Sally asked fourteen-year-old Elizabeth "to try your taste and skill in the purchase of a handsome rocking chair, I wish it gilt and finished suitably for a Parlour." One of Sally's nieces was at hand to help if Elizabeth required advice. All of the family depended on advice from Philadelphia in matters of taste. Charles relayed a message from his aunt to his mother of a kind that frequently passed down the Delaware River. Writing to Elizabeth, Charles said, "Aunt desires you to tell Mother, that She has ordered the blinds to be painted yellow with black trimmings, this is a new fashion, and is more tasty for a drawing Room or parlour than the green." There was no hint of presumption in the aunt's advice on the color and trim of the blinds. Charles and the aunt knew that Sally wanted the information. In the same spirit, he passed along information on hat styles for Elizabeth. Sally in turn asked Elizabeth to let her know "are plain gingham's worn by grown persons?"[19]

Although an everyday inquiry, the question about ginghams was telling, and in some respects pitiful. Here was a mature, intelligent woman asking for authorization from Philadelphia to wear ginghams in Dover. The question implied that what was done in Philadelphia sanctioned and supported Sally's practice in Dover, defining what was fitting and proper. A hundred miles away in a little rural village, the refined tried to carry on to some degree a Philadelphia existence. Their own idea of themselves, tied to a perception of urban superiority on the scale of civilization, required that the question about the ginghams be asked lest an error be committed and the support for one's conduct undermined. The Ridgelys were not Philadelphians, but they wished to be members of the society that Philadelphia represented, polite society. Dover being what it was and the Ridgelys what they were, the family lived, from one perspective, as aliens in their own town. They blended easily in Philadelphia because though they dwelt in Dover, they took their instructions from Philadelphia. Like many who pursued refinement, they found the capital of their culture in another place.

COUNTRY TOWNS

ALTHOUGH disparaging dull little Dover, the Ridgely letters actually record a substantial growth in vernacular gentility in the town and in nearby villages. Compared with Philadelphia or Wilmington, the life crept on at a petty pace, but Dover had changed a great deal by 1850, compared with the town in the time of Charles Greenberry Ridgely, and the same was true for surrounding towns. Sally herself admitted at one point in 1831 that "Dover is very gay, the Morris family give a very large party this evening, great preparations are making, on Friday our girls give a very large party." Court time, when the legislature met, was always busy. As she said, the "Town is now really filled with genteel Strangers."

The coming of the dancing master for his series of lessons was another occasion for balls. Charles George, at age ten a student in the classes, considered the balls news to pass on to his father in Washington. Later, Charles scoffed at Dover social life. He wrote to Elizabeth, on receiving reports of a round of parties, that "however numerous may be the parties, of a similar nature to those, which you mentioned in your letter, they certainly are not suited to you, from the very want of accomplishment, and I may even say of the common courtesies of life, which appears in them. The mere assemblage of persons of a different Sex, is excessively unpleasant, when not improved and ornamented by talent and elegance."

By city standards, Dover entertainments did fall short, but their recurrence indicated that people introduced fashions in entertaining as best they could. Ann learned from her brother in 1843 that "Dover has been quite lively of late; we have had parties in abundance, almost every evening. We had 'Tableauxs' at some and dancing at all." City pleasures soon found their way to the country. Charles teased Elizabeth about the fashionable ice cream he enjoyed in Philadelphia, a luxury "that you poor devils in the country can only feast on in imagination." A few years later Dover had its own ice-cream shop.[20]

Dover elementary schools had improved considerably from the 1770s, when Nathaniel Luff said that the poorly trained teachers did more harm than good to the unsuspecting students. As might be expected, the Ridgelys helped to advance education. Chancellor Nicholas Ridgely signed the petition to the Assembly for an academy charter in 1810, and the legislature designated Henry Moore Ridgely as a trustee. The charter authorized the trustees to raise $10,000 by lottery to purchase a lot and erect a building. Even after the town organized a public school in 1832 under the Public Education Act of 1829, a private classical school met in the upper room of the academy building and a school for girls in the rooms below. A few miles south in Camden, the Union Academy was organized in 1815, and for forty-two years was reputed to offer one of the best classical educations in the state. These select little schools sprang up in town after town, despite the emergence of the free public school system. In 1852, the pastor of the Dover Presbyterian Church opened a school for girls, teaching English, Latin, French, music, and drawing, and he attracted eighteen or twenty young ladies each year. The debating society provided advanced students, and especially the young men, an opportunity to speak in public; lecturers informed the interested public of the latest developments in topics like astronomy for a quarter a person. Schools, debating societies, and lecturers all nurtured that literary culture which the Ridgelys felt was vital to personal improvement.

William Huffington, Charles's literary friend and Elizabeth Ridgely's onetime suitor, attempted a monthly magazine, *The Delaware Register and Farmers' Magazine,* in 1838 and 1839. The publication, a combination of historical sketches, reports on agricultural methods, and general essays and fiction, failed for lack of subscribers, but Huffington's belief that it might find an audience, added to the appearance of educational institutions, suggests the rising level of literary culture in this predominantly rural society. The Ridgelys were not alone in their commitment to books, learning, and knowledge.[21]

These educational and social activities occurred in a town whose physical face gradually grew more graceful, especially in the center. At the heart of the town lay the square with the statehouse anchoring the east side and the Ridgely house nearby on the north. King Street passed through the center of the square from north to south. Many businesses were located along the southern extension of King between the square and the landing at St. Jones Creek, but shops were also scattered throughout the town.

George Purnell Fisher, who spent boyhood years in Dover, reconstructed the order of the buildings along King and around the square in 1824. His memories enable us to see how mixed the buildings were as of that date, with little effort as yet to create a whole neighborhood of elegant dwellings. The order of buildings on the south side of the square opposite the Ridgelys indicates the indiscriminate placement of businesses near residences, with little thought for the ambience of the whole:

Furbee Tavern
Brick office
One-story structure with barbershop
Story-and-a-half structure with candy shop
Printing and post office
Old frame house
Two-story brick lawyer's office
Chew-Sykes house with garden

This was the most ragged stretch. Elsewhere on the square stood the Farmers' Bank, two-story brick and frame residences, and one three-story brick house.

The same mixture of elegance and simplicity occurred throughout the town. Fisher remembered Dr. Morris's two-story brick mansion on the north end of King as the best house in Dover. Next to it stood a one-story frame house occupied by an African-American and on the other side a two-story frame house. A genteel person's sense of the zone of beauty and polish extended to the limits of his own lot rather than to the neighborhood as a whole, probably in the belief that little could be done outside those limits. In the large lot behind her house, Sally Ridgely cultivated a lovely garden, much admired. Yet immediately next door to the east, between the Ridgelys and the statehouse, stood the ramshackle one-and-a-half-story house of a widow. What could the Ridgelys do about that?[22]

They could notice the incongruity and wish for improvement, and the town as a whole could take some steps toward overall beautification. In 1841 Nicholas wrote Ann of an "improvement to the appearance of the town" when an old stable attached to the next-door tavern was taken down. The awareness of ugliness and the wish for improvement was the beginning of a broader neighborhood beautification.

In 1829 some rudimentary steps were taken by letting a contract to lay pavement in front of the statehouse and then ordering the neighbors on either side to pave the walks in front of their houses. By 1835 many people in town were expected to pave the walks before their houses, and in 1837 the principal street crossings were flagged. A few years later, in 1846, an order was issued to plow the public square, probably in preparation for planting grass, and iron posts and chains were ordered to enclose the square. From that time on, the square could properly be called a green, its present name. In 1849 a whitewashed oak post and rail fence replaced the chains, and elm trees were planted. An enclosed and tree-lined green now united the mansions and stores around the square. By 1850 Dover was achieving a measure of refinement and grace, becoming a fitting site for the gay parties, the learning, the lectures, and the debates that now and then occupied its more refined populace.[23]

Dover was not the only hub of culture in the region. As capital of the state and county seat, the town attracted educated and polished people to live and do business there. Throughout the nineteenth century, Dover led the towns of Kent County in marks of refinement. But Dover does not seem to have served as cultural capital for the county or to have monopolized cultural improvements. Wherever economic growth occurred, the signs of incipient refinement soon followed.

Duck Creek Cross Roads, fifteen miles north of Dover, near a landing on Duck Creek, was one of a half dozen exchange points where grain from Kent County and Maryland farms began the journey up the Delaware River to the Philadelphia market. As a sign of local ambition, the name was changed in 1806 to Smyrna, after the great Turkish port. Still, it was not until 1817, when the population was little more than 250 inhabitants, that a group of commissioners, including Henry Moore Ridgely, laid out and regulated the streets. The grain trade steadily improved and with it the level of cultural aspiration.

In the first quarter of the nineteenth century, the Friends opened their Southern Boarding School in Smyrna, a group of young ladies ran a Sunday school, Samuel Priestly taught at a private school, and two charitable free schools were organized. Later on, in 1857, Smyrna had a library—ahead of Dover, which did not organize one until 1885. In keeping with the interest in learning, shops and manufacturers sprang up to serve the needs of the cultivated portion of the populace who valued books and the schools. A piano manufacturer advertised the commencement of business in 1824, though he seems not to have survived long. The Indian King Hotel opened in 1827, and by 1857 among the shops in town were a china store, two jewelry shops, three coach shops, and two hotels, along with twelve dry-goods and grocery stores to serve 1,800 residents. A select private school survived to that date in competition with the free public schools. While no cultural metropolis, midcentury Smyrna had the institutions of refinement essential to the self-respect of the aspiring middle class.[24]

Little Smyrna, not large enough in 1850 to count as an urban place in the federal census, can stand for the innumerable villages across the country where cultural light flickered in the nineteenth century, signaling a broadening stratum of people interested in select schools, lectures, carriages, or pianos. Throughout middle Delaware, the record of an academy carrying on for a decade or two, of a ball or a dancing master, of a china shop or piano manufacturer tells of little centers forming where once there were only crossroad taverns and smith's shops, centers for transmission and realization, where people with ideas of respectability taken from larger centers could bring refinement to their lives in remote rural places. These were forming everywhere across the Delmarva Peninsula in these years, in Elkton, Newark, St. George's, Odessa, Camden, Milford, every fifteen or twenty miles in the settled areas.[25]

Farther north, in Wilmington and New Castle, the intensity and complexity of activity increased. Paintings were on display in Wilmington, and Sally Banning, while she lived there, benefited from the instruction of a drawing master and music master. For a time in the 1830s there was a theater with a resident company. Outside the city at Brandywine Springs a large hotel with a 250-foot portico, a hundred sleeping rooms, and elegantly laid-out gardens served as a resort for a fashionable clientele. Wilmington had nurserymen to provide rare plants for city gardens and an active subscription library.

Ten miles to the south on the Delaware River, New Castle, the county seat and one of the oldest settlements in the state, seems to have led Dover by fifteen or twenty years in achieving improvements. New Castle called for paved sidewalks in 1803, rather than 1829, had streetlamps by 1807, and the streets themselves were paved between 1811 and 1826. The town had a flourishing academy by 1800 and a literary society in 1801, "to receive and communicate useful information, by the reading of Essays, and the discussion of Questions of a Moral, Political, Philosophical, Agricultural, and Literary nature." In 1811 a group of public-spirited gentlemen formed the New Castle Library Company, which one of the organizers hoped "by furnishing books to the young will give them a Taste for literature and promote the general improvement." For their own benefit, twenty gentlemen organized an atheneum to help each other become better informed through the cooperative purchase of newspapers to be kept in a reading room. In common with many small towns elsewhere in the state but in greater concentration here, cultural enterprises of many sorts sprang up on all sides, like green shoots through the earth in the spring. Some of the enterprises, like New Castle's Haydn Society, quickly faded, leaving evidence of much aspiration but of less commitment. Other institutions persisted for many years, sustaining the desire of the townspeople for refinement and cultural respectability.[26]

The flourishing of this culture in rural villages is one measure of the spread of vernacular gentility to the middle range of Delaware society, where earlier farming, religion, and family had circumscribed the purposes and routines of most lives. Within the villages themselves only a fraction of the people sent their children to the dancing master or purchased china for their tables and mantels, but the dancing class in Dover or the china shop in Smyrna is evidence that more families were interested in the appearances of gentility than earlier when Philadelphia or Wilmington supplied genteel things. Dover and Smyrna could never provide all that a cultivated family required, as the Ridgely correspondence abundantly shows. But by midcentury those towns had become minor cultural nodes where respectable families could connect with the network of information and supplies necessary for a modest genteel existence. Recent recruits could link themselves through Dover and Smyrna to the larger worlds of Wilmington and Philadelphia and begin to acquire the goods, the practices, and the outlook that went into refined lives.

HOUSES

THE practical effects of this cultural distribution system were evident in Kent County estate inventories by the decade of the 1840s, although the process of acquiring the proper household furnishings began much earlier. In the third quarter of the eighteenth century there were clear signs in the estate inventories that middling people would acquire small genteel possessions—knives and forks or teacups and saucers—at a time when gentility was still the possession of the gentry and still foreign to common people. This piecemeal acquisition accelerated as the years went by. Middle-class acquisition of polite behavior occurred gradually, but little by little the commitment to these material goods grew more intense. By the middle of the nineteenth century, everyone who claimed to be among the respectable members of the community—a much larger group than the eighteenth-century gentry—occupied a house with a parlor and furnished it in some semblance of the genteel style.

Estate inventories, the detailed lists of possessions made at the time of death as part of probate proceedings, enable us to measure these changes, though somewhat less accurately than at first appears. Since the smallest items, down to those worth a few pennies, appear on the lists, we are tempted to believe we can visualize virtually everything in Kent County households. Unfortunately, there are too many omissions. The problem does not lie in the absence of inventories from poor households. Although better-off people were more likely to go through probate than the poor, we have enough inventories with total personal estates adding up to less than $100— the lowest in the 1842–50 sample was $7.45—to be sure we are getting into many poor households. Other kinds of omissions create the problems. Every now and then an inventory turns up with an elegant mirror and silver plate and no beds, or the total value may be far lower than seems right for the estate of a person living at the standard implied by the listed items. These exceptional inventories compel us to realize that particular circumstances sometimes caused portions of the household furnishings to be removed before death—perhaps by gift or by family agreement during a protracted illness—resulting in a partial inventory of the actual belongings of the person. These instances remind us that inventories can only depict general tendencies and are most trustworthy when we deal with statistical distributions that do not depend on the complete accuracy of each inventory.

The table on page 229 represents tabulations taken from random samples of Kent County inventories in the 1770s and again in the 1840s, bridging the period when cultural developments in the country towns suggest an awakened interest in polite living among country people. The figures represent the percentage of inventories that list each of the items. This is a crude measure, because the condition of the item as suggested by the assigned value and the number of items of a given type in the individual inventories are omitted. The table shows the absence or presence of at least one example of the specified type in inventories ranging in total value of personal estate from £8 4s. 6d. to £888 18s. 6d. in the earlier group and from $7.45 to $14,425 in the later group. The median in the two samples fell between £98 14s. 4d. and £111 7s. 10d. for the first, and between $269.28 and $276.50 for the second group.

The table's most significant point is the obvious one, that across the seventy-year span from the 1770s to the 1840s the proportion of households containing items roughly associated with refined living increased tremendously. Furniture made of superior woods, mainly walnut and mahogany and to a lesser extent cherry, was unknown in poor rural households in the earlier period. These were expensive materials that signified pretensions

COMPARATIVE PERCENTAGES OF HOUSEHOLD ITEMS
IN A RANDOM SAMPLE OF KENT COUNTY ESTATE INVENTORIES

1770–74 (A) AND 1842–50 (B)

A: N = 48　　B: N = 50

Rank by Value of Pers. Estate	Mahog., Walnut, Cherry Furn.		Ceramics		Bed Linens*		Looking Glasses		Carpets		Clocks		Presentation Furn.†		Carriage	
	A	B	A	B	A	B	A	B	A	B	A	B	A	B	A	B
Lowest Quartile	0	31	33	62	8	8	0	46	0	31	0	31	0	31	0	8
Lower Middle Quartile	0	50	25	75	8	58	15	42	0	42	0	50	15	50	0	33
Upper Middle Quartile	15	83	58	92	25	67	67	100	0	67	0	58	25	83	0	33
Highest Quartile	33	85	58	100	25	62	58	77	0	100	0	85	67	85	0	92

*Bed linens = sheets, comforters, counterpanes, pillowcases, spreads.
†Presentation furniture = desks, dining-room tables, cupboards, secretaries, sideboards, buffets.
Source: Kent County Probate Inventories, Hall of Records, Dover.

utterly foreign to ordinary people. Only a third of the *wealthiest* households owned such items in the 1770s. By the 1840s walnut and mahogany furniture had been in production for so long that used items were trickling down to the lowest level. Nearly a third of the *poorest* households owned some walnut or mahogany form in the 1840s, and nearly every household in the upper half of the estates had something made of these woods. In the later period, these forms were more than simple utilitarian chairs, tables, chests, and bedsteads, the staples of the eighteenth-century inventory. They took more complicated shapes like desks and cupboards or forms for specialized use like dining tables. Ceramics—dishes, plates, bowls, and so forth—made of more refined materials than simple earthenware were fairly widely distributed in the 1770s, but they nearly doubled in frequency over the next seventy years.

Moreover, the simple measure of frequency does not show the proliferation of forms. Take the median household of Margaret Wilson of Mispillion Hundred, who died in 1843 with a personal estate valued at $276.50. Under the heading of ceramics, her inventory listed vegetable dishes, a cream pourer, sugar dish, cups and saucers, pitchers, glass tumblers, wineglasses, decanters, a punch bowl, pickle dishes, mugs, and dining plates.

Where did all these things come from? Ceramic production must have shot up to supply this immensely enlarged usage, but probably mostly outside Kent County. There are no figures on Kent County potters, no pottery traditions, and no extant local pottery. The dishes must have been coming down the river from Philadelphia for purchase in country stores. As to furniture, the number of furniture makers in Kent County is known to have increased roughly two and a half times between 1800 and 1850, from eleven active between 1796 and 1800 to twenty-six between 1846 and 1850. But that number does not account for the massive increase in consumption, especially when only three or four of the makers in 1850 ran shops large enough to take apprentices. While the heightened demand for better household furnishings stimulated production within Kent County, much of the business went to the emerging furniture factories in Philadelphia. Carriages seem to be the one fashionable item that was manufactured close to home. In the 1860 census, flour milling and lumbering were the two largest Kent County industries, but carriage making was one of just three others valued at over $50,000 annually.[27]

What did the profusion of new objects mean for their owners? Carpets, household items nearly unknown in the 1770s, were present at every wealth level by the 1840s. Nearly a third of the households in the lowest quartile had some kind of rug, and literally all households in the uppermost quartile. These were not all luxurious pile carpets. In many of the poorer inventories, the appraisers describe simple rag rugs of very little value. But in this instance, the market value does not measure the significance. Though inexpensive, the simplest rug implied a new idea, covering floors and placing a fabric pad underfoot. To most people in the 1770s, walking with street shoes on a woven fabric of any kind would have been sacrilege. The later use of carpets suggested a sharp change in sensibility having to do with dirty shoes and outdoor and indoor surfaces. This transformation of sensibility gives the rugs significance.

To some extent, the same is true for the other items. They suggest that the purchasers envisioned another way of living that gave meaning to the walnut dining-room tables and sets of plates and dishes. These people were not only imitating the wealthy. They independently perceived a higher mode of existence that called for improvements in the household environment. A carpet or a cupboard implied that at certain moments and in certain places, people chose to be polite, to elevate themselves to a more refined mode of living that elsewhere in their lives was impossible to attain. The furnishings were linked with the dancing masters and debating societies in the country towns as aspects of the broader culture of refinement now enveloping many lives.

At the same time, the intermittent nature of this commitment must always be kept in mind. A looking glass and bed sheets did not imply that a household had converted to total refinement and entered into an entirely new kind of life. A household was more likely to have a few nice things strategically located as signs that certain moments and places were refined. Had more been required, the cost would have barred the middle and lower classes from ever assimilating gentility. Many of the inventoried items must still have existed in a rough environment. Judging from a sample taken from tax evaluations in Duck Creek Hundred, one of the county's more prosperous regions, fully a quarter of all houses at midcentury were built of logs. This substantial proportion was an improvement from 1797, when 43 percent of the houses were log. Although log houses could be spacious, they ordinarily lacked external ornament and went unpainted. We can envision a piece or two of walnut furniture, a small collection of ceramics, and rag rugs sitting in log houses that were otherwise quite plain, occupied by inhabitants who, to a genteel visitor, would appear entirely unpretentious.[28]

CLASS LINES

A VAST distance separated log or simple frame houses from Henry Moore Ridgely's brick mansion on the square next to the statehouse, raising the question of the relationship between the people in one and the other. Ridgely died in 1847 with personal possessions valued at $5,464.46, more than any other estate in the 1840s sample except John Reed's at $14,425. What did Henry Moore Ridgely think of people with estates of $200 or $500, and they of him? Certainly possessions set them apart. The number and quality of Henry Ridgely's furnishings would have given the interior of his house an entirely different aspect from the rooms in most Kent County houses. He owned some items that had no equivalent in lesser houses. Only a tiny handful of people in this rural society possessed sofas or any upholstered furniture. No one else in the sample, including John Reed, owned a piano or an astral lamp as Ridgely did. Washstands were still relatively uncommon, limited, with one exception, to less than half of the people in the top quartile. Each of these individual items marked Ridgely's distinctive status.

And the differences went beyond individual items. His parlor had a different atmosphere than comparable rooms lower in society. Curtains and blinds, like washstands, were limited to houses in the upper ranks, and these combined with the astral lamp enabled Ridgely to modulate the light in his room as others could not. The eighteenth-century mansions had introduced the large windows that flooded rooms with light; in the nineteenth century owners of the finest houses tried to moderate the light to create a glow through the room. Venetian blinds, curtains, and drapes provided that control in the daytime; the astral lamp radiated enough light at night to achieve a comparable glow, lightening the deep shadows that candles made.

The regulation of the light made the Ridgely parlor different, and so did its contents. His parlor was set apart by its simple elegance, not only from those of lesser neighbors but from the parlor of his own father, Charles Greenberry Ridgely. The Charles Ridgely parlor, judging from the estate inventory of 1785, contained many more things than Henry's parlor in 1847. Charles Ridgely's room had held eleven china plates, four china dishes, a blue-and-white china bowl, two dozen small queensware plates, a double glass cruet, and so on and on. All this was gone sixty years later.

The creation of a parlor had long implied the removal of work tools first and then of beds. Beyond these, the Henry Ridgely parlor was emptied of all the dinnerware ceramics that previously stood proudly on display. Dominating the parlor were the important furniture pieces—the sofa, the piano, a table, a dozen chairs, the mantel with three decorative vases, and a mirror, the single most expensive item in the room and doubtless large and probably gilt. All the other items were simple decorative touches, like the piano cover and the matting, there in place of a rug because the inventory was taken in August. It was a restrained parlor, stripped of the ornate fuss of the ceramic display (though still cluttered with fourteen chairs and two stools) and so featuring its larger furniture in sculptured outline.[29]

Unusual furnishings, the modulated light, the restrained parlor furnishings, all distinguished the Ridgely house from most others in Dover and elsewhere in the county. Did those material facts reflect a social reality? Should we conclude that material culture still set apart a gentry class despite the rapid acquisition of refined parlor goods all up and down the social scale? While we are inclined to believe that the elite always manages to remain elite, we should keep in mind how much the gap had closed since the eighteenth century. Then the mansions with their grand staircases, smoothed parlor walls, and rooms dedicated to entertainment were a different species from the one-room houses or the traditional hall-and-parlor houses where work, eating, and social life mingled in a hurly-burly conglomeration. Many of the middling people of Kent County now claimed parlors of some kind, and those in the upper half of society filled them with many of the proper furnishings: mirrors, carpets, walnut tables, looking glasses, clocks, and dining tables. Although more primitive in both possessions and manners, these ordinary people of the upper half embraced the same culture as the Ridgelys', at least in its fundamental points. However different in scale, the houses all aspired to refinement. In the face of these facts, could the people of Kent County still sustain a sense of division comparable to that fundamental break between gentlemen and the rest in the eighteenth century? The cultural boundary that once coincided with the social and political boundary now had moved downward in society to encompass a much larger group. In the face of that enlargement, could the nineteenth-century gentry still conceive of themselves as a separate class, or was cultural democracy erasing the old lines?

The Ridgely letters do not address the question of class directly, nor do family members betray assumptions about class character in tangential asides as Charles Greenberry Ridgely did in the eighteenth century. But the letters are revealing. The Ridgelys frequently express their dismay with Dover society. Sally Ridgely, it will be remembered, told Elizabeth at school in Philadelphia not to yearn for home; "the Society of Dover is so bad there are scarcely any I should feel willing for you to associate with." Sally Ridgely seemed to feel the Ridgelys themselves were the only people worth knowing in the town. "There is nothing out of your own immediate family to interest," she told Elizabeth. Even Henry Moore Ridgely, whose wife accused him of undeserved devotion to the town, advised his daughters against attendance at dances and parties. "They are not proper places for

The reduced decoration in this interior was a more sophisticated version of Henry and Sally Ridgely's parlor as revealed in their estate inventory.

Ladies who have a just feeling of self respect and honest pride." But the use of the word "society" in the letters implied the existence of a circle that pretended to gentility and observed the rituals of genteel entertainment; it only fell short of Ridgely standards. Charles's observation to his sister that "in Philadelphia the Company which we so often meet, is so much superior to that which we only rarely find in Dover," acknowledged a society that occasionally satisfied him. The town was not entirely a wilderness. Behind these phrases is the awkward middling society of the probate inventories, a society of people attempting refinement with inadequate means and little experience. The Ridgelys' attitude suggests how the old gentry felt about this vernacular gentility. The Ridgelys do not relegate these parvenus to another class entirely, using words like "coarse" or "rude"; they simply regard the local gentility with disdain.[30]

The emerging middle class could be scorned, or they could be ignored. The reminiscences of a woman raised in Indian River Hundred, fifty miles to the south of Dover in a less well-developed area, suggests the possibilities for other forms of social analysis in this period of rapid change. Mary Parker Welch was born in 1818, and many years later described her life as a girl in the 1820s and 1830s. Peter Parker, her father, grew up on a plantation near Lewes, the major port town of Sussex County. The estate went to the eldest son, John, who paid a small portion of the farm income to Peter as his share until he finally settled with his brother for a cash payment of $1,374.53. Peter opened a store in nearby Milford and then moved from place to place keeping store, doing construction, and occupying farms. He married twice, lived in seven different locations, mainly in Indian River Hundred, and ran at least four different farms.

Despite the rather ordinary commercial career of her father, Mary Welch was determined to assimilate her people into the cavalier tradition of aristocratic English families carried to America. She devoted many of the early pages to the story of her English roots and to the style of her first ancestors in America. The Parkers, she claimed, came from the landed aristocracy in England, and the first Parker in America bore the title "gentleman," which, she reminds her readers, "carried with it in early days an admission of high respectability, and indicated that its possessor was well-born." She pictured her ancestors as "cavalcades of horsemen and ladies on horseback, their flowing skirts wavering in the winds, as with song and laughter they threaded the forest aisles, bent on pleasure." Her mother's ancestors, she said, held a country seat, "Horn-Castle" in Lincolnshire, and received favors from the king in return for their services. Of the Parkers' American plantation, Mary Welch said, a son "inherited the old mansion and the broad demesne about it," using words associated with feudal manors. It is as if she wished to make her ancestors into characters in a novel by Sir Walter Scott.[31]

She described her family's circle in Delaware, as the "best families," the ones invited to the finest entertainments, and living in "ancient manor houses." Her father moved from Herring Creek to Bundick's Branch in Indian River Hundred to be nearer company for his wife. "There were many fine old families living here," Mary Welch said, "and some of the homes dated back to the seventeenth century." Although her own family moved constantly from place to place, she compensated by explaining that they moved into the Burton mansion at Bundick's Branch, "being the colonial mansion belonging to Robert Burton, first of that name, who had a grant of six hundred acres of land in 1682." She wished us to know that it was an imposing house.

This was a very large house, with many rooms, and wide porches and extensive grounds. The lane leading from the Kings' Highway was lined on each side with tall Lombardy populars [sic], like the one we had left. In fact, these glistening, picturesque trees were the ornaments about most of the homes of any pretence, in the early days.

Not only the homes but the way of life was pretentious. There were dances, where her sister Ann excelled, and books. In her mother's line, an ancestor "taught her children the love of the books that had been brought from England." Mary's own mother, an accomplished horsewoman and many other things, "was a great reader, and had a judicious, penetrating mind, and she was a sprightly conversationalist, full of humor and repartee." These were the leaders of society, people of "social prominence," Mary Welch called them, and leaders of government. She recounted tales of many who became governor or held other high office, and spoke of some who would have risen higher if they had not died prematurely.[32]

Quite remarkably for a nineteenth-century American, Mary Welch pictured her circle of associates not only as classic American gentry, leaders in society and government, but as an extension of the European aristocracy, carrying on in an American form a style of life originating in the country seats of England. Furthermore, in contrast to the aristocrats, she saw no middling farmers, living respectable lives of modest gentility. There were only peasants. At Springfield Cross Roads, the family seemed to have settled for a while, and Mary was old enough to visit neighboring families. She showed some disapproval of the crowd that gathered at a tavern and made merry late into the night, "their loud laughter and rude songs jarring upon the night." But of most of the rustics she was humorously tolerant. She enjoyed "Old Jimmie Johnston's" family, who lived in a two-room house with loft, attached to the original house, an old log cabin. Here "in two big rooms and the low lofts above lived the swarthy old farmer and his thin, dreary wife, eleven children and a maiden aunt." They worked 150 acres of thin soil, growing corn and a "scraggly apple orchard."

On the wide hearth in the glow of the pine coals intermixed with the children would lie a number of gaunt hounds, dozing and dreaming, or lifting their long muzzles to watch the grimy table for the beginning of the family meal. On Sunday mornings it became rare sport for Theodore and me to steal over to the low house, and sit upon the loom bench, to watch the Johnsons at their late breakfast. On this day they had the rare treat of wheat bread on their table, and each little Johnson, his biscuit held tightly in his fist, his elbow planted on the table, would look triumphantly at us and rigidly hold aloft his wheaten morsel. Between them, ranged round in order, stood the hounds, greedily devouring with their eyes the coveted bread.

Mary told at some length of Jimmie Johnston's belief that witches tried to ride him every night. He hung a screen above the bed in the belief that it kept them away. She and her friends listened to the stories with great interest, and fifty years later she remembered many of them. Yet she claimed never to have believed in witches. "Scarcely any of the acquaintances and friends that we had, would tolerate such delusions." This superstition was one of the divides in her society. "The lower classes were steeped in these beliefs," while "even the children of the better class regarded the stories of mysticism with amusement and incredulity." There were many such divides: the rough dialect of the rustics, their use of oxen rather than horses, their loud laughter and rude songs. Her family would not tolerate disparaging comments about these country people. Her father showed only contempt for one of the better families who referred to the rustics as "corn-crackers." Yet the scorn for their coarseness and superstition is as surely present in Mary herself. At least in retrospect, she depicted her brother and herself watching the Johnston children at breakfast among the dogs as if they were looking at animals in a zoo. In Mary Welch's mind the rustics and the better families possessed entirely different cultures, and tolerant disdain for her lowly neighbors or at best warmhearted amusement was the greatest measure of respect she could muster.[33]

The two groups, best families and rustics, made up the whole of Indian River society in Mary Welch's telling. No middle class attempted to be polite and live respectably, without pretense to gentry status. The Parkers themselves may have lived modestly; they certainly had no deep roots in any of the houses they occupied. Around them people achieved gentility with varying degrees of success. Yet Mary Welch refused to think of any of her acquaintances as in the middle ranks. They were either superstitious, naïve, coarse rustics or socially prominent families tied by descent and inclination to the country seats of old England. Words like "demesne" and "manor house" and references to royal favors and embassies bolstered the claims for the "fine old families" she admired. She could not or would not think of a middle class that was neither peasant nor aristocratic.

By the mid-nineteenth century, the idea of a middle in society had taken form and was given expression in political discourse and literature. But Mary Welch's convoluted efforts suggest that for many there were difficulties in arriving at a satisfactory formulation. It was hard for her to conceive of a class with the culture of the gentry but without their power or wealth. The Ridgelys were not much more successful; the middle class troubled them. Although the Ridgelys did not see their Dover neighbors as rustics, the family repudiated Dover people as dull and untalented, unworthy company for their children. The Ridgelys ridiculed the middle for its failed pretensions. Only the gentry received their respect.

The difficulty of conceiving a satisfactory middle class complicated life and politics in a society where the emergence of a broad middle class was an indisputable fact. For all those who, like Mary Welch, could not find a place for the emerging middle, politics oscillated between rule by aristocrats and rule by the mob. The genteel yearned for the triumph of the gentry and endured when the mob gained power. For the Ridgelys social life was a trial. People with pretensions to gentility but lacking the proper finish made unwonted claims on the family's attention.

While the spread of gentility now appears natural for a republican society, the democratization of culture perplexed those who lived through the refining process, blurring their conceptions of social class. What was to be made of people who were touched with gentility and yet not engaged in the public roles of the traditional gentry, who were polite but not polished? Or still worse, what of middling men without polish or breeding who ran for office as if they were gentry? The confusion and intermingling of marks of social position that had once cohered in clear patterns, made the precise definition of class difficult to achieve.

CHAPTER VIII

The Comforts of Home

JOHN DICKINSON loved the house his father, Samuel, built in 1741 on the family's plantation near Dover. Even when other responsibilities kept him away, Dickinson superintended the management of the Kent County farms in scrupulous detail. Much to his regret, he lived there only intermittently. Public responsibilities detained him, and his wife did not share his affection for Kent County. Mostly he resided in Philadelphia or Wilmington, where, to support a life in keeping with his position, Dickinson thoroughly remodeled one house and built two others.

After his marriage to Mary Norris in 1770, he remodeled Fairhill, the country estate she inherited from her father, and erected a large town house on a prime lot in Philadelphia, suitable for a fashionable family, diagonally across Chestnut Street from the statehouse. In Wilmington, where he later moved to finish out his days, Dickinson purchased a house and lot on Market and Kent, now Eighth, and in 1798 designed a new structure to add to the one already there.

While making plans, Dickinson studied Abraham Swann's *Book of Architecture*, wrote for advice to the builder who had worked on the Philadelphia house, and picked out details from distinguished standing houses. In his directions to the contractors, Dickinson said to examine doors, windows, chimneys, mantels, and staircases in the Philadelphia houses of William Bingham, Henry Hills, George Clymer, Thomas Fitzsimmons, and others. A family friend and amateur architect, William Thornton, designed the fanlight for the front door. The finished house, forty-five feet square, three stories high with four large rooms on the first floor, was a monumental residence on Wilmington's Market Street from 1799 until purchased by the Wilmington Institute library late in the nineteenth century.[1]

Dickinson's Wilmington town house was one of thousands of extravagant residences that went up in American cities and across the countryside through the nineteenth century. The compulsion to build mansions that first inspirited the American gentry in the 1720s and resulted in the erection of an ever larger number of great houses before the Revolution, continued without abatement in the new republic. Public figures like Dickinson, professional men, merchants, and later industrialists devoted substantial portions of their fortunes to the construction of polished and ornamented residences befitting their achievements and wealth.

The nineteenth-century gentry and people with newly acquired wealth were as determined to present themselves as refined members of polite society as their eighteenth-century predecessors, and as before, the great house was the most forthright statement of a person's cultural condition. The appearance of these houses is the palpable evidence that American elites continued their pretensions to the refinement that the eighteenth-century gentry had so warmly embraced. Indeed, with greater wealth at their disposal, the nineteenth-century upper class achieved levels of elegance and grandeur unattainable earlier.

John Dickinson's Wilmington town house was one of his four residences in Delaware and Pennsylvania.

Thomas Handasyd Perkins, the Boston merchant and philanthropist, purchased five different Boston town houses between 1788 and 1833. In an effort to create the right house, he added a ballroom to his third mansion on Pearl Street before purchasing another Pearl Street house in 1810. In the 1820s the center of Boston fashion moved to the mansions lining the Common, but Perkins failed to purchase a lot in time and moved instead in 1833 to Temple Place. Meanwhile he purchased sixty-one acres in nearby rural Brookline for a country seat, erected a house with piazzas on both first and second floors looking out over Boston Harbor, and filled his extensive gardens with exotic plants imported from all over the world.[2]

Many of the finest rural residences served as country estates for people with primary residences in town. These houses increased steadily on the fringes of American cities through the early decades of the nineteenth century, just as they did around London, Birmingham, Gloucester, and Leeds.[3] Mostly they were retreats for businessmen and public officials. Few farmers, whose income came exclusively from the land, could afford the elaborate villas that merchants, professional men, and public figures could erect as country houses. Andrew Jackson Downing defined a villa as a country house requiring three or more servants, and with few exceptions additional sources of income beyond farming were required to build and maintain what Downing called "the most refined home of America," "enriched without and within by objects of universal beauty and interest," where we could look for "the happiest social and moral development of our people."[4]

Built before the turn of the century, the nineteen-room mansion of Henry Knox, a land speculator and politician, enabled him, as a friend said, to "live in the style of an English nobleman."

One way or another, grand houses did go up in rural areas. Rather than appearing exclusively on fashionable city streets or on the hills overlooking the largest cities, nineteenth-century mansions were constructed everywhere. Eighteenth-century North Carolina was noticeably lacking in distinguished Georgian mansions, because of its relative poverty, but in the nineteenth century scores of elegant houses in the latest styles arose in little towns all over the state. Some were erected by migrants from Virginia who grew rich in Warren and Halifax, the prime tobacco counties. One such person, William Williams, owned three plantations spread over 6,000 acres and built Montmorenci with the fabulous curving staircase that now stands in the Winterthur Museum. Other houses were built by merchants and professional men who sometimes derived part of their income from farming. James Johnston, a lawyer and landowner, was one of these. Johnston sent the architect William Nichols to New York City to purchase steps, railings, fanlights, and mantels, as well as furniture for his house at Hayes near Edenton, North Carolina. More than twenty Palladian farmhouses with two-story central blocks presenting their gable ends to the front and one-story wings on each side still stand in North Carolina. By the middle of the century, nearly every town across the northern and eastern regions of the state had a mansion of some proportions, and some had a half dozen or more. These houses stood as evidence that gentility and polite society had come to country towns.[5]

The refinement of upper-class Americans, as exemplified by Sarah Morton, grew ever more aristocratic and sophisticated after 1800.

ARCHITECTS AND THE RAGE TO BEAUTIFY

THE most splendid of these houses can be understood as the direct successors to the eighteenth-century mansions erected by the American gentry after 1720. The owners of the later mansions, although not always involved in public office like the eighteenth-century gentry, were without exception the elite of their districts, successful professional men, merchants, industrialists, high military and government officials, and large planters. The houses embodied their wealth, achievements, and cultural aspirations, notably the desire for genteel culture.

But while there were continuities, there were changes too, for the nineteenth-century mansions came into existence in a different cultural and social setting than their eighteenth-century predecessors. More splendid than ever, the nineteenth-century mansions were less isolated outposts of civilization than leading examples of a broad cultural movement. The eighteenth-century gentry mansions had risen like bright sentinels of culture above the surrounding rough, dark houses of common people. The great houses set their residents apart from everyone else. Gradually through the first half of the nineteenth century, the architectural environment was transformed. Gentility brought refinement to dwellings at nearly every level. Rather than embodying the culture of a distant and foreign world, the great houses represented the best and highest of a culture claimed by many and present in some degree in houses all around the mansions.

This diffusion came about partly because the campaign to beautify, one of the deepest urges within genteel culture, burst out of its eighteenth-century limits. In the earlier time there were certain exalted places where polite society assembled and where cultivated spirits showed their powers, notably in parlors, formal gardens, assembly rooms, and city promenades. Within all was beauty, ease, and elevation. Outside those privileged precincts, life was dirty, rude, or at least plain. Gentility drew much of its strength from the striking differences between the coarse and the refined, the large brick mansions of the gentry and the unpainted frame and log houses of commoners, or the rooms where cards, music, and dancing were marks of cultivation and the rooms in inns and taverns where they were vulgar and debased. Most of the world was plain and rough; only in a few privileged areas was it smooth and brilliant. Gentility can be seen as an effort to create beautiful places, in Edmund Burke's sense of the word, and in the eighteenth century only a few privileged locales were properly adorned for the society of polished people who knew how to conduct themselves with genteel ease and grace.

In the nineteenth century, gentility's beautification campaign extended its reach far beyond the limited precincts where it had prevailed before. Indeed, by midcentury some writers denied all limits and sought to make virtually everything in the world beautiful. Prominent among these aesthetic enthusiasts were the architects who created the plans for upper-class mansions and were themselves products of the mansion-building boom of the nineteenth century.

Before 1800 there were no professional architects as we understand the term. In the eighteenth century, masons and carpenters for the most part designed as well as constructed houses guided by instructions from the owner and help from builders' manuals. In 1798 John Dickinson studied an architecture book and then told the builder what he wanted in his Wilmington house. Only a few gentlemen amateurs like Peter Harrison or extremely skilled builder/designers like William Buckland came close to acting like architects.

Beginning with Benjamin Latrobe, who designed the Bank of Pennsylvania in Philadelphia in 1799 and the reconstruction of the United States Capitol after the British burned it in 1814, professional architects took over the design of government and church structures and large private houses. Professionals like Alexander Jackson Davis, based in New York, received commissions all over the country; Davis designed some twenty buildings in North Carolina. Others had practices of similar national scope: Isaiah Rogers, Robert Mills, Thomas U. Walter, Richard Upjohn, William Strickland, James Renwick, and Ithiel Town.

Besides these favored few, a host of lesser-known architects served a regional clientele. William Nichols practiced in North Carolina from 1800 to 1819 until moving to the Southwest, where he supervised buildings in Alabama, Louisiana, and Mississippi; William Percival designed houses in Raleigh in the 1850s. What was true for North Carolina was true for every section. Skilled local architects, aware of current styles and the work of national practitioners, met the need for gracious, fashionable mansions for the parochial gentry.[6]

Quite a number of these architects, some with distinguished practices, wrote books. Between 1797 and 1860, there were 188 architectural books published in the United States, 93 of them in the decade before 1860. At first, skilled builders wrote most of the books. North Carolina used Owen Biddle's *Young Carpenter's Assistant* (1805), John Haviland's *Builder's Assistant* (1818), Asher Benjamin's *Practical House Carpenter* (1830) and *Practice of Architecture* (1833), and William Ranlett's *The Architect* (1847).[7] In the 1840s and 1850s, the professional architects began to write, and the books changed character. From being concerned with decorating houses, they became guides for beautifying the landscape.

In the earlier books, builders like Benjamin focused attention on details, a stair baluster, the design of a door, or a mantel. Turning the pages, we encounter detailed drawings of the classical orders or a pattern for a cornice. Sketches of the arrangement of roof trusses interspersed with highly technical directions were included in the text, but no plans for the overall construction of the house. The authors seemed to understand the process of house design as a matter of assembling beautiful features and applying them to the surfaces of the house. Floor plans and façade compositions were included as well, but the books assumed that carpenters and masons knew how to erect the basic structures and needed most help with the design of the embellishments. The eye of the discerning observer, it was implicitly assumed, looked to these details, not to the floor plan, to measure the elegance of the house. Actual houses from the earlier period bear out the books' assumption; the grandest of them, beginning with the mansions of the 1720s, are notable for the plasterwork on the ceilings, mantel carvings, cornice moldings, and pedimented doorframes. After the basics of smooth walls, a higher ceiling, a smaller fireplace, and enlarged sash windows were in place, these embellishments measured grandeur and refinement.

In contrast, the books that came out in such profusion in the 1840s and 1850s played down architectural details. The books show elevations and floor

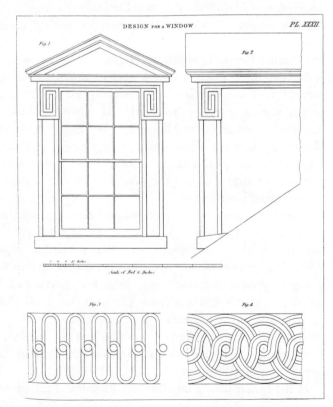

Early architectural books focused on specific design elements in a building rather than on the overall appearance.

plans with virtually no attention to the details that so preoccupied their predecessors. Moreover, the elevations are presented differently than before. The earlier books showed the façade in a stark two-dimensional frontal view to provide dimensions and design details. After 1840 the houses are drawn three-dimensionally as an approaching observer would see the structures, and they are placed in landscapes with trees and shrubs surrounding the buildings and suggestions of walks or drives and sometimes fences sketched in. In short, the houses are depicted as if the total effect of the scene, rather than the elegance of the decorative detail alone, interested the architect. The later books train the eye to look at houses differently. Instead of narrowing the focus to the telling intricacies, the eye is led to survey the entire setting and to see the house as part of a broad picture.

In the much more discursive texts of the later books, the architectural authors explicitly told readers to look at the entire scene. These authors thought of themselves more as artists than as builders and wrote under the influence of the picturesque aesthetic with its interest in composing natural and man-made features into harmonious wholes. In a characteristic passage on siting the farmhouse, Lewis Allen, an upstate New York architect who published his *Rural Architecture* in 1852, urged his readers to take into account lakes, streams, and every attractive natural feature "in such manner as to combine all that is desirable both in beauty and effect, as well as in utility, to make up a perfect whole in the family residence." Allen wanted his readers to view the entire scene, not just the house.

In that scene, neither the natural features nor the house should predominate. "A single object should not control, but the entire picture, as completed, should be embraced in the view." "A farm with its buildings, or a simple country residence with the grounds which enclose it, or a cottage with its door-yard and garden, should be finished sections of the landscape of which it forms a part." The landscape should be interesting and attractive from every angle. "General appearance should not be confined to one quarter alone, but the house and its surroundings on every side should show completeness in design and harmony in execution." The nearby orchard and woods should "connect the house and out-buildings with the fields beyond, which are of necessity naked of trees, and gradually spread the view abroad over the farm until it mingles with, or is lost in the general landscape." The aim of these authors was to turn the world into pictures.[8]

Viewing the house so broadly brought under the architect's eye structures once thought to be beneath his attention. The architecture books now included designs for barns, stables, dovecotes, fences, and bridges. As part of a larger picture, these lesser buildings became objects of taste and had to be, in their own way, beautiful. The great country estates of the late eighteenth century that took their lead from the French *ferme ornée* and flourished in

England as rural retreats for affluent bankers and businessmen provided precedent for this broadened realm of beauty. On such estates, the owners considered the beauty and elegance of the whole composition, houses, outbuildings, and fields, as much as their functional efficiency. Joseph Barrell, a Boston businessman, among two dozen or more fellow citizens with an interest in country estates, laid out such a villa farm in Charlestown, complete with a Bulfinch-designed mansion, a magnificent cattle barn, coach house, greenhouses, and a picturesque landscape that stretched from the house to the Charles River.

At first only rich gentlemen could indulge in such estates. Speaking of Christopher Gore's large estate in Waltham, an 1818 article in Massachusetts commented that "farmers may perhaps be disposed to treat with levity these efforts to adorn our country." The author wistfully hoped that they might be brought around: "In truth if they knew the interesting and important effects of this taste in Great Britain they would materially alter their opinions." John Adams must have spoken the feelings that commonly prevailed at the beginning of the century when he warned Abigail against "all expensive ornaments" on their barn. Practical farmers must have scoffed at the

PERSPECTIVE VIEW.

After about 1840 architectural books depicted entire structures in their overall settings, as if the houses were to be seen as pictures.

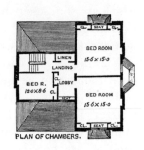

effeminacy of painting a barn, much less decorating one. She gaily replied that the President's horses would be the best-housed creatures in the town and proved to be more prescient than he. By the 1850s architectural authors who claimed to offer sensible advice for ordinary farmers were urging more strongly that they consider "correct taste" in barn architecture. The writers specifically opposed elaborate decoration on any farm buildings and recommended simplicity for the farmhouses themselves. But they insisted that every farm building, woodshed, stable, and barn, came under the jurisdiction of taste and by proper siting and design could become an object of beauty.[9]

By midcentury, the improvers among ordinary farmers were responding to the idea of a tasteful farm layout. The nineteenth century was an era of barn building as well as house building, and the plans for the large handsome barns, so admired today, were often taken from designs offered in agricultural periodicals. The most striking practical response came in southern Maine and eastern New Hampshire, where farmers moved their outbuildings from various scattered locations to join them into a single, ordered line. The advantages for improved efficiency and protection from the weather played a part in motivating this strenuous effort, but those benefits do not account for painting the trim to match the house and installing lights above the barn door and in general bringing the farm buildings into harmony with the architecture of the house. One large white barn was ornamented in the same Greek Revival style as the house. The *Third Annual Report of the*

The architect authors who designed this house said of it: "Nestling in a sunny nook upon the hill-side, guarded and sheltered by tall old trees, painted of a cheerful color, and decorated with vines and flowers, this cottage would have charms for the dullest eyes."

Secretary of the Maine Board of Agriculture in 1858 gave the reasons for these decorative changes. "A cultivated taste requires that all the appointments, out buildings, grounds, shade and fruit trees, flower and vegetable gardens, should be arranged as to please the eye." Farmers had adopted taste as one of the principles of farm management. Thomas Hubka, who has written most powerfully about the connected farmstead, concludes it was the "genteel, town-influenced" great estate houses of gentlemen farmers and merchants— like Joseph Barrell—who provided models for the farmers and led them to move their buildings into orderly lines. Paintings of farm scenes elsewhere show great painted barns standing proudly beside the farmhouses, made into things of beauty by the owners.[10]

The architects thus broadened the refinement of the environment to include virtually every visible object. In turning the entire world into pictures, they broke down the lines around the grand house and garden, once the primary precinct of genteel beauty, and made outbuildings and fields aspects of the scene in view. The intensity of taste was diluted as it spread outward from house and garden. Paint on the barns, windows in the style of the house, and a simple strong design was about all that correct taste required. But these humble structures nonetheless came under the influence of gentility's overall beautification campaign, showing that nothing was exempt. A manual admonished farm wives to give heed to their dairy by pointing out that "at some of the noblemen's country houses in England, the dairies are arranged with great taste, and finished off in the handsomest manner. Placed in the circuit of the ornamental grounds, guests are taken to see them, and are often charmed with the fresh and cool as well as elegant air which prevails in them."[11]

Gervase Wheeler, in his *Rural Homes,* went through an entire village in his mind's eye converting virtually every object into a fitting element of a picture. "In a few years," he remarked, "how beautiful may this country be made by its rural architecture! There are bye places, and nooks and lanes, fertile valleys and rich knolls, that only want the hand of taste and the clear eye to invest with the sentiment of beauty." Beginning with the houses, "now but assemblages of white boxes thrust as near as may be upon the street," the villages may be beautified in every detail. The church, the schoolhouse, the rural inn, and on the outskirts the blacksmith shop, the tollhouse, the covered bridge, "how pretty and yet how simple might they all be made." Wheeler recognized that no single supervising taste could direct the changes, but if all worked together, he romantically assumed, "the result of the collected whole will show one harmonious design."[12]

As taste beautified the rural environment, it also implanted gentility's anxieties. In the hands of the architects, the farm became a performance. It was no longer sufficient to ask how well it worked; also of concern was how well it looked. Lewis Allen, in advocating better breeds of cattle, claimed they improved profits, but his emphasis was on how they looked. He was surprised that people with "an eye for a fine house, pleasant grounds, beautiful trees, and all the surroundings which such a place might command" would stock their farm with "the veriest brutes, in the way of domestic animals." Allen felt people should be as self-conscious about their animals as about the decorations in their houses. A country dweller knew that an inferior picture "would be laughed at by his friends," yet would drive into his grounds "the meanest possible creature, in the shape of a cow, a pig, or a sheep."

Allen wanted his rural residents to feel the same shame about parading the wrong animals as about hanging the wrong picture. He considered it pitiful for a person with a fine lawn before his house to "go and get a parcel of mean scrubs of cattle, or sheep, to graze it, surrounding his very door, and disgracing him by their vulgar, plebeian looks." Anyone with "true taste in such matters" will buy the best stock, not just to yield the most milk and flesh but to "embellish his grounds" and "arrest the attention of those who visit him, or pass by his grounds." His establishment was to be looked at, not just worked. Once the farm came under the sway of taste, the animals themselves were on display and in danger of shaming their owner with their "vulgar, plebeian looks."[13]

Writing in 1858, three years after the publication of his first book, Gervase Wheeler felt that the efforts of the "lovers of art" were bearing fruit. "Already this fair land has been, within the last three years, plentifully dotted with tasteful dwellings, in a progressive numerical increase, far beyond that of preceding times." The "rage to 'beautify,' " as he called the campaign, had touched "myriad buildings" across the land. Besides extending across the countryside, he and the other authors hoped that beautification would also reach down through the social scale. All of the architectural authors included small cottages among their designs with explicit notification that appropriate taste could rule there too. "A true taste may be as fully displayed in a five hundred dollar cottage as in a fifty thousand dollar mansion, and by use of the same means," Wheeler insisted.

The books customarily gave the cost of building the house or even specified the right property level for the owner. Allen showed a farmhouse "suitable for a farm of twenty, fifty, or an hundred acres," with a parlor, sitting room, kitchen, and bedroom on the first floor. He offered another plan of a house actually built for a Mr. Ryan, a plumber, on a suburban lot in Newburgh, New York, for $1,500 or $1,600, an amount not beyond the reach of established mechanics. The main idea was that none of these residences, and by implication none of the residents themselves, was beyond the circle of taste. Gervase Wheeler claimed that one of his houses in the "Rural

DESIGN FOR A LOG-HOUSE.

The architect attempted to beautify a log house by giving it a porch and shrubbery. By calling the all-purpose room in the center a living room rather than a hall, he implied the possibility of more refined activities occurring there.

Italian" taste could be constructed for $1,400 with "an appearance of symmetry and refinement that adapts it to the occupancy of a family of elegance and taste." A family's modest means need not imply an absence of refinement.

To show the extent of beauty's reach, the architecture books frequently included a log house among the tasteful designs. Lewis Allen claimed he had seen many primitive houses, among them log cabins, that "under the hands of taste, and a trifle of labor, [were] made to look comfortable, happy, and sufficient." For those log houses still going up, Calvert Vaux urged the owners to give "some thought to the *beauty* as well as to the *utility* of the homes they erect." These lovers of art were determined that no dwelling remain outside the realm of taste. The beautification campaign was to envelop everything. These new conditions gave the grand houses of the elite a new context. Indisputably they still stood on a social and cultural peak, but they did not stand alone. They were the most elegant expressions of a culture that in theory belonged to everybody and everything.[14]

HOUSES IN THE MIDDLE

THE ambitions of the architectural authors were not to be fully realized in the nineteenth century. Simple two-room-plan houses and even one-room houses with loft, both harking back two centuries, continued to be constructed nearly everywhere, at least through the first half of the century.

In Kent County, at the middle of the century, a quarter of the houses were still of log construction, probably with only minimal decorative touches. Even houses that aspired to beauty disappointed some of the architects. Pleased as he was with the improvements in architecture, Gervase Wheeler blamed the rage to beautify for houses "adorned with costly gingerbread," in "amusing contrast to the quiet but elegant structures, that those of better taste erect."[15]

Yet the awkward efforts at beautification point to a broadly based urge to improve domestic architecture. The upgrading of vernacular houses seems to have been the natural extension of the earlier purchases of silver spoons and sets of teacups. Sensing the scorn of the gentry for vulgar simplicity, ordinary people resolved to appropriate for themselves the marks of polite life, beginning with the genteel objects and then going on to patterns of conduct. The widespread improvement in vernacular architecture reflected a continuing desire to acquire what was incessantly represented as high and refined, much of which was coming within reach of many more people in a time of increasing prosperity. A large proportion of the population was still left out altogether, but the number who moved into houses with parlors and painted exteriors grew every year.

The crucial characteristic of a refined house was a parlor, free of work paraphernalia and beds, and dedicated to formal entertainment and the presentation of the family's most decorative possessions. Ordinary families, from most accounts, used the room infrequently for its designated purpose, formal entertainment, but that seems to have been true of many eighteenth-century mansions as well. The presence of the room was a testament of the family's refinement, proof that they understood how to be polite, that they had a front to their lives as to their houses, where the rough ways of work and family intimacy were concealed, and that they could appear as polished beings capable of grace, dignity, and propriety. After the parlor, a stair passage and broad stairs with balusters and newel post provided a formal entry to the house, and held out the promise that in the chambers above the family continued to live with dignity. When compromise was required for want of space, the stair passage could be left out; the parlor was essential.

At the beginning of the century, the parlor was still emerging in many middling houses. Estate inventories in southern New Castle County, Delaware, in which the contents of each room were listed, show that the larger houses with side or center passages had a clearly defined parlor and strictly formal furnishings. But about half the time, the occupants of smaller three-room-plan houses kept fiber-working equipment in the best room, and two-thirds of the old-style hall-and-parlor houses still had beds in the parlors.[16]

Over the next fifty years, more and more of these people learned that parlors were essential and moved the beds upstairs and the work equipment into other rooms, leaving only good furniture and the accoutrements of gentility in the family's formal best room.[17] By the middle of the nineteenth century, floor plans of all the houses in the architectural books, with rare exceptions, included parlors. An 1857 agricultural annual assumed that even a farmer of modest means would not be satisfied without a kitchen, parlor, bedroom, entry, upstairs bedrooms, and a cellar. Gervase Wheeler put a parlor into his plans for a city tenement, and Lewis Allen into "a farm house of the simplest and most unpretending kind."[18]

Over the course of the nineteenth century a number of vernacular house forms emerged to serve the purposes of the respectable middle class. The best-documented form is the I house, which appeared in virtually every section of the country as a residence for prosperous farmers. The I house was a simple variation of the older hall-and-parlor house, with two rooms side by side on the first floor and two chambers (or more) above. The difference in the nineteenth century was that many of the I house plans inserted a passage and stair between the two first-floor rooms, providing an entrance hall and enabling the owners to treat one of the rooms off the hall as a parlor.

In the cities, small row houses went up in great numbers in the first half of the century, virtually all with parlors, many with dining rooms behind, and some with stair passages. Even the plans of two-bay urban row houses where the door entered directly into the front room called that room the parlor.

Many variant plans can still be seen along country roads. In New England and the Midwest, the temple-form house, as Henry Glassie has called it, presented the gable end of a two-story block to the street and added a cross-gable wing to the side. These vernacular Greek Revival dwellings were extremely common. Less common idiosyncratic houses turn up too, the products of local ingenuity, spread by communal loyalty to local styles, and capable of serving middle-class aspirations. All had parlors.[19]

In addition to the construction of new middling housing stock with parlors and open stairs, the owners of older houses redecorated and remodeled their existing dwellings. Architectural historians have found that virtually every house in some areas underwent substantial change in the first half of the century. One example has received the attention of the archaeologists and historians at Old Sturbridge Village, who meticulously worked over every scrap of written and material evidence in preparation for moving the Emerson Bixby house from Barre Four Corners in central Massachusetts to a site at Old Sturbridge. They found that Bixby, a blacksmith and small landowner in this little community at the northern edge of Barre, purchased a house in 1826, shortly after moving to the neighborhood with his wife and daughter. Remote as the neighborhood was, Bixby was not out of touch with sources of cultural information. Barre's town center, sustained by dairying, cattle raising, and grain production, augmented subsequently by small in-

In the first half of the nineteenth century, brick and frame versions of the I-house proliferated in the Middle Atlantic states, the Midwest, and the South. Wings were sometimes added to the back, as at Fairview in New Castle County, Delaware.

dustries, throve in the 1830s, resulting in the construction of a new town hall, churches, and four Greek Revival dwellings attributed to a local Worcester architect, Elias Carter.

The Bixby house in 1826 showed signs of having already been touched by the refining impulse. This idiosyncratic three-room house, twenty-six feet on each side, did not fall into any of the usual patterns for New England houses, though four other houses of nearly identical plans were found in the neighborhood. The rooms were used as kitchen, sitting room, and best room, and the last especially showed signs of the former owners' aspirations. They had redecorated the best room sometime before 1826 to introduce Prussian blue wainscoting with a molded chair rail around the room, and above it wallpaper over the only plastered walls in the house. On the applied mantelpiece at the fireplace opening, there was Federal-style detailing. The sitting room did not come up to the best room's decor, but it had wallpaper over the board walls and the wall around the fireplace was painted to suggest a mantel.

These were admirable improvements, but when the Bixbys moved in, the house, for all of the efforts to introduce fashionable touches, had only a veneer of refinement. The staircase going up from the kitchen was still enclosed in the old-fashioned way and would remain so for lack of space to do anything more. Much worse, the family took their meals in the best room, and in it stood a bed. It was more like the seventeenth-century parlor with the parents' bed and the family's best possessions, even though the room had mantel, wainscoting, and chair rail, all genteel touches from the eighteenth century.[20]

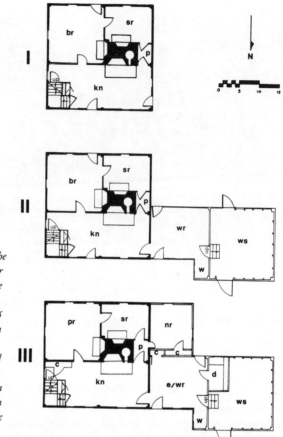

The plans show the expansion of the house as the Bixbys improved their parlor and added rooms. Dates are I: c. 1807; II: c. 1813–1820; III: 1844–1845. Restored to its 1826 condition, the house now stands in Old Sturbridge Village. The important feature the Bixbys could not install when they changed the bedroom (br) to parlor (pr) was an unenclosed staircase. Improvisation and compromise were characteristic of vernacular gentility.

In the late 1830s, as the oldest of the Bixbys' three daughters entered young womanhood, the family made changes in the house. They closed up the exterior door into the best room, so that people coming from the outside would not tramp in directly. They plastered the walls in the house to give them that desirable smooth finish and either painted them gray or, as in the best room and sitting room, papered them with fashionable gray paper. They added a ground-floor room, which became the parents' bedroom. The bed then left the best room, clearing it for its true function of formal entertaining and transforming it into a proper nineteenth-century parlor.

Archaeological investigations also showed that after the remodeling period the area immediately around the house was treated differently. The Bixbys pulled down a barn that stood close to the house and made an older structure at a distance from the house into a barn. They also stopped throwing refuse into the yard. Earlier, broken dishes, glass, household utensils, ashes, and food scraps were thrown from the door openings all over the yard. By the 1840s, very little refuse was discarded in the front yard; most of it went into collection areas out of public sight. At the same time, the Bixbys removed the unpainted clapboards on the house and painted the new ones white. It is not hard to imagine a fence and a lawn going in, as happened commonly elsewhere. By 1845, the Bixbys' house, though not a finished mansion by any means, made reasonable pretensions to gentility and afforded the daughters suitable entertainment spaces. Perhaps the parents felt they had no choice. Virtually every house in the neighborhood underwent changes between 1810 and 1840, and the Bixbys were among the last to remodel.[21]

The Bixbys and Barre Four Corners were not unique. In southern New Castle County, another intensely studied area, the same thing was going on in the same period; virtually every house underwent changes much like those at the Bixbys'. Simple one- or two-room-plan houses, with the entry directly into the main room, had rooms added to create central passages and parlors off them. Often the walls and ceilings were then plastered and a mantel and trim added. Larger houses, already respectable mansions when constructed in the eighteenth century, were made more elaborate. Geraldsville, built as a two-story, side-passage-plan brick house, had a room added alongside the hall to form a center-passage plan; the new room was adorned with mantels and chair rails. In Alabama, single-room two-story log houses with simple sheds on the back were enlarged to create a reasonable semblance of a Georgian mansion with central passage and parlor and Federal- or Greek Revival-style trim. A broad spectrum of the population had the desire and the means to bring their houses up to a modest standard of respectable gentility.[22]

INWARD AND OUTWARD REFINEMENTS

IN countless other middling houses, as at the Bixbys', the organization of a formal parlor was the leading edge of improvement, but it was only the beginning. Beyond the parlor, the most significant new addition to modest house plans was the addition of a sitting room or library and later a dining room, all of them implying new living patterns. These rooms brought family activities back to the front part of the house, from which entertainment had excluded them, but in a new form. Cooking, working, and everyday eating did not come forward again. The life of the seventeenth-century hall was still banished to the rear. The sitting room and library implied another kind of activity and a new kind of family life.

In these rooms people gathered, during leisure hours, to read books or to write letters, sew, or converse. The family did not work in these forward portions of the house. The humdrum functions of keeping up a household were relegated to the rear, to some extent repressed or hidden and certainly restricted to the back. In the front, they did not merely relax; they improved their minds. "It is an odious sight to witness a family idle of a winter evening: and a no less beautiful spectacle when a circle surround a table, employing their needles, while one reads aloud. Let one of the party provide a map and dictionary for reference, and the knowledge obtained in an evening will be surprising." These were activities worthy of the better rooms to the front. Here the family presented itself in repose, though not idle, engaged in refined activities in keeping with the cultivated spirit of the environment. These people, whose private activities as well as entertainments were refined, could benefit from a house, as Downing had said, "enriched without and within by objects of universal beauty and interest."[23]

The provision of libraries and sitting rooms in prominent positions on the first floor reveals again the inexorable tendency of refinement to spread its influence, this time abetted by the architects. The eighteenth-century parlor implied gatherings of polite society where, on formal occasions, people attempted to reach that condition of perfect ease and polish that was the ideal of genteel culture. The sitting room and library extended the genteel ideal. These rooms implied that in its leisured moments the family conducted itself with equal refinement, not in the stiffly formal parlor mode but in the relaxed, easy, cordial style that was increasingly favored, and for this they could gather in adorned rooms adjacent to the parlor. In Catharine Sedgwick's *Home*, the Barclays gathered in the evening "round a well-lighted table." Mr. Barclay read, Mrs. Barclay sewed, "Charles and Wallace were seated on each side of her, drawing, acquiring at a leisure hour some knowledge of an art for which a man in almost every pursuit has some occasion. Alice was basting hems and ruling copy-books for the little girls' next day's work. Mary was dressing a doll for her youngest sister."[24] Stories and pictures showed the refined family engaged in sewing, letter writing, conversing, and especially reading, all genteel activities worthy of performance on upholstered chairs, sitting at mahogany tables near draped windows with pictures on the walls.[25]

At the same time as genteel improvements moved deeper into the house, the exterior of the improved houses had to be refined too. In the eighteenth century, the mansion with garden and grounds acted a part for all who approached to see, and the same came to be true for modestly genteel houses in the nineteenth century. A house in open view on the landscape was a continuing performance meant for the eyes of every passerby, just as parlor behavior was a performance for the assembled company and the family in cultivated repose was a scene of refined living meant to be admired. To dress up the exterior, the Bixbys painted their house and stopped throwing garbage in the yard at the same time as they improved their parlor. Middling houses tended to change on the outside at about the same time as formal parlors came into being on the inside.

In the first four decades of the nineteenth century, white frame houses with green shutters (or blinds, as they were often called) came to characterize New England townscapes and to appear nearly as commonly in other sections of the country. In the eighteenth century, pretentious buildings like

In the middle-class house, refinement enveloped the family in its relaxed, informal moments in the sitting room, as well as during formal entertainments in the parlor.

churches or great mansions were sometimes white but more often yellow, sand-colored, red, or green. Other structures with no paint at all on their log or board exteriors weathered to a gray-brown. By the middle of the nineteenth century, the white-and-green combination had become almost a cliché for middling houses, and men of advanced taste were beginning to disparage it. "We are not among those who cast off, and on a sudden condemn, as out of all good taste, the time-honored white house with its green blinds, often so tastefully gleaming out from beneath the shade of summer trees," wrote one architect in 1852. It seemed to him that "for a century past white has been the chief color of our wooden houses, and often so of brick ones, in the United States." Although he extended the reign of white too far into the past, its dominance at midcentury was beyond question.[26]

White was dominant both in the sense of prevalent and in its power to elevate houses on the landscape. White houses gleamed from amidst the trees as once only mansions had done, when most dwellings huddled against the ground, lost in the landscape, garbed in colors not much different from those of the fields and forests themselves. By midcentury the middling house stood its ground, rose up and spoke out in brisk white as once only mansions dared do. The picturesque architects, in fact, felt that white spoke too loudly. They wanted houses to blend with the countryside, to be an element in the picture, not to stand alone in the spotlight. White paint, Calvert Vaux thought, "protruded from the surrounding scenery." A white house, "instead of grouping and harmonizing with [the landscape], asserts a right to carry on a separate business on its own account; and this lack of sympathy between the building and its surroundings is very disagreeable to an artistic eye."[27] Architects like Vaux recommended pale earth tones to subdue the house and return it to harmony with the natural landscape.[28]

More than white paint marked the presence of vernacular gentility in a dwelling. The eighteenth-century mansions, predecessors of the middling genteel houses, were set in gardens, with approach drives and sometimes fenced courtyards guarding the front doors. Out of that array of possibilities, the fenced foreyard emerged as the most common feature of the nineteenth-century house exterior. John Warner Barber meant to compliment the citizens of Waterbury, Connecticut, when he observed that "some of the private dwellings may be called splendid, and a majority of them are neat, convenient, with handsome court yards in front." A simple white picket fence with gate was sufficient to create the "court yard," to demark the zone of domestic refinement from the dirt of the street, or, in a rural setting, from the fields and animals. To heighten the effect, square posts with caps could be set at regular intervals. Fences served the practical purpose of keeping animals out of the foreyard, but an inexpensive field fence would have been equally effective against animals. The painted fence kept out animality as well as animals and established the realm where taste and gentility were meant to reign.[29]

The fenced courtyard was a remnant of an obsolete gardening style. The fenced yard with gate and a straight path to the door recalled the formal gardens of seventeenth-century country houses with their rigorous geometrical lines formed by graveled paths and parterres. In the great houses of that time, fenced courtyards stood before the main entrances with formal gardens to the side or rear. In the eighteenth century, the leading gardeners turned away from formal to landscape gardening, to play up the natural features in the entire sweep surrounding the house rather than ordering only the gardens immediately adjacent to it. Natural curves and irregularities replaced strict geometrical figures. In this aesthetic, the sharp boundary formed by a fence had no place. The house and its grounds were to blend imperceptibly with fields, streams, and woods. These principles, taken from eighteenth-century landscape gardening, underlay the admonitions of American picturesque architects of the 1840s and 1850s to blend the house and landscape. These architects did not advocate fences for country houses, and as their viewpoint took hold, fences began to come down.[30]

The effect on owners of middling houses, however, was not to make picket fences unfashionable. By the middle of the nineteenth century, both fenced and unfenced foreyards could be seen before modestly genteel houses, as if they were indiscriminately acceptable. People mixed styles, oblivious to the injunctions of gardening's leading lights. The aim of vernacular gentility, it seems, was less to incorporate up-to-the-minute fashion than to achieve dignity and respectability. Middling people borrowed from

By 1840 modest houses commonly had a fenced yard in front with trees and shrubs before the house.

the upper ranks of society, but less by exact imitation than by assembling impressions of refinement and propriety from many sources, incorporating elements that suited them. Though derivative, the result represented their own taste, not a simpleminded aping of the rich and powerful. A fenced courtyard carried an air of dignity and charm, and ordinary people valued that style long after leading gardeners and architects had abandoned it. The unfenced yard, with lawn, trees, and shrubs, appealed to others, based on images of American estates and English country houses landscaped according to informal principles.[31]

Whether fenced or unfenced, front yards were required to present shrubs and trees. Early-nineteenth-century scenes show many houses rising starkly from the street or the landscape, bare of fence or softening plant life. That blank look satisfied neither formal nor landscape gardening principles, and plantings began to appear before an increasing proportion of middling houses. In 1836 John Warner Barber noted of Middletown, Connecticut, that "much taste is displayed by the citizens about their residences, in the collection of choice shrubs and plants"; by implication any residence lacking shrubs and trees failed to show taste.[32]

Lyman Beecher understood this principle when he took his new bride, Roxana, to East Hampton on Long Island in 1799, to a town desolate of culture, lacking even a store for purchasing supplies. Back in Guilford, Connecticut, where she had been raised, Roxana was deeply immersed in eighteenth-century genteel culture. With her friends, she read the latest novels, and at one time announced that her husband must be another Sir Charles Grandison. In East Hampton she spun cotton to make a carpet and painted flowers on it, the first carpet in the town. Later she opened a select school for girls where she taught French, drawing, music, and needlework.

A person of her taste would naturally attack the dooryard. She planted flowers and shrubs; Lyman remembered snowball and catalpa specifically. The minister's wife's example caught the attention of the town. "Others saw this and did the same. The wood-piles were cleared away from the street in front of the houses, and door-yards made pretty, and shade-trees set out. And now you will not find many places prettier in summer than East Hampton." With the help of his wife, Beecher the Christian preacher became an apostle of gentility and the beautification campaign.[33]

The grooming of the foreyard and the painting of the house extended the culture of the parlor outward into the space before the house. With snowballs and catalpa in front, going from the yard outside to the parlor within met no offensive disruptions. Later-nineteenth-century engravings of large farmhouses show ladies with parasols strolling with gentlemen in the paths before the house or approaching in carriages, demonstrating how the grounds around the house had been claimed for gentility. By that time virtually every house had a large piazza on the front of the house, serving as an outdoor parlor with furniture for supporting conversation. By midcentury, piazzas were as fashionable as picket fences or landscaped yards. The obstreperous Widow Bedott, the comical creation of Miriam Berry Whicher, demanded of her hapless new husband, Mr. Sniffles, that he immediately improve his house to make it "fit for ginteel folks to live in." She hated its "humbly yaller" color and wanted it "all painted white, with green winder blinds." Then he was to "build a piazzer in front with four great pillars to't." "*That* would look something *like,* and then I shouldent feel ashamed to have ginteel company come to see me, as I dew now."[34] Less expensive substitutes for piazzas were possible. Andrew Jackson Downing put in "little rustic arbors or covered seats" under the bay windows of a small cottage "to answer in some measure in the place of a veranda, and convey at the first glance, an impression of refinement and taste."[35]

The urge to improve houses in keeping with genteel taste transformed the appearance of once respectable houses that had grown obsolete with the passage of time. William Corbit's grandfather, William Brinton, had constructed a two-story, plain-front brick house in southern Chester County, Pennsylvania, in 1704 that was an immense advance over the cabin his father lived in all his life. But what was an imposing house in 1704 had to be upgraded after a century. Photographs from 1864 and immediately prior to the house's twentieth-century restoration to its 1704 condition show the changes wrought by nineteenth-century taste. The owner in 1820 added a porch that went the full length of the house. By 1864 the porch wrapped

William Brinton's 1704 house went through many transformations in the nineteenth century to make it a respectable dwelling for a middle-class family. The porch and fenced yard extended the refined space outward from the parlor while fixing a boundary between the genteel portions of the house and the working barnyard to the rear.

around two sides of the house, the brick had been painted white, windows had been enlarged, shutters added, and a picket fence enclosed the fore-yard.[36] While no mansion, the house was a fitting residence for a respectable family, displaying the family's undoubted commitment to refined living.

CONTRADICTIONS

TO the scene created by the house, its porch, and its surrounding trees and shrubbery, the architectural authors attributed a mood of calm and retreat. Trees soften the outlines of a house, one claimed, and give an air of protection and retirement. Shrubberies, observed another, "at once the orna-ment most effective to all domestic buildings," were "delightful in the repose they offer in hours of lassitude or weariness." The simple refined house with "moderate court-yard in front," "should wear a most domestic look, and breathe an air of repose and content." On the side of the house should be a porch with lattice "over which vines, by way of drapery, may run; thus combining that sheltered, comfortable, and home-like expression so desir-able in a rural dwelling."[37]

Work went on elsewhere in the house and on the farmstead, but not in the refined parts of the house. One architect recommended an end door for a farmhouse to serve as "the business entrance," to keep that kind of activity away from the front door. The end door was to come off the farm lane, "which should also lead to the barns and shed beyond, not far distant." Another path led to the house. The business part of the farm was not to be hidden; the pictures of the great farmhouses showed the outbuildings and barnyard stretching out behind the house as if the working end of the farmstead was an essential part of the prosperity and respectability the picture conveyed. But the front yard with lawn, trees, and shrubs, the porch, and the house itself were not the regions of business and effort. They were a domestic zone of repose and peaceful contentment.[38]

In all genteel houses, in city and country, the same division occurred. The work of the house, whether done by servants or the mistress of the establish-ment, moved to the rear and the back, out of sight of visitors. Only genteel occupations like sewing, reading, or visiting went on in the parlor and sitting rooms. On the outside, the barns might stand in view of the house, but not immediately adjacent. In their remodeling, the Bixbys moved their barn to the back of their lot away from the house. A generous zone of repose and refinement had to exist at the front, emanating from parlor and stair hall to the porch and then to the foreyard with its softening trees and shrubs. The refined dwelling obviously was the product of work, but business was not to show itself in the genteel portions of the house. Domestic refinement was in this sense a façade that gave to the family an appearance of ease, as if they were truly ladies and gentlemen who had no need to work, while the creation and maintenance of the house was known by all to be the result of intense labor. The parlor and the piazza in effect represented half of the double lives led by the middling people who embraced vernacular gentility.

In actual fact, the calm of the genteel parlor lay at the vortex of a whirlwind of economic activity reaching far beyond the house itself. It began with the farmer, professional man, or merchant who labored to pay for the house, and with the wife and domestics who labored to keep it up. Activity circled out to the builders who constructed the house and the storekeepers and artisans who provided the furnishings, and then to the rising industrial organizations with their armies of workers that came to life to supply the hundreds of thousands of genteel dwellings built, remodeled, and furnished in the first half of the nineteenth century. There were, of course, the huge textile factories that provided the draperies, sheets, napkins, tablecloths, and upholstery stuffs. Beyond these the furnishing of parlor, porch, and yard stimulated scores of lesser enterprises involving carpets, clocks, ceramics, furniture, books, pictures, flowers and shrubs, paint, glazing, wallpaper, tableware, and so on.[39]

One contemporary architectural historian, with only slight exaggeration, traced the economic consequences of one "superior" house in a community. The neighbors look with new eyes on their own houses, he wrote.

> The teaching influence soon shows its effects. The furniture, the internal plenishing and details take a tone from the dwelling. Articles in improved taste are demanded from the country store, or perhaps sent for from the distant city. There are some inquired for by others, and the building of one moderately good house (good in artistic sense) will often occasion the introduction of a thousand commodities of a better taste into a rural community.[40]

With orders coming in from a thousand country towns, merchants and then industrialists soon found cause to step up production and trade, and the domestic market became an object of great interest to the nation's businesses. A large segment of the country's mighty economic machinery started into motion to serve the parlor and its refined surroundings.

Through it all, the genteel house in its idealized conceptualization remained resolutely oblivious to business and work. The parlor and porch, in the rhetoric of refinement, were regions of repose where ease ruled in defiance of the exertions of the economy. The very power of the parlor depended on its naïve purity. The walnut chairs and tables, the finished porcelains, the gilt clocks, the carpets, the flowers and shrubs had no functional use in the world of business. Their productive value was nil. They existed to sustain a life whose virtues contradicted the virtues of work and business. Parlor furnishings stood for repose, polish, economically useless knowledge, beauty, and decorative activity, all pointless in the marketplace and factory. Yet to create a realm where those values presided, vast sums were laid out by hundreds of thousands of families. Regiments of merchants, industrialists, and intellectuals, backed by armies of shopkeepers, artisans, laborers, and peddlers, worked assiduously to meet the parlor's demands.

How did this strange disjuncture come about? What sustained these placid havens of economic inutility? The contradiction between parlor culture and the business culture of the enveloping national economy grew out of the history of the parlor, a history that introduced a deep-seated ambivalence into parlor life. The reason for the disjuncture was that parlors were borrowed from another culture, from royal courts and aristocratic drawing rooms, and did not grow organically from the everyday experiences of the ordinary people who inhabited them.[41] By so borrowing, the middle class introduced into their houses a culture that was alien to their ordinary lives, a culture that valued polish and repose and repudiated work in contrast to the homely, middle-class regard for industry and efficiency. In the aristocratic drawing room, polished manners were the means to advancement in a world of real power; in the middle-class parlor they were an adornment,

Even modest forms of gentility required the accumulation of large numbers of goods. This household, while lacking a carpet and elaborate furniture, has accumulated lots of ceramics, pewter, knives and forks, a clock, and a few books and pictures.

irrelevant to the world of business in farmyard, shop, and factory. Though aristocratic house culture was diluted and transformed in the adaptation to more modest circumstances, the contradictions remained, making the middle-class dwelling under parlor influence a house divided against itself.

The contradiction manifests itself in a hundred details of ordinary life. The transformation of one surface, the floors, for example, suggests the broader ambiguities people constantly endured. Until around 1800, uncarpeted and unfinished broad plank boards served as floors in most houses. Many of the most meticulous housekeepers scattered sand and swept it into patterns with brooms made of twigs bound to sticks. Speaking of her early life in Philadelphia in the eighteenth century, a woman told John Fanning Watson that "a white floor sprinkled with clean white sand, large tables and heavy high back chairs of walnut or mahogany, decorated a parlour genteelly enough for any body."[42]

Around 1800, a new kind of broom came into use that gave a new feel and look to floors. In 1797, Levi Dickinson, an enterprising farmer in Hadley, Massachusetts, planted a small field in broom corn, and after harvest stripped off the seeds and bound the stalks to sticks to sell for brooms. Sales went briskly and by 1833 Hadley manufactured a half million brooms annually. By 1850, Massachusetts broom makers made several million and still fell behind New York's production.[43] Distributed by storekeepers and peddlers, these brooms changed the households they entered. The twig brooms merely swept off larger clods and leaves, leaving a fine silt of dirt on the floor; the broom corn broom swept away everything, leaving a clean surface and establishing a new standard of cleanliness.

Then, in the 1830s and 1840s, the American carpet industry suddenly accelerated its growth.[44] Soft, woven fabric was laid on floors of rooms where there had been only bare planks before. The new floors compelled feet to relate to the surfaces below them in new ways. A carpeted floor was a fitting surface for a gentleman's fine shoe, not for a farmer's boots; a meticulously swept floor, and still more one with a carpet, repelled muddy feet. Feet crossing that threshold had to be transformed as they entered an alien zone of domestic space. The farmer, as a workman wearing muddy boots, was not at home in his own house. In the name of taste and cultivation, an artificial barrier had been erected at the door of his parlor. An 1840 correspondent to *The Cultivator*, an Albany agricultural journal, complained of the expense of the houses whose plans were published in the journal. These costly dwellings did not really serve their residents, for after one was built, the correspondent reported, "we must have a shed behind it, to live in, for we here don't think of living in the front part of our houses, not even to go in at the front door."[45]

A cliché of popular fiction was the fanatic housekeeper, who made life miserable for the men in the family by imposing what Edward Eggleston sardonically called "the wretchedness of civilization."⁴⁶ The humor betrayed the persisting tensions in houses invaded by parlors, a tension that set off an ongoing domestic battle between men and women, but fundamentally grew out of the contradiction between aristocratic parlor refinement and middle-class work.

In Harriet Beecher Stowe's *Oldtown Folks*, the parlor was the preserve of Aunt Lois, a stiff and demanding housekeeper in the bounteous family of her well-to-do farmer father. The house, of course, had "a best room, else wherefore were we on tea-drinking terms with the high aristocracy of Oldtown?" The young boy who narrates the story said the room was "as cold, as uninviting and stately, as devoid of human light or warmth, as the most fashionable shut-up parlor of modern days."

It had the tallest and brightest pair of brass andirons conceivable, and a shovel and tongs to match, that were so heavy that the mere lifting them was work enough, without doing anything with them. It had also a bright-varnished mahogany tea-table, over which was a looking-glass in a gilt frame, with a row of little architectural balls on it; which looking-glass was always kept shrouded in white muslin at all seasons of the year, on account of a tradition that flies might be expected to attack it for one or two weeks in summer.

The family much preferred the kitchen to the best room. "In the kitchen each member of the family had established unto him or her self some little pet private snuggery, some chair or stool, some individual nook,—forbidden to gentility, but dear to the ungenteel natural heart,—that we looked back to regretfully when we were banished to the colder regions of the best room." In the parlor a dozen cherry chairs "with upright backs and griffin feet, each foot terminating in a bony claw, which resolutely grasped a ball," were so high and slippery that "no mortal could ever occupy them except in the exercise of a constant and collected habit of mind." The chairs "preached decorum in the very attitudes which they necessitated."⁴⁷

Aunt Lois wanted to move the family out of the kitchen to the parlor to be ready for high-toned guests should they turn up. "One reason why I wanted to sit in the best room to-night," Aunt Lois insisted when the family resisted, "was that every old tramper and queer object sees the light of our kitchen fire, and comes in for a lounge and a drink; and then, when one has genteel persons calling, it makes it unpleasant." "We all know you're aristo-cratic, Lois," says Bill, a nephew back from college, "but, you see, you can't be indulged." Instead, he teases her, he will take the genteel guests into the parlor, "and show 'em our best chairs, andirons, and mahogany table, and then we can come out and be comfortable."⁴⁸

Aunt Lois nurtured a vision of a genteel society mingling in elegantly furnished rooms purged of vulgar clowns who were capable only of base behavior. This vision of a purely polite society grew from a cultural memory out of an aristocratic past. The whole family shared enough of the vision and memory to create a room filled with the current tokens of genteel culture—mahogany table, brass andirons, gilt mirror, and stuffed and claw-footed cherry chairs—but the incongruities with their ordinary friends and everyday existence made them shun the parlor in favor of the kitchen. They rarely mingled in a polite society and felt ill at ease when they did. The parlor was the pledge of their allegiance to refinement, and they hoped this token gentility would relieve them of the pain of actually sitting there. "They all know we've got a best room," the college boy says jokingly, "and that's enough."[49]

In Stowe's story, the parlor was an alien realm within the otherwise inviting farmhouse, a cold, forbidding place of decorum, stiff formality, and aristocratic pretense. The allure of the aristocratic drawing room was irresistible even for a hearty, down-to-earth family in a small New England village, who knew they must install a parlor to complete the house. But they also knew the best room was foreign territory. Presumably not every family suffered from so much antipathy as the characters in Stowe's exaggerated account. But enough people felt that way for the issue to require resolution.[50] The parlor could not stand in the house like an undigested lump deposited in middling dwellings as an unwonted remnant of another class and culture. The forbidding formality of the room had to be softened, warmed, and made compatible with its surroundings.

In writings on the house, the single pervasive word representing the desired direction of change was "comfort." Let's visit the parlor, Bill said to Aunt Lois, see the "chairs, andirons, and mahogany table, and then we can come out and be comfortable." That one word summed up the lack in Aunt Lois's parlor. Comfort and fashion stood at opposite poles in the domestic moral economy, and the aim of parlor reform was to introduce comfort into the best and least inviting room in the house. John Fanning Watson caught up the issue in a sentence when he observed that "the fact is, we are ashamed to be comfortable, lest we should appear ungenteel."[51]

COMFORT

NINETEENTH-CENTURY critics did not invent the word "comfort." It came into common usage in reference to houses in the late eighteenth century when the English gentry extolled the pleasures of comfortable country living in contrast to the glitter of life at court.[52] Comfort was a gentry value before adoption by the middle class. The word seemed suitable to set the tone of ordinary houses in the nineteenth century, because from the start comfort was placed in opposition to the brilliance of aristocratic drawing rooms. Beyond the physical side of comfort—warmth, good food, restful chairs, and accessible conveniences—comfort implied a moral condition achieved through retirement from the bustle of high life and retreat into wholesome domesticity. An observer of the Philadelphia social scene in the 1790s, when the federal government resided in the city, complained of the profligacy of entertainments. "There have been a good many delightful parties, and I have been at Chew's, McKean's, Clymer's, Dallas's, Bingham's, and a dozen other houses lately," he wrote an acquaintance. "Among your more particular friends," he observed, however, "there is more quiet and comfort, and it is not impossible that the most truly respectable people are least heard of." Quiet and comfort, he implied, were superior to the endless round of parties.[53]

Abigail Adams did not use the word "comfort," but referred to the same idea when she wrote John:

> I well know that real, true and substantial happiness depend not upon titles, Rank and fortune; the Gay coach, the Brilliant attire, the pomp and Etiquet of Courts, rob the mind of that placid harmony, that social intercourse which is an Enemy to ceremony. My Ambition, my happiness centers in him, who sighs for domestick enjoyments, amidst all the world calls happiness—who partakes not in the jovial Feast, or joins the Luxurious table, without turning his mind to the plain unadulterated food which covers his own frugal Board, and sighs for the Feast of reason and the flow of soul.[54]

Comfort drew its power from association with the substantial happiness of domestic enjoyments contrasted to pomp, rank, fortune, etiquette, and ceremony. The middle class seized upon the word fortuitously, for in the name of comfort the humble and obscure could present their claims to an honorable existence against the overwhelming pretenses of the polite assemblages that shone so brilliantly in the palaces of the mighty.

In nineteenth-century usage, comfort was the antidote to aristocratic pretense and to all forms of fashionable display. An article in *Ballou's Pictorial Drawing-Room Companion* in 1855 featured a picture of a homely New England sitting room and applauded the many homesteads "which yet exist, remote from cities and large towns, in all their primitive purity and attractiveness. . . . We do not look with jaundiced eyes upon a brilliant ball-room, crowded with graceful forms . . . but it is a relief sometimes to turn away from the contemplation of the highest social refinement and splendor, and see how comfortable and happy people may be with a few wants and no luxuries."[55]

In Solon Robinson's *How to Live: Saving and Wasting, or, Domestic Economy Illustrated by the Life of Two Families of Opposite Character, Habits, and Practices*, the misled Doolittle family left their little farm "surrounded with country comforts" for the city, where they bought an overdecorated house at a price they could not afford and ruined themselves and their children. They enjoyed none of the comforts that the Saverys, their counterparts on the good side, acquired at little expense by industry and rational planning.[56] In Robinson's account, city life was the antithesis of sensible and comfortable living.

Lewis Allen, in *Rural Architecture*, told of a family that moved from city to country, but mistakenly took the city with them. On the floor in the parlor "was a Wilton carpet, too fine to stand on; around the room were mahogany sofas and mahogany chairs, all too fine to sit on—at all events to *rest* one upon if he were fatigued." "On the center and side tables were all sorts of gimcracks, costly and worthless. In short, there was no *comfort* about the whole concern." Allen rebuked his friend for assembling "all your town nonsense about you," and urged him to give away the furniture to some of his "town friends," and "get some simple, comfortable, cottage furniture." Why "ape the fashion, and the frivolity of the butterflies of town life?" Allen asked. "It is a folly into which many are imperceptibly gliding, and which, if not reformed, will ultimately lead to great discomfort to themselves, and ruin to their families."[57]

In Allen's account and in virtually all the discourse on these themes, "comfort" was a punishing word, with a double-edged hostility attached to it. The idea of comfort was used to disparage the frivolities of "butterflies of the town" and empty aristocratic grandeur, and at the same time to rebuke the pretenses of plain people who foolishly tried to imitate the fashionable. Though meaning to promote the true worth of middle-class life over the shallow pleasures of gay society, the critics as often as not turned against middle-class people themselves for exceeding their proper bounds. Stowe did not write against the aristocracy, but against Aunt Lois, who tried to imitate them.[58] Comfort defined both the merits and the limits of vernacular gentility.

All beauty and gentility need not be removed from the parlor to make it comfortable. The Saverys in Solon Robinson's story practiced every economy and conformed their lives perfectly to the logic of comfort, yet when the father came home in the evening, they immediately sat down to tea using a service that "was rich, though very plain. The sugar bowl, cream jug, spoons, and forks were all silver." The Savery parents valued teatime with their children as "a proper place to teach them politeness." When Salinda, the heroine of the story who learned housekeeping from Mrs. Savery, married and moved to a house of her own, she quickly ordered a carpet for the parlor.[59] "Your house ought not to look mean and common," said Harriet Beecher Stowe's Christopher Crowfield, "your house ought to look beautiful."[60] The advice manuals did not repudiate gentility altogether, but showed how to achieve it at moderate cost without sacrificing comfort. They aimed toward a modest and fitting gentility, purged of fashion and pretense, and so made suitable for ordinary people.

The ideal of comfort assumed that the parlor served a different purpose from its predecessor, the drawing room. No one had talked of making drawing rooms comfortable. Drawing rooms were intended to be the settings of entertainments, teas, and polite conversation, never as places for relaxed leisure. People were to be at ease, to be sure, but not relaxed. At polite entertainments people strove to shine, showing to best advantage their wit, complaisance, physical grace, and fine manners. They held themselves erect precisely as the claw-footed cherry chairs in Aunt Lois's parlor demanded. Decorum governed all.

Comfort, on the other hand, imbued the parlor with the spirit of repose. Lewis Allen objected to the town furniture in his friend's country house because it did not invite one to rest if he was fatigued, implying that comfortable parlors were for physical ease, not the practiced ease of manner that the eighteenth-century gentry valued. The nineteenth century substituted the word "repose" for the eighteenth-century "ease" as the desired ambience of genteel spaces in ordinary houses. Parlor reformers wished to shift the parlor from a place of entertainment toward a room for living during one's leisure moments. They sometimes called it a living room. Calvert Vaux said that "all that appears to be necessary for real comfort in a villa or cottage residence, exclusive of the bedrooms and offices, is a parlor of tolerable size, which shall be the general living-room of the family, and another apartment contiguous to, or connecting with it, to be used as a breakfast and dining room."[61]

Vaux's statement reveals the tendency for family to displace company as the primary users of the genteel rooms in the house. The family objected to Aunt Lois's stiff parlor because it was reserved for company and had no appeal for the family itself. Many people considered it foolish to set aside a company room in an ordinary household. Vaux complained of the elaborately decorated best room with the door tightly shut, "always ready for— what? for daily use? Oh, no; it is in every way too good for that. For weekly use? No, not even for that—but for *company* use; and thus the choice room, with the pretty view, is sacrificed, to keep up a conventional show of finery that pleases no one." In his opinion, "all this is absurd. No room in any house, except, perhaps, in a very large mansion, ought to be set apart for company use only. If a reception-room for strangers is needed, it should be a small, unpretending room, certainly not the most agreeably situated apartment in the house, *which should be enjoyed daily.*"

Writing in 1856, Vaux, the architectural reformer, spoke as if many disagreed with his preference for a family living room, and likely the ideal of a formal company parlor prevailed in most middle-class houses to the end of the century and beyond. Vaux told of a tenant who shocked his landlady when he proposed to use a back parlor for a dining room. " 'All the best families,' she said, 'lived in the basement. Why use such a beautiful parlor merely for an *eating* room.' "[62] In the same spirit, Solon Robinson's Salinda put her best carpet in the parlor and then furnished another room on a slightly lesser scale for the family to occupy most of the time.[63] But under the influence of the comfort ideal there was a pull toward opening the parlor to the family. A properly regulated family could feel as much at home in the parlor as they did in the sitting room or library, especially if limited means made both a parlor and a sitting room impractical. Because gentility had enlarged its sphere to include refined family activities, it was not incongruous for children and parents to sit around the table in the parlor with an astral lamp lighting the room. Reading and sewing harmonized with the refined decorations of the best room.

In fact, the family circle, gathered to write letters, read, sew, sing, or talk, came to be thought of as the characteristic genteel gathering for the middle class in the nineteenth century. These homey gatherings were in marked contrast to the select company of the eighteenth-century gentry assembled for polite entertainments. Even in informal moments, this refined family was worthy of a beautiful environment. The older ideal of a room dedicated solely to formal entertainment gave way to the combination of the comfort ideal and refined family activity and so opened the parlor door to family life.

The critics specified surprisingly few actual changes to make parlors more comfortable. Sofas and chairs were commonly attacked for being too high, hard, and slippery. Formal rooms were criticized if they lacked ventilation, warmth, and light. But the main complaint was that the formal rooms were not inviting. The carpets were too fine to stand on, the chairs too fancy to sit on, the "gimcracks" on tables and mantels too costly and fragile. The very polish and refinement of the room required a stiff decorum unnatural for middling people. The remnants of the old courtly style kept ordinary people from relaxing in their own parlors.[64]

The one specific furniture form that came to symbolize the relaxation of parlor decorum under the domesticating influence of comfort was the rocking chair. The rocker was a nineteenth-century and primarily American contribution to parlor furnishings. The eighteenth-century turn toward comfort resulted in the easy chair, the upholstered, padded armchair that appeared in a few American inventories in the first half of the century and then more commonly among the wealthiest in the second half. Because of its expense, the easy chair was beyond the means of ordinary people in the first part of the nineteenth century, but the rocking chair served the same purpose.

Both the easy chair and the rocking chair implied a relaxation of the stiff upright stance earlier required of ladies and gentlemen. The two chair types allowed the legs to be crossed, one of the marks of the new easiness cultivated in the eighteenth century.[65] The rocker and the easy chair permitted sitters to lean back or slump slightly, forbidden indulgences by the older standard. Because the easy chairs were so far out of keeping with standard postures, historians once thought that they were reserved for the elderly or convalescent and used mainly in bedrooms in the eighteenth century. Initially they were, but evidence indicates that later in the eighteenth century they appeared in parlors and enjoyed a wider usage.[66]

The rocking chair, which came after the easy chair, allowed further relaxation of posture.[67] Leaning back and totally relaxing the spine, along with the lulling back-and-forth motion of the rocker, were anathema to the posture code of the earlier dancing masters. In 1838, Harriet Martineau, the caustic English traveler, thought rocking despicable. "How this lazy and ungraceful indulgence ever became general, I cannot imagine; but the nation seems wedded to it."[68] Initially the rocker does seem to have been reserved for the elderly and the ill, whose bodily decrepitude gave them license to let their bodies give way. The immense popularity of rockers after 1830—the Boston rocker may have been the most popular chair style ever known in America—suggests they were used much more widely soon after that time.[69] In Jacob Abbott's 1839 volume, *Rollo Learning to Read*, Rollo, hearing that his father will soon be home, "went and took hold of the great rocking-chair, to pull it to the fire for his father."[70] Even so, in portraits and pictures of domestic interiors, rockers were reserved for the elderly. Adults in their prime wished not to appear in rockers, which suggests that some shame was still associated with such bodily indulgence.[71]

Rocking chairs eventually found their way into the parlor despite the contradiction with older genteel codes. In 1827, Mrs. Henry Ridgely, it will be remembered, asked her daughter in Philadelphia to order one. "I wish you to try your taste and skill in the purchase of a handsome rocking chair, I wish it gilt and finished suitably for a Parlour."[72] The combination of gilt and rocking seems incongruous, combining the most high-toned finish and the most relaxed posture, but the rocker was actually a representative form. A gilt rocking chair embodied the melding of the two ideals that were flowing together in middle-class parlors, comfort and gentility.

Advertisements for rockers played upon both values. A Washington, D.C., ad in 1830 said the maker's rockers "combine in a peculiar manner, both Elegance and Ease," and another promoted patented spring-seat rocking chairs, "combining comfort and splendor."[73] The refined rocker stood for the changes going on in the vernacular parlor as the American middle classes, guided by the ideal of comfort, tried to assimilate parlor culture into the modest domestic economies of ordinary people.

PARLORS AND CLASS

THE spread of parlor culture was one of the great democratic movements of the nineteenth century. In making parlors for themselves, great
masses of people laid claim to cultural power never accessible before. In
the eighteenth century, the purchase of scattered items like teacups or
silver spoons connected their owners with the high culture of the gentry
and reflected an urge to participate in the cultural life of the rulers of
society. But the mass of the people beyond the scattering of gentlemen
and ladies in each place still looked in on genteel society as outsiders.
Genteel culture was not theirs, but the culture of their superiors in society
and government. Everyone else observed, admired, envied, or resented the
elite, powerless to do more.

The construction of parlors in ordinary houses in the nineteenth century
changed this relationship. A parlor set off as a place for company with even
rudimentary parlor furnishings meant that the people in the house were
attempting to embrace gentility as their own, to possess it rather than to
observe it. They invariably fell short of the mark, assimilating genteel values
only sporadically, sometimes resisting the awkward constrictions, and often
looking ridiculous to the more practiced elites above them. But at those
times when middling people strove to be refined, however awkward and
reluctant the effort, they made the culture of the court, the aristocracy, and
the colonial gentry their own. In making parlors in their houses, the people
implicitly claimed the right to live like rulers.[74]

The presence of a parlor did not make the modest cottage dweller the
equal of the resident of a great villa. The midcentury architectural authors
who included a parlor in virtually every house plan, for mechanics and
farmers as well as for merchants and lawyers, were acutely conscious of
levels of housing. They organized their books by social rank, usually going
from bottom to top, and labeling each plan according to the social class for
which it was designed. They were quite explicit about what was appropriate
for the rich and what for the poor, as if houses were meant to mark social
ranks rather than to amalgamate people into a single unified society.

Andrew Jackson Downing divided country houses into three clear ranks,
cottages for mechanics and workingmen, farmhouses for well-off farmers
whose accommodations "must be plain but more spacious," and villas for
"the man of easy income, who builds a villa as much to gratify his taste, as
to serve the useful purposes of a dwelling."[75] The architectural authors
brushed aside the undemocratic implications of ranked housing. "A man of
mark," Lewis Allen wrote, "should, if he live in the country, occupy a
dwelling somewhat indicating the position which he holds, both in society
and in public affairs. By this remark, we may be treading on questionable

ground, in our democratic country; but, practically, there is a fitness in it which no one can dispute."[76]

Notwithstanding the existence of ranks, these divisions in society did not imply a division in culture. The architectural books are equally explicit about the common values binding top to bottom. The rich man's villa stood on a larger property, was adorned with more elaborate decorations, and was elaborated into many more rooms. But all the houses in the book shared one value—beauty. The realm of beauty and taste knew no bounds. The farmer's cottage could exhibit taste as surely as the rich man's mansion, and in the end be as pleasing in its own way.

In designing a cottage, the architect was "bound down by rigid notions of economy, and must bring all the accommodation within very narrow limits," Downing wrote. "It does not follow, however, that tasteful cottages cannot be designed." "There are tens of thousands of working-men in this country, who now wish to give something of beauty and interest to the simple forms of cottage life; there are many of these who are desirous to have their home of three rooms tasteful and expressive, no less than among those whose dwellings number thirty rooms."[77]

The architectural critics seem to have derived as much pleasure from proving that a simple house could be beautiful as in displaying the magnificence of the most elaborate residence. The very inclusion of the cottage plans in the same book with mansion plans indicated the author's conviction that both participated in a single culture, that of beauty and refinement. "Every artisan, cultivator, or trader, may, if he think fit," Calvert Vaux wrote, "not only be an honest, industrious republican, but a thoughtful, noble, and refined worker." An "all-encircling civilization" was "within reach of every class."[78]

The great divide in American society as refinement diffused into the middling ranks lay not between the small and great parlor houses, but between houses with parlors and those with none. The confidence of the architectural authors that no house was too humble to be beyond the reach of good taste did not mean that parlor culture had entered into every dwelling in the land. Vaux thought that people's houses frequently showed that their "capacity of enjoyment, and the appreciation of what is really desirable in life," was wanting. "Each of these bare, bald, white cubes tells its monotonous story of a youth passed with little or no cultivation of the higher natural perceptions, and of a system of education in which the study of the beautiful in its most simple elements is neglected and apparently despised."[79]

While so vague an idea as refinement, even when measured by the presence of a parlor, is probably beyond accurate quantification, it is entirely possible that half the houses in the country fell outside the realm of vernacular gentility at midcentury. Olmsted's description of southern cabins, Edward Eggleston's depiction of Hoosier country, Timothy Flint's western record, and innumerable novels, journals, and travel accounts fill the land with plain cabins devoid of elaborate furnishings and inhabited by people with little desire for refinement. Living in such quarters, the inhabitants were beyond the pale, the people of another order, truly the lower class, excluded from the national culture enveloping the middling orders of America.

This benighted group was not forgotten by those who rose to the simple refinements of vernacular gentility. A vulgar population in the back streets and backcountry presented a problem to the enlarging middling orders in American society. Coarse living in rude dwellings repelled people who were trying to bring refinement into their homes and their lives. The boorish people in cabins and tenements stood for all that people on the lower edges of refinement were trying to escape and consequently hated most.

On the other hand, crude cabin dwellers were recognizable as their own neighbors or as family—of a previous generation or a collateral line. They were the offensive country cousins, but cousins nonetheless. Managing this ambiguous relationship called for delicacy and tact. An essay originally published in *The American Agriculturalist* on how to eat with a fork rather than a knife suggested the restraint that was required. "Now in polite society," the

This scene of domestic happiness in a modest house without carpet or curtains includes touches of refinement—the flowers at the window and a bookshelf on the wall, sure signs that gentility was to be found in these humble circumstances.

essay gently informed farm readers, "it is considered . . . an offense against propriety to use the knife for any other purpose than to cut the food." "To use the knife and not the fork betrays want of association with refined life." The author addressed these instructions to the young, but at the same time cautioned readers not "to be troubled because your father or mother choose to retain the habits of their childhood. They have a right to do so, and no child has a right to treat them with any less respect or reverence because of it." The young reader was asked to put aside the vulgar practice of eating with a knife without scoffing at his own parents who followed the old ways.[80] And so with the middle class generally; as they moved toward refinement themselves, they could not without pain of conscience turn their backs on the vulgar populace.

In the contest of conflicting impulses, the desire to flee vulgarity was for some overcome by a stronger urge to reform the lower orders. Rather than widening the distance between themselves and the coarse population below them, these apostles of refinement sought to proselytize the lower orders. As they came to recognize the deepening cultural divide in American society, middle-class social critics transmuted genteel conventions into universal moral principles and tried to convert everyone.

The task of instructing the unenlightened poor took on the air of a crusade. Refinement and moral improvement were blended into a single gospel of beauty, manners, and good order and taken to the rough population that had not yet learned polite conduct and the value of beauty. The architectural authors wrote as emissaries of good taste, bringing beauty and comfort to mechanics, farmers, and even laborers at the lowest levels of society, through house plans that facilitated the practice of parlor culture.

Even more evangelically, Catharine Maria Sedgwick, in three immensely popular novels published in 1835, 1836, and 1837, *Home, The Poor Rich Man, and the Rich Poor Man,* and *Live and Let Live,* tried to persuade readers that simple refinement was within the reach of everyone. *Harper's* observed at the time of Sedgwick's death in 1867 that the three volumes were "one of the most popular series of works ever published," suggesting the widespread interest in the issue among the literate middle class, if not the poor themselves.[81]

Sedgwick regretted that gentility was dividing society in contradiction to the American principle of equality. "There is nothing that tends more to the separation into classes," Mr. Barclay, the hero of *Home,* tells an acquaintance, "than difference of manners. This is a badge that all can see." Differences in manners weighed on children because manners were so visible. "There is no sort of inferiority about which young people suffer more than that of manners. There are other things certainly far more important, but this is for ever before their eyes, pressing on their observation,—is seen and felt at every turn." Mr. Barclay dreamed of a "new state of things," where differences were erased and society was thoroughly egalitarian. Although he believed that "genteel" was "a vulgar word that ought to be banished from an American's vocabulary," equality was not to be achieved by overlooking gentility. The point of the book was to spread refinement.

Through Barclay, the manager of a printing shop in New York City, Sedgwick showed that gentility was within reach of everyone. In the model household that he and his wife set up in New York, all the key elements of refined living were achieved on a modest budget. By practicing frugality and avoiding ornamental furniture, Barclay furnished his house with all that was needed for comfort and with plenty of good books. His children not only read, they played the flute and piano, studied with a drawing master, and took dancing lessons. When an acquaintance queried Barclay on the advisability of dancing for children of a printer, Barclay at first said it was good exercise for children confined by city living, but then betrayed his interest in less practical matters by adding that "there is nothing that conduces more to ease and grace, than learning to dance." "I do not wish my boys to suffer as I have from blundering into a room," Barclay goes on, "and feeling when I had to bow to half a dozen gentlemen and ladies, as if I had to run a muck." Far from laying aside gentility, Barclay's picture of his boys entering a room went back to the guidebooks for courtiers and gentlemen of two centuries earlier. In his little house in New York, Barclay was making gentlemen of his sons.[82]

The Barclay girls made the beds, swept the floors, and cooked with energy and goodwill, taking on these tasks not as onerous duties to be patiently borne but as fulfilling and interesting work. Still, when the evening came, and the family assembled around the table in the parlor, the girls took up parlor activities with the same alacrity. "Nor were they in the least disqualified by these household duties for more refined employments; and when they assembled in the evening, with their pretty work-boxes and fancy-work, their books and drawing, they formed a group to grace any drawing-room in the land."

It was a fantastic republican vision of every parlor in every American house training young ladies to grace drawing rooms, while the young men learned how to enter such rooms like gentlemen. The Barclays' parlor was scarcely large enough to turn around in, as they admitted themselves when they moved in, yet Sedgwick believed that under proper management it could serve as a training ground for young Americans to become ladies and gentlemen.[83]

In *The Poor Rich Man, and the Rich Poor Man*, the Aikin family, worthy members of the "lower orders," lived so poorly they could not afford a parlor. The front room in the house was kitchen, bedroom, and parlor combined. Yet they put up a bookshelf and tried to "cultivate their own and their children's minds." In the climax of the story, a wealthy philanthropist offers the Aikins what Sedgwick believed to be the most useful of all bequests, a better house, which is to say one with a true parlor. The Aikins were ready. "Parlour!" exclaims one of the children when they hear the news; "are we going to have a parlour? Oh, that's what mother has been making the new carpet for?" When they come upon books in a bookcase, "the children crowded round, and eagerly took down the books." They had long been holding small "sociables" in their old tenement, ready for transfer to the new dwelling. " 'How nice,' exclaimed Anne, 'this parlour will be for our "sociables!" ' "[84] The Aikins were a parlor family before they had a parlor, and thus Sedgwick demonstrated that manners need not divide America. Refinement could seep to the bottommost layers of society and erase the differences that divided people into classes. An egalitarian society could be achieved through refinement.

By opening vernacular gentility to everyone, Sedgwick's democratic vision of a ubiquitous parlor culture seemingly laid to rest her anxiety about growing class divisions. In one sense it was a generous, inclusive vision; in another it was severely exclusive. It would have been more tolerant and inclusive if Sedgwick could have taken to heart Mr. Barclay's opinion that gentility should be banished from the American vocabulary. But that was impossible. The lower orders could be accepted into American society only after they learned good manners. "I cannot blame a gentleman for not asking a clown to his table," Barclay says, "who will spit over his carpet, and mortify himself and annoy every body else with his awkwardness."

In the country where Barclay moved after retirement, society was more open than in the city, but even there Barclay would admit an ignorant man to his company only "provided he does not offend against the usages of civilized society." He offered the example of a common farmer who merited admission to polite society because he had "some acquaintance with science, draws beautifully, and writes graceful verses." Sedgwick had characters in the novel raise objections about the scarcity of such accomplished mechanics and farmers, to which she spoke of better home education and the refining influence of a few good families. But mainly she laid the responsibility on the lower orders themselves. "It will be our own fault," Barclay told his friend, "if, in our land, society as well as government is not organized upon a new foundation. But we must secure, by our own efforts, the elevations that are now accessible to all."

The consequence of claiming that refinement could be achieved at any income level was to place the blame for vulgarity on the vulgar themselves. "It is the fault of the mechanic, if he takes a place not assigned to him by the government and institutions of his country. He is of the *lower orders,* only when he is self-degraded by the ignorance and coarse manners, which are associated with manual labor in countries where society is divided into castes."[85]

Despite Sedgwick's egalitarian and compassionate impulses, she could not overcome her conviction that gentility was founded on universal and eternal principles. She admitted that whether one ate with a fork or a knife was mere convention, but picking one's teeth and leaning back in a chair were intolerable, actions in which the Barclay children would never in the world indulge. She could not possibly envision an America where egalitarianism required the toleration of rude behavior at such extremes.[86] Her prescription for ending class inequalities was not to moderate the influence of parlor culture but to enhance it, to bring parlor virtues to every family in the land. In the meantime, while the difference in manners still existed, the people without refinement were rightfully and necessarily excluded.

Ironically, the diffusion of parlors created a homogeneous and roughly democratic national culture for those who subscribed, and at the same time excluded the broad mass of people who did not. People who spat upon carpets or handled themselves awkwardly had no place in the parlors of people who had learned good manners.

Never had the coarse population enjoyed significant access to polite society, no more in the eighteenth than in the nineteenth century. But in the eighteenth, when gentility was the culture of the elite, the middling and lower orders looked on together from the outside. The great divide between polished and crude left everyone below the rank of gentleman with a common culture. In the nineteenth century, as refinement spread downward and the middling orders assimilated a diluted refinement of their own, the great divide between polite and coarse isolated the lower orders on the margins of American culture. Cultural class lines were not more severely drawn, but because they separated the lower from the middling orders rather than the gentry from all the rest, they were more humiliating.

Catharine Sedgwick's well-meaning attempt to show compassion for the lower orders only betrayed her scorn for "self-degrading" mechanics and farmers who failed to raise themselves to her standards of refinement. Because parlor ideals commanded the middle-class moral imagination so completely, it was difficult for anyone who had been touched by refinement not to shun those who failed to appreciate the beauties of parlor life. Without anyone so intending, the unwonted consequence of the democratic movement to spread parlor culture was to draw an indelible line between the middle and lower classes in American society and to make rudeness a cause for shame.

CHAPTER IX

Literature and Life

IN Catharine Maria Sedgwick's novel *Home*, Mr. Barclay, the artisan who moved with his family into a modest house in the city, resisted the temptation to purchase a fancy Swiss clock and with the savings bought books. This was the "one luxury," Sedgwick wrote, "which long habit and well cultivated taste had rendered essential to happiness,—a book-case filled with well selected and well bound volumes." Later the story looked in on the Barclays gathered "round a well-lighted table." While Mrs. Barclay sewed and the children drew and worked on projects, Mr. Barclay "was reading aloud the Life of Franklin, and making now and then such remarks as would tend to impress its valuable instruction on his children."[1]

Books had long had a place in refined households. A particular species of books—courtesy books—had for centuries helped the refining population to polish their personalities. The handbooks of behavior listed the rules of proper conduct for the benefit of people who were unable to learn directly from the examplars of refinement at court. But in Mr. Barclay's household, other books were read and for another purpose: they expressed a cultivated taste, Sedgwick noted, and likely were also intended to develop that taste. The choice of Franklin's *Autobiography* suggests that Barclay (and Sedgwick) wished to instruct the character of the children as much as cultivate their minds, but refined households placed equal emphasis on mental culture, a term that came into frequent use after 1800. The primary reason for refined people to read, beyond all practical benefits, was to enhance their mental culture.

The reading matter to aid this endeavor vastly increased in the first half of the nineteenth century. Authors multiplied their efforts, printers turned out inexpensive editions, libraries were organized in big cities and small towns, and periodicals were distributed throughout the land. There was an explosion of print, and much of it was intended to help the improving population better their minds.

Of all the forms of print pouring from the presses, sentimental fiction played the most critical part in the extension of refinement to the middle class. The influence of sentimental fiction was not a new development in the propagation of refinement; in the eighteenth century, novels had joined forces with courtesy books to spread information about genteel behavior. Richardson's *Sir Charles Grandison, Pamela,* and *Clarissa* were handbooks of refinement for American readers. If anything, nineteenth-century fiction was less influential as compared with the earlier novels, largely because of the later authors' own ambivalence. Did fiction elevate its readers or not? Sedgwick would not have given Mr. Barclay a novel to read to his children; they required more meaty fare. And yet Sedgwick herself was a novel writer. The contradictions were there to perplex readers, but they did not stanch the flow of sentimental fiction. The volume increased immensely in the first half of the century, continuing the Richardson tradition of instruction in genteel conduct.

Sentimental fiction moved immediately to the center of the refining process. The stories engaged the central problem of the period: how to adapt genteel values to middle-class life. In these years, architects and carpenters installed parlors in ordinary houses, bringing a faint touch of the aristocratic drawing room to middle-class dwellings. In the same fashion, fiction writers redesigned genteel manners and values for use by housewives, farmers, businessmen, and clerks.

Their efforts at adaptation can be summed up in the word "domestication." Authors of sentimental fiction made aristocratic gentility accessible by domesticating it. The stories transplanted refinement from balls and assemblies, the sites of brilliant entertainments, to homes. Refined lives were lived in parlors and sitting rooms like Mr. Barclay's, occupied by children and friends rather than by assemblages of brilliant women and notable men. The writers infused refinement with love and moral values, just as the architectural authors had placed comfort above polish in furnishing houses. By domesticating refinement, the writers were able to make gentility an essential element of the respectability for which every middle-class family yearned.

The domestication of gentility had the effect of putting women at the center of genteel performances. Women wrote much of the sentimental fiction, and women were the leading characters. Their upbringings, their courtships, their motherhood, while not driving men from the scene, figured more prominently than before. Women became leading figures in the stories just as they were taking over leadership of domestic affairs in the house. The writers of sentimental fiction thus confronted the constraints, the contradictions, and the promises of life for refined women in the first half of the nineteenth century, and ultimately, as we shall see, did battle for them in the plots of the stories.

MENTAL CULTURE

ALL the guides to respectable living put books on the shelves and had people reading alone or to each other. In a common scene from a well-ordered household, "William Hamilton is reading aloud, and the soft light of the astral lamp falls upon a circle of young faces, that gather round the centre table." The Savery children in Solon Robinson's *How to Live* loved books, and the heroines of virtually every romance were notable not only for beauty and grace but for minds cultivated by reading.[2] A writer in an agricultural almanac confronted farmers with the fact that compared with members of the learned professions and merchants, the farmer was "looked upon as an inferior man." The reason was simple: "Ignorance, ignorance; nothing but ignorance of the grossest kind has caused their elevation and our shame." The writer understood "how hard it is to earn one's bread and make any progress in literary pursuits at the same time," but he thought that the farmer might read during some wasted moments.[3] In the same vein, housewives were told they "must find time to read." "If she finds herself pressed for time, she can put one flounce less on her dress, or economize her fancy needle-work in some other way."[4]

No single item was more essential to a respectable household than a collection of books, and no activity more effectual for refinement and personal improvement than reading.[5] Good books left a mark on a person that could never be mistaken. A turn of the plot in a story printed in a Wilmington, Delaware, newspaper required Frederick, the hero, to disguise himself as a simple peasant with a red wig and a slouch hat. He happened into the cottage of a learned gentleman in reduced circumstances and asked for a night's lodging. Hearing but two sentences from the hero's lips, the gentleman penetrated the disguise. Noting the gentleman's glance, "Frederick knew it was too late to affect ignorance of literature."[6] Books had so shaped Frederick's manners that his refinement could not be concealed from a knowing observer, no matter how rustic the appearances.

Salinda, Solon Robinson's heroine, meets Sam Whitlock fresh from work on his farm. He was rough as a bear with long beard and dirty from his farm work, "yet when introduced to Salinda, in her eyes, he dropped all the roughness of the farm, for she only saw and heard, a most polite well-bred gentleman, well read, and full of intelligence upon every subject."[7] Reading and manners made Sam a gentleman no matter how he looked, a hopeful thought for farmers ashamed of their rude appearance.

Like so much else in nineteenth-century vernacular gentility, the exaltation of books came from earlier traditions of cultivation. Reading was not exclusively or primarily a genteel value growing out of life at the Renaissance courts, but it early blended with those cultural influences. By the eighteenth century, reading had become an inseparable part of refinement. Isaac Watts's 1741 volume, *On the Improvement of the Mind*, contained a chapter entitled "Of Books and Reading."[8] One of the nineteenth century's perennial favorites, going through thirty-five editions between 1800 and 1850, was an eighteenth-century story, "Little Goody Two-Shoes," first published in 1765 and attributed to Oliver Goldsmith. Goody Two-Shoes was a little girl impoverished and left to the mercies of the world when her parents died prematurely; her name came from her delight at having two shoes after a time with no shoes or one. But her chief accomplishment was learning to read. By virtue of what she learned from books, she rose to become a schoolteacher and eventually the wife of a gentleman. By the late eighteenth century it seemed perfectly plausible that by reading alone a little girl could so refine herself that she would be worthy of marrying a fine gentleman.[9]

With so much being said in their favor, books, more than any other possessions, came to identify cultivated people, rivaling parlors as symbols of refinement. To own books implied sensibility, taste, even polish. Books placed and defined their owners. Literature, it was believed, ingrained refined habits into the minds, hearts, and speech of readers, making books the purest symbols of true refinement. Portrait painters depicted their sitters with their fingers in the pages of books, as if they had just looked up from reading; or the painters placed books on the tables, where they were easily accessible to the sitters.

One measure of serious devotion to books was the purchase of a bookcase, not just to hold books but to display them. Though doubtless many more households possessed books than owned bookcases, in Chester County, Pennsylvania, the proportion of houses with bookcases rose sharply over a century. In the decade from 1750 to 1759, less than 1 percent of the estates inventoried listed a bookcase or desk with bookcase. In the years from 1840 to 1849, over 8 percent did, nearly a ninefold increase.[10] Visitors to these houses knew at a glance of the family's commitment to mental culture. In 1860 the Bureau of the Census considered books a sufficiently significant index of civilization to ask for the number of libraries in each state and the number of books each possessed.[11]

Among a number of economic offshoots of the exaltation of reading, the gift-book industry turned the devotion to books into a profitable business aimed at the young-woman market. Following English and still earlier

French and German models, Carey and Lea, the Philadelphia publishers, brought out *The Atlantic Souvenir* in 1825, an annual containing sentimental poetry, fiction, and moral essays, liberally illustrated with elaborate engravings. The annuals were intended initially as Christmas or New Year's gifts but soon were advertised for all seasons. *The Atlantic Souvenir* was immensely successful, rising to a circulation of 10,000 by 1832 and soon widely imitated.

Ralph Thomson, the bibliographer of gift-book annuals, listed 469 of them, but estimated that there were actually over 1,000 different annuals published between 1825 and 1860. A number of these annuals sold as many as 7,500 copies per issue. Some annuals cost as little as thirty-seven and a half cents; others went as high as twenty dollars. Ordinarily they were priced between two and three dollars, a high price for a book at that time. The gift-book annuals were among the finest examples of nineteenth-century printing. The steel or copper engravings and occasional lithographs were printed on high-quality paper, and they were commonly bound in heavy, embossed covers, and later in varnished paper-mâché with inlaid mother-of-pearl. Presumably the books deserved lavish attention because belles lettres were so highly valued. The contents were rarely distinguished, but giving such a book, with its "Gems of Prose and Poetry," implied the giver's commitment to refinement through literature and a presumption of the recipient's taste for the pleasures of mental culture.[12]

In this elegant sitting room, the married pair occupy their evening by reading to each other.

Perhaps because reading held so much promise for improvement and advancement, middle-class authors gave it nearly an unconditional endorsement. No matter what other personal gifts a woman had, she was not complete without "mental culture" achieved through study. In an 1839 story in *Godey's Lady's Book*, a young girl from a remote village was so beautiful and gracious and so accomplished a musician that she won the heart of a distinguished older gentleman. Realizing at once the deficiencies of her education, she applied herself to the books in his study, and "at the end of two or three years, she had changed from a childish, thoughtless, though lovely girl, to a woman of refinement and intelligence."[13]

One of the guiding principles of the immensely popular *Godey's Lady's Book* under the editorship of Sarah Josepha Hale was that every young woman must undergo intellectual cultivation through reading. The beautiful, talented girl without an interest in books was invariably doomed to disappointment, while the young woman with mental culture always won the heart of the most attractive man. The ideal mother says of her ideal child in a *Godey's* story:

> To cultivate her mind, to form her manners, to improve the accomplishments she had acquired at school, was the task I had proposed for myself, when I should be settled beneath my paternal roof. But the dear child needed not my instructions, the prompting of her own ardent thirst for knowledge was sufficient to carry her forward in the path of improvement. She loved all that was graceful, good, and beautiful, and pursued study with as much avidity as the generality of youth pursue amusement.[14]

Of course, it was not women alone who benefited from mental cultivation. A biographical sketch of the publisher George Graham told of his life as cabinetmaker's apprentice in Philadelphia. "His first object was to discipline his mind, to improve his tastes, and to enlarge his stores of knowledge. For this purpose he began a course of literary study, and, for three years, prosecuted it with undiminished ardor," working ten to twelve hours a day and studying six. Later he went on to publish *Graham's Magazine*, a rival to *Godey's*.[15]

Reading was almost invariably associated with that most powerful of nineteenth-century ideas, improvement. There was laid out before each person, as the ideal mother said, a "path of improvement." Books and knowledge carried a person along that path. Judging from the endless stories on the theme, improvement led to position in the world whether in business as in Graham's case or as the wife of a gentleman as in Little Goody Two-Shoes'. The conviction that reading was the key to success underlay the proliferation of mechanics' libraries in the nineteenth century. Reformers believed that contact with books would empower a worker to rise in his trade or beyond it. No particular course of study was laid out for the patrons of workers' libraries, although there was a clear hierarchy among books, some valued far more than others. But the important thing was reading, not the courses or instructors. Books and knowledge in themselves would develop workers' minds for general improvement. One of Catharine Sedgwick's idealized images was of a worker who spoke out in a public meeting and by displaying familiarity with books won the admiration of hearers from all social classes.[16]

But advancement in the world does not tell the whole story about books. Reading was promoted for something beyond its instrumental value in helping one acquire a job or a husband. The ultimate was the achievement of intellectual culture. An essay in *Godey's* described a young woman in her prime, beginning with her personal beauty: "Her form was beauty's self. Her step was light as that of the fairy queen. Her carriage graceful as the movements of Venus, and her smiles as benignant as the blushes of Aurora." But physical beauty was not enough.

> If her figure was beauty personified, her intellectual qualifications were perfection almost deified. In these consisted her chief excellence. *Her mind* was the sparkling gem set in a golden coronet. . . . Intelligence beamed from her eyes in all the effulgence of mind itself, while the sweetness of her disposition, joined with the most perfect amiability of character, afforded a shining mark to the keen darts of envy.[17]

This combination of physical grace, amiability of character, and "effulgence of mind" brought a person to perfection, and the achievement of that combination was the goal of improvement. Worldly success in the form of wealth or marriage was a secondary reward; more important, reading carried the diligent student to a higher level of existence.[18]

One component of mental culture was knowledge useful in conversation. The cultivated mind had a fund of information that permitted a person to display one's "parts," as it was put in the eighteenth century. Advice books told young people to prepare in advance for occasions when they would be called upon to converse, so as to have something to say. The picture of witty, well-informed people exchanging information and opinions around the circle continued to inspire people of refinement in the nineteenth century as it did the gentility a hundred years earlier.[19] Thousands of books, newspapers, and lectures fed the voracious appetite for miscellaneous information that could be used in conversation among people devoted to the pleasures of good talk. The cultivated person knew something of virtually everything.

The experienced old salt Captain Truck in Cooper's *Home As Found* announced after a discussion with the gracious hostess Mrs. Hawker that she knew as much about ships as he did. In the same drawing room the amazing Mrs. Bloomfield discoursed learnedly on punishments, not to advance Cooper's plot but to demonstrate the wide-ranging powers of a cultivated mind.[20]

In a temperance story, Henry Hervey, a promising young man, meets a beautiful and accomplished girl and surprisingly does not at once excuse himself, as was his custom with other young ladies. Instead he

> entered into conversation with the fascinating Amanda. They talked of history, philosophy, botany, and the arts and sciences generally; of the great names of antiquity, and compared them and their works with the moderns. They discoursed of the mighty productions of the Creator of the universe, from the starry Heavens to the simple flower of the valley; and with all these subjects he was surprised and delighted to find the lovely Amanda acquainted.[21]

The mind of the well-read young woman encompassed the universe.[22]

While reading supplied the mind with knowledge, one writer believed the aim was to create mind. Some people, he said, "overlook the only important office of reading and study, which plainly is the accelleration of our faculties through an increase of mind." And how was mind made to grow? "Mind is increased by receiving the mental life of a book, and assimilating it with our own nature, not by hoarding up information in the memory." A stock of knowledge was mere "mechanical" learning. Books properly read "enrich and enlarge the mind, stimulating, inflaming, concentrating its activity." "The greatest genius is he who consumes the most knowledge, and converts it into mind."[23] The proponents of reading usually were thinking of something like this enhancement of luminescent intellectual powers when they spoke of mental culture. Taste, sensibility, perspicacity, and breadth of vision all grew out of the cultivation of mind through reading.

THE LITERARY TURN

IN the prescriptive texts on good reading, fiction was not given the prize for its contribution to mental culture. History and biography always headed the list of recommendations, with moral essays and science close behind; Mr. Barclay read Franklin's *Autobiography* to his children. Fiction came much lower, and the approved novels were restricted to highly moralistic books like the temperance stories.

But the reading public did not always heed the recommendations. From the evidence of what was published, fiction ranked high with readers. The quantity of fiction alone indicates that it captured the public's interest despite the animadversions of moralists and literary critics. "There never was a time," Caroline Kirkland wrote, "when there was such a mania for novel-reading, or a country in which it was as freely indulged as our own."[24] Sentimental fiction appeared in the most popular magazines like *Godey's, Graham's,* and *Peterson's,* as well as in gift books; it was published in farm journals, and even ran serially in newspapers. Readers consumed vast amounts of it as short stories or novels, and got more of the same notions from the poetry that was nearly as widespread. Whatever the prescriptive texts called for, the people were reading fiction.[25]

Their choices were significant for the refining process because the writers of sentimental fiction so warmly embraced genteel values. By invariably making the heroes and heroines refined, the stories taught people to pursue mental culture and the rest of the genteel virtues. We cannot know for certain, of course, that people got the message. The influence of fiction on the reading public in the nineteenth century is as difficult to pin down as the effects of television on society today, and the possible effects are all the more problematic because the books carried mixed messages. Novel reading itself, to take an obvious example, was condemned in the pages of novels. Equally perplexing, women's subordination to men, the benefits of religion, and obedience to rules were simultaneously enjoined and subverted.[26]

But in their own day such contradictions were not the concern of social critics. They worried that the messages were all too plain, especially the messages of bad fiction. They thought that stories corrupted readers and that fictional values too readily transferred to real life. Readers were tempted to become like the characters in the stories, whether for good or ill. Young girls, a class of readers "whose vivid imagination makes a fictious example nearly as influential as an actual one," would dream of romantic marriages rather than accept the limitations of their actual lives, and so become susceptible to seduction or grow discontent with tedious housework.[27] As Janet Todd has written, "in all forms of sentimental literature, there is an assumption that life and literature are directly linked, not through any notion of a mimetic depiction of reality but through the belief that the literary experience can intimately affect the living one."[28]

One way to conceive of the influence of fiction is to recognize that people thought of their own lives as stories, following narrative lines like the ones they so frequently read. They intermingled literature and life. Diarists, letter writers, and memoir writers, in describing their experiences, lapsed into prose that seemed to be taken from books. They would sketch scenes that could easily have taken place in stories. "The day is fast declining, the sun has sunk beneath the western sky, at such an hour how gratifying to hold delightful converse with an absent friend," wrote Elizabeth Banning to Nicholas Ridgely in 1840. "The soft, the melancholy hours of twilight, there is to me, something peculiarly interesting and tranquilizing in this hour." Describing Williamina Ridgely's unsuccessful romance with a medical student, a midcentury biographer noted that "the result was quite as touching as the veriest lover of romance could well desire."[29] The handful of girls at Lowell who contributed to the *Lowell Offering* were moved by the same impulse. They wrote poetry, essays, and stories to prove that mental culture could be found in mills, and in so doing turned their lives into literature.

An entire letter or memoir did not fall into a fictional form. The contrivances of sentimental fiction were too artificial for anyone but the most abandoned romantic to impose them on life as a whole. But a remembered plot sometimes echoed real experience, showing a deeper meaning and justifying the use of story language. Then the person could play a role, or perhaps replay it in memory, acting like a storybook character and thinking of a storybook ending. In this fashion, sporadically and partially to be sure, fiction took command of character and imagination as readers stepped from real life into the plot lines of the stories.[30] If the refining impulse led people to turn their houses and yards into pictures, it also moved them to make their lives into stories.

Exercising these powers, sentimental fiction to a great degree took over the responsibility of inculcating gentility in the nineteenth century. Fiction was better suited than the etiquette books to reach a broad public if only because the authors told stories about real life.[31] This is not to say that the stories were realistic; like the etiquette books, sentimental stories were elevated well above the tedium of the ordinary. The heroes and heroines were idealized stereotypes, and the secondary figures were caricatures set up as foils to make a point. Yet for all their unreality, the characters in the stories lived in recognizable villages where people worked, married, sickened, and died, making them far more appealing than the list of rules in the etiquette books. Just as architecture books after 1840 created entire scenes as backgrounds for houses, rather than simply giving design details, fiction embedded courtesy-book rules in life settings with complete characters who underwent lifelike experiences.

A RISTOCRATIC E TIQUETTE

IN taking up the task of teaching gentility, sentimental fiction inherited the problems that went with disseminating genteel culture in America. The difficulties arose because gentility was essentially aristocratic and America was not. Sentimental fiction carried a culture that was at heart aristocratic into a society that was striving to be republican. Every effort to promulgate gentility became involved in the conflicts between the two systems of value. Underlying much of the cultural work that sentimental fiction had to perform in the first half of the nineteenth century was the anomaly of aristocratic gentility exercising vast influence in a democratic, middle-class society.

Fiction was not alone in this undertaking. The etiquette books did their part in conveying aristocratic attitudes to the middle class. Manuals like *The Lady's Guide to Perfect Gentility* or *A Guide to Politeness* stood in a direct line of descent from the courtesy literature of the medieval period, beginning with the mirrors for princes and continuing to the manuals for courtiers and the lesser gentry. Rooted in that tradition, the books were a medium for conveying centuries-old aristocratic practices into the nineteenth century. Chesterfield retained his popularity well into the century, and others of the classics never went out of favor. In 1813 while in Washington, Henry Ridgely purchased *The whole duty of woman by a Lady written at the desire of a noble Lord,* a seventeenth-century courtesy book, and after a brief perusal said he was "thus far very much pleased with it."[32]

In more modern etiquette books deference received less emphasis than in earlier works, but regard for superiors still found a place.[33] The books also encompassed the same limited range of human life implied in older courtesy books. The modern works described a world made up of polite conversations, walks, entertainments, and formal correspondence, the leisured life of ladies and gentlemen; work, business, and family relationships had no place. The nineteenth-century books enlarged the genteel world in only one dimension. They contained rules for conducting oneself on city streets and while shopping. But even then the rules mainly concerned responses when meeting other ladies and gentlemen, as if the only moments on the street that mattered were encounters with the polite. The rest of the human population was largely neglected.[34]

The qualities of refined people changed little from the eighteenth to the nineteenth century; the personal skills and the moral virtues were the same, none of them republican or middle-class. High value was placed on conversation, letter-writing, penmanship, needlework, and dancing. The refined mind was characterized by delicacy, taste, and sensibility. The Barclay children studied drawing, music, and French, enjoyed the beautiful, and were highly sensitive to the feelings of others. They ate with forks, though by then more emphasis was laid on laying the table with exact precision, putting each knife, fork, and spoon in place with plummet and line as Mrs. Barclay insisted.[35] The usual bodily postures and movements were forbidden: holding knees between locked hands, crossing legs, placing the hand on a person while conversing, rolling the eyes, beating time with feet or hands, rubbing face or hands, and of course leaning back in a chair. All these were "in the highest degree displeasing."[36]

Refinement still consisted of a hundred details of behavior that only well-bred persons could adequately comprehend. Jarvis, a middle-class businessman in Cooper's *Home As Found* recognized that despite the aristocratic Mr. Effingham's condescension, this highly cultivated gentleman might not fully enjoy his company. As he explained to his wife, "refinement is a positive thing, Mrs. Jarvis, and one that has much more influence on the pleasures of association than money. We may want a hundred little perfections that escape our ignorance, and which those who are trained to such matters deem essential."[37] One can be sure that all hundred of them were conventional court manners.

The aristocratic nature of the etiquette books went still deeper than the innumerable details of courtly conduct. The books were aristocratic at their very core. The organization of moral authority was based on the existence of an aristocratic order. Like the long line of courtesy books that preceded them, etiquette books presented the reader with a set of rules to be obeyed— how to set a table, how to use a napkin, how to eat with a fork. They functioned like a dancing master, correcting the position of the foot or the angle of the arm in order to achieve the most pleasing effect. But what gave these rules their authority? Why should anyone comply? Behind the rules was the presumption of an unseen authority that put the rules in force, an authority that was essentially aristocratic in form.

The rules assumed the existence of a right society, one where people knew how to behave correctly, and where goodness originated. "Now in polite society," one instruction went, "it is considered as a great offense against propriety to use the knife for any other purpose than to cut the food." That was why one ate with a fork—to "be at home in good society." Success was to shine in that company, to win its favor by complying. The authority behind the rules was this distant yet powerful "polite society" whose disapproval was the punishment for infractions. "To use the knife and not the fork betrays want of association with refined life," the instructions said, as if separation from "refined life" was a shameful ignominy too painful to bear.[38]

We cannot help wondering what this idea of right society could have meant to ordinary people living in little towns across America. In an earlier time, readers of the courtesy books knew exactly where this good society was to be found. Society existed at court and in the palaces and mansions of the aristocracy and gentry. Society was anchored by titles, wealth, and political power. Good society, cultural authority, and political office were concretely embodied in actual assemblages of known people who set the standard of refinement. To enable a young person to shine in that society was a practical and significant goal. Its disapproval had concrete repercussions.

One would think that in America's little villages this society would be an amorphous and fleeting reality at best. Aunt Lois wanted the family to move into the parlor in case genteel visitors came to visit, but their numbers were exceedingly few among the "Oldtown folks," and when they did drop by, they were content to sit in the kitchen. The moral authority of a handful of great people and a scattering of parvenus seems scarcely powerful enough to generate fear. "Society" operated in full force in great cities. In country towns, only the tattered fragments of this society were to be seen, making polite society and the authority of etiquette-book rules seemingly artificial and hopelessly abstract.

And yet a sense of a best society of refined and honorable people had to exist even in tiny villages for etiquette books to have had any credibility. A story in the *The Delaware Register and Farmers' Magazine* spoke of "a limited but highly refined and intelligent circle of ladies and gentlemen" in a small country town.[39] The words imply that tiny circles like this one believed that they were a branch of a greater refined society that held forth in cities and at court. All who read and complied with the etiquette books implicitly accepted the authority of this invisible but immensely powerful world.

Perhaps one of the most important changes wrought by the spread of gentility was for these little village groups to link themselves to other best societies stretching in a vast network from the centers of cultural power into the remote corners of the land. Not the least of the benefits of practicing gentility was the accrual of authority and significance to small-town elites through their implied association with larger circles of refinement in the great world. Where no actual courts existed, the etiquette books implicitly manufactured them. The books created in the readers' imaginations an aristocratic or best society with branches in every place where the rules of refinement were observed. The books overlaid an aristocratic order on republican society.

That implied connection with a higher society must have been part of the allure of refinement. The continued popularity of etiquette books based on centuries-old courtesy books suggests the appeal of anything with an aristocratic flavor. The adoption of gentility for middle-class usage did not require a vetting of every aristocratic flourish. Far from it. The faint air of aristocracy in gentility was the source of its attractiveness. That sentimental heroes and heroines resembled the shadowy figures who had inhabited courtesy books for generations made them all the more desirable. The evocation of a distant best society held open the possibility of ascent or thrilling interventions from a greater world beyond.

The flirtation with aristocracy went to an extreme in a few instances, and the extremes illuminate a broader tendency in refinement. In *Oldtown Folks*, Harriet Beecher Stowe created two models of refinement in the persons of Tina and Harry Percival. Thrown on the mercies of the Oldtown villagers after their reprobate father abandoned their mother, who subsequently died, the two young orphans embodied all the qualities of refined temperament. For one thing, both were exceedingly well-spoken. Miss Mehitable, herself well-bred and aristocratic, noted of Tina that "one can tell, by the child's manner of speaking, that she has been brought up among educated people. She is no little rustic." Harry was notable for "his refined and quiet habits."

Although first put in the keeping of Miss Asphyxia, an unfeeling house-keeper, Tina soon "showed the unquenchable love of beauty." She collected tiny pretty things, bits of colored glass, some red berries, and a few smooth pebbles. The sight of flowers thrilled her, whereas Asphyxia dismissed them as "little weeds that put on obtrusive colors." Later at Miss Mehitable's house, Tina would ramble in the fields and return laden with flowers to fill every vase in sight. She knew how to sew, as every lady did, but not to knit, a more plebeian task.

Tina's natural gift was to entertain, in the sense of pleasing everyone she met. She was the very model of eighteenth-century complaisance, the wish to please and be pleased. "Her strongest instinct . . . was to entertain and please." Both she and Harry had "a considerable share of artistic talent," and they sketched and painted. Impatient with the tedium of study, Tina none-theless read books. She loved history, took delight in dramatizing Plutarch's *Lives*, and translated Latin and Greek poetry so proficiently as to win the commendation of a demanding schoolmaster. Along with her natural genius for entertaining and creating beauty, she "cultivated her literary tastes and powers," in keeping with the requirements of perfect refinement. Having the taste, delicacy, sensibility, and accomplishments of a "well-cultivated mind," she was a lady.[40]

Where Stowe went further than most with these two precious children was in making their refinement grow out of physiology. She credited the mother of the two children, the daughter of an English curate, for the children's precocious polish, but her moral influence alone did not account for their admirable traits. Stowe said that Harry was "of a delicate and highly nervous organization,—sensitive, aesthetic,—evidently fitted by nature more for the poet or scholar than for the rough grind of physical toil." Harry was by physical nature refined. The mother made a biological contribution to the children's refinement.

Beyond their blond, curly-haired beauty, Stowe associated the children's sensibility with their biology and ultimately with their descent. Harry's "finely formed head, with its clustering curls of yellow hair, his large, clear blue eyes, his exquisitely delicate skin, and the sensitiveness betrayed by his quivering lips, spoke of a lineage of gentle blood." Tina's "wilderness of curls of a golden auburn, and the defined pencilling of the eyebrows, and the long silken veil of the lashes that fell over the sleeping eyes, the delicate polished skin, and the finely moulded limbs, all indicated that she was one who ought to have been among the jewels, rather than among the potsherds of this mortal life."

Miss Mehitable recognized that the children's refinement rested in their bodies well before their minds had undergone cultivation. No sooner had she met them than she declared, "Depend upon it, those children are of good blood." Their father was the younger son of an English baronet who, after mistreating their mother, subsequently succeeded to the title and repented. Though a reprobate himself, in mating with the daughter of an English curate he bestowed on the children a bloodline that produced polished skin, finely formed heads, and delicate nervous organization.[41]

Stowe's emphasis on innate physiology was hardly unique among fiction writers. Other authors commonly fixed refinement in physical attributes, if not explicitly in aristocratic blood, suggesting the importance of descent. The forehead received great attention from many of these writers. Stowe described a civilized man on his deathbed with "hair clinging in damp curls round his high white forehead." In one story after another, people who were noted as elegant, especially men, enjoyed the benefits of a "broad, white forehead." The description of a sailor boy as having "a profusion of rich, dark

FATHER'S PRIDE.   MOTHER'S JOY.

These exaggerated depictions of refined children gave them high foreheads, tiny feet, curls, and soft skins. The girl's feet scarcely touch the floor, and the ground the boy sits on seems to be covered with a carpet.

brown hair; his forehead, broad and intellectual," was a sure sign that, being refined by nature, he was destined to figure as a hero. By the same token, Stowe foreshadowed the evil in Ellery Davenport's otherwise brilliantly polished person when she gave him a "low Greek forehead." Ultimately he proved to be base of heart as well as of head. Among women, a high forehead was less the mark than the presentation of a "fairness of a brow where intelligence and sensibility now sat enthroned."[42]

Authors were even more fascinated with tiny hands and feet, or, as they put it, "hands and feet delicately small." In the exaggerated lithographs of the period, children minced on cruelly shrunken feet, in keeping with their luscious skin, luxurious curls, and large eyes. Emily Thornwell observed in *The Lady's Guide to Perfect Gentility* that "an elegant hand is regarded by many as betokening evident prestige in its possessor," some gentlemen going so far as to "make the hand the test of beauty, calling a lady pretty, however ugly she may be otherwise, if she can display a beautiful hand." One of Cooper's aristocratic characters associated beautiful hands and feet with the nobility. He was surprised to find an American girl with "such feet and hands" as he "fancied could only belong to the daughter of peers and princes." Conversely, large feet in clodhopper shoes conventionally marked the low origins of a person. An inept serving girl in a *Godey's* story was described as "a great staring Dutch girl in a green bonnet with red ribbons—mouth wide open, and hands and feet that would have made a Greek sculptor open *his* mouth too." An editorial in the *Lady's Book* berated women for wearing thin-soled slippers and silk stockings outside on cold days, but the writer knew full well that "many a lovely girl has sacrificed her life, rather than wear abroad what would disfigure her beautiful foot."[43]

This attempt to identify refined body types in keeping with some imagined notion of aristocratic elegance gained strength from the congruence with genteel delicacy. Tiny feet, for example, were associated with a wish for delicacy in touching the earth, and may be linked with the impulse to cover floors with carpets and the ground outside with paving stones. The same impulse made travel in carriages above street level more desirable than walking. Small feet physically expressed the wish to purify sensual experience, limiting contact with the raw earth.

With small feet went delicacy and a feathery lightness in every movement. In a story in *Graham's,* a country girl who had been away to boarding school showed what she had learned by the way she moved. "Poising one little foot up the hub of the cart-wheel, Lucy sprang lightly to the side of her father, gave him a hearty smack upon each sunburned cheek, and then alighted again like a bird upon the soft, green turf." Her lighting "like a bird" and the "soft, green turf" that received her tell the right story; the little feet had to be protected from the soiling effect of raw earth. So in an urban scene the heroine's "little foot twinkled upon the pavement."⁴⁴ A muddy city street would have dirtied her beauty as well as her shoes. Even inside houses with carpeted floors, nineteenth-century women lifted their delicate little feet onto padded footstools to make all connections with the world as soft and smooth as possible.

This preoccupation with the motions and attributes of refined bodies bespeaks the thrilling possibilities of gentle blood. It is as if these middling intellectuals were fascinated with the lingering mystery of class, going back to the time when the aristocracy occupied a higher and unreachable world, one of glory and power touched with magic. Implanting refinement in physical nature may seem to have put it out of the reach of less favored children. But on the other hand, the appearance of a high forehead or delicate hands in a child suggested that a trace of noble blood had found its way into one's offspring. By mimicking supposedly aristocratic gestures one might claim qualities of innate aristocracy for oneself. The yearning to lay claims to aristocracy turns up in fashion plates featuring children clothed in concoctions meant to resemble court dress. If few mothers costumed their children in that way, it was one of the dreams of an aristocratic past that the magazines let play across middle-class imaginations.

There were other means to associate oneself with aristocracy. The eighteenth-century American gentry had painted coats of arms on their carriages, and even after the Revolution, people used crests of one sort or another. Claims of noble descent were always credible, since the distribution of bloodlines meant that, statistically, virtually everyone was related to a noble family at some point in the past. Later in the century when genealogical research was institutionalized, many white Northern Europeans, with a little diligence, traced their families back to Charlemagne.

Many more took advantage of the simplest form of claiming aristocratic lineage: assigning the right name to their offspring. In New England the seventeenth-century practice of using biblical names faded away and a new set of names came into use between 1761 and 1820. John, Thomas, and Samuel, once the most common boys' names, gave way to George, Charles, and William, the names of the most recent English monarchs. In the early nineteenth century, the assignment of middle names began among the middle class, a practice that had been restricted to the aristocracy in the eighteenth century. The most common kind of legal name change (a practice unknown before 1790) was to add a middle name. In the ring and rhythm of these new names were heard echoes of more pretentious family origins than the actual circumstances of the children suggested. About the same time, parents began to stop giving their own names to their children. The parents assumed the responsibility of assigning identities to their offspring that transcended the parents' circumstances.⁴⁵ The Finneys, modest Con-

*The children's attire faintly associates
them with life in an Eastern court.*

*The picture indulges the fantasy of
children on a throne, in royal
dress, surrounded by luxury, as if
life in a royal court would be
desirable for children.*

necticut people themselves, must have had high ambitions for their son when they named him Charles Grandison Finney after the paragon of gentility in Richardson's novel. Each newborn presented an opportunity to make such extravagant and imaginative selections. The full name of Tina Percival, Stowe revealed, was Eglantine. Would a daughter be more refined if named something like that?

Harriet and Catharine Beecher were both given aristocratic English, not family, names. Harriet was the name of Charles Grandison's wife, a woman fully equal to his surpassing refinement, and Catharine was the famous Russian queen. An editorial in *Godey's* made fun of people who went too far with elegant names, but the editor complained about his own name. "It is no small evil to be called by a harsh, disagreeable name a hundred times in a day; as I have known by experience. I never dared to write a love-letter, nor appear sentimental, nor could I hope that any woman of refinement would ever be induced to call me dear Zechariah!—no wonder I am an old bachelor." He urged parents to think twice about names. "I wish that parents would cultivate this taste for the beautiful in that department of their child's destiny over which they have uncontrolled power."[46] If parents could not actually redo bloodlines, they could modify the child's name, the traditional indicator of descent, to impart a flavor of favored birth and refined disposition.

THE TROUBLE WITH REFINEMENT

THIS reaching for aristocratic connections could not long escape criticism in republican America, and sentimental writers were among those to recognize the incongruities. The abandonment of family names in favor of borrowed aristocratic names suggests how much gentility was an artifice for people just learning to be refined. Refinement did not grow naturally from their own upbringing and culture. It came from outside, the rightful property of another people. It often seemed like a contrivance and imposition, and how could it be otherwise when gentility was first devised for courtiers and brought to culmination at Versailles? It was not created for farm families and rising artisans and shopkeepers who worked hard for their living. One of the tasks of sentimental fiction was to face up to this artificiality and to redesign gentility for an American setting.

The writers did not hesitate to ridicule the fruitless efforts of ordinary people to appear more genteel than they were. Harriet Beecher Stowe herself expressed mild amusement at the aspirations of ordinary people, even while noting the power of gentility in the little New England towns she knew from birth. "Then, as now, even in the simple and severe Puritanical village, there was much incense burnt upon the altar of gentility,—a deity somewhat corresponding to the unknown god whose altar Paul found at Athens, and probably more universally worshipped in all the circles of this lower world than any other idol on record." Though a practitioner of the genteel arts and the creator of numerous refined heroes and heroines, Stowe considered the devotion of common country people to gentility to be sometimes more comical than brave.

Writing in the same vein, Royall Tyler turned his satire on his own mother in the semi-autobiographical fragment called "The Bay Boy," written in 1824 and 1825 at the end of his life. In *The Contrast* in 1787, Tyler had castigated imported fashions in manners and dress; in "The Bay Boy" he belittled the fashionable fruits of female education in America. His mother, Miss Molly Anvil in the story, had the best education her father, a Boston merchant, could buy. "She was taught every accomplishment then deemed necessary to qualify a young lady to adorn the first circles in society." She could "cut paper into all sorts and shapes" of useless trivia, sew every conceivable stitch—backstitch, cross-stitch, tent stitch, nun's stitch, seed stitch, and on and on—and make artificial flowers "with the aid of silk and linen threads, floss silk, cap wire, gum arabic, gamboge and verdigris." "The crown and cap sheaf of all her accomplishment was her performance on the spinet," as notable for the figure she cut as for the music she rendered. She sat on her stool "as erect and attractive as a polished shaft from the quiver of Cupid, her hair craped on her lovely head—an operation which required the labor of the barber for only five hours—but no time was lost in the process, as the hair thus fashionably craped would continue for five months without the application of a comb."

> Her hair was turned up behind and secured to the back of her head by a tortoise shell comb resplendent with French paste, excepting one lock, called by the ladies a "favorite" and by the beaux a "love lock," which was suffered to stray over the left shoulder, and wanton down her lovely neck—this with a black patch as big as a pea stuck under her right eye and another at the corner of her mouth gave an air of smartness to the fair one altogether irresistible to the eye of taste.[47]

Despite her graces, Molly Anvil inexplicably failed to marry until she met Tyler's father, a bachelor of forty working his father's farm in a Massachusetts village. Molly turned on her charm and gaiety, and casually let it be known that she was worth £3,000 old tenor independent of her father. The pair were soon wed and her husband took over the farm.

Shortly after the wedding, a marvelous transformation took place. "As if suddenly awakening as from a dream of girlish fancy, she hastened to assume the matronly character." She combed out the crape of her hair, donned a mop cap, deposited her brocaded negligee in a trunk, and changed her high-heeled shoes for flat heels. "In fine she became an excellent housewife, was expert in all the mysteries of the dairy and superintended her household with such economy and decorum that she obtained the respect of all her neighbors and her husband's entire confidence."

Considering how it all turned out, Tyler thought he had reason to question the efficacy of female education. Why teach women "what is seldom practiced in married life"? Why, for example, "is thrumming the piano forte held so indispensible to polite education"? "How soon is the instrument abandoned while the new married lady is learning housekeeping and the culinary arts from her own domestics. How many, like my good mother, in their egress into married life have to commence their education anew and to substitute the useful for the ornamental"? For Tyler the story turned out happily. His mother put aside the useless frivolities she had learned as a girl and came into her own as a farm housewife. Why not train a woman in the first place to fulfill her true destiny, he asked, "to become in a word, a good wife and mother which comprehends all that is excellent in female character?" Even daughters of the opulent, while learning history and geography, would do well to "sometimes stray from the boarding school into the kitchen and obtain some insight into the domestic arts that they may know how to direct others."[48]

By Tyler's time, castigation of female boarding schools was already a stock critique of gentility. The schools were accused of teaching girls supercilious manners and extravagant behavior that totally unfitted them for the actual lives they had to live. Ostrich plumes, heavy carpets, footstools, and pianos were the visual symbols of the frothy, haughty, insipid manners of the boarding-school product. "Poor Mr. McArthur," one story lamented on behalf of a father. "It was a sad day for him that saw his conclusion to place his motherless daughters at Madame Herville's boarding-school. They entered good-natured, unaffected, sprightly girls; they emerged, after three years' seclusion, fashionable young ladies." And with what accomplishments? One could hit high C when singing Italian songs, the other could crochet purses. They insisted that he redecorate the house at great expense, throwing out the furniture he loved because associated with their mother. Everything they touched was artificial and superficial. Above all, the schools failed young women by neglecting the practical work skills needed for household management, and even fostering an aversion to work.[49]

In a story in *Graham's Magazine,* young Isabel (with her queenly name) asks her aunt why she troubles herself to make a shirt. " 'Pray, aunt, why do you bother yourself with such things,' I said, for I was full of boarding-school notions on the dignity of *idleness.* 'Why don't you leave it for a seamstress.' "

The wealthy Mrs. Lovewell in Solon Robinson's *How to Live* wisely apprentices her daughter Salinda to the practical housekeeper Mrs. Savery, knowing "a quarter's tuition from Mrs. Savery, will be worth more than any quarter she ever had at boarding-school, or from her music master or French teacher." Boarding schools were "expensive experiments to cramp reason out of its natural purpose," teaching music, drawing, and history to no effect, and "needle-work that is utterly impracticable and useless all through life. Such is fashionable education."[50]

The attacks on female education opened to view the lumpy seam where middling people tried to blend gentility into their lives. The pretensions of boarding-school girls were so out of keeping with reality as to be laughable. That disparity, added to Stowe's notion of real refinement residing in blood and breeding, suggests that middling people felt that gentility really was an alien culture. Either they could not rise to the purity of the Percival children or they scoffed at the pettiness of the trifling genteel arts. The incongruity of assimilating aristocratic refinements devised for an idle class that disparaged common work into lives where labor was a necessity was too much for many writers on middle-class life to tolerate.

Lydia Maria Child, in the pointedly titled advice book *The American Frugal Housewife*, castigated the respectable mechanic who mistakenly married "a thoughtless, idle, showy girl." The daughter of the pair "dressed in the fashion; learned to play on the piano; was taught to think that being engaged in any useful employment was very ungenteel," and the chief end in life was to marry. Because of her extravagance, the father died bankrupt, and "the weak and frivolous mother lingered along in beggary, for a while, and then died of vexation and shame." Mrs. Child almost agreed with Tyler that genteel accomplishments were irrelevant to middling people, their pursuit a wild-goose chase, and the yearning for them misplaced. In school, Child wrote, girls acquire the "*elements* of a thousand sciences, without being thoroughly acquainted with any," or learn "a variety of accomplishments of very doubtful value to people of moderate fortune." "As soon as they leave school, (and sometimes before,) they begin a round of balls and parties, and staying with gay young friends." "What time have they to learn to be useful?"[51] If Stowe's attention to gentle blood made true refinement biologically unattainable, Mrs. Child's devotion to household work, so alien to aristocratic life, made gentility among the middle classes completely impractical.

Yet even the hardheaded Mrs. Child could not relinquish all hope for refinement. After her indignant condemnation of genteel superficiality, she concluded by saying "by these remarks I do not mean to discourage an attention to the graces of life. Gentility and taste are always lovely in all situations." It was all a matter of balance, she said, despite her previous disparagement of everything about a genteel education. "When accomplishments and dress interfere with the duties and permanent happiness of life, they are unjustifiable and displeasing; but where there is a solid foundation in mind and heart, all those elegancies are but becoming ornaments."[52] After throwing the refinements out with the trash, she in effect invited young women to bring them back if they could, betraying a fascination of her own with the beauty of good manners and graceful living.

Tyler had thought his mother better off for casting aside all the trivialities of her early education and settling down to plain housekeeping. She fulfilled herself only when she forgot her paper cutouts, craped hair, and the piano. Child's ambivalence about gentility was more characteristic of prevailing opinion. Impatient with girls who failed to learn practical skills while devoting themselves to dress and the piano, she eventually admitted the desirability of taste and grace in a measure fitting to one's means. The middle class should acquire this alien aristocratic culture, but take care not to forsake industry and frugality, the indigenous and necessary middle-class virtues, in the frantic pursuit of refinement.

Despite the contradictions, nearly all the authors seemed to agree that the two cultures should be blended. The gentry, and beyond them the glittering nobility, had so long defined what was desirable that the attempt to achieve refinement could not be abandoned. Emulation of the upper ranks had become as much a middle-class trait as industry itself. How else was one to know how to live after industry and frugality had brought one wealth? To halt the pursuit of refinement would destroy one reason for being. Refinement defined middle-class purpose nearly as significantly as wealth or Christian faith. And yet the difficulties remained—the expense of refinement, its seeming incongruity with work, its superficiality and uselessness, its focus on entertainment above family.

DOMESTIC REFINEMENT

THE responsibility for resolving this dilemma was assumed by sentimental fiction. Authors turned the perplexities of refinement into stories. Heroines and heroes were made to bridge the gulf between the two cultures and both character and plot turned on issues emerging from the conundrums and possibilities of middle-class gentility. To meet the cultural needs of the period, the nature of sentimental plots shifted as the eighteenth century moved into the nineteenth. Seduction of innocence or paternal intervention in romantic love, standard story lines in eighteenth-century fiction, gave way after 1820 to the war of fashion versus modesty, a plot that exposed and resolved the dilemmas of middle-class refinement.

In many stories the strains between fashion and modesty were faced directly through the leading characters, two sisters or two girls in the same village, one devoted to dress, dancing, the piano, beaux, and all forms of gaiety, the other more studious and retiring, devoted to family, flowers, books, and kindly service. Caroline Edwards "lived to herself and the world—the fashionable world. To dress, see company, exhibit herself in public places, and feel that she was the model after which humbler pretenders to distinction copied, was the highest aim, the highest happiness of this immortal being." Mary Howard, in the same story, cared little for dress, company, or fashionable amusements and devoted herself to her family. The point of the story was to show how right Mary Howard was and how wrong Caroline Edwards. Eventually, after passing through adversity, Caroline acknowledged the emptiness of the fashionable life. "I have no cultivation of mind—and no time for it. I have no capacity for order and system—I have no energy—in short, I am nothing at all." Mary then taught her to be useful, strong, and loving.[53]

The seat of fashionable life in the stories remained, as it was in actual life in the eighteenth century, the ballroom and the parlor. The characteristic event, the natural setting for fashion and the place that showed its true character, was the grand entertainment. At the ball, the fashionable girl was at her best. Anna, the fashionable sister in one story counterposed to Emilia, the thoughtful, modest girl, shone like a star at Saratoga. Anna "entered with more zest into the fashionable gayeties of the day than Emilia. She danced like a sylph, floated in the waltz like a gossamer, played and sung with a spirit and finish that made her the center of attraction to all that gay and glittering throng, and many hearts, hands, and fortunes were offered for her acceptance."[54]

Sentimental fiction partly did its work of reconciliation by rebuking entertainments of this sort and those who loved them too dearly. More than the world of work and business, also a vexed and dangerous sphere, the beau monde, the brilliant balls and fashionable teas, lay at the opposite pole from home. The allure and danger of fashion was much more the problem in the stories than greed and oppression in business. The grand entertainments were not depicted as scenes of vice and depravity. The standard phrase for them was "innocent amusements." But they were superficial, glittering events, ultimately unsatisfying, while those who shone at them were revealed to be shallow, weak, or vicious. The point of the stories was to stop susceptible young people, especially young women, from being drawn in and burned like moths in a flame.

Through this polarity of ballroom and home, brilliance and virtue, fashion and modesty, sentimental fiction dealt with the perplexities of middling people trying to live genteel lives. Simple imitation on a lesser scale would have been the most straightforward way to reconcile refinement and domesticity, and in real life assembly rooms did appear in country towns; there were dancing classes, balls, assemblies, and tea parties everywhere and at every level. The stories could have shown lovely country girls shining at dances in village hotels without evoking anxiety or recrimination. But a long history of tension and animosity between domesticity and gentility (or bourgeois and aristocratic) did not permit that kind of wholehearted embrace. The authors had to say that the genteel aristocracy wasted their lives for want of meaningful work and deep personal relationships. Descriptions of social life, although usually avoiding direct attacks, implicitly condemned the round of amusements as inconsequential. "Evening after evening dancing and various plays, and during the day, walking parties and riding parties, seemed to form the sum total of the happiness of Mrs. Almy and her daughters, enlisting all the gentlemen, who chose to be caught by her well thrown out baits."[55] Though the elite as a class were never attacked, the heart of the aristocratic social world, formal entertainment, was indicted and chastised.[56]

The judgment passed on genteel entertainments was preliminary and preparatory and not the ultimate achievement of the sentimental stories. The greater aim was to relocate the characteristic site of the refined life from the ballroom to the home. The stories domesticated gentility, bringing refinement securely within the orbit of conventional middle-class life. The authors showed the modest heroines at their best with their families by the fireside. The beautiful Amanda, in a story in *The Delaware Register*, was

The beautiful, modest, refined young woman was the central figure in innumerable sentimental stories and pictures.

entirely devoted to her father, a Revolutionary soldier, then seventy years old. "Her mother died while Amanda was an infant, and she had never known but one parent, her now aged father, upon whom all her deep and fond affections centered; and she never appeared so happy as when ministering to his ease and comfort." She was most happy, most at ease, most in her element with her father. "It was a beautiful sight, and one that angels might look upon with admiration, to behold the tall and symmetrical form of the daughter giving support to the feeble steps of her idolized parent, as they wended their way to the house of prayer, or strolled through the gardens and pleasure grounds attached to their dwelling."[57]

Within the humble confines of the home, Amanda could live a fully refined life. She did not forgo her natural refinement to stay with her father; she was fully as refined there as at an elegant entertainment. In domesticating refinement, ordinary houses were invested with beauty and refinement. A fictional diary of a model mother in *The Family Circle* magazine recorded a day's activities in which the pedestrian tasks were intermingled with touches of beauty.

> To-day I have been doing ever so much, and the very nature of engagement is to make one happy. I helped Hannah with her ironing— mended the linens—had my rose-sprouts and bulbus-roots planted out—and the mignonnette sown—wrote out that music for Clara— and heard Annie and Mary's lessons.

Flowers, music, and mental culture alternated with ironing and mending. On Saturday the good housewife went to market to purchase flowers and a vase, and returned contemplating the joys of her life.

> O that magic word HOME. How sacred, how dear to every honest heart are its sweet associations, and how laudable is that industry, that neatness, that taste, yea and also that elegance, which has for its object the improvement of this hallowed spot.[58]

That was the goal, to blend neatness, order, and industry with taste and elegance.

In her *Treatise on Domestic Economy*, Catharine Beecher confronted the apparent incongruity of combining the life of a hardworking housewife with the genteel grace of a lady. She aimed for that blend in her school, where students combined domestic duties with academic studies, although she knew that ambitious mothers would protest. But "let not the aristocratic mother and daughter express their dislike of such an arrangement," she instructed, "till they can learn how well it succeeds." She acknowledged the real problem of delicate hands. "Is it asked, how can young ladies paint, play the piano, and study, when their hands and dresses must be unfitted by such drudgery?" After all, aristocratic ladies never worked and their delicate hands proved it. Never fear, Beecher insisted. "A young lady, who will spend two hours a day at the wash-tub, or with a broom, is far more likely to have rosy cheeks, a finely-moulded form, and a delicate skin, than one who lolls all day in her parlor."

To bring refinement and domesticity together, Beecher believed, basic attitudes must change. American women must make "a decided effort to oppose the aristocratic feeling, that labor is degrading; and to bring about the impression, that it is refined and lady-like to engage in domestic pursuits." It was a matter of association. "In past ages, and in aristocratic countries, leisure and indolence and frivolous pursuits have been deemed lady-like and refined, because those classes, which were most refined, patronised such an impression. But as soon as ladies of refinement, as a general custom, patronise domestic pursuits, then these pursuits will be deemed lady-like."

Beecher acknowledged that some believed that "it is impossible for a woman who cooks, washes, and sweeps, to appear in the dress, or acquire the habits and manners, of a lady; that the drudgery of the kitchen is dirty work, and that no one can appear delicate and refined, while engaged in it." The key was to establish order and system. Once housework was brought under control, the housekeeper could fill both roles. "It is because such work has generally been done by vulgar people, and in a vulgar way, that we have such associations; and when ladies manage such things, as ladies should, then such associations will be removed." Beecher was determined to refine every detail of housework and to remove every obstacle to housekeepers living like ladies.[59]

Housework could indeed turn women into drudges. That was the curse on Asphyxia, the ironfisted housekeeper in *Oldtown Folks*, who blighted the life of young Tina Percival. Asphyxia was suffocating in work; it had taken command of her life, hardened her heart, and blinded her to beauty. In many of these stories, fanatical housekeepers are held up to scorn. The Beecher women promulgated a different vision of household life, where refinement and elegance were found along with industry and order. The heroines of the sentimental stories attained their superlative graces in such households.[60]

THE LINGERING ALLURE OF ARISTOCRACY

BY disparaging fashion and the gay society of formal entertainment, and by making home the scene of true refinement, intermingling elegance and delicacy with pedestrian household work, nineteenth-century authors tried to domesticate gentility for the benefit of the middle class. But sentimental authors never totally repudiated aristocracy in the process of appropriating gentility; they aimed to purge the dross and adapt it to middle-class circumstances, not to abandon it altogether. For sentimental authors to discredit aristocracy would be to destroy their own hearts' desire. They revealed their lingering affection for grand entertainments in their unwillingness to let their heroines fail in polite society. Their simple country girls, with no education, often managed to outshine the greatest belles of the ball. The beautiful "Amanda was universally admired, and sought for on all festive occasions, to grace with her presence the assemblies of beauty, wit and fashion." In keeping with her preference for home, "had she consulted her own feelings alone, she would never have left the side of her father, for any pleasures such places of amusement could afford her." When her father insisted,

> she would sometimes suffer herself to be prevailed upon to enter the social circles among her compeers. No ball or party was ever held in the neighborhood to which she was not invited; and whenever she attended, all eyes were bent upon her, and every ear opened to catch the slightest sound that escaped from her lips. She seldom danced, but when she did condescend to tread a measure, the admiration at her agile and graceful movements was general and unbounded. The best performers thought it wonderful that she should equal or surpass them, when they well knew she had never taken a lesson from a teacher of the art.[61]

Although casually entered as an aside as if the admiration of the assembly meant nothing, Amanda's accomplishments in the "assemblies of beauty, wit and fashion" validated the authenticity of her natural refinement. Her success there proved she was the real thing.

Emilia, the modest Stanhope sister contrasted to the gay Anna, danced beautifully at Saratoga too, but then, to show that her tastes led elsewhere, would "wander by the lake, and watch its placid waters and joy in the whisperings of the spirit of nature." She preferred "amid the festive hour of song and dance, to steal out in the calm moonlight and indulge in the companionship of her own willing thoughts."[62] Though more at home with nature, Emilia would not have served as a true heroine had she cut a poor figure at the Saratoga dances.

The disparagement of gay life in the beau monde, the natural habitat of polite society, would seem implicitly to condemn aristocrats themselves. But that was not the intent of the stories. Virtually every middle-class author believed in the existence of aristocrats who transcended the glitter of the ballroom and practiced true refinement. In the purest form, these aristocrats came from noble lines in Europe, but such figures blended with people of great wealth or learning in America whose advantages enabled them to incorporate aristocratic qualities. Harriet Beecher Stowe described descendants of Jonathan Edwards as virtually of royal blood in an American mode.[63] People from this world were the final arbiters of taste and good living. The ultimate vindication of the modest girl who shunned the ballroom to stay with her father was the approval of an aristocrat or refined gentleman from a distant place who brought into the orbit of the local society the higher standards of the great world beyond.[64]

True aristocracy could take the form of a woman whose tastes had been refined in a distant city or, better yet, in Europe, and who was acknowledged by all to live by a higher standard. More often the aristocrat was a man, perhaps only a rich merchant from a great port, but as often as not a man of gentle blood with the aura of a title and European courts about him. It was not necessary that the heroine marry this fine gentleman, only that she win his heart and his approbation and so validate her refinement and worthiness. With surprising frequency in the stories, thousands of times more frequently than could ever have occurred in real life, the heroine actually married the aristocrat and moved to his mansion abroad. The frequency of that improbable outcome bears witness to the dependence of middle-class culture on aristocracy. Only through aristocratic validation could the middle class fulfill its dreams. Not conquest or purchase, but marriage, the marriage of the modest refined girl and the gentleman of surpassing refinement, was the middle-class metaphor for the desired relationship with the aristocracy they had so long resented, envied, and emulated.

Out of Obscurity

FASHIONABLE refinement confronted middle-class virtue on the surface of sentimental stories, with characters and plots that placed the issue squarely before the reader. No one misunderstood the point when, in the competition for attention from a polished city gentleman, a flirtatious girl in fashionable dress lost out to a young woman with a well-stocked mind and a kind heart. The moral of the story never needed to be stated. But the stories carried less obvious messages too. Authors and readers may have been less conscious of a related theme that ran just below the surface of the stories, bearing an implied moral that was the silent partner of the explicit point of the story and equally important for readers' lives.

This theme, also based on an aspect of refinement, grew out of the stories' settings. The stories commonly began in an obscure place, one specifically identified as out of the way, off the main street, away from the center, at a distance from the city. The descriptions have the peculiar quality of actually describing two locations at once. "Elissa Waldron," begins one story, "was the only daughter of an honest and intelligent farmer, who resided a few miles from one of our largest cities. Their humble, but neat cottage stood a little distance from the principal avenue leading out of the metropolis."[65] While setting the scene in an out-of-the-way place, the description draws attention in the same breath to the city, where the story is not taking place. In calling a village remote, the meridian for measuring the distance of this place is at once established; it is the city or a central place of some kind. A side street in a town implies a main street. In a sense the action is being viewed from the central place looking out toward a periphery. The author herself writes as one who knows life at the center and brings urbane sophistication to the story she is to tell, and assumes the reader has the same perspective. In other stories, the action begins in a mansion, a place of wealth and culture, but the plot takes the characters into the country, away from the center and toward obscurity.[66]

With either beginning, an axis between center and periphery is established, and the reader's attention is swung from one to the other as the characters move along the axis. In the obscure setting there is always a person of note, not just a strong, comical, or fierce person, but one of refinement. It may be a child, but more often a lovely modest young lady of beauty and grace. "Among the fair portion of our race, with whom it is our fortune to become acquainted," began the story of Amanda, "in every town and neighborhood, there occasionally appears a being transcendently beautiful, and endowed with manners and accomplishments, precluding all comparison with those by whom she is surrounded. Such an one was Amanda Moreton; born, raised, and educated in an obscure village in one of the Atlantic States."[67] She is surrounded by humble people who may prize her as a magnificent beauty or, alternatively, scoff at her, not appreciating the jewel in their midst.

The plots of these stories may be conceived as bringing this notable person out of obscurity, moving her along the axis from periphery to center. The plot turns on the troubles she encounters as she is put in touch with these centers—through a visitor from afar, or a visit herself to a city, or any number of other devices. In Caroline Lee Hentz's story "The Shaker Girl," the young heroine begins in a Shaker village, through circumstances is elevated to ladyhood in the city, and is returned to the village; her gentleman lover must pursue her to each locale and recognize her virtues in varying circumstances.[68]

What may be read as a romantic plot—will the refined gentleman find and love her?—may also be understood as a story of emergence—will the heroine rise from obscurity? The excitement of the story comes from the successive revelations of her involvement with the great world and her triumphs or her failures. She may, as in Stowe's *The Minister's Wooing*, marry locally and live happily in her village, but not before receiving attention and validation from people of the great world. Or things may go the other way around: A woman from a center of fashion and refinement will be taken to the village, by the failings of a husband or father or some other twist of fate, and there she will thrive through her strength of character. Usually she will be raised once again to a place of honor, but not necessarily. The point seems to be that women of refinement often flourish in a village.

What is the meaning of these stories of movement and exchange between center and periphery, the beau monde and the simple life, the city and the provinces? At one level the stories may simply fulfill the promises implicit in the culture of refinement. From the beginning the aim of gentility was to enable a person to shine in the best society. The meaning of complaisance, a primary genteel virtue, was to please and be pleased. Anyone who cultivated the sensibility, the manners, and the presence of refinement was implicitly preparing to shine in polite society as the culmination and fulfillment of the entire discipline. The stories established that young women of surpassing refinement might be found behind cottage doors or living in obscure side streets, and they must by virtue of their refined natures be brought into polite society. That was the promise of even vernacular gentility. Refinement that was made in an ordinary home connected with the civilities of the best societies everywhere. Refinement permitted one to conjure fantastic dreams and to feel that one could rightfully claim a place in the most exalted society. The importance of shining impelled subscribers to seek a route to the best society, and the sentimental authors simply plotted the course from obscurity to honor.

At another level, the stories may be read to say there are marvelous women buried in obscurity who deserve to be released, raised up, and honored. The stories speak for a prevailing sense of undeserved neglect and wrongfully concealed virtue. The stories rarely blame anyone for this oversight, except occasionally a loved but flawed husband or father. Nor are the women despondent or embittered. They are patient, cheerful, affectionate. Yet it is obvious that they deserve better. Their qualities transcend their circumstances. The reader would be disappointed if no one of note appeared to validate these women, or if the polished gentleman foolishly passed one of them by.

We know that the women who wrote the stories used writing to bring themselves out of obscurity. The lovely, modest heroines of the stories recapitulated the authors' own escape from obscurity to recognition. Although beauty, virtue, and refinement were the fictional means rather than publishing, the direction was the same. Heroines, like the authors, moved along the axis from periphery to center. The immense popularity of the stories shows that their predicament and their hopes were recognizable. Readers, it must be assumed, understood the yearning to be acknowledged, to leave a limited, backward place, and ascend—if only for a moment—into a bright, graceful, elegant world where they would be recognized and admired. The stories offered reassurance that the worthy would not be left to languish in obscurity. Refinement was the key to unlocking the door, the quality that would bring worthy women to the attention of the great world. Refinement promised each one that light might shine on her house, her room, and her place, turning an obscure setting into a stage watched from afar. Through refinement, a reader could become a person in a story.[69]

How did the popularity of this endlessly repeated plot reflect on the lives of the readers? Why did they go again and again to stories that brought beautiful, gracious, but unrecognized young women out of the obscurity of a village to the bright splendor of the great world? What was the readers' sense of their own unappreciated virtues, what their longing for acknowledgment and validation, their hidden regrets? If the reading was related to women's circumscribed roles and their subjection in the household and the world, as we naturally think today, one would expect more recrimination and bitterness in the stories, more searching for culprits. Why were husbands and fathers not more commonly attacked? Instead they are honored and loved, and women are depicted as entirely devoted. If there was anger, and surely it was there somewhere, it was buried below the surface of the stories. It would seem that the stories spoke more for impossible yearnings and the desire for magical release found in fairy stories. The stories created women of flawless virtue and led them to glory along a chain of entirely improbable events. The magical ascent seems to accentuate the powerlessness of women. They yearned for romance as peasants dreamed of pots of gold.

But both the writing and the reading of the stories tell us that women were not entirely impassive in their confinement. Granted that the tales exalted domesticity and made the women await valorization by a noble man. But more prominent than romance itself is the implied moral right of the worthy woman to acknowledgment in the great world. The heroes are often shadowy figures, who enter the scene intermittently or only at the end. At center stage is the modest, refined woman of surpassing virtue, and the reader is made above all to feel her worthiness. If the heroine herself is not assertive, the writer is assertive on her behalf. The stories cry out that this woman deserves acknowledgment. The happy endings that now seem insipid in their predictability grew out of the moral structure of the characterization; the good qualities of the woman required recognition. The happy endings were in effect an assertion of right, a repeated insistence on attention and acknowledgment. Although written primarily by women and for women, they nonetheless hammered home a demand as well as a hope.

An urge so powerful would have found expression under any circumstance. But the culture of refinement provided a channel and direction. The discipline of refinement, as noted before, by its very nature prepared people to come out of obscurity. Refinement posited a polite society of gracious, polished people and then taught believers how to shine there. Refinement thus offered a ready-made plot to writers—the beautiful girl who has prepared in obscurity comes at last into deserved renown. Her refinement gives her a moral claim on recognition at the highest levels. According to the rules of gentility, polish and grace qualified anyone for acceptance. A truly refined person of the most humble origins rightfully belonged in cultivated society. The culture of refinement gave the improbable events of the sentimental tale plausibility, and so fostered dreams of emergence.

What the stories only glimpsed was the peril of this indulgence in unreality. Immersion in the pleasures of sentimental fiction committed readers to a culture dangerously removed from the actualities of life in middle-class America and ultimately worsened women's predicament rather than offering an enduring resolution. A subsequent generation of women recognized that they must take another course. They discarded the false hopes nurtured by the stories and embraced values more in keeping with the realities of middle-class life.

CHAPTER X

Religion and Taste

FOR all its sweetness and beauty, refinement troubled middle-class America. While people could not resist gentility's tantalizing allure, they often said it was a temptation better resisted. They were pulled first one way and then the other. They acknowledged the beauty of a refined life, but objected to its extravagance and vanity. A parlor was the center of family pride, as the expensive furnishings amply demonstrated; yet it seemed forbidding and comfortless, a place where no one felt at home. To measure up, modest heroines in the stories had to prove themselves at fashionable balls and tea parties that were portrayed in the same stories as shallow and heartless. Middle-class fathers paid high fees to educate their daughters in private schools and were unhappy when the girls turned up their noses at housework. Looking at instances like these, genteel culture and the middle class appear to have suffered a contentious marriage of unlike minds.

Religion could not escape this turmoil. Gentility set off conflicts in nearly every branch of Protestant Christianity. The clergy who fought the battles could not see that the turbulence arose from the meeting of two great cultural streams, Protestantism and Renaissance civility. They understood the conflicts more simply as a struggle between faith and worldliness, seeing in gentility a formidable competitor for the hearts and minds of their congregations. The pretension of high-style fashion was a vain and empty show that pulled people away from God.

But religious people also felt the magnetic attraction of refinement, its nobility and grace, and felt the need to incorporate refinement into religion. Some came close to making a religion of refinement. The Christian lady and the Christian gentleman were meant to embody the finest of both cultures. Although reconciliations were made, religious leaders, as a group, were as ambivalent about refinement as people in every other cultural realm.

EVANGELICAL RESISTANCE

THE struggle was not a peculiarly American problem: European intellectuals argued over refinement with equal vigor and much greater sophistication. In 1799, the German theologian Friedrich Schleiermacher, in *On Religion: Speeches to Its Cultured Despisers*, addressed himself to the "class that have raised themselves above the vulgar, and are saturated with the wisdom of the centuries," and so have entirely neglected God. He acknowledged that "the life of cultivated people is far from anything that might have even a resemblance to religion."

> In your ornamented dwellings, the only sacred things to be met with are the sage maxims of our wise men, and the splendid compositions of our poets. Suavity and sociability, art and science have so fully taken possession of your minds, that no room remains for the eternal and holy Being that lies beyond the world. I know how well you have succeeded in making your earthly life so rich and varied, that you no longer stand in need of an eternity.[1]

Although numbered among the foremost theologians of his time, Schleiermacher had to deal with the same sort of worldliness that disturbed popular evangelical preachers in the small towns of America.

Lorenzo Dow, the untutored American evangelist who converted thousands over a long career at the turn of the nineteenth century, expressed comparable apprehensions in his eccentric essay "Journey from Babylon to Jerusalem; or, the Road to Peace." Among the "Schools of Babylon" which the Christian must escape as he took his departure for Jerusalem were the "Dancing School," where people were taught "the important art of hopping and jumping about," and the "school of Music" that sought to "divert the mind and touch the passions" and was "admirably calculated to be a substitute for penitence." The school for the "promotion of Polite Literature" offered lectures on the "barbarity and folly displayed by the writers of the Old and New Testament" and promoted the "sublimity, beauty, elegance, taste and morality, which are every where found in a choice collection of Romances and Novels." Inquirer, Dow's pilgrim, perceived "that there were many things in Babylon, which were opposed to the nature" of the Supreme Being.[2]

The shedding of genteel trappings became a standard episode in evangelical conversion narratives. The accoutrements of the fashionable life came to stand for pre-conversion worldliness. Giving up hats, jewelry, balls, and tea parties signaled the convert's turn of heart. Mary Mason, daughter of an

Irish shoemaker who prospered after settling in Philadelphia in 1794, was reared by her parents to shine in fashionable society. She graduated in 1808 from the Young Ladies' Academy in Philadelphia, where she learned ornamental needlework and landscape painting. Her biographer wrote that "the ambition of Mary's parents was to see her elegant and refined, and for this purpose she was encouraged to attend balls, and to dress in gay attire."

But Mary's Uncle John, a Methodist preacher, blighted these hopes when he began to talk to her about salvation. Coming under religious conviction, she fainted one evening while dancing at a ball. When consciousness returned, her first thought was: "If I should die, what would become of my soul?" In the midst of a long ensuing illness, Mary obtained peace; when she recovered, she was a converted Christian. Besides going from house to house to tell her experience, "Mary now felt it her duty to leave off her jewelry and gay clothing, to cease attendance on vain amusements, and to lead a new life." Her parents objected to this renunciation, having high social ambitions for their daughter. They forbade her attendance at religious meetings, and to obtain their permission, Mary offered to work as a servant in their house. In time she married and conducted a pious Christian school for young women.[3] For her, as for many evangelical converts, the repudiation of gentility marked her renunciation of the world and a spiritual change of heart.

Pious writers, crafting stories of the fashionable girl and the modest girl, easily gave their work an evangelical turn. Since the point of the stories was to show the failings of fashion and to bring the fashionable girl to her senses, her enlightenment could take the form of a religious awakening. In a sketch called "The Sisters. A Tableau Vivant," published in *The Christian Parlor Book* for 1855, Laura, famed for her beauty and gaiety, "was the bright particular star of that brilliant galaxy of beauty and fashion which she graced," but her "character wanted depth and spiritual beauty. She lived wholly in the outward world of enjoyment, action, and endeavor. The inner life of the soul, its high sentiment and deep feeling, were wanting to the completeness of her nature." Her sister Annie, by contrast, had a "serene and wise, yet gentle and loving nature." The deep spiritual difference between the two was signified by their dress.

> The *faces* of both were beautiful, and the costume of each equally elegant, tasteful and appropriate; yet so entirely different in *style*, that the most careless observer would have recognized the soul-difference, which robed the one beautiful and queenly figure in the elaborate fold, and flounce, and frill, decked with gorgeous ribbons, and flashing with costly gems; and the other less queenly and commanding, but as gracefully symmetric, in the plain silk or muslin robe, the severely

simple style of which is somewhat relieved by a single well-selected ribbon, or a few elegant ornaments, or, in their absence, by a fragrant new-blown flower.

Laura's appearance eventually came to be a crucial issue in her conversion. She was first troubled by her lack of sincerity in worship and by the reproving gaze of a handsome young man at a ball. One afternoon she was arranging her hair while Annie was silently meditating nearby. Opening her eyes, Annie "observed that Laura still stood before the glass with toilette all complete, save one stray curl wanting that elegant and nice adjustment which was to give the grace of perfect finish to her face." Without thinking, Annie said that she wished Laura would not always wear curls. She immediately apologized for the impetuous request, but the arrow had struck home. Laura "saw herself just then, not with her *own* eyes in the looking-glass where she had so long studied her outward image, but with the soul's eyes in the clearer mirror of Annie's nobler heart and purer mind." Overcome with remorse, "Laura wept, oh! what bitter tears of wounded self-love and mortified pride!" In her humility a blessed spirit came over her and filled her with great peace. "Her tears were sweet and soothing like an earnest prayer." Then she turned once more to her hair. "She rose and dressed her hair again; and while she smoothed with comb and brush and hand the spoiled and tangled ringlets of her wavy hair, she shuddered at the touch, as though in every glossy, shining coil a serpent lay concealed with deadly sting." When she rejoined the family after a time at her toilette, both Annie and the girls' mother noted that Laura's "hair was plainly shaded on her brow, and fastened up in graceful braids and 'bandeau à la Grecque,'" and they recognized that a transformation had occurred. Laura had been given a new heart that showed itself in a new hair arrangement of smoothed ringlets and simple braids.[4] The real Mary Mason and the fictional Laura lived out the same story, leaving the world and coming to God by casting off the vain symbols of a fashionable life.

How did ringlets come to have serpents concealed in them or dancing become an evil pastime at a scene of wickedness? What was the evil in these seemingly innocent matters? In some passages the fashionable life was depicted as the first step on a downward path to ruin. In a Baptist youth magazine, the caption beneath a picture of a well-dressed gentleman in a parlor asked its readers to "mark the sinful course, the miserable end, and awful destiny of the *thoughtless young sinner*." He began his descent when "he adopted the manners, echoed the conversation of his gay witty companions," and then plunged through extravagance and dissipation to his final end in prison or dying of disease, "forsaken by his former gay companions."[5] His ruin was complete.

More often the warning was less melodramatic, more vague, and yet still ominous. In *The Sunday School Advocate,* Mary asks a friend about dancing school. "Many of the most respectable people speak in favor of sending girls and boys to dancing school," Mary noted. "You judge of people's respectability, Mary, I fear by the figure they cut in society," Eliza replied. "The most respectable people, in my judgment, are those that strive hardest to love and serve God. You don't hear such persons speak well of dancing schools." Good people just knew that dancing school was wrong. Eliza admitted that dancing itself was not intrinsically evil. "I suppose, Mary, there is no harm in the mere act of dancing; but the practice is deemed sinful on account of the follies and vices with which it is associated now-a-days."[6] Something in the ambience, perhaps flirtation and the threat of seduction, was dangerous, but the actual nature of the follies and vices was not specified. Evil beyond any specific sin hovered about modish living.

The conversion stories most often spoke of the fashionable life, not as viciously evil in itself, but as a rival to Christian belief. Rather than dwelling on the specific dire consequences of dancing or fancy dress, the narrators of conversion stories, both fictional and actual, told them as conflicts between two cultures. In the story of Widow B.'s conversion in *The Sunday School Magazine,* places and things are framed as opposites, delineating two paths, two ways of life. Widow B. "was of the elite and à la mode, the devotee of fashion—the sine qua non to every party of amusement. The ball room was her glory. There she figured the 'gayest of the gay.' " After her conversion, "she laid aside her gay attire. Instead of the ball room, she visited the sanctuary of her God. Her constant companions were those who loved the Saviour." Fancy attire and plain clothes, ballroom and sanctuary, lively company and lovers of the Savior stood opposed to one another as emblems of opposing systems of belief and conduct. When she met "her former companions in vanity and fading pleasures" on the street, she told them, "you once attended me to the ball room, I'll now conduct you to a far better place."[7] So conceived, the fashionable life was a path leading away from God. The emblems of genteel living were evil because, as rival loves, they prevented the transfer of the heart to Christ.

Peter Cartwright told of a conversion in 1810 at a period when fashionable men wore ruffled shirts. Wearing such a shirt, a wealthy man came under conviction and, much engaged, was brought to the altar. "But it seemed there was something he would not give up. I was praying by his side, and talking to him, when all on a sudden he stood erect on his knees, and with his hands he deliberately opened his shirt bosom, took hold of his ruffles, tore them off, and threw them down in the straw; and in less than two minutes God blessed his soul, and he sprang to his feet, loudly praising God."[8]

Another wrong was that gentility imposed a hierarchy of rank, allowing the lovers of fashion to claim a superior position for themselves. Even children sensed the difference. The father of James in *Youth's Penny Gazette* sent his sons to "the most expensive schools, and could indulge them in many things which most boys have to do without." James knew he was better than his friends. "James felt his importance, put on many airs, became quite vain of his dress, and showed plainly enough that he regarded himself as much above the common run of boys."9 The author of this pious story obviously disapproved. The Missouri clergyman who furnished the story of Widow B. felt the same way. Before conversion, he wrote, she "felt herself above the 'vulgar herd,' her equals few, her superiors none."10

In the congregations of believers, only one stood above the rest—the preacher. Fashionable people, swishing into meetings with the emblems of superiority emblazoned in their posture and clothing, challenged the minister's preeminence. Charles Finney told of a young woman entering the meetinghouse who "had two or three tall plumes in her bonnet, and was rather gayly dressed." Finney sat in a slip awaiting the start of the meeting and watched her advance.

> I observed, as soon as she came in, that she waved her head and gave a very graceful motion to her plumes. She came as it were sailing around, and up the broad aisle towards where I sat, mincing as she came, at every step, waving her great plumes most gracefully, looking around just enough to see the impression she was making. For such a place the whole thing was so peculiar that it struck me very much. She entered a slip directly behind me, in which, at the time, nobody was sitting. Thus we were near together, but each occupying a separate slip. I turned partly around, and looked at her from head to foot. She saw that I was observing her critically, and looked a little abashed. In a low voice I said to her, very earnestly, "Did you come in here to divide the worship of God's house, to make people worship you, to get their attention away from God and his worship?" This made her writhe; and I followed her up, in a voice so low that nobody else heard me, but I made her hear me distinctly. She quailed under the rebuke, and could not hold up her head. She began to tremble, and when I had said enough to fasten the thought of her insufferable vanity on her mind, I arose and went into the pulpit.11

Finney recognized in her a competitor for the congregation's attention. When he asked if the young woman came to "make people worship you, to get their attention away from God and his worship," he implied that she distracted people from Finney, the spokesman for God. The tale ended triumphantly for Finney with the conversion of the young woman and evangelical order restored to the disrupted meetinghouse.

Peter Cartwright made refinement the central principle of his jeremiads to the Methodists. Cartwright, who was born in 1785, received his first circuit assignment in Kentucky when he was seventeen, and he preached continuously until the end of his life. In his *Autobiography,* published in 1856 when he was seventy-one, he chastised the Methodists for departing from the simplicity of their early faith. "The Methodists in that early day dressed plain; attended their meetings faithfully, especially preaching, prayer and class meetings; they wore no jewelry, no ruffles; they would frequently walk three or four miles to class-meetings and home again, on Sunday; they would go thirty or forty miles to their quarterly meetings, and think it a glorious privilege to meet their presiding elder, and the rest of the preachers." Cartwright associated the absence of jewelry and ruffles with faithful attendance at meetings and respect for preachers. Like Finney, he saw that worldly refinement diluted regard for the ministry. "Parents did not allow their children to go to balls or plays; they did not send them to dancing-schools." "But O, how have things changed for the worse in this educational age of the world! I do declare there was little or no necessity for preachers to say anything against fashionable and superfluous dressing in those primitive times of early Methodism; the very wicked themselves knew it was wrong, and spoke out against it in the members of the Church. The moment we saw members begin to trim in dress after the fashionable world, we all knew they would not hold out."

His was the classical lament of a Jeremiah: we have departed from the purity of our fathers. The early Methodists knew fashionable dress was the enemy, and now the enemy was winning. In the old days, members "wore no jewelry, nor were they permitted to wear jewelry, or superfluous ornament, or extravagant dress of any kind, and this was the rule by which we walked, whether poor or rich, young or old." The contradiction was obvious. "We then knew and know now that extravagant dress and superfluous ornaments engender pride, and lead to many hurtful lusts, directly at war with that humility and godly example that becomes our relation to Christ." And yet the Methodists were weakening. "Are there not a great many worldly-minded, proud, fashionable members of our Church, who merely have the name of Methodist," and who rarely attend class meetings? Cartwright saw the course of Methodist history over his lifetime as movement along the axis from simplicity to refinement, allowing fashion and pride to undermine faith and worship.[12]

Refined Christians

CARTWRIGHT used the word "superfluous" to describe fashionable dress. Fashionable dress had "superfluous ornament." In the old days, there was no "fashionable and superfluous dressing." "If the Methodists had dressed in the same 'superfluity of naughtiness' then as they do now," he wrote at one point, "there were very few even out of the Church that would have any confidence in their religion." The word "superfluous" implied that fashion was a contrived addition. One gave up fashion by stripping it away, tearing off a ruffle, taking off jewelry, removing plumes. When two young sisters in Baltimore were converted, they "took off their gold chains, ear-rings, lockets, etc., and handed them to me, saying, 'We have no more use for these idols.' "[13] Underneath these golden ornaments was the natural, true person. Gentility was an affectation, an artificial show.

Cartwright, a son of the Kentucky frontier, experienced refinement as alien, not human or natural. As he came into his manhood at the beginning of the nineteenth century, gentility was still just making its entry into the broad middle class on the eastern seaboard; on the western fringes of settlement, it was still more foreign, the property of a few gentlemen and an effeminate elite, not the culture of the broad masses of plain people reared in log houses. It was natural for Cartwright to consider the artifices of fashion the "superfluities of naughtiness."

Yet even Cartwright, the rough-and-ready frontier preacher, who was not above physically intimidating his opposition when he needed to, eventually learned to be polite. His wide popularity as a preacher brought him occasionally into the houses of refined people, where he received a little polish. When he visited Governor Tiffin in Chillicothe, Ohio, along with Brother Axley, another Methodist preacher, his comments showed how far he had come. Brother Axley and I "were both raised in the backwoods," Cartwright recalled, "and well understood frontier life. Brother Axley was truly a child of nature; a great deal of sternness and firmness about him as well as oddity. He knew nothing about polished life," had been "raised almost in a cane brake, and never been accustomed to see anything but log-cabins, [and] it was a great thing for him to behold a good house and sleep in a plastered room."

Although Cartwright loved Axley, he found him an embarrassment on this occasion. When Mrs. Tiffin offered him a fried chicken leg, Axley "took it in his fingers, and ate it in that way; and when he had got the flesh from the bone, he turned round and whistled for the little lap-dog, and threw the bone down on the carpet." The governor nearly burst out laughing, but the impeccably polite Mrs. Tiffin made no sign.

Cartwright was mortified. He lit into Axley as soon as he got him alone. "Brother Axley, you surely are the most uncultivated creature I ever saw. Will you never learn any manners?" Axley was mystified. "What have I done?" he protested. When Cartwright explained his mistakes, Axley burst into tears and pleaded that "I didn't know any better." Cartwright forgave him, and telling the story many years later, turned it into a humorous anecdote, revealing that he himself was leaving behind his canebrake culture and learning to be polite.[14]

If Cartwright himself was learning manners, many of his listeners were, too. Gentility was becoming more and more a part of their lives rather than a superfluous addition. The question was, would dancing and fancy dress continue to seem sinful as it became more natural, more an unconscious assumption of middle-class upbringing? When many middle-class children were reared in plastered rooms rather than rough-boarded cabins like Brother Axley, would they still feel they must strip off their jewelry and rip away ruffles in order to come to Christ? Cartwright's jeremiads made clear that by the end of his life the Methodists were giving up the rigors of the old-time religion. What part would gentility play in religion as refinement became second nature to the broad masses of middle-class Americans?

The gradual change in popular religion can be followed in the vast outpouring of the religious presses after 1820. Periodicals addressed to children frequently offered directions for good living that touched on manners and cultivation. For two decades after Sunday-school publications began to come out in the 1820s, however, many of the newspapers and magazines made no mention of gentility. Those under Baptist and Methodist influence and the publications of the American Sunday School Union went month after month without a single reference to refinement for either good or ill. Concentrating on the promotion of piety and traditional Christian virtues, periodicals like the American Sunday School Union's *Youth's Friend* made no mention of the dangers of dancing or, on the other hand, the benefits of cultivating good taste. The magazine did now and then recommend good manners to young people, but for use at home rather than in polite society.[15] The implied settings for the moral tales and essays on the Christian virtues were homely locations among ordinary people with no reference to beautiful objects, fashionable people, fine clothing, or even flowers in the garden or vines on the house. Books and study were recommended as preparation for a useful life, not to cultivate the mind.[16]

Congregational, Episcopal, and Unitarian children's periodicals, on the other hand, incorporated refinement from their beginnings in the 1820s, and gradually the bastions of plain Christianity began to give way, too. The pressures on the conservative magazines grew because refinement itself was spreading among the population, especially the reading, magazine-buying public. As Cartwright lamented, the Methodists, who were among the most restrained Christians at first, were wearing fashionable clothing by the 1850s, signifying an absorption of genteel values. Would they not expect the children in their magazines to dress and act the same?

The Youth's Cabinet was among the plain magazines through the early

1840s. Then, in 1846, the editor changed the format. In the first issue of the new series, the editor conducted an imaginary talk with a young reader, who exclaimed, "We hardly knew it when it came in, it was dressed up so elegantly. Why what a change they have made in it. What a beautiful cover; and how much the pictures are improved." More pictures and a more elaborate cover signaled the change. The dress of the magazine and the dress of the readers were linked, but, the editor hastened to assure his readers, the heart was not changed. Continuing the conversation, a reader in defense of the new format says that "for my part I love to see a person dress with taste. But the Cabinet has got a good heart as well as a handsome coat." The change did not signify a betrayal of the old religion, only the adoption of a more graceful demeanor.

As if to assure readers, the editor said in his own voice that "we shall not forget that the great purpose of life should be higher and holier than mere entertainment—that we as well as our readers are accountable to our God, and that virtue and religion are more to be coveted than much fine gold." Yet as he listed the magazine's purposes, new elements were introduced. "We shall deem our work well done, only when it tends to instruct the intellect—to refine the taste—to bind stronger the golden chains of domestic and social life," and "to raise higher the standard of morality, and virtue, and purity, and holiness." A few years earlier, "refine the taste" would never have found a place alongside morality, purity, and holiness.[17]

As the purposes changed, contributors shifted the places in their essays from plain homes to refined dwellings. The stories did not have to take place in mansions to introduce refinement. In a story of kindness and charity, the poor family lived in a cottage which, though very small, had "honey-suckle and roses trained over the porch and windows," guaranteeing the inhabitants' refinement and not incidentally their worthiness for the visitors' largesse.[18] But fashionable, wealthy children began to come onstage too. The American Sunday School Union's *Youth's Friend* began a new series in 1844, and changes soon followed. An illustration in an early edition showed Arthur Singleton, a man in a top hat, entering a door flanked with pillars, accompanied by his two children, Mary and Arthur; they were visiting their cousins, William and Ellen Swan. The author noted that the holidays are a "season of travel," and the children, with their fancy names, must not forget to read their scriptures as they visit relatives in their father's carriage. The story of a young child's death introduced the doomed hero, George, as, quite blatantly, a good little boy. "If you had seen him, with his white pinafore and his snowy collar round his neck, I am sure you would have felt a great interest in him." Young persons like these took over center stage, becoming the ones worthy of stories. Ordinary farm kids or blacksmith's children accustomed to playing around the forge are seen from behind refined eyes as characters in stories that were essentially about refined children.[19] In the editors' minds, the intended audience had shifted from plain to cultivated, and the heroes and heroines of the stories moved with them.

The editors went by small steps from the beautification of the magazine itself to improving the settings in the pictures and to the cultivation of the characters in the stories, ending up, as Cartwright would have known, locked in the embrace of gentility. Ultimately, refinement became a part of religion, virtually an expression of godly morals. So artificial a gesture as entering a room, left over from the etiquette of courtiers at Versailles, merited discussion as a Christian practice. The boisterous entrance of young Henry, drowning all conversation with his loud talk and rushing up to the fire, where he blocked his mother's exposure to the warmth, prompted a little lesson on the morals of entering a room. His fault was that he "came into the room as if he did not care for any body but himself." "Henry, go out of the room and come in again," his mother tells him, "as a boy should do, if he loved us all as well as himself." It was not just proper, but moral, to enter a room in polite fashion. "Don't forget to enter a room in this manner," the mother tells them all. "Come in politely, and come in cheerfully. Those who

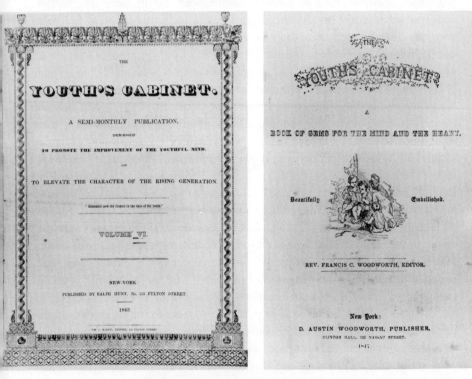

The change in the masthead reflects the magazine's effort to reach a more refined audience after 1844.

love God often think of him, and it makes them smile to think how good he is." Even the pleasing manner of the polite person comes from a love of God. Some think, the essay goes on to say, "that a person who has not good manners may get them by going to a dancing school. I have known persons who could dance, bow, talk, &c., who had no true politeness at all. They had not that love to God or for other people from which it grows." The article transmuted manners that were leftovers from fashionable drawing rooms into acts of piety by connecting them to religious principles.[20]

These stories from the pages of more conservative denominational publications came decades after popular religious periodicals became active. The editors of *The Christian Spectator,* the voice of Connecticut Valley high Congregationalism, caught the vision of the refined Christian in its very first issue in 1819. On the opening pages, the magazine lauded Julia Strong, the daughter of Governor Caleb Strong of Massachusetts. Julia died at age twenty-six, according to her eulogist, with all the Christian virtues; she was devout, believing, and notable for charitable work among the poor. In addition to all this, "she was peculiarly sedulous to take from the refined and intellectual, all excuse for the rejection of religion; by stripping it of degrading associations, showing its inherent dignity and making taste and intellect subservient to its cause." As she neared death, Julia told a friend to "cultivate, my dear N. your manners, refine your taste, mature your judgment, be not negligent of your dress, render yourself and your religion, in every way, as amiable as you can, if by any means you may win some."[21]

The melding of religion and taste in people like Julia Strong meant that religious conversion itself could come to be depicted as part of the refining process. Instead of stripping people of their gentility, conversion could burn away vulgarity and elevate the spirit to higher levels of sensibility and good taste. An Englishwoman, writing in the 1850 *Family Circle,* told of her attraction to religion through Emily, a beautiful young girl. "I found myself strongly affected by the discourse of the little Emily. There was an elegance and a refinement in her ideas which I never before observed about a child." At first the writer attributed this polish to education. "Being totally ignorant of the power of the Holy Spirit of God in producing these beautiful effects, I attributed them to the more than ordinary care of a refined and well-instructed mother in the direction of her early studies." But Emily's precocious piety, rather than her education, accounted for her elegance.

The point of this article was to persuade parents that religion would not prevent the proper refinement of their children. People who believed this wrong idea evinced an "ignorance in regard to the influence of the Gospel in refining and beautifying the intellectual, moral, and social character." They wrongly thought "that the first acceptable offerings to piety are personal refinement and social enjoyment." Stories like Mary Mason's, of abandoning balls and fashionable company at conversion, misled parents. The *Family Circle* author promised parents that early piety would make children all the more attractive in polite company, because love of the beautiful came from God. "The benevolence of the Deity is strikingly displayed in that inherent love of the beautiful, which he has so kindly made a part of the common nature of man." Refined religious writers came near to saying that sanctification intensified the love of beauty as it did every other godly virtue.[22]

For people of this outlook, all the refined virtues were rooted in Christian principles and improved with compliance to God's law. Catharine Maria Sedgwick's Barclay children may have erred in technicalities such as the proper use of forks, but they would never "be found wanting in the weightier matters,—in the gentle courtesies of the social man,—in that politeness which comes from the heart, like rays from the sun,—nor in the very soul of good breeding, Christian grace and gentleness." Christian grace, a pure heart, and the gentle courtesies of the social man intermingled in their minds. All were grounded in the most fundamental Christian teachings, so that a true Christian was perforce polite. "He who should embody and manifest the virtues taught in Christ's sermon on the Mount, would, though he had never seen a drawing-room, nor ever heard of the artificial usages of society, commend himself to all nations, the most refined as well as the most simple."[23]

The absorption of refinement into faith went so far as to turn believers like Sedgwick against religion that lacked refinement. Impolite religion offended the more delicate sensibilities of polite Christians. News in 1829 that Elizabeth Ridgely was attracted to Methodism disturbed Charles Ridgely. He objected to "that enthusiasm, that bigottry, which lead unhappy professors totally to disregard exterior form, and the social intercourse of the world—that monastic reserve which leads us to believe that every thing must be disregarded save the one engaging subject. No, we have duties to perform, and duties too among our fellow creatures; and the performance of these duties frequently brings us upon the stage of society." Besides neglecting the exterior forms of social intercourse and staying off the stage of society, Methodist worship was itself ungainly. "Religion is always represented as clothed in mildness and in benignity, how then can she assume the dress, which she certainly wears in the Methodist Church, where your ears are stunned by the cries, the jumping of those poor credulous creatures around you. If these modes of worship are unpleasant even to the limited good sense of man, how much more disgusting must they appear in the eye of all wise Deity."[24] For Charles Ridgely, Methodist worship was not beautiful; it certainly was not graceful, and because not refined was unworthy of the Deity.

There was a suspicion that the harsh rigor of religions like Methodism actually hardened the heart and made a person less Christian. The intolerance toward dancing and fashionable company made straitlaced religionists intolerant of all human weakness. *Godey's Lady's Book,* always the advocate of genteel faith, published the story of two women dealing with a milliner. Martha accused her friend Caroline of living too much for society, "following after its fashions, and entering into its pleasures." Martha thought dancing, playgoing, and opera were sinful. Caroline found nothing wrong in "a mere fondness for dress or in a desire for innocent pleasure." In the end Caroline proved the better Christian. When a poor, sickly milliner was unable to finish Martha's hat in time for Sunday, she insisted on completion, driving the poor woman to despair and worsening her illness. The more easygoing Caroline understood the milliner's condition and charitably came to her aid.[25] The ease and gentleness of refinement comported better with Christian charity and mildness than what the New York Episcopalian John Pintard called "the severity of austere rigid piety."[26] Not only did refinement grow out of Christianity; a lack of refinement stunted Christian love.

THE THEOLOGY OF TASTE

HORACE BUSHNELL, the leading thinker among Connecticut Valley Congregationalists in the middle of the nineteenth century, felt great pain at the crudeness of unrefined religion. Born in 1802, Bushnell grew up on a farm in New Preston in the northeast corner of Connecticut. His Methodist mother intended him for the ministry and urged him to go to college. Bushnell loved farm life and resisted, but when the growth of manufacturing threatened his father's carding and cloth mill, Bushnell recognized he had no future in New Preston and entered Yale. Twenty-one and older than most students when he arrived dressed in the family's homespun, which he agreed to wear through college for the sake of economy, he saw himself as an awkward country boy lost among the "great folk" of the college.

He never shone at Yale, but he did try to polish his rural manners. He wrote a tragedy and essays on dancing and oratory, compensating for the deficiencies of his upbringing. "I was brought up in a country family," he later wrote, "ignorant of any but country society, where cultivated language in conversation was unknown." After graduation he taught school in Norwich, Connecticut, where his mother recognized his desire to "convert himself into a gentleman." In an essay on his childhood meant as a tribute to his mother, Bushnell noted that "the mothers of the homespun age had a severe limit on their culture and accomplishments." While he honored his mother, it was a simple fact, he wrote, that "we demand a delicacy and elegance of manners impossible to them." Bushnell tried journalism and thought of law before returning to Yale as a tutor (at his mother's urging), finally to enter Yale Divinity School in 1831. He so far succeeded in burnishing his manners and speech that Hartford's North Church, the city's most urbane congregation, called Bushnell to its pulpit in 1833, and there he remained as pastor for the rest of his life.[27]

Bushnell began his ministry at a moment when New England Congregationalism suffered from a peculiar combination of contorting strains. The revival tradition coming down from Jonathan Edwards through the First and Second Great Awakenings still made evangelical conversion the measure of a minister's success. Congregationalism distinguished itself from more liturgical religions by its insistence on new birth as the mark of a true Christian. Bushnell felt pressure for a revival in his own congregation, and his failure after years of effort undermined his confidence in his powers as a preacher.

At the same time, Congregationalists, especially of the kind who populated the North Church, doubted the propriety of revivals. The church was founded as a division from the First Church when the minister there conducted revival meetings that offended the sensibilities of some of his parishioners. The methods of the great national revivalist Charles Finney seemed coarse to refined Christians. Bushnell faced the difficult task of convicting his congregation of their sins without plunging them into emotional turmoil that would appear unseemly.[28]

Although still a small commercial port on the Connecticut River, Bushnell's Hartford sported an elite of merchants and professionals who claimed every form of refined behavior as their own. They sponsored dancing assemblies, literary circles, concerts, libraries, academies, and lecture series to entertain the polite society that moved about the city in carriages and gathered in their elegant parlors for conversation. By Bushnell's time, these people and the less pretentious middle class that formed below them had assimilated gentility into their personal culture. A *Christian Spectator* review of two religious novels noted that "nothing is admitted which should wound the finest feelings, or disgust the most delicate taste," and consequently the interest in New England would be high. The novels were "decidedly calculated to raise the tone of thought, and to refine the minds of those readers, whose previous attainments are such, as prepares them duly to appreciate their worth. And we believe that in our country, such a degree of mental cultivation is very extensively diffused; and consequently, that these volumes are adapted for very extensive circulation and usefulness."[29]

In such a society, refinement was less and less experienced as an artificial imposition, at war with the natural person hidden behind the masquerade of fashionable dress. Refinement was a personal quality like courage or kindness, ingrained in one's character and among the most admirable of the virtues. One could not dismiss the objections of refined sensibility to coarse religion any more than one could brush aside a charge that preaching was uncharitable. A perfect religion must necessarily appeal to taste. "The Christian religion, being adorned with every excellence that either moral subjects can contain, or the mind is capable of conceiving, has been presented to men by its author under every form of inviting grace and beauty," wrote a contributor to *The Christian Spectator*. Naturally, then, Christianity appealed to taste. "The taste that has been raised to high refinement by long acquaintance with the objects of its delight" will find its greatest pleasure in the works of God. People of taste, in fact, will embrace the Gospel more avidly than others. "A mind whose faculties are cultivated, whose feelings are chastened and whose sympathies are active, is capable of receiving the truth of God with a clearer and more lively interest, than one of which the apprehensions are more dull and the taste less exercised." By the same token, the religion of tasteful people would understandably be more beautiful. "It is easy to see how the taste that is conversant with the most refined pleasures, and employs its thoughts in the most noble and just views of common subjects, will gain a propriety of feeling—a superior harmony and proportion to its religion."[30] The physical antics that Charles Ridgely found distasteful in the Methodists, and that made Finney suspect, could never be part of a religion that appealed to the highest and best in people.

While that conviction dampened enthusiasm for revivals, it put Congregationalists in danger of losing members to religions that directly appealed to refinement. If taste was the measure of religion, then the faith that refined its members most fully was the one to embrace. In Boston, the Unitarians occupied that ground, and in Connecticut, the Episcopalians. Congregational periodicals were surprisingly blunt about the danger and conducted a campaign to discredit Unitarian refinement. A correspondent from New York derided the Unitarian claims on the grounds that their congregations in New York City were feeble and not notable for fashionable adherents. "Unitarianism is not fashionable in New York; it does not, as in Boston, attract to itself the men of high pretensions to taste and cultivation, the men of wealth and fashion, the more elevated classes of society." At the same time, the writer had to admit the attractions of Unitarianism. "We concede to Unitarians as a class a high degree both of intellectual and moral culture: we recognize among them many of the brightest ornaments of literature and of social life. Their general urbanity, courtesy and refinement are the appropriate result of the cultivation of certain good natural traits of character as Christian virtues."

The writer's defense was that rebirth through divine grace, Congregationalism's trademark as an evangelical religion, could refine a person with equal effect. "The same result is often reached with far less cultivation where the heart is renewed and sanctified by divine grace." Other compensations made up for Unitarian refinements. "In some points of mere esthetics, Unitarianism does, indeed, compare advantageously with the old Orthodoxy of New England. But can it show us the severe simplicity, the massive nobleness of the old Puritan race?"[31] Much could be said on behalf of Congregationalism, but in the circles that read *The New Englander* and *The Christian Spectator,* Unitarianism and the Episcopal Church clearly posed a threat. At the same time as Congregationalists strove to promote Evangelical conversion they had to protect themselves against high-toned religion, so that while poor and humble converts were coming in through one door the wealthy and refined would not be leaving through another.[32]

Swimming in these crosscurrents, Bushnell made his own statement on religion and taste in an 1843 essay in *The New Englander* called "Taste and Fashion." Though the aesthetic attractions of other religions troubled the atmosphere in which he wrote, he chose not to address the problem of the Unitarians and Episcopalians directly. Their presence might have moved him to write, but once on the topic, he chose to discuss a broader issue. He implicitly answered the question of Congregationalism's relationship to refinement by completely incorporating taste into his conception of religion. Explicitly, he turned to the problem that preoccupied sentimental authors: how to distinguish true beauty from superficial fashion. The sentimental authors had domesticated religion. They created a gentility that flourished in the home among family members, apart from the glitter of balls and assemblies, and purged of its aristocratic dross. Bushnell's solution was to ground refinement in religion by making good taste an attribute of God, and then to condemn everything associated with the trappings of aristocratic gentility. His essay gave refinement a secure genealogy that bypassed European courts and so removed any inhibitions about the pursuit of tasteful religion.

Bushnell's first effort was to tear taste out of the hands of the aristocracy, where it had securely rested for so long. The European nobility, he insisted, were the purveyors of fashion, not of beauty. Totally oblivious to the descent of the genteel tradition from Renaissance courts to palaces of the nobility and then to the lesser gentry, Bushnell saw only a crass love of caste in the European aristocracy, not real taste. Defense of a social position, not love of beauty, underlay the aristocratic addiction to fashion. "In its higher and more sovereign manifestations, fashion is rooted in a desire of caste." Fearing that the vulgar herd below will overtake them, the upper classes see "that the only way to keep distance, is to lead off in a perpetual round of change in the dress, equipage, and social forms of life." They cannot get off the whirligig of fashion because each innovation is rapidly imitated. "The new style soon grows common," descending through the ranks of society, obliging the caste at the top to take up something new again. Pride and slavish imitation lay behind fashion, not taste or love of beauty.

The origin of true taste, to Bushnell's mind, was God himself and the model to emulate was the Creation. "The highest known example of taste is that of the Almighty, when he invents the forms, colors and proportions, of this visible creation." Refined people should not look to European palaces for inspiration, but to the natural world all about them. "The whole fabric of creation is an exertion of taste." By so saying, Bushnell came close to claiming that taste was the foundation principle of the universe. Furthermore, this divine taste did not exist in some exalted sphere far above the realms of man. "Taste, in man, is every way resembled to this power of form displayed in creation, except that it is a capacity slowly cultivated and matured, and not inherently complete like the divine." Humans had to cultivate their taste. "But, when awake, it is as truly original as the taste of God, and is one of the highest points of resemblance to him in our nature."

The creations of human taste, he went on to say with astounding confidence, were extensions of the original divine creative act. "Architecture, gardening, music, dress, chaste and elegant manners—all inventions of human taste—are added to the rudimental beauty of the world, and it shines forth, as having undergone a second creation at the hand of man." Through taste, people participated in God's great work of beautifying the world. The Hartford merchant who erected a fine house and surrounded it with a pleasure garden and invited elegantly dressed friends to dine was on God's errand. All of this made the cultivation of taste one of man's divine duties. "Taste is God's legacy to him in life, which legacy he can not surrender, without losing the creative freedom and dignity of his soul."[33]

The moral for Americans, of course, was to cultivate taste and avoid fashion. "Fashion is an eminently unrepublican influence." Wherever it appeared, it grew from the aristocratic principle of caste. Regrettably that held true for America too. "We certainly have the genuine spirit—a spirit as ambitious of caste, as can be found in any country. It has the genuine impudence and vulgarity. Its pretensions are as hollow as in the old world; the distinction it assumes as fictitious; its principles as rotten; its heart as cold." Rather than pursue fashion, Americans should seek beauty, for taste was not the property of class or wealth and so was intrinsically republican. "Taste is possible to all. The humblest and poorest man may look on the face of beauty with as much freedom, and love it with as high a relish, as the most favored." Besides merely valuing the beauty he can see, "the poor man's house can be as tasteful as the rich man's; for taste does not consist in the abundance of the things that it possesseth, but in the use which is made of what it has."

Like the architectural writers who designed beautiful cottages, barns, and dovecotes, and Catharine Sedgwick's rich poor man, Bushnell envisioned a total landscape suffused with beauty where taste ruled over all, rich and poor alike. "Every common man's house or cottage, might be more than a palace,—a little abode of tastefulness and refined happiness." He dreamed of an American empire of beauty, the fruit of ubiquitous republican taste. "Would now that we could bring this subject near to all our countrymen, and fill their minds with the beautiful spectacle our country ought to exhibit." Social abuses would end under the softening influence of beauty. "We would declare to them the universal possibility of taste, and show them how it would soften our asperities, if all classes were thus engaged to adornment and grace to life."

> Look, what a spectacle this great nation will exhibit, when it is occupied as a realm of taste—when the neat cottages sprinkled over the hills, and blended with the elegant mansions of the rich—when the graceful dress of our people, their fine truthful manners, the genial glow of their society, their high-toned liberty and tasteful piety, combine to show the dignity of our institutions.

Bushnell lived at a time when the refining process was nearing its zenith, and a limitless confidence in taste could generate utopian visions. It seemed possible for a moment that taste cleansed of fashion could create a world of blissful beauty, and that in republican America, where aristocratic fashion had no natural home, a millennium of genteel beauty could be brought to pass.[34]

RELIGIOUS FICTIONS

BUSHNELL'S essay resolved the conflict between gentility and piety by completely blending them. Rather than telling Christians to strip away jewelry, hats, and ruffles as Cartwright and Finney did, Bushnell said fine houses, handsome dress, and gracious manners were simply divine. Gentility's campaign to beautify the world was a "second Creation," carrying on the work of the Author of all natural beauty. Later in his life Bushnell envisioned a large public park for Hartford in what must have seemed like divine and human cooperation on a grand scale. The identification of worldly and divine beauty meant that refined taste ranked among the Christian virtues. His theology licensed believers to pursue refinement in domestic life and taste and sensibility in personality as part of their salvation.

But a theological resolution of the conflict did not necessarily bring peace to the believers in tasteful religion. Quite the opposite. They found themselves at odds more than ever with a world that was neither wholly refined nor wholly pious. Within the Hartford North Church, worshippers may have agreed on the divinity of refinement; beyond its gates, vulgarity and worldliness still abounded to irritate and rebuff refined Christians. On every side there were occasions to take offense, to be repulsed, or to suffer in the presence of barbarism. For Christians of taste and sensibility the world was filled with sin.

One of the best-sellers of the 1850s, Susan Warner's *The Wide, Wide World*, caught up these conflicts in the person of little Ellen Montgomery, one of the most delicate and sensible creatures in nineteenth-century fiction and one who strove mightily to be religiously submissive and worshipful. Blessed with both refined and pious impulses, Ellen found only two secluded places in all the world where she was truly at home. Her sensitive spirit simply could not abide the vulgar world of coarse farm work, nor was it at ease in polished houses where God was not honored. In a book so long and complex as *The Wide, Wide World*, the tens of thousands of readers doubtless found many things to capture their interest, but the pilgrimage of a godly and delicate child in search of a haven that was both pious and refined must have seemed poignant to many.

The Wide, Wide World could have been read as a manual for refined living. The delicacy of Ellen's sensibilities were established at once in the opening scenes, in which she was about to part from her languishing mother and wept gallons of tears at the prospect of separation. The regularity and volume of weeping in the book was excessive even by the standards of sentimental fiction, but the tears established the intensity of Ellen's responses to poignant circumstances, a requisite for a refined character in whom any form of dullness or torpidity would have been a damning flaw. On the positive side, Ellen demonstrated her sensibility by her exultant responses to nature, and especially flowers, whose delicacy and beauty reflected the refined viewer's own character. "Do you love flowers, Ellen?" asked a cultivated friend. "I love them dearly, Miss Alice," Ellen replied.

Probably the warmth and intensity of Ellen's responses accounted for her attractiveness. The convention in sentimental fiction for demonstrating the radiance of the refined personality was to surround such people with awe-struck admirers. Although Ellen had her enemies, wherever she went she won the love of her acquaintances. A grand lady concluded that "there is a grace in her politeness that can only proceed from great natural delicacy and refinement of character." Even the housekeeper in a great mansion said Ellen was a "blessing of the house."

She had, moreover, all the skills of a well-bred young woman to match her innate sensibility. A wealthy family considered her the "best-bred child in the world." The test came at the end of the book when she was carried off to an aristocratic household in Edinburgh and successfully met the most exacting standards. Not only did she have perfect manners, but she had read history, including Scottish history, carried her body with perfect dignity, and overwhelmed her French riding master with her equestrian skills. Conversation, letter writing, drawing, music, French were all within her powers. Anyone looking for a model of perfect ladyhood could rely confidently on Ellen Montgomery.[35]

In spite of and partially because of these splendid qualities, Ellen rarely felt at home. Her mother's illness and her father's unnamed business problems forced Ellen to leave her happy New York home while still a young girl of about ten, and after that she was at ease only in certain rarefied places. She was perfectly happy with her lovely mother, who turned out to be the daughter of an aristocratic Scottish family. The New York apartments were one of the two congenial environments in her peregrinations. Even the clerk in a fancy New York shop offended Ellen when she was sent off to make a purchase for her sick mother. Warner repeatedly confronted Ellen with coarse characters, as if her revulsion at vulgarity proved her own refinement.

She was repelled by Aunt Fortune, her father's sister, who made Ellen part of the aunt's farm household. For one thing, Ellen's room was distasteful. "The floor was without a sign of a carpet; and the bare boards looked to Ellen very comfortless. The hard-finished walls were not very smooth nor particularly white." The worsted white-and-blue coverlet "came in for a share of her displeasure," and under the good wool blanket were cotton sheets and a cotton pillowcase. She was chagrined to learn she would have no basin in her room and must wash at the spout in the yard. At breakfast "her tea-spoon was not silver; her knife could not boast of being either sharp or bright; and her fork was certainly made for anything else in the world but comfort and convenience, being of only two prongs, and those so far apart that Ellen had no small difficulty to carry the potato safely from her plate to her mouth." The presence of one of the hired help at the table surprised Ellen, though she passed it off as a mere trifle. Aunt Fortune humiliated her when she learned the little girl had only white stockings and dyed them all a color fitting for the country.

Warner so perfectly created in Ellen a stereotypical effete city snob encountering wholesome country life that one expects a conversion somewhere in the story, but it never happened. While she came to love a few country characters, most of them remained colorful boors to the end. Ellen dutifully took on chores around the house but never enjoyed them, as if her temperament was too fine for base labor. "After spending the whole morning with Miss Fortune in the depths of housework, how delightful it was to forget all in drawing some nice little cottage with a bit of stone wall and a barrel in front; or to go with Alice, in thought, to the south of France, and learn how the peasants manage their vines and make the wine from them." Art and learning were more suitable to Ellen's character than work.[36]

On the other hand, Ellen was not perfectly at ease in more refined settings. When her travels brought her to Ventnor, an elegant country mansion with rich furniture and polite company, Ellen was seemingly in her element. She loved the dignified, gracious Marshmans and they loved her. But the happiness was not to last. A few brattish children grated on Ellen's sensibilities, but even more their Sunday play offended her when she preferred to curl up with the Bible.

At the end of the novel, when Ellen returned to her mother's relatives in Scotland, she was unhappy again. They were immensely gracious and aristocratic people with a country house on the Tyne and a town house on Georges Street in Edinburgh. The houses themselves pleased Ellen. One was "comfortably, luxuriously furnished; but without any attempt at display. Things rather old-fashioned than otherwise; plain, even homely, in some instances; yet evidently there was no sparing of money in any line of use or comfort; nor were reading and writing, painting and music, strangers there." From the house, Ellen instinctively "formed a favourable opinion of her relations." They welcomed her warmly as a daughter and were astounded at her accomplishments. "It is extraordinary," said Lady Keith, "how after living among a parcel of thick-headed and thicker tongued Yankees she could come out and speak pure English in a clear voice." They were equally amazed at her French, history, and riding, all the aristocratic genteel arts.

It was Ellen's piety that occasioned a falling out. The trouble began when she announced that she sang only hymns and "Hail, Columbia." It soon appeared that she had no taste for balls and assemblies, and an intense desire for worship. Her predilections enraged her otherwise affectionate kinsmen. "I would like to see you a little more gay," said her uncle, "like other children." They were soon locked in a battle of wills over scores of little things, from drinking wine, which she stiffly refused until compelled, to attending church twice on Sunday, to rising early to pray. Ellen, Mrs. Lindsay said indignantly, "was spoiling herself for life and the world by a set of dull religious notions that were utterly unfit for a child." All the culture and wealth of the Lindsay household failed to satisfy her.

After leaving her mother, Ellen was truly at home only with the Humphreys, the household of an English clergymen and his daughter and son, who were the ones to train Ellen in both gentility and piety. In that house "there was an atmosphere of peace and purity," where both sides of her character flourished and grew together. In that delicately balanced and rare mixture, Ellen found perfect happiness in "long evenings of conversation and reading aloud, and bright firelights, and brighter sympathy and intelligence and affection." The Humphreys provided a gloriously happy existence—but one that was achieved only by their self-seclusion in a country retreat away from the worldlings who fell short of their elevated standards. At the end of the book, John Humphrey resolved Ellen's fate by rescuing her from the Lindsays in Edinburgh and promising a return to the isolated purity of the Humphrey country home. After all her travels in the wide, wide world, Ellen could find no other refuge where her Christian and her genteel sensibilities were at peace.[37]

BEAUTIFUL CHURCHES

ELLEN MONTGOMERY'S troubles would have evaporated had she listened to the instruction of the old-time evangelists. They admonished their audiences to slough off gentility as an unwonted excrescence and find salvation through simple piety. But a girl with Ellen's sensibilities could never rest content with plain religion and a plain life. As gentility grew into a second nature among people in urban congregations, refinement and religion intertwined as values of nearly equal standing. The needs of urbane parishioners compelled ministers to seek a reconciliation of some kind. Preachers like Bushnell had to integrate piety and gentility or risk losing their most eminent members to the polished worship of the Episcopal churches or to the civilized preaching of the Unitarians. Urbane worshippers insisted on viewing religion through refined eyes, and that cast everything in a new light. What had once been good, under the scrutiny of refinement appeared cruel, harsh, or, worst of all, uncivilized. Preachers were compelled to reassess everything from worship to church architecture and the Puritan past and conform religion to refined tastes.

In her religious stories, Harriet Beecher Stowe spoke as one who found the burden of Puritanism too much to bear and who took refuge ultimately in the Episcopal Church. There were more important issues than a lack of refinement to disturb Stowe. She suffered mainly under the seemingly unreasonable demand for a change of heart as a requirement for salvation when conversion was impossible to achieve without divine aid. The death of Catharine Beecher's fiancé before conversion and then the loss of Harriet's own son in the same condition drove home the cruelty of a religion that condemned people for shortcomings that were beyond their capacity to rectify. Stowe populated her stories with individuals frozen in rage and despair by this impossible contradiction, the obligation, as Charles Foster put it, to climb a rungless ladder to heaven.

Alongside this conundrum, the cultural poverty of Puritan worship and architecture was a relatively minor objection, and yet significant because so similar to the austerity of the doctrine. The "severe bareness and rigid restriction" of the Congregational funeral services corresponded to the severity of the doctrine of New Birth. The meetinghouses were "huge, shapeless, barn-like structures," with "two staring rows of windows, which let in the glare of the summer sun, and which were so loosely framed" that in winter there "poured in a perfect whirlwind of cold air." The frosty winds were not the result of primitive carpentry: "it was a part of the theory of the times never to warm these buildings by a fire." The "desolate plainness" of these buildings was matched by the "barbarous" and "primitive" psalmody that gave utterance to an undertone of "doubt, mystery, and sorrow."[38] The building and the music created an ambience suitable for the demanding theology of the Puritan divines.

In *The Minister's Wooing* of 1859, Stowe had found surcease from the sorrows of rigid doctrine through the spontaneous warmth of female love. Women reconciled alienated souls to divine judgment by giving God a human face; people who thought God could never love them were persuaded otherwise by the love of a pious woman. After her conversion to Episcopalianism, Stowe offered her new religion as another alternative to despairing Puritans. In *Oldtown Folks,* Harry and Tina Percival learned their Anglicanism from their mother, the daughter of an English curate. The imperturbable Harry, who grew up to be an Anglican priest, never wavered under the onslaughts of Puritan logic. He simply refused to believe that a change of heart was necessary to know God, and yet by his implacable piety proved his spiritual superiority to every Puritan in sight. Tina's happy, childlike love won over the sorrowing heart of Mehitable Rossiter, who had long since given herself up as damned. Through these elegant, believing children Stowe showed her Congregational readers an accessible, human, and yet equally devout way to God.

With this kindly religion went worship in churches whose beauty ministered to the spirit. After the bare plainness of the Congregational church in Oldtown, "the architecture of the Old North and its solemn-sounding chimes, though by no means remarkable compared with European churches, appeared to us a vision of wonder," wrote the youthful narrator in *Oldtown Folks.* "We gazed with delighted awe at the chancel and the altar, with their massive draperies of crimson looped back with heavy gold cord and tassels, and revealing a cloud of little winged cherubs." "Then there was the organ, whose wonderful sounds were heard by me for the first time in my life."[39]

Little Dolly in another Episcopalian novel, *Poganuc People,* was a surrogate for Harriet Beecher growing up in Litchfield. Dolly stole away to Christmas Eve services in the tiny Episcopal church, enthralled by the mystery and beauty of the worship. Stowe spoke her mature mind when she observed that "it was in truth a very sweet and beautiful service, and one calculated to make a thoughtful person regret that the Church of England had ever

expelled the Puritan leaders from an inheritance of such lovely possibilities."
The Episcopal Church offered repose for those bruised by Puritanism. The
comfort of its doctrines and the beauty of its churches went together. They
both accounted for the growth of little Episcopal congregations in the
heartland of Puritanism. "There came to them gentle spirits, cut and bleeding by the sharp crystals of doctrinal statement, and courting the balm of
devotional liturgy and the cool shadowy indefiniteness of more aesthetic
forms of worship." Stowe never claimed that Episcopal preaching shone or
that its logic exceeded the Puritan's, but in the soft beauty of Episcopal
worship troubled souls found peace.[40]

Conversion to Episcopalianism was not required to make Congregationalists aware of their barren houses of worship and harsh doctrines. In his
memoir of Quabbin, Massachusetts, at the beginning of the century, Francis
Underwood lamented the suppression of everything beautiful and enlightened under the doleful weight of Puritan religion. Give the clergy their way,
complained a visitor, "and there would not be a poet, novelist, painter or
composer." With deep bitterness Underwood had the fictional character
assert that "let the best and purest man say a word in favor of light, life, and
beauty, he is the target of arrowy texts." In a more cheerful vein, Underwood
noted the subsequent lifting of this repressive influence as manifest in the
Quabbin meetinghouse. Earlier painted a "dingy sulphur color, and without
a steeple," it stood sideways to the road flanked by decrepit horse sheds. As
the years went by and the people grew more polite, "a steeple was set astride
the roof; the building was painted white, furnished with green (outside)
blinds, and turned with its end to the street." Inside there was an organ, once
the feature solely of Episcopal worship. Indeed the first of Quabbin's ministers would be astounded and probably appalled at the changes. "Strange to
him and his people would have appeared the antiphonal reading of the
psalm in the morning service, and the profuse floral decoration of the pulpit
and communion table. The disciples and contemporaries of Cotton Mather,
or of Jonathan Edwards, would find little to please them in the worship or
sermons at Quabbin, or elsewhere in Massachusetts" at this latter day.[41] For
Underwood, of course, the changes meant progress.

That kind of progress went on everywhere in New England after 1800. In
the years when Stowe was growing up, hundreds of Congregational
churches improved their meetinghouses. Edmund Sinnott, who studied 200
of the 509 extant early meetinghouses in New England, concluded that
"almost every town in New England, in the first quarter of the nineteenth
century, either built a church of the new type or achieved the same end by
modernizing an earlier meetinghouse."[42] By "new type" Sinnott meant
buildings with the main doors at one end of a long axis and the pulpit at the
other, and usually with a porch or portico on which was mounted a tower

and steeple—in short, the meetinghouses familiar in New England towns to this day.

They were the successors to the oblong buildings of the eighteenth century, barnlike structures with the pulpit on the long side and a door opposite, and as often as not lacking a tower and belfry. After 1825 a Greek Revival version of the "new type" appeared in New England with more elaborate classical columns and an entablature on the portico or at least classical pilasters. In his intensive study of Connecticut churches, J. Frederick Kelly found only seven remaining structures that were originally of the older variety, and all of these had been remodeled to meet the new standards.[43] All of the meetinghouses commonly but mistakenly associated with colonial New England took their places on the village greens in the early nineteenth century as part of this massive rebuilding.

In addition to the reorientation of the axis, the construction of tower and steeple, and an exterior painted white instead of a "dingy" yellow (or red,

In 1774, the East Haven meetinghouse had a tower, but, like the Old South meetinghouse of 1729, kept the main entrance on the long side. A steeple was added by 1797, but not until after 1850 was the long-side entrance closed and the church given a fully longitudinal orientation.

blue, or brown), the new meetinghouses took on a new air on the inside. More than appearance was involved; the entire ambience was changed. The coming of stoves after 1815 warmed an atmosphere that previously was mercilessly cold when temperatures dropped below freezing. To the warmth in the air were added new sounds—from an organ or, when a congregation could not afford that extravagance, from a bass viol.[44] The changes in furnishings complemented the music and the warmth in the air. Red silk draperies hanging behind the pulpit dignified the preacher and added a bright touch of color. Carpets on the floors and cushions on the pew seats in more affluent congregations hovered on the edge of luxury. By comparison to meetinghouses of a century earlier, the entire space sent a message of welcoming comfort.[45]

But comfort was not the only value guiding changes in the meetinghouses. The builders thought fully as much about beauty. They wanted tasteful churches in keeping with the growing refinement of the worshippers. How much architectural taste meant to the Congregationalists came out when the General Convention asked a committee to establish a policy for sending building aid to struggling western churches. The General Congregational Convention meeting at Albany in 1852 charged the committee on aid to procure suitable plans "with a view to promoting convenience, economy and good taste, in the design and execution of the work." The implication was that receiving aid depended on the selection of a suitable plan.

The resulting volume, *A Book of Plans for Churches and Parsonages. Published under the Direction of the Central Committee, Appointed by the General Congregational Convention, October, 1852. Comprising Designs by Upjohn, Downing, Renwick, Wheeler, Wells, Austin, Stone, Cleveland, Backus, and Reeve,* recommended right off that churches employ an architect who knew how to erect a building "in a tasteful and proper manner." A skillful builder might erect a workable meetinghouse, but only an architect could make it look right.

> The difference between a building made up of patchwork features, stolen piecemeal from one and another existing structure, and one whose every feature has been determined by a competent and comprehensive knowledge of architectural principles, though it may not be apparent at once to every eye, will sooner or later reveal itself, and that difference is wide almost as the poles. And if architecture should either be satisfactory to good taste, or be the means of cultivating it, then surely attention to its quality in this respect is not out of place or unimportant.

The authors of the book had enlisted in the campaign to introduce beauty into every corner of the landscape with no exceptions for churches. Not even impecunious churches were exempted from the requirements of taste.

The principles of architecture apply to one structure as well as to another; to the humblest and simplest, as well as to the most imposing and elaborate. They have place as truly in the building of the plainest cottage as in the erection of a palace; in the shaping of the garden fence or the kitchen chimney, as truly as in the arrangement of a portico or the hanging of a dome.

The ambition of gentility's beautification campaign was to conquer the entire world, and no meetinghouse on the desolate western prairies was to be forgotten.

Church builders also had to take into account that the taste of their parishioners was rising like a tide to drown ugly buildings. That was why village mechanics could not be trusted with the contract. Carpenters patched together Gothic windows, Grecian pediments, something from here, something from there, without understanding how the elements were intended to harmonize. A building of such eclectic confusion, though serviceable, would in time fail the congregation. "As those who use the building grow in taste, while the building itself remains the same from year to year, the latter becomes more and more unsatisfactory, and instead of being cherished the more the longer it stands, is soon despised, and ere long deserted or pulled down to make room for a better." The committee offered this warning mindful of "the rapidity with which our villages become towns and cities, and how fast the demands of taste and convenience advance in a country moving onward so swiftly as ours, in the acquisition of wealth and in general culture."[46]

In fulfilling its charge, the committee looked wherever it could for exemplars of good architecture. The title of the volume listed ten architects whose buildings the committee considered tasteful models for Congregational parishes. It was a broad-bottomed, ecumenical group, by no means restricted to architects with New England or Congregational practices. Richard Upjohn was most noted for his design of Trinity Church in New York City, the preeminent example of Gothic church architecture in the 1840s, and James Renwick designed New York's Grace Church. Although Trinity was the foremost symbol of Episcopalianism in America, Upjohn's identification with another denomination did not inhibit the committee. It was looking for tasteful buildings, not orthodox ones, and Upjohn's architectural achievements qualified him beyond any question. Standards of taste took precedence over parochial denominational culture.

Since the early eighteenth century, Congregationalists had borrowed from Anglican churches in the effort to beautify their meetinghouses, turning the axis to follow the long dimension of the building and adding steeples. To emulate the best of Episcopal architecture now was not a sudden departure. In that spirit, the title of the book abandoned the traditional term "meetinghouse" that had long distinguished Congregational places of worship from Anglican churches. The volume offered Congregational parishes *A Book of Plans for Churches*. The title was not likely to disturb readers; the old "meetinghouse" usage by this time was disappearing from parish minutes in country towns anyway.[47]

There were other reasons why a book on church architecture in 1852 could not disregard Episcopal influences. For the preceding twenty years the Anglican Church in England and the Episcopal Church in America had undergone a renaissance in church architecture. In 1836 Augustus Welby Northmore Pugin (1812–52) had launched his campaign for Gothic as the only true Christian architecture with a publication that lamented the decay of taste since the fifteenth century. Five years later, in *The True Principles of Pointed or Christian Architecture*, Pugin insisted that nothing but Gothic was suitable for churches. The Cambridge Camden Society, organized in 1839, was less dogmatic than Pugin but no less determined to improve architectural taste and to restore the place of ritual in worship. To achieve that end, the Camden Society recommended plans with enlarged chancels. In the seventeenth and eighteenth centuries chancels had shrunk under the Protestant emphasis on preaching, and the society wished to restore the place for the traditional liturgy.[48]

American bishops took an interest in the movement almost from the beginning. By 1841 literature from the Camden Society was widely available in the United States, and in 1836 John Henry Hopkins, bishop of Vermont, had published a book of his own on Gothic ecclesiastical architecture with an American audience in mind. George Washington Doane, bishop of New Jersey, toured England viewing churches in 1841 and was inducted into the Camden Society. He returned to sponsor a number of eminent Gothic structures. In 1847 the New York Ecclesiological Society was organized and the next year began publishing *The New York Ecclesiologist*, offering help with the design of churches. Already by 1846 ten Gothic churches had been erected in New York City, nine of them Episcopal. In the 1840s, Episcopal Gothic churches were widely considered the most beautiful churches in America, the standard for others to emulate. The *Ecclesiologist* took upon itself to spread information on Gothic to inland cities and country churches.[49]

The *Book of Plans for Churches and Parsonages* was in a sense a Congregational answer to this Episcopal campaign. The book gave little western churches the same kind of help the *Ecclesiologist* afforded Episcopal parishes. Elegantly designed Episcopal churches threatened to steal away the most refined parishioners, and the Congregationalists could not remain defenseless in this cultural competition. Since the Episcopalians set the industry standard of taste, the Congregational committee had to offer compatible or at least equivalent architecture.

Although the Congregationalists were clearly under Episcopal influences, pure imitation would not do. The architectural struggle with the Episcopalians was only one aspect of an unhappy relationship between the churches in the 1840s, and the Congregationalists were not in a mood for unreserved neighborly borrowing. Congregational intellectuals attacked Episcopal worship and doctrine on many fronts. Episcopalianism was a religion of forms, the Congregationalist critics said, not a religion of experience; it sacrificed conversion to the liturgy. It gave up the Bible in favor of tradition and creeds. The revival of Gothic architecture only proved the point. The Gothic church explicitly created spaces for ritual and emphasized liturgy over the word.

Unfortunately, a religion of ritual and forms appealed to cultivated worshippers. "Some will love its imposing formalities," Bushnell wrote, "and praise it as a tasteful religion." One Congregationalist essayist in *The New Englander* believed that Episcopalianism was attracting even more cultivated

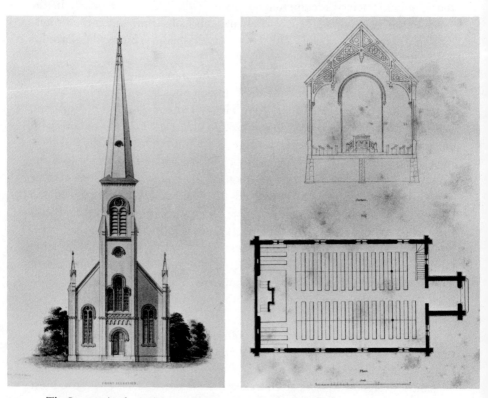

The Congregational committee on church architecture recommended plans that could scarcely be distinguished from those for Anglican churches.

worshippers than Unitarianism. Unitarians were migrating to Episcopalianism, anomalously giving up unfettered freedom of thought for obeisance at the feet of a hierarchy. Whether or not that was true, the appeal to the opulent threatened a terrible loss to Congregationalism. "Sad indeed would it be to see the seats of learning, the cabinets of science and art, the accumulated capital, the cultivated intellect of New England, laid at the feet of a church, unknown to our fathers except as a persecutor, and uncongenial to the institutions planted by them."[50] Obviously the Congregationalists had to do battle for their most cultivated members, and attention to architecture was one line of defense.

With such bad blood running, Congregational advocates of tasteful architecture could not advocate exact duplication of Episcopal churches. Distinctions had to be drawn. The *Book of Plans* explicitly repudiated the exclusive claims of Gothic "ecclesiastical and even Christian architecture, as if no other style had been appropriated, or reckoned suitable by the world at large, for ecclesiastical or Christian use." That was sectarian special pleading. "The Gothic is not, and never has been, the prevailing style of architecture in Christendom at large. It belongs mainly to England and parts of France and Germany." The *Book of Plans* took the high ground on the question of Christian taste, kicking a little sand in the faces of the Episcopalians as it climbed. "We are sure that a catholic liberality of sentiment ought to prevail on this subject as really as on any other, and will conduce more to improvement in church building, than any exclusive or bigoted preference adopted by a fashionable *clique* or religious sect."[51]

More important by far than style, in the Congregational view, was the plan of the church. Pugin and the Episcopalians tried to make the pointed style the only true expression of Christian belief. The *Book of Plans* said Greek or Gothic or other styles had equal affinities with Christian doctrine. What mattered more was how the church functioned, and above all whether it was suitable for preaching.

> In all the churches which Christianity, as reformed and brought back to its spiritual simplicity, has constructed for its own use, so working out a natural manifestation of its own ideas, the most conspicuous thing in the temple, the central point of attention for the assembly, is the pulpit for the living ministry of the living word, and before it, as convenience dictates, the table for the commemorative bread and wine.

The error in the decayed Christianity of the Roman apostasy was the prominence of ritual and the diminishment of the word.

> In the temples of a corrupt and superstitious Christianity, where the grand idea of the place is not preaching and praying, but sacrifice, you

see the pulpit diminished, and thrust as it were into a corner, while the focus of attention is the altar, and the high and holy place around it, where the priest pretends to renew Christ's expiation for sin, and according to his own showing, crucifies the Son of God afresh.[52]

The issue came down to altar versus pulpit. Was the chancel, the site for the altar, the focus of the church, or was the place of preaching the center of attention.

Henry Martyn Dexter, the eminent historian of Congregationalism at midcentury, in a lengthy treatise on church architecture, confessed his admiration for what he called the cathedral churches of Europe, but noted that "the voice of a preacher half hidden behind clustering pillars, is lost adown the 'long drawn aisle,' and confused among the reverberations that are thrown back from the 'fretted vault.' " American imitations of the cathedral style like New York's Trinity, "the most respectable in design and size, and every way the finest of the imitations of the cathedral style, which we have in this country . . . are not, and in the nature of the case cannot be, well adapted to the purposes of that form of Sabbath worship which centers its interest in the preaching and hearing of the Gospel."[53] The Congregationalists believed a Christian church had to be above all an auditory rather than a site for processions and ritual celebrations.

When Dexter wrote, Protestant churches had been built on the auditory principle for centuries; he enunciated the idea that had guided Dissenting church architecture from the beginning of the Reformation. But the Congregationalists of his generation gave the principle a peculiar twist. Earlier the emphasis on preaching had simplified churches, stripping down the plan and the decoration to the bare bones of pulpit and pews in an acoustic space. In the middle of the nineteenth century, the auditory principle reversed this process. With the pulpit firmly in place, Protestants felt justified in making churches more extravagant. The pulpit became a foundation on which to elaborate church architecture, to adorn buildings, and to authorize liberal adoption of traditional forms.

In churches built for preaching, the pulpits themselves grew more magnificent, with elaborate draperies in the French taste, including many-layered swags and tails, double stairways approaching from each side, an upholstered mahogany table with rich carvings as pulpit, and a Grecian sofa for the minister.[54] And beyond that natural outgrowth of a preaching emphasis, the auditory principle permitted Congregationalists to copy virtually anything else in High Church architecture. By anchoring a distinctive architectural identity in preaching, the Congregationalists thought they foreclosed the danger of sliding into popish corruptions. After that there were few limits.

Looking back on the early Puritan churches, Dexter thought they were needlessly averse to Anglican influences. He noted that the first Puritans continued to erect simple barnlike meetinghouses when they had the means to do better because the "feeling against the English Church and all its belongings, appears to have been still too great to permit our fathers, generally, even to attempt to approximate toward the external style of Church edifice which had been left behind in England." But those feelings gave way with time and the improvement of taste. "As the general culture improved, it began to be felt that God might be quite as acceptably worshipped in houses that should have a comelier aspect, and that should even suggest some of the old associations which had been left behind in the fatherland." Hence the turning of the church axis and the addition of towers and steeples. Dexter did not lament this return to English ways; it was a sign of an improving culture. He found nothing to fear in the explicit imitation of Episcopal churches. "There is nothing in a church spire, or a general outward church-ly look, which suggests anything inappropriate to the severest simplicity of our Denominational system."[55] So long as the churches held to the auditory principle they could go as far as they liked in imitation of traditional Anglican architecture.

The *Book of Plans*, also building on the fundament of preaching churches, set a cross on the tower of one model church. Just as a spire marked a building as a church, so did a cross, and Congregationalists should not bridle.

The fear or the dislike of Popery which forbids the use of this hallowed and most significant symbol in such a position, is a fear or a dislike, in our judgment, both unenlightened and harmful. The cross, in which the great apostle gloried and which is endcared to all Christians as the symbol of the atonement, it would seem, might safely crown our Christian temples, holding its place undisturbed and without giving offence, wherever the Savior is honored or his truth believed. There is no good reason why every little chapel of the Mother of Harlots should be allowed to use what appeals so forcibly and so favorably to the simplest understanding, and we be forbidden the manifest advantage which its use would often give us; or why, in this respect, we should suffer in comparison with other Christian denominations.[56]

There were seemingly no limits on Congregational architecture once the pulpit was given its due. Virtually any style, any decor, any period could be drawn on. So it was that in the larger towns where growth required new structures after the middle of the nineteenth century, Congregationalists built Romanesque, Gothic, and English country churches as often as they replicated the more familiar styles of the New England villages.[57]

For over a century Anglican churches had set the standards of taste for American churches. Congregationalists with refined aspirations looked to Anglican models for inspiration. By the middle of the nineteenth century, cultural competition brought the Congregationalists close to outright imitation, save for the ever important auditory principle. Distinguishing churches by their architecture became nearly impossible. In *Home As Found,* James Fenimore Cooper scoffed at this competitive emulation among the churches. A visiting lady to the village of Templeton in upstate New York inquired about a Presbyterian church standing next to St. Paul's, a newly constructed Episcopal church. "Pray, sir, what building is this nearly in a line with New St. Paul's, and which resembles it a little in color and form?" A local man, a Mr. Bragg, explained that the two were nearly identical, "windows excepted; it has two rows of regular square-topped windows, Miss, as you may observe." There was one other important difference in Bragg's view. The Presbyterians had gained the advantage over his own Episcopal church by reason of their bell. "Their new bell weighs quite a hundred more than that of New St. Paul's, and has altogether the best sound."[58] If it were not the bell, then the organ, or the height of the steeple. And so the churches drove themselves to ever greater exertions in the struggle for elegance and cultural superiority.[59]

The Methodists lagged only a step or two behind the Congregationalists and Presbyterians in this cultural competition. By the middle of the century they were beginning to upgrade the plain-style worship that was a point of pride for Cartwright. The early Methodist chapels resembled the barn meetinghouses of New England, devoid of tower and steeple and lacking in ornamentation. In 1858 the Methodists erected St. Paul's Methodist Episcopal Church in New York in a classic Gothic form, their entry in the swelling ranks of elegant Gothic churches in that city. In 1876 the Board of Church Extension started to offer plans for churches and parsonages and in 1883 alone sold 428 sets of plans for churches with estimated construction costs ranging from $1,000 to $12,000. The board warned churches against reliance on local carpenters, who were sure to produce "an awkward, ill-proportioned, inconvenient structure not likely to awaken devotional feelings." The catalogue contained ads for stained-glass windows, and the board itself recommended paper imitation stained glass.[60]

In the latter half of the nineteenth century all the mainstream Protestant churches erected great stone, brick, and wooden buildings in vast numbers patterned after one form or another of English churches. The plebeian beginnings of the Methodists and Baptists made the construction of tasteful churches all the more urgent for a later generation of cultivated members. Writing at the moment when the Methodists were beginning to put up refined churches, Cartwright looked back longingly to the time when the

ABOVE. *Like Methodist churches in England, this early structure in New York had little on the outside to make it apparent it was a church.*

RIGHT. *The Methodist church in Saratoga was located near the magnificent Grand Union Hotel and was judged by a guidebook author to be the "most elegant and conveniently located edifice" of all the town's churches. By this date Methodists were competing with all the other denominations to excel in the grandeur and beauty of their churches.*

Methodists "had no pewed churches, no choirs, no organs; in a word, we had no instrumental music in our churches anywhere," just as the people dressed plainly and "Methodist preachers were called by literary gentlemen illiterate, ignorant babblers."[61] But his dispirited lament seemed to acknowledge that the tide of tasteful religion could not be stopped. As in every other denomination, Methodist churches came to be made up of well-dressed worshippers, sitting in beautiful structures, listening to educated ministers.

REVERSING THE COURSE OF HISTORY

DEXTER wrote about church architecture historically, beginning with the simple meetinghouses of the first settlers and coming up to the embellished churches of the present. Although useful for understanding architectural change, the Congregational story told through buildings cast church history in a new light. In the traditional way of recounting the Puritan past, religion in New England declined from its first founding. The heroic piety of the founders weakened as the years passed. The task of the ministry was to revive religion, to restore the churches to their original purity and devotion. With the meetinghouses as indicators, the course of church history was reversed; New England religion appeared to have improved over time. The first meetinghouses were primitive structures, rude shelters from the elements, erected "without regard to much comeliness of aspect." The addition of towers and steeples, the embellishment of interior decoration, the reorientation of the axis came with the improvement of economic conditions and the elevation of general culture. Churches with a "comelier aspect" were signs of progress in society and in religion.[62]

Dexter was not alone in rewriting Congregational history from an architectural perspective. Noah Porter, a leading figure among the New Haven intellectuals through the middle years of the nineteenth century, was equally scornful of the first Puritan churches.[63] The only excuse for their homely appearance was the comparable deformity of Anglican houses of worship. The first King's Chapel (built in 1689) "was ugly enough to match any of the ugliest churches of the Puritans, and effectually to redeem the Puritan principles and tastes from any special responsibility for the defective architecture of the times." From such a low beginning, there was nowhere to go but up.

Porter did not wish to discredit the first settlers entirely, but in searching for redeeming qualities he put the old religion in a new light. "Uncouth as were their manners, and harsh their speech," he said on their behalf, "the spirit of courtesy and reverence animated their precise and decorous life." Porter's address shocks a reader accustomed to the appeals to history in earlier sermons. He and Dexter not only reversed the direction of history from decline to progress; they judged the past by a new standard: the earlier generation's degree of refinement. Disregarding the piety of the founders, Porter found early Puritan worship lacking because it was rude and uncouth. Looking for virtues in the early churches, he valued them not as centers of faith but as centers of culture and schools of good manners, struggling along in a primitive age. "There was nothing the New England minister so much deplored as ignorance and barbarism in his flock," he argued in defense of the clergy. The churches were to be admired as outposts of civilization. "Every meeting house was of necessity a center of culture, a school of good manners, a training place for decorum, an enforcement of order, in the name of the living God and in the interests of the kingdom of Christ."

The faith of the founders disappears from this account. The past was judged for the level of civilization it had achieved; progress was marked by refinement, not piety. Urging toleration, Porter emphasized that while "the worship might perhaps seem rude to us, and the sermons unfinished and uncouth, and the culture and education from both to have been of a negative value," still they did their best with what they had. "We should remember as we drag through the old sermons, and the books of ghostly counsel, and the poetry of doubtful inspiration, that the first preachers of New England were two generations and more earlier than Locke, three before Addison, and five before Johnson."[64] So much for the glories of pristine Calvinism. What New England lacked in the seventeenth century was instruction in Augustan gentility.

Dexter and Porter interpreted change as Francis Underwood did in his native Quabbin. The improvement in the churches reflected the improvement in every aspect of culture and worship—in music, for example. "In the first generations of New England," Porter wrote, "the poetry and singing were rude enough and very little of culture could come of either." With the acceptance of Isaac Watts and the new way of singing, "separate choirs triumphed, and with these came in that cultivation of sacred music, which for nearly a century at least has made the New England meeting house so efficient an incitement to the musical culture and incidentally to the refinement of the community."[65] That was progress. Cartwright's jeremiad on the decline of Methodist worship, marked by the introduction of choirs and organs, sounded only retrograde to the ministers of tasteful religion. Decline for him was progress for them. Culture, in the sense of beauty, refinement, and taste, was the measure of human development, and religion had advanced as it measured up to these universal standards.[66]

WORLDLY RELIGION

THE advocates of taste were not unaware of the untoward consequences of refining religion. They knew, for one thing, that the cost of church membership in sophisticated congregations excluded the poor. Payment for the beautiful buildings erected at ever greater expense came more and more from the sale of pews, and the cost was more than many could bear. The prices sometimes stretched the budgets of middle-class people. When St. Thomas surpassed Grace Church as an up-to-date and fashionable New York Episcopal church, John Pintard sold his Grace Church pew and hoped he would realize enough to pay for a more costly place at St. Thomas. He was willing to go as high as $500 and was delighted when the prime location he desired went for $400.[67] Poor people could not afford a fraction of that price.

In 1846 a religious periodical reported a philanthropic effort "to erect a church edifice in which the poor might enjoy an equal opportunity with the rich in the privileges of the sanctuary." The idea was "to make a trial how far a church can be maintained without having recourse to the pew system." The trouble was that by this time, with elegant churches going up on every side, a plain church for the poor would arouse their ire rather than win their gratitude. "It was necessary," the magazine commented, "that the building should not be behind in point of architecture, lest it should be regarded as designed *only* for the humbler classes of the community, who on that account would be likely to avoid it."[68] Elaborate buildings had so corrupted the churches that the poor could not afford membership, and yet segregation into a plain church offended them.

On top of pew costs, worshippers had to wear clothes in keeping with the splendor of the building, and the style of the congregation became an insurmountable barrier for many. A century earlier a common farmer could dress up for church by putting on a blue check shirt. In the genteel atmosphere of the new beautiful churches, more was required. Two little du Pont girls felt shabby at church because they lacked new bonnets.[69] Though easily dismissed as a whiff of girlish vanity, the sense of being personally shabby in the environment of worship was more serious for those who lacked the means of improving their appearance. Churches could become alien environments like formal parlors or concert halls, where plainspoken, commonly dressed people marred the scene. Stowe observed that everyone in Oldtown felt "obliged to appear in decent apparel, and to join with all the standing and respectability of the community in a united act of worship."[70] Her intent was to draw a happy scene of village harmony, except that linking decent apparel to the communion of respectable worshippers excluded people without the right dress. An advocate of beautiful churches warned about

drawing aesthetic standards to such a fine point that shabby worshippers had
no place. "Too often it is true that pride would exclude poverty; that, while
ostensibly the wealthy erect beautiful and costly church edifices for religion's sake, it is in reality only for pride's sake; and hence whatever in the
garb of poverty and lowliness offends the eye must be excluded."[71]

The books on church architecture had to meet the charge of extravagance
that went along with this pride. Drawing on Ruskin, they argued that houses
of worship merited at least the same degree of elegance as the residences
of the worshippers. Members slighted God by giving Him a plainer house
than the dwellings they built for themselves. "I do not understand the
feeling," they quoted Ruskin as saying, "which would arch our own gates
and pave our own thresholds, and leave the church with its narrow door and
footworn sill; the feeling which enriches our own chambers with all manner
of costliness, and endures the bare wall and mean compass of the temple."

The *Book of Plans for Churches* offered as a simple rule of thumb in
determining internal adornment that "the church should correspond in style
to the better class of the dwellings possessed by those who are to occupy the
church." It seemed like a good idea to synchronize church adornment with
the decor of nearby houses.

> If the people are generally poor, so as to be able to have only the
> plainest houses and the most necessary articles of furniture in them,
> then it is not to be expected that their place of worship will be other
> than plain. But if the people indulge in carpets and lounges, in furni-
> ture made of rare and costly woods, in mirrors and marbles, and
> ingenious carvings and hang their walls with pictures, then it is rightly
> expected that their house of worship will show something besides bare
> floors and the array of plain rectangular spaces of unadorned walls.[72]

The Congregational committee may not have realized that this seemingly
reasonable suggestion meant that class divisions were incorporated into the
very bricks and mortar of the churches. One glance would tell a visitor about
the wealth and culture of the people who worshipped in a building and
whether or not poor or rich belonged there. In their very appearance,
churches explicitly stated the level of refinement achieved by a congregation
and so of their social class. In their ambition to elevate the culture of the
churches, the advocates of improved architecture forgot the effect on the
people who lagged behind and rarely asked whether the resulting invidious
comparisons were in keeping with their own Christian values.

The spread of refinement among the middle classes necessarily ensnarled
religion in contradictions like this one. The old-time evangelists instinctively
recognized the incompatibility of religion and gentility without understanding what lay behind it. They did not see that gentility had originated in royal

courts; it was a culture formed around power, hierarchy, and worldly ambition. The contradictions were not always evident in the simplified, domesticated gentility adopted by the American middle class. In the skillful hands of
Bushnell, refinement of mind blended imperceptibly with purification of
spirit; beauty in houses, dress, and manners extended the beauty that God
invested in His creations. Those appealing ideas obscured the underlying
clash between the two traditions. The advocates of tasteful religion lost sight
of gentility's fundamental commitment to court hierarchies and the cultural
elevation of a superior class, hardly the aim of Christianity.

Only on closer examination does the justice of the evangelists' instinctive
antipathy toward gentility become clear. In one of the innumerable sentimental stories with a Christian message, a gentle little girl visits an old
gardener to learn the spiritual truths of plants. This innocent account of a
child's thirst for heavenly truths was meant to offend no one, and yet it
clearly implied the social inferiority of the gardener who must cater to the
little princess dancing among his plants. Although he was the teacher, she
was the center of the story, her growth was the matter of consequence.

Not just the recognition of class and the acknowledgment of social inferiority was significant in stories like this one; more important, the genteel
people were the only ones who counted. The little girl was worthy to
occupy the center because she was refined. The others—the farmers who
spoke in dialect, the kindly people in simple dress, the beggar girls on the
streets—stood at the margins, in one way or another serving the significant
ones at the center. Even acts of charity by benevolent gentlemen focused on
the goodness of the genteel. The stories illustrated the gentlemen's power
to uplift the poor more than the changes in the lives of the benighted. For
the poor to become significant, they had to become genteel. Working from
that same perspective, the architects of grand churches easily overlooked the
danger of excluding the poor from beautiful buildings because the beautiful
worshippers were the ones who counted.

The moving force behind all of this was the spread of gentility through
middle-class America and the resulting blend of personal refinement with
traditional Christian values. As people embraced gentility, how could they
fail to make refinement a virtue like faith, charity, or humility, adding to the
Christian creed provisions that were not there at the beginning? Once the
two traditions were joined, the stories of genteel Christians and marginal
inferiors naturally came into existence—just as tasteful religion created
beautiful churches that inadvertently expelled the shabby. It was not a
repulsive combination. With all its radiance and elevation, tasteful religion
engaged the sympathies of a large segment of the Protestant clergy, who in
their desire to sanctify genteel culture overlooked the contradictions and
cruelties introduced into the very heart of their churches.

CHAPTER XI

City and Country

B Y the middle of the nineteenth century, gentility had left innumerable traces on the American landscape. Fashionable houses, imposing public buildings, elegant churches, fancy shops, tree-lined streets, hotels and theaters, landscaped squares, pleasure gardens, and vacation resorts were erected to meet the needs of the growing genteel population. Taken together, these structures made up a geography of refinement, a map of places where genteel people could feel at ease, places marked by beauty and frequented by mannerly people in proper dress, engaged in elevated activities. On this map, boundaries divided greater from lesser areas of gentility and regions of civilization from areas of barbarism. Travelers passing from one zone to another noted signs of gentility or rudeness, measuring in their minds the levels of refinement in each place.

"City" and "country" were the words used to designate the broadest cultural regions. The terms divided the world in half, implying refinement and polish in the city and coarseness in the country. The usage was inaccurate if taken as an actual description of the two places. In reality polished and coarse culture could be found in both city and country. Within urban households there was even a difference in refinement going from kitchen to parlor or from stable to house, and still sharper distinctions from street to street. In rural villages, the level of refinement differed from house to house and certainly from country town to outlying farms. Refinement and vulgarity took innumerable forms within city and country and were not a simple distinction between the two.

More than an objective measure of reality, city and country were a cultural and social polarity in a mental geography. The words were categories of a simple but useful vernacular sociology. Fashion, refinement, and excitement were at one pole, and simplicity, rudeness, and torpor at the other. City and country represented the extremes of two contrasting ways of life. The words organized the social world spatially, attributing levels of culture to place, even while people recognized the far more complex boundaries of cultural difference in the real world. For us, looking back on the first half of the nineteenth century, city and country are a reminder that refinement had a geographic dimension, and they prompt us to explore how gentility left its imprint on American space.

CULTURE AND URBAN SPACE

DESPITE the explosive expansion of cities in the nineteenth century, their cultural organization continued to follow patterns laid down earlier when the tangled medieval city gave way to Renaissance order. In forming the geography of refinement within the city, the seats of civic authority retained their magnetic power as primary centers of urban gentility at least through the first half of the nineteenth century. Not every great house could look out on a city hall or statehouse, but such buildings exercised a gravitational pull that drew fine houses, shops, and hotels toward them, just as the royal palaces attracted aristocratic residences to the West End of London away from the commercial center in the City.

The Massachusetts statehouse in Boston, at the summit of Beacon Hill facing the landscaped Boston Common, anchored a district of elegant houses down the slopes on both sides and around the Common. The Pennsylvania statehouse (later Independence Hall), standing in a park extending from Chestnut to Walnut in Philadelphia, set the tone for the grand houses and genteel shops that eventually filled Walnut and Chestnut. City Hall in New York, in a park at the juncture of Broadway and Park Place, stood at the center of the city's finest shops and hotels and, until midcentury, of many elegant residences. Richmond's great houses were erected in the "Court End" north of the capitol. Gentility basked in the aura of the political power radiating from civic buildings, as it had done at Versailles and Europe's Renaissance courts.[1]

Civic centers surrounded by grand residences and elegant hotels, promenades and parks for fashionable walkers, and the wide boulevards flaring from such bases—the standard elements of polished European cities—were focal points of the genteel city. But more room was needed for the growing numbers who were coming under the influence of refinement. The campaign to make the world safe for gentility had to bring more and more of the city under its control, claiming areas far removed from the civic centers, and thus enlarging the spaces on the map that were part of the genteel realm.

In the nineteenth century, this expansion was less the work of city planners like Francis Nicholson, who dominated urban design in the eighteenth-century Chesapeake, and more the result of private initiatives to profit from gentility. Elizabeth Blackmar has shown how developers and contractors, aided by a few government advocates of city beautification, created sections of elegant housing at many locations in Manhattan. As they gained control of properties scattered through the city, developers devised means for creating a refined aura other than by location near a civic institution.

The best was a small park in front of the houses, preferably ringed with an iron fence as at Gramercy Park and Union Square. In 1831, the New York's Street Committee, noting the advantages, agreed to "facilitate enterprising individuals in laying out private squares," and the parks proliferated, heightening the values of the adjoining lots.[2] A statue in the square added to the attraction, perhaps because a national hero or major public figure brought some of the aura of governmental authority to the space, as street names like Duke or Queen had added civic honor to the plain grids of commercial southern cities in the eighteenth century.

Where a park was impossible, a setback from the street had a similar effect. A developer of Bleecker Street row houses in 1828 introduced a covenant in the titles to leave ten feet between the street and the housefront as "open court or space and not appropriated or occupied by any edifice or wall nor in any manner obstructed otherwise than by an ornamental fence

Union Square, at the time the largest and most elaborate park in New York City, attracted major cultural institutions and fine residences to this area of Broadway.

or railing enclosing the same."[3] Improved circulation of air, considered important to health when most disease was attributed to miasma, combined with the slight parklike air of the open courtyards, made it possible for the developer to ask $12,000 for his houses.

Where there was no space for courtyards, trees in front of the house or, better still, before a row of houses accomplished the purpose. Hillhouse Avenue in New Haven, where James Hillhouse began planting trees before the turn of the century, set a standard for aspiring avenues throughout the country.[4] The aesthete and gentleman Sidney George Fisher thought "the quantity of trees in squares and in the streets is a great charm in Philadelphia."[5] Pictures of early city streets frequently showed newly planted young saplings encased in protective boxing, a sure sign that the urge to beautify and refine was at work.

The Bleecker Street developer in New York received permission to rename his section of the street Leroy Place, a privilege granted to developers of Lafayette Place, Waverly Place, Irving Place, and others.[6] The localized street designations were meant to be indicators of fashionable housing, a little rise in the cultural elevation at that point in the street, so that the standing of a person could be determined from an address alone. Giving a shop clerk one's address on Leroy Place brought a person a little tingle of pride denied a resident of a more plebeian street.

Using all of these devices—squares, courtyards, trees, and street names— developers planted patches of elegance here and there in the city like naturalized bulbs. Everywhere the map of gentility became something of a patchwork, with many rather than a few focal points and fashionable areas interspersed among plainer residences. In Philadelphia the best houses lined the squares and certain east-west streets, Chestnut, Walnut, and Spruce among them; in the nearby alleys and on side streets just around the corner, artisans lived in cramped quarters. One-room hovels in Providence's "Snowtown" were only a few yards away from the larger houses of merchants and craftsmen.[7] On the back side of Boston's fashionable Beacon Hill, servants and workmen lived in tiny houses, a fraction of the size of the nearby mansions. The only long New York streets that were fashionable from beginning to end were Broadway and, as midcentury drew near, Fifth Avenue. In Boston, Hanover, Franklin, Washington, and State were the favored avenues.[8] In James Fenimore Cooper's *Home As Found*, a visiting English aristocrat asked about social divisions in New York City, and an American lady interpreted his questions spatially. "Sir George Templemore, if I understand him, wishes to know if we estimate gentility by streets, and quality by squares."[9] And of course they did.

In the eighteenth century other sites besides residences were identified as areas of refinement. The best taverns contained long rooms for assemblies

ABOVE: *Although not blessed with a park, Boston's Franklin Street did have the advantage of a widened street formed by Franklin Crescent to the right, and trees, lights, and an urn in the center.* Ballou's Pictorial Drawing-Room Companion *noted that the houses were occupied by "some of our wealthiest citizens."*

LEFT: *Trees in protective casings appeared along city streets wherever the residents or proprietors wished to introduce a note of refinement.*

where polite society met for dancing, cards, and talk. At the end of the century some taverns adopted the name "hotel" to add French sophistication and to distinguish themselves from the lower range of taverns. In the nineteenth century, hotels were situated at central places in the geography of gentility to attract the best society. Boston's Tremont Hotel faced the Common and the capitol; New York's Astor House faced City Hall Park, both near to elegant residences and eminent public buildings. Over the century hotels set a standard of decoration and furnishings that was rarely matched in the grandest residences.[10] The magazine publisher Frederick

Gleason linked hotels to "the advancements of civilization and refinement in our growing country."[11]

On a more modest scale, cultural institutions did the same. The New Theatre went up in 1793 in Philadelphia, next to Oeller's Hotel and across from the statehouse on Chestnut at Sixth, the architecture copied after the theater in Bath, England.[12] Other cultural institutions—concert halls, pleasure gardens, museums, colleges, atheneums—became part of the genteel architectural assemblage. Miss Leslie's famed behavior guide listed among the acceptable places of amusement theater, opera, concerts, and meetings of the legislature. The existence of galleries for the unvarnished population did not discredit theaters for genteel patronage, and by midcentury certain theaters had become the exclusive resort of the gentility.[13]

These elevated environments provided settings and activities suitable for refined people who circulated along the genteel routes in the city, from mansion to mansion, along fashionable streets and promenades, and on to theaters, churches, museums, libraries, and hotels. Respectable people required houses with parlors, dining rooms, and the other spaces in which genteel activities occurred, with trees in the pavement before the house if possible, but besides this, when the family left the house, their paths had to follow a genteel route to places where their refinement would not be besmirched. Reuben Vose, an enthusiast for fashionable gentility, wrote in 1859 of New York's Fifth Avenue Hotel that "a seat may be occupied in the hotel,

Away from the fashionable streets, much more modest houses without trees or front yards intermingled with stores and industrial shops.

and before him will pass more of the real beauty and wealth of the nation than in any other spot in the city."[14] The comment would have pleased the patrons, because the presence of all that beauty and wealth reassured them that they were located on an established passage for the city's genteel population.

Genteel spaces had immense authority because being there—at the right moment in the right dress—identified a person as genteel. Having a room at the Fifth Avenue Hotel, with the related right to pass regularly through its parlors, made a public claim to personal refinement. Such environments offered constant reassurance of one's gentility. On the other hand, locating an establishment on the paths of genteel movement gave a place a great advantage in attracting the best customers. The owners of the Fifth Avenue Hotel benefited greatly from its location on that fabled street, and countless other establishments sought the same good fortune. Barnum located his New York museum at a prime Broadway location and his Philadelphia establishment on Chestnut Street and Seventh in hopes that the places would shed luster on his entertainments.[15] The need to remain securely within the orbit of gentility and the concomitant desire to exploit that need commercially were the major forces generating the urban geography of refinement.

The commercial possibilities of gentility led to the chief nineteenth-century contribution to the geography of refinement, the genteel shop. In the eighteenth-century European capitals, such shops did business near the royal palaces or residential squares.[16] Some faint imitations appeared in Philadelphia and Boston by the end of the century. Before 1800 American shop architecture showed less influence of refinement than did the advertisements of the owners. The ads commonly addressed their customers as "gentlemen and ladies" and invited them to view the most recent imports from London. The implication was that anyone who entered the store and purchased its goods was gentry. The lure of the fashionable shop was that the very act of buying goods there helped one to establish a genteel social identity.[17]

In the nineteenth century, architecture enhanced the illusion. John Fanning Watson said that before 1800 Philadelphia shops occupied regular houses with signs to distinguish them. Sometimes wares, suspended from chains, were displayed on shutters. The first shop with bulk windows, in contrast to smaller house windows, was one at Market and Front streets that sold penknives, buttons, and scissors. A more striking departure from the old way was the shop of the Londoner Mr. Whiteside at 134 Market, done up, it was said, in Bond Street style. In the two large shop windows with uncommonly large panes "fine mull-mull and jaconet muslins, the chintses, and linens" were "suspended in whole pieces, from the top to the bottom, and entwined together in puffs and festoons." Inside, the shopman stood "behind the counter, powdered, bowing and smiling." Mr. Whiteside's was "all the stare" for a while, Watson said. But at the time the "pouncet-box" atmosphere and the bow to the ladies seemed "rather too civil by half for the (as yet) primitive notions of our city folks."[18]

By the 1830s, when Watson wrote, retailers had gone miles beyond Whiteside's with their elegant façades and interiors. Bulk windows gave way to full plate glass and inside the store were long aisles with mahogany cases, marble floors, and formally dressed clerks who could not be distinguished from their most eminent patrons. By the 1850s dry-goods and department stores exceeded the decor of domestic drawing rooms, even in mansions, and adopted the name "palace" to suggest the ambience they sought to re-create. Their extravagant architecture and decoration made them the marvels of the city—Philip Hone called A. T. Stewart's "one of the 'wonders' of the Western World"—an irresistible magnet for genteel customers.[19]

Watson published a poem that claimed the beauties of Chestnut Street outshone the splendors of Bond Street, the Rialto, and New York's Broadway, making it the "pride and honour of our land."[20] The streets of shops, once ancillary to residential squares, promenades, and civic buildings, became centers of genteel life. Promenading on Broadway or Chestnut Street became more fashionable than on the Battery or one of the graveled walks in a park. A *Godey's* story of 1850 complained of girls who delayed dinner six days in seven "by their Chestnut Street promenades." Watson said that in

John Jacob Astor built his hotel on Broadway at the south end of City Hall Park, in the heart of the district encompassing the city's civic institutions, fashionable shopping, and many fine residences.

his time it had become the chief street as a "fashionable walk."[21] Shop-lined streets were the central routes for genteel traffic.

This kind of commercial activity failed to drive away genteel residences. Philip Hone, the wealthy and cultivated connoisseur of the arts and of New York life, lived at 345 Broadway across from City Hall Park until 1838 and then moved to another Broadway location farther north. On the traditional visiting day, January 1, he said, "Broadway was thronged with male pedestrians," visiting the fashionable houses on the street.[22] But the energy behind the creation of shops could not be contained. Hotels and residences of a previous generation gave way year after year to more "splendid stores." In 1850 Hone noted that "the mania for converting Broadway into a street of shops is greater than ever. There is scarcely a block in the whole extent of this fine street of which some part is not in a state of transmutation."[23]

That energy reached into side streets as well. Entrepreneurs installed commercial parlors in unlikely locations in hopes of attracting customers. The daguerreotype studios that mushroomed with the development of photography in the late 1840s, as Katherine Grier has discovered, were furnished with waiting rooms like drawing rooms in mansions. With a business estimated at three million daguerrotypes a year, the studios drew in customers with the promise of luxurious reception rooms as much as with camera skill. A Rochester daguerreotypist advertised that his rooms were "fitted up in a style of unusual splendor" and "supplied with every thing the extravagant could desire, the luxurious sigh for." Lush carpets, marble Italian statuary, divans, and French chairs were among the attractions. A Cincinnati gallery had a piano to amuse waiting patrons.[24] The daguerreotypists hoped to envelop photographic portraits in the refinement attached to paintings.

The same impulse brought parlors to steamboats and railroad cars. Wall-to-wall carpets, rosewood furniture, marble-topped tables, mirrors, stained glass, gilt moldings, and chandeliers were installed on passenger steamboats running the Great Lakes, the Mississippi and Ohio rivers, and Long Island Sound from New York to Newport. These mobile spaces served as havens of refinement so that genteel people could occupy reassuring environments even on long journeys.[25]

Not every enterprise was successful in achieving gentility. Along the edges of the refined spaces, businesses struggled to meet the high standards while maintaining industrial plants. The industrial side of tailoring or hatmaking could be relegated to the back or an upper story while the ground floor was fitted out with marble floors and mahogany cases. Cutting gravestone markers, or other heavy manufacturing, was less easily disguised. Yet the lithographed advertisement cards that became plentiful in the 1840s

Daguerreotypists fitted their waiting rooms out as elegant drawing rooms to create an aura of aristocratic refinement around the new form of portraiture.

Like the daguerreotype galleries and dry goods stores, I. M. Singer and Company wished to establish a genteel environment for retailing its machines.

often pictured ladies and gentlemen in carriages drawing up to the front door of a business while the industrial activity lay to the back.

John Fanning Watson watched the gentrification of blacksmithing with some amusement. Blacksmith shops, he wrote in the 1840s, "used to be low, rough one story sheds, here and there in various parts of the city, and always fronting on the main streets." Now they "have been crowded out as nuisances, or rather as eyesores to genteel neighbourhoods." But instead of disappearing, they were disguised in a new garb. "They are seen to have their operations in genteel three story houses, with warerooms in front, and with their furnaces and anvils, &c, in their yards or back premises." Watson, skeptical of the supposed advance of civilization, noted this advance "among the remarkable changes of modern times."[26] Proprietors had to refine their premises to bring customers to their doors.

Merchant's exchanges, where deals were struck, warranted elegant architecture befitting the wealth and cultural pretensions of the merchants who came there. In New York the exchange was considered "one of the ornaments of the city."[27] But at the beginning of the nineteenth century, docks

Although an industrial enterprise, the Keystone Marble Works appealed to the genteel population in its advertisement by placing a carriage and a lone lady before the building and encasing all of the scenes in a decorative framework.

The grandeur of the Second Merchants' Exchange Building, by Martin E. Thompson, spoke for the honor accorded commerce, setting merchants' exchanges firmly on the path to gentility. The building burned in the great fire of 1835 and was replaced by Isaiah Rogers's even grander Exchange at the current site of the New York Stock Exchange.

and countinghouses, where the merchants usually worked, stood at the opposite pole from the center of civic refinement. Countinghouse furniture did not warrant the interest of master craftsmen. The desks and bookcases now in our museums occupied the front rooms of mansions, not the merchant's place of work near his warehouse. The countinghouse as a place of work was off the map of refinement.

In the first half of the nineteenth century, the office, meaning the workplace of businessmen, began the gradual transformation that culminated in the elegant office towers of the late nineteenth century. The buildings that went up along the East River wharves in New York City, for example, received touches of dignity. The four-story brick building constructed in 1811 for Peter Schermerhorn on Fulton Street in New York City, though housing storage space and requiring a hoist on the front, had rusticated Georgian archways and a hip roof. In 1829, not far away on Coenties Slip, simple three- and four-story warehouses and stores with space for offices were constructed in a plain version of Greek Revival. But at this stage the elegance was restrained; they were not designed for a fashionable clientele. A guide to proper behavior noted that "in the countingroom and office, gentlemen wear frock-coats or sack coats. They need not be of very fine material."[28] The buildings had a heavy entablature on the ground-floor granite piers and a simple cornice, but little more. Richard Webster has termed the style utilitarian classicism. The structures represented the work world, where businessmen went when they left their mansions each day; they were not meant to glorify that work or to make high cultural claims for it. That came later.[29]

How the Other Half Lives

THESE buildings along the margins of refinement were a reminder that the entire city did not belong to gentility. Although at certain sites its claims were predominant, vast regions were given over to tawdry, rude, and dangerous society. An etiquette book noted that the extremes of society inhabited the cities: they were "the home of the most highly cultivated people, as well as of the rudest and most degraded." George Templeton Strong, a resident of New York's Gramercy Park, halted his chase of a fire alarm up Lexington Avenue in 1857 when he passed "beyond the bounds of civilization into desert places where Irish shanties began to prevail" and the area became "lonely and suspicious."[30]

In the heart of the city, in the jungle of cut-up and added-on houses extending into backyards and growing along alleys, was another kind of degeneration. A report in a children's magazine told of a philanthropic gentleman searching for the mother of a New York beggar girl. He found the number on an alley house off Centre Street. "I went in, and asked for the person who was sick. No one knew such a person. I entered room after room, without finding her. At last, after winding through a dark passage, I reached an apartment where the wretched invalid lay."[31]

Beyond the "bounds of civilization," whether on the outskirts or in the dark tunnels of the dense inner city, the dangers were far greater than the likelihood of having one's sensibility offended. Besides the presence of disease, vice, and suffering, riots and fighting broke out in these regions. In the Northern Liberties, just outside the formal boundary of Philadelphia, fighting erupted every Saturday night between the ship carpenters from Kensington and the butchers from Spring Garden. After the Tompkins Square riots in New York City in 1857, a gentleman walking the area at night risked being "knocked on the head." Strong said most of his friends were "investing in revolvers and [they] carry them about at night, and if I expected to have to do a great deal of late street-walking off Broadway, I think I should make the like provision."[32] His comment implied that in the night, in a time of trouble, gentility could call only a few places in the city its own.

The refined could not even feel completely secure in their own houses.

In 1855 after demagogues harangued unemployed New York workmen, rumors flew. "Friday night it was rumored that a Socialist mob was sacking the Schiff mansion in the Fifth Avenue, where was a great ball and mass meeting of the aristocracy." When a fire ravaged the tip of Manhattan in 1835, Philip Hone was aghast at "the miserable wretches who prowled about the ruins, and became beastly drunk on the champagne and other wines and liquors" they found there. He despaired of the "poor deluded wretches" who rejoiced in the sufferings of the "aristocracy, as their instigators teach them to call it."[33] At least in the imaginations of the wealthy gentility, this horde of discontented back-street barbarians threatened to invade the genteel city whenever suffering or disaster stirred them.[34]

The low-grade environments off the genteel routes fenced in the movements of the genteel population, especially women. The threat of physical violence or sexual molestation and, beyond that, the loss of dignity inhibited even simple activities. Charles du Pont forbade his wife to enter the railroad ticket office in New York City because it was "no place for a lady." Just being there amidst the stares of the vulgar population was degrading. For a long time railroad travel was off-bounds for genteel girls. Ann Ridgely thought it daring to propose a fifty-mile trip by herself in 1840; in 1855 she put her eleven-year-old niece on the cars from Wilmington to Farmington without hesitation. In the interval the railroads had installed "ladies' apartments" in the cars, just as steamboat lines had put in ladies' parlors. Women could venture out of their secure orbits only in spaces that excluded vulgar eyes and met the standards of genteel decor.

For the same reason Miss Leslie advised women to choose their shopping companions carefully. Some will have a "predilection for bargain-seeking in streets far off, and ungenteel." "There are ladies who will walk two miles to hustle in the crowd they find squeezing toward the counter of the last new emporium of cheap ribbons; and, while waiting their turn, have nothing to look at around them but lots of trash, that if they bought they would be ashamed to wear."[35] Better to stay with the genteel shops on the genteel streets where one did not have to weary one's eyes with trashy merchandise.

The trouble was that no site was entirely secure against invasions by the vulgar multitude. Miss Leslie warned her readers that the first-come, first-served rule in American shops compelled a lady to wait patiently for "a servant-girl, making a sixpenny purchase."[36] The coin of the realm gave anyone access to exclusive shops. In Dickens's *Nicholas Nickleby*, an English hairdresser refused the business of a coal heaver who wandered in for a haircut. When the customer expressed surprise, the hairdresser explained that he had to draw the line somewhere or his genteel customers would desert him. American shopkeepers could not be so overtly snobbish, however much they wanted to keep out vulgar intruders. A photographer lamented that customers entered his plushly decorated waiting room, and "having approached the middle of the room, wipe their feet on the Brussels carpet." While waiting their turns in the studio, they roughly handled the artwork in the parlor, "especially selections framed in gold-leaf," and then sat down, "elevating their muddy *under-standings* (which are suitable for a Connecticut River fishing smack) into the best and most expensive upholstered chair."[37]

Rude people could not always be kept out of private parlors. Samuel Seabury III told of the discomfort he caused his New York City aunt when she invited him to visit. Seabury, the grandson of the first Episcopal bishop in America, was apprenticed to a Manhattan cabinetmaker after the boy's father fell on hard times. On working days Samuel labored amidst the dust and shavings of the shop and carried finished pieces through the streets to their destinations in the fine houses of the city gentry. On the weekends he sat beside these customers at his aunt's dinner table. He was aware of the utter anomaly of moving back and forth across the line in the city's social geography and of his aunt's well-intentioned efforts to explain his presence when he was actually an embarrassment. She asked questions in a way to "help her company to understand that I was a poor connexion at a trade whom she in the midst of her splendor was not ashamed to disown." These excursions across the border wounded Seabury; "to one of my temperament it was agony."[38] He doubtless was equally troublesome to her.

Politics opened doors in the same way. Philip Hone reported the miseries of New York's mayor during the traditional open house at the beginning of 1837. In previous years a few gentlemen dropped by for a greeting, a hand-shake, and a morsel of cake; in 1837 his doors were

> beset by a crowd of importunate *sovereigns,* some of whom had already laid the foundations of *regal* glory and expected to become *royally* drunk at the hospitable house of His Honor. The rush was tremendous; the tables were taken by storm, the bottles emptied in a moment. Confusion, noise, and quarreling ensued, until the mayor with the assistance of his police cleared the house and locked the doors.

Hone blamed the mayor's involvement in party politics for his troubles. "Every scamp who has bawled out 'Huzza for Lawrence' and 'Down with the Whigs' considered himself authorized to use him and his house and furniture at his pleasure; to wear his hat in his presence, to smoke and spit upon his carpet, to devour his beef and turkey, and wipe his greasy fingers upon the curtains." The mayor was helpless. Hone predicted that Lawrence was too much of a gentleman to put up with such treatment for long. But the minute he kept the crowd out they would throw him over "for somebody of their own class less troubled than him with aristocratical notions of decency, order, and sobriety."[39]

The most constant source of irritation for the genteel population was urban street life. In European cities guards stood at the gates of certain walks to keep out slovenly people, but there were no gates to Broadway or Chestnut Street, and anyone could walk there. Cartmen had to trundle their vehicles up and down the street with merchandise and supplies for the shops; lithographs from the period make cartmen fixtures of the scene. Beggars, thieves, and urchins were drawn to the best streets to ply their trades, and the curious of every class came to look in the shop windows. John Pintard worried about "the multitudes of poor Children, who are turned out like pigs into the streets" while their parents worked.[40] He had the children's interest in mind, but their presence on the best streets was not pleasing either. Strong complained that

> no one can walk the length of Broadway without meeting some hideous troop of ragged girls, from twelve years old down, brutalized already almost beyond redemption by premature vice, clad in the filthy refuse of the rag-picker's collections, obscene of speech, the stamp of childhood gone from their faces, hurrying along with harsh laughter and foulness on their lips.

Besides disgusting Strong, they troubled his conscience. He swore to help at least "one dirty vagabond child out of such a pestilential sink" before he died.[41] These inhabitants of another world were both a moral and an aesthetic hazard for genteel Broadway strollers.

Given this social patchwork, how were refined people to conduct themselves on the streets? On the one hand, they had to steer clear of the vulgar population and not let themselves be thrown in with the wrong company. Miss Leslie advised ladies never to share a hack. If a woman did, she was likely to "have for her riding-companions persons of improper character and vulgar appearance, and to be carried with them to their places in remote parts of the city, before she is conveyed to her own home." (Genteel people thought of their places as the center and the doubtful parts of the city as remote.)

On the other hand, fashionable streets were a genteel stage where a performance was required. Miss Leslie reminded her readers that they were always under scrutiny in public places. "Strangers, knowing you but slightly, or not at all, will naturally draw their inferences for or against you from what they see before their eyes; concluding that you are genteel or ungenteel, patrician or plebeian, according to the coarseness or the polish of your manners."[42] The city sections of conduct books instructed readers on how to greet one's genteel friends and to relate to genteel strangers, as if such people were the street's chief denizens.

The major aim was to make a favorable impression. Should a lady carry a package through the streets, for example? In a humorous sketch in *Godey's* called "Signs of Gentility," a wife scoffs at the idea of bringing a bundle containing a purchase of gloves and handkerchiefs through Broadway. "What was to distinguish them from any vulgar people?" A good address on a genteel street put one under the obligation of proceeding unencumbered. "Bundles were not to be carried by those who were not ashamed to give their address to a fashionable shopboy." Carrying a package with music was an exception. "A roll of music looks so perfectly *genteel.* It announces that you can not only play, but can also afford to get all the novelties as they appear."[43] Although written as a caricature, the fiction had real-life equivalents. In 1829 a Philadelphia mother sent her daughter to a southern town to school mainly because "she is too much grown to walk through our streets with her school Books." After a certain age, a young lady would be embarrassed to walk with so much in her hands.[44]

The ideal was to move about the streets in carriages, which protected the occupants from the vulgar crowd by encasing them in genteel boxes. The lady in the *Godey's* story who worried about packages, envied a wealthy acquaintance who lived on one of New York's squares. She "need not set foot on the pavement except to cross it to her carriage," the perfect arrangement. Going about the streets in a carriage was far different from going by foot. One conduct book thought that "American ladies dress too richly and elaborately for the street. You should dress well—neatly and in good taste, and in material adapted to the season; but the full costume, suitable to the carriage or the drawing-room, is entirely out of place in a shopping excursion, and does not indicate a refined taste." A carriage, because it elevated a person above the street, was like a drawing room and called for a different costume entirely.[45]

Few people with a desire to be refined could afford carriages, and so they were left to cope with the perplexities of street life in the patchwork city. Like little Ellen Montgomery in *The Wide, Wide World,* they were not completely at ease in the mixed population of vulgar and genteel. Efforts to create refined routes and havens, to install parlors everywhere, including rooms on steamboats and railroads, could never fully insulate the genteel population from all the others. Everywhere the realms of refinement bordered on the realms of vulgarity, and the borders could not be sealed.

The miseries of the poor who came continually under their gaze disturbed the consciences of many in the genteel population. Innumerable plans and organizations to ameliorate the sad condition of beggar girls, drunkards, and fallen women grew out of their urban encounters. At the same time, the urge to withdraw, to purify genteel neighborhoods, and to shut out the vulgar was equally powerful. As the geography of refinement enlarged, the boundaries between gentility and barbarism grew more rigid in a vain attempt to end the tensions between the two cultures in the nineteenth-century city.

VILLAGE CULTURE

THE mythic cities in the United States in 1850 were Boston, New York, and Philadelphia. Country people thought fashionable life reached the pinnacle there. The provincials granted cultural authority to anyone from the great cities. Even a single visit to one of the fashionable cities gave a tourist a cultural advantage upon his or her return to small-town society.

So functioned the myth of city and country. In actuality, genteel culture throve vigorously in many secondary cities. State capitals like Hartford, Providence, Richmond, and Annapolis were organized spatially according to urbane city-planning principles and sustained a flourishing polite society. In the 1796 tax list Hartford showed 90 carriages when the list contained just 784 polls. (New Haven, a county seat and college town, had 109 carriages with 622 polls.)[46] Hartford had its civic center and a street of fine houses. A visitor to Hartford in 1808 noted that "within a few years, the stile of building has almost totally changed. The dwelling-houses, stores, etc. erected of late, are generally in a stile of superior taste and elegance. The gothic and clumsy appearance which marked the buildings thirty years ago is entirely done away with." Another visitor counted twenty-two three-story shops.[47]

The same kind of urban refinement was found in county seats and secondary ports like Wilmington, Delaware; Salem, Massachusetts; and Cincinnati. These towns bore all or most of the marks of urbane planning principles: a civic center or square, a major street (or two) extending from the square with fine shops and grand houses, a scattering of upscale hotels and cultural institutions like libraries, museums, and churches, and trees along sidewalks to refine and soften the streetscape.

As these smaller cities grew larger, areas of refinement appeared away from the central axis, usually anchored by a church or a cultural institution. In Providence, Rhode Island, Benefit was the preeminent street of fine homes in the early nineteenth century. The old statehouse and the First Baptist Church within a block of one another on Benefit established the claims of the street (along with its route along the bluff overlooking the harbor). The Atheneum, the focal point for the intellectual and literary life of the city, was housed in a Greek Revival building on Benefit Street, constructed by the Philadelphia architect William Strickland in 1838. Brown

University rose up nearby, and John Carter Brown built his mansion just off Benefit; the most fashionable shops occupied a stretch of North Main just a block away from the street.

But a decade or two into the nineteenth century, Westminster Street across the harbor attracted fine residences, perhaps drawn by the theater and the Episcopal church. The Episcopal bishop saw to the erection of a Richard Upjohn church in 1845–46. To complete the picture, a sketch showed trees set in the sidewalks along Westminster. In a sense, Benefit was the Baptist street of refinement, and Westminster the Episcopal.[48]

Now and then, a passage from a historical document allows one to observe the diffusion of these urban cultural forms from provincial centers into country villages. The appearance of New Haven entranced Oliver Wolcott of Litchfield, Connecticut, when at age thirteen he visited Yale. "It took a long time to recount all the wonders I had seen," he later wrote. Along with the vessels at the Long Wharf, he admired "the grandeur of New Haven, its numerous Streets, beautiful Trees, Shrubbery and Flowers in the House Yards." Impressed with the elms James Hillhouse had planted, Wolcott started a tree-planting campaign in Litchfield after he returned from college. First he set out thirteen sycamores along South Street to commemorate the thirteen colonies. When these died, elms from the swamps replaced them. John C. Calhoun later joined the effort. While a student at Tapping Reeve's law school in Litchfield, Calhoun planted trees in front of every house where he boarded.[49]

All the planting baffled an older inhabitant. "We have worked so hard in our day, and just finished getting the woods cleared off, and now they are bringing the trees back again." That was a natural reaction from someone of the older culture. But by the end of the eighteenth century, a few people in Litchfield acknowledged the higher culture of the cities and wanted it for themselves. Colonel John Pierce sent his sister to New York to prepare to open a school for young ladies in Litchfield. In 1784 he urged her to make the most of her time.

> The short time you have and the many things you have to learn, occasions me to wish you would employ every moment for the purpose, I hope you will not miss a single dancing school, and that you will take lessons from Capt. Turner at other times, pray get him and Katy your friend, to instruct you in every thing in walking standing and sitting, all the movements of which tho' they appear in a polite person natural, are the effects of art. while [sic] country girls never attend to and which you had best take the utmost pains, or you will never appear natural and easy in. I am somewhat fearful that your old habits at your age can not be so thoroughly removed, as to give

place to a natural careless genteel air, and which totally hides all the art of it.⁵⁰

The consciousness of deficiency and the yearning for improvement preceded the acceptance of genteel culture from the cities. Sarah Pierce, the young woman in question, had that sense, learned the lessons a country girl needed, and returned to establish the famous school for young women that was the pride of the town. In the same spirit, Wolcott was ready to see beauty and grandeur in New Haven, and so the trees made their impression on him.

Backed by the growing genteel population, town leaders were prepared for major steps to beautify Litchfield by the early nineteenth century. The success of a small ballroom on the second floor of a local tavern convinced another tavernkeeper in 1787 to devote his entire second floor to a ballroom. Litchfield had 6 carriages in 1796 for its 678 polls, a trifle compared with Hartford's 90, but a start. By 1800 the town had a hotel and a public library.⁵¹ By 1810 among the businesses in town were two carriage makers, three goldsmiths, and two bookstores. South Street, the main avenue in Litchfield, gradually became a street of fine houses. The eighteenth-century unpainted or yellow, red, brown, or blue houses without lawns gave way to white houses with fenced front yards standing behind the rows of elms Wolcott had planted in 1790. A visitor in 1820 thought it a stunning scene:

> One principal street extends more than a mile and contains a collection of very handsome houses with gardens and courtyards. The houses and appendages are generally painted white. And it is rare to see so considerable a number of houses in a country town where nearly all apparently belong to gentry . . . it presents a very interesting and gratifying spectacle.⁵²

The residents along South Street doubtless were the ones to back improvements in the central park or square. Before 1780 the meetinghouse, courthouse, jail, tavern, and schoolhouse stood in the middle of the town's chief intersection. At that time geese, turkeys, and ringed hogs still ran free in the streets. In the center of the streets were loose stones and brush with mounds of whortleberry bushes. After 1820 the town cleaned all this up. The buildings, including the Second Congregational Church, were moved out of the main intersection, leaving an open space. In that decade, for the first time the church was painted white. In 1835 the town began to create parks. The old militia parade in the center of town was turned into Central Park; it was graded and fenced, and trees were planted. The expenses grew so high that people living in outlying areas who benefited little from the improvements complained, and in 1870 a Village Improvement Society was organized to carry on the work outside the structure of town government. By dint of great effort, Litchfield made itself into a civilized town, with a central civic square, a long boulevard of elegant residences, and parks.[53]

Litchfield was notable but not unique among New England towns. Of all the regions, New England had been the least influenced by Renaissance urban design in the eighteenth century. Inspired by another tradition, the towns had resisted rectangular grid plans and civic squares. In the first half of the nineteenth century, one little village after another made up for lost time. At the central intersection where a church, a tavern, and a militia training ground had haphazardly come together, a new vision of civic order took over. The church was often turned to face directly onto the square or green or a new one was built with tower and steeple foremost.[54] The central space was fenced, a lawn planted, and a row of trees heeled in. A barren space once occupied by stumps, stagnant pools, and stones gave way to beauty and order. Around the green the town's civic buildings gathered: church, hotel, schoolhouse, bank, and town house all in proper white and many in Greek Revival style.[55]

J. W. Barber's sketches of these towns, published in 1836 for Connecticut and 1839 for Massachusetts, celebrated their achievement. Of Westfield, Massachusetts, a typical town, he observed that "a small enclosed common, oval in its form, is in the central part of the area, around which the public buildings are situated; it is newly set out with shade trees, and will add to the beauty of the place." Scores of towns had made the same improvements. The finest greens appeared in the most prosperous towns. Salem's Washington Square had all the elements: "This common is a beautiful plot of eight and a half acres, almost perfectly level, enclosed by a neat railing, bordered by a large number of elms, and traversed by gravel walks." Many other towns had taken preliminary steps to clear space, plant trees, and bring the town's civic buildings into order around the green.[56]

In his books of sketches of New York and New Jersey towns, published in 1841 and 1844, Barber found fewer signs of civic improvement. Houses tended to be scattered, with fewer fenced yards and trees, and civic squares less in evidence. Middle states' improvements occurred more commonly in larger towns, often ones with state or county government buildings. Newark, New Jersey, had a "beautiful Public Ground," as Barber and Howe called it, with a broad open green, rows of trees, and an Episcopal church. The green was situated on Broad Street, a wide avenue of shops, churches, hotels, trees, and residences. Dover, Delaware, fenced its green and planted lawns and trees, as a hotel, a bank, and fine houses went up around it. In West Chester, Pennsylvania, people began setting their houses back from the streets in the early nineteenth century, and planting trees and shrubs. In 1823, the town government ordered sidewalks to be graded, curbed, and paved. An 1827 visitor said she "found more taste, talent and refinement in West Chester, in proportion to the number of inhabitants than in any town, without exception, I have visited." The town's ambitions culminated in the construction of the courthouse in 1848 at the central intersection from a design by the notable architect Thomas U. Walter. A remarkable row of linked town houses fronted by trees went up the same year.[57]

This depiction of Concord, Massachusetts, on the eve of the Revolution shows how disorganized the town center was. The large building to the left is the Congregational church and the house-like structure in the center foreground was an inn. Later a green was laid out in the open space between the cemetery and the town, and the buildings were grouped more regularly.

Even before its streets were paved, Pittsfield enclosed a central green and planted trees. Churches, hotels, schools, banks, and fine residences gathered around the green.

Even towns with modest civic aspirations planted trees. In bird's-eye views of cities and towns, the roofs and spires of the buildings came to look as if they floated on a sea of trees. Shaded walks were the boast of every city. Looking back on West Chester's improvements, the authors of an 1881 county history said that until the trees were "planted which now render the streets of West Chester so umbrageous and pleasant, our pedestrians found nothing to intercept the glare of the summer sun, save here and there, at long intervals, a straggling relic of a decaying Lombardy poplar."[58]

These refinements in the appearance of country towns proved that genteel culture was not sequestered in large cities. Gentility had given a new eye for beauty to town fathers in remote villages who dutifully appropriated tax moneys for clearing greens, putting in fences, and planting trees. Vernacular gentility also changed the villagers themselves. James Fenimore Cooper, who knew upstate New York from personal experience, had one of the characters in *Home As Found* observe the changes in fashion by 1840.

Such a thing as a coat of two generations was no longer to be seen; the latest fashion, or what was thought to be the latest fashion, being as rigidly respected by the young farmer or the young mechanic, as by the more admitted bucks, the law student and the village shop-boy. All the red cloaks had long since been laid aside to give place to imitation merino shawls, or, in cases of unusual moderation and sobriety, to mantles of silk. As Eve glanced her eye around her, she perceived Tuscan hats, bonnets of gay colors and flowers, and dresses of French chintzes, where fifty years ago would have been seen even men's woollen hats and homely English calicoes.[59]

Although less common in New Jersey than in New England, enclosed greens did appear in larger towns. In Newark, trees not only lined the green but stood before the houses surrounding it.

To entertain this fashionable crowd, hotels went up in tiny villages. A three-story brick hotel was erected across the street from William Corbit's house in Odessa, Delaware (earlier called Cantwell's Bridge), about the same time as the village imposed a grid plan to guide future building construction.[60] Country town hotels were centers of village social life. The assembly room in Litchfield's Phelps's tavern, where the law students from Tapping Reeve's school sponsored balls for the girls at Miss Pierce's school, had a high arched ceiling under the mansard roof with a music balcony at one end and red moreen divans around the walls.[61] Besides the frequent dances, beaux and belles in some places gathered nightly in the town hotel for conversation and flirtation.[62]

For the serious, lyceum lecturers came on tour and small subscription libraries made books available for modest fees. Villages were not to be deprived of mental culture. Francis Underwood thought the change he witnessed in his native Quabbin ran deep. "The change was not simply a matter of dress, of speech, or of tone,—there was a growing refinement in these externals,—it was something deeper: no less than an overturning of old habits of thought."[63]

Country towns must be entered on the map of refinement, earning places by virtue of their public squares with fenced greens and lines of elms, their shaded avenues of fine residences with lawns and white fences, and their hotels, balls, libraries, and public lectures. Outside of those locations, where did gentility reside in the country? Some factory owners attempted to bring their mills within the orbit of gentility. The du Ponts built a mansion on the bluff looking directly down on their black powder mills on the Brandywine River in Delaware. As the years went by they planted elaborate gardens on the hillside that came within a few feet of the buildings where the water-

The Brick Hotel in Odessa, Delaware, was erected directly across the street from William Corbit's house in the former Cantwell's Bridge. More elaborate in their architecture than small-town taverns of the eighteenth century, the hotels by the change of name suggested their wish to entertain genteel travelers and become the center of town social life.

Kirk Boott's cotton mills. The mill owners tried to draw the mills within the sphere of genteel respectability by planting a small green with trees in front of them and showing ladies and gentlemen gazing at them admiringly.

wheels turned the huge grindstones. Lithographs of mill housing sometimes show trees lining the streets with mills standing in geometrical precision nearby. Kirk Boott built his mansion with a Greek portico and large yard immediately adjacent to the entrance to the Lowell mills. Trees lined both sides of Dutton Street, which led to one mill entrance. In North Brookfield the shoe factory stood across the street from the green with walks and encircling trees and the church and fashionable houses on all sides. The cupolas on mill buildings, the cornices and moldings around windows and doors suggest efforts to turn mills into quasi-public buildings like hospitals and jails, making them ornaments of the town even though their purposes fell outside the bounds of refinement.[64]

That effort only occasionally succeeded. Mills were more often located away from the town's main street and public square, in remote mill villages near water sites. Worker housing could not consistently come up to refined standards when many owners lacked the capital to stabilize their industrial enterprise much less provide stylish residences for their workers. Despite attempts to reverse the drift, mills gravitated away from the centers of refinement, toward the commercial and business end of the cultural axis, the workers falling outside the bounds of gentility.

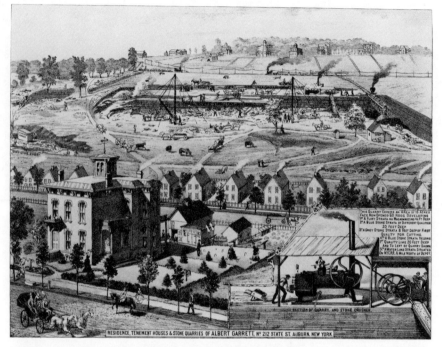

Entrepreneurs did not at first attempt to separate their residences from their industrial works. This fancy house with ladies holding parasols was put next to tenement houses and the owner's stone quarries, just as estate houses stood in front of barns and fields. The refined house was the front for the working rear, but the two parts made a single whole.

The sharpest boundary in country towns was between the villagers and the farmers, who by common agreement were rude and coarse beyond redemption. The merciless ridicule of this population by people of otherwise broad sympathies stuns a modern reader. In one edition of *Walden,* Thoreau commented on the outlying farmers who drove their carts into town.

How often in years gone by have I seen a country man come into town a-shopping, in a high-set wagon, whose clothes looked as if they were made before the last war by a maiden sister,—no reproach to her! His coat hung so high that you could see the whole of his waistcoat pockets beneath it; while the scant coat-tail hastened to a speedy conclusion, like a frog couchant on a bank; the funnel-shaped sleeves halting at a respectful distance from his victorious palms, and the collar, hard-rolled and round like a boa-constrictor, prompting you to run to his rescue.

And so on and on through his "waistcoat striped like the zebra's skin," and pants "straight and round like a stove-pipe," and his hat "towering straight and round, like a column, to meet the sun in his rising."[65] Thoreau, no advocate of the fancy life, had nothing but scorn for the appearance of the plain farmer.

Francis Underwood in his reminiscence of a boyhood in Quabbin, Massachusetts, near the end of the century thought the hill farmers outside his village beyond reprieve. He saw nothing picturesque in their houses, "one story, always of wood, clapboarded, rarely painted, and dusky with weatherstain." "Nature's gray is picturesque," he conceded; "so are dirt and rags, in the eyes of artists; but a dwelling that is gray or dingy with neglect, and rifted or 'chinky' with dilapidation, is no more comfortable for being in harmony with a low-toned landscape." Gentility had not made the slightest inroads there. "The old manners naturally survived longest in districts remote from the village and its modernizing influences," Underwood wrote, leaving the hill people behind in an unbelievably coarse existence. "The difference between these people and those in the social centre," Underwood said, "was like a gulf between centuries; and the rooted antipathy on the part of the hill people toward the better-dressed villagers was almost past belief." The hill people dressed in old blue frocks and went barefoot in the summer. They could sign their names and keep accounts but had no books or newspapers. They used obsolete words and spoke with "a universal drawl and *twisting* of accent." Distance and their "repugnance to the village set" kept them away from church; they preferred to listen now and then to unlettered preachers who poured contempt upon book learning and hireling priests. In town meetings they opposed public schools and road and bridge improvements. Underwood had no great admiration for the Quabbin villagers either, but "if they were not illuminated, their faces were turned toward the light." The hill people lived in cultural darkness.[66]

Underwood reported bitter resentment along the border between civility and barbarism in Quabbin, a "rooted antipathy" in the hill people toward the villagers. Suspicion, mistrust, and resentment must have commonly embittered these relationships. A well-meaning farmer who tried to start a school in the South Farms parish of Litchfield to reform the young people who seemed to him "clownish, ignorant and uncivil" was brought before the church by their parents for disturbing the public peace. Miss Pierce's students kept up a constant warfare with the Litchfield farm girls who came to work as hired help in town mansions. They fought over the best pews on Sundays and looked for every opportunity to show their disdain for one another.[67]

Ralph Hartsook, the hero of Edward Eggleston's *The Hoosier School-Master,* got the same treatment in Flat Creek, only a few miles outside Lewisburg, the little southern Indiana town where Ralph was raised. Lewisburg had its tokens of civilization; Flat Creek was pure degradation. As schoolmaster,

Ralph lived with the Means family, where, to his misfortune, the daughter Mirandy fell in love with him. She was, Ralph lamented, "the ugliest, the silliest, the coarsest, and the most entirely contemptible girl in Flat Creek district." While having a morning smoke from her pipe, the girl's mother made a proposal to Ralph. They sat before the fire, where

> the poplar table, adorned by no cloth, sat in the floor; the unwashed blue tea-cups sat in the unwashed blue saucers; the unwashed blue plates kept company with the begrimed blue pitcher. The dirty skillets by the fire were kept in countenance by the dirtier pots, and the ashes were drifted and strewn over the hearth-stones in a most picturesque way.

The proposal that Ralph marry Mirandy nearly felled him, but when he refused, the Means clan turned on him, and eventually drove him from Flat Creek, threatening to jail him or have his life. Ralph cordially disliked them and they returned the hatred.[68]

The resentment and distrust of country people for the village set—or for city people—sometimes turned to shame. If farmers hoped to elevate themselves in social rank, crude manners and awkward appearance embarrassed them. At age seventeen Samuel Seabury III was offered the position of usher in his New York aunt's boarding school. Being thrown into the middle of a half dozen young ladies in New York City made Seabury see himself in a new light. His feet, he realized to his embarrassment, were "long and sprawling" and "covered with a pair of substantial thick soled cow hide shoes" that had long gone without blacking. His coat and pantaloons of "course grey cloth" were too small, the pants not reaching to his ankles. "My hat too which had become rounded at the top and quite peaked, owing to my *capital* expansion, caused me as I stood bolt upright to present an object which . . . an army of lilliputians would have taken for a liberty pole." His aunt rushed him off to the hatter, shoemaker, and tailor, adding "as she looked at my long, stiff unbrushed hair, that though I had little marks of *civilization* to spare she would nevertheless recommend me to be *barbarized*." Looking back, Seabury recognized that the "stiffness of manner which I then possessed . . . utterly at variance with the easy lubricity which something of this world's polish" gave people, caused him to stumble in simple tasks like buying a book.[69] Seeing themselves through civilized eyes caused country people to feel awkward, inept, ugly, and foolish.

Levels of refinement varied in the countryside just as they did in the city. Underwood's crude farmers were the hill people, occupying only a certain quarter of the township. Scattered across the landscape elsewhere were prosperous farmers whose houses "were neat and comfortable, though invariably plain."[70] Seabury's family must have fallen into this general category, though his father was the minister of the town. Such people were not isolated from the currents of civilization or hostile to refinement, but they lacked the wealth and the incentive to black their boots and brush their hair.

Alongside these simple farmers, gentility sometimes seated itself in great elegance. By the middle of the nineteenth century a few gentlemen established country estates and erected mansions of the highest order. In 1840 James Fenimore Cooper told Sidney George Fisher that "handsome country establishments are found now everywhere in New York, and that the taste for rural life is increasing rapidly."[71] The numerous architectural books that proposed house designs for common farmers invariably culminated in designs for the villas of country gentlemen. Andrew Jackson Downing offered fourteen plans in his 1850 volume, *The Architecture of Country Houses*. He defined a villa as a country house for a person of sufficient wealth "to build and maintain it with some taste and elegance," with a staff of at least three servants. "The villa, or country house proper," he asserted with perfect confidence, "is the most refined home of America—the home of its most leisurely and educated class of citizens." "It is in such houses that we should look for the happiest social and moral development of our people."[72]

Although the villa was not meant for actual farmers who took their living from the soil, the most prosperous of farm families doctored and adorned their houses to give them a modest genteel air. Thomas Hubka has documented the incredible exertions of Maine farmers to turn their houses around to face the road, to paint and enlarge them, to turn kitchens into proper parlors, to plant trees and put white fences around the front yards— borrowing these ideas from genteel estates in city and country.[73]

David Goodale, who took over the management of his father's Marlborough, Massachusetts, farm in 1819, was another farmer who improved his standard of living while improving farm production. Goodale's 165-acre farm put him among the top 10 percent of farmers in Marlborough. He built an icehouse, an aqueduct system, and a new barn, and subscribed to *The American Banker*, all signs of his improving mentality. In 1841 he turned to the aesthetics of his farm. The 140-year-old house was painted white, and flower beds were planted along the horseshoe-shaped drive leading to the front door. During a remodeling of the house that year, designs were stenciled on the walls of the five upstairs bedrooms. In 1848 and 1849, when more remodeling went on, the downstairs rooms were papered. Goodale bought a sofa, an organ, and carpets; his children had music, drawing, and painting lessons. He subscribed to *Harper's Magazine* and *The Atlantic Monthly*; a son took *The Youth's Companion*. Besides conducting his farm in the most approved modern fashion, Goodale was determined to rear his children with some gentility. They received names like Lucy, Harriet, and Charles, as compared with

Abner, Nathan, Timothy, and Patience for the previous generation. One daughter attended Mount Holyoke. The family had daguerreotype portraits made for their missionary son in the Sandwich Islands. The Goodales represent the indigenous rural gentry, rooted in the farm life of their town, committed to its basic religious values, making no pretense to fashion, and yet ready to embrace a modest form of vernacular gentility suitable to their standing in the town.[74]

The success of prosperous farmers like the Goodales in acquiring a semblance of gentility is visually attested in county histories published in the last third of the nineteenth century. These histories almost always included engravings of the most attractive farm spreads in the county. There the houses stand, surrounded by trees with well-trimmed barns and outbuildings to the rear and drives running up to the front doors. Sometimes carriages or couples appear to give the reader a glimpse of the life of the residents. These are idealized pictures, but they document the cultural aspirations of prosperous farmers and the existence of outposts of refinement all across the rural landscape.

County histories of the late nineteenth century were profusely illustrated with pictures of farms with mansion houses standing in front of barns and fields. The houses had all the marks of refined mansions—fenced yards, shrubs, walks, porches, and commonly carriages. Their selection as prominent illustrations suggests that these refined country houses, fronting prosperous farms, were thought to represent the highest style of life in the county.

WESTERN CULTURE

CITY and country were European stereotypes; when transmuted into the polarity of East and West the terms took on a peculiarly American cast. East and West exaggerated the qualities of city and country. The American West extended the backwardness of the country pole toward the outright barbarism associated with untamed nature and ferocious primitive savagery. Going beyond simple rudeness and torpor, life in the West could descend into satanic superstition, animal violence, and unfeeling cruelty. Some eastern intellectuals thought the degeneration so extreme that the West endangered American society, threatening to tear down all that civilization had erected. The decision in 1787 to admit western states on an equal basis with the East took considerable courage on the part of Congress in light of their uncertainty about western character. For the next half century, Easterners watched the West with apprehension, fearful that the whole section would be lost to civilization. Cooper's Ishmael Bush in *The Prairie* stood at the far end of the spectrum, representative of the depths to which the immigrants might fall. Bush learned nothing of natural law from his immersion in frontier nature. He simply shed all forms of civilization, degenerating into rude and vicious savagery.[75]

The coarseness of the West was not just more extreme than the backwardness of simple farmers in the country. The West was complicated by its entanglement in history. Like many other intellectuals of his time, Cooper believed that going west through space carried a traveler back through time.

> The gradations of society, from that state which is called refined to that which approaches as near barbarity as connexion with an intelligent people will readily allow, are to be traced from the bosom of the states, where wealth, luxury and the arts are beginning to seat themselves, to those distant and ever-receding borders which mark the skirts and announce the approach of the nation, as moving mists precede the signs of the day.[76]

A Southerner observed in an 1818 guide for emigrants that "a journey from New Orleans to the mouth of the Sabine, exhibits man in every stage of his progress, from the palace to the hut." New Orleans enjoyed "all that luxury and learning can bestow," while in the far western extremes of the territories "are found those pastoral hunters who recall to our imagination the primitive times of history." The progress of man from its rude beginnings to the refined present was laid out before the traveler's eyes. "On a space of three hundred miles can be found human beings from the most civilized to the most savage."[77]

The widely accepted idea of passing through time while moving through space, while helpful for understanding the West, had treacherous implications. What happened to the emigrants who went West to stay? Did they regress through history and return to a primitive state? The idea implied that westward migration stripped away civilization. The possibility was strong enough in many people's minds to set the agenda for their western travel. Some travelers went West to measure the decay of civilization or to

The sequence from first winter clearing to the next summer and then to ten years and to forty-five years later lays out the course of progress expected of a

note countervailing signs of refinement. Their preconceived cultural geography was to be confirmed or overthrown.

Even sympathetic travelers believed in western degeneracy. When Timothy Flint published his *Recollections of the Last Ten Years in the Valley of the Mississippi* in 1826, he had to deal with "the horror, inspired by the term 'backwoodsman,'" among the people of New England. Flint admitted he had had the same prejudices when he first went West. "In approaching the country, I heard a thousand stories of gougings, and robberies, and shooting down with the rifle." Flint wanted to say that his experience did not support

farm family. The rude beginnings were honorable, but only if they culminated in the comfortable mansion.

the common prejudice. "The backwoodsman of the west, as I have seen him, is generally an amiable and virtuous man." But in defending the Westerner, Flint had to deal with eastern prejudices. He acknowledged that the backwoodsman's "manners are rough. He wears, it may be, a long beard," and "he carries a knife, or a dirk in his bosom," but for all that, Flint insisted, he was warmhearted and hospitable.[78] Flint had good intentions, but he could not help noting the rough manners, the beard, and the knife, betraying his awareness of these telltale signs of degeneracy.

The eastern clergy did little to dispel the idea of declining civilization in the West. It was in their interest to confirm the historical-geographical map of cultural regression, since belief in a western crisis opened the pocketbooks of potential donors to missionary societies and western colleges.[79] Lyman Beecher sought support for the Lane Seminary in Cincinnati, after he took over the presidency, by arguing in *A Plea for the West* that the West was in danger of falling into the hands of Roman Catholics.[80] In 1847 Horace Bushnell gave a talk entitled "Barbarism the First Danger" in support of the Home Missionary Society.

Of the two, Bushnell's dealt more directly with the dynamics of western cultural geography. Roman Catholicism was not the primary threat, Bushnell said. Barbarism was the first danger and the spread of Catholicism in the West a secondary effect. Migration to the frontier was the root cause of both, and only institutions like the Home Missionary Society could counteract the evil tendencies. Bushnell's essay shows how an immensely sophisticated mind, imbued with the idea of historical stages, conceived of the West at midcentury.

He tied the problem of the West into a general historical process that could be found in the Bible. His text from Judges 17:13, he told his audience, was written when the Jewish nation was "passing through the struggles incident to a new settlement, a time therefore of decline towards barbarism." The consequences were severe: "Public security is gone. The people have run wild. Superstition has dislodged the clear sovereignty of reason." All the dire effects feared for the West occurred in the Bible in a time of new settlement. Bushnell italicized the general conclusion that "*emigration, or a new settlement of the social state, involves a tendency to social decline.*" Even cultivated professional men would decay on the frontier. "The immense labors and rough hardships necessary to be encountered, in the way of providing the means of living, will ordinarily create in them a rough and partially wild habit." "The salutary restraints of society being, to a great extent, removed, they will think it no degradation to do before the woods and wild animals, what in the presence of a cultivated social state, they would blush to perpetrate."

New England had gone through the same decay in its migration. The highly cultivated first generation could not perpetuate itself in the wilderness. Their dress, houses, furniture became "coarse and rude." Education was defective. "And, more than all, society, that indefinable but powerful something, which gives a tone of refinement to literary tastes, and without which, feeling cannot rise to its highest dignity—this was a want, which no industry or care could supply." Everything declined; civility, manners, even "character had fallen to a lower type." "We feel, in short, that we have descended to an inferior race."[81]

The example of New England offered hope. In Bushnell's judgment, civilization there revived after about 1750. New England still has "a raw, unfinished aspect," he thought, "which it remains for the next century to civilize and bring into full ornamental perfection," but "we are rising steadily into noon, as a people socially complete." Would not the course of history in time elevate the West? Bushnell did not think the revival was inevitable. "Commonly nothing but extraordinary efforts in behalf of education and religion will suffice to prevent a fatal lapse of social order." The degenerative forces had to be stopped; they would not reverse themselves on their own. Bushnell saw few hopeful signs.

Is it not well understood that a partially wild race of men, such as cannot be properly included in the terms of civilization, is already formed? I speak of what is sometimes called the pioneer race. They roll on like a prairie fire, before the advance of regular emigration. . . . These semi-barbarians too, are continually multiplying in numbers, and becoming more distinct in their habits. Ere long, there is reason to fear, they will be scouring in populous bands, over the vast territories of Oregon and California, to be known as the pasturing tribes—the wild hunters and robber clans of the western hemisphere—American Moabites, Arabs and Edomites!

Unless halted in their course, the pioneers would put large areas of western America under the domain of violent and ignorant barbarism. The advent of Roman Catholicism among these superstitious people would actually be a blessing.[82]

The real West, not the West of Bushnell's imagination but the one occupied by actual people making their livelihood on the land, had to form its culture within the demeaning constraints of ideas like these. The presumption was always against western culture. John Pintard thought the accomplishments of a visitor from Tennessee worth mentioning in a letter to his daughter. He marveled "that a young miss from the interior of Tennessee (Paris) was endowed with all the elegant accomplishments of polished society. She is amiable and modest, pretty but not handsome and genteel in person and deportment."[83] Flint showed less surprise, but still thought the refinements of Kentuckians worth recording. Many houses in Frankfort showed "taste and opulence"; in Lexington "in the circles where I visited, literature was most commonly the topic of conversation." "There was generally an air of ease and politeness in the social intercourse of the inhabitants of this town, which evinced the cultivation of taste and good feeling."[84] Refined Westerners were not exactly talking dogs, but marks of civilization were not taken for granted.

In actuality, civilization spread through the West almost concurrently with the population. Scarcely a corner of the land could be found without some refinement, even at the extremities of the frontier. Bushnell had hopefully noted the "dispensation of railroads and telegraphs." They so compacted space that in a sense, he said, "there is no emigration left." The frontier was present in Boston and New York, "touched by all the refinements, principles, high sentiments of society."[85]

George Caleb Bingham experienced the strange mixture of crude violence and valiant attempts at refinement when he moved with his parents to Franklin, on the western boundary of Missouri, in 1819. Franklin had not been laid out until 1816, when it became the county seat of Boon's Lick County and the location of the General Land Office. The Binghams moved there after they lost their farm in Virginia. Located on the Missouri River, the town frequently entertained the boatmen coming downstream with loads of furs. Duels and murders were not uncommon, and once drunken boatmen tried to tear down the jail.

Yet one aspiring resident reported to a Washington, D.C., newspaper in 1819 that while Franklin lacked elegant buildings it offered "an agreeable and polished society." In keeping with that polish, the town had been laid out on the classic grid pattern with a two-acre public square and a courthouse, jail, and market house plus a collection of shops and taverns. Of the houses in town, 120 were built of logs, mostly one story; only two were frame and two brick. Yet in one, the home of the receiver of public moneys for the region, a visitor in 1820 found a daughter playing a piano. During the next decade Franklin stores stocked silk lace, satin gauze, silk shawls, and silk and kid gloves. In the paper that began in 1819, schoolteachers advertised to teach Latin and all the "ordinary branches of a classical or polite Education on the most approved principles." Young ladies could be "finished" with the ornamental branches of female education, painting on velvet, drawing landscapes, embroidery, and needlework. The newspaper published excerpts from the novels of Scott, Cooper, and Irving. A few years later someone founded a library and someone else opened a bookstore. All the while squatters lived nearby in crude cabins furnished with rough furniture and rougher manners.[86]

In 1819 Franklin was at the very edge of western settlement. Provisioning wagon trains for the Santa Fe trek provided major town business. Yet even before railroads and the telegraph, some residents of this remote outpost were in touch with genteel culture. Despite the difficulties, people who wanted pianos, silk shawls, and a little Latin for their children found ways to obtain those precious commodities, perhaps treasuring them all the more because of the circumstances. The genteel population, a thin upper crust of society, was vigorous enough to keep a young portrait painter alive. Bingham's miraculous emergence in this primitive farm community is itself a testimonial to the strength of gentility in Missouri. The painter Chester Harding visited Franklin once when the Binghams were there, but he did not linger long enough to give lessons. Bingham's artistic gift was recognized and encouraged by local people.

First apprenticed to a cabinetmaker, Bingham turned to painting around 1833 when he was twenty-two. In 1834 and 1835 he was turning out more-than-respectable portraits for local dignitaries along the Missouri near his home, in Columbia, and later in St. Louis. As the years went by, he traveled farther afield, but he kept coming back to Missouri, where he always found business.[87] Missouri alone provided ample evidence that civilization did not disappear along the frontiers of settlement. The pioneers carried genteel values West with them, and thousands of entrepreneurs were quick to supply the materials to meet their cultural needs.

Westerners themselves still felt the power of the stages-of-civilization idea. They firmly denied their own degeneracy, but they still accepted eastern culture as the standard of civilization. The newspapers that advertised Bingham's presence in town betrayed the self-conscious uneasiness of people living in the shadow of presumed cultural inferiority. The editor of the Columbia *Missouri Intelligencer* visited Bingham's temporary studio in 1835 and reported what he found. "We are unacquainted, save to a degree, with the work of Eastern Artists," he began, with the usual deference to the nation's metropolitan centers, "but it is tho't that the portraits of Mr. Bingham might be placed along side the finest specimens of Harding, Catlin, and Duett [Jouett], and receive honor from the comparison." The native western artist measured up to the eastern standard, but he was always compared.

> If the young artist, who has called forth these remarks, possesses the talents which we conceive, let them be excited and drawn out by liberality of encouragement at home, and ere long, the country shall see with delight, and hear with pleasure, the productions and the praises—to borrow a title of Rubens—of a Western "meteor of the art."[88]

With these sentiments the editor laid on patrons the responsibility for development of the arts. Bingham's artistic talent put the West on trial.

Would Westerners support an artist and so launch an artistic meteor of their own? Would they rouse themselves from the lethargies of frontier living and the coarse satisfactions of the wilderness to value the refined pleasures of the arts? Implicitly the editor asked the question that the historical-stages theory posed: Was the West capable of civilization?

Bingham himself addressed the question in his paintings and gave two answers. The portraits from which he made his living depict a conventional genteel society in Missouri, furnished with men and women of the proper facial posture, refined dress, ease, taste, and complaisance. Seeing those pictures, John Pintard would conclude that he could feel at home in Columbia, Missouri.

The genre paintings, which gave Bingham the modest fame he enjoyed in his lifetime, depicted another society, one nearly devoid of ladies and gentlemen. Common farmers, tavernkeepers, boatmen, local politicians, and squatters occupy this world. The best of them show only the slightest touches of gentility; most were quite plain. But not one shows an Ishmael Bush or Bushnell's scouring bands of Edomites. These are placid, gentle, unassuming people. Sometimes cheerful, more often melancholy or contemplative, they are not fierce or eccentric. The genre paintings reassure Bushnell that the West will not give way to savagery. Nor will it rise to the heights of refined sensibility. The West is a calm, a happy, and a safe land. In his genre paintings Bingham broadened the middle range between refinement and vulgarity to create a space for simple, plain people who neither aspire to fashion nor teeter on the brink of barbarism, a space for unassuming middling people.[89]

THE SOUTH

IN contrast to the West, the South was traditionally genteel. The great Virginia mansions had been among the first architectural embodiments of refinement in the colonies. Northern critics in the eighteenth century had complained that the South carried refinement too far toward aristocratic hauteur, to the point of trespassing on republican equality. The nineteenth-century mansions increased in elegance as cotton and sugar production provided funds to erect large Greek Revival residences on the land or in cities like Natchez, Mississippi.

To match the residences, post-Revolutionary southern towns complied with the standard format of a well-ordered city. A resident of Providence, Rhode Island, or Litchfield, Connecticut, could immediately read the social structure of Lynchburg, Virginia. The 1813 courthouse faced down broad Water Street to the commercial activity on the James River. Fine residences clustered around this center, and another locus of refinement formed along Federal Street a few blocks away. The layout would have assured visitors of a familiar small-town urbanity.

The founders of Savannah laid the city out in squares that attracted fashionable residences in the manner of London, New York, and Philadel-

LEFT. *George Caleb Bingham's portrait of Mary Darby is one of a large number of portraits which testify to the existence of polite society in Missouri. His portrait sitters contrast with the rough-spun farmers and boatmen whom he pictures as part of another culture entirely.*

BELOW. *Bingham's frontier people make no pretense to gentility, but their gentle, melancholy demeanor does not imply savagery either. They are simple, homely people.*

phia. A visitor in 1810 reported that white cedar posts joined by a chain surrounded each square, and walks were laid out, trees planted, and grass sown. Other towns in Georgia—Milledgeville, Augusta, Macon—had their public squares, and in these places the great planters built their mansions.[90] Southern gentlemen understood how to create urban environments suitable for refined living. To accompany the outward signs of refinement, there sprang into existence schools and academies where drawing, French, and ornamental needlework were taught to the daughters of planters and Latin and Greek to their sons. By 1850 there were 2,700 academies in the South compared with 1,000 in New England. Inside some great houses were libraries to nourish a taste for literature.[91]

At the time none of these refinements were perceived as evidence of a pure genteel culture in a southern setting. Southern gentility had its own peculiar character, and for many observers it seemed sadly decayed. As the stages of history colored the geography of refinement in the West, making migration to the frontier seem like a return to the primitive, so slavery colored the southern cultural map, infecting the region with another kind of degeneracy. In the minds of cultural critics, the slave work force influenced everything—the great houses, the cities, even the personalities of southern gentlemen. From the perspective of many Northerners, slavery corrupted masters by bringing them wealth without labor, and a genteel veneer could not hide the inner rot.

As Bushnell observed of the South, "while the northern people were generally delving in labor, for many generations, to create a condition of comfort, slavery set the master at once on a footing of ease." Southerners had the advantage of "leisure for elegant intercourse, for unprofessional studies, and seasoned their character thus with that kind of cultivation which distinguished men of society." But the result of enjoying "a condition of ease which is not the reward of labor" was the deterioration of character. "It nourishes imperious and violent passions" and fails to sustain churches and schools. "Education and religion thus displaced, the dinner-table only remains," and "however highly we may estimate the humanizing power of hospitality, it cannot be regarded as any sufficient spring of character." Southern refinement suffered from a "mock quality," having "about the same relation to a substantial and finished culture that honor has to character." It was "expense without comfort," "airs in place of elegance, or assurance substituted for ease."

As time passed, this shell of refinement steadily crumbled. The westward movement carried pioneers through space into primitivism; the passage of time, Bushnell thought, depressed the level of southern civilization. The great generation of American founders gave way to lesser men. "Violence and dissipation bring down every succeeding generation to a state continually lower." The exhaustion of the soil and moral decay proceeded together, reaching their culmination in the Southwest.

> Thus, at length, has been produced what may be called the bowie-knife style of civilization, and the new west of the South is overrun by it—a spirit of blood which defies all laws of God and man ... educated to ease, and readier, of course, when the means of living fail, to find them at the gambling-table or the race-ground, than in any work of industry—probably squandering the means of living there, to relieve the tedium of ease itself. Such is the influence of slavery, as it enters into our American social state, and imparts its moral type of barbarism through emigration, to the new west.[92]

Bushnell was not alone in his jaundiced views; many writers found deep, constitutional defects in southern gentility.[93] Frederick Law Olmsted, who grew up under Bushnell's preaching in Hartford, traveled the South with a similar outlook. Already committed to the antislavery cause when he began his journey in 1852, Olmsted believed that southern claims to superior aristocratic refinement were more than counterbalanced by the primitive condition of the mass of people. Although an astute observer and basically fair, he noted the signs of false show among the gentry or of crudity in ordinary households. In Mississippi, he credited the planters for their comely gardens. "The plantation residences were generally of a cottage class, sometimes but not usually, with extensive and tasteful grounds about them." But when he arrived at the court town of Woodville and stopped at a "small but pretentious hotel," he first observed the gentry in the public rooms wearing black cravats and silk or embroidered waistcoats, and then looked at the disgusting conditions in the bedrooms. The sheets on his bed were soiled and the pillow greasy, and one towel had to serve both occupants. The flashy appearance downstairs and the filth upstairs summed up southern aristocracy for him. "Where there is one true gentleman, and to be respected, at the South," he later concluded, "there are two whose whole life seems to be absorbed in sensualism and sickly excitements."

In Virginia, Olmsted enjoyed the hospitality of a planter who invited him into a parlor in the great house.

> It was a square room, with a door from the hall on one side, and two windows on each of the other sides. The lower part of the walls was wainscoted, and the upper part, with the ceiling, plastered and white-washed. The fire-place and mantel-piece were somewhat carved, and were painted black; all the wood-work lead colour. Blue paper curtains covered the windows; the floor was uncarpeted, and the only furniture

in the room was some strong plain chairs, painted yellow, and a Connecticut clock, which did not run.

The house represented the decay of culture under the slave regimen. "The house," Olmsted went on, "had evidently been built for a family of some wealth, and, after having been deserted by them, had been bought at a bargain by the present resident, who either had not the capital or the inclination to furnish and occupy it appropriately."[94]

The ultimate indictment of the slave system, in Olmsted's mind, was the impact on ordinary people. The small farmers made no pretense of gentility. Late one rainy night he asked for shelter at a cabin typical of many he had seen that day. Although the family had no slaves, cotton was planted in a large area behind the house and Olmsted saw a horse and wagon. The occupant did not take in travelers, he said, and his wife was ill, but he offered Olmsted lodging anyway.

> The house was all comprised in a single room, twenty-eight by twenty-five feet in area, and open to the roof above. There was a large fireplace at one end and a door on each side—no windows at all. Two bedsteads, a spinning-wheel, a packing-case, which served as a bureau, a cupboard, made of rough hewn slabs, two or three deer-skin seated chairs, a Connecticut clock, and a large poster of Jayne's patent medicines, constituted all the visible furniture, either useful or ornamental in purpose. A little girl, immediately, without having had any directions to do so, got a frying-pan and a chunk of bacon from the cupboard, and cutting slices from the latter, set it frying for my supper. The woman of the house sat sulkily in a chair tilted back and leaning against the logs, spitting occasionally at the fire, but took no notice of me, barely nodding when I saluted her. A baby lay crying on the floor. I quieted it and amused it with my watch till the little girl, having made "coffee" and put a piece of corn-bread on the table with the bacon, took charge of it.[95]

This is not a purely objective description. The sullen tone of the household was likely Olmsted's own reading of the situation; that bright little girl bustling around to cook supper and care for the baby suggests there was more happiness here than Olmsted saw. But discounting for Olmsted's prejudices, the description surely shows that these people did not pretend to gentility. Nothing in the furniture, save perhaps the clock, or in the manner of the woman tilted back in her chair and spitting into the fire gave a hint of cultural aspiration. Sidney George Fisher, reading Olmsted's published letters in 1856 in the comfort of his Philadelphia house, was astonished at Olmsted's "picture of the South": "I had no idea of the ignorance, poverty, and barbarism that slavery had produced among the *whites*."[96]

Olmsted concluded that the non-slaveholding Southerner was both culturally and economically inert. "So far as they can be treated of as a class, the non-slaveholders are unambitious, indolent, degraded and illiterate—are a dead peasantry so far as they affect the industrial position of the South."[97] A chorus of other voices backs up his observations of southern culture, including his views on the primitive living conditions of middling and well-off planters. A recent arrival in Mississippi saw that the planters there "don't care much about show, a great many wealthy people live in log houses, some few have them well furnished, some don't seem to care." In southern Virginia a traveler found slaveholders' homes "dirty, and comfortless in the extreme."[98]

These observers circumscribe the geography of southern refinement within extremely narrow limits. Gentility was to be found in infrequent plantation mansion houses, in the town residences of planters and professional men, and in select neighborhoods in southern cities. In the Olmsted cartography, there lay between these bright spots vast dreary stretches of benighted cabin people and decaying mansions. Far from being the heartland of American refinement, the South was a desert sprinkled with a few oases.

The caricature suggests the jaundiced northern view of plain people in the South. The rough cabin, the crude woman with her pipe, and the lean dogs imply that no refinement had reached these people.

Was this picture exaggerated by antislavery ideology? The candor of Olmsted's photograph-like descriptions is disarming, yet artfully selective. Did he and the other travelers focus on crude conditions to prove the ill effects of the slave system? The architectural record modifies their observations in one respect. The firsthand accounts fail to note one of the fixtures of the southern landscape around 1850, the I house, the dwelling form most typical of middling farmers in the upland South. Two stories high, one room deep and one or two rooms wide, often with a stair hall, the I house was the preferred form for comfortable planters who spilled over the Appalachians from the Tidewater and settled along the Ohio River and southward. (In the Deep South, a one-story house with four first-floor rooms was more common.)

The I house was certainly a step above the plain log cabin, and bore a few modest signs of fashion. Henry Glassie has hypothesized that the form combined a traditional vernacular plan with the Georgian style of the eighteenth-century American gentry. I houses commonly had central hallways with rooms opening on each side, the basic Georgian plan, or in a smaller version they followed the two-thirds Georgian plan with a stair hall adjoining a parlor. The stairs ascended in a straight run to a landing, a cardinal mark of genteel housing. I houses with stair halls imply that a substantial segment of the population was in touch with genteel culture.[99] Where do these people fit into Olmsted's picture?

The accounts of southern hospitality at the middling level often describe a bare shell of a house, meagerly furnished, with wainscoted rooms, a few hard chairs and no carpets, as if a memory of gentility hung about the dwelling while the spirit had departed. The I houses had the simplest decoration—dadoes, beaded boards on internal walls, moldings at doors and around the fireplaces—and very little more. Southern vernacular housing seemed wholly isolated from the currents that made Greek Revival and Italianate architecture fashionable in the North.[100]

An idea of the meaning of the houses can be glimpsed in an experience of Fanny Trollope's when she was invited to take tea with a family who owned three slaves and had three hundred acres under cultivation. They lived in a two-room house furnished with "one heavy huge table, and about six wooden chairs." Yet before sitting down with her visitor the woman of the house changed into a "smart new dress." A slave laid the table with "cups of the very coarsest blue ware, a little brown sugar in one, and a tiny drop of milk in another," and no butter. The woman attempted to engage in refined conversation. "She ambled through the whole time the visit lasted, in a sort of elegantly mincing familiar style of gossip, which, I think, she was imitating from some novel." She claimed to have married "a first cousin, who was as fine a gentleman as she was a lady," and she called her slave Lycurgus.

This performance amused and disgusted Trollope, who compared it with the simple plenitude of English farmhouses and considered it a mockery of real refinement. The farm wife herself showed no embarrassment at the shortcomings of her house or table. She seemed secure in her pretensions as if she had no idea how far she fell short.[101] The smart dress, a little fashionable talk, and a family name supported her claims to gentility.

An I house with a stair hall and a dadoed parlor was such a token. That may have been enough for people with aspirations, and for the rest, no pretense was made. A visitor to Mississippi marveled at the living conditions on a thousand-acre farm in the pine woods, manned by slaves worth $10,000. In the house,

> wooden benches were used in the place of chairs, one iron spoon answered for the whole family, and the mother added the sugar ... to the coffee with her fingers, and tasted each cup before sending it round to ascertain if it was right. Such things as andirons, tongs, and wash-basins were considered useless; and the bedstead upon which we slept was a mere board. . . . All [twenty members of] the family, excepting the parents and two sons, were barefooted, and yet the girls sported large finger rings in abundance, and wore basque dresses of calico.[102]

One can only guess what the rings and the calico dresses meant to the girls, but whatever vanity they expressed, they apparently did not clash with bare feet and wooden benches.

After duly weighing in the I houses, the burden of testimony still upholds the image of southern culture as a desert with oases—judged by the canons of genteel geography. A small number of mansions, primarily in cities and towns but also on farms, upheld by libraries, academies, and concert halls, were the oases of refinement on a culturally bleak landscape. The modest vernacular culture that permeated the northern middle class scarcely touched the South.

Samuel Perkins Allison, the southern planter who engaged Olmsted in debate on the issue of sectional culture, made no attempt to claim any gentility for ordinary Southerners; his case rested solely on the superiority of the aristocracy.[103] Southern farmers may have owned blue teaware like the Means family in *The Hoosier School-Master*, or houses with stair halls, or smart new dresses, or large finger rings like the Mississippi girls, but the southern middle class did not grasp the total genteel discipline. They did not understand that the objects were tokens of an inward cultivation of the senses and the emotions. They had little idea of gentility's beautification campaign and its attempt to turn entire environments into scenes from pictures. The Mississippi lady may have borrowed her conversation from a novel; she did not see that she must conduct her life like the novel's heroines, heightening her sensibilities, refining her movements, cultivating her mind, and sweetening her spirit. The material traces of refinement among the southern middle class resemble the scattering of silver teaspoons in eighteenth-century estate inventories, indicating a mild urge to emulate genteel ways without embracing the fullness of the genteel gospel.[104]

The southern middle and lower classes embarrassed the region's intellectuals, who were horrified by the violence along the edges of cracker culture. They thought that only by the most rigorous personal self-discipline could the southern gentry keep the ubiquitous ruffians from mayhem.[105] For the others, southern intellectuals followed Bingham. Rather than pretending that the bulk of the people enjoyed a modest gentility as Olmsted claimed for the North, southern intellectuals showed plain people to be warmhearted and colorful.

August Baldwin Longstreet depicted southern scenes resembling Bingham's genre pictures. At a country dance held in the local squire's one-room log house, he admired the "bouncing, ruddy-cheeked girls," who were "attired in manufactures of their own hands." He considered it a virtue that "the refinements of the present day in female dress" had not reached the country. He admired their free and easy movements, unhampered by corsets, and their willingness to dance with everyone there. The happy scene of good humor and good food was unspoiled by civilization.[106] Like Bingham, Longstreet approached the problem of refinement by taking a large segment of the population off the map and grading them by a different standard. Self-conscious as Longstreet was about his own gentility, by this device he tried to redeem the South, as Bingham did the West, from the reproaches of its critics.

SPACE AND CULTURE

THE geography of refinement can be viewed from two perspectives. From the first, the more mechanical of the two, gentility is seen as a spreading culture, reaching downward through the social structure and outward through space. Its presence or absence can be measured by material evidence of cultural aspiration: parlors, stair halls, front lawns with white fences, hotels with assembly rooms, landscaped town squares, academies, and so on.

This is the simpler of the two perspectives, requiring only diligence in research to answer the key questions. We can measure gentility the way we count television sets or bathtubs. Though conceptually simple, the results of pursuing this perspective would not be trivial. Counting items would measure the formation of a national culture with similar values and practices in every region. As that happened, people recognized the gentility in one another, as Pintard appreciated the refinement of the Tennessee girl visiting New York. That tiny flash of recognition had large implications, signifying that a single culture was overriding regional differences and uniting people of the same social class.

That broad common culture in turn created a national market for genteel goods and fashions, a market large enough to power industrialization. From the rough sketch in this chapter, we can imagine this national genteel culture concentrated in cities, spreading to towns virtually everywhere, turning up in farmhouses especially in the Northeast, and thinning out in rural areas in the West and South. As it spread, manufacturers and storekeepers came to bank on the belief that people of this culture would respond similarly to fashionable goods, warranting large capital investments in machinery and factories and the creation of far-flung distribution networks. Bingham left Missouri for a time to paint portraits in Washington, D.C., knowing he could find customers wherever there was a genteel society. Makers and sellers of hats, of magazines, of wallpaper, of furniture, of carpets began to operate on the same assumption.

From the second perspective, city and country, East and West were elements of an intellectual geography. These conceptions for understanding culture and society were ways of seeing and judging based on location rather

Thousands of small entrepreneurs stood to benefit from the spread of gentility and so inadvertently facilitated its expansion. Although the purchasers are obviously plain people, the vine over the porch signifies their budding taste.

than categories like wealth or race. To say a person was a country man or a place was a country town bestowed predictable qualities on a subject. "It is an opinion far too prevalent among those engaged in the more active occupations of our people," a book on rural architecture confidently asserted, "that everything connected with agriculture and agricultural life is of a rustic and uncouth character."[107] The country was a cultural condition, and on the scale of civilization often presumed to be a lower one.

Even among the genteel, life was conducted differently in the country. "The white or pale yellow gloves, which you must wear during the whole evening at a fashionable evening party in the city, on pain of being set down as unbearably vulgar," an etiquette book declared, "would be very absurd appendages at a social gathering at a farm-house in the country. None but a *snob* would wear them at such a place."[108] Apart from any considerations of cost or understanding, place transformed behavior.

The division of city and country into contrasting cultural regions did not mean that the relationship was precisely polarized and easy to understand. In common speech, "country" was almost a synonym for "rude and plain," and "city" for "fashionable and polished." But that clarity did not extend to the actual relationships between their respective populations. City and country were like social classes, separate but engaged, and the engagement had many moods: resentment, suspicion, envy, awe. The tension between the two poles was an enduring source of conflict and strain that took many twists and turns.

When John Pierce of Litchfield, Connecticut, wrote to his sister Sarah at school in New York City in 1784, the complexity of his feelings about city and country disrupted his brotherly instructions.

> You must take care also not to get your ideas of Happiness from a City, you know you are not to live there, and ought therefore to be cautious of the refinement and pleasures attending your situation. You must endeavor to obtain such a versatility of disposition, as to really reconcile yourself not only to the solitude of the country, but also to the manner of it so that you may not be unhappy in the one case, nor appear proud or vain in the other.

The excitement of the city compared with rural solitude worried him. Would Sarah be satisfied with simple country pleasures once she returned to Litchfield? Would she offend her country neighbor with city vanities? "You may expect on your return a great many ill natured observations made on you and the only way to prevent the effect intended or indeed to keep your sisters easy will be to be very unassuming in your deportment."[109]

Country people resented pretentious city folks and punished them when they could. John was uncertain about his sister's ability to reconcile the two manners of life. Yet he sent his sister to New York for schooling and planned for her to open a school in Litchfield to educate country girls in city ways. Such ironies, such doubts and contradictions beset the commerce between city and country wherever gentility spread across the land.

CHAPTER XII

Culture and Power

THE proposal to map gentility in the United States brings us finally to the question of dynamics. What motor drove the refinement process? Mapping makes us realize how much the analysis of refinement depends on the word "spread." The overriding image in the preceding chapter was of gentility spreading across the land, from focal points in the cities down long, elegant avenues, into more modest side streets, through space to smaller country towns, out to prosperous farmhouses and estates in the countryside, and then across great distances to western cities and outposts on the frontier. Starting from independent bases in plantation houses in the Tidewater, it moved westward to other southern mansions and perhaps in reverse of the usual direction into southern towns.

That expansion in turn was a branch of a movement that began much earlier in Europe. The spread across America continued the flow of gentility outward from fifteenth-century Italian cities and country villas to European Renaissance courts, across the Channel to the English aristocracy, into the upper reaches of the English middle class, and in the eighteenth century across the Atlantic to the great houses of the American gentry. In the nineteenth century gentility spread downward through the social structure to large segments of the middle class and, in small doses, into the lives of working-class people. And besides spreading through space and the social structure, gentility entered hearts and minds, taking control of personality, establishing a standard of human worth, and defining large segments of personal identity.

For four centuries genteel culture expanded in many dimensions, claiming new populations and taking new material forms. It was diluted, adulterated, and reshaped as it went, so that by 1850, in its middle-class variant, gentility had become an aspect of bourgeois respectability. And yet, while more comfortable, religious, and domestic than when it set forth centuries earlier, nineteenth-century American gentility was still recognizable as an honest descendant of its Renaissance ancestor and even held on to its name. Why did this happen? How was gentility able to cross national boundaries, to extend from class to class, to enter into hearts? What propelled the refining process?

THE UTILITY OF EMULATION

THE evidence in the artifacts of genteel culture compels us to make emulation the starting point for an explanation. In the words and objects of refined culture, the signs of gentility's origins in European courts are everywhere present. We can hardly doubt that people on the provincial periphery borrowed their culture from aristocratic centers. The books that fixed the rules for genteel behavior in America were only slightly revised versions of handbooks for courtiers; eighteenth-century mansions copied the styles of English country houses; American city plans were adaptations of Renaissance conceptions of civic space; artisans and shopkeepers promoted their goods by claiming they were the latest London fashions. Stamped on every form of genteel culture was the mark of its origin in Europe and more specifically in aristocratic English society. Later people in country towns took their cues from American metropolitan centers, following the pattern of emulation but transferring the source.

Given this evident emulative impulse, the methods of cultural transmission are not hard to envision. We know that the eighteenth-century American gentry desired to have the latest from Europe, and the stream of immigrant artisans supplemented by design books supplied the details. Provincial gentlemen in smaller towns in turn looked to models in Philadelphia or New York. John Dickinson told his carpenters to build a house in Wilmington, Delaware, modeled after great Philadelphia mansions; the decor of William Corbit's house in Cantwell's Bridge strongly resembled the carving in Samuel Powel's Philadelphia town house. Such transfers, multiplied a thousand times, were the basic mechanism for the spread of culture. The practice of emulation, replicated at every level with every cultural good, created innumerable networks of influence along which gentility flowed from European style centers to remote American outposts.[1]

Despite the compelling evidence in its favor, we hesitate before this explanation. While unmistakably embodied in genteel materials, imitation as an explanation seems shallow, as does imitation as a practice. Emulation falls short of our expectations for explanation. We want to know why the

American gentry fastened their attention on London fashions and expended vast sums to copy English models. What need did a Georgian house fulfill in the life of a Dover physician? What did a parlor mean to a New England blacksmith? Our instincts lead us toward the condition of society. We look for some contradiction, some tension or conflict, some struggle for power, some damaging weakness that gentility remedied or resolved. We want to know how the spread of gentility met the unfulfilled needs of American society.

Gentility, it seems safe to assume, served just such purposes—many of them—for the populations that strove for refined respectability. In the eighteenth century, gentility supported class authority. It established a discernible line between the gentlemen of the place and ordinary citizens. Great mansions, books, fine dress became instruments of power, a superior culture to parade before the eyes of a deferential population whose compliance was necessary to the continuation of authority.[2] In the nineteenth century, southern planters used gentility to distinguish themselves from dollar-mad Yankees, whom they both resented and envied. Gentility put a glossy surface on lives that in reality were equally committed to gain.[3] At different times and different places the desire for refinement met varied needs.

For one large group, gentility stabilized identity amid the social confusion of the early nineteenth century. Both Karen Halttunen and John Kasson have observed how etiquette books and genteel conduct helped individuals make their way from a traditional society of entrenched personal connections into a world of constantly shifting relationships. As traditional communities broke up and people were cast adrift, status and identity lost their footing. Established hierarchies dissolved, and strange faces replaced familiar ones. Strangers had no preconceived idea of each other's places in the world, especially in the flux of the city. They could only judge by appearances and manners. Gentility enabled the wanderers to claim a place, forge an identity, and establish a recognizable hierarchy.[4] Skyrocketing urban growth between 1820 and 1860, increasing at three times the rate of the general population, brought more and more Americans into the world of strangers. Genteel guidebooks introduced some ordered security into this confusing melee.[5]

Gentility was particularly useful in securing one's identity along the lower boundary of the middle class, where people were emerging from a cruder traditional culture and were uneasy about the validity of their refinement. Had they truly cast off their simple and rude pasts? Did they accurately understand the principles of refinement? Did they betray their own uncertain claims to gentility by mistakes in speech or decorum? The embarrassments of the parvenu were a staple of satire, from John Trumbull's

"Progress of Dulness" to Alice Mowbray's popular drama *Fashion*, suggesting a prevalent social insecurity. By insisting on precise compliance with the punctilios of etiquette, by keeping up to the minute with fashion, and by joining in the ridicule of newcomers' genteel pretensions, an uneasy population who had themselves only recently risen into the middle class could bolster their confidence.

We must acknowledge all of the uses to which gentility was put in the course of its travels over four centuries without losing sight of the emulative impulse that ran through them all. For, given its many uses, we still must ask why gentility served its multiple purposes so well. There are so many ways of asserting power, reconciling conflicts, stabilizing identity, bolstering confidence; how did gentility come to have the power to perform so well under so many circumstances? Why century after century did one population after another call upon gentility to serve their varied purposes? Why was gentility thought to have the cultural power to intimidate, sustain, and exclude? When we seek to locate gentility's continuing force, we are brought back again to emulation.

Yet we still hold back because emulation goes against the grain of our democratic instincts. Diffusion by emulation implies that culture is created at the top for those lower down. Our egalitarian impulses make us want to believe that cultural exchanges between the powerful and weak go both ways, that high culture and low culture borrow from one another in more or less equal portions.[6] We want to hear ordinary people talk back to their pretended superiors.

But the spread of gentility in America is a reminder that our democratic instincts may not always be right. The exchange between high and low is anything but equal. The most obvious social fact about power is that it exercises influence, not just physical coercion, but influence over hearts and minds. It compels attention. The surest sign of the end of power is unselfconscious neglect; then power no longer matters. So long as an institution is powerful, it stands at the center of attention as well as at the center of authority and force. Culture may indeed percolate up from below, and in emulating people adapt what they borrow and make it their own; but the fact remains that people at the top have an immense advantage in influencing cultural forms. To believe otherwise is to misunderstand the nature of power.

Provincials paid heed to the English upper classes in their town and country houses, parading the streets, or posing in public places because so much power was focused in their persons. Their conspicuous wealth, their offices, their acknowledged eminence in society made them fascinating. Moreover, they exercised that most compelling of human authorities, the power to confirm identity. They determined who and what was worthy.

Tradesmen yearned for the custom of a great aristocratic house because it confirmed the worth of their product. Artists sought the patronage of great lords, not only for their favor but for their praise. To live under the gaze of power was to live meaningfully. All of this came together to empower gentility. The mighty influence of Europe's ruling classes stood behind the values of genteel culture and drove the emulative impulse.[7] When gentility was transferred to America, it was the culture of the gentry, the classes who combined the greatest wealth, political authority, and social prominence. Gentility was always most fully realized at the pinnacles of power.

But the word is emulation, not imitation. The impulse was not to copy, but to partake—of power and of the glory, strength, and beauty that were believed to inhere in those who stood at the peak of society and government. The underlings never expected to equal the aristocracy; the guidebooks sternly warned against trying. They hoped to join in their power, to dignify their own existence with a portion of the glory that radiated from the highest and best circles. At its best, emulation went deeper than external splendors of mansions and capitols. Emulation meant acquiring a refinement of spirit, a sensitivity to beauty, a regard for the feelings of others, a wish to please, all long associated with aristocracy at its best.

The emulators could not simply imitate, because no specific individual embodied the perfection of refinement. Gentility was an ideal—of a perfect king or queen, a most gracious and benevolent lord or lady, an imaginary Sir Charles Grandison or Harriet Byron, a polished and wealthy urban gentleman, whose elevated surroundings reflected their exquisitely cultivated spirits. Elevated spaces and refined persons were invested with the hopes of people for truly gracious rulers, for disciplined and beautiful greatness, for something like salvation. The courtesy books envisioned a society that never was and never could be except in the imaginations of the subjects of power. But the ideal, interwoven with the actual authority and power of the aristocracy, drove the refining process for four centuries.

Gentility and Commerce

THE irony and incongruity of this exalted impulse is that it was so fully put to the service of commerce in the eighteenth and nineteenth centuries. Capitalism joined forces with emulation to spread gentility wherever the lines of commerce could reach. Without the mass production of genteel goods, ordinary people with limited incomes could not have afforded the accoutrements of refinement. Entrepreneurs responded to every sign of increasing demand for fabric, furniture, parlors, clothing, and ingeniously provided them at affordable prices.

At the same time, gentility did its part in advancing capitalism. A large market for consumer goods was a prerequisite for industrialization. Industrial capitalism could not come into existence in America until workers willingly spent all they earned to purchase the products of the factories. Gentility served the vital role of turning producers into consumers, helping to form the national market on which industrialization rested. Gentility and capitalism collaborated in the formation of consumer culture, gentility creating demand and capitalism manufacturing supply. All the participants in the emerging industrial system had a vested interest, understood or not, in the promotion of gentility.

The process can be viewed in microcosm in one industry in Chester County, Pennsylvania, where Barry Kessler has studied the growth of the furniture industry. Kessler uncovered a steep rise in the number of small-time cabinetmakers and chairmakers going into business in the two decades from 1790 to 1810, at the very time when a much larger proportion of the population began to install parlors in their houses and to furnish them with respectable tables and chairs. The shops were scattered all over the countryside in virtually every township. Many of the makers had identified themselves as farmers on the tax lists a decade earlier. The rise in demand after 1790 moved them to spend more effort on furniture making and so change their primary occupational identity.

For a few decades they met the need; then these small producers faded from the record, and larger makers and retailers began to appear along the main roads and in the larger Chester County towns. Some of the town cabinetmakers in time began large-scale production, using powered machinery; others retailed furniture manufactured in Philadelphia. Apparently the local furniture people, who had done the work as a sideline to farming, could meet the increased demand initially. When the furniture market was better defined, the established demand warranted larger investment in production. Increasing demand called ever larger production systems into existence.[8]

If we extrapolate from Chester County, we can imagine thousands of ambitious artisans, storekeepers, and peddlers manning their stations along the commercial and industrial networks, seeking customers for their goods. In time, to these small operators were added industrialists whose vast investments committed them to the enhancement of demand for their products. All these people, small merchants and artisans along with great entrepreneurs, joined their energies to spread gentility. The commercialization of gentility in the nineteenth century, like the commercialization of leisure in eighteenth-century England, became a major business. The livelihoods of countless individuals on both sides of the Atlantic depended on it. These people understandably exerted themselves to promote the material forms of genteel culture in the widest possible market, selling paintings, books, carpets, brooms, furniture wherever and to whomever they could.[9]

But these promoters of gentility were neither its inventors nor the source of its power. They exploited genteel culture; they did not create its magnetic appeal. The spread of gentility in America coincides so closely with the period of industrialization that we may give all credit to capitalism and overlook the power of the older tradition. We commonly think of industrial capitalism and the widening market as the preeminent developments in American society in the first half of the nineteenth century. It follows that the spread of any cultural values must be attributable to those forces, when in actuality capitalism could not have devised or propagated the culture of refinement all on its own. In our preoccupation with the coming new order we may wrongly neglect the persistent influence of the old. The spread of gentility reminds us that the *ancien régime* still had a grip on the social imagination of Americans. The market that drove the industrial machinery arose initially from the ideal of a higher life taken from the old regime. In the absence of the magnetic attraction of refined living, the demand for parlors, for clothing, for carriages would not have come into existence.

That is transparent in the career of Josiah Wedgwood. Underlying his success was an ability to interweave genteel ideals and capitalist enterprise. Wedgwood's strategy for selling his ceramics was to invest them with the aura of aristocracy. He did not compete in price; his wares cost more than his competitors'. He aimed to attract the interest and the patronage of nobility and then, with their favor glorifying his products, to market them to the middle classes.

Wedgwood's greatest commercial success was queensware, named for the pottery he manufactured for Queen Charlotte. He wondered himself whether the quality of his wares or the quality of the patrons figured more in their success. "If a Royal, or Noble Introduction be as necessary to the sale of an Article of Luxury, as real Elegance and beauty, then the Manufacturer, if he consults his own interest will bestow as much pains, and expence too, if necesary, in gaining the former of these advantages, as he would in bestowing the latter." He gladly accepted a money-losing commission from Catherine the Great for a table service of 952 pieces requiring a thousand original paintings, knowing the honor would enhance the value of his other products. He painted the country houses of the English nobility on the plates and then invited them to his London showrooms to see the service. He did not regret for a second the expense of the display, which he believed would "fully complete our notoriety to the whole Island and help us greatly, no doubt, in the sale of our goods, both useful and ornamental." He excluded common people from these great exhibits to protect the exalted atmo-sphere—admission was by ticket only to the nobility and gentry—and then manufactured quantities of cheaper versions of his wares to market among the middle classes, who bought them in vast quantities.[10] The greatest profits were made in this middling market, not among the tiny handful of aristocratic patrons whose patronage was essential for controlling the mass market.

Wedgwood's experience is a model for the spread of gentility generally in the eighteenth century. His skill as a promoter explains the distribution of his wares all over the Western world, but his success depended on the force emanating from his aristocratic patrons. Wedgwood prospered because he harnessed the influence of aristocracy for commercial purposes. Every shopkeeper who advertised the latest fashions from London did the same in a milder way. It was the provincials' fascination with the glorious life in the capital that sold the goods. Gentility spread in America because people longed to be associated with the "best society" that they imagined to exist in the metropolitan centers.

REFINEMENT AND DEMOCRACY

THE collaboration of capitalism and gentility in the formation of consumer culture seems at first sight an unlikely partnership. Surprisingly, the interplay of an old order with the coming new order in the end lent strength to both. Still more curious was the seemingly incongruous overlay of aristocratic gentility on democracy. That combination presents a second major problem to go with the initial question of why gentility spread. How did it come about that the leading republican nation in the modern world should warmly incorporate gentility into its national values at the very moment when its civic culture had wholly discredited aristocracy? Gentility had obvious uses for a colonial gentry struggling to establish its authority in the new world and still dependent on the English gentry for models of behavior. But after the Revolution repudiated monarchical government and made "aristocrat" a term of political opprobrium, how could the culture of courts and country houses envelop an America ostensibly devoted to republican equality?

One reason is that both middle-class gentility and democracy came out of the democratic revolutions of the eighteenth century. The political upheaval of 1776 coincided with a more quiet cultural revolution proceeding at the same time in connection with the spread of refinement. Adam Smith identified the crucial change while pursuing the sources of the wealth of nations. Smith noticed that the English aristocracy had committed itself to genteel culture in all its material forms and that jeopardized their political power. Once cultural power was invested in chairs and carpets, rather than armies and castles, Smith argued, the aristocracy was vulnerable. He scolded the gentry for foolishly redirecting the income from their estates away from the older forms of power. At one time, a landlord's wealth supported tenants and retainers whose allegiance was unquestioned because of their dependence on the lord. Then foreign commerce and manufacture tempted the ruling classes to purchase baubles instead. "For a pair of diamond buckles perhaps, or for something as frivolous and useless, they exchanged the maintenance, or what is the same thing, the price of the maintenance of a thousand men for a year, and with it the whole weight and authority which it could give them." In other words, they sacrificed patronage for personal splendor. "Having sold their birth-right, not like Esau for a mess of pottage in time of hunger and necessity, but in the wantonness of plenty, for trinkets and baubles, fitter to be the play-things of children than the serious pursuits of men, they became as insignificant as any substantial burgher or tradesman in a city."[11]

Smith did not pursue the point to its conclusion, but he implied that the investment of lordly power in baubles put that power up for auction. Burghers and tradesmen could buy trinkets and live like lords. Whereas common people before had contented themselves with observing power or submitting to it in order to partake of its strength, they could now participate more directly in the cultural aspects of power. Genteel culture was not an inheritance; it could be acquired by purchase. Smith may not have understood this himself, but the implication was that one could enjoy aspects of the power of kings by living like a king, or in some reduced version of the kingly life.

In this context, the purchase of a Wedgwood vase became an act of cultural usurpation. Bearing all the associations sedulously cultivated by Wedgwood, the vase installed a tiny fragment of aristocratic culture in the owner's parlor. The owner acquired power by purchase. Adorned with other objects, with houses, dress, and manners, the lives of the emulators recognizably resembled their aristocratic models. Though far removed in levels of splendor and display, not to mention actual political authority, the refined middle class nonetheless laid claim to the same culture as the aristocracy and so to a portion of its power. In a certain way the Wedgwood vase was a revolutionary presumption, an invasion of aristocratic circles by an excluded class. Genteel consumerism was a form of cultural revolution.

But if these resemblances, parallels, and collaborations brought gentility and republicanism together, there was more that drove them apart. Although advancing the democratic revolution in some respects, the spread of gentility ran at cross-purposes in others. The revolution through emulation and acquisition had a different purpose from the political revolution that took place in America in the eighteenth century. The political revolution displaced aristocratic power in the colonies, making the people sovereign in place of the king. Ideologically, aristocracy was the enemy of the republic; "aristocrat" was a despised title. The inner impulse of republicanism was to destroy aristocracy.

Middle-class gentility was no less a claim on another kind of aristocratic power, but a claim laid without repudiating aristocracy itself. Indeed the middle-class acquisition of gentility honored aristocracy by the sincerest form of praise—emulation. Rather than liberating people from aristocratic cultural power, the spread of gentility left Americans more in its thrall than ever. Every effort to behave like the best people was a tribute to the superiority of the aristocratic circles where the best people were known to reside; delight in Wedgwood's queensware did honor to the queen's taste. Americans were caught in the perplexing contradiction of a democratic government presiding over the spread of an aristocratic culture.

The contradiction was all the more severe because gentility was at odds with older middle-class values. Gentility envisioned an existence free of work, devoted to conversation, art, and the pursuit of pleasure. By contrast, industry lay at the heart of middle-class life and was rightly enjoined upon all who wished to succeed in the middle-class world. Nothing in the courtesy books told people how to work harder or better. Parlors and formal dining rooms were not furnished to facilitate labor. They were places explicitly dedicated to leisure and to higher pleasures of the mind. Moreover, genteel spaces and activities were redolent of luxury, the adornment of a world with superfluous ornaments wholly lacking in productive purpose. Genteel adornments squandered the fruits of labor rather than conserving or encouraging them. Gentility was the culture of a leisured governing class, not of hardworking farmers and artisans. In its pure form, gentility not only contradicted the inner spirit of republican government; it undermined the values that were functionally necessary to the perpetuation of middle-class life. In the revolutionary effort to plunder the finest fruits of aristocratic existence, the middle class committed itself to values potentially subversive of their indigenous culture.[12]

The consequences of these contradictions have shown themselves on many of the preceding pages. People sought to reconcile principles that in many respects were irreconcilable. Horace Bushnell's search for a religion of taste untainted by aristocratic fashion and Catharine Beecher's prescription for refined housewives unafraid of work were but two attempts to create a place for aristocratic culture in a republican and middle-class society. Bushnell and Beecher were two among many who formulated compromises for reconciling the differences.

But there was no way to escape some degree of alienation and contradiction. The standing joke about forbidding parlors was one mild expression of middle-class alienation from the culture it was so avidly seeking. People felt uncomfortable in the parlors which they made such an effort to create. The guidebooks constantly pleaded for greater simplicity that would end the contradiction:

There is in some houses such a difference between things used every day, and those which are kept for company, that . . . an unexpected ring at the doorbell produces the greatest consternation. . . . Now would it not be more refined and dignified, as well as more honest and comfortable, to live a little better every day and make less parade before company.[13]

Underlying the consternation of the surprised householders was the artificiality of the company culture; in their natural state people did not live up to company standards; it was a life outside of their own. But it would be more humiliating still not to be genteel, and so people went on with the act.

For some the tensions were agonizing. Sidney George Fisher, the Philadelphia gentleman who desperately yearned to devote himself wholly to mental culture, mourned the necessity of his involvement in business. "Business and moneymaking to one who has tasted this intoxicating pleasure are loathsome," he wrote. Businessmen "live in a very base and inferior world."[14] Refinement and commerce were oil and water, and Fisher could find no way to mix them. The aesthetic impulses died in the world of business, an architectural author wrote. Aesthetics must be cultivated in youth, for there was no hope for their growth "after the heart has become worn by the business-experiences of the struggling life of a prosperous merchant, or professional man."[15] The admission was damning, for it meant that business, the very engine of middle-class life, destroyed the love of beauty, the heart of gentility.

One impulse was to repudiate gentility, condemning it for its artificiality, extravagance, and aristocratic origins. John Fanning Watson lamented Philadelphia's progress in luxury during the half century before 1840, invoking bourgeois criticisms of court culture that went back a hundred years and more. While the increase in comfort and beauty was admirable, he deplored the extravagance as "kingly pride and exotic vain-glory—not becoming either our profession or our wants." Americans should not be "the servile and debased imitators of *courtly modes and forms,* from which our fathers so earnestly and devotedly divorced themselves and their posterity." Yet even in Watson's mind the courtly modes were inextricably interwoven with the progress of civilization and refinement in Philadelphia.[16] In sphere after sphere gentility was experienced as alien, at odds with the natural life and business of the middle class, the servile imitation of aristocracy. Yet people could never cast it off entirely for fear of losing the precious refinement they had stolen from the gentry.[17]

The reasons for gentility's influence are clear: plain people needed a vocabulary of honor and glory and were compelled to find one where they could.[18] They had no appropriate markings of their own to signify their elevation when they came to power in government or rose to prominence through wealth. They could only turn to the elites of the preceding regime. They required the splendors of palaces and mansions to honor their own achievements. How could an ascendant middle class display its newfound strength but in forms borrowed from their former rulers? They could invent no more extravagant word to dignify a building than "palace," and thus the innumerable palaces of commerce, art, and pleasure. In the very moment when they were attempting to eradicate aristocratic rule from government, they were compelled to cover themselves with an aristocratic veneer—to ratify their new authority. While at first it may seem like gross negligence on their part to have entangled themselves in the contradiction of democratic government rising amid the forms of an aristocratic culture, their cultural position left them no alternative.

THE ARISTOCRATIC REVIVAL

HAVING made that commitment, middle-class Americans in the nineteenth century faced a number of perplexing difficulties growing out of the contradictions in their culture. Among the discomforts and embarrassments, they were left with a truncated culture whose zenith and ultimate realization lay outside their borders. Republicanism cut off the top of American society by forbidding an American aristocracy. Aristocratic bloodlines, traditionally the bearers of the highest culture, could not be tolerated. In republican society, the absence of an aristocracy was a blessing; in genteel society, it was a grave loss. It meant that the best people and the best circles, the models for others to follow, were always elsewhere.

Even the best societies of the greatest cities lived in the shadows of still more refined aristocratic society in Europe. In *Home As Found,* Cooper ridiculed pretentious New Yorkers who bowed to the judgments of hajjis, Americans who had visited Europe and returned home hallowed by the experience. He scoffed at New Yorkers' willingness to settle every question of social usage by citing European precedent. His bluff Captain Truck raised a stir when he lighted a cigar in a drawing room. The resulting discussion of his daring move turned on the question of whether "smoking is ungenteel in England." Judgments of the simplest matters turned on the opinions of people in a distant land. Cooper had no trouble in making these sycophantic Americans look ridiculous. Being a hajji, as one character put it, entitled the pilgrim to wear anything, "green, blue, or yellow, and to cause it to pass for elegance."[19]

Although the points of reference changed, the same structure carried over to little towns. The practitioners of gentility, as the stories related over and over, lived by the standards of the "best people," who always existed else-where. If they did not always think of European courts, they had the characteristic provincial habit of envisioning some superior society in a grand metropolis that embodied the highest in cultural achievement. They were fixed in a colonial mentality of periphery and center. In villages they thought of Boston or New York with the same awe as New York regarded London or Paris. In village and city, the structure was the same; ultimate authority lay in a distant place. The genteel lived by a standard outside themselves and their own circle. They could not break the colonial and provincial habit of looking upward and outward for leadership.

The arrival of a visitor from one of the centers of authority could be unsettling. Commonplace practices in the village lost validity when the visitor did otherwise. A woman who refused to carry packages in the street lost confidence in her superiority when she saw an acknowledged aristocrat with a package in hand. The village social leaders could be displaced in an instant. When the stranger looked with favor on a wallflower, as so often happened in the stories, the former belles instantly faded. The authority of the outsiders enabled neglected heroines to rise suddenly to glory, in the favorite plot devices of sentimental novels, but these reversals suggested the instability of a truncated society, insecure within itself. Snide comments about American refinement in the published travel journals of European visitors like Frances Trollope or Captain Basil Hall infuriated Americans. Yet readers could not dismiss their judgments as trifles; the writers' familiar-ity with European standards gave them too much authority.

Genteel guidebooks frequently disparaged dependence on European models and claimed to offer advice for Americans. "We have had enough of mere imported conventionalism in manners," one etiquette book declared. "Our usages should not be English or French usages, further than English and French usages are founded on universal principles." Yet this very book recommended that "if we are writing to a superior, we should leave large spaces between the lines. Also, commence the letter quite down low upon the sheet, and be particular not to crowd the writing, as it is considered disrespectful." Those instructions had nothing to do with universal princi-ples; they came from courtesy books originating at Versailles 150 years earlier. American writers had no place to turn for guidance except to the European aristocracy.[20]

Troubled by the contradictions, some Americans came to believe that America had to have an aristocracy of its own. Constant imitation of Euro-pean fashions and deference to the judgment of every English traveler who published a word on American manners was too painful for a nation that purported to lead the world in enlightened government and to exceed everyone in entrepreneurial energy. Responding to the need, a few literary people tried to envision an American elite in the nineteenth century. They were helped by the place given to an aristocracy of virtue within classical republican political thought, an elite in keeping with America's explicit political principles and quite distinct from Europe's old order. Jefferson expected an educated elite to lead the nation and founded the University of Virginia for the very purpose of training such a body of men. John Adams had based his defense of the American Constitution on the belief that an aristocracy of superiors would naturally emerge in any society. Even the more egalitarian democracy of the Jacksonian era failed to dissolve completely these classical ideas of broad democratic participation under a select leadership. The remnants of classical republicanism in the background gave the literary people encouragement as they tried to conceive an American aristocracy that would complete our independence from Europe.[21]

The memory of a republican elite was preserved in the stereotype of the gentleman of the old school, a frequent figure in fiction and in real life who reminded Americans of the aristocracy that had once governed the nation. Chancellor Nicholas Ridgely of Kent County, Delaware, who lived until 1830, was described, it will be remembered, as such a person. "Although constantly thrown among gay and fashionable society," Ridgely was said to have "adhered strictly to the manners and customs and fashions of his youth. In speaking, he used the old mode of pronunciation, without regard to Walker's Diction; and in writing, employed the same number of capital letters as were used in the days of Addison and Pope. The cut of his coat was the same for fifty years; and he constantly wore short breeches with kneebuckles and long fair-top boots to correspond."[22]

These nostalgic evocations of old-style aristocrats seemed to suggest that at the nation's founding a class of true gentlemen had commanded our destiny. Harriet Beecher Stowe's Parson Lothrop in *Oldtown Folks* "was a stately, handsome, well-proportioned man, and had the formal and ceremonious politeness of a gentleman of the old school." He "was one of the cleanest, most gentlemanly, most well bred of men,—never appearing without all the decorums of silk stockings, shining knee and shoe buckles, well-brushed shoes, immaculately powdered wig, out of which shone his clear, calm, serious face, like the moon out of a fleecy cloud."[23] Old-school gentlemen were depicted as quaintly out of style, and yet admirable. The evocations betrayed a longing for a better world now passing, as well as establishing a tradition on which to ground an American aristocracy.

Rufus Wilmot Griswold's *Republican Court*, published in 1854, was a full-scale evocation of this lost world. Griswold, a Vermont-born New York editor and all-purpose literary figure, conceived of the book as a serious work of historical research, based on extensive documentation. Much of it consisted of lengthy passages from late-eighteenth-century letters and diaries about high-end social life in the founding years, especially during George Washington's two terms as President. But the topic and the book's title suggested that Griswold was offering an editorial comment on American society. Griswold chose the word "court" intentionally, to show that the social rituals practiced during the Washington administration paralleled and possibly equaled the assemblies, levees, and banquets of a royal court. The ladies were as beautiful, the company as brilliant, the decorum as circumspect, and all was sanctioned by the President. The father of the country was a patron of a court society. The book could have been read as a seditious slander of the republic's most eminent founder, but it was not. Favorable reviews appeared everywhere. "*The work* excites attention and is of a nature to command prolonged sales," a friend wrote. Second and third editions appeared in 1855 and 1856, followed by others.[24] Griswold's reviewers accepted his demonstration that a fullness of gentility had been realized in Washington's court. The book asked implicitly if comparable leadership could be found in 1854.

Griswold's book was one artifact in a midcentury aristocratic revival. In paintings, books, and poetry, artists sketched out the lives of American aristocrats, praising their virtues. The architectural books on rural culture included extravagant country villas intended for families of superior wealth and refinement. The architectural authors hoped that stable families, anchored in these mansions, would establish standards of honor and virtue.[25]

Huntington's painting pictures Martha Washington as a grand lady, in keeping with the painting's anomalous title, Lady Washington's Reception, *and turns the assembled group into courtiers. Huntington imagined an aristocratic court forming at the beginning of the American republic.*

Sentimental writers peopled their landscapes with aristocratic residences to set the proper tone for their stories. "Here and there was a gentleman's seat, with its handsome grounds to diversify the scene," said one in describing a village countryside.[26] The democratic extremes of Jacksonian politics made the vestiges of aristocracy all the more pleasurable. A popular manners book even favored honoring the differences of birth.

> A man or woman of good stock or breed, has the same superiority in consequence that a horse or dog has. A man may be born rich, handsome, smart, elegant, and noble; there is no more doubt of this, than that a horse may be born with similar qualities and advantages. Another may be born poor, ugly, stupid, awkward, and base. There is therefore an aristocracy of birth, which it is a great folly to deny, and the denial of which is as useless as it is false.[27]

Americans pursuing their genealogical roots prized every connection with European nobility. Mary Parker Welch, in her reminiscences of life in Delaware, emphasized her English ancestor with the title of "gentleman" opposite his name. "The title, 'gentleman,' " she reminded her readers, "carried with it in early days an admission of high respectability, and indicated that its possessor was well-born. The Norman word was, as the French now is, gentilhomme."[28] In democratic America, she shamelessly refined her own bloodlines by establishing aristocratic connections.

James Fenimore Cooper campaigned for an American aristocracy as energetically as anyone, though never without ambivalence, for he was at the same time devoted to republican principles. Like the New Yorkers whom he ridiculed, Cooper was an admirer of the hajjis. The heroine of *Home As Found*, Eve Effingham, acquired her unmatched grace by frequenting European drawing rooms. Her experience allowed Eve to excel her beautiful cousin Grace Van Cortlandt, who had never resided abroad. A European background gave Eve superior taste on every subject from houses to mountains to the management of servants. Yet rather than deprecating the American gentry as pale imitations of the authentic European article, Cooper was at pains to demonstrate their absolute equality with their transatlantic counterparts. Eve had seen her father and cousin John Effingham "moving in the best circles of Europe, respected for their information and independence, undistinguished by their manners, admired for their personal appearance, manly, courteous, and of noble bearing and principles, if not set apart from the rest of mankind by an arbitrary rule connected with rank." With some passion, she insisted that such men merited the best of European titles. "Earls, counts, dukes, nay, prince! These are the designations of the higher classes of Europe, and such titles or those that are equivalent, would belong to the higher classes here." Old American families deserved the same honor as European old families.

> There are two great causes of distinction everywhere, wealth and merit. Now if a race of Americans continue conspicuous in their own society through either or both of these causes for a succession of generations, why have they not the same claims to be considered members of old families, as Europeans under the same circumstances?

It made no difference that the American polity forbade hereditary rank. "A republican history is as much history as a monarchical history." Only the absence of official recognition distinguished the two. "Sentiment is at the bottom of our nobility, and the great seal at the bottom of yours."[29] Behind Eve's comment was a devoted republicanism, an insistence that the best of America, despite the absence of a titled nobility, was every whit the equal of Europe's best. With such an elite at the head of society, Americans could declare their cultural independence of Europe.

But American republicanism defeated every effort of this elite to assume its rightful place at the head of society. Aristabulus Bragg, the upstart land agent for Mr. Effingham, assumed that he was as worthy of the hand of Eve Effingham as anyone. He could not see the vast gulf that separated them. Her dignified austerity rebuffed him without dashing his hopes. He persisted in the belief that they were equals. Mr. Jarvis, the "plain, pains taking, sensible man of business," understood perfectly that John Effingham, "in education, habits, association, and manners, was, at least, of a class entirely distinct from

William Warner Major, a Mormon convert from Britain, wished to identify Brigham Young's family with the life of the English nobility. In addition to creating an extravagant architectural setting, he puts a book in Brigham Young's hand, places flowers on the table, and sets Young's wife's feet on a cushion, making the scene one of exalted domestic refinement in an aristocratic house.

his own," and "without a feeling of envy or unkindness of any sort" made no claims to social equality. Cooper wanted the land to be filled with Mr. Jarvises; unfortunately, the Mrs. Jarvises prevailed. Mrs. Jarvis thought her husband's opinions "very spiritless, and as particularly anti-republican." "I am sure they have no right to pretend to be our betters," she proclaimed, "and I feel no disposition to admit the impudent claim." "All I ask is a claim to be considered a fit associate for anybody in this country—in these United States of America."

Cooper saw in that belief the glory of America and its bane. Common people refused to grovel and aspired instead to a modest respectability. Sir George Templemore was astounded at the dress and beauty of ordinary women. But at the same time, none of them reached the heights.

> The women strike me as being singularly delicate and pretty; well dressed, too, I might add; but while there is a great air of decency, there is very little high finish; and what strikes me as being quite odd, under such circumstances, scarcely any downright vulgarity or coarseness.

John Effingham confirmed Templemore's judgment. "Of the coarseness that would be so prominent elsewhere, there is hardly any." Republican equality elevated virtually everyone. "So great is the equality in all things in this country, so direct the tendency to this respectable mediocrity, that what you now see here to-night may be seen in almost every village in the land." But that was the fault in the society: its respectable mediocrity. Republicanism elevated everyone but bound down the superior. Failure to acknowledge its own aristocracy deprived America of high finish. "Much is wanting that would add to the grace and beauty of society." Mediocrity was America's great achievement and its preeminent failure.[30] Without an aristocracy of its own, America could not reach the heights of refinement promised by its genteel culture.

The obstacles to a republican aristocracy did not discourage a succeeding generation of Americans. In the half century after Cooper wrote, American magnates accumulated wealth to equal the estates of the European nobility. Buoyed by their fantastic success, Americans cast off all constraint and claimed, as Cooper had wished, to be the complete equals of Europe's titled lords. They married their daughters to dukes and earls. They erected palaces to equal in grandeur Europe's great houses. They entertained in lavish style and patronized the arts in the best aristocratic tradition.

While their expenditures now appear egregiously extravagant and their mansions hopelessly pretentious, these American lords and ladies were in actuality the logical fulfillment of the refining process. Gentility required a top for society, a dwelling place for the best people, a center of beauty, a court society. After George Washington that court society departed from the capital of government. American court society moved to the great cities, and especially New York, and then to the country estates of the nation's wealthy magnates. The self-appointed aristocrats of the post–Civil War era took upon themselves the task of forming a top for American society, a place where the architecture, the decor, the manners, and the art achieved the grandeur and high finish Cooper had hoped for. If their claims to aristocratic polish now seem overinflated and their taste questionable, they cannot be faulted for trying. Their mansions, their airs, their pretensions were the natural outgrowth of the aristocratic genteel culture that the American middle class had appropriated from its former rulers.

LOCATING THE LOWER CLASS

THE creation of an elite for American society implied the existence of a lower class, and there lay another problem for a refined republic: reconciling republican equality with the divisions inherent in aristocratic gentility. Genteel culture assumed a gulf between polite people and the nameless and faceless masses in the dull world of work and service. They were the "parcel of impolite, yet honest and worthy men" of Charles Ridgely's Kent County, or the superstitious and ragged peasants of Mary Welch's Sussex, eating biscuits in their old log cabin.[31] By fixing standards of polite conduct for the elite, gentility marked more humble people just as distinctly, with their contrasting disheveled clothes, rough houses, and coarse manners. Tavern-keepers sized up the social rank and culture of their customers at a glance; Thoreau noted the details of a backwoods farmer's oversized hat, tight-fitting coat, and lumbering wagon, instantly placing him socially and cultur-ally; George Templeton Strong thought the rude manners of the New York City crowds wholly disqualified them to enter the mayor's house on New Year's Day. Gentility gave visible expression to social class and was meant to do so. In aristocratic societies, genteel conduct distinguished the superior people, who were destined to rule, from ordinary people, who were to be ruled.

But what was the proper demeanor of the vulgar masses in republican America, where no class was destined to rule and the whole people were sovereign? James Fenimore Cooper, advocate of an American aristocracy, took pride in the modest refinement of ordinary villagers. His John Effing-ham was bragging up America when he observed that "of the coarseness that would be so prominent elsewhere, there is hardly any." He was pleased that the level of mediocre gentility that he and Templeton saw in New York "may be seen in almost every village in the land."[32] Cooper wished for a society with a top and a middle but no bottom.

But was that possible? One American observer thought not. *The Sunday School Magazine* for 1845 insisted that "we cannot all be 'lords' and 'gentlemen'; there must be a large part of us, after all, to make and mend clothes and houses, and carry on trade and commerce." Yet that seemingly obvious argument did not persuade everyone. Despite the need for a working class, "so strong is the propensity to be thought 'gentlemen' " that "thousands upon thousands" of young people hoped for a life without labor.[33] Except in slave regions, the idea of a lowest class was not acceptable for American republicans.

Driven by republican logic, reformers looked for ways to make everyone polite, to invite everyone into the drawing room. In Catharine Sedgwick's popular trilogy of novels published in the 1830s, her hero Mr. Barclay said that "there is nothing that tends more to the separation into classes than difference of manners. This is a badge that all can see." To give everyone the right badge, Sedgwick's novels showed ordinary working people reading books, teaching their children to draw, treating people politely, even learning to dance, and so erasing the marks of their lower-class status. Sedgwick was trying to prove that a degree of gentility was accessible to everyone, making it "the fault of the mechanic, if he takes a place not assigned to him by the government and institutions of his country."[34]

A similar vision inspired Frederick Law Olmsted. In 1852 on one of his southern journeys, Olmsted debated the merits of northern and southern societies with Samuel Perkins Allison. Allison argued that the southern labor system permitted the flowering of true aristocratic gentility impossible to achieve in the North. Olmsted replied that the superior culture of the ordinary people in the North more than compensated for the deficiencies of the northern elite. Allison scornfully pointed to the ruffians and rowdies of the North to deflate Olmsted's claims. Stung by the exchange, Olmsted resolved to work for "the *general* elevation of all classes," to vindicate free republican society. "We need institutions that shall more directly *assist* the poor and degraded to elevate themselves," he wrote. That meant people like himself had to "get up parks, gardens, music, dancing schools, reunions which will be so attractive as to force into contact the good and bad, the gentlemanly and the rowdy," so as to polish the common people.[35]

Olmsted was influenced by Horace Bushnell, the preacher of his family church in Hartford, and by the landscape architect Andrew Jackson Downing. Olmsted extended Bushnell's analysis of frontier influences to the city. He felt that the barbarism that arose where the frontier dissolved social bonds also occurred in cities. Nowhere on the western frontier did people live "so isolated from humanizing influences and with such constant practice of heart-hardening and taste-smothering habits as that to be found in our great Eastern cities." The eastern population required elevation as much as the western. Olmsted believed that Downing had prescribed the right rem-

edy in his essay "The New York Park" in an 1851 issue of *The Horticulturalist.*
The essay had a profound effect on Olmsted. When he proposed a memorial
statue to Downing in Central Park, Olmsted submitted a passage from the
essay for the inscription:

> The higher social and artistic elements of every man's nature lie
> dormant within him, and every laborer is a possible gentleman, not by
> the possession of money or fine clothes—but through the refining
> influence of intellectual and moral culture. Open wide, therefore, the
> doors of your libraries and picture galleries, all ye true republicans!
> Build halls where knowledge shall be freely diffused among men, and
> not shut up within the narrow walls of narrower institutions. Plant
> spacious parks in your cities, and unloose their gates as wide as the
> gates of morning to the whole people.[36]

That conception of republican refinement inspired Olmsted's own work for
four decades: "The poor need an education to refinement and taste and the
mental and moral capital of gentlemen."[37] Olmsted constructed parks in the
1850s as an American aspect of the worldwide struggle to establish republicanism. In Europe, revolutions against monarchical tyranny were still taking
place; in America, the battle had shifted away from government. He aimed
for "the encouragement of a democratic condition of society as well as of
government."[38]

Olmsted realized that aristocratic elements in American society were
cynical about elevating the democratic masses. An editorial in the New York
Herald in 1857 cast doubt on the elevating influence of Central Park, then
under construction. The problem in America, the *Herald* argued, was that
"nobody has any 'superiors'; we know no 'nobility and gentry.' " "Sam the
Five Pointer is as good a man as William B. Astor or Edward Everett." The
result will be that "when we open a public park, Sam will air himself in it.
He will take his friends, whether from Church street or elsewhere. He will
enjoy himself there, whether by having a muss, or a drink at the corner
groggery opposite the great gate," and the immensely expensive park "will
be nothing but a huge bear garden for the lowest denizens of the city."[39]
That outcome would have defeated all of Olmsted's hopes. He disparaged
the moanings of crypto-aristocrats as the "fallacy of cowardly conservatism,"
and made plans to discipline park visitors to keep up the proper tone and
to make park life a civilizing influence.[40] He insisted on the historic importance of Central Park in refining democratic culture: "It is of great importance as the first real park made in this country—a democratic development
of the highest significance and on the success of which, in my opinion, much
of the progress of art and esthetic culture in this country is dependent."[41]

Sentimental writers similarly assumed responsibility for the refinement of the rude. Their repeated depiction of characters with meager means but refined lives underscored the idea that the lowliest of Americans could be refined. A description of a "plain brown frame house, with nothing to relieve its unsightliness but a luxuriant morning-glory vine," with curtains inside and "a neat rag carpet on the floor," said plainly that a refined soul could dwell in the humblest circumstances.[42] For these writers there was no inescapable culture of poverty. In one story, the poor but pious Brainard family lived in small, perfectly clean rooms with honeysuckle and roses over door and windows, revealing the telltale love of flowers and trees. "The yard was beautiful—a handsome mound in the middle, ornamented and bordered by dahlias and other choice flowers. It was an Eden of beauty. The tall elms and poplars completely embowered their dwelling." Naturally the children in such a home did not suffer in the least from the parents' poverty. Mr. and Mrs. Brainard were great readers. "Poor people have often a greater taste for reading, than the rich; and it is this that constitutes their chief source of enjoyment." The Brainards read history to their children and during the long winter evenings instructed them in all the right academic subjects. "Charles and Susan were well acquainted with geography, were very good at figures, and spent many a merry hour over their slates. They had a small table on which they kept their maps, books, and such things, all in perfect order."[43] Children with names like Charles and Susan would of course spend merry hours over their slates, while their parents read history to them. The virtues of such a household assured readers that the lower orders could be perfectly happy—and refined—in their humble homes. The differences in wealth did not imply a difference in culture.

Even romance between genteel and rude was not out of the question. Linda, a genteel city girl, chanced upon Paul, a childhood sweetheart, in the street; as they walked together "her little foot twinkled upon the pavement close to him," and "her robe brushed his coarse garments." Miss Lofty, Linda's companion, scorned Paul with his monstrous green jacket (green was the sure sign of rude taste), and Paul himself wondered at the gulf between them. "Was it because, as Miss Lofty had said, he wore a green jacket, and worked with his hands, while Linda sat in her delicate robes of muslin or silk, and with slender fingers wrought at her embroidery-frame, or airily swept the piano?" But readers had no apprehensions of danger, because the sensible Paul could easily learn manners and so become worthy of Linda.[44] Good-hearted country boys fell in love with lovely city girls all the time in the stories. Part of the excitement of the romance was devising ways for the rude to show that they actually had noble hearts and so were worthy of refined love. Rather than acting as an insurmountable barrier, cultural differences made romance more poignant.

Some observers believed so confidently in the effectiveness of democratic elevation that they pronounced republican refinement to be an accomplished fact. In his centennial oration on July 4, 1876, Henry Ward Beecher insisted that, despite the influx of immigrants, the United States had raised ordinary people far above the levels of culture at the founding. At the beginning "there were here and there notable mansions, here and there notable households of intelligence and virtue." A century later "the ordinary workman's house" had in many respects outdistanced the old mansions. "If there be one thing that has grown in solidity and grandeur, in richness and purity and refinement, it has been the American household." A workman with a virtuous upbringing who avoided whiskey should own an unmortgaged house. A workman "who has not in that house provided carpets for the rooms, who has not his China plates, who has not his chromos, who has not some picture or portrait hanging upon the walls, who has not some books nestling on the shelf . . ." had only himself to blame.[45]

Beecher could not report that every house in America had a carpet. He knew that in 1876 a large proportion of the population could afford few such luxuries and might not care about having them. American society was not entirely refined then and never would be. His concern was where to place the blame for the deprivations of workmen who lacked unmortgaged houses with books on the shelves, and he pointed to the workmen themselves who gave way to whiskey or fell short in diligence. Worthy workmen could become refined if they tried, just as Sedgwick's novels had shown. Rude workingmen in her stories were blamed for being content to live in disorder, resisting Mr. Barclay's genteel household regimen. Mr. Barclay and her other heroes were living proof that improvement was within reach if only workers were sensible and diligent.

Fixing responsibility for the condition of the poor relieved the middle class of its guilt and enabled the polite population to scorn the vulgar, who could scarcely expect invitations into the parlor when they refused to better themselves. Beecher and Sedgwick were democratic within limits. In principle, they accepted men and women from any wealth stratum who adopted the rudiments of genteel culture, and they conscientiously showed the benighted how to improve. After that they justifiably excluded those who clung to rude ways. The Beecher-Sedgwick resolution of the contradiction between gentility and republicanism was to welcome everyone into society, but only on genteel terms. Genteel culture could not tolerate dirty feet tracking mud on parlor carpets.

Calvert Vaux, the architectural reformer, believed every farmer deserved a house with a parlor, but the farmers were at fault if they failed to use their houses properly. Unfortunately, "it is the custom with some farmers to make a constant practice of taking all meals in the kitchen." Kitchen dining disgusted Vaux: "this habit marks a low state of civilization." Vaux thought farming "ought to be made a refined and noble pursuit," but farmers who insisted on eating in the kitchen remained in the cellar of civilization, not enjoying "every grace that belongs to rural life."[46] For all his supposed respect for farm life, Vaux was scornful of real farmers who refused to observe the protocols of cultivated living.

These middle-class promoters of refinement could not rid themselves of genteel scorn for the vulgar despite a strong sentiment in favor of republican egalitarianism. They wanted the lower classes to live in genteel poverty, and if they refused to learn manners, they could not expect to come to the mayor's home on New Year's Day. In the last analysis, the principles of culture overcame the principles of politics; genteel exclusion overrode republican equality. When it came to society, only the polite were created equal.

POLITICS AND CULTURE

THE social tensions growing out of this patronizing attitude could not be permanently restricted to occasional scuffles on village streets and the exchange of slighting remarks in taverns. Eventually the anxiety and resentment growing out of continuous invidious comparisons was bound to break out in major public controversy. That happened in the Log Cabin Campaign of 1840, when the aristocratic Whigs, acknowledging the realities of democratic politics, made refinement versus vulgarity a campaign issue. For once democracy had the advantage in the struggle. Temporarily and superficially, men of high culture had to speak a homespun language and at least feign regard for log cabin virtues. Whig politicians, converts by political necessity to equality, were forced to work out their own compromise with the vulgar masses, and offer an alternative solution to the problem of the lower orders in a republic.

Well before 1840, the log cabin had come to stand for rude living. The rough, unpainted exterior, the absence of a stairway, the unfinished ceiling, the small windows, the lack of decoration set life within log walls apart from life in the mansions. Since a house was the primary site of genteel existence, a rough dwelling enveloped its inhabitants in an aura of rudeness and shame. The vast energy released in the Log Cabin Campaign came from the cultural tension encapsulated in the log cabin as a symbol of a crude existence.

Lucy Mack Smith, the mother of the prophet Joseph Smith, experienced the humiliation of log cabin life shortly after the Smith family moved to Palmyra, New York, in 1816. They purchased land in 1817 and constructed a standard small cabin with a lean-to and moved in with their family of nine. While living there Lucy was invited to tea with a few women of the town, "some wealthy merchants wives and the minister's lady." The time passed "quite pleasantly," she said, until one lady observed, "Well I declare Mrs. [Smith] ought not to live in that log house of her's any longer she deserves a better fate and I say she must have a new house." The seemingly innocent and well-meaning remark stirred Lucy's wrath. Interpreting the comment as a slight, she turned on the women in a fury. To the wives of the merchants she admitted her family lacked property, but the little they enjoyed "has not been obtained at the expense of the comfort of any human being." "We never distressed any man which circumstance almost invariably attends the Mercantile life." As for the minister's wife, she was "kept awake with anxiety about your sons who are in habitual attendance on the Grog Shop and gambling house," while Lucy's children were all sober and upright. Having established her moral superiority to all others present despite her residence in a log house, Lucy ended her account.

But in the very next sentence in the memoirs she noted that "we still continued felling timber and clearing land and about this time we began to make preparations for building a house." The family hired a carpenter to construct a frame house with parlor and central hall and staircase, in keeping with local styles. They greatly enjoyed the house, but at an expense they could not afford. Not having paid off the mortgage on the land, they were unable to meet the payments on house and land, and in 1825 lost them both. The humiliation of log cabin life drove them to exceed their resources, with disastrous results.[47]

Other log cabin dwellers were doubtless satisfied with their houses, but for families who had adopted middle-class values like the Smiths, conscious-

Simple log houses remained a common residence for many Americans in virtually every section of the country through the middle of the nineteenth century.

ness of inferior housing was a painful reminder of their exclusion from respectable society. Log cabins divided the polite from the vulgar, inviting invidious comparisons and publicly identifying the inferior classes. The Democratic newspaper reporter who ridiculed William Henry Harrison as a man happy to retire to a log cabin with a jug of cider invoked a common stereotype about log cabin people. Their rough houses were outward signs of inferior character; they were unpolished, unambitious, and simple. The reporter forgot that a large proportion of the American population still lived in log cabins. A correspondent to the *Genesee Farmer* in 1842 assumed that "a goodly portion of your readers" were "like myself, yet the tennants of primitive log cabins."[48] To deride Harrison for his log cabin life was to denigrate all the log cabin people.

Whig political managers immediately saw that they could benefit from the gibe. Harrison, a war hero and Indian fighter, had been nominated in the first place to win votes "among the Log Cabins." Seizing the opportunity, his supporters reprinted the attack everywhere: "Give him a barrel of hard cider, and settle a pension of two thousand a year on him, and my word for it, he will sit the remainder of his days in his log cabin by the side of a 'sea coal' fire, and study moral philosophy."[49] The Whig politicians did not counter with a reminder of Harrison's birth in an aristocratic Virginia family or his actual residence in an elegant mansion on the Ohio River. They happily left him in the log cabin and turned the reporter's derisive comment into an attack on honest poverty. "After having spent many a year of toil and danger for the defence of this land against foreign and savage foes, and having sat down in poverty in his cabin, General Harrison is to be made the object of a scornful and contemptuous jest."

The Whigs kept the limelight on Harrison personally and expounded on

The Joseph Smith family began construction of this house in 1823 immediately after Lucy Smith was subjected to the neighbors' ridicule of the family's log cabin.

the injustice of the attack on him, but Harrison was surrogate for all the other log cabin people. The Whigs played upon the resentments of millions of Lucy Smiths who had suffered the shame of log cabin living amidst a refining society. The Whigs said of Harrison that "he is a man of substance, not of show—plain in his dress and manners; a practical farmer; works with his own hands, and treats every honest man as his equal." The same could be said of all the others in this abused class.⁵⁰ Their virtues warranted full acceptance without benefit of gentility. They did not have to put parlors in their houses and their children in dancing school to be respectable. On July 4, 1840, the Whigs toasted "Democracy: Shame upon those who, professing democracy, would slander the occupants of Log cabins, and scoff at the honest yeomanry, whose only beverage is plain hard cider."⁵¹ In political society, men and women from log cabins stood on an equal basis alongside people from mansions.

In the course of the campaign, the Whigs wavered a little in their defense of log cabin society. They promoted Harrison as a man of culture as well as a simple farmer, saying that "although a working man and not a lawyer, he has talents of a high order, is a 'scholar and a ripe and good one.'—is one of the best read men in the country—and thinks well—speaks well—writes well, and fights well." Like Sedgwick and Olmsted, the Whigs wanted their poor man's candidate to have familiarity with books.

They wavered just as much in their descriptions of John W. Bear, "the Buckeye Blacksmith," a genuine blacksmith from South Bloomfield, Ohio, whom the Whigs sent to campaign for John Tyler, the vice presidential candidate, to whom they hoped to give a little of the log cabin aura. An editorial in support of Bear as a campaigner willingly admitted that "he is a very illiterate man, without any education, and that his language is not by any means classical"; he was not "skilled in the ornamental elegancies of language." Those shortcomings were all in his favor. Locofoco criticism of Bear was actually an attack on all plain men:

> Every insinuation against his character and abilities is an indirect insult to the working classes of this country; it is at once saying that mechanics and manual laborers have not, and cannot attain, that portion of knowledge of the English tongue, the collection of facts, and the ability of reasoning, that fit a man for expressing his thoughts and feelings before a public audience.

Nevertheless, Bear had to be well informed and well spoken. The Whigs introduced into politics a truly virtuous plain man, not the virtuoso of ornate speech, but not the dull and torpid peasant either. Bear was an exemplar of a new democratic politician. "His is the eloquence of the reason and

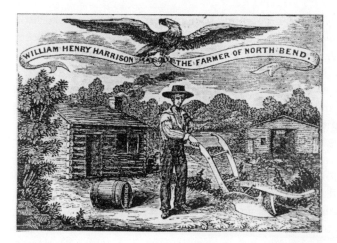

William Henry Harrison's campaign managers used every device they could think of to identify their candidate with the log-cabin people. That strategy lowered Harrison from his actual social station, but it also raised the residents of log cabins to new dignity.

Lincoln's progress was measured by the quality of his houses.

understanding, in which the gorgeous trappings of fancy have very little existence.... His language is that of the common conversation in workshops, and every workman will understand the words and grasp the ideas."[52] Bear, the virtuous plain man, was the direct descendant of Charles Ridgely's "impolite, yet honest and worthy men." In 1840 the republicans brought these people fully into the political arena as candidates and orators, insisting that they belonged there.

The political elevation of log cabin people blurred the line between rude and refined, giving many plain people a measure of respectability they had not previously enjoyed. Referring to Bear and the host of imitators who sprang up in his wake in 1840, one of the Whig campaign managers said there was "a large measure of this unpolished but effective oratory, from men unknown before." In many instances, the rude men drove the polite from the field. "The contest of 1840 soon became too uproarious for gentlemen of . . . refined taste." To gain a hearing, gentlemen had to affect a taste for log cabin life themselves. The aristocratic South Carolinian Hugh Swinton Legaré donned rough clothes and a coonskin cap when he went on the campaign trail and substituted frontier idioms for classical allusions.[53] Snobbery toward log cabin people became politically dangerous. The Whig campaigners could too easily expose the aristocratic, anti-republican principle underlying refinement. One of the Whig July 4 toasts honored "Log Cabins—Emblems of republican simplicity; none but aristocrats despise, none but despots fear them."[54]

Too much must not be made of this democratization of culture. Whig politicians talked up log cabins and cider out of political expediency, not because of a newfound respect for lower-class culture. Many must have reacted to the democratization of their party like the woman in a *Godey's* story in 1839, the wife of a politician. To her dismay her house was the resort of "citizens of all classes." "*Exclusiveness*, once my pride, was turned out of doors; and the motley crowd admitted. It is a wretched system, but I suppose in a government like ours, an unavoidable one."[55] She bluntly noted the opposition between aristocratic gentility's inherent exclusivity and republicanism's equality for all male voters within political society, and she doubtless was not alone. Isaac Mickle, a wealthy young Philadelphia Democrat, lamented in 1842 that "coarse and irregular persons" would laugh anyone to scorn who brought into their company "a refined and fastidious taste and style." A politician had to learn to "drink and roar and talk roughly."[56]

But however secretly cynical, after the campaign of 1840 Whigs and Democrats alike had to moderate any repugnance born of fastidious sensibilities. Lewis Allen, the author of *Rural Architecture*, was, like Catharine Maria Sedgwick, devoted to the elevation of the mass of citizens before granting them equality. Like so many middle-class reformers, he could not believe that humanity could fulfill itself in a degraded dwelling. "A squalid, miserable tenement, with which they who inhabit it are content, can lead to no elevation of character, no improvement in condition, either social or moral, of its occupants." Yet when he came to log cabins he had to tread lightly. "A log cabin, even,—and I speak of this primitive American structure with profound affection and regard, as the shelter from which we have achieved the most of our prodigious and rapid agricultural conquests,—may be so constructed as to speak an air of neatness, intelligence, and even refinement in those who inhabit it." The phrase "log cabin, even" and the adjective "primitive" revealed Allen's views, yet he had to show deference for the merits of log cabin life. Although his purpose was to refine the log cabin people and move them to better homes, he had to affect a regard for their simple houses.[57]

The softening of attitudes toward the log cabin people in Allen and many like him was not a small achievement. It was at least partly responsible for the log cabin people's great triumph in 1860, when one of their own claimed the most honored mansion in the land without repudiating his humble origins. Lincoln's rise from a log cabin to a modest parlor house became part of his appealing life story. His election offered hope for a moment that democratic politics could reconcile the two cultures and bring rude and refined together in a truly republican society.

THE CONFUSION OF CLASS

THIS courting of the log cabin people, while complimentary, was confusing on the question of social divisions. Was there a lower class or not? The ambiguity in the conceptions of the vulgar working class had the effect of obscuring the very nature of class in the United States. Certainly there were poor people, but were they a distinct class, set apart by a culture of their own as well as by their poverty? The difference between refined and rude, the most powerful cultural signs of class, should have marked the lower class in the nineteenth century as it set apart the gentry in the eighteenth century. But the contradictions in American culture worked to obfuscate class clarity.

The Whigs of the Log Cabin Campaign made an effort to draw a line. While accepting plain farmers into political society through the exaltation of the log cabin, they did not imply that ordinary people had achieved the same level of culture. Log cabins merited respect and the inhabitants had their role in politics, but these people were not genteel and did not belong in drawing rooms. The political paintings of George Caleb Bingham, an active Missouri Whig politician, present a population of ordinary people, devoid of gentility, voting at the polls or listening intently to stump speakers.

The scenes reassure observers that unpolished men can be trusted with the vote. Even drunken, ignorant, simple men vote safely in the benign "County Election." In a sense Whigs like Bingham were more democratic than Sedgwick and Beecher in acknowledging the dignity of plain men who lived plain lives without any of the benefits of refinement.

But Bingham's picture of an egalitarian political society implicitly left room for a genteel polite society made up of the refined people pictured in his portraits. They lived a genteel life in their mansions while the rest of the voters returned to their cabins. One political scene, "Stump Speaking," places a member of the local gentry prominently in the front of the audience, sitting comfortably among the listeners, no more than an equal in the assembled political society while obviously superior to all in dress and manner. The Whigs solved the problem of class in 1840 by projecting an egalitarian political society while preserving inequality in culture and so in private life.

The readers of Sedgwick's popular novels were told differently. They were instructed not to tolerate social and cultural inequalities. Republican government demanded a republican society, Sedgwick thought, and a funda-

All levels of society here gather peacefully for political deliberation, though obviously the white-suited man to the right with the tall hat occupies a higher social position than the others. Painter Bingham's message seems to be that cultural and social differences are compatible with harmonious democratic politics.

mental social equality could be achieved. Sedgwick did not advocate an equalization of wealth or standard of living; the crucial distinctions were in manners and culture, not property or work. She wished to imbue every American with vernacular gentility so that a single culture encompassed all. Absorption into a common culture would give the poorest person equal standing in a republican society. All that was needed was for every family to occupy a parlor with chromos on the walls. The large readership of her books suggests she was not alone in this opinion. While those who suffered from poverty may have better understood the difficulties of achieving gentility on a low income, they found no formal barriers to aspiration in Sedgwick's work. No sumptuary laws or attitudes condemned the acquisition of genteel goods. Scores of books insisted that modest gentility could be achieved on modest incomes. A vine and flowers, a rag carpet, a book or two brought a family within the circle of respectability.

These two alternatives, while reasonably clear in themselves, did little to clarify the meaning of class overall. The question of a distinctive lower class was left unanswered. Many Whigs found a permanent place for a simple, plain class of workers and farmers, but others like Catharine Sedgwick bent their efforts to upgrade the lower class, inviting, instructing, insisting on a change of culture. In keeping with Sedgwick's campaign, thousands of peddlers, storekeepers, and industrialists promoted vernacular gentility with an intense devotion born of self-interest. On top of all this, politicians across the

This temperance picture, which shows a poor household saved from the devastation of drink, assumes that even at this level of society, curtains, ceramics, a Windsor chair, and a pedestal table would be found among the furnishings.

land dinned the ears with the language of republican equality. How could working people sustain a belief that they were a separate class when on every side they were told otherwise? The contradictions in American culture prevented the hardening of class consciousness and instead, in the face of repeated rebuffs and exclusions, spread a belief in the right of every American to be middle-class.[58]

THE REFINEMENT OF RACE

THE confusion about class made treacherous footing for any who tried to rise in American society. Reformers, politicians, hucksters held out the promise of respectability to anyone of good character who underwent the proper education and practiced a little self-discipline. But was the promise to be believed? Was polite society ready to admit anyone with good manners and a little mental culture? Or were common people meant to stay in their places, segregated and excluded from the houses of the refined? There were many who believed the promises, among them the most underprivileged and abused elements of the population, free black people living in larger cities. Their efforts to achieve refinement tested the ultimate meaning of gentility in American society.

By the second or third decade of the nineteenth century in virtually every large city in both North and South, a small number of free black people had achieved a degree of respectability that made the pursuit of refinement a practical goal. The black elite did not come from the professional and

The vine over the door, the woman with a child in the front, and the fenced yard express the belief that the rudiments of refinement could be achieved in the simplest settings.

mercantile classes, as was true for the rest of the population. The leading black figures were primarily barbers, carpenters, and other artisans, plus ministers and teachers, who managed to accumulate property—some in substantial amounts; a few were valued at as much as $40,000 in the tax lists. They purchased houses, sent their children to school, organized societies, and ran churches.[59] Joseph Willson, born in Georgia and educated in Boston, followed the printing trade in Philadelphia before studying dentistry and moving to Cincinnati. In his book *Sketches of the Higher Classes of Colored Society in Philadelphia*, published in 1841, he observed that black society divided into three levels, much like the rest of the population. At the top, people of color were to "be seen in ease, comfort and the enjoyment of all the social blessings of this life," just as they were to "be found in the lowest depths of human degradation, misery, and want," and "in the intermediate stages—sober, honest, industrious and respectable—claiming neither 'poverty nor riches,' yet maintaining, by their pursuits, their families in comparative ease and comfort."[60]

The families at the top adopted all the forms of respectability that middle-class whites were bringing into their lives in the same period. The black elite emphasized education, moral restraint, industry and frugality, the development of skills, and religious faith, all the standard middle-class traits. They also paid heed to manners and parlor furnishings, the marks of the prevalent vernacular gentility. Cyprian Clamorgan, a St. Louis barber, who published *The Colored Aristocracy of St. Louis* in 1858, sketched the character of the personalities who comprised the elite of black society in his city. One was noted for being "extremely polite in his intercourse with his equals and inferiors, and quite aristocratic in his feelings." Another was "very genteel in his manners," and the description of one belle rang all the changes on female gentility. Mrs. Sawyer, Clamorgan wrote, "is fond of society, gay and sparkling, while her lively sallies of wit spread cheerfulness around her, and her beauty, like a summer flower, awakens the liveliest admiration. Her mind is equally gifted with her person, and she is the bright star of all social parties."[61]

Other accounts tell of houses fitted with the necessary emblems of genteel life. William Johnson, the remarkable Natchez barber who loaned money to black and white clients and knew everything that went on in town, furnished his house with a large sofa, mahogany chairs, large mirrors, and bookcases, and frequently recarpeted the rooms. He hung pictures on the walls; owned piano, guitar, flute, and violin; subscribed to New York newspapers; and owned copies of Shakespeare.[62] Joseph Willson said of the Philadelphia higher society that it went without saying that "their parlors are carpeted and furnished with sofas, sideboards, card-tables, mirrors, &c. &c., with, in many instances, the addition of the piano forte."[63]

Willson gave the most complete description of this elite society. Even if we allow for his wish to promote the black upper class in the eyes of whites, his account leaves no doubt of their adoption of the genteel code. He observed young ladies who showed "much taste and skill in painting, instrument music, singing, and the various departments of ornamental needlework, &c." They also had mastered the supreme art of the genteel life, conversation. At their evening entertainments, playing musical instruments, singing, and conversing occupied the company. "The character of the conversation is usually varied, interesting and instructive. All the current topics of the time, appropriate and of sufficient interest, are elaborately discussed in a mild, dignified and becoming manner, in which the ladies mostly take part and contribute their full quota."[64]

Willson also emphasized that higher society was exclusive, and he considered this discrimination a virtue. "Visiting *sans cérémonie* does not obtain to a very great extent with the higher classes of colored society. Even among those who are otherwise intimate acquaintances, the order of unceremonious visits is but limited. They are mostly by familiar or formal invitation, or in return for others previously received." He offered the classic genteel reason for the exclusions. The wrong company was "detrimental to the harmony of social intercourse." By taking care, the elite "manage to collect a very agreeable company, all perhaps on terms of perfect agreement and intimacy."[65]

The black elites rounded out their program of refinement by seeking mental culture for themselves and their children. Leonard Curry estimates that free blacks organized over twoscore literary societies in American cities in the second quarter of the nineteenth century. The societies collected books and newspapers, wrote poetry and essays, held debates, and sponsored lectures. The study of literature was integrated with more immediately practical purposes like learning a skill and developing self-discipline. The 1833 constitution of the Phoenix Society of New York stated that the condition of the "people of colour" can "only be meliorated by their being improved in *morals, literature,* and the *mechanic arts.*" [66]

Much of the effort went into the elementary education necessary to raise the population from abject poverty, but higher goals were kept in mind too. In his address to the Moral Reform Society of Philadelphia in 1836, William Watkins ended his talk by evoking the image of the cultivated person.

> The educated man—the man of cultivated taste, whose mind is enriched with stores of useful knowledge, has, within himself, an inexhaustible source of refined pleasure. On the contrary, the uneducated man lives in a sort of embryo; he has eyes, sir, but sees not, ears, but hears not; his spiritual senses are sealed; his intellectual powers, for the most part, dormant. But when a flood of mental and moral light is

poured upon his benighted vision, his slumbering energies are awakened, and called forth into vigorous exercise; he now enters into a new world and beholds, with effable delight, scenes new, beautiful, and grand.

Watkins told his hearers that the pleasures of the man of taste were beyond compare. "He gazes upon the works of genius—the painted canvass or the sculptured marble—and discovers beauties to which others are strangers; beauties that afford him the most exquisite delight." Books, orations, conversations fill him "with feelings of pleasure inexpressible, and, to the illiterate, incommunicable." Once one is educated, "the attractions of the gambling table and the ale house are not, in his view, to be compared with those to be found in his own domicile, in the rich volumes of a well selected library." He shuns the "whirlpools of vice," and all forms of "licentiousness and gross sensuality," and spends his hours in the "hall of science, the lecture room, the moral lyceum." On this premise, Watkins could conclude that "a good education is the great *sine qua non* as it regards the elevation of our people."[67]

In every respect the black elite bought into the culture of refinement. They doubtless sought refined pleasures for all the reasons that moved the middle class everywhere. But they had the added need to win respect in a society that denied them many of its ordinary privileges. The Phoenix Society noted in its preamble that while no one in New York could hold another person as property, the people of color "labour under much greater disadvantages than any other class of people." The society was formed to overcome these obstacles. Watkins told his audience that education would lift black people from their peculiarly degraded position. "Give them this and they cease to grovel; give them this and they emerge from their degradation, though crushed beneath a mountain weight of prejudice; give them this and they will command respect and consideration from all who respect themselves and whose good opinions are worth having." Refinement had the double purpose for blacks of elevating them into the pleasures of beauty and taste and also of breaking down the racial prejudices that closed avenues of growth and economic improvement. Through education, Watkins said, "they acquire a moral power that will enable them to storm and batter down that great citadel of pride and prejudice."[68]

The black elite thus was in a position to test Sedgwick's proposition that only manners separated the classes. Her novels presented artisans and poor families whose refined lives made them worthy of general respect. If not intimates of the wealthy and fashionable, they could stand on an equal cultural plane, having read books, developed their minds, and learned polite behavior. Would blacks who followed Sedgwick's program win the regard which her stories promised?

Willson aimed for just that regard when he wrote about Philadelphia high society. Yet he had doubts from the start. At the outset he observed that "the idea of 'Higher Classes' of colored society is, it must be confessed, a novel one; and will, undoubtedly, excite the mirth of a prejudiced community on its annunciation." He had good reason to expect scorn. A decade earlier black society had been the object of outright attacks and demeaning caricatures of their activities. In 1828 some Philadelphia thugs had assaulted black women as they stepped from coaches outside a dancing assembly, insulting them, tearing their gowns, and throwing some into the gutter. Instead of condemning the ruffians, the *Pennsylvania Gazette* made fun of the "sable divinities" and the *Philadelphia Monthly Magazine* published a long satiric account of the event. The article carried on in the spirit of caricatures drawn by David Claypool Johnston, William Thackera, and Edward Clay, ridiculing black pretensions. They depicted black people in the rituals of genteel life, at balls or calling on one another, but in awkward poses, in fantastic costumes, mouthing unconsciously ridiculous comments.[69] Apparently white response to black gentility had changed very little a decade later, when Willson wrote that there were those "who like to see their neighbor's merits caricatured, and their faults distorted and exaggerated." In reading the book, they "will expect burlesque representations, and other laughter exciting sketches, and probably be thereby led to procure this little volume for the purpose of gratifying their penchant for the ludicrous."[70]

The reaction to black efforts at self-improvement established the limits of Sedgwick's hope for a democracy of gentility. Manners, education, well-furnished parlors, exclusive entertainments, none of the genteel virtues won respect for the black population. Instead of honoring the black elite for their progress toward refinement, the more general reaction was to turn the standard aristocratic critique of middle-class pretensions against blacks. Caricaturists had long openly scorned the ungainly attempts of the white middle class to imitate the entertainments and manners of the gentry. This same set of stereotyped clichés was now directed against black refinement. At times, it seemed as if they were moving backward despite the opposition to slavery and growing abolitionist sentiment. In 1838 the Philadelphia legislature revoked free blacks' right to vote. After the Civil War, in 1873, *Harper's Weekly,* supposedly an agent of civilization, satirized an upper-class black wedding with a cartoon on the marriage of "Mr. Leon de Sooty, the distinguished Society Man," and "Miss Dinah Black, the beautiful heiress."[71]

The attacks on the black elite provide a clear example of middle-class sensitivity to invasions from below. Not all of the middle-class population opened their arms like Sedgwick to poor artisans who had a parlor and taught their children manners. The readers of the Philadelphia newspapers in 1828 or *Harper's Weekly* in 1873 were more interested in guarding the

boundaries of gentility against untoward incursions. Their aim was to separate themselves from the lower classes, not to assimilate them. Of all black
people, aspiring blacks were the most threatening. Nothing could anger this
middle-class population more than for people from the lower orders to lay

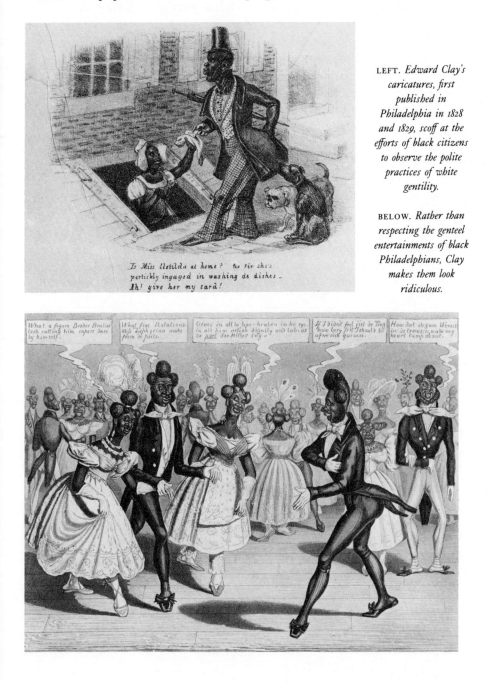

LEFT. *Edward Clay's
caricatures, first
published in
Philadelphia in 1828
and 1829, scoff at the
efforts of black citizens
to observe the polite
practices of white
gentility.*

BELOW. *Rather than
respecting the genteel
entertainments of black
Philadelphians, Clay
makes them look
ridiculous.*

claim to refinement and so to undermine the hard-won claims of those who had preceded them.

Thoughout most of his book, Joseph Willson was a model of restraint and cool analysis. But at one point he broke out in rage and frustration at the opposition that the black population faced every day of their lives.

> The exceedingly illiberal, unjust and oppressive prejudices of the great mass of the white community, overshadowing every moment of their existence, is enough to crush—effectually crush and keep down—any people. It meets them at almost every step without their domiciles, and not unfrequently follows even there. No private enterprise of any movement,—no public movement of consequence for the general good,—can they undertake, but forth steps the relentless monster to blight it in the germ.

And yet he saw no recourse but to seek patiently for respect through rigorous and unrelenting self-improvement. The black community, he said, "in the face of all this . . . not only bear the burthen successfully, but possess the elasticity of mind that enables them to stand erect under their disabilities, and present a state of society of which, to say the least, none have just cause to be ashamed."[72]

WOMEN

THE confusion at the top of American society about the need for an American aristocracy matched confusion at the bottom about the existence and place of a lower class. In between, no group was wrenched about more than middle-class women. On the one hand, the widespread adoption of gentility was a triumph for women. They were thought to be the exemplars of refinement's highest virtues—taste, sensibility, and delicacy—models for men to conform to. Partially because of their refinement, women took over management of the house, the primary site of genteel activity. All this strengthened their positions in society. On the other hand, women's gentility cut them off from other vital centers of middle-class power: the workplace, the marketplace, and the government. Women were denied the wealth and power available in those places, and the confidence and energy they bestowed. Superior gentility both exalted and restricted them.[73]

The idea of a superior feminine nature was inherited from the eighteenth century, when it was repeatedly asserted that women had a natural affinity for genteel culture. Women were "distinguished from the robust Make of *Man* by that *Delicacy,* express'd by *Nature* in their *Form*," one guidebook confidently informed its readers. "Superior delicacy" and "natural softness and sensibility" predisposed women toward complaisance and a taste for beauty.[74] Nineteenth-century commentators continued to believe that women were drawn to beauty as a reflection of their own natures, delighting, for example, in flowers as an inheritance from Eve. "Certain it is that her taste for these fair creations has descended to her daughters with very few exceptions," a gift book told its readers. The poorest women with no genteel training took pleasure in blooms. "How many a poor seamstress finds her hours of labor sweetened by the pot of dear mignonette at her elbow, whose odors she can inhale even when she dare nor [sic] spare the time to lift her eyes and feast them on its delicate beauties."[75] Nicholas Ridgely gave full credit to his mother for the family's beautiful garden in Dover. "Men have little . . . taste in such matters and where there is no female there is not often a pretty garden."[76]

The genteel creature was one of the best-defined of women's roles in the nineteenth century, publicly declared, universally acknowledged, and repeatedly honored.[77] Women did not have to struggle for equality within genteel culture or fight neglect and obscurity. They occupied the seats of honor as the finest examples of the refined virtues. To add to their triumph, women were given full responsibility for the household, although they were still dependent on financial support from their husbands. Wives took primary responsibility for rearing children, managing day-to-day affairs, and beautifying the house. The home became woman's sphere, the parlor her peculiar domain. In the eighteenth century Washington and Franklin took the lead in ordering household furniture; in the nineteenth century women became responsible for house decoration.

There they expressed their taste and exercised influence. Female company had always polished men; in the nineteenth century women were believed uniquely qualified to refine children. "The lamp of taste is lighted at the mother's knee," an architectural adviser noted, "and if unlit then, the light of after-years will but dimly supply its place."[78] Women supervised entertainment, the central social preoccupation of genteel culture. Lydia Sigourney thought it a truism that "most of the refined nations of our time entrust the usage of hospitality to the keeping of the gentler sex."[79] In the household, women's influence was dominant.

And yet these victories did not bring the gains that earlier would have gone with control of the house. Houses in the eighteenth century were places where many forms of power were exercised. Drawing-room society often brought together influential people to create relationships over dinner or at tea that played directly into alliances in business and politics. The friendships cemented in eighteenth-century parlors carried over into all the serious affairs of life. Houses served as power centers because few other business sites existed. The architecture of the merchant's exchanges and of a few public buildings implied important work going on within, but governors conducted their everyday business at home, having no offices in public buildings except the council chambers. Merchants had their countinghouses, but these were undistinguished spaces, and they commonly worked at home. Fine eighteenth-century furniture was not made for commercial offices. Few paintings depict merchants at work in their offices. Much of the work of the world went on in houses, where dignified settings reflected the importance of the relationships formed there. Command of the house signified command of all its power functions, and understandably men retained control of these places where significant business occurred.

In the nineteenth century, business moved out of the house. Governors and their minions began to conduct business in the new imposing state capitols. The houses of officials continued to figure in their conduct of affairs, but the center of political activity gradually shifted out of the house. In the new republic, only the White House functioned both as an officeholder's residence and as a center of political activity, combining functions that had traditionally been united in the palaces of kings.

Commercial and industrial power shifted even more dramatically. One of the major architectural developments of the nineteenth century was the emergence of the office building, a structure dedicated to the conduct of business and exhibiting an increasingly pretentious architectural presentation. Factories with cupolas and bell towers claimed some dignity, but offices and banks strove for the greatest elegance. The Hayden, Gere and Company Brass Works in Williamsburg, Connecticut, erected an elegant Second Empire structure resembling a house but given over to the company's offices and to a bank. The Haydens thought it entirely appropriate to install inlaid marble floors and rosewood and mahogany cabinetry to honor the business conducted within the building.[80] The building offered space for the conduct of business that once would have been reserved for the owner's residence and announced with a flourish that important work was proceeding there.[81]

The construction of commercial office buildings and state capitols was a measure of the relocation of power in American society. Power once concentrated primarily in houses was distributed elsewhere. The construction of these new buildings also reflected the decreasing significance of the house in the management of power. As one went up, the other went down. As work implements and beds had moved out of the parlor in the eighteenth century, so commercial and political dealings moved away from the house in the nineteenth century. The home was gradually emptied of its commercial and political functions and devoted mostly to family and culture.

That seeming advancement in refinement, accruing to the benefit of women's activities, also marked their separation from the sites of economic and political activity. The standing of the middle class rested ultimately on its productive capacities, its ability to manufacture and grow, and so to make money. Middle-class virtues were shaped to advance that work, just as aristocratic virtues were formed to enhance the power to govern. Middle-class husbands could believe sincerely in the values of genteel culture, contribute vast sums to the construction of elegant houses, and devote themselves to reading and art. But finally, they must heed the main chance—work and business—or their lives would crumble to dust. When business moved out of the house into offices and factories, strength departed. Women could be vested with control of the house because the events there were little by little reduced in significance. Respectable men needed grand houses, and they valued the culture of their wives, but the centers of their dominant values lay in their offices. The refined women in command of elegant houses conveyed less authority than they had a hundred years before. It required strenuous ideological and organizational exertion on the part of the defenders of domestic culture to uphold the importance of home against the countervailing weight of capitalist endeavor.

Men were overtly and doubtless sincerely committed to the values of home. But in numerous little ways they conveyed a sense that the household existed on the margins of life's serious work. The stereotypical caricatures of women and women's work offer clues to male thinking about household gentility. The humorous comments often assumed that efforts at refinement were frills. Genteel women were charged with a slavish devotion to fashion, an excessive love of balls and fine clothes, a squandering of their husband's money on needless fripperies.[82] Male ambivalence came out in descriptions of shuttered parlors where "the master of the house fidgets from one seat to another as if he were anywhere but at home."[83] The "master's" wealth had created a space that was foreign to his tastes, and his wife had turned the house into a place where he was not at home. All the jokes, though warmhearted, were patronizing and ultimately demeaning.

One example can serve for many. In Edward Eggleston's *The Hoosier School-Master*, Matilda White was a small-town housekeeper renowned for the cleanliness of her home. "How white the table-cloth, how bright the coffee-pot, how clean the wood-work, how glistening the brass door-knobs, how spotless everything that came under the sovereign sway of Mrs. Matilda White." But the very thoroughness of her housekeeping made the house uninhabitable for her husband. "No member of Mrs. White's family ever staid at home longer than was necessary." And where did Mr. White go for relief from "the wretchedness of extreme civilization"? "Her husband found his office—which he kept in as bad a state as possible in order to maintain an equilibrium in his life—much more comfortable than the stiffly clean house at home." That tone of humorous disdain for the conscientious efforts of Mrs. White was possible only if her work was considered essentially trivial. Eggleston puts the reader on the side of Mr. White in his flight from a "house too neat to be habitable," assuming the reader will concur in the humor.[84] In Mr. White's office retreat, important work gets done despite the clutter. Eggleston disregarded the feelings of female readers who kept house and who were expected to enjoy the joke on themselves. They were expected to acknowledge men's secret belief that household work, including the beautification of the interior, was of secondary importance, and that the real work went on elsewhere.[85]

Catharine Beecher and Harriet Beecher Stowe understood the underlying disrespect for housework when they wrote *The American Woman's Home.* In the opening sentence they announced that the "disabilities and sufferings of their sex" came from "the fact that the honor and duties of the family state are not duly appreciated." They implied that the competition of business affairs was too much for the home. "Women are not trained for these duties as men are trained for their trades and professions, and that, as the consequence, family labor is poorly done, poorly paid, and regarded as menial and disgraceful." For housekeeping to be respected, it had to be regarded as a profession, to match the other professions. They aimed "to render each department of woman's true profession as much desired and respected as are the most honored professions of men."[86] Ultimately they sought to show that household work was part of the productive economy like any profession and thus worthy of regard.

Beecher and Stowe were among the women who heroically stood against the expanding capitalist economy. They were less concerned with economic injustices or social tensions than with the tendency of the economy to crush or absorb all other cultural values. Did anything else really matter besides the production of wealth or the exercise of political power? Their vision of an efficient, Christian, and refined home was placed squarely in the path of capitalist expansion as a center of countervailing values. And their efforts were not entirely futile. Their success was measured by the commitment of millions of women to their vision and to the continued allocation of wealth to the creation of such homes. Men paid lip service to the values of refined, Christian homes and paid the bills. Women spent their lives managing such homes and making them places of beauty and love.

But occasionally a woman felt that her "duties were too numerous and varied, and none sufficiently exhilarating or intellectual to bring into play my higher faculties." Elizabeth Cady Stanton posed the problem as a matter of "practical difficulties," and of tedium rather than marginality. But she did speak of woman's sphere as "the isolated household" and felt "the impossibility of woman's best development if in contact, the chief part of her life, with servants and children." Life in the isolated household lacked the compelling purpose that made tedium and difficulties worthwhile. Instead a woman's labors only left her with a "wearied, anxious look."[87]

Stanton's personal solution, suitable for a critic ahead of her times, was a Woman's Rights Convention and then a campaign for women. Her efforts had many purposes, but one was to break through into politics and give women the vote. Women would at least enjoy the dignity of the log cabin people and have a recognized role in government. Voting was a strange solution for the problems of weary, anxious housekeepers, but Stanton understood instinctively that a connection with forms of power that were valued in society would somehow enliven suffering women.

Gentility played a small part in Stanton's housekeeping in Seneca Falls. Part of her lament was the absence of refinement in her life. "Cleanliness, order, the love of the beautiful and artistic, all faded away in the struggle to accomplish what was absolutely necessary from hour to hour."[88] The Beechers' directions for combining ladylike refinement with the hard work of keeping house seemed impossible in Stanton's struggles with children and innumerable chores.

Earlier she had tasted the other kind of life. In Boston when first married she had enjoyed some of the pleasures of beautifying a house. Mr. Stanton had told her "that his business would occupy all his time, and that I must take entire charge of the housekeeping." She enjoyed the commission. "It is a proud moment in a woman's life to reign supreme within four walls." She trained herself to be an efficient housekeeper and brought both order and beauty to her little kingdom, thinking of herself as an artist making a picture.

Surely a mother and child, tastefully dressed, and a pretty home for a framework, is, as a picture, even more attractive than a domestic scene hung on the wall. The love of the beautiful can be illustrated as well in life as on canvas. There is such a struggle among women to become artists that I really wish some of their gifts could be illustrated in clean, orderly, beautiful homes.[89]

In Boston she embraced the values of middle-class gentility and enjoyed its pleasures.

Yet when the clouds of household care closed over her in Seneca Falls, Stanton did not advocate a return to the peaceful, beautiful Boston days, though doubtless the happy involvement of those times would have helped. A refined and orderly household, however satisfying, was not her answer to women's problems. She chose instead to strike for power, in one of the realms where she knew power lay. Only when validated by participation in the central activities of their society could women stabilize their identities and be assured of their worth. Stanton was a minority voice when she spoke in 1848, but one that rang true for more and more women in the ensuing century and a half.[90]

In Conclusion

THE discontent of the women at Seneca Falls in 1848 can be read as a sign of the weakness of nineteenth-century genteel culture compared with the cultural systems of capitalism and republican government. The inability of these women, though small in number, to find confidence and hope in lives based on household refinement, housekeeping, and the rearing of children suggests the weakness of genteel culture over against the countervailing claims of other spheres of power. Gentility lacked the cultural strength to sustain women's labors and sufferings in the absence of a place in the money economy or in government. Overall, gentility doubtless had less cultural strength than Christianity; a Christian mother was more apt to feel secure in her life at home than a woman who relied solely on refinement.[91] Gentility was only one of three or four major cultural systems in nineteenth-century America and not the most powerful.

Still, the strength of gentility is remarkable. Considering its tainted origins in the discredited royal courts, gentility exercised unlikely influence in republican America. Knowing that gentility took its rise among the European nobility and achieved its fullest realization in their palaces and mansions did not inhibit the refining process; middling American citizens in every corner of the land made a dilute version of gentility necessary for self-respect. Individuals measured themselves and everyone around them by their refinement. Parents labored to instill genteel qualities in their children, aware that manners were a necessary part of rudimentary respectability. Once adopted, gentility transformed life into a performance in which one's beauty and grace were constantly on display. Houses, yards, carriages, costume, posture, manners were all part of the show, part of the seeking for applause, part of the dread of scorn.

Genteel values spread so widely in the population and infiltrated so deeply into religion and the organization of neighborhoods that gentility shaped the structure of society. Refinement and vulgarity became the most palpable signs of class, for many the very definition of class. More than wealth or kind of work, manners and style of life divided people in their everyday exchanges with one another. To a degree, gentility reflected economic condition: clerks, schoolteachers, engineers, government officials, and bank tellers were more likely to have parlors with pictures than farm laborers or journeymen shoemakers. But gentility was also an independent variable in the class equation. Poor refined people distanced themselves from the vulgar poor and elicited different treatment. A poor man who read books and planted flowers before his door received respect not granted to an uncouth workingman. In a telling sign of gentility's power, poor people gave aristocratic names to their children, taught them to say please and thank you, furnished their houses with carpets, and occasionally bought pianos. By small gestures people in all classes incensed the air around them with refinement. The promise of respectability contained in simple genteel objects and gestures lured ever more Americans into the toils of consumer culture, hopelessly blurring the boundaries of class.

What has happened to gentility in our century? Did the attacks on genteel culture at the end of the nineteenth century deal a mortal blow? Has the subsequent onslaught of rival cultural systems in the twentieth century erased gentility from our social consciences? While lords and ladies and country houses have been fading from the American social imagination, have we also abandoned genteel habits and values?

The answer, of course, is no. Whatever the particular signs of barbarism in today's world, the more evident fact is that gentility is ingrained into our lives. We assume that house lots will have yards with lawns and shrubbery, that houses will make space for formal entertainment, that everyone will own books, take baths, carry handkerchiefs, eat with knife and fork, forgetting that all this once had to be learned. Gentility is not at the top of the self-improvement agenda, as it was in 1850. But the refinement of America succeeded in making the practices of genteel culture second nature.

Gentility remains with us to this day, with all its pleasures and pains. Our love of beauty, our sensitivity, the kindness and amiability of society are qualities we prize, and these come from the desire to be refined. At the same time, gentility divides us and makes us anxious. Gentility separates us from one another on meretricious grounds: our clothes, our speech, our manners. We suffer embarrassment from the necessity to please, the sense of constant performance, the fear of scorn. Through it all, we struggle to distinguish true gentility from vanity and superficial fashion.

The failings of refinement do not limit our sacrifices in its behalf. Gentility has commanded our resources ever since Americans first undertook to refine themselves nearly three hundred years ago. Elevation above the drab reality of ordinary life has seemed worth the cost. Here in republican America, inspired by a distant court's dream of an unattainable beauty, we have suffered gentility's injustices, its expense, and its pains, in the hope of refining and thus exalting our streets, our houses, and ourselves.

Notes

INTRODUCTION

1. This theme figures heavily in John F. Kasson, *Rudeness and Civility: Manners in Nineteenth-Century Urban America* (New York, 1990).
2. The effect of culture on demand and industrialization is discussed critically with references to the growing literature on the subject in Ben Fine and Ellen Leopold, "Consumerism and the Industrial Revolution," *Social History,* 15 (May 1990), 151–80.

1. THE GENTRIFICATION OF RURAL DELAWARE

1. The story of William Corbit and his house are told in full detail in John H. Sweeney, *Grandeur on the Appoquinimink: The House of William Corbit at Odessa, Delaware* (Newark, Del., 1959). His early life and ancestry are recounted on pp. 4–22. Population figures are from Sally Schwartz, "Cantwell's Bridge, Delaware: A Demographic and Community Study," *Delaware History,* 19 (Spring–Summer, 1980): 20–38.
2. Expenses are calculated from accounts published in Sweeney, *Grandeur on the Appoquinimink,* 45, 86–93.
3. For discussion of the unusual similarities to Philadelphia houses, see ibid., 42–43, 49.
4. Sweeney describes those possibly constructed by Robert May, William Corbit's carpenter, in ibid., 57–62.
5. Wealth estimates are from John J. McCusker and Russell R. Menard, *The Economy of British America, 1607–1789* (Chapel Hill, N.C., 1985), 57.
6. Margaret Berwind Schiffer, *Survey of Chester County, Pennsylvania, Architecture, 17th, 18th, and 19th Centuries* (Exton, Pa., 1984), 20; George E. Stetson, "The 1704 House Built in Chester County, Pennsylvania, by William Brinton the Younger" (M.A. thesis, University of Delaware, 1961), 25–26; Jack Michel, " 'In a Manner and Fashion Suitable to Their Degree': A Preliminary Investigation of the Material Culture of Early Pennsylvania," in Glenn Porter and William H. Mulligan, Jr., eds., *Working Papers from the Regional Economic History Research Center,* 5 (1981): 72. Michel emphasizes the greater pretensions of Philadelphia housing. Sweeney explains the relationship to the Brintons through William Corbit's mother in *Grandeur on the Appoquinimink,* 14–15.
7. Nicholas Ridgely, Dover, to Charles Greenberry Ridgely, Philadelphia, Jan. 12, 1754, folder 156; May 12, 1752, Sept. 29, 1752, and Dec. 16, 1752, folder 154; Dec. 4, 1753, folder 156; Charles Greenberry Ridgely, Philadelphia, to Nicholas Ridgely, Dover, June 21, 1753, folder 279, Ridgely Collection, Hall of Records, Dover, hereafter cited as Ridgely Collection. The Ridgely papers are calendared in Leon deValinger, Jr., and Virginia E. Shaw, *A Calendar of Ridgely Family Letters 1742–1899 in the Delaware State Archives,* 3 vols. (Dover, Del., 1948–61). A selection is reprinted in Mabel Lloyd Ridgely, ed., *What Them Befell: The Ridgelys of Delaware and Their Circle in Colonial and Federal Times: Letters 1751–1890* (Portland, Me., 1949).
8. Nicholas Ridgely, Dover, to Charles Greenberry Ridgely, Philadelphia, Oct. 28, 1751; March 20, 1753; Dec. 6, 1752, all folder 154, Ridgely Collection.
9. Charles Greenberry Ridgely, Philadelphia, to Nicholas Ridgely, Dover, Nov. 2, 1752, folder 276; June 21, 1753, folder 279, Ridgely Collection.
10. For an explication of the gratitude ethic in the larger political realm, see Richard L. Bushman, *King and People in Provincial Massachusetts* (Chapel Hill, N.C., 1985), 17–25.

11. The background on the Ridgely family is sketched in deValinger and Shaw, *A Calendar of Ridgely Family Letters,* 1:12–16, 66–67, and Ridgely, ed., *The Ridgelys of Delaware,* xvii–xx.
12. Harold B. Hancock, *History of Kent County, Delaware* (Dover, Del., 1976), 4–5, 7.
13. Harold B. Hancock, "Description and Travel Accounts of Delaware, 1700–1740," *Delaware History,* 10 (1962): 150.
14. Charles Inglis, Dover, to the Secretary of the Society for the Propagation of the Gospel, May 10, 1760; June 21, 1761; July 2, 1765, in William Stevens Perry, ed. *Historical Collections Relating to the American Colonial Church,* 5 (Hartford, 1870–78): 102, 103–4, 118. For similar references, see also ibid., 90, 94, 121, 127.
15. G. Daniel Blagg, *Dover: A Pictorial History* (Virginia Beach, Va., 1980), 5; Thomas Scharf, *History of Delaware, 1609–1888* (Philadelphia, 1888), 132, 136; Harold Donaldson Eberlein and Cortlandt D. Hubbard, *Historic Houses and Buildings of Delaware* (Dover, Del., 1963), 54, 56–57; George Frazer, Kent County, to the Secretary, the Society for the Propagation of the Gospel, Nov. 12, 1733, Perry, ed., *Historical Collections,* 5:70–71.
16. Nicholas never said explicitly that he came to Kent to enlarge his estate for the next generation, but the patriarch of another gentry family, Samuel Dickinson, had that purpose in mind. Dickinson, born in 1689 and just five years older than Nicholas Ridgely, also migrated from Maryland to Kent County, arriving in 1741. Dickinson also was a third-generation American. His grandfather, Walter Dickinson, came first to Virginia and then to Talbot County on Maryland's Eastern Shore, where he accumulated 1,200 acres in Delaware and Maryland. His son William purchased even more. At age twenty-eight Samuel Dickinson inherited 2,500 acres in five separate farms in three Maryland counties. Still not satisfied, Samuel went on purchasing and then consolidating his lands. By the time he moved to Kent County he had accumulated 9,000 acres in Maryland, which he designated for a son and daughter by his first marriage. He came to Delaware to provide for two other sons, John and Philemon, by his second wife, Mary Cadwalader of Philadelphia. During the 1730s Samuel bought out smaller farmers and put together a huge estate of over 3,000 acres on St. Jones Neck. To reserve these lands for John and Philemon, he docked the entail so that the eldest son on the Maryland plantation could make no claim on the Delaware lands. These measures gave Samuel some assurance that he had secured the fortunes of his offspring for at least two generations. Having completed his large brick mansion, in the winter of 1741 Dickinson moved his family seventy miles across the peninsula from Talbot to Kent. He had been appointed a justice of the Court of Common Pleas even before the family moved and so immediately assumed the place in society to which his wealth and background entitled him. Though a Quaker, Samuel Dickinson set a standard in houses, manner, and dignity to which the Ridgelys and the other gentry families in the county might aspire. J. H. Powell, *The House on Jones Neck: the Dickinson Mansion* (n.p., 1954).
17. Eberlein and Hubbard, *Historic Houses and Buildings of Delaware,* 65, 68–69; Emil G. Sammach and Don O. Winslow, eds., *Dover: The First Two Hundred and Fifty Years, 1717–1967* (Dover, Del., 1967), 15; Annie Jump Cannon, "The Loockermans Manor House Near Dover," *Delaware History,* 3 (1948–49): 97–104; Leon deValinger, Jr., *Calendar of Kent County, Delaware Probate Records* (Dover, Del., 1944). As an indication of the imperfections of the probate records, Samuel Chew's will and inventory are not among the records.
18. deValinger and Shaw, eds., *Calendar of Ridgely Family Letters,* 33.
19. Powell, *House on Jones Neck,* 20.
20. Pictures of façades and a few floor plans are found in Eberlein and Hubbard, *Historic Houses and Buildings of Delaware,* 167–227.
21. Information on houses comes from the National Register of Historic Places nominations in the Kent County Cultural Resources Survey Files, Bureau of Archaeology and Historic Preservation, Delaware Division of Historical and Cultural Affairs, Dover, Del.
22. Nicholas Ridgely's inventory along with other estate papers is filed under his name and the date of 1755 in the Hall of Records, Dover, Del.
23. Ann Ridgely to Henry and Charles Ridgely, May 21, 1797, folder 227, Ridgely Collection.
24. Nathaniel Luff, *Journal of the Life of Nathaniel Luff, M.D., of the State of Delaware* (New York, 1848), 12–13.
25. For an analysis of the social meaning of great houses in the Connecticut Valley, see Kevin M. Sweeney, "Mansion People: Kinship, Class, and Architecture in Western Massachusetts in the Mid Eighteenth Century," *Winterthur Portfolio,* 19 (Winter 1984): 231–55.
26. The most complete story of the Rodneys is William P. Frank, *Caesar Rodney, Patriot* (Wilmington, Del., 1975). Information on Caesar Rodney, Sr., can also be found in Harold Hancock, ed., " 'Fare Wether and Good Helth': The Journal of Caesar Rodney, 1727–1729," *Delaware History,* 10 (April 1962): 33–70.
27. Hancock, " 'Fare Wether and Good Helth,' " *Delaware History,* 10:33, 40.
28. Ibid., 40–45.
29. Ibid., 40–45, 48–49, 65.
30. Ibid., 43, 46–48.
31. Sammach and Winslow, eds., *Dover,* 15.

32. William P. Frank and Harold B. Hancock, "Caesar Rodney's Two Hundred and Fiftieth Anniversary: An Evaluation," *Delaware History*, 18 (Fall–Winter, 1978): 66, 71.
33. William Tod, Philadelphia, to Caesar Rodney, Nov. 19, 1767, Harold Hancock, ed., "Letters to and from Caesar Rodney: The Personal Side," *Delaware History*, 20 (Spring–Summer, 1983): 220–21.
34. Ibid., 221.
35. Frank and Hancock, "Caesar Rodney's Two Hundred and Fiftieth Anniversary," *Delaware History*, 18:68. For a more general study of Caesar Rodney, Jr., see Frank, *Caesar Rodney Patriot*.
36. For evidence of political cooperation, see Henry Bickerton, Dover, to Charles Ridgely, Philadelphia, Sept. 2, 1755, folder 156, Ridgely Collection.
37. Sweeney, *Grandeur on the Appoquinimink*, 13–16.
38. For the children's lives, ibid., 75–76.
39. Charles Inglis, Dover, to the Secretary of the Society for the Propagation of the Gospel, Sept. 26, 1760; Thomas Crawford, Dover, to the Secretary for the Propagation of the Gospel, April 3, 1706; Mr. Becket, Lewes, to the Secretary for the Propagation of the Gospel, Sept. 1, 1722, in Perry, ed., *Historical Collections*, 5:2, 36, 102–3.
40. Luff, *Journal of a Life*, 4–5.
41. Charles Ridgely, Dover, to Charles Inglis, New York, March 17, 1767, folder 100, Ridgely Collection.
42. Luff, *Journal of a Life*, p. 6.

II. THE COURTESY-BOOK WORLD

1. Oliver H. Leigh, ed., *Letters to His Son by the Earl of Chesterfield: On the Fine Art of Becoming a Man of the World and a Gentleman* (New York, 1937), 292.
2. Eleazar Moody, *The School of Good Manners*, 5th ed. (New London, 1754), 53.
3. Moody, *School of Good Manners*, 9, 18, 19. For a traditional Puritan book for children, see [Cotton Mather] *A Token for the Children of New England . . . added as Supplement unto the Excellent Janewayes Token for Children Upon the Reprinting of it, in this Country* (Boston, 1700).
4. Charles Moore, ed., *George Washington's Rules of Civility and Decent Behaviour in Company and Conversation* (Boston and New York, 1926), 3, 11.
5. Douglas Southall Freeman, *George Washington: A Biography. Vol. 1: Young Washington* (New York, 1948), 200, 202, 229, 230.
6. R. W. G. Vail, "Moody's School of Good Manners: A Study in American Colonial Etiquette," *Studies in the History of Culture: The Discipline of the Humanities* (Freeport, N.Y., 1969 [orig. pub., 1942]), 261–71.
7. Moore, ed., *George Washington's Rules of Civility*, x–xiv; Esther B. Aresty, *The Best Behavior: The Course of Good Manners—from Antiquity to the Present—as Seen through Courtesy and Etiquette Books* (New York, 1970), 113; John E. Mason, *Gentlefolk in the Making: Studies in the History of English Courtesy Literature and Related Topics from 1531 to 1774* (Philadelphia, 1935), 39.
8. My understanding of courtly ideals before the Renaissance relies heavily on C. Stephen Jaeger, *The Origins of Courtliness: Civilizing Trends and the Formation of Courtly Ideals, 939–1210* (Philadelphia, 1985), and Nicholas Orme, *From Childhood to Chivalry: The Education of the English Kings and Aristocracy, 1066–1530* (London and New York, 1984). On the mirror literature, see Jean-Philippe Genet, ed., *Four English Political Tracts of the Later Middle Ages*, Camden Fourth Series, 18 (London, 1977).
9. Aresty, *Best Behavior*, 109; Jaeger, *Origins of Courtliness*, 108.
10. Mason, *Gentlefolk in the Making*, 292.
11. Edwin Ramage, *Urbanitas: Ancient Sophistication and Refinement* (Norman, Okla., 1973); Jaeger, *Origins of Courtliness*, 115–19, 264–68, and passim.
12. Jaeger, *Origins of Courtliness*, 258; Norbert Elias, *The History of Manners. Vol. 1: The Civilizing Process*, tr. Edmund Jephcott (New York, 1978 [orig. pub. 1939]), 151, and *The Court Society*, tr. Edmund Jephcott (New York, 1983 [orig. pub. 1969]).
13. Jaeger, *Origins of Courtliness*, 108; Ruth Kelso, *The Doctrine of the English Gentleman in the Sixteenth Century, with a Bibliographical List of Treatises on the Gentleman and Related Subjects Published in Europe to 1625* (Urbana, Ill., 1929), 17; A. G. Dickens, ed., *The Courts of Europe: Politics, Patronage and Royalty, 1400–1800* (London, 1977). On the transition from medieval to Renaissance ideals of education, see Orme, *From Childhood to Chivalry*, 220–38. J. R. Woodhouse, *Baldesar Castiglione: A Reassessment of The Courtier* (Edinburgh, 1978), 38–58, discusses the classical and Renaissance sources of Castiglione's educational ideal. The best survey of the courtesy literature is still Mason, *Gentlefolk in the Making*. For eighteenth-century purges of warrior virtues, see Margaret Anne Doody, *A Natural Passion: A Study of the Novels of Samuel Richardson* (Oxford, 1974), 242–43.
14. Mason, *Gentlefolk in the Making*, 35, 39, 187, 227, 259, 261, 291–92; Gertrude E. Noyes, *Bibliography of Courtesy and Conduct Books in Seventeenth-Century England* (New Haven, 1937), 2; Peter W. Thomas, "Charles I of England: The Tragedy of Absolutism," in Dickens, ed., *The Courts of Europe*, 191–212; Noyes, *Bibliography*

of Courtesy and Conduct Books, 1, 5; Antoine de Courtin, *The Rules of Civility; or, The Maxims of Genteel Behaviour, As They Are Practis'd and Observ'd by Persons of Quality, upon Several Occasions* (London, 1703), 185.

15. Mason, *Gentlefolk in the Making*, chaps. 7 and 9; Hunter Dickinson Farish, ed., *Journals and Letters of Philip Vickers Fithian, 1774–1774* (Williamsburg, Va., 1957), 50, 66; Ethel Armes, ed., *Nancy Shippen, Her Journal Book: The International Romance of a Young Lady of Fashion of Colonial Philadelphia with Letters to Her and about Her* (Philadelphia, 1935), 171, 178; Doody, *A Natural Passion*; Gerald R. Barker, *Grandison's Heirs: The Paragon's Progress in the Late Eighteenth-Century Novel* (Newark, Del., 1985). Other popular courtesy books reprinted in America were James Forrester, *The Polite Philosopher: or, An Essay on that Art, Which Makes a Man Happy in Himself, and Agreeable to Others* (Tarrytown, N.Y., 1922 [orig. pub. London and New York, 1758]); Abbé d'Ancourt, *The Lady's Preceptor* (Woodbridge, N.J., 1759); Dr. Gregory, *A Father's Legacy To his Daughters* (New York, 1775); and Pierre Joseph Boudier de Villemert, *The Ladies' Friend: Being a Treatise on the Virtues and Qualifications which Are the Brightest Ornaments of the Fair Sex and Render Them Most Agreeable to the Sensible Part of Mankind* (Philadelphia, 1771); [Hester Chapone] *Letters on the Improvement of the Mind* (Boston, 1772). There are eighteen entries for Samuel Richardson's *Pamela* in Shipton and Mooney's catalogue of eighteenth-century American imprints, eight entries for *Clarissa*, and eight for *Sir Charles Grandison*. Some of the Shipton and Mooney entries come from ads noted by Charles Evans and do not necessarily represent a new American edition; they do indicate the currency of the book. Clifford K. Shipton and James E. Mooney, eds., *National Index of American Imprints Through 1800: The Short-Title Evans* (n.p., 1969). For the development of polite society in England, see Paul Langford, *A Polite and Commercial People: England, 1727–1783* (Oxford, 1989), 59–123.

16. "Philip Dormer Stanhope, fourth Earl of Chesterfield," in Leslie Stephen and Sidney Lee, eds., *The Dictionary of National Biography* (London, 1917 ff.), 18:911–24. For the American editions of Chesterfield, see Shipton and Mooney, eds., *National Index of American Imprints Through 1800*.

17. On Versailles, see Jacques Levron, *Daily Life at Versailles in the Seventeenth and Eighteenth Centuries*, tr. Claire Elaine Engel (New York, 1968).

18. Thomas Hunter, *Reflections Critical and Moral on the Letters of . . . Chesterfield*, 3rd ed. (Boston, 1780).

19. Courtin, *Rules of Civility*, 14, 40–41, 81–82, 114, 119.

20. Ibid., 12, 15; Joan Wildeblood, *The Polite World: A Guide to the Deportment of the English in Former Times*, rev. ed. (London, 1973), 124–25; Moore, ed., *George Washington's Rules of Civility*, 7, 9, 13, 17, 21. The word "clown" in the civility manuals usually meant peasant.

21. Moody, *School of Good Manners*, 8.

22. Melvin Yazawa, *From Colonies to Commonwealth: Familial Ideology and the Beginnings of the American Republic* (Baltimore, 1985), 59–69.

23. Quoted in Aresty, *Best Behavior*, 143.

24. Elias, *The History of Manners*; James L. Axtell, ed., *The Educational Writings of John Locke* (Cambridge, Eng., 1968), 133–36.

25. Rodney quote in John U. Munroe, *Federalist Delaware* (New Brunswick, N.J., 1954), 155; Moore, ed., *George Washington's Rules of Civility*, 5.

26. Moore, ed., *George Washington's Rules of Civility*, 3, 5, 11, 19.

27. Courtin, *Rules of Civility*, 89–90; Moore, ed., *George Washington's Rules of Civility*, 3, 5, 11, 19, 21.

28. Mark Girouard, *Life in the English Country House: A Social and Architectural History* (New Haven, 1978), 144–50; Levron, *Daily Life at Versailles*, 40–42.

29. Moore, ed., *George Washington's Rules of Civility*, 9.

30. Ibid., 3.

31. Ibid., 5.

32. Ibid., 3, 5, 15, 17. A century earlier, coming from court society, Courtin was more concerned about affability and condescension of superiors toward inferiors. *Rules of Civility*, 7.

33. John Locke, *Some Thoughts Concerning Education*, 5th ed. (London, 1705), in Axtell, ed., *The Educational Writings of John Locke*, 162, 247.

34. Ibid., 190–91, 246; Leigh, ed., *Letters to His Son by the Earl of Chesterfield*, 137.

35. For excellent evocations of this society from other perspectives, see Richard D. Brown, *Knowledge Is Power: The Diffusion of Information in Early America, 1700–1865* (New York, 1989), chap. 2, and Philip Greven, *The Protestant Temperament: Patterns of Child-Rearing, Religious Experience, and the Self in Early America* (New York, 1977), chaps. 6–7.

36. Moore, ed., *George Washington's Rules of Civility*, 9.

37. Armes, ed., *Nancy Shippen, Her Journal Book*, 141–42, 171, 244; Rufus Wilmot Griswold, *The Republican Court; or, American Society in the Days of Washington* (New York, 1868), 376–77; Farish, ed., *Journals and Letters of Philip Vickers Fithian*, 94; [Richard Hill] *An Address to Persons of Fashion, Containing Some Particulars Relating to Balls: And a Few Occasional Hints Concerning Play-Houses, Card-Tables, &c. In Which Is Introduced The Character of Lucinda, A Lady of the Very Best Fashion, and of Most Extraordinary Piety* (Boston, 1767), 21.

38. Griswold, *Republican Court*, 271, 381; *The Diary of Matthew Patten of Bedford, N.H.* (Concord, N.H., 1903); Ann Ridgely to Charles Ridgely, Dover, April 12, 1785, in Mabel Lloyd Ridgely, ed., *What Them Befell:*

The Ridgelys of Delaware and Their Circle in Colonial and Federal Times: Letters 1751–1890 (Portland, Me., 1949), 39.

39. Alexander Graydon, *Memoirs of His Own Time*, ed. John Stockton Littell (New York, 1969 [reprint of 1846 ed.; orig. pub. as *Memoirs of a Life*, 1811]), 105–6, 298; Marian Dickson Terry, ed., *Old Inns of Connecticut* (Hartford, 1937), 84; Kym S. Rice, *Early American Taverns: For the Entertainment of Friends and Strangers* (Chicago, 1983), 108; *The Journal of Nicholas Cresswell, 1774–1777* (New York, 1924), 57–58; Farish, ed., *Journal and Letters of Philip Vickers Fithian*, 57, 62, 64, 66, 76, 82, 90, 91.

40. Norman Arthur Benson, "The Itinerant Dancing and Music Masters of Eighteenth-Century America" (Ph.D. diss., University of Minnesota, 1963), 72.

41. Ridgely, ed., *What Them Befell*, 248–49, 260–62, 265–68; L. H. Butterfield, Wendell D. Garrett, and Marjorie E. Sprague, eds., *Adams Family Correspondence* (Cambridge, Mass., 1963), 1:4, 382.

42. Girouard, *Life in the English Country House*, 30–34; Robert W. Malcomson, *Popular Recreations in English Society, 1700–1850* (Cambridge, Eng., 1973), 52–74; Alice Morse Earle, *Customs and Fashions in Old New England* (Rutland, Vt., 1973 [orig. pub. 1893]), 214–33; Philip Alexander Bruce, *Social Life of Virginia in the Seventeenth Century* (Lynchburg, Va., 1927), 225–27; L. H. Butterfield, Leonard C. Faber, and Wendell D. Garrett, eds., *The Diary and Autobiography of John Adams* (Cambridge, Mass., 1962) 1:173.

43. Bruce, *Social Life of Virginia in the Seventeenth Century*, 186–88. On Rodney, see above, chap. 1.

44. Thomas Balch, *The Philadelphia Assemblies* (Philadelphia, 1916), 93, 95; Armes, ed., *Nancy Shippen, Her Journal Book*, 248; Griswold, *Republican Court*, 95.

45. Balch, *Philadelphia Assemblies*, 48, 50, 51; Esther Singleton, *Social New York under the Georges, 1714–1776: Houses, Streets and Country Homes, with Chapters on Fashions, Furniture, China, Plate and Manners* (New York, 1902), 301–3; Rice, *Early American Taverns*, 50, 51, 126; Benson, "Itinerant Dancing and Music Masters," 129, 144, 225, 337–38, 370–72; Gerald W. R. Ward, "The Assembly House," *Essex Institute Historical Collections*, 111 (Oct. 1975): 241–65.

46. Balch, *Philadelphia Assemblies*; Benson, "Itinerant Dancing and Music Masters," 129, 337–38, 370–72; Rice, *Early American Taverns*, 126.

47. The classic study of the objects associated with formal dining is Louise Conway Belden, *The Festive Tradition: Table Decorations and Desserts in America, 1650–1900* (New York and London, 1983); for tea it is Rodris Roth, "Tea Drinking in 18th-Century America: Its Etiquette and Equipage," *Contributions from the Museum of History and Technology*, Paper 14 (Washington, D.C., 1961), 61–91.

48. Gerald W. R. Ward, " 'Avarice and Conviviality': Card Playing in Federal America," in Benjamin A. Hewitt, Patricia E. Kane, and Gerald W. R. Ward, eds., *The Work of Many Hands: Card Tables in Federal America, 1790–1820* (New Haven, 1982), 17, 21; Rice, *Early American Taverns*, 107; *Journal of Nicholas Cresswell*, 57.

49. Griswold, *Republican Court*, 19–20, 158.

50. Ibid., 19–21, 158, 270–71; Farish, ed., *Journal and Letters of Philip Vickers Fithian*, 63, 64–65.

51. Pierre Rameau, *The Dancing Master*, tr. Cyril W. Beaumont (New York, 1970 [orig. pub. Paris, 1725]), 39; Griswold, *Republican Court*, 157; Benson, "Itinerant Dancing and Music Masters," 337–38.

52. Armes, ed., *Nancy Shippen, Her Journal Book*, 141–42, 166, 178.

53. [Hill] *Address to Persons of Fashion*, 22.

54. John C. Fitzpatrick, ed., *The Writings of George Washington from the Original Manuscript Sources, 1745–1799*. Vol. 2: *1757–1769* (Washington, 1931), 342; *Journal of Nicholas Cresswell*, 57–58; Josiah Quincy, *Memoirs of the Life of Josiah Quincy, Junior, of Massachusetts, 1774–1775* (Boston, 1824), 105.

55. Armes, ed., *Nancy Shippen, Her Journal*, 173.

56. Farish, ed., *Journal and Letters of Philip Vickers Fithian*, 123; Griswold, *Republican Court*, 257–58; Abigail Smith to John Adams, Weymouth, April 12, 1764, Butterfield et al., eds., *Adams Family Correspondence*, 26.

57. D'Ancourt, *Lady's Preceptor*, 9.

58. Lord Chesterfield [Philip Dormer Stanhope], *Principles of Politeness, and of Knowing the World; by the late Lord Chesterfield. Methodised and Digested under Distinct Heads, with Additions, by the Reverend Dr. John Trusler: Containing Every Instruction Necessary to Complete the Gentleman and Man of Fashion, to Teach Him a Knowledge of Life, and Make Him Well Received in All Companies* (Portsmouth, 1786), 8.

59. Robert Hunter, *Quebec to Carolina in 1785–1786, Being the Travel Diary and Observations of Robert Hunter, Jr., a Young Merchant of London*, ed. Louis B. Wright and Marion Tinling (San Marino, Calif., 1943), 206–8; Griswold, *Republican Court*, 20, 259.

60. M. Ridgely to Henry Ridgely, Philadelphia May 9, 1798, and Ann Ridgely to Henry Ridgely, May 27, 1785, in Ridgely, ed., *What Them Befell*, 120, 124; Graydon, *Memoirs of His Own Time*, 102.

61. Courtin, *Rules of Civility*, Foreword; Chesterfield, *Principles of Politeness*, 7.

62. Arthur Meier Schlesinger, *Learning How to Behave: A Historical Study of American Etiquette Books* (New York, 1946), 9; Noyes, *Bibliography of Courtesy and Conduct Books*, 7, 21, 22.

63. [Richard Allestree] *The Whole Duty of Man, Laid down In a Plain and Familiar Way, for the Use of All, but especially the Meanest Reader* (London, 1728), 208–10, 266.

64. Noyes, *Bibliography of Courtesy and Conduct Books*, 4, 7; d'Ancourt, *Lady's Preceptor*, 31.

III. BODIES AND MINDS

1. "Genteel," J. A. Simpson and E. S. C. Weiner, eds., *The Oxford English Dictionary*, 2nd ed. (Oxford, 1989), 6:447.
2. George Francis Dow, *The Arts and Crafts in New England, 1704–1775: Gleanings from Boston Newspapers Relating to Painting, Engraving, Silversmiths, Pewterers, Clockmakers, Furniture, Pottery, Old Houses, Costume, Trades and Occupations*... (Topsfield, Mass., 1927), 25, 119, 122–25, 135, 162; John C. Fitzpatrick, ed., *The Writings of George Washington from the Original Manuscript Sources, 1745–1799*. Vol. 2: *1757–1769* (Washington, D.C., 1931), 351; Kym S. Rice, *Early American Taverns: For the Entertainment of Friends and Strangers* (Chicago, 1983), 42. For a compact list of many uses of the world "genteel," see *The Oxford English Dictionary*, 6:447.
3. Rice, *Early American Taverns*, 55; Carl F. Bridenbaugh, ed., *Gentleman's Progress: The Itinerarium of Dr. Alexander Hamilton, 1744* (Chapel Hill, N.C., 1948), 13.
4. Alexander Graydon, *Memoirs of His Own Time*, ed. John Stockton Littell (New York, 1969 [reprint of 1846 ed.; orig. pub. as *Memoirs of a Life*, 1811]), 102.
5. Abbé d'Ancourt, *The Lady's Preceptor* (Woodbridge, N.J., 1759), 6.
6. Thomas Chippendale, *The Gentleman and Cabinet-Maker's Director: Being a large Collection of the Most Elegant and Useful Designs of Household Furniture, In the Most Fashionable Taste* (London, 1762), plates 52, 54, 55, 63, 114, 118, 119; Brock Jobe and Myrna Kaye, *New England Furniture: The Colonial Era* (Boston, 1984), 180–94. For the history of bathing, see Richard L. Bushman and Claudia L. Bushman, "The Early History of Cleanliness in America," *Journal of American History*, 74 (March 1988): 1213–38.
7. Antoine de Courtin, *The Rules of Civility; or, The Maxims of Genteel Behaviour, As They Are Practis'd and Observ'd by Persons of Quality, upon Several Occasions* ... (London, 1703, from the 12th French ed.), 89–90; Charles Moore, ed., *George Washington's Rules of Civility and Decent Behaviour in Company and Conversation* (Boston and New York, 1926), 3, 5, 11, 19, 21.
8. Lord Chesterfield [Philip Dormer Stanhope], *Principles of Politeness, and of Knowing the World; by the Late Lord Chesterfield. Methodised and Digested under Distinct Heads, with Additions, by the Reverend Dr. John Trusler: Containing Every Instruction Necessary to Complete the Gentleman and Man of Fashion, to Teach Him a Knowledge of Life, and Make Him Well Received in All Companies* (Portsmouth, 1786), 18, 55–56. See also Courtin, *Rules of Civility*, 44; *Youth's Behavior, or Decency in Conversation Amongst Men* ..., tr. Francis Hawkins, 8th printing (London, 1663), 18–19.
9. Authors of the detailed instructions on how to hold the body properly often insisted that the artificial postures were the natural ones. The elaborate directions as to the angle of the head, the position of the shoulders, the upright torso, the set of the legs, the splay of the feet were meant to put the body into its natural as well as its most graceful posture. In a book on dancing and posture, Rameau instructed young women that "a lady should carry the head erect, the shoulders low, and the arms bent and held backwards close to the body, while the hands should be in front, one over the other, clasping a fan. But remember, above all, no affectation." Pierre Rameau, *The Dancing Master*, tr. Cyril W. Beaumont (New York, 1970 [orig. pub. Paris, 1725]), 31.
10. Alicia M. Annas, "The Elegant Art of Movement," in *An Elegant Art: Fashion and Fantasy in the Eighteenth Century: Los Angeles County Museum of Art Collection of Costumes and Textiles* (Los Angeles and New York [1983]), 31–58; Wendy Hilton, *Dance of Court and Theater: The French Noble Style, 1690–1725*, ed. Caroline Gaynor (n.p., 1981), 66–67.
11. Courtin, *Rules of Civility*, 208; Norman Arthur Benson, "The Itinerant Dancing and Music Masters of Eighteenth-Century America" (Ph.D. diss., University of Minnesota, 1963); Edward Warwick, Henry C. Pitz, and Alexander Wyckoff, *Early American Dress: The Colonial and Revolutionary Periods*. Vol. 2 of *The History of American Dress*, ed. Alexander Wyckoff (New York, 1965), 257. For the Ridgelys' dance instruction, see above, chap. 1.
12. The standard works on early American dress are Claudia B. Kidwell and Margaret C. Christman, *Suiting Everyone: The Democratization of Clothing in America* (Washington, D.C., 1974); Warwick et al., *Early American Dress*; and Elisabeth McClellan, *History of American Costume 1607–1870* (New York, 1937). But costume usage for the genteel classes can best be understood through their portraits. The best work on colonial portraits are Wayne Craven, *Colonial American Portraiture: The Economic, Religious, Social, Cultural, Philosophical, Scientific, and Aesthetic Foundations* (Cambridge, Eng., 1986), and Richard H. Saunders and Ellen G. Miles, *American Colonial Portraits: 1700–1776* (Washington, D.C., 1987).
13. Portraits of Matthew Pratt and Mrs. Thomas Gage (Margaret Kemble) can be conveniently found in Saunders and Miles, *American Colonial Portraits*, 267, 241, and of John Hancock in Craven, *Colonial American Portraiture*, 325.
14. Quoted in Benson, "Itinerant Dancing and Music Masters," 237–38.
15. Rice, *Early American Taverns*, 84. John Lewis Krimmel, "Interior of an American Inn," oil, Philadelphia, 1813, shows two workingmen with aprons and loose-fitting frocks on underneath. The eighteenth century read character as well as class into posture. Rameau observed of a young woman that "if she holds her head erect and her body upright, without affectation or boldness, it will be said: 'There goes a fine lady.'"

If she carry herself carelessly, she will be regarded as indifferent; if she hold herself too far forward, she will be termed indolent; finally, if she stoop, she will be looked upon as dreamy or shy." Rameau, *Dancing Master*, 31.

16. Chesterfield, *Principles of Politeness*, 23. "A man need not, for example, fear to put his hands in his pockets, take snuff, sit, stand, or occasionally walk about the room; but it would be highly unbecoming to whistle, wear his hat, loosen his garters, or throw himself across the chairs. Such liberties are offensive to our equals, and insulting to our inferiors. Easiness of carriage by no means implies inattention and carelessness. No one is at liberty to act, in all respects as he pleases; but is bound by the law of good manners, to behave with decorum." Ibid., 13.

17. Rufus Wilmot Griswold, *The Republican Court; or, American Society in the Days of Washington* (New York, 1868), 311–32.

18. Quoted in Stephen Decatur, Jr., *Private Affairs of George Washington: From the Records and Accounts of Tobia Lear, Esquire, his Secretary* (Boston, 1933), 48–49.

19. N. B. Harte, "State Control of Dress and Social Change in Pre-Industrial England," in *Trade, Government and Economy in Pre-Industrial England: Essays Presented to F. J. Fisher*, ed. D. C. Coleman and A. H. John (London, 1976), 132–65. A seventeenth-century Virginia law forbade the importation of silk pieces save for hoods and scarves and the wearing of silver, gold, and bone lace. Philip Alexander Bruce, *Social Life of Virginia in the Seventeenth Century* (Lynchburg, Va., 1927), 168–70.

20. Anne Buck, *Dress in Eighteenth-Century England* (New York, 1979), 189, 197.

21. "Let your Dress be always agreeable to your Condition, by exceeding that you'll only make yourself the Jest of your Equals, and the Scorn of your Superiors." D'Ancourt, *Lady's Preceptor*, 51.

22. A Hartford merchant in 1825 had 389 dozen buttons in stock plus an additional forty-four bags of them. Barbara McLean Ward, "Metalwares," in Gerald W. R. Ward and William N. Hosley, eds., *The Great River: Art and Society of the Connecticut Valley, 1635–1820* (Hartford, 1985), 274. See also Darrett B. and Anita H. Rutman, *A Place in Time: Middlesex County, Virginia, 1650–1750* (New York and London, 1984), 229. Matthew Boulton, the English industrialist, considered buttons the "Sheet Anchor" of his enterprises and debated whether to leave them for steam engines. Neil McKendrick, "The Commercialization of Fashion," in Neil McKendrick, John Brewer, and J. H. Plumb, eds., *The Birth of a Consumer Society: The Commercialization of Eighteenth-Century England* (Bloomington, Ind., 1982), 70. An extravagantly adorned figure stood out, as when Fithian noted the glittering dress of a guest at the Carters'. "He was drest in black superfine broadcloth; Gold-laced hat; laced Ruffles; black Silk Stockings; and to his Broach on his Bosom he works a Majors Badge inscrib'd 'Virtute and Silentio' cut in Golden Medal! Certainly he was fine!" Hunter Dickinson Farish, ed., *Journals and Letters of Philip Vickers Fithian, 1773–1774* (Williamsburg, Va., 1957), 113. Copley's portraits of Mr. and Mrs. Jeremiah Lee are exceptional for their extravagance. Mr. Lee's coat sported gold brocade trim, and Mrs. Lee wore a gold satin gown and a cape trimmed with ermine. Craven, *Colonial American Portraiture*, 345–47.

23. Clean linen, well-brushed cloth coat, and shining shoes became the "foppery" of the lesser tradesmen. Roderick Random in Smollett's novel had one suit of clothes when he came to London, but a half dozen ruffled shirts and as many plain. Buck, *Dress in Eighteenth-Century England*, 92; see also ibid., 65, 138, 197.

24. Ibid., 124. "Stockings were a carefully graded item of dress, the grading based partly but not entirely on practical considerations. There was no simple distinction between wool and silk, but a progression from coarse yarn to finer worsted and silk." Ibid., 138. In the eighteenth century a velvet suit was the best suit of a rich man; cotton lined with linen was the best suit of a man of humbler circumstances. Kidwell and Christman, *Suiting Everyone*, 33.

25. Kidwell and Christman, *Suiting Everyone*, 23.

26. Edmund Burke, *A Philosophical Enquiry into the Origin of our Ideas of the Sublime and Beautiful*, ed. James T. Boulton (London, 1958 [reprinted 1968; rev. ed., Oxford, 1987]), 114.

27. He listed other qualities of beauty, among which gradual variation was central. By this he meant that a curve was more beautiful than a straight line, sharp angle, or jutting edge. (In later editions Burke acknowledged the similarities with Hogarth's line of beauty.) But gradual variation was a form of smoothness in its aversion to abrupt edges and related to softness, another Burkean quality, as well. Softness and smoothness resembled one another in offering no resistance to the touch as fingers engaged a surface. Ibid., 115.

28. John F. Watson, *Annals of Philadelphia and Pennsylvania, in the Olden Time . . .* ([Philadelphia], 1850 [orig. pub. 1843]), 184–85, 187, 189, 191.

29. Spoon meals, the name given to soups, gruels, porridges, and similar infusions, were well liked and prepared the year around. The more important ones, made with cereal grains, were porridge, gruels, and brose. Oat porridge when boiled until a thick, stiff jelly was called flummery and was highly esteemed. A similar dish made out of whole wheat was called frumenty. Gruel was made from thick dark water poured off the grains after they had been steeped but not yet boiled into porridge and then allowed to ferment slightly in a wooden bowl. It was drunk straight with a dash of liquor or ale or thinned down and heated. The high tables, by contrast, provided strange mixtures of spices, mashed meats, and

sometimes vegetables in "made dishes." The wealthy also served foods sweetened with one of the most prized of spices, sugar, and in addition featured a banquet course of nuts, raisins, and fruits at the end of the meal. These refinements set upper-class dining apart, but meat remained the important difference. Jay Allan Anderson, " 'A Solid Sufficiency': An Ethnography of Yeoman Foodways in Stuart England" (Ph.D. diss., University of Pennsylvania, 1971), 75, 153–54, 173–75, 185, 245–49, 260, 262; Jack Goody, *Cooking, Cuisine and Class: A Study in Comparative Sociology* (Cambridge, Eng., 1982), 133–39; Stephen Mennell, *All Manners of Food: Eating and Taste in England and France from the Middle Ages to the Present* (Oxford, 1985), 48, 51, 52, 63.

30. On the college student menu (for Brown) and the Boston family diet, see Richard J. Hooker, *Food and Drink in America: A History* (Indianapolis, 1981), 67, 68. On military diets, consult Series Z 195–212, *Historical Statistics of the United States: Colonial Times to 1970,* part 2 (Washington, D.C., 1975), 1175. On upscale meat consumption, see Jane Carson, *Colonial Virginia Cookery: Procedures, Equipment, and Ingredients in Colonial Cooking* (Williamsburg, Va., 1985 [orig. pub. 1968]), 3–8. In the period from 1653 to 1795, McMahon found meat in 37 to 57 percent of inventories through all seasons of the year, and 68 to 83 percent with swine or fat cattle on the hoof. Sarah F. McMahon, "Provisions Laid Up for the Family: Toward a History of Diet in New England, 1650–1850," *Historical Methods,* 14 (1981): 14, 17. On meat in country stores, see Daphne L. Derven, "Wholesome, Toothsome, and Diverse: Eighteenth-Century Foodways in Deerfield, Massachusetts," in *Foodways in the Northeast,* Dublin Seminar for New England Folklife: Annual Proceedings 1982 (Boston, 1984), 56–57. On food theft, see Laurel Ulrich, "It 'went away she knew not how': Food Theft and Domestic Conflict in Seventeenth-Century Essex County," in *Foodways in the Northeast,* 96–97, 99–100.

31. Kevin M. Sweeney, "Furniture and the Domestic Environment in Wethersfield, Connecticut, 1639–1800," *The Connecticut Antiquarian,* 36 (Dec. 1984): 12, 15; Joan M. Jensen, *Loosening the Bonds: Mid-Atlantic Farm Women, 1750–1850* (New Haven, 1986), 218.

32. David D. Hall, ed., *Witch-Hunting in Seventeenth-Century New England: A Documentary History, 1638–1692* (Boston, 1991), 40; Phillip R. Shriver, ed., *A Tour to New Connecticut in 1811: The Narrative of Henry Leavitt Ellsworth* (Cleveland, 1985), 66–67.

33. Fernand Braudel, *The Structures of Everyday Life: The Limits of the Possible.* Vol. 1 of *Civilization and Capitalism: Fifteenth to Eighteenth Centuries,* tr. Sian Reynolds (New York, 1981 [orig. pub. 1979]), 205; Anderson, "A Solid Sufficiency," 236, 239; George Francis Dow, *Every Day Life in the Massachusetts Bay Colony* (New York, 1977 [orig. pub. 1935]), 11, 37, 41.

34. James Deetz, *In Small Things Forgotten: The Archeology of Early American Life* (New York, 1977), 56.

35. Bridenbaugh, ed., *Gentleman's Progress,* 8.

36. Sweeney, "Furniture and the Domestic Environment in Wethersfield," *Connecticut Antiquarian,* 36: 12, 15; Jensen, *Loosening the Bonds,* 218, 220; Anna Hawley, "The Trappings of Gentility: A Brief Analysis of Some Items from a Sample of Probate Inventories, Kent County, Delaware, 1727–1767," unpublished paper based on Richard L. Bushman and Anna Hawley, compilers, *A Random Sample of Kent County, Delaware, Estate Inventories, 1727–1775* (Newark, Del., 1987).

37. Marley R. Brown, "Ceramics from Plymouth, 1621–1800: The Documentary Records," in Ian M. G. Quimby, ed., *Ceramics in America* (Charlottesville, Va., 1973), 60; Jensen, *Loosening the Bonds,* 218, 220; Carole Shammas, *The Pre-Industrial Consumer in England and America* (Oxford, 1990), 184; Hawley, "The Trappings of Gentility"; Lois Green Carr and Lorena S. Walsh, "Changing Life Styles and Consumer Behavior in the Colonial Chesapeake," in *Of Consuming Interests: Styles of Life in the Eighteenth Century* (Charlottesville, Va., forthcoming 1992), tables 1 A–F. Knives and forks were still rare in English provincial estate inventories by 1725. Lorna Weatherill, *Consumer Behaviour and Material Culture in Britain, 1660–1760* (London, 1988), 153.

38. Deetz, *In Small Things Forgotten,* 25, 30, 33, 58–60; Brown, "Ceramics from Plymouth, 1621–1800," 45, 48–51, 56, 58; Hawley, "The Trappings of Gentility"; Shammas, *Pre-Industrial Consumer in England and America,* 184. The absence of plates in the inventory of a Yorktown, Pennsylvania, potter suggests the market was not strong enough to bring backcountry kilns into plate production. Norman F. Barka, "The Kiln and Ceramics of the 'Poor Potter' of Yorktown: A Preliminary Report," in Quimby, ed., *Ceramics in America,* 303, 306–9.

39. Charles F. Montgomery, *A History of American Pewter* (New York, 1973), 145; Benjamin Franklin, *The Autobiography of Benjamin Franklin,* ed. Leonard W. Labance, Ralph L. Ketcham, Helen C. Boatfield, and Helene H. Fineman (New Haven, 1964), 145.

40. John Locke, *Some Thoughts Concerning Education,* 5th ed. (London, 1705) in James L. Axtell, ed., *The Educational Writings of John Locke* (Cambridge, Eng., 1968), 160.

41. D'Ancourt, *Lady's Preceptor,* 11.

42. Dr. Gregory, *A Father's Legacy To his Daughters* (Portsmouth, N.H., 1786) [bound with Chesterfield, *Principles of Politeness*], 102, 104. In *The Plan of an Essay upon Delicacy* (n.p., 1748), Nathaniel Lancaster defined delicacy as "good Sense refined; which produces an inviolate Attachment to Decorum and Sanctity, as well as Elegance of Manners, with a clear Discernment and warm Sensibility of whatever is pure, regular and polite; and, at the same Time, an Abhorrence of whatever is gross, rustic, or impure, of unnatural,

effeminate, and over-wrought Ornaments of every kind. It is, in short, the graceful and the beautiful added to the just and the good." Quoted in John E. Mason, *Gentlefolk in the Making: Studies in the History of English Courtesy Literature and Related Topics from 1531 to 1774* (Philadelphia, 1935), 276.

43. Quoted in "Sensibility," *The Oxford English Dictionary*, 14:981–82.

44. Ethel Armes, ed., *Nancy Shippen, Her Journal Book: The International Romance of a Young Lady of Fashion of Colonial Philadelphia with Letters to Her and about Her* (Philadelphia, 1935), 169, 246; Susanna Rowson, *Charlotte Temple: A Tale of Truth*, ed. Clara M. and Rudolph Kirk (Schenectady, N.Y., n.d. [orig. pub. 1791]), 45–46. For a discussion of feeling as related to sensibility, see Jan Lewis, *The Pursuit of Happiness: Family and Values in Jefferson's Virginia* (Cambridge, Eng., 1983), 209–30.

45. Farish, ed., *Journals and Letters of Philip Vickers Fithian*, 77–78.

46. Elise Pinckney, ed., *The Letterbook of Eliza Lucas Pinckney, 1739–1762* (Chapel Hill, N.C., 1972), xv–xvi.

47. Gregory, *A Father's Legacy*, 103; Armes, ed., *Nancy Shippen, Her Journal Book*, 175.

48. *The Polite Arts, or, a Dissertation on Poetry, Painting, Musick, Architecture, and Eloquence* (London, 1749), 8. Montesquieu quote from Peter Gay, *The Enlightenment: An Interpretation*. Vol. 2: *The Science of Freedom* (New York, 1969), 300. For the aversion to boredom and a guide to avoiding it, see A. F. B. Deslandes, *The Art of Being Easy at all Times and In all Places*, tr. Edward Combe (n.p., 1724). D'Ancourt told his charge to "talk little, but never appear speechless and disconcerted, like your young Creatures just come to Town from a Welsh Boarding-School, who resemble Birds got loose from a Cage, that know not where they are, or how to dispose of themselves." D'Ancourt, *Lady's Preceptor*, 9.

49. D'Ancourt, *Lady's Preceptor*, 9; *Art of Complaisance*, quoted in Rice, *Early American Taverns*, 78–79; Gertrude E. Noyes, *Bibliography of Courtesy and Conduct Books in Seventeenth-Century England* (New Haven, 1937), 11; Courtin, *Rules of Civility*, 69–75. See also Herbert Davis, "The Conversation of the Augustans," in *The Seventeenth Century: Studies . . . by Richard Foster Jones and Others Writing in His Honor* (Stanford, Calif., 1951), 181–97.

50. The American editions of English and American works are listed in Charles Evans, *American Bibliography. A Chronological Dictionary of All Books, Pamphlets and Periodical Publications Printed in the United States of America from the Genesis of Printing in 1639 Down to and Including the Year 1820*, 12 vols. (Chicago, 1903–55), and Roger P. Bristol, *Supplement to Charles Evans' American Bibliography* (Charlottesville, Va., 1970).

51. *The Weekly Rehearsal* (Boston) is quoted in David H. Flaherty, *Privacy in Colonial New England* (Charlottesville, Va., 1972), 111. Armes, ed., *Nancy Shippen, Her Journal Book*, 170, 176, and Chastellux quoted on 309; Griswold, *Republican Court*, 79–80.

52. Henry Peacham, *The Complete Gentleman*, ed. Virgil B. Heltzel (Ithaca, N.Y., 1962 [orig. pub. 1622; this is from the 1634 ed.]), 117, 121.

53. Chesterfield, *Principles of Politeness*, 10 (quote), 71–72.

54. Ibid., 35; Jacques Levron, *Daily Life at Versailles in the Seventeenth and Eighteenth Centuries*, tr. Claire Elaine Engel (New York, 1968), 61; Bonnin quote from Rice, *Early American Taverns*, 117; Courtin, *Rules of Civility*, 32–33; New York newspaper quote from Esther Singleton, *Social New York under the Georges, 1714–1776: Houses, Streets and Country Homes, with Chapters on Fashions, Furniture, China, Plate and Manners* (New York, 1902), 323.

55. Courtin, *Rules of Civility*, 68–75.

56. Josiah Quincy, *Memoirs of the Life of Josiah Quincy, Junior, of Massachusetts, 1774–1775*, 2nd ed. (Boston, 1874), 116, 138. See also Benson, "Itinerant Dancing and Music Masters," 143–44, 220.

57. *Youth's Behavior*, 3.

58. Emerson's epigrammatic and slightly enigmatic sentences reflect one version of a genteel conversational style and Dr. Johnson's endless witty judgments another.

59. Philomusus, *The Academy of Complements. Wherein Ladyes, Gentlewomen, Schollers, and Strangers May Accomodate Their Courtly Practice with Most Curious Ceremonies, Complementall, Amorous, High Expressions, and Formes of Speaking, or Writing* (London, 1640), preface; Thomas Goddard Wright, *Literary Culture in Early New England, 1620–1730*, edited by his wife (New York, 1966), 122, 230.

60. Henry Fielding, "An Essay on Conversation," in *Miscellanies by Henry Fielding, Esq.; Volume One*, ed. Henry Knight Miller ([Middletown, Conn.] 1972), 123, 150; Chesterfield, *Principles of Politeness*, 34. Jonathan Swift's *Treatise on Good Manners and Good Breeding*, published in 1754 but written around 1731, opened with the statement "Good manners is the art of making those people easy with whom we converse." Quoted in Mason, *Gentlefolk in the Making*, 277. He records supposed polite banter from genteel drawing rooms in an effort to expose its poverty and vanity. *A Complete Collection of Genteel and Ingenious Conversation, According to the Most Polite Mode and Method Now Used at Court, and in the Best Companies of England. In Three Dialogues* (London, 1738), in *Polite Conversation*, ed. Eric Partridge (London, 1963).

61. Swift, *A Complete Collection of Genteel and Ingenious Conversation*, 23.

62. Bonamy Dobree, ed., *The Letters of Philip Dormer Stanhope, 4th Earl of Chesterfield* (n.p., 1932), Nov. 24, 1749, 4:1442–43. Benjamin Rush quoted in Craven, *Colonial American Portraiture*, 396.

63. William Henry Irving, *The Providence of Wit in the English Letter Writers* (Durham, N.C., 1955), 22, chaps. 3–6, passim; *The Complete Letter-Writer, Containing Familiar Letters, on the Most Common Occasions in Life. Also,*

A Variety of Elegant Letters for the Direction and Embellishments of Style, on Business, Duty, Amusement, Love, Courtship, Marriage, Friendship, and Other Subjects (New York, 1793). For letters as a literary genre and the books on how to do it, see Katherine Gee Hornbeak, *The Complete Letter Writer in English, 1568–1800* (Northampton, Mass., 1934). See also Ruth Perry, *Women, Letters, and the Novel* (New York, 1980).

64. Abigail Adams to Mercy Otis Warren, Boston, July 16, 1773, and Mercy Otis Warren to Abigail Adams, Plymouth, July 25, 1773, in L. H. Butterfield, Wendell D. Garrett, and Marjorie E. Sprague, eds., *Adams Family Correspondence* (Cambridge, Mass., 1963), 1: 84–87.

65. Abigail Adams to Mercy Otis Warren, Boston, Dec. 11, 1773, in ibid., 1:89.

66. Sally Fisher, Duck Creek Cross Roads, to Deborah Norris, Duck Creek Cross Roads, March 1780, and Deborah Norris to Sally Fisher, Philadelphia, May 6, 1780, in John A. H. Sweeney, ed., "The Norris-Fisher Correspondence: A Circle of Friends, 1779–82," *Delaware History,* 6 (March 1955): 200, 204. For the tension between formal and emotive expression in Southern love letters, see Steven M. Stowe, *Intimacy and Power in the Old South: Ritual in the Lives of Planters* (Baltimore, 1987), 88–96.

67. Graydon, *Memoirs,* 102; Bickham quoted in Ambrose Heal, *The English Writing-Masters and Their Copy-Books, 1570–1800: A Biographical Dictionary and a Bibliography* (Hildesheim, 1962 [orig. pub. 1931]), x; Chesterfield quoted in Wilfrid Blunt, *Sweet Roman Hand: Five Hundred Years of Italic Cursive Script* (London, 1952), 33; also in Chesterfield, *Principles of Politeness,* 60; Ray Nash, *American Writing Masters and Copybooks: History and Bibliography Through Colonial Times* (Boston, 1959), 23; Moore, ed., *George Washington's Rules of Civility,* xii, xiii; Armes, ed., *Nancy Shippen, Her Journal,* 282–83. The Ridgely children studied writing and penmanship in Philadelphia in 1799. Mabel Lloyd Ridgely, *What Them Befell: The Ridgelys of Delaware and Their Circle in Colonial and Federal Times: Letters: 1751–1890* (Portland, Me., 1949), 241.

68. The history of handwriting since the Renaissance is conveniently summarized in Stanley Morison, "The Development of Hand-Writing: An Outline," in Heal, *The English Writing-Masters,* ix–xxi.

69. Morison, "The Development of Hand-Writing," xxv, xxviii, xxxiii; Nash, *American Writing Masters,* 11, 23–25; Stanley Morison, *American Copybooks: An Outline of Their History from Colonial to Modern Times* (Philadelphia, 1951), 15–19.

70. Nash, *American Writing Masters,* 8, 12, 16, 18, 25.

71. For a discussion of one collection of desks, Brock Jobe and Myrna Kaye, *New England Furniture: The Colonial Era: Selections from the Society for the Preservation of New England Antiquities* (Boston, 1984), 103–8, 220–57. Residential desks likely contained business correspondence in many instances, but we forget women's correspondence and friendship letters if we associate the desk form solely with business.

72. Samuel Richardson, *The History of Sir Charles Grandison,* ed. Jocelyn Harris, 3 vols. (London, 1972), part I, 182.

73. Joseph Addison, "No. 409," June 19, 1712, *The Spectator,* ed. Donald F. Bond, 3 (Oxford, 1965): 527; *The Polite Arts, or, a Dissertation on Poetry, Painting, Musick, Architecture, and Eloquence* (London, 1749), 5. The broad outlines of the concern about aesthetics are sketched in Gay, *The Science of Freedom,* 290–318.

74. Burke, *Philosophical Enquiry,* 124.

75. *The Polite Arts,* 9. Speaking of the aim of the artistic genius, the same author proposed that "all his Efforts must necessarily reduce him to make choice of the most beautiful Parts of Nature, to form one Exquisite whole which should be more perfect than mere Nature, without ceasing however, to be natural" (p. 8). For a discussion of the kinds of nature known to the eighteenth century and the place of beautiful nature, see Roger Turner, *Capability Brown and the Eighteenth-Century English Landscape* (New York, 1985), 68–78.

IV. HOUSES AND GARDENS

1. The infusion of Renaissance styles into English residential architecture is worked out in Daniel D. Reiff, *Small Georgian Houses in England and Virginia: Origins and Development through the 1750s* (London and Toronto, 1986), chaps. 1, 2 passim. For the same process in a provincial city, see Andor Gomme, Michael Jenner, and Bryan Little, *Bristol: An Architectural History* (London, 1979), 75, 81. The Summerson quote is from John Summerson, *Georgian London,* rev. ed. (Harmondsworth, Eng., 1978), 27.

2. Reiff, *Small Georgian Houses,* 174–75 and chaps. 3, 4 passim. The Harris quote is on p. 174. Gomme et al., *Bristol,* 94–106, with quote from p. 94. Peter Smith, "Rural Building in Wales," in *The Agrarian History of England and Wales.* Vol. 5: *1740–1750: II. Agrarian Change,* ed. Joan Thirsk (Cambridge, Eng., 1985), 738–41, 774; Maurice Craig, *Classic Irish Houses of the Middle Size* (London, 1976). There is evidence that the building boom peaked in the 1720s and fell off for the two succeeding decades, in contradiction to John Harris's estimation of continued construction. M. W. Barley, "Rural Building in England," in Thirsk, ed., *Agrarian History,* 600–3, 621. For an analysis of urban houses in the classical taste, see Peter Borsay, *The English Urban Renaissance: Culture and Society in the Provincial Town, 1660–1770* (Oxford, 1989), 47–60.

3. Porches are most extensively discussed in William N. Hosley, Jr., "Houses," in Gerald W. R. Ward and William N. Hosley, eds., *The Great River: Art and Society of the Connecticut Valley, 1635–1820* (Hartford, 1985), 63–64, 73. See also Abbott Lowell Cummings, *The Framed Houses of Massachusetts Bay, 1625–1675* (Cambridge,

Mass., 1979), 35–39; Fraser D. Neiman, "Domestic Architecture at the Clifts Plantation: The Social Context of Early Virginia Building," in Dell Upton and John Michael Vlach, eds., *Common Places: Readings in American Vernacular Architecture* (Athens, Ga., and London, 1986), 297; Darrett B. and Anita H. Rutman, *A Place in Time: Middlesex County, Virginia, 1650–1750* (New York and London, 1984), 67–69; Cary Carson, Norman F. Barka, William M. Kelso, Garry Wheeler Stone, and Dell Upton, "Impermanent Architecture in the Southern American Colonies," *Winterthur Portfolio,* 16 (Summer–Autumn 1981): 145, 152. Upton says that the frequency of external tower porches or internal porch entries increased at the end of the seventeenth century. Dell Upton, "Vernacular Domestic Architecture in Eighteenth-Century Virginia," in *Common Places,* 322. On brick houses in New England, see Hugh Morrison, *Early American Architecture: From the First Colonial Settlements to the National Period* (New York, 1952), 72.

4. The important regional variations in single-cell houses are explained in the recent literature on vernacular housing from which this picture is derived: Cummings, *Framed Houses of Massachusetts Bay,* chap. 3; Robert Blair St. George, " 'Set Thine House in Order': The Domestication of the Yeomanry in Seventeenth-Century New England," in *New England Begins: The Seventeenth Century: Mentality and Environment* (Boston, 1982), 159–87; Jack Michel, " 'In a Manner and Fashion Suitable to Their Degree': A Preliminary Investigation of the Material Culture of Early Rural Pennsylvania," *Working Papers from the Regional Economic History Research Center,* 5 (1981); Carson et al., "Impermanent Architecture," 135–96; Douglas Swaim, ed., *Carolina Dwelling: Toward Preservation of Place: In Celebration of the Vernacular Landscape,* Student Publication of the School of Design, vol. 26 (Raleigh, N.C., 1978); Gloria L. Main, *Tobacco Colony: Life in Early Maryland, 1650–1720* (Princeton, N.J., 1982), chap. 4; William N. Hosley, Jr., "Architecture," in *The Great River,* 63–135.

5. The sources cited in note 4 also discuss the double-cell house.

6. Margaret Berwind Schiffer, *Survey of Chester County, Pennsylvania, Architecture, 17th, 18th, and 19th Centuries* (Exton, Pa., 1984), 26–29; Robert Potter and Virginia S. Johnson, "The John Chad House" (April 1975), Chadds Ford Historical Society, Chadds Ford, Pa., hereafter cited as Chadds Ford Historical Society.

7. Schiffer, *Survey of Chester County, Pennsylvania, Architecture,* 24–25; Virginia S. Johnson, "The Barns-Brinton House" (Oct. 1979), Chadds Ford Historical Society.

8. Cummings, *Framed Houses of Massachusetts Bay,* 22–23, 27, 35, 47, 159, 177, 190; Morrison, *Early American Architecture,* 54–55.

9. Cummings, *Framed Houses of Massachusetts Bay,* 158–88.

10. Michel, " 'In a Manner and Fashion Suitable to Their Degree,' " 7; Upton, "Vernacular Domestic Architecture in Eighteenth-Century Virginia," 316–17.

11. Carole Shammas, *The Pre-Industrial Consumer in England and America* (Oxford, 1990), 165–68.

12. "Dover Orphans," "Duck Creek Orphans," and "Mispillion Orphans," Computer Printouts, Center for Historic Architecture and Engineering, University of Delaware, Newark, Del.

13. On the continuation of the most frail kind of seventeenth-century housing, hole-set, impermanent architecture, into the eighteenth century, see Carson et al., "Impermanent Architecture," 161–63. On New England, see Hosley, "Architecture," 65; and Kevin M. Sweeney, "Mansion People: Kinship, Class, and Architecture in Western Massachusetts in the Mid Eighteenth Century," *Winterthur Portfolio* 19 (Winter 1984): 242. On the southside, see Richard R. Beeman, *The Evolution of the Southern Backcountry: A Case Study of Lunenburg County, Virginia, 1746–1832* (Philadelphia, 1984), 39, 75, 182. See also Lee Soltow, "Housing Characteristics on the Pennsylvania Frontier: Mifflin County Dwelling Values in 1798," *Pennsylvania History,* 47 (1980): 57–70.

14. Walter Kendall Watkins, "The Hancock House and Its Builder," *Old-Time New England,* 17 (1926–27): 3–19; Walter Kendall Watkins, edited by Richard M. Candee, "The Province House and Its Occupants," *Old-Time New England,* 62 (April–June 1972): 95–106; Nancy H. Schless, "The Sergeant and Foster-Hutchinson Houses: Dutch Palladianism in Boston," *Journal of the Society of Architectural Historians,* 28 (Oct. 1969): 218; Abbott Lowell Cummings, "The Foster-Hutchinson House," *Old-Time New England,* 54, no. 3 (Jan.–March 1964): 59–76; Morrison, *Early American Architecture,* 73–75, 475–77, 514; Albert Cook Myers, *Narratives of Early Pennsylvania, West New Jersey, and Delaware, 1630–1707* (New York, 1912), 273n., 290, 330; William H. Pierson, Jr., *American Buildings and Their Architects: The Colonial and Neo-Classical Styles* (Garden City, N.Y., 1976 [orig. pub. 1970]), 72–74; Reiff, *Small Georgian Houses,* 234–35. Susan Mackiewicz provided the references on Robert Turner, Jr., and Richard Whitpaine.

15. For Virginia's great houses, see Thomas Tileston Waterman, *The Mansions of Virginia: 1706–1776* (Chapel Hill, N.C., 1946). For the Hancock house and New England eighteenth-century mansions, see Watkins, "The Hancock House and Its Builder," and Sweeney, "Mansion People." The standard architectural surveys tend to concentrate on these great houses: Morrison, *Early American Architecture,* and Pierson, *American Buildings and Their Architecture.* There is a vast, uneven literature, profusely illustrated, for the admirers of eighteenth-century architecture, all of it valuable in one way or another. Among the surveys, besides Pierson and Morrison, are Fiske Kimball, *Domestic Architecture of the American Colonies and of the*

Early Republic (New York, 1966 [orig. pub. New York, 1922]); Thomas Tileston Waterman, *The Dwellings of Colonial America* (Chapel Hill, 1950); and Alan Gowans, *Images of American Living: Four Centuries of Architecture and Furniture as Cultural Expression* (Philadelphia, 1964). Among the regional studies in addition to those already cited are Antoinette Forrester Downing, *Early Homes of Rhode Island* (Richmond, 1937); Alan Gowans, *Architecture in New Jersey: A Record of American Civilization* (Princeton, 1964); J. Frederick Kelly, *Early Domestic Architecture of Connecticut* (New York, 1963 [orig. pub. 1924]); Mills Lane, *Architecture of Old South Carolina* (Savannah, 1984); Marcus Whiffen, *The Eighteenth-Century Houses of Williamsburg: A Study of Architecture and Building in the Colonial Capital of Virginia* (Williamsburg, 1960); John Mead Howells, *The Architectural Heritage of the Merrimack: Early Houses and Gardens* (New York, 1941); James L. Garvin, "Portsmouth and Piscataqua: Social History and Material Culture," *Historical New Hampshire,* 26 (Summer 1971): 3–48; Bernard Herman, *Architecture and Rural Life in Central Delaware, 1700–1900* (Knoxville, Tenn., 1987); Catherine W. Bishir, Charlotte V. Brown, Carl R. Lounsbury, Ernest H. Wood, *Architects and Builders in North Carolina: A History of the Practice of Building* (Chapel Hill, N.C., 1990); Harold Donaldson Eberlein, *The Manors and Historic Homes of the Hudson Valley* (Philadelphia, 1924) and *Historic Houses and Buildings of Delaware* (Dover, Del., 1962); George B. Tatum, *Philadelphia Georgian: The City House of Samuel Powel and Some of Its Eighteenth-Century Neighbors* (Middletown, Conn., 1976); Van Jones Martin, *Landmark Homes of Georgia, 1733–1783: Two Hundred and Fifty Years of Architecture, Interiors, and Gardens* (Savannah, 1982).

16. Upton, "Vernacular Domestic Architecture in Eighteenth-Century Virginia," 315–35.

17. Sweeney, "Mansion People," 248–49. Of thirty houses built between 1719 and 1776 and analyzed in one study of Connecticut dwellings, twelve had central passages, while sixteen had central chimneys with a front entry between door and chimney pile; only three of the thirty, however, still had the plain or enclosed stairway of seventeenth-century houses. The rest were open stairs with rails, balusters, and posts and usually paneling on the wall below. Bertha Chadwick Trowbridge and Charles McLean Andrews, *Old Houses of Connecticut from Material Collected by the Committee on Old Houses of the Connecticut Society of the Colonial Dames of America* (London, 1923), 117–388. See also Downing, *Early Homes of Rhode Island,* 77, 126, 129, 169–75.

18. Schiffer, *Survey of Chester County, Pennsylvania, Architecture,* 44, 52, 58, 69.

19. Downing, *Early Homes of Rhode Island,* 25, 39–41, 175.

20. Frank E. Sanchis, *American Architecture: Westchester County, New York: Colonial to Contemporary* (n.p., 1977), 32.

21. Quote from Mifflin's journal in John A. Munroe, *Federalist Delaware, 1775–1815* ([Newark, Del.] 1987 [orig. pub. 1954]), 41–42.

22. Smith, "Rural Buildings in Wales," 738. See also pp. 773, 779

23. Mark R. Wenger, "The Central Passage in Virginia: Evolution of an Eighteenth-Century Living Space," in Camille Wells, ed., *Perspectives in Vernacular Architecture,* 2 (1986): 137–49; Mark Girouard, *Life in the English Country House: A Social and Architectural History* (New Haven, 1978), 93 (Burghley quote), 118; Isaac Ware, *A Complete Body of Architecture Adorned with Plans and Elevations, from Original Designs* (London, 1767), 326.

24. Girouard, *Life in the English Country House,* 194–95; Cummings, *Framed Houses of Massachusetts Bay,* 162–67.

25. Catherine Thomas Masetti, "Bed Form and Placement in Chester County, Pennsylvania, 1683–1751" (M.A. thesis, University of Delaware, 1987), 34.

26. Ibid., 30, 34.

27. Abbott Lowell Cummings, *Rural Household Inventories 1675–1775* (Boston, 1964), passim. On value of bedroom furnishings, St. George, " 'Set Thine House in Order,' " 354–55.

28. Waterman, *Mansions of Virginia,* 50; Charles A. Hammond, "Producing, Selecting, and Serving Food at the Country Seat, 1730–1830," in *Foodways in the Northeast,* Dublin Seminar for New England Folklife, Annual Proceedings 1982 (Boston, 1984), 84–85; Margaret Henderson Floyd, "Measured Drawings of the Hancock House by John Hubbard Sturgis: A Legacy to the Colonial Revival," in *Architecture in Colonial Massachusetts: A Conference Held by the Colonial Society of Massachusetts, September 19 and 20, 1974* (Boston, 1979), 90; Tanya Boyett, "Thomas Handasyd Perkins: An Essay on Material Culture," *Old-Time New England,* 70 (1980): 54; Masetti, "Bed Form and Placement in Chester County, Pennsylvania," 34–37; Julie Riesenweber, "Order in Domestic Space: House Plans and Room Use in the Vernacular Dwellings of Salem County, New Jersey, 1700–1774" (M.A. thesis, University of Delaware, 1984), 62–63. On the sash window in England, see Borsay, *English Urban Renaissance,* 51.

29. For standard seventeenth-century surfaces, see Cummings, *Framed Houses of Massachusetts Bay,* 162, 169–83, 190–97; Neiman, "Domestic Architecture at the Clifts Plantation," 297.

30. Alice Morse Earle, *Home Life in Colonial Days* (Stockbridge, Mass., 1974 [orig. pub. 1898]), 32, 34, 43, 70–71; William Thomas O'Dea, *The Social History of Lighting* (London, 1958), 25–26; Elisabeth Donaghy Garrett, "The American Home: Part VI: The Quest for Comfort: Housekeeping Practices and Living Arrangements the Year Round," *The Magazine Antiques,* 128 (Dec. 1985): 1220.

31. Arthur Devis, "Mr. and Mrs. Richard Bull in Their House at Ongar in Essex," English, 1747, in Peter Thornton, *Authentic Decor: The Domestic Interior, 1620–1920* (New York, 1984), 120. For other examples, Edgar deN. Mayhew and Minor Myers, Jr., *A Documentary History of American Interiors: From the Colonial Era to 1915*

(New York, 1980), 84, 90. Rodris Roth, *Floor Coverings in 18th-Century America*, United States Museum Bulletin 250, Contributions from the Museum of History and Technology, Paper 59 (Washington, D.C., 1967), 11. In "A Family Group," English, about 1740, in the collections of Colonial Williamsburg, four women and four men appear in a room with a carpet entirely on one side of the room occupying only a quarter of the floor space. One couple are dancing on the open floor. All the others stand or sit on the carpet around a table. Brock Jobe and Myrna Kaye, *New England Furniture: The Colonial Era: Selections from the Society for the Preservation of New England Antiquities* (Boston, 1984), 290, 296.

32. Henry J. Kauffman, *The American Fireplace: Chimneys, Mantelpieces, Fireplaces and Accessories* (New York, 1972), 197–211, 223–36; Leonard W. Labaree, Whitfield J. Bell, Jr., eds., *The Papers of Benjamin Franklin: vol. 2, January 1, 1735 through December 31, 1744* (New Haven, 1960), 424–25.

33. James Ward Thorne, *American Rooms in Miniature* (Chicago, 1962), plate 2; Kenneth M. Wilson, "Window Glass in America," in Charles E. Peterson, ed., *Building Early America: Contributions toward the History of a Great Industry* (Radnor, Pa., 1976), 156; Thornton, *Authentic Decor*, 100; Earle, *Home Life in Colonial Days*, 42.

34. Carl Bridenbaugh, *Cities in Revolt: Urban Life in America, 1743–1776* (London, 1971 [orig. pub. 1955]), 170–71; Cummings, *Framed Houses of Massachusetts Bay*, 153–57; O'Dea, *Social History of Lighting*, 60–61; Harold F. Williamson and Arnold R. Daum, *The American Petroleum Industry: The Age of Illumination 1859–1899* (Evanston, Ill., 1959), 28–29; John Rogers Williams, ed., *Philip Vickers Fithian: Journals and Letters, 1767–1774* (Princeton, N.J., 1900), 73.

35. Anne Buck, *Dress in Eighteenth-Century England* (New York, 1979), 17; O'Dea, *The Social History of Lighting*, 32, 34, 45, 48–49. The quotation is from p. 40. Lori S. Russell, "Early Nineteenth-Century Lighting," in Peterson, ed., *Building Early America*, 191.

36. Roy Strong, *The Renaissance Garden in England* (London, 1979). The story for France, a constant source of influence on English gardens, is told in Kenneth Woodbridge, *Princely Gardens: The Origins and Development of the French Formal Style* (New York, 1986). For gardening books for gentlemen, Gertrude E. Noyes, *Bibliography of Courtesy and Conduct Books in Seventeenth-Century England* (New Haven, 1937), 11. Formal gardens of seventeenth-century English houses are depicted in John Harris, *The Artist and the Country House: A History of Country House and Garden View Painting in Britain 1540–1870* (London, 1979), 8–87.

37. John Reps, *The Making of Urban America: A History of City Planning in the United States* (Princeton, 1965), 151. A second map, "A Description of the Towne of Mannados or New-Amsterdam," of 1661, shows a garden design in the same place as the first one, "Afbeeldinge van de Stadt Amsterdam in Nieuw Neederlandt," and labels an adjoining site "Governours Garden." I. N. Phelps Stokes, *The Iconography of Manhattan Island, 1498–1909* (New York, 1915), plates 10, 10A-b. Peter Martin, " 'Long and Assiduous Endeavours': Gardening in Early Eighteenth-Century Virginia," in Robert P. Maccubbin and Peter Martin, eds., *British and American Gardens in the Eighteenth Century: Eighteen Illustrated Essays on Garden History* (Williamsburg, Va., 1984), 107; Elizabeth McLean, "Town and Country Gardens in Eighteenth-Century Philadelphia," ibid., 137; James D. Kornwolf, "The Picturesque in the American Garden and Landscape before 1800," ibid., 95.

38. Martin, " 'Long and Assiduous Endeavours,' " 108, 112–14 (Bartram quotation on p. 113); Alan Emmet, "The Codman Estate—'The Grange': A Landscape Chronicle," *Old-Time New England*, 71 (1981): 6 (Hancock quotation); Abbott Lowell Cummings, "Eighteenth-Century New England Garden Design: The Pictorial Evidence," in Maccubbin and Martin, eds., *British and American Gardens*, 130; McLean, "Town and Country Gardens," 138–39; George C. Rogers, "Gardens and Landscapes in Eighteenth-Century South Carolina," in Maccubbin and Martin, eds., *British and American Gardens*, 148–50.

39. Kornwolf, "The Picturesque in the American Garden and Landscape before 1800," 93–106, with helpful pictures to illustrate the mixture, plates 1–6, 12–15, 17–23, 27–30.

40. Ethel Armes, ed., *Nancy Shippen, Her Journal Book* (Philadelphia, 1935), 139, 154–55; Williams, ed., *Fithian: Journal and Letters*, 77; Martin, " 'Long and Assiduous,' " 109–11.

41. Quotation in William M. Kelso, "Landscape Archeology," in Maccubbin and Martin, eds., *British and American Gardens*, 162.

42. Harris, *The Artist and the Country House*, 2, chaps. 3, 4.

43. Rogers, "Gardens and Landscapes in Eighteenth-Century South Carolina," 151–52 (quotation), 153. For self-conscious associations of gardens with literature and theater, see John Dixon Hunt, *The Figure in the Landscape: Poetry, Painting, and Gardening during the Eighteenth Century* (Baltimore, 1976); Maynard Mack, *The Garden and the City: Retirement and Politics in the Later Poetry of Pope, 1731–1743* (Toronto, 1969); and John Dixon Hunt, "Pope's Twickenham Revisited," in Maccubin and Martin, eds., *British and American Gardens*, 26–35.

44. Cummings, *Framed Houses of Massachusetts Bay*, 201; Richard M. Candee, *Housepaints in Colonial America: Their Materials, Manufacture and Application* (New York, n.d.); orig. pub. as "Housepaints in Colonial America," *Color Engineering* (Sept.–Oct. 1966; Nov.–Dec. 1966; Jan.–Feb. 1967; March–April 1967), 4, 5; Butler, "Another City upon a Hill: Litchfield, Connecticut, and the Colonial Revival," in Alan Axelrod, ed., *The Colonial Revival in America* (New York, 1985), 24, 29 (quotation), 30 (quotation), 31, 39.

45. Daniella Pearson, "Shirley-Eustis House Landscape History," *Old-Time New England*, 70 (1980): 3, 8, 11;

Rogers, "Gardens and Landscapes in Eighteenth-Century South Carolina," 151 (quotation); John Flowers, "People and Plants: North Carolina's Garden History Revisited," in Maccubbin and Martin, eds., *British and American Gardens,* 125 (quotation).

46. Cummings, *Framed Houses of Massachusetts Bay,* 200; Charles Arthur Hammond, " 'Where the Arts and the Virtues Unite': Country Life Near Boston, 1637–1864" (Ph.D. diss., Boston University, 1982), 81, 83; Emmet, "The Codman Estate," 6 (Faneuil quotation); Butler, "Another City upon a Hill," 24, 25, 31; Cummings, "Eighteenth-Century New England Garden Design," 134 (1794 quotation); Maccubbin and Martin, eds., *British and American Gardens,* plates 15, 18, 19, 22.

47. By the end of the century, the wealthiest farmers were attempting to civilize the farm outbuildings and form an array of structures that at least included house and horse barn. Outbuildings were painted, placed symmetrically in the yard, and cupolas mounted on the roofs. While John Adams was in Washington, Abigail suggested the construction of a new horse barn. Adams called it "a Moment of Foppery," but she built it anyway. Hammond, "Producing, Selecting, and Serving Food at the County Seat, 1730–1830," 83. Dell Upton, "New Views of the Virginia Landscape," *The Virginia Magazine of History and Biography,* 96 (Oct. 1988): 403–70, is a lengthy review essay of the work on Virginia architecture and gardening since 1970 that includes judgments on what we now know and do not know.

V. CITIES AND CHURCHES

1. Josiah Quincy, *Memoirs of the Life of Josiah Quincy, Junior, of Massachusetts, 1774–1775,* 2nd ed. (Boston, 1874), 95, 124–37. For a collection of comments on one city, Williamsburg, see John W. Reps, *Tidewater Towns: City Planning in Colonial Virginia and Maryland* (Williamsburg and Charlottesville, Va., 1972), 183–85.

2. John Arlott, ed., *England: A Coloured Facsimile of the Maps and Text from the Theatre of the Empire of Great Britaine,* 4 vols. (London, 1953–54 [orig. pub. 1611]); John W. Reps, *The Making of Urban America: A History of City Planning in the United States* (Princeton, 1965), 124–28, 131–50.

3. Quincy, *Memoirs,* 137; Anthony N. B. Garvan, *Architecture and Town Planning in Colonial Connecticut* (New Haven, 1951), 44–49; Reps, *Making of Urban America,* 130, 175–83; Reps, *Tidewater Towns,* 65–91; Sylvia Doughty Fries, *The Urban Idea in Colonial America* (Philadelphia, 1977), 65–68, 88–107. Fries speculates (pp. 64–68) that ideally Winthrop would have laid out a regular city for the capital of Massachusetts, using biblical models as prototypes.

4. Helen Resenau, *The Ideal City: Its Architectural Evolution* (New York, 1972), 48–73; Reps, *Making of Urban America,* 9–24.

5. Mark Girouard, *Cities and People: A Social and Architectural History* (New Haven, 1985), 119–21, 171–74, 178–79; John Summerson, *Georgian London,* 3rd. ed. (Cambridge, Mass., 1978), 29–37.

6. A. J. Youngson, *The Making of Classical Edinburgh: 1750–1840* (Edinburgh, 1975); Peter Borsay, *The English Urban Renaissance: Culture and Society in the Provincial Town, 1660–1770* (Oxford, 1989).

7. Girouard, *Cities and People,* 28, 140–41, 153. For examples of views of American cities with the shipping emphasized in the foreground, see John A. Kouwenhoven, *The Columbia Historical Portrait of New York: An Essay in Graphic History in Honor of the Tricentennial of New York City and the Bicentennial of Columbia University* (Garden City, N.Y., 1953), 45, 48–49, 52–53, 61.

8. Hugh Phillips, *Mid-Georgian London: A Topographical and Social Survey of Central and Western London about 1750* (London, 1964), 52–53.

9. Ibid., 215, 236; Girouard, *Cities and People,* 169, 172, 203; Resenau, *Ideal City,* 50.

10. Girouard, *Cities and People,* 151, 156; Reps, *Making of Urban America,* 11; Josef W. Konvitz, *Cities and the Sea: Port City Planning in Early Modern Europe* (Baltimore, 1978), 170–74; Summerson, *Georgian London,* 52–64.

11. Bordeaux had its Place Royale looking out directly on the docks, and the huge Place des Quinconces at the spatial center of the city. Frederick R. Hiorns, *Town-Building in History: An Outline Review of Conditions, Influences, Ideas, and Methods Affecting 'Planned' Towns Through Five Thousand Years* (London, 1956), 242. For port development, see Konvitz, *Cities and the Sea.* Dell Upton suggested the T-shape term as a description of regular town plans.

12. Reps, *Tidewater Towns,* 117–28. For Nicholson, see Dorothy Louise Noble, "Life of Francis Nicholson" (Ph.D. diss., Columbia University, 1958).

13. Ibid., 141–42; "Speeches of Students of the College of William and Mary Delivered May 1, 1699," *William and Mary Quarterly,* 2nd ser., 10 (1930): 323–27, 329.

14. Reps, *Tidewater Towns,* 146, 148, 177, 179.

15. Quotation from *A Short Advertisement upon the Situation and Extent of the City of Philadelphia and the Ensuing Plat-form thereof, by the Surveyor General* (London, 1683) in Fries, *Urban Idea in Colonial America,* 90–91; William Penn, *A Further Account of the Province of Pennsylvania* (London, 1685), in Albert Cook Myers, *Narratives of Early Pennsylvania, West New Jersey, and Delaware, 1630–1707* (New York, 1912), 242–44, 261–73; Reps, *Making of Urban America,* 161, 167, 169.

16. Reps, *Tidewater Towns,* 195 (quote), 196, 197, 198 (quote), 199, 201, 210, 211, 231, 194–230, passim; Richard Robbie Pillsbury, "The Urban Street Patterns of Pennsylvania Before 1815: A Study in Cultural Geography" (Ph.D. diss., Pennsylvania State University, 1968), 127.

17. Reps, *Making of Urban America*, 158, 180–82; Reps, *Tidewater Towns*, 233–38. For Dover town plan see figure 7 above.

18. Edward M. Riley, "The Independence Hall Group," in Luther P. Eisenhart, ed., *Historic Philadelphia from the Founding Until the Early Nineteenth Century: Papers Dealing with Its People and Buildings with an Illustrative Map*, Transactions of the American Philosophical Society, 43 (Philadelphia, 1953) I:7 (quote), 8, 9 (quote), 10, 16.

19. Walter Muir Whitehill, *Boston: A Topographical History*, 2nd ed. (Cambridge, Mass., 1968), 13–14, 20, 26, 27, 59–66; William DeLoss Love, *The Colonial History of Hartford Gathered from the Original Records* (Hartford, 1914), 221, 222, 224; John Hutchins Cady, *The Civic and Architectural Development of Providence, 1636–1950* (Providence, 1957), 37–38, 47, 19. Carl Bridenbaugh, *Cities in the Wilderness: The First Century of Urban Life in America, 1625–1742* (London, 1971 [orig. pub. 1938]), 326 (quote). New York erected its town hall in 1699 at the terminal point of Broad Street facing down the street toward the harbor. Work began on the new city hall in 1803, a building whose plan was believed to do "no less credit to the taste and talents of the architects, than it reflects honor on the judgement of the Corporation." Quoted in I. N. Phelps Stokes, *The Iconography of Manhattan Island, 1498–1909* (New York, 1915), 1:463. In Charleston the public buildings were first placed directly on the water, disregarding the open square provided in the original plan. In the 1750s a new Anglican church and the statehouse were built on the square, reviving its original civic importance. Frederick R. Stevenson and Carl Feiss, "Charleston and Savannah," *Journal of the Society of Architectural Historians*, 10 (Dec. 1951): 3–9; George C. Rogers, Jr., *Charleston in the Age of the Pinckneys* (Norman, Okla., 1969), 58. In Marblehead, Massachusetts, the market square was located at the head of King Street, which ran directly to the town wharf in almost exact imitation of Boston. A classically symmetrical town house was built there in 1727. Sidney Perley, *Marblehead in 1700* (Salem, Mass., 1912); Robert F. Trent, "Architecture and Society in Marblehead, Massachusetts, 1630–1820" (senior honors thesis, Boston University, 1972), 153, 157.

20. J. Smith Futhey and Gilbert Cope, *History of Chester County, Pennsylvania, with Genealogical and Biographical Sketches* (Philadelphia, 1881), 215 (quote); quote from *The Daily Advertiser* (New York), Nov. 23, 1790, in Stokes, *Iconography of Manhattan Island*, 1:381.

21. Gerald W. R. Ward, *The Assembly House* (Salem, Mass., 1976), 8 (quote), 9, 10; Hugh Morrison, *Early American Architecture: From the First Colonial Settlements to the National Period* (New York, 1952), 383.

22. Dell Upton, *Holy Things and Profane: Anglican Parish Churches in Colonial Virginia* (Cambridge, Mass., 1986), 219; Esther Singleton, *Social New York under the Georges, 1714–1776: Houses, Streets and Country Homes, with Chapters on Fashions, Furniture, China, Plate and Manners* (New York, 1902), 301, 302, 310, 311.

23. Massachusetts and Pennsylvania quotations in Kym S. Rice, *Early American Taverns: For the Entertainment of Friends and Strangers* (Chicago, 1983), 26, 29–30; L. H. Butterfield, Leonard C. Faber, and Wendell D. Garrett, eds., *Diary and Autobiography of John Adams. Vol. 1: Diary 1755–1770* (Cambridge, Mass., 1961), 129; Robert Earle Graham, "The Taverns of Colonial Philadelphia," in Eisenhart, ed., *Historic Philadelphia*, 318.

24. Stokes, *Iconography of Manhattan Island*, 6:616; Rice, *Early American Taverns*, xv; Cady, *Civic and Architectural Development of Providence*, 37; M. S. Ball, *Pathways of the Puritans* (Framingham, Mass.), 100, 101. On the culture of common taverns, see Peter Clark, "The Alehouse and the Alternative Society," in D. Pennington and K. Thomas, eds., *Puritans and Revolutionaries* (Oxford, 1978), 47–72; and David W. Conroy, "In Public Houses: Drink and Community in Colonial and Revolutionary Massachusetts" (Ph.D. diss., University of Connecticut, 1987).

25. Graham, "Taverns of Colonial Philadelphia," in Eisenhart, ed., *Historic Philadelphia*, 320–21; Stokes, *Iconography of Manhattan Island*, 1:618.

26. Rice, *Early American Taverns*, 32, 33; Graham, "Taverns of Colonial Philadelphia," 322–24; Stokes, *Iconography of Manhattan Island*, 1:195, 422, 611. For a view of Broadway near Trinity Church in 1799, ibid., 1: plate 68a.

27. Harold E. Davis, *The Fledgling Province: Social and Cultural Life in Colonial Georgia, 1733–1776* (Chapel Hill, N.C., 1976), 191; Henry Wansey, *An Excursion to the United States of North America in 1794* (Salisbury, 1798), 119, quoted in Graham, "Taverns of Colonial Philadelphia," 323–24; Stokes, *Iconography of Manhattan Island*, 6:611, 618; Cady, *Civic and Architectural Development of Providence*, 55. The first two great hotels in America, Tremont House in Boston (1829) and the Astor in New York (1836,) raised the standard to a still higher level. Both fashioned magnificent public rooms off grand entry halls, and both were situated at the most glamorous locations, the Astor on Broadway and Tremont House facing the Common across from the Massachusetts capitol amidst the city's finest residences. Jefferson Williamson, *The American Hotel: An Anecdotal History* (New York, 1930), 13–37.

28. Girouard, *Cities and People*, 124, 175, 178, 186, 189–93.

29. Norman Arthur Benson, "The Itinerant Dancing and Music Masters of Eighteenth-Century America" (Ph.D. diss., University of Minnesota, 1963), 177 (quote); Reps, *Making of Urban America*, 141; Fries, *Urban Idea in Colonial America*, 97; Stokes, *Iconography of Manhattan Island*, 1:195 (quote).

30. Stokes, *Iconography of Manhattan Island*, 1:372, 373, 382, 384–85, 400, 425; 6:517; Whitehill, *Boston: A Topographical History*, 15; John Drayton, "View of the Battery, 1793," in Kouwenhoven, *Columbia Historical Portrait of New York*, 88. The larger trees in Bowling Green, seen in Archibald Robertson's drawing of New York in 1791, suggest it had been landscaped a decade or so longer than the Battery. Ibid., 87. The unfinished

state of the Battery is evident from a 1793 engraving, but the presence of a dozen or more genteel strollers in the scene clearly identifies the park's purpose. The Trinity churchyard in New York City had railed walks, benches, and lamps in the trees for evening promenades. Stokes, *Iconography of Manhattan Island*,, 1: plate 55b, 328. In Edinburgh, the equivalent of Broadway in New York or Bond Street in London was High Street, where Smollett in 1776 saw "all the people of business in Edinburgh, and even the genteel company . . . standing in crowds every day, from one to two in the afternoon." Quoted in Youngson, *The Making of Classical Edinburgh*, 53.

31. For scenes of life on genteel streets and the mingling of classes in the city, see Kouwenhoven, *Columbia Historical Portrait of New York*, 83, 102, 107, 108, 119; William Birch, *The City of Philadelphia in the State of Pennsylvania North America; as it appeared in the Year 1800* . . . (Philadelphia, 1800). On mobs in the best streets, see Stokes, *Iconography of Manhattan Island*, 1:310, 311; Riley, "The Independence Hall Group," 10, 25n.

32. Alexander Graydon, *Memoirs of His Own Time. With Reminiscences of the Men and Events of the Revolution*, ed. John Stockton Littell (Philadelphia, 1846), 82.

33. Ann Ridgely, Dover, to Ann Ridgely, Philadelphia, Jan. 24, 1799, folder 134, Ridgely Collection, Hall of Records, Dover, Del.; John Gay, *Trivia: or, the Art of Walking the Streets of London* (London, 1716), tells of the various characters to be met on the street and the precautions to be taken with each. William Burgis's 1717 view of New York depicts two genteel couples on the ferry dock in Brooklyn. Kouwenhoven, *Columbia Historical Portrait of New York*, 54, 83.

34. Robert W. Shoemaker, "Christ Church, St. Peter's, and St. Paul's," in Eisenhart, ed., *Historic Philadelphia*, 190, 193. A visitor to New York in 1716 claimed there were but two coaches in the entire province. Kouwenhoven, *Columbia Historical Portrait of New York*, 55. In fashionable London and Bath sedan chairs and hackney cabs were available for hire after midcentury. P. J. Corfield, *The Impact of English Towns, 1700–1800* (Oxford, 1982), 171. The separation of polite and vulgar cultures in English provincial towns is discussed in Peter Borsay, " 'All the Town's a Stage': Urban Ritual and Ceremony, 1660–1800," in Peter Clark, ed., *The Transformation of English Provincial Towns, 1600–1800* (London, 1984), 246–52.

35. Girouard, *Cities and People*, 143, 167, 175, 176, 187, 189, 190, 191. For the Brooklyn street front, see Francis Guy, "View from No. 11 Fulton Street," in Kouwenhoven, *Columbia Historical Portrait of New York*, 108; Futhey and Cope, *History of Chester County*, 215. Paving was not common in smaller towns in the colonial period. The main street of Hartford was unpaved until 1790 or 1791, when the town voted to cover it with stone. John Warner Barber, *Connecticut Historical Collections* (New Haven, 1836), 50.

36. George Francis Dow, *The Arts and Crafts in New England, 1704–1775: Gleanings from Boston Newspapers Relating to Painting, Engraving, Silversmiths, Pewterers, Clockmakers, Furniture, Pottery, Old Houses, Costume, Trades and Occupations* . . . (Topsfield, Mass., 1927), xvi; John W. Reps, "Boston by Bostonians: The Printed Plans and Views of the Colonial City by Its Artists, Cartographers, Engravers, and Publishers," Massachusetts Colonial Society Publication, *Boston Prints and Printmakers, 1670–1775* (Boston, 1973), 33–55; Stokes, *Iconography of Manhattan Island*, 1: plates 25, 31.

37. Marian Card Donnelly, *The New England Meeting Houses of the Seventeenth Century* (Middletown, Conn., 1968), 16, 18, 66, 74–77, 79, 92.

38. Morrison, *Early American Architecture*, 430–31; Abbott L. Cummings, "Meeting and Dwelling House: Interrelationships in Early New England," in Peter Benes and Philip Zimmerman, eds., *New England Meeting House and Church: 1630–1850* (Boston, n.d.), 6; Bettina H. Norton, "Anglican Embellishments: The Contributions of John Gibbs, Junior, and William Price to the Church of England in Eighteenth-Century Boston," ibid., 70.

39. Morrison, *Early American Architecture*, 433–34; Harold Wickliffe Rose, *The Colonial Houses of Worship in America Built in the English Colonies before the Republic, 1607–1789, and Still Standing* (New York, 1963), 114–29, 149–57, 202–58, 400–19. The transition in church architecture was worked out by Charles A. Place in three articles: "From Meeting House to Church in New England," *Old-Time New England*, 13 (Oct. 1922): 69–77; "From Meeting House to Church in New England. II. The Eighteenth Century Meeting House," *Old-Time New England*, 13 (Jan. 1923): 111–23; "From Meeting House to Church in New England: III. Eighteenth Century Churches," *Old-Time New England*, 13 (April 1923): 149–64. See also Edmund W. Sinnott, *Meeting House and Church in Early New England* (New York, 1963). On seventeenth-century decoration, see Robert F. Trent, "The Marblehead Pews," in Benes and Zimmerman, eds., *New England Meeting House and Church*, 101–11; Stokes, *Iconography of Manhattan Island*, 1:415 (*New York Magazine* quote). The first New England meetinghouses to follow the longitudinal orientation were the second Brattle Street meetinghouse, 1772–73, and the First Baptist Church in Providence, 1775. Place, "From Meeting House to Church in New England: III," 155, 159.

40. Morrison, *Early American Architecture*, 414, 442–44, 537, 552; S. Charles Bolton, *Southern Anglicanism: The Church of England in Colonial South Carolina* (Westport, Conn., 1982), 42 (quote); Harley J. McKee, "St. Michael's Church, Charleston, 1752–1762," *Journal of the Society of Architectural Historians*, 23 (March 1964): 39–42.

41. Clifford K. Shipton, *Biographical Sketches of Those Who Attended Harvard College in the Classes 1690–1700 with*

Bibliographical and Other Notes: Sibley's Harvard Graduates, Volume IV, 1690–1700 (Cambridge, Mass., 1933), 13 (quote), 124, 128 (quote). For the organization of the Brattle Street Church against the background of provincial doubt, see David D. Hall, *The Faithful Shepherd: A History of the New England Ministry in the Seventeenth Century* (Chapel Hill, N.C., 1972), 271–73; Robert Middlekauf, *The Mathers: Three Generations of Puritan Intellectuals, 1596–1728* (New York, 1971), 219–20; and Perry Miller, *The New England Mind: From Colony to Province* (Cambridge, Mass., 1953), 240–42.

42. Clifford K. Shipton, *Biographical Sketches of Those Who Attended Harvard College in the Classes 1701–1712 with Bibliographical and Other Notes: Sibley's Harvard Graduates, Volume V, 1701–1712* (Boston, 1937), 344 (quote), 346 (quote).

43. Donald Richard Friary, "The Architecture of the Anglican Churches in the Northern American Colonies: A Study of Religious, Social, and Cultural Expression" (Ph.D. diss., University of Pennsylvania, 1971), xcv, 376–77 (quote); John Frederick Woolverton, *Colonial Anglicanism in North America* (Detroit, 1984), 89; Shoemaker, "Christ Church, St. Peter's, and St. Paul's," 188 (quote from *Pennsylvania Packet*, Jan. 13, 1772); John Tyler, *The Sanctity of a Christian Temple: Illustrated in a Sermon, At the Opening of Trinity-Church, in Pomfret, On Friday, April 12, 1771* (Providence, 1761 [sic]), 13–14 (quote). For further tabulations of church buildings, see Frederick V. Mills, Sr., *Bishops by Ballot: An Eighteenth-Century Ecclesiastical Revolution* (New York, 1978), 12.

44. Herbert and Carol Schneider, eds., *Samuel Johnson, President of King's College: His Career and Writings* (New York, 1929), 1:5 (quote), 7 (quote); Shipton, *Biographical Sketches, IV,* 127; Miller, *The New England Mind,* 334–35, 469–70, 473. For Samuel Johnson, see Joseph J. Ellis, *The New England Mind in Transition: Samuel Johnson of Connecticut, 1696–1772* (New Haven, 1973).

45. Ola Elizabeth Winslow, *Meetinghouse Hill: 1630–1783* (New York, 1952), 150–67; Gilbert Chase, *America's Music: From the Pilgrims to the Present,* 3rd ed., rev. (Urbana, Ill., 1987), 19–34; Benson, "Itinerant Dancing and Music Masters," 332, 343–47, 383; Friary, "The Architecture of the Anglican Churches," 222. Stiles did not include German and Dutch churches in his survey, for they installed organs from early in the century. Benson, "Itinerant Dancing and Music Masters," 184, 191, 192, 222, 272, 279. On organs, see Barbara Owen, *The Organ in New England: An Account of Its Use and Manufacture to the End of the Nineteenth Century* (Raleigh, N.C., 1979).

46. Chase, *America's Music,* 38–39; Sinnott, *Meeting House and Church in Early New England,* 37. On architectural changes in general, see G. W. O. Addleshaw and Frederick Etchells, *The Architectural Setting of Anglican Worship: An Inquiry into the Arrangements for Public Worship in the Church of England from the Reformation to the Present Day* (London, 1948), 15–120.

47. Jane C. Nylander, "Toward Comfort and Uniformity in New England Meeting Houses, 1750–1850," in Benes and Zimmerman, eds., *New England Meeting House and Church,* 93, 96, 97; Trent, "The Marblehead Pews," 110; Sinnott, *Meeting House and Church in Early New England,* 6, 32, 34, 44, 48, 54; Place, "From Meeting House to Church in New England," 76; Place, "From Meeting House to Church in New England, II," 112–14, 117–20; Peter Benes, "Sky Colors and Scattered Clouds: The Decorative and Architectural Painting of New England Meeting Houses, 1738–1834," in Benes and Zimmerman, eds., *New England Meeting House and Church,* 59, 67; Nathaniel Shurtleff, *A Topographical and Historical Description of Boston* (Boston, 1871), 69–70. Pulpits had first become universal in English parish churches in the seventeenth century. The Providence Presbyterian church in Louisa County, Virginia, built in 1750, and lovingly but plainly decorated, originally had no pulpit. Upton, *Holy Things and Profane,* 50, 191–92.

48. Abbott Cummings argues that churches and meetinghouses in Boston lagged behind the houses stylistically in the first part of the eighteenth century. Cummings, "Meeting and Dwelling House: Interrelationships in Early New England," in Benes and Zimmerman, eds., *New England Meeting House and Church,* 4–17.

49. Upton, *Holy Things and Profane,* 12, 39, 61, 83, 108–10, 160 (quote), 164 (quote). The William Burgis view of the newly constructed New Dutch Church in New York City, 1731, with a high tower and spire, suggests how urban churches in other cities responded to the challenge to erect spires. Kouwenhoven, *Columbia Historical Portrait of New York,* 56.

50. The Fayerweather quote is in Sinnott, *Meeting House and Church in Early New England,* 184; the Robin quote is in Shurtleff, *Topographical and Historical Description of Boston,* 71; Jane C. Nylander, "Textiles, Clothing, and Needlework," in Gerald W. R. Ward and William N. Hosley, eds., *The Great River: Art and Society of the Connecticut Valley, 1635–1820* (Hartford, 1985), 374–77. On genteel theatricality in Virginia churches, see Upton, *Holy Things and Profane,* 204–5.

VI. AMBIVALENCE

1. [James Forrester] *The Polite Philosopher: or, an Essay on that Art, which Makes a Man happy in Himself, and agreeable to Others* (London, reprinted New York, 1758), 7.

2. Steven R. Pendery, "The Archeology of Urban Foodways in Portsmouth, New Hampshire," in *Foodways in the Northeast,* Dublin Seminar for New England Folklife: Annual Proceedings 1982 (Boston, 1984), 27; Charles Woodmason, *The Carolina Backcountry on the Eve of the Revolution: The Journal and Other Writings of Charles Woodmason, Anglican Itinerant,* ed. Richard J. Hooker (Chapel Hill, N.C., 1953), 6; Douglas Southall Freeman,

George Washington: A Biography (New York, 1948), 1:238; George Francis Dow, *The Arts and Crafts in New England, 1704–1775: Gleanings from Boston Newspapers Relating to Painting, Engraving, Silversmiths, Pewterers, Clockmakers, Furniture, Pottery, Old Houses, Costume, Trades and Occupations . . .* (Topsfield, Mass., 1927), 162.

3. Adams quote from Merrill Jensen, *The Founding of a Nation: A History of the American Revolution, 1763–1776* (New York, 1968), 428.

4. Benjamin Franklin, *The Autobiography of Benjamin Franklin*, ed. Leonard W. Labaree, Ralph L. Ketcham, Helen C. Boatfield, and Helene H. Fineman (New Haven, 1964), 145.

5. Lois Green Carr and Lorena W. Walsh, "Changing Life Styles in Colonial St. Mary's County, Maryland," *Working Papers from the Regional Economic History Research Center*, 1 (1978); Lois Green Carr and Lorena S. Walsh, "Changing Life Styles and Consumer Behavior in the Colonial Chesapeake," in *Of Consuming Interests: Styles of Life in the Eighteenth Century* (Charlottesville, Va., forthcoming 1992), tables 1A, 1E, 1F; Carole Shammas, "The Domestic Environment in Early Modern England and America," *Journal of Social History*, 14 (Fall 1980): 12, 13. See also Carole Shammas, *The Pre-Industrial Consumer in England and America* (Oxford, 1990), and Lorna Weatherill, *Consumer Behaviour and Material Culture in Britain, 1660–1760* (London, 1988), 80.

6. L. H. Butterfield, Wendell D. Garrett, and Marjorie E. Sprague, eds., *Adams Family Correspondence* (Cambridge, Mass., 1963), 1:49.

7. Kym S. Rice, *Early American Taverns: For the Entertainment of Friends and Strangers* (Chicago, 1983), 100, 101, 113; L. H. Butterfield, Leonard C. Faber, and Wendell D. Garrett, eds., *The Diary and Autobiography of John Adams* (Cambridge, Mass., 1961), 1:47.

8. Statement from the Committee on the Theater to the Massachusetts General Court, 1791, quoted in Norman Arthur Benson, "The Itinerant Dancing and Music Masters of Eighteenth-Century America" (Ph.D. diss., University of Minnesota, 1963), 364. The degree of gentility divided Freemasonry into Ancient and Modern orders. Steven C. Bullock, "The Revolutionary Transformation of American Freemasonry, 1752–1792," *William and Mary Quarterly*, 3rd. ser., 47 (July 1990): 347–69.

9. *Columbian Centinel*, Dec. 8, 1792, quoted in ibid.

10. Gertrude E. Noyes, *Bibliography of Courtesy and Conduct Books in Seventeenth-Century England* (New Haven, 1937), 4.

11. Benson, "Itinerant Dancing and Music Masters," 214, 336–37 (quote), 350–51 (quote), 351–53 (quote, Boston *Gazette*, Nov. 20, 1732); S. Charles Bolton, *Southern Anglicanism: The Church of England in Colonial South Carolina* (Westport, Conn., 1982), 51; Edmund Hayes, "Mercy Otis Warren Versus Lord Chesterfield, 1779," *William and Mary Quarterly*, 40 (Oct. 1983): 616–21.

12. John Trumbull, "The Progress of Dulness," in *The Satiric Poems of John Trumbull*, ed. Edwin T. Bowden (Austin, Tex., 1962), 53, 56–57.

13. Ibid., 58–59, 63.

14. Dr. Gregory, *A Father's Legacy To His Daughters* (Portsmouth, N.H., 1786), 97; *The American Museum* (Philadelphia), Jan. 1787, 12–13; June 1787, 550–52.

15. John Trumbull, "The Progress of Dulness: Part Third: The Adventures of Miss Harriet Simper," in Bowden, ed., *The Satiric Poems of John Trumbull*, 77–80.

16. Ibid., 66–67.

17. *Sans Souci, Alias Free and Easy: or an Evening's Peep into a Polite Circle, an Intire New Entertainment: In Three Acts* (Boston, 1785). For the Sans Souci controversy, see Charles Warren, "Samuel Adams and the Sans Souci Club in 1785," Massachusetts Historical Society, *Proceedings*, 3rd ser., 60 (1926–27), and Gordon S. Wood, *The Creation of the American Republic, 1776–1787* (Chapel Hill, N.C., 1969), 421–23.

18. *Sans Souci*, 3, 4, 7, 9, 11–12, 20.

19. Ibid., 4, 18, 19.

20. *The American Museum* (Philadelphia), Jan. 1787: 11–13, 66–67, 119; June 1787: 536–37, 549–52. Discussions of the anti-luxury literature can be found in Neil Harris, *The Artist in American Society: The Formative Years, 1790–1860*, rev. ed. (Chicago, 1982), 30–33; and Kenneth Silverman, *A Cultural History of the American Revolution: Painting, Music, Literature, and the Theatre in the Colonies and the United States from the Treaty of Paris to the Inauguration of George Washington, 1763–1789* (New York, 1976), 505–16.

21. Timothy Dwight, "Greenfield Hill: A Poem in Seven Parts" (New York, 1794), in *The Major Poems of Timothy Dwight (1752–1817) with A Dissertation on the History, Eloquence, and Poetry of the Bible*, ed. William J. McTaggart and William K. Bottorff (Gainesville, Fla., 1969), 384, 385, 389, 399, 401, 412, 513.

22. Ibid., 382–83, 402, 411, 414, 415, 523. For the tradition lying behind pastoralism, see Leo Marx, *The Machine in the Garden: Technology and the Pastoral Ideal in America* (New York, 1964).

23. Dwight, "Greenfield Hill," 402.

24. Pittsfield *Sun*, Aug. 5, 1809; Edward Augustus Kendall, *Travels*, 3:10, quoted in Charles Arthur Hammond, "'Where the Arts and the Virtues Unite': Country Life Near Boston, 1637–1864" (Ph.D. diss., Boston University, 1982), 125.

25. Hammond, " 'Where the Arts and the Virtues Unite,' " passim; William N. Hosley, "Architecture," in Gerald W. R. Ward and William N. Hosley, eds., *The Great River: Art and Society of the Connecticut Valley, 1635–1820* (Hartford, 1985), 66–68, 118; *Connecticut Courant*, Mar. 2, 1808 (quote); William N. Hosley, Jr., "Architecture and Society of the Urban Frontier: Windsor, Vermont, in 1800," in *The Bay and the River: 1600–1900*, Dublin Seminar for New England Folklife: Annual Proceedings, June 13 and 14, 1981, ed. Peter Benes (Boston, 1982), 73–86; Elizabeth M. Kornhauser and Christine S. Schloss, "Paintings and Other Pictorial Arts," in Ward and Hosley, eds., *The Great River*, 137; George S. Roberts, *River Towns of the Connecticut River Valley* (Schenectady, N.Y., 1906), 185 (quote).

26. John Adams to Abigail Smith, Braintree, Feb. 14, 1763, and Boston, May 7, 1764; Abigail Smith to John Adams, Weymouth, May 9, 1764; John Adams to Richard Cranch, Sept. 23, 1767, in Butterfield et al., eds., *Adams Family Correspondence*, 1:3, 44–47.

27. John Adams to Abigail Adams, Falmouth, July 7, 1774; John Adams to Abigail Adams, York, June 29, 1774; John Adams to Abigail Adams [Philadelphia], April 14, 1776; John Adams to Abigail Adams, Falmouth, July 5–6, 1774, in ibid., 1:130–31, 114, 382, 125.

28. Abigail Adams to John Adams, Braintree, Mar. 16, 1776; John Adams to Abigail Adams, Aug. 4, 1776, in ibid., 1:359; 2:75–76. John apparently discouraged Abigail's interest in Chesterfield, as she wrote a month later that "I give up my Request for Chesterfields Letters submitting intirely to your judgment." Abigail Adams to John Adams, April 21, 1776, in ibid., 1:389.

29. John Adams to Abigail Adams, Passy, April 12, 1778, in L. H. Butterfield, Marc Friedlaender, and Mary-Jo Kline, eds., *The Book of Abigail and John: Selected Letters of the Adams Family, 1762–1784* (Cambridge, Mass., 1975), 210.

30. John Adams to Abigail Adams, Passy, April 25, 1778; John Adams to Abigail Adams, Passy, June 3, 1778; John Adams to Abigail Adams, Passy, July 26, 1778; Abigail Adams to John Adams [Braintree], Feb. 13, 1779; John Adams to Abigail Adams, Passy, Feb. 13, 1779; John Adams to Abigail Adams, Passy, Feb. 21, 1779, in ibid., 211, 217, 222, 236, 238, 240.

31. John Adams to John Quincy Adams, Amsterdam, Dec. 28, 1780; John Adams to John Quincy Adams, Paris, May 14, 1783, in Butterfield et al., eds., *The Book of Abigail and John*, 284, 349. In 1771 he was pleased when his wife's sister and her husband decided against dancing lessons for their children, since, as Adams said, "I never knew a good Dancer good for any Thing else." On the other hand, he held back judgment for himself. "I would not however conclude, peremptorily, against sending Sons or Daughters to dancing, or Fencing, or Musick," so long as they did not grow overfond of them. L. H. Butterfield, Leonard C. Faber, and Wendell D. Garrett, eds., *Diary and Autobiography of John Adams.* Vol. 2: *Diary 1771–1781* (Cambridge, Mass., 1961), 46.

32. Ada Lou Carson and Herbert L. Carson, *Royall Tyler* (Boston, 1979), 15–17; Abigail Adams to John Adams [Braintree], Dec. 23, 1782, in Butterfield et al., eds., *The Book of Abigail and John*, 334.

33. John Adams to Abigail Adams, Paris, Jan. 22, 1783; John Adams to Abigail Adams, Paris, Jan. 29, 1783, in Butterfield et al., eds., *The Book of Abigail and John*, 338, 340, 390; Carson and Carson, *Royall Tyler*, 17–18 (quote), 19–20 (quote).

34. John Adams to Abigail Adams, Philadelphia, Aug. 14, 1776; John Adams to Abigail Adams [Paris, April–May 1780], in Butterfield et al., eds., *The Book of Abigail and John*, 156, 256.

35. John Adams to Abigail Adams, June 17, 1780, in Butterfield et al., eds., *The Book of Abigail and John*, 260, 261; Wilhelmina S. Harris, *Adams National Historic Site: A Family's Legacy to America* (Washington, D.C., 1983), 6, 7, 9, 47, 50.

36. *The American Museum* (Philadelphia), Jan. 1787: 11–13, 66–67 (quote); June 1787: 549–53.

VII. VERNACULAR GENTILITY IN RURAL DELAWARE

1. *The Delaware Register and Farmers' Magazine* (Dover), 2 (July–Jan. 1839): 186.

2. *The Delaware Register and Farmers' Magazine*, 1 (Feb.–July 1838): 195, 196; Kevin M. Sweeney, "Mansion People: Kinship, Class, and Architecture in Western Massachusetts in the Mid Eighteenth Century," *Winterthur Portfolio* 19 (Winter 1984): 250–54; Robert Blair St. George, "Artifacts of Regional Consciousness in the Connecticut River Valley," in Gerald W. R. Ward and William N. Hosley, eds., *The Great River: Art and Society of the Connecticut River Valley, 1635–1820* (Hartford, 1985), 35–37; Ronald Dale Karr, "The Evolution of an Elite Suburb: Community Structure and Control in Brookline, Massachusetts, 1770–1900" (Ph.D. diss., Boston University, 1981), 100–11.

3. Leon deValinger and Virginia Shaw, eds., *A Calendar of Ridgely Family Letters, 1742–1899, in the Delaware State Archives* (Dover, Del., 1948–61), 2:12, 17–18, 87–88.

4. J. Thomas Scharf, *History of Delaware: 1609–1888* (Philadelphia, 1888), 2:1031; Kent County Probate Records, Henry M. Ridgely, 1847–49, Hall of Records, Dover; deValinger and Shaw, eds., *A Calendar of Ridgely Family Letters*, 2:263, 267.

5. DeValinger and Shaw, eds, *Calendar of Ridgely Family Letters*, 2:87–89; Chancellor Nicholas Ridgely,

Dover, May 11, 1827, to Elizabeth Ridgely, Philadelphia, folder 217, and Mrs. Henry M. Ridgely, Dover, Jan. 20, 1828, to Elizabeth Ridgely, Philadelphia, folder 218; Charles George Ridgely, Philadelphia, to Elizabeth Ridgely, Dover, May 7, 1829, folder 219; Charles George Ridgely, Lebanon, to Elizabeth Ridgely, Dover, Aug. 12, 1829, folder 219, Ridgely Collection, Hall of Records, Dover, hereafter cited as Ridgely Collection.

6. deValinger and Shaw, eds., *A Calendar of Ridgely Family Letters*, 2:260–61; Lover, Philadelphia, to Elizabeth Ridgely, Sunday, Nov. 1828, folder 218; Chancellor Nicholas Ridgely, Dover, May 11, 1827, to Elizabeth Ridgely, Philadelphia, folder 217; Elizabeth Ridgely, Philadelphia, to Henry M. Ridgely, Washington, Feb. 2, 1828, folder 253; anonymous love poem to Elizabeth Ridgely, folder 219; William Huffington, New Castle, to Elizabeth Ridgely, Dover, May 10, 1830, folder 219, Ridgely Collection.

7. deValinger and Shaw, eds., *A Calendar of Ridgely Family Letters*, 3:62–64; Nicholas Ridgely, Dover, to Mrs. Charles du Pont, Wilmington, May 25, 1841, folder 44; Henry Ridgely, Dover, to Ann du Pont, Wilmington, June 10, 1841, folder 44; Mrs. Charles du Pont, Wilmington, to Nicholas Ridgely, Greensborough, Dec. 8, 1843, folder 295; Henry Ridgely, Dover, to Mrs. Charles du Pont, Wilmington, June 5, 1841, folder 44; Mrs. Mary B. Couper, New Castle, to Nicholas Ridgely, Dover, Jan. 14, 1842, folder 292, Ridgely Collection.

8. Nicholas Ridgely, Dover, to Mrs. Charles du Pont, Wilmington, May 25, 1841, folder 44, Ridgely Collection; deValinger and Shaw, eds., *Calendar of the Ridgely Family Letters*, 2:262–68; 3:140–47.

9. Quoted in deValinger and Shaw, eds., *Calendar of Ridgely Family Letters*, 2:66.

10. Ibid., 3:191; Henry M. Ridgely, Washington, to Sally Ridgely, Dover, Nov. 17, 1811, folder 266; Charles George Ridgely, Philadelphia, to Elizabeth Ridgely, Dover, May 7, 1829, folder 219; Charles George Ridgely, Philadelphia, to Elizabeth Ridgely, Dover, March 21, 1829, folder 219, Ridgely Collection.

11. deValinger and Shaw, eds., *The Calendar of Ridgely Family Letters*, 2:167, 168; Charles George Ridgely, Dover, to Henry M. Ridgely, Washington, Dec. 12, 1812, folder 244; Charles G. Ridgely, Dover, to Henry M. Ridgely, Washington, Jan. 3, 1812, folder 242; Henry M. Ridgely, Washington, to Sally Ridgely, Dover, April 12, 1812. folder 268; Sally Ridgely, Dover, to Henry M. Ridgely, Washington, July 21, 1813, folder 246; Sally Ridgely, Dover, Dec. 19, 1827, to Elizabeth Ridgely, Philadelphia, folder 218; Sally Ridgely, Dover, to Elizabeth Ridgely, Philadelphia, Feb. 24, 1828, folder 218, Ridgely Collection.

12. Charles George Ridgely, Dover, to Henry M. Ridgely, Washington, March 1, 1812, folder 243; Charles G. Ridgely, Dover, to Henry M. Ridgely, Washington, Jan. 3, 1812, folder 242; Aunt Morris, Dover, to Charles George Ridgely, Baltimore, Sept. 30, 1816, folder 150; Sally Ridgely, Dover, to Miss Flizabeth Ridgely, Philadelphia, March 26, 1877, folder 217, Nicholas Ridgely, Dover, to Mrs. Charles du Pont, Wilmington, May 25, 1841, folder 44; Daniel M. Bates, Wilmington, to Nicholas Ridgely, Dover, April 29, 1840, folder 289, Ridgely Collection.

13. Henry M. Ridgely, Washington, to Charles George Ridgely, Dover, July 18, 1813, folder 150; Mrs. Henry Ridgely, Dover, to Elizabeth Ridgely, Philadelphia, Sept. 1827, folder 217, Ridgely Collection.

14. Mrs. Henry M. Ridgely, Dover, to Elizabeth Ridgely, Dover, Jan. 13, 1828, folder 218; Henry Moore Ridgely, Washington, to Charles George Ridgely, Dover, Nov. 29, 1812, folder 150; Henry Moore Ridgely, Washington, to Ann Ridgely, Dover, Feb. 27, 1827, folder 140; Henry Moore Ridgely, Washington, to Charles George Ridgely, Dover, March 29, 1812, folder 150; Henry M. Ridgely, Washington, to Charles George Ridgely, Dover, July 18, 1813, folder 150, Ridgely Collection. Henry purposely misspelled "Iliad" as an exercise for Charles to catch the error.

15. Henry Moore Ridgely, Washington, to Charles George Ridgely, Dover, Nov. 29, 1812, folder 150; Henry Moore Ridgely, Washington, to Charles George Ridgely, Dover, June 27, 1813, folder 150; Henry Moore Ridgely, Washington, to Charles George Ridgely, Dover, Feb. 23, 1812, folder 150; Mrs. Henry Ridgely, Dover, to Elizabeth Ridgely, Philadelphia, Nov. 19, 1827, folder 217; B. B. Comegys, Philadelphia, to Nicholas Ridgely, Dover, May 8, 1840, folder 289; Elizabeth Wilson, Wilmington, to Sally Banning, Camden, Dec. 27, 1800, folder 5, Ridgely Collection; Kent County Probate Records, Henry Moore Ridgely, 1847–49, Hall of Records, Dover.

16. Sally Ridgely, Dover, to Henry M. Ridgely, Washington, Dec. 15, 1811, folder 242; Sally Ridgely, Dover, to Henry M. Ridgely, Washington, July 21, 1813, folder 246; Henry M. Ridgely, Dover, to Sally Ridgely, Wilmington, Sept. 25, 1808, folder 265; Ann Ridgely, Dover, to Elizabeth Ridgely, Philadelphia, Dec. 19, 1827, folder 218; Ann Ridgely, Dover, to Elizabeth Ridgely, Philadelphia, Dec. 19, 1827, folder 218; Sally Ridgely, Dover, to Henry M. Ridgely, Washington, Feb. 23, 1812, folder 242; Sally Ridgely, Dover, to Elizabeth Ridgely, Philadelphia, Dec. 12, 1827, folder 218; Sally Ridgely, Dover, to Elizabeth Ridgely, Philadelphia, Jan. 4, 1828, folder 218, Ridgely Collection.

17. S[ally] R[idgely] to Henry M. Ridgely, Dover, June 14, 1805, folder 237; Henry M. Ridgely, Washington, to Sally Ridgely, Dover, Feb. 21, 1815; Henry M. Ridgely, Washington, to Sally Ridgely, Dover, Jan. 29, 1815, folder 270; Charles G. Ridgely, Philadelphia, to Elizabeth Ridgely, Dover, Dec. 18, 1828, folder 218, Ridgely Collection; Nicholas Van Dyke to Mrs. Delia Stockton, Nov. 7, 1816, and Dorcas M. du Pont to Alfred W. Van Dyke, Jan. 15, 1825, quoted in Constance M. Cooper, "A Town Among Cities: New Castle, Delaware, 1780–1840" (Ph.D. diss., University of Delaware, 1983), 285.

18. Charles George Ridgely, Philadelphia, to Elizabeth Ridgely, Dover, March 5, 1829, folder 219, Ridgely Collection.
19. Elizabeth M. Davy, Philadelphia, to Sarah Ridgely, Dover, Oct. 6, 1834, folder 272; Mrs. Henry M. Ridgely, Dover, March 26, 1827, to Miss Elizabeth Ridgely, Philadelphia, folder 217; Charles George Ridgely, Philadelphia, to Elizabeth Ridgely, Dover, Dec. 12, 1828, folder 218; Sally Ridgely, Dover, to Elizabeth Ridgely, Philadelphia, April 27, 1831, folder 220, Ridgely Collection.
20. Sally Ridgely, Dover, to Elizabeth Ridgely, Philadelphia, June 14, 1831, folder 220; Charles G. Ridgely, Dover, to Henry M. Ridgely, Washington, Dec. 29, 1813, folder 247; Charles G. Ridgely, Dover, to Henry M. Ridgely, Washington, Jan. 30, 1813, folder 247; Charles George Ridgely, Philadelphia, to Elizabeth Ridgely, Dover, March 21, 1829, folder 219; E. Ridgely, Dover, to Mrs. Charles du Pont, Wilmington, Jan. 4, 1843, folder 48; Henry Ridgely, Philadelphia, to Ann Ridgely, Dover, June 3, 1837, folder 143, Ridgely Collection; deValinger and Shaw, eds., *A Calendar of Ridgely Family Letters*, 3:180.
21. Scharf, *History of Delaware*, 2:1064, 1066, 1134; Henry Ridgely, Dover, to Ann Ridgely, New Castle, June 14, 1833, folder 141; Henry Ridgely, Baltimore, to Ann Ridgely, Dover, Nov. 11, 1833, folder 141; Ridgely Collection; William Huffington, *The Delaware Register and Farmers' Magazine*, 2 vols. (Dover, 1839).
22. George Purnell Fisher, *Recollections of Dover in 1824*, ed. Joseph Brown Turner, Papers of the Historical Society of Delaware, 55 (Wilmington, n.d.).
23. Nicholas Ridgely, Dover, to Mrs. Charles du Pont, Wilmington, May 25, 1841, folder 44, Ridgely Collection; Scharf, *History of Delaware*, 2:1050, 1051.
24. Scharf, *History of Delaware*, 2:1068, 1099, 1104–5, 1106, 1114.
25. Charles G. Ridgely, Dover, to Henry M. Ridgely, Washington, March 6, 1814, folder 247, Ridgely Collection; deValinger and Shaw, eds., *Calendar of Ridgely Family Letters*, 2:83; Scharf, *History of Delaware*, 2:1119, 1195; George Theodore Welch, *Memoirs of Mary Parker Welch, 1818–1912*, ed. Dorothy Welch White (n.p., 1947), 91–92; Harold B. Hancock, *Bridgeville: A Community History of the Nineteenth Century* (Bridgeville, Del., 1985), 170.
26. Sally Ridgely, Wilmington, to Henry M. Ridgely, Dover, July 7, 1809, folder 239; Elizabeth McKee, Wilmington, to Sally Ridgely, Dover, Nov. 29, 1803, folder 264, Ridgely Collection; *Delaware State Journal* (Wilmington), July 14, 1840; William H. Conner, "The Life and Death of Wilmington's First Theatre," *Delaware History*, 5 (1952–53): 3–41; W. Emerson Wilson, ed., "Phoebe George Bradford Diaries," *Delaware History* 16 (1974–75): 8–9; Cooper, "A Town Among Cities," 195, 202, 204, 210, 258, 290, 291, 304, 309.
27. Figures on furniture makers tabulated from Harold B. Hancock, *Delaware Furniture Craftsmen, 1655–1800: A Directory* (Westerville, Ohio, 1980); Harold B. Hancock, *A History of Kent County, Delaware* (Dover, 1976), 22.
28. Kent County Tax Assessments, Duck Creek Hundred, 1852, Reel 1, Record Group 3535, Hall of Records, Dover; Document 20-06/78/4/4, Laura Gehringer, "Final Summary—1797 Tax Assessments for Kent County," Bureau of Museums, Division of Historical and Cultural Affairs, Dover.
29. Inventories of Charles Ridgely, Dec. 16, 1785, and Henry Moore Ridgely, Aug. 1, 1847, Kent County Probate Records, Hall of Records, Dover.
30. Mrs. Henry M. Ridgely, Dover, to Elizabeth Ridgely, Philadelphia, Dec. 17, 1827, folder 218; Mrs. Henry M. Ridgely, Dover, to Elizabeth Ridgely, Philadelphia, Jan. 4, 1828, folder 218; Henry Moore Ridgely, Washington, to Ann Ridgely, Dover, Feb. 27, 1827, folder 140; Charles G. Ridgely, Philadelphia, to Elizabeth Ridgely, Dover, Dec. 18, 1828, folder 218, Ridgely Collection.
31. White, ed., *Memoirs of Mary Parker Welch, 1818–1912*, 3, 7, 17.
32. Ibid., 25, 76, 88, 101, 120.
33. Ibid., 91, 101–2, 110, 118.

VIII. THE COMFORTS OF HOME

1. Milton E. Flower, *John Dickinson, Conservative Revolutionary* (Charlottesville, Va., 1983), 86–90, 282–84.
2. Tanya Boyett, "Thomas Handasyd Perkins: An Essay on Material Culture," *Old-Time New England*, 70 (1980): 45–62. For a circle of republican aristocrats in federal Boston, see Eleanor Pearson DeLorme, "The Swan Commissions: Four Portraits by Gilbert Stuart," *Winterthur Portfolio*, 14 (Winter 1979): 361–95.
3. For the development of high-class English suburbs in the early nineteenth century, see David Cannadine, *Lords and Landlords: The Aristocracy and the Towns, 1774–1967* (Leicester, 1980), 402–3; Peter Clark, "The Civic Leaders of Gloucester, 1580–1800," in Peter Clark, ed., *The Transformation of English Provincial Towns, 1600–1800* (London, 1984), 333. For American suburbs and country estates in the first half of the nineteenth century, see Henry C. Binford, *The First Suburbs: Residential Communities on the Boston Periphery, 1815–1860* (Chicago, 1985); Tamara Plakins Thornton, *Cultivating Gentlemen: The Meaning of Country Life among the Boston Elite, 1785–1860* (New Haven, 1989); and Charles Arthur Hammond, " 'Where the Arts and the Virtues Unite': Country Life Near Boston, 1637–1860" (Ph.D. diss., Boston University, 1982).
4. Andrew Jackson Downing, *The Architecture of Country Houses, Including Designs for Cottages, and Farm-Houses, and Villas, with Remarks on Interiors, Furniture, and the Best Modes of Warming and Ventilating* (New York, 1969 [orig. pub. 1850]), 257–58.

5. Catherine W. Bishir, Charlotte V. Brown, Carl R. Lounshunx, Ernest H. Wood, *Architects and Builders in North Carolina: A History of the Practice of Building* (Chapel Hill, N.C., 1990); Thomas T. Waterman and Frances Benjamin Johnston, *The Early Architecture of North Carolina* (Chapel Hill, N.C., 1947); Mills Lane, *Architecture of the Old South: North Carolina* (Savannah, Ga., 1985), 111, 137, 146.

6. Lane, *Architecture of the Old South*, 8, 150, 152, 220, 239–49. For the emergence of the architectural profession, see Dell Upton, "Pattern Books and Professionalism: Aspects of the Transformation of Domestic Architecture in America, 1800–1860," *Winterthur Portfolio*, 19 (Summer–Autumn, 1984): 107–50.

7. Upton, "Pattern Books and Professionalism," *Winterthur Portfolio* 19:108; Lane, *Architecture of the Old South*, 9, 181, 214. On the most notable of the builder authors, see Jack Quinan, "Asher Benjamin and American Architecture," *Journal of the Society of Architectural Historians*, 38 (Oct. 1979): 244–56. The books are listed in Henry Russell Hitchcock, *American Architectural Books* (Minneapolis, 1962).

8. Lewis F. Allen, *Rural Architecture. Being a Complete Description of Farm Houses, Cottages, and Out Buildings, Comprising Wood Houses, Workshops, Tool Houses, Carriage and Wagon Houses, Stables, Smoke and Ash Houses, Ice Houses, Apiary or Bee House, Poultry Houses, Rabbitry, Dovecote, Piggery, Barns and Sheds for Cattle, &c, &c. Together with Lawns, Pleasure Grounds and Parks; the Flower, Fruit and Vegetable Garden. Also, Useful and Ornamental Domestic Animals for the Country Resident, &c, &c, &c. Also, the Best Method of Conducting Water into Cattle Yards and Houses* (New York, 1852), 31–34.

9. Hammond, " 'Where the Arts and the Virtues Unite,' " 85–88, 145 (quote), 180 (quote). Allen, *Rural Architecture*, 13. On the *ferme ornée* in England, see John Martin Robinson, *Georgian Model Farms: A Study of Decorative and Model Farm Buildings in the Age of Improvement, 1700–1846* (New York, 1984), 77.

10. Bernard L. Herman, *Architecture and Rural Life in Central Delaware, 1700–1900* (Knoxville, Tenn., 1987), 146; Thomas C. Hubka, *Big House, Little House, Back House, Barn: The Connected Farm Buildings of New England* (Hanover, N.H., 1984), 185 (quotes), 211; Thornton, *Cultivating Gentlemen*, 38, 41, 72, 107, 120, 127, 152, 196.

11. *The Housekeeper's Annual and Ladies' Register for 1844* (Boston, 1843), 44.

12. Gervase Wheeler, *Rural Homes: or Sketches of Houses Suited to American Country Life with Original Plans, Designs, &c.* (Auburn, N.Y., 1855), 289, 290, 293; Hubka, *Big House, Little House, Back House, Barn*, 133–34.

13. Allen, *Rural Architecture*, 346, 347, 348.

14. Gervase Wheeler, *Homes for the People, in Suburb and Country; the Villa, the Mansion, and the Cottage, Adapted to American Climate and Wants. With Examples Showing How to Alter and Remodel Old Buildings. In a series of One Hundred Original Designs* (New York, 1858), 359, 360; Wheeler, *Rural Homes*, 148; Allen, *Rural Architecture*, 72, 83; Calvert Vaux, *Villas and Cottages. A Series of Designs Prepared for Execution in the United States*, 2nd ed. (New York, 1864), 121–23, 124–25.

15. Wheeler, *Homes for the People*, 361. For Kent County log houses, see chap. 8, note 28.

16. Beth Ann Twiss-Garrity, "Getting the Comfortable Fit: House Forms and Furnishings in Rural Delaware, 1780–1820" (M.A. thesis, University of Delaware, 1983).

17. Ibid., 24–29.

18. Vaux, *Villas and Cottages*, 54; Wheeler, *Homes for the People*, 310; Allen, *Rural Architecture*, 72.

19. Fred Kniffen, "Folk Housing: Key to Diffusion," *Annals of the Association of American Geographers*, 55 (Dec. 1965): 549–77; Ernest Allen Connally, "The Cape Cod House: An Introductory Study," *Journal of the Society of Architectural Historians*, 19 (May 1960): 47–56; Henry Glassie, *Pattern in the Material Folk Culture of the Eastern United States* (Philadelphia, 1968), 48–55, 56–59, 64–69, 80–83, 96–98, 107–12, 124–35; Mary Ellen Hayward, "Urban Vernacular Architecture in Nineteenth-Century Baltimore," *Winterthur Portfolio*, 16 (Spring 1981): 33–64; Gwendolyn Wright, *Building the Dream: A Social History of Housing in America* (Cambridge, Mass., 1981), 27–37. For more imposing houses, but not architect-designed, see Catherine W. Bishir, "Jacob W. Holt: An American Builder," *Winterthur Portfolio*, 16 (Spring 1981): 1–32. For the plans of English row houses, see Stefan Multhesius, *The English Terraced House* (New Haven, 1982), 79–146.

20. Myron O. Stachiw, "Tradition and Transformation: Rural Society and Architectural Change in Nineteenth-Century Central Massachusetts," *Perspective in Vernacular Architecture, III*, ed. Thomas Carter and Bernard L. Herman (Columbia, Mo., 1987).

21. Ibid., 141–45.

22. For the remodeling of rural Delaware, see Herman, *Architecture and Rural Life in Central Delaware*, 148–86, and for southern Maine at somewhat later dates, see Hubka, *Big House, Little House, Back House, Barn*, 86–112. For Alabama, see Robert Gamble, *The Alabama Catalog: Historic American Buildings Survey: A Guide to the Early Architecture of the State* (University, Alabama, 1987), 27–28, 30, 32, 37.

23. *The Delaware Register and Farmers' Magazine* (July–Jan. 1839), 2:390. For a stereotypical pictorial example, see Gwendolyn Wright, *Building the Dream: A Social History of Housing in America* (Cambridge, Mass., 1981), 79.

24. [Catharine Maria Sedgwick] *Home* (Boston, 1835), 87.

25. Edgar deN. Mayhew and Minor Myers, Jr., *A Documentary History of American Interiors: From the Colonial Era to 1915* (New York, 1980), 107, 113, 127, 130, 133.
26. Allen, *Rural Architecture*, 42.
27. Vaux, *Villas and Cottages*, 66.
28. Roger W. Moss, *Century of Color: Exterior Decoration for American Buildings, 1820–1920* (Watkins Glen, N.Y., 1981), 9, 11.
29. John Warner Barber, *Historical Collections of the State of Connecticut* (Hartford, 1836), 261. The adoption of picket fences is best charted through paintings and prints such as Barber's, e.g., ibid., 116, 129, or those in Jay E. Cantor, *The Landscape of Change: Views of Rural New England, 1790–1865* (n.p., n.d.), such as figure 8.
30. Christopher Hussey, *English Gardens and Landscapes, 1700–1750* (London, 1967); Roger Turner, *Capability Brown and the Eighteenth-Century English Landscape* (New York, 1985). Cities, with the danger of vagrant invasions of unwanted visitors, were more inclined to keep fences.
31. The best discussion of the fenced yard is Hubka, *Big House, Little House, Back House, Barn*, 70–80. For complaints about the stark New England house, hard upon the road, without protecting trees and shrubbery, see "Scenes in New England," *The Lady's Book* (Godey's), 18 (Jan. 1839): 7.
32. Barber, *Historical Collections of the State of Connecticut*, 144, 509; Allen, *Rural Architecture*, 125; *The Lady's Book* (Godey's), 18 (Jan. 1839): 7.
33. Barbara M. Cross, ed., *The Autobiography of Lyman Beecher* (Cambridge, Mass., 1961), 1:86–87, 91 (quote).
34. [Miriam Berry Whicher] *The Widow Bedott Papers* (New York, 1856), 227–28.
35. Downing, *Architecture of Country Houses*, 80–81.
36. George E. Stetson, "The 1704 House Built in Chester County, Pennsylvania, by William Brinton the Younger" (M.A. thesis, University of Delaware, 1961), 44, 120.
37. Wheeler, *Rural Homes*, 279.
38. Allen, *Rural Architecture*, 31, 75, 80.
39. Chauncey M. Depew, ed., *One Hundred Years of American Commerce, 1795–1895* (New York, 1915); Chauncey Jerome, *History of the American Clock Business for the Past Sixty Years* (New Haven, 1860); Arthur H. Cole and Harold F. Williamson, *The American Carpet Manufacturers* (Cambridge, Mass., 1941); Charles E. Peterson, *Building Early America: Contributions Toward the History of a Great Industry* (Radnor, Pa., 1976); Barry Kessler, "Of Workshops and Warerooms: The Economic and Geographic Transformation of Furniture Making in Chester County, Pennsylvania, 1780–1850" (M.A. thesis, University of Delaware, 1987); David Jaffee, "'One of the Primitive Sort': Portrait-Makers in the Rural North, 1760–1860," in Jonathan Prude and Steven Hahn, eds., *The Countryside in the Age of Capitalist Transformation: 1780–1900, Essays in Social History* (Chapel Hill, N.C., 1985), 103–38.
40. Wheeler, *Rural Homes*, 276.
41. Downing, *Architecture of Country Houses*, 410–11.
42. John F. Watson, *Annals of Philadelphia and Pennsylvania, in the Olden Time . . .* ([Philadelphia] 1844 [orig. pub. 1830]), 1:204, 205. Watson's *Annals* grew by accrual. He published a primitive version in 1823; by 1830 it approximated its later form.
43. *Documents Relative to the Manufacture in the United States*, 22nd Congress, 1st Session, House Document no. 308 (Washington, D.C., 1833), 1:298–99; Charles Jones, "The Broom Corn Industry in the Counties of Franklin and Hampshire, and in the Town of Deerfield in Particular," *History and Proceedings of the Pocumtuck Valley Memorial Association, 1897–1904* (Deerfield, Mass., 1905), 4: 105–11; Gregory H. Nobles, "Commerce and Community: A Case Study of the Rural Broommaking Business in Antebellum Massachusetts," *Journal of the Early Republic*, 4 (Fall 1984): 287–308.
44. Cole and Williamson, *The American Carpet Manufacturers*, 12–16.
45. *The Cultivator, a Consolidation of Buel's Cultivator and Genesee Farmer, Designed to Improve the Soil and the Mind* (Albany), 7 (1840): 93.
46. Edward Eggleston, *The Hoosier School-Master* (Bloomington, Ind., 1984 [orig pub. 1871]), 157; see also Christopher Crowfield [Harriet Beecher Stowe], *House and Home Papers* (Boston, 1865), 34–47, 64–67.
47. Harriet Beecher Stowe, *Oldtown Folks*, ed. Dorothy Berkson (New Brunswick, N.J., 1987 [orig. pub. 1869]), 63–64.
48. Ibid., 65–66.
49. Ibid.
50. For real-life examples of closed parlors, see Katherine C. Grier, *Culture and Comfort: People, Parlors, and Upholstery, 1850–1930* (Rochester, N.Y., 1988), 73–76.
51. Watson, *Annals of Philadelphia*, 1:251–52. This tension and its resolution is the central theme of Grier, *Culture and Comfort*; see especially pp. 91–102. See also Vaux, *Villas and Cottages*, 95–97.
52. Witold Rybczynski, *Home: A Short History of an Idea* (New York, 1986), 83, 104, 118, 120; John Cornforth, *English Interiors, 1790–1848: The Quest for Comfort* (London, 1978).

53. Quoted in Rufus Wilmot Griswold, *The Republican Court, or, American Society in the Days of Washington* (New York, 1856), 272.

54. Abigail to John Adams, April 7, 1783, in L. H. Butterfield, Marc Friedlaender, and Mary-Jo Kline, eds., *The Book of Abigail and John: Selected Letters of the Adams Family, 1762–1784* (Cambridge, Mass., 1975), 345.

55. Quoted in Grier, *Culture and Comfort*, 101.

56. Solon Robinson, *How to Live: Saving and Wasting, or, Domestic Economy Illustrated by the Life of Two Families of Opposite Character, Habits, and Practices, in a Pleasant Tale of Real Life, Full of Useful Lessons in Housekeeping, and Hints How to Live, How to Have, How to Gain, and How to be Happy; Including the Story of a Dime a Day* (New York, 1860), 41, 50.

57. Allen, *Rural Architecture*, 59–61, 242; Downing, *Architecture of Country Houses*, 409–11.

58. Stowe's *House and Home Papers* is an extended admonition to readers of the *Atlantic* to live more modestly.

59. Robinson, *How to Live*, 66, 77–78, 259.

60. [Stowe] *House and Home Papers*, 82.

61. Vaux, *Villa and Cottages*, 55. The word "office" did not refer to business offices but to work spaces like the kitchen and washroom. Downing's description of the "living-room" of a small cottage for a workingman as "the kitchen, sitting-room, and parlor of this family" harked back to the seventeenth-century hall. But in the next level up he included a back kitchen "for the rough-work" so that "the living-room can be made to have the comfortable aspect of a cottage parlor, by confining the rough-work to the kitchen proper." Even in a simple house, work had to be separated from the parlor. Downing, *Architecture of Country Houses*, 73, 81.

62. Vaux, *Villas and Cottages*, 96–97.

63. Robinson, *How to Live*, 261. See also Allen, *Rural Architecture*, 52, for a similar grading of decoration from the presentation spaces down through family occupancy to the workrooms. Allen divided the house into "a parlor for their friends; a library, or sitting-room for their own leisure and comfort," and then bedrooms and a kitchen. Harriet Beecher Stowe's Christopher Crowfield thought of the parlor in a sensible home as the elegant place where "pappa and mamma sit and receive their friends." *House and Home Papers*, 67–68.

64. Vaux, *Villas and Cottages*, 95–96; Allen, *Rural Architecture*, 58–60; Downing, *Architecture of Country Houses*, 409–11.

65. Rybczynski, *Home*, 84. A French example of the lounging stance is depicted in a 1728 painting, "The Reading from Molière," by Jean-François de Troy, illustrated in Peter Thornton, *Authentic Decor: The Domestic Interior, 1620–1920* (New York, 1984), 116.

66. Brock Jobe and Myrna Kaye, *New England Furniture: The Colonial Era: Selections from the Society for the Preservation of New England Antiquities* (Boston, 1984), 366; Ellen and Bert Denker, *The Rocking Chair Book* (New York, 1979), 19–23, 37.

67. Rocking chairs are found in American inventories by the 1740s but came into their own in the next century. Denker and Denker, *The Rocking Chair Book*, 13–14.

68. Quoted in Denker and Denker, *The Rocking Chair Book*, 38.

69. The sudden jump in rockers is measured in Margaret B. Schiffer, *Chester County, Pennsylvania, Inventories, 1684–1850* (Exton, Pa., 1974), 133.

70. Jacob Abbott, *Rollo Learning to Read* (New York, 1839), 81.

71. Denker and Denker, *The Rocking Chair Book*, 28, 40–42, 53; Mayhew and Myers, Jr., *Documentary History of American Interiors*, 121, 127.

72. Mrs. Henry M. Ridgely, Dover, to Miss Elizabeth Ridgely, Philadelphia, March 26, 1827, folder 217, Ridgely Papers, Hall of Records, Dover. On rockers in parlors, see also Denker and Denker, *The Rocking Chair Book*, 60, 62.

73. Quoted in Denker and Denker, *The Rocking Chair Book*, 59–60.

74. Downing, *Architecture of Country Houses*, 410–11; Vaux, *Villas and Cottages*, 28–30.

75. Downing, *Architecture of Country Houses*, 40.

76. Allen, *Rural Architecture*, 167.

77. Downing, *Architecture of Country Houses*, 70–71.

78. Vaux, *Villas and Cottages*, 37, 38; see also 50–51, 262–63; Wheeler, *Homes for the People*, 271, 274, 331, 360.

79. Vaux, *Villas and Cottages*, 48.

80. Quoted in E. G. Storke, *The Family and Householder's Guide; or, How to Keep House; How to Provide; How to Cook; How to Wash; How to Dye; How to Paint; How to Preserve Health; How to Cure Disease; etc. etc.: A Manual of Household Management* (Auburn, N.Y., 1859), 30, 31.

81. Quoted in Edward Halsey Foster, *Catharine Maria Sedgwick* (New York, 1974), 124.

82. [Catharine Maria Sedgwick] *Home* (Boston, 1835), 35–36, 39.

83. Ibid., 6, 110 (quote).

84. [Catharine Maria Sedgwick] *The Poor Rich Man, and the Rich Poor Man* (New York, 1837), 104, 106, 173–74.
85. [Sedgwick] *Home*, 38 (quote), 39–40 (quote), 42, 120 (quote), 121.
86. Ibid., 48–49.

IX. LITERATURE AND LIFE

1. [Catharine Maria Sedgwick] *Home* (Boston, 1835), 8, 87, 85.
2. *The Lady's Book* (Godey's), 18 (March 1839): 122; Solon Robinson, *How to Live: Saving and Wasting, or, Domestic Economy Illustrated by the Life of Two Families of Opposite Character, Habits, and Practices, in a Pleasant Tale of Real Life, Full of Useful Lessons in Housekeeping, and Hints How to Live, How to Have, How to Gain, and How to Be Happy; Including the Story of a Dime a Day* (New York, 1860), 38, 39.
3. G. W. Marshall, "Intellectual Improvement of Farmers Necessary," from *The Illustrated Agriculturist's Almanac for 1852*, in *The Family Circle and Parlor Annual*, 11 (1851): 207–8.
4. *The Housekeeper's Annual and Ladies' Register for 1844* (Boston, 1844), 42–43.
5. To show the quality of her ancestry, Mary Parker Welch said of one of the first women in her line to settle in Delaware that, along with felling trees and clearing fields, "the mother taught her children the love of the books that had been brought from England." George Theodore Welch, *Memoirs of Mary Parker Welch, 1818–1912*, ed. Dorothy Welch White (n.p., 1947), 24. For her own devotion to books, see ibid., 98–99.
6. *The Delaware State Journal* (Wilmington), Dec. 3, 1839.
7. Robinson, *How to Live*, 181–82.
8. "Of Books and Reading" is chap. 4 in Isaac Watts, *On the Improvement of the Mind*, in D. Jennings and P. Doddridge, eds., *The Works of the Late Reverend and Learned Isaac Watts, D.D.* 5 (London, 1753): 185–356.
9. Wilbur Macey Stone, "The History of Little Goody Two-Shoes," *Proceedings of the American Antiquarian Society*, new ser., 49 (April–Oct. 1939): 332–70.
10. Margaret B. Schiffer, *Chester County, Pennsylvania, Inventories, 1684–1850* (Exton, Pa., 1974), 1, 132, 139.
11. The data are analyzed in Edgar W. Martin, *The Standard of Living in 1860: American Consumption Levels on the Eve of the Civil War* (Chicago, 1942), 435. For the growth of libraries, see Jesse H. Shera, *Foundations of the Public Library: The Origins of the Public Library Movement in New England, 1629–1855* (Chicago, 1949). See also William Charvat, *Literary Publishing in America, 1790–1850* (Philadelphia, 1859), and William Gilmore, *Reading Becomes a Necessity of Life: Material and Cultural Life in Rural New England, 1780–1835* (Knoxville, 1989).
12. Ralph Thomson, *American Literary Annuals and Gift Books, 1825–1865* (New York, 1936), 1, 3, 7–9, 35, 50; *The Young Ladies' Offering, or Gems of Prose and Poetry, by Mrs. Sigourney and Others* (Boston, 1848); Katherine Martinez, "Messengers of Love, Tokens of Friendship: Gift-Book Illustrations by John Sartrain," in Gerald R. Ward, ed., *The American Illustrated Book* (Charlottesville, Va., 1987), 89–112. For a discussion of English gift books, see Anne Renier, *Friendship's Offering: An Essay on the Annuals and Gift Books of the 19th Century* (London, 1965, 1964).
13. *The Lady's Book* (Godey's) 18 (Jan. 1839): 38. A young woman in another story took up reading and writing when disappointed in love and in time "the dignity of intellect diffused a higher charm over her beautiful features than mere youth could impart." *The Family Circle*, 10 (1850), 210.
14. *The Lady's Book* (Godey's), 18 (May 1839): 215.
15. *Graham's Magazine*, 37 (July 1850): 43.
16. [Sedgwick] *Home*, 40; Sidney H. Ditzion, "Mechanics' and Mercantile Libraries," *Library Quarterly*, 10 (1940): 192–219.
17. *The Lady's Book* (Godey's), 18 (March 1839): 131.
18. The blending of motives is illustrated in the story of Paul, who though lacking wealth and education fell in love with an accomplished young woman. He watched her beautiful graceful form from afar and then "resolved to improve his mind by study and application, that he might at least raise himself above her contempt; and so, by the midnight lamp, the poor fellow went to work, and for two years every leisure moment was spent in study, and every penny he could save, employed in procuring books for his thirsting mind. His perseverance did not go unrewarded; his employer soon took note of his talents, and Paul became assistant editor of a popular weekly journal." *Graham's Magazine*, 37 (July 1850): 102.
19. *The Young Man, or Guide to Knowledge, Virtue and Happiness* (Lowell, Mass., 1845), 138; Eliza Leslie, *The Behaviour Book: A Manual for Ladies*, 4th ed. (Philadelphia, 1854), 185, 186.
20. James Fenimore Cooper, *Home As Found* (New York, 1860 [orig. pub. 1838]), 72, 73.
21. *The Delaware Register and Farmers' Magazine* (Dover), 2 (July–Jan. 1839): 153. See also Mrs. Maberly, *The Art of Conversation, with Remarks on Fashion and Address: Together with General Rules to Be Observed in Intercourse with Society* (New York, 1845), 20.
22. On the importance of conversation in improving young men, see Richard D. Brown, *Knowledge Is Power: The Diffusion of Information in Early America, 1700–1865* (New York, 1989), 221, 229.
23. *Graham's Magazine*, 37 (July 1850): 5. For a discussion of "mind" and civilization, see Peter Borsay, *The English Urban Renaissance: Culture and Society in the Provincial Town 1660–1770* (Oxford, 1989), 263–67.

24. Caroline Matilda Kirkland, *A Book for the Home Circle; or, Familiar Thoughts on Various Topics, Literary, Moral and Social. A Companion for the Evening Book* (New York, 1853), 28.
25. For the spread of novel reading before 1820, see Cathy N. Davidson, *Revolution and the Word: The Rise of the Novel in America* (New York, 1986), 15–29. My own sampling of the vast body of sentimental fiction has gone on at three levels: well-known novels such as those by Harriet Beecher Stowe, Catharine Sedgwick, and Susan Warner; the stories in two popular ladies' journals, *Godey's Lady's Book* and *Graham's Magazine*, from 1839 to 1860; and fiction encountered in local newspapers and farm periodicals.
26. For a reading of these contradictions, see Jane Tompkins, *Sensational Designs: The Cultural Work of American Fiction, 1790–1860* (New York, 1985).
27. Kirkland, *A Book for the Home Circle*, 31–32.
28. Janet Todd: *Sensibility: An Introduction* (London, 1986), 4.
29. Elizabeth Banning, to Nicholas Ridgely, Dover, April 4, 1840, folder 289, Ridgely Collection, Hall of Records, Dover, hereafter cited as Ridgely collection; Samuel Miller, *The Life of Samuel Miller, D.D., LL.D., Second Professor in the Theological Seminary of the Presbyterian Church, at Princeton, New Jersey* (Philadelphia, 1869), 73. See also White, ed. *Memoirs of Mary Parker Welch, 1818–1912*, 59, 97, 99, 117–18, 120, 124, and passim.
30. Caroline Kirkland believed novels misled readers because "ignorance of society and the lack of a just taste in manners and conversation are exhibited by a large proportion of novel-writers." The errors were understandable: "It is hardly possible for a person whose own habits and associations are coarse, to avoid giving a tinge of coarseness to fictions intended as pictures of society." She urged that the young never be allowed "to associate in books with persons whose sentiments would be sufficient to close our doors against them if they attempted entrance in bodily shape." Kirkland, *A Book for the Home Circle*, 31–32.
31. For the turn to fiction to teach religion, see David S. Reynolds, *Faith in Fiction: The Emergence of Religious Literature in America* (Cambridge, Mass., 1981).
32. Henry M. Ridgely, Washington, to Sally Ridgely, Dover, June 27, 1813, folder 269, Ridgely Collection.
33. Emily Thornwell spoke of precedence in going up stairs and in seating. Places near the window of the fireplace were reserved for superiors over seats directly before the fire. Emily Thornwell, *The Lady's Guide to Perfect Gentility, in Manners, Dress, and Conversation, in the Family, in Company, at the Piano Forte, the Table, in the Street, and in Gentlemen's Society . . .* (New York, 1856), 85.
34. Francis D. Nichols, *A Guide to Politeness; or, A System of Directions for the Acquirement of Ease, Propriety and Elegance of Manners. Illustrated by a Large Number of Figures, Representing Graceful Attitudes . . .* (Boston, 1810); *How to Behave: A Pocket Manual of Republican Etiquette, and Guide to Correct Personal Habits . . .* (New York, 1857); *The Illustrated Manners Book: A Manual of Good Behavior and Polite Accomplishment* (New York, 1855); Thornwell, *The Lady's Guide to Perfect Gentility.*
35. [Sedgwick], *Home*, 28, 48–49.
36. Emily Thornwell even advanced the old notion of leaving space at the heading of a letter in proportion to the rank of the recipient. Thornwell, *The Lady's Guide to Perfect Gentility*, 87–88 (quote), 159.
37. Cooper, *Home As Found*, 56. Cooper's critique of American society cast in the form of a novel is a handbook on the graces of true aristocratic refinement compared with the ungainly pretensions of American parvenus.
38. E. G. Storke, *Family and Householder's Guide* (Albany, N.Y., 1859), 30.
39. *The Delaware Register and Farmers' Magazine*, 2 (July–Jan. 1839), 477.
40. Harriet Beecher Stowe, *Oldtown Folks*, ed. Dorothy Berkson (New Brunswick, N.J., 1987 [orig. pub. 1869]), 100, 102, 103, 197, 204, 257, 269, 397, 401, 499, 509.
41. Ibid., 89, 91–92, 110, 204, 393.
42. Ibid., 13–14, 299, 349; *Graham's Magazine*, 37 (Sept. 1850): 177; *The Lady's Book* (Godey's), 18 (Feb. 1839): 52–53; *Graham's Magazine*, 37 (July 1850): 8. See also *The Lady's Book* (Godey's), 18 (April 1839): 169.

   This attention to the physicality of refinement partly reflected the influence of the phrenologists and, to a lesser extent, the physiognomists, whose writings were in vogue in the United States from the 1830s through the 1850s. Johann Kaspar Spurzheim, the follower of Franz Joseph Gall, the founder of phrenology, took Boston by storm during his lecture tour in 1832. George Combe, the Scottish phrenologist, spoke to large upper-class and intellectual audiences during his American tour in 1838–40. In the following decade phrenology was popularized by Orson Squire Fowler and his brother Niles; they lectured incessantly, spawned hundreds of imitators, organized societies, started a journal, and founded a college. Leading American literary men, with Poe and Whitman among the most enthusiastic, accepted the validity of phrenology and introduced its notions into their writings. Harriet Beecher Stowe's brother, Henry Ward Beecher, was converted to phrenology at Amherst College in 1833 at the same time as his classmate Orson Fowler. (John D. Davies, *Phrenology Fad and Science: A 19th-Century American Crusade* [New Haven, 1955], 16–20, 29, 31–32, 33–40.) Physiognomy enjoyed less of a vogue in the United States but had a wide influence on European literature. (Graeme Tyler, *Physiognomy in the European Novel: Faces and Fortunes* [Princeton, N.J., 1982].) This buzz of interest, apart from any specific commitment to phrenological doctrines, drew attention to the bodily manifestations of character, especially in the head and face. Authors expected parts of the body to signify the presence of civilization.

Phrenology focused attention on the forehead. One popular diagram of the heads of beasts and men ranked the levels of their intelligence according to the slope of the foreheads, ascending from snakes and dogs through human idiots and the Bushman to "uncultivated," then to "improved," "civilized," "enlightened," and "Caucasian—Highest Type." (Davies, *Phrenology Fad and Science,* frontispiece.) Good-hearted people might have sloping foreheads, but not refined and intellectual persons. That general ideal carried over into fiction.

Though the quasi-sciences of the era had their effect on these descriptions, the attributes of refined bodies in sentimental fiction went beyond the particulars of phrenological doctrine. Refinement did not reside in foreheads and faces alone, the focus of the phrenologist's attention.

43. *The Delaware Register and Farmers' Magazine,* 2 (July–Jan. 1839), 239; "Mother's Joy," no. 48671, and "Father's Pride," no. 48671-A, Harry T. Peters Collection, National Museum of American History, Washington, D.C.; Thornwell, *The Lady's Guide to Perfect Gentility,* 54; Cooper, *Home As Found,* 51, cf. 353; *The Lady's Book* (Godey's), 18 (Jan. 1839): 5; 18 (March 1839): 142.
44. *Graham's Magazine,* 37 (July 1850): 38, 102.
45. Elsdon C. Smith, *The Story of Our Names* (New York, 1950), 15–17; Daniel Scott Smith, "Child-Naming Practices, Kinship Ties, and Change in Family Attitudes in Hingham, Massachusetts, 1641 to 1680," *Journal of Social History,* 18 (Summer 1985): 556–59.
46. *The Lady's Book* (Godey's), 18 (Feb. 1839): 82.
47. Royall Tyler, "The Bay Boy," in Marius B. Peladeau, ed., *The Prose of Royall Tyler* (Montpelier and Rutland, Vt., 1972), 50–53.
48. Ibid., 57, 59.
49. *Godey's Lady's Book,* 40 (May 1850): 332.
50. *Graham's Magazine,* 37 (Sept. 1850): 159; Robinson, *How to Live,* 22, 193. On the same theme, see [Catharine Maria Sedgwick] *The Poor Rich Man, and the Rich Poor Man* (New York, 1837), 77; Kirkland, *A Book for the Home Circle,* 102.
51. Lydia Maria Child, *The American Frugal Housewife,* new ed., ed. Alice M. Geffen (New York, 1972 [orig. pub. 1829]), 93, 112–13.
52. Ibid., 93.
53. *The Lady's Book* (Godey's), 18 (Jan. 1839): 9; 18 (March 1839): 121.
54. *The Family Circle,* 10 (1850): 142.
55. *The Lady's Book* (Godey's), 18 (Jan. 1839): 19.
56. The criticism of fashion was not an invention of the middle class; it was endemic to gentility almost from the outset. But the consistency and conviction of sentimental stories about fashion suggests that middling people were working out problems of their own when they took up the theme. For a direct attack, see Anna Cora (Ogden) Mowatt (Ritchie), *Fashion; or, Life in New York: A Comedy in Five Acts* (New York, 1854).
57. *The Delaware Register and Farmers' Magazine,* 2 (July–Jan. 1839): 150. The success of the middle-class campaign to domesticate refinement was measured by the growing inclination of monarchy, especially English monarchs, to have themselves portrayed in domestic settings. Simon Schama, "The Domestication of Majesty: Royal Family Portraiture, 1500–1800," in Robert I. Rotberg and Theodore K. Rabb, eds., *Art and History: Images and Their Meaning* (Cambridge, Eng., 1986).
58. *The Family Circle,* 10 (1850): 73, 77.
59. Catharine Beecher, *A Treatise on Domestic Economy for the Use of Young Ladies at Home, and at School,* ed. Kathryn Kish Sklar (New York, 1977 [orig. pub. 1841]), 32–33, 39.
60. Along with genteel housekeeping, there was equal attention given to genteel Christian motherhood and the proper way to raise young ladies and gentlemen. For a lengthy account of such a mother by Sarah Pierce, founder of the Litchfield Academy, see Emily Noyes Vanderpoel, *Chronicles of a Pioneer School from 1792 to 1833 Being the History of Miss Sarah Pierce and her Litchfield School,* ed. Elizabeth C. Barney Buel (Cambridge, Mass., 1903), 215–16. See Colleen McDannell, *The Christian Home in Victorian America, 1840–1900* (Bloomington, Ind., 1986).
61. *The Delaware Register and Farmers' Magazine,* 2 (July–Jan. 1839): 150–51.
62. *The Family Circle,* 10 (1850): 142. Harriet Beecher Stowe's heroine Mary Scudder, for all her simplicity, dazzles the assemblage at the first grand entertainment she attends and captures the attention of the most polished gentleman there, Aaron Burr. Harriet Beecher Stowe, *The Minister's Wooing* (Ridgewood, N.J., 1968 [orig. pub. 1859]), 118–28. See also *The Lady's Book* (Godey's), 18 (Jan. 1839), 37.
63. Stowe, *Minister's Wooing,* 122.
64. *Godey's Lady's Book,* 40 (May 1850): 338.
65. *The Lady's Book* (Godey's), 18 (Jan. 1839): 24.
66. The stories were equally careful to note the refinement of the obscure cottage. The houses in one village

destined to be the scene of a story were "for the most part humble and unpretending, yet so embosomed among fruit and forest-trees as to render each cottage of itself a coup d'oeil of beauty." *Graham's Magazine*, 37 (July 1850): 37.

67. *The Delaware Register and Farmers' Magazine*, 2 (July–Jan. 1839): 149, 150.
68. *The Lady's Book* (Godey's), 18 (Feb. 1839): 52.
69. Mary Kelley, *Private Woman, Public Stage: Literary Domesticity in Nineteenth-Century America* (New York, 1984).

X. RELIGION AND TASTE

1. Friedrich Schleiermacher, *On Religion: Speeches to Its Cultured Despisers*, tr. John Oman (New York, 1958 [orig. pub. 1799]), 1–2.
2. "Journey from Babylon to Jerusalem; or, the Road to Peace," in *History of Cosmopolite: Lorenzo Dow: Containing His Experiences and Travel from Childhood to 1814* . . . (Pittsburgh, 1849), 477–79.
3. *Consecrated Talents: or, the Life of Mrs. Mary W. Mason* (New York, 1870), 11, 12–16.
4. *The Christian Parlor Book. Devoted to Science, Literature, and Religion. With Numerous Embellishments* (New York, 1853), 17, 18, 23, 24.
5. *The Baptist Tract and Youths' Magazine* (Philadelphia), 2 (Oct. 1829): 229.
6. *The Sunday School Advocate: A Semi-Monthly Periodical, Devoted to the Interests of Sunday Schools in the Methodist Episcopal Church* (New York), 4 (Sept. 2, 1845): 183.
7. *The Sunday School Magazine* (New York), 1 (1845): 53–54.
8. Peter Cartwright, *Autobiography of Peter Cartwright*, ed. Charles L. Wallis (New York, 1956 [orig. pub. 1856]), 63.
9. *Youth's Penny Gazette* (Philadelphia), 12 (Feb. 1, 1853).
10. *The Sunday School Magazine* (New York), 1 (1845): 53.
11. Charles G. Finney, *Memoirs of Rev. Charles G. Finney. Written by Himself* (New York, 1876), 115–16.
12. Cartwright, *Autobiography*, 5, 61–62 (quote), 334, 336–37 (quote).
13. Ibid., 61–63. There are similar instances of stripping away or giving up superfluities in Finney, *Memoirs*, 249, 287.
14. Cartwright, *Autobiography*, 72–73.
15. *The Youth's Friend* (Philadelphia), New Series, 2 (Jan. 1845): 99.
16. Among the periodicals with this character were *The Baptist Tract and Youths' Magazine* (Philadelphia), the Methodist *Sunday School Advocate* (New York), and the American Sunday School Union's *Youth's Cabinet* (New York) (before 1846) and *Youth's Penny Gazette* (Philadelphia).
17. For the comparison, see *The Youth's Cabinet. A Semi-monthly Publication, Designed to Promote the Improvement of the Youthful Mind, and to Elevate the Character of the Rising Generation* (New York), 6 (1843), and Rev. Francis C. Woodworth, ed., *The Youth's Cabinet: A Book of Gems for the Mind and the Heart, Beautifully Embellished* (New York), 1 (1846); quotations on pages 6, 7.
18. *The Baptist Tract and Youths' Magazine* (Philadelphia), 5 (June 1832): 123.
19. *The Youth's Friend* (Philadelphia), New Series, 2 (Jan. 1845): 102, 109, 147.
20. *The Sunday School Magazine* (New York), 1 (1845): 45–47.
21. Barbara M. Cross, *Horace Bushnell: Minister to a Changing America* (Chicago, 1958), 89, 90, 103; *The Christian Spectator* (New Haven), 1 (Jan. 1819): 2.
22. *The Family Circle and Parlor Annual*, 10 (1850): 11, 45, 47, 49.
23. [Catharine Maria Sedgwick] *Home* (Boston, 1835), 49. Sedgwick believed that her Barclays' charity and refinement put them on the path to salvation. "Their labors and their pleasures were transitory, but the vivifying spirit of love and intelligence that informed them was abiding, and was carrying them on to higher and higher stages of improvement, and preparing them for that period to which their efforts and hopes pointed, when the terrestrial shall put on the celestial." Ibid., 110–11.
24. Charles George Ridgely, Lebanon, to Elizabeth Ridgely, Dover, Dec. 18, 1829, folder 219, Ridgely Collection, Hall of Records, Dover, Del.
25. Anna Wilmot, "The Spring Bonnet," *Godey's Lady's Book*, 36 (June 1850): 381–84.
26. John Pintard, New York, May 24, 1820, in Dorothy C. Barck, ed., *Letters from John Pintard to His Daughter, Eliza Noel Pintard Davidson* (New York, 1940), 1:293–94.
27. Quotations from Cross, *Horace Bushnell*, 4, 5, 9.
28. Ibid., 42–43, 53–56.
29. Ibid., 33–36; *The Christian Spectator* (New Haven), 6 (Dec. 1, 1824): 629–30, 632.
30. *The Christian Spectator*, 6 (Dec. 1, 1824): 629–30.
31. *The New Englander* (New Haven), 5 (Jan. 1847): 22.
32. Cross, *Horace Bushnell*, 88–92.
33. [Bushnell] "Taste and Fashion," *The New Englander*, 1 (April 1843): 155–57.

34. Ibid., 166–68. For a discussion of the Unitarians and refinement, see Daniel Walker Howe, *The Unitarian Conscience: Harvard Moral Philosophy, 1805–1861* (Cambridge, Mass., 1970), 201–4.
35. Elizabeth Wetherell [Susan Warner], *The Wide, Wide World* (New York, 1987 [orig. pub. 1850]), 164, 498, 520.
36. Ibid., 102, 106, 336.
37. Ibid., 501, 505, 508, 542–43.
38. Harriet Beecher Stowe, *Oldtown Folks* (Boston and New York, 1911), 44, 49–50, 68–69; Harriet Beecher Stowe, *Poganuc People* (Hartford, 1977 [orig. pub. 1878]), 70.
39. Stowe, *Oldtown Folks*, 126, 130, 248, 292, 259 (quotation).
40. Stowe, *Poganuc People*, 27 (quotation), 38 (quotation). In an effort to redeem her ancestors, Stowe tried to argue that seventeenth-century Puritans were really just slightly reformed Anglicans; Jonathan Edwards was responsible for the break with the Episcopal Church. Charles H. Foster, *The Rungless Ladder: Harriet Beecher Stowe and New England Puritanism* (Durham, N.C., 1954), 179–89. Harriet Hanson Robinson as a child reported being drawn to the Episcopal Sunday school "because their little girls were not afraid of the devil, were allowed to dance, and had so much nicer books in their Sunday-school library," many of them dealing with English lords and ladies. Quoted in Claudia L. Bushman, *"A Good Poor Man's Wife": Being a Chronicle of Harriet Hanson Robinson and Her Family in Nineteenth Century New England* (Hanover, N.H., 1981), 54.
41. Francis H. Underwood, *Quabbin: The Story of a Small Town with Outlooks upon Puritan Life* (Boston, 1986 [orig. pub. 1893]), 7, 337–38, 341.
42. Edmund W. Sinnott, *Meeting House and Church in Early New England* (New York, 1963), 110.
43. J. Frederick Kelly, *Early Connecticut Meetinghouses: Being an Account of the Church Edifices Built before 1830 Based Chiefly upon Town and Parish Records* (New York, 1948), 1:34.
44. Jane C. Nylander, "Toward Comfort and Uniformity in New England Meeting Houses, 1750–1850," in Peter Benes, ed., *New England Meeting House and Church: 1630–1850* (Boston, n.d.), 86–89. Kelly, *Early Connecticut Meetinghouses*, 1:249.
45. Nylander, "Toward Comfort and Uniformity," 93, 97–99.
46. *A Book of Plans for Churches and Parsonages. Published under the Direction of the Central Committee, Appointed by the General Congregational Convention, October, 1852. Comprising Designs by Upjohn, Downing, Renwick, Wheeler, Wells, Austin, Stone, Cleveland, Backus, and Reeve* (New York, 1853), 2, 4, 5, 6.
47. Calder Loth and Julius Toursdale Sadler, Jr., *The Only Proper Style: Gothic Architecture in America* (Boston, 1975), 60; H. M. Dexter, *Meeting-Houses: Considered Historically and Suggestively* (Boston, 1859), 14; Kelly, *Early Connecticut Meetinghouses*, 1:250–51.
48. James F. White, *The Cambridge Movement: The Ecclesiologists and the Gothic Revival* (Cambridge, Eng., 1962), 2–3, 9–11, 203.
49. Phoebe B. Stanton, *The Gothic Revival and American Church Architecture: An Episode in Taste, 1840–1856* (Baltimore, 1968), 41–43, 45, 56, 160–61; Loth and Sadler, Jr., *The Only Proper Style*, 56, 62.
50. For general attacks on Episcopalianism, see *The New Englander*, 7 (Jan. 1844): 66–80, 113–42, 143–75; 3 (July 1845): 333–73. The quotations are at *The New Englander*, 2 (Jan. 1844): 166; 3 (Oct. 1845): 557–59.
51. *A Book of Plans for Churches and Parsonages*, 13, 15.
52. Ibid., 6–7.
53. Dexter, *Meeting-Houses*, 11, 14.
54. Nylander, "Toward Comfort and Uniformity," 94–96.
55. Dexter, *Meeting-Houses*, 4, 7, 17.
56. *A Book of Plans for Churches and Parsonages*, 11.
57. Richard Upjohn designed a Gothic church for the Central Congregational Church in Boston in 1865. Loth and Sadler, Jr., *The Only Proper Style*, 61.
58. J. Fenimore Cooper, *Home As Found* (New York, 1860 [orig. pub. 1838]), 168, 169.
59. For competition among Episcopal churches based on the worth of the organ, see Barck, ed., *Letters from John Pintard* 3:153–54.
60. Board of Church Extension of the Methodist Episcopal Church, *Sample Pages of Catalogue of Architectural Plans for Churches and Parsonages for the Year 1884* (Philadelphia, n.d.), 1–2.
61. *Autobiography of Peter Cartwright*, 61, 64. One Methodist preacher complained that the fancy new churches interfered with the sound of the preacher's voice, trespassing on the auditory principle. Daniel Wise, *Earnest Christianity Illustrated: or Selections from the Journal of the Rev. James Caughey*, 9th ed. (Toronto, 1856), 397–402.
62. Dexter, *Meeting-Houses*, 2–7.
63. The views of the circle around Noah Porter are analyzed in Louise L. Stevenson, *Scholarly Means to Evangelical Ends: The New Haven Scholars and the Transformation of Higher Learning in America, 1830–1890s* (Baltimore, 1986).

64. Noah Porter, *The New England Meeting House* (New Haven, 1933; originally read before the New England Society of Brooklyn, N.Y., Dec. 5, 1882, and printed in *The New Englander* for May 1883), 7, 15, 20.

65. Ibid., 22, 23.

66. John Pintard, New York, Feb. 20, 27, 28, 1826, in Barck, ed., *Letters from John Pintard*, 2:231, 235, 236.

67. Woodworth, ed., *The Youth's Cabinet*, 1 (1846): 112.

69. Leon deValinger, Jr., and Virginia E. Shaw, eds., *A Calendar of Ridgely Family Letters 1742–1899 in the Delaware State Archives* (Dover, Del., 1961), 3:30–31.

70. Stowe, *Oldtown Folks*, 59.

71. George Bowler, *Chapel and Church Architecture with Designs for Parsonages* (Boston, 1856), 8. *The Sunday School Advocate* of 1845 simply assumed elegant dress as a prelude to worship. "On Sunday morning, before going to church, what a dressing there is among all classes, and what a stir to be gay and pleasing!" This writer said nothing of those unable to appear in gay dress; the only concern was preoccupation with externals instead of with internal preparation. "Curls may be arranged, fine shell combs fixed, sparkling ear-rings hung, splendid garments displayed. And yet, perhaps, the gay fair one's mind may be poisoned with conceit, troubled with rivalry, and kept on the torture by ignorance and vanity." *The Sunday School Advocate*, 5 (Dec. 2, 1845): 39.

72. *A Book of Plans for Churches and Parsonages*, 11–12. For an example of the same line of reasoning, also relying on Ruskin, see Bowler, *Chapel and Church Architecture*, 8.

XI. CITY AND COUNTRY

1. Harry M. Ward, *Richmond: An Illustrated History* (Northridge, Calif., 1985), 59. For other capital neighborhoods, see Walter Muir Whitehill, *Boston: A Topographical History*, 2nd. ed. (Cambridge, Mass., 1968), 59–66; E. Digby Baltzell, *Philadelphia Gentlemen: The Making of a National Upper Class* (Glencoe, Ill., 1958), 175.

2. Quoted in Elizabeth Blackmar, *Manhattan for Rent, 1785–1850* (Ithaca, N.Y., 1989), 166. See also Charles Lockwood, *Bricks and Brownstones: The New York Row House, 1783–1929, a Guide to Architectural Styles and Interior Decoration for Period Restoration* (New York, 1972).

3. Quoted in ibid., 164.

4. Calvert Vaux, *Villas and Cottages: A Series of Designs Prepared for Execution in the United States*, 2nd ed. (New York, 1864), 254. John Fanning Watson credited William Hamilton at Woodlands outside the city and William Bingham with bringing Lombardy poplars to Philadelphia. John F. Watson, *Annals of Philadelphia and Pennsylvania, in the Olden Time . . .* ([Philadelphia] 1844 [orig. pub. 1830]), 1:223. They were the classic marking tree for three or four decades and then went out of style in the city; western country towns planted them much longer.

5. Nicholas B. Wainwright, ed., *A Philadelphia Perspective: The Diary of Sidney George Fisher Covering the Years 1834–1871* (Philadelphia, 1967), 101.

6. Quoted in Blackmar, *Manhattan for Rent*, 164.

7. Stuart M. Blumin, *The Emergence of the Middle Class: Social Experience in the American City, 1760–1900* (Cambridge, Eng., 1989), 163–79; Jack Larkin, *The Reshaping of Everyday Life, 1790–1840* (New York, 1988), 113–14.

8. Edgar W. Martin, *The Standard of Living in 1860: American Consumption Levels on the Eve of the Civil War* (Chicago, 1942), 108.

9. James Fenimore Cooper, *Home As Found* (New York, 1860 [orig. pub. 1838]), 44.

10. For nineteenth-century hotels, see Katherine C. Grier, *Culture and Comfort: People, Parlors, and Upholstery, 1850–1930* (Rochester, N.Y., 1988), 29–38, and Jefferson Williamson, *The American Hotel: An Anecdotal History* (New York, 1930).

11. Quoted in Grier, *Culture and Comfort*, 25.

12. Harold Donaldson Eberlein and Cortlandt Van Dyke Hubbard, "Music in the Early Federal Era," *Pennsylvania Magazine of History and Biography*, 69 (April 1945): 103, 124–25.

13. Eliza Leslie, *The Behaviour Book: A Manual for Ladies*, 4th ed. (Philadelphia, 1854), 87–91; Lawrence W. Levine, *Highbrow/Lowbrow: The Emergence of Cultural Hierarchy in America* (Cambridge, Mass., 1988), 24–25, 56–60.

14. Quoted in Grier, *Culture and Comfort*, 26.

15. Neil Harris, *Humbug: The Art of P. T. Barnum* (Boston, 1973), 38–39; Wainwright, ed., *A Philadelphia Perspective*, 238.

16. Mark Girouard, *Cities and People: A Social and Architectural History* (New Haven, 1985), 169, 199–204.

17. Richard L. Bushman, "Shopping and Advertising in Colonial America," in Ronald Hoffman and Cary Carson, eds., *Consuming Interests: Styles of Life in the Eighteenth Century* (Charlottesville, Va.: forthcoming 1992).

18. Watson, *Annals of Philadelphia*, 1:222.

19. Allan Nevins, ed., *The Diary of Philip Hone, 1828–1851* (New York, 1969 [orig. pub. 1927]), 897.

20. Watson, *Annals of Philadelphia*, 230. The development of nineteenth-century retail architecture is analyzed in Blumin, *The Emergence of the Middle Class*, 93–107.
21. *Godey's Lady's Book* 40 (May 1850): 332–33; Watson, *Annals of Philadelphia*, 230.
22. Nevins, ed., *Diary of Philip Hone*, viii, xvii, 295 (quote); Eleanor Ewart Southworth, "Mirrors for a Growing Metropolis: Printed Views of Broadway, 1830–1855" (M.A. thesis, University of Delaware, 1985), 21, 65.
23. Nevins, ed., *Diary of Philip Hone*, 896. John Fanning Watson mourned the destruction of the grand residences on High Street above Fourth to make way for shops. *Annals of Philadelphia*, 226. The best analysis of the coming of shops to Broadway is Southworth, "Mirrors for a Growing Metropolis," 69–82.
24. Grier, *Culture and Comfort*, 44, 45 (quote), 46.
25. Ibid., 38–44.
26. Watson, *Annals of Philadelphia*, 242.
27. Nevins, ed., *Diary of Philip Hone*, 187.
28. *How to Behave: A Pocket Manual of Republican Etiquette, and Guide to Correct Personal Habits* . . . (New York, 1857), 35.
29. Donald Martin Reynolds, *The Architecture of New York City: Histories and Views of Important Structures, Sites, and Symbols* (New York, 1984), 75–77, 98–103. The escalation of commercial architecture in Philadelphia is discussed in Richard J. Webster, *Philadelphia Preserved: Catalog of the Historic American Buildings Survey* (Philadelphia, 1976), 43–51.
30. *How to Behave*, 126; Allan Nevins and Milton Halsey Thomas, eds., *The Diary of George Templeton Strong*, 4 vols. (New York, 1952), 2:349 (July 16, 1857).
31. Rev. Francis C. Woodworth, ed., *The Youth's Cabinet: A Book of Gems for the Mind and the Heart, Beautifully Embellished* (New York, 1847), 86.
32. Watson, *Annals of Philadelphia*, 282–83; Nevins and Halsey, eds., *Diary of George Templeton Strong*, 2:320, 349.
33. Nevins and Halsey, eds., *Diary of George Templeton Strong*, 2:209; Nevins, ed., *Diary of Philip Hone*, 1:189.
34. The dark side of the nineteenth-century city has been illuminated in John F. Kasson, *Rudeness and Civility: Manners in Nineteenth-Century Urban America* (New York, 1990), 74–111; Susan G. Davis, *Parades and Power: Street Theatre in Nineteenth-Century Philadelphia* (Philadelphia, 1986); Karen Halttunen, *Confidence Men and Painted Women: A Study of Middle-Class Culture in America, 1830–1870* (New Haven, 1982), 1–55.
35. Leon deValinger and Virginia E. Shaw, eds, *A Calendar of Ridgely Family Letters 1742–1899 in the Delaware State Archives*, 3 (Dover, Del., 1961): 39–40, 45, 175; Leslie, *Behaviour Book*, 80.
36. Leslie, *Behaviour Book*, 77.
37. Quoted in Grier, *Culture and Comfort*, 46.
38. Robert Bruce Mullin, ed., *Moneygripe's Apprentice: The Personal Narrative of Samuel Seabury III* (New Haven, 1989), 69.
39. Nevins, ed., *Diary of Philip Hone*, 1:235–36. Politics forced Sidney George Fisher to tolerate the "vulgarity of my associates" when he acted as judge of elections in Philadelphia. Wainwright, ed., *A Philadelphia Perspective*, 104.
40. Dorothy C. Barck, ed., *Letters from John Pintard to His Daughter, Eliza Noel Pintard Davidson*, 2 (New York, 1940): 272 (June 3, 1826).
41. Nevins and Halsey, eds., *Diary of George Templeton Strong*, 2:57. For images of mixed crowds on Broadway, see Southworth, "Mirrors for a Growing Metropolis," 85, 88.
42. Leslie, *Behaviour Book*, 98, 101.
43. *Godey's Lady's Book*, 40 (June 1850): 370–71.
44. Elizabeth Wright, Philadelphia, to Sally Ridgely, Dover, Jan. 1829, folder 271, Ridgely Collection, Hall of Records, Dover, Del.
45. *Godey's Lady's Book*, 40 (June 1850): 371; *How to Behave*, 103.
46. "Grand List of the Polls and rateable Estate of the several Towns in the State of Connecticut for August 20th. 1796," Connecticut State Archives, Hartford.
47. Quoted in William N. Hosley, Jr., "Architecture," in Gerald W. R. Ward and William N. Hosley, eds., *The Great River: Art and Society of the Connecticut Valley, 1635–1820* (Hartford, 1985), 68.
48. Patrick T. Conley and Paul R. Campbell, *Providence: A Pictorial History* (Norfolk, Va., 1982), 40, 44, 53, 63, 79.
49. Alain C. White, *The History of the Town of Litchfield, Connecticut, 1720–1920* (Litchfield, 1920), 95, 96, 97, 121, 123, 138, 144 (quotation), 168, 169, 170.
50. Emily Noyes Vanderpoel, *Chronicles of a Pioneer School from 1792 to 1833, Being the History of Miss Sarah Pierce and her Litchfield School*, ed. Elizabeth C. Barney Buel (Cambridge, Mass., 1903), 347.
51. White, *History of the Town of Litchfield*, 95, 96, 97, 121, 123, 138.
52. William Butler, "Another City upon a Hill: Litchfield, Connecticut, and the Colonial Revival," in Alan Axelrod, ed., *The Colonial Revival in America* (New York, 1985), 30, 32–33.
53. White, *History of the Town of Litchfield*, 169, 171, 173, 175, 232; Butler, "Another City upon a Hill," 27–28.

54. Francis Underwood, *Quabbin: The Story of a Small Town with Outlooks on Puritan Life* (Boston, 1986 [orig. pub. 1893]), 7.

55. Hosley, "Architecture," 9; David Brodeur, "Evolution of the New England Town Common," *The Professional Geographer*, 19 (1967): 315; Joseph Sutherland Wood, "The Origin of the New England Village" (Ph.D. diss., Pennsylvania State University, 1978), 282.

56. John Warner Barber, *Historical Collections . . . of Every Town in Massachusetts . . .* (Worcester, 1839), 88, 140, 192, 225 (quote), 266, 282, 288, 301 (quote), 359, 388, 434, 443, 457, 460, 483, 552, 554. Barber had previously performed the same service for Connecticut: John Warner Barber, *Connecticut Historical Collections . . . of Every Town in Connecticut . . .*, 2nd ed. (New Haven, 1836). For a general discussion of New England town improvements, see Rudy Favretti, "The Ornamentation of New England Towns: 1750–1850," *Journal of Garden History* (Oct.–Nov. 1983), 325–42.

57. John W. Barber and Henry Howe, *Historical Collections of the State of New Jersey . . . with the Geographical Descriptions of Every Township in the State* (New York, 1844), 176. J. Smith Futhey and Gilbert Cope, *History of Chester County, Pennsylvania, with Genealogical and Biographical Sketches* (Philadelphia, 1881), 215; Margaret Berwind Schiffer, *Survey of Chester County, Pennsylvania, Architecture: 17th, 18th and 19th Centuries* (Exton, Pa., 1984), 150–52.

58. Futhey and Cope, *History of Chester County*, 215. The change can be seen in the contrasting townscapes painted of "Globe Village" in 1822 and "Waterbury Green" in 1851 in Jay E. Cantor, *The Landscape of Change: Views of Rural New England, 1790–1865* (n.p., n.d.), figures 2, 5.

59. Cooper, *Home As Found*, 352.

60. Bernard L. Herman, *Architecture and Rural Life in Central Delaware, 1700–1900* (Knoxville, Tenn., 1987), 146.

61. White, *History of the Town of Litchfield*, 121–22.

62. *The Lady's Book* (Godey's), 18 (Jan. 1839): 17, 19. Harriet Hanson Robinson attended eight balls in Concord in the winter of 1854, when she and her husband were newcomers to the town. Claudia L. Bushman, "*A Good Poor Man's Wife": Being a Chronicle of Harriet Hanson Robinson and Her Family in Nineteenth-Century New England* (Hanover, N.H., 1981), 88.

63. Underwood, *Quabbin*, 30.

64. Claudia B. Kidwell and Margaret C. Christman, *Suiting Everyone: The Democratization of Clothing in America* (Washington, D.C., 1974), 66; Gwendolyn Wright, *Building the Dream: A Social History of Housing in America* (Cambridge, Mass., 1981), 68–69; J. H. Temple, *History of North Brookfield, Massachusetts* (North Brookfield, 1887), 264; John R. Stilgoe, *Common Landscape of America, 1580 to 1845* (New Haven, 1982), 328

65. Philip Van Doren Stern, ed., *The Annotated Walden: Walden; or, Life in the Woods by Henry D. Thoreau* (New York, 1970), 297–98.

66. Underwood, *Quabbin*, 19, 128–30. A despairing and disgusted depiction of farm life appeared in N. G. Holland, "Farming Life in New England," *Atlantic Monthly*, 2 (1858): 334–41.

67. White, *History of the Town of Litchfield*, 116, 182 (quote).

68. Edward Eggleston, *The Hoosier School-Master: A Novel* (Bloomington, Ind., 1984 [orig. pub. 1871]), 28.

69. Mullin, ed., *Moneygripe's Apprentice*, 103–5.

70. Underwood, *Quabbin*, 19.

71. Wainwright, ed., *A Philadelphia Perspective*, 94.

72. Andrew Jackson Downing, *The Architecture of Country Houses, Including Designs for Cottages, and Farm-Houses, and Villas, with Remarks on Interiors, Furniture, and the Best Modes of Warming and Ventilating* (New York, 1968 [orig. pub. 1850]), 257–58.

73. Thomas C. Hubka, *Big House, Little House, Back House, Barn: The Connected Farm Buildings of New England* (Hanover, N.H., 1984), 16, 70–79, 87–93, 106–12, 127.

74. Gail Emily Nessell, "The Goodale Family: Seven Generations of Continuity and Change in Marlborough, Massachusetts," (M.A. thesis, University of Delaware, 1985), 52, 57, 61–65, 67, 71, 73, 138.

75. James Fenimore Cooper, *The Prairie: A Tale*, ed. James P. Elliott (Albany, N.Y., 1985 [orig. pub. 1827]), 66, 341–64.

76. Quoted in Henry Nash Smith, *Virgin Land: The American West as Symbol and Myth* (Cambridge, Mass., 1950), 220. In the pages that follow, Smith discusses the implications of this view of historical regression for literature. Although Cooper used the word "refinement" to identify the high end of the spectrum, writers usually had a larger conception of civilization in mind when they spoke of the West. Besides refinement of manners and the arts, civilization encompassed economic progress, law and order, and religion.

77. William Darby, *The Emigrant's Guide to the Western and Southwestern States and Territories* (New York, 1818), 61, quoted in Paul W. Gates, *The Farmer's Age: Agriculture, 1815–1860* (New York, 1960), 16.

78. Timothy Flint, *Recollections of the Last Ten Years in the Valley of the Mississippi*, ed. George R. Brooks (Carbondale, Ill., 1968 [orig. pub. 1826]), 128–29.

79. For a diary report of the hardships experienced by a refined Connecticut couple who braved the western

wilderness to teach religion, see "Diary of Flavel Bascom, Yale, 1828," in William Warren Sweet, *Religion on the American Frontier, 1783–1850.* Vol. 3: *The Congregationalists: A Collection of Source Materials* (Chicago, 1939), 236–52.
80. Lyman Beecher, *A Plea for the West,* 2nd ed. (Cincinnati, 1836).
81. Horace Bushnell, "Barbarism the First Danger," in *Work and Play* (New York, 1883), 226, 229, 232, 241, 242.
82. Ibid., 229, 246, 255.
83. Barck, ed., *Letters from John Pintard,* 3:75 (New York City, April 23, 1829).
84. Flint, *Recollections of the Last Ten Years,* 49, 51.
85. Bushnell, "Barbarism the First Danger," 260.
86. John Francis McDermott, *George Caleb Bingham: River Portraitist* (Norman, Okla., 1959), 4–7, 10.
87. Ibid., 18–21.
88. Quoted in ibid., 18.
89. Bingham's vision of American society in the genre paintings resembles Timothy Dwight's Greenfield Hill, the New England village of cheerful, competent, and virtuous farmers, the classic republican society.
90. S. Allen Chambers, Jr., *Lynchburg: An Architectural History* (Charlottesville, Va., 1981), 40–41, 44, 46; Frederick Doveton Nichols, *The Early Architecture of Georgia* (Chapel Hill, N.C., 1957), 12, 20, 21, 53–108, 117. In inland towns, the courthouse and the market occupied the same square. See Edward T. Price, "The Central Courthouse Square in the American County Seat," in Dell Upton and John Michael Vlach, eds., *Readings in American Vernacular Architecture* (Athens, Ga., 1986), 124–45.
91. Clement Eaton, *The Growth of Southern Civilization, 1790–1860* (New York, 1961), 115–17, 119–24; Richard Beale Davis, *Intellectual Life in Jefferson's Virginia, 1790–1830* (Knoxville, Tenn., 1972), 34–46, 77–84.
92. Bushnell, "Barbarism the First Danger," 248–51.
93. William R. Taylor, *Cavalier and Yankee: The Old South and American National Character* (New York, 1961), 129–40.
94. Charles Capen McLaughlin, ed., *The Papers of Frederick Law Olmsted.* Vol. 3: *Slavery and the South, 1852–1857,* ed. Charles E. Beveridge, Charles Capen McLaughlin, and David Schuyler (Baltimore, 1981), 244–45, 310; Frederick Law Olmsted, *Cotton Kingdom: A Traveller's Observations on Cotton and Slavery in the American Slave States . . .* (New York, 1861) 2: 178, 147–48.
95. Olmsted, *Cotton Kingdom,* 2:105–6.
96. Wainwright, ed., *A Philadelphia Perspective,* 255.
97. Beveridge, McLaughlin, and Schuyler, eds., *Slavery and the South, 1852–1857,* 252.
98. Quoted in James Oakes, *The Ruling Race: A History of American Slaveholders* (New York, 1982), 83, 85.
99. Henry Glassie, *Folk Housing in Middle Virginia* (Knoxville, Tenn., 1975), 91, 101, and *Pattern in the Material Folk Culture of the Eastern United States* (Philadelphia, 1968), 64–69, 75, 99–101, 109–12; Fred B. Kniffen, "Folk Housing: Key to Diffusion," in Upton and Vlach, eds., *Readings in American Vernacular Architecture,* 3–26.
100. Glassie, *Folk Housing in Middle Virginia,* 153, 157–58.
101. Frances Trollope, *Domestic Manners of the Americans,* ed. Richard Mullen, (Oxford, 1984 [orig. pub. 1832]), 195.
102. Grady McWhiney, *Cracker Culture: Celtic Ways in the Old South* (Tuscaloosa, Ala., 1988), 243–44, and for more in the same vein, 233–44.
103. Beveridge, McLaughlin, and Schuyler, eds., *Slavery and the South, 1852–1857,* 234.
104. For Olmsted's comparison of vernacular gentility in North and South, see *Cotton Kingdom,* 2:283–86.
105. Kenneth S. Lynn, *Mark Twain and Southwestern Humor* (Boston, 1959).
106. A. B. Longstreet, *Georgia Scenes: Characters, Incidents, etc., in the First Half Century of the Republic* (New York, 1957 [orig. pub. 1835]), 6 (quote), 7–9.
107. Lewis F. Allen, *Rural Architecture. Being a Complete Description of Farm Houses, Cottages, and Out Buildings . . .* (New York, 1852), x.
108. *How to Behave,* 127. "It is a mistaken and mischievous opinion that a sermon must be composed in one style for the city, and in another for the country,—that our large and populous towns require a learned and polished discourse, while 'a plain country congregation' demand one of humbler merit." "On Preaching," *The Christian Spectator,* 7 (Dec. 1, 1825): 642.
109. John Pierce, Philadelphia, to Sarah Pierce, New York, June 8, 1784, in Vanderpoel, *Chronicles of a Pioneer School,* 348–49.

XII. CULTURE AND POWER

1. The most sophisticated discussion of the emulation explanation is Neil McKendrick, "Commercialization and the Economy," in Neil McKendrick, John Brewer, and J. H. Plumb, eds., *The Birth of a Consumer Society: The Commercialization of Eighteenth-Century England* (Bloomington, Ind., 1982), 9–196.
2. Rhys Isaac, *The Transformation of Virginia, 1740–1790* (Chapel Hill, N.C., 1982).

3. William R. Taylor, *Cavalier and Yankee: The Old South and American National Character* (New York, 1961), chap. 5.

4. John F. Kasson, *Rudeness and Civility: Manners in Nineteenth-Century Urban America* (New York, 1990); Karen Halttunen, *Confidence Men and Painted Women: A Study of Middle-Class Culture in America, 1830–1870* (New Haven, 1982), 34–37, 192–95. Halttunen's chief concern is not the spread of gentility, but the vulnerability of migrants to predators and the need for established marks of true virtue.

5. The public benefit of assigning identity and status to strangers was the imposition of some degree of order on this turbulent society. Kasson, *Rudeness and Civility*, 58–63.

6. For a discussion of upward borrowings, see Lawrence W. Levine, *Highbrow/Lowbrow: The Emergence of Cultural Hierarchy in America* (London, 1988).

7. E. P. Thompson, "Patrician Society, Plebeian Culture," *Journal of Social History*, 7 (Summer 1974): 382–405.

8. Barry Allen Kessler, "Of Workshops and Warerooms: The Economic and Geographic Transformation of Furniture Making in Chester County, Pennsylvania, 1780–1850" (M.A. thesis, University of Delaware, 1987). The same chronology of demand preceding supply holds true for textile production. Rolla M. Tryon, *Household Manufactures in the United States, 1640–1860* (New York, 1966 [orig. pub. 1917]); Robert Zevin, "Cotton Textile Production after 1815," in Robert Fogel and Stanley Engerman, eds., *The Reinterpretation of American Economic History* (New York, 1971), 122–47. For a similar argument concerning soap, see Richard L. Bushman and Claudia L. Bushman, "The Early History of Cleanliness in America," *Journal of American History*, 74 (March 1988): 1213–38.

9. For small-town cultural entrepreneurs in the northeast, see David Jaffee, "Peddlers of Progress and the Transformation of the Rural North, 1760–1860," *Journal of American History* 78 Sept. 1991): 511–35; " 'One of the Primitive Sort': Portrait-Makers in Rural America, 1760–1860," in Jonathan Prude and Steven Hahn, eds., *The Countryside in the Age of Capitalist Transformation: 1780–1900, Essays in the Social History of Rural America* (Chapel Hill, N.C., 1986), 103–38; and "The Village Enlightenment in the Rural North, 1760–1860," *William and Mary Quarterly*, 47 (July 1990): 327–46. For England, see J. H. Plumb, "The Commercialization of Leisure," in Neil McKendrick, John Brewer, and J. H. Plumb, eds., *The Birth of a Consumer Society*, 265–85.

10. Neil McKendrick, "Josiah Wedgwood and the Commercialization of the Potteries," in ibid., 100 (quote), 108–12, 121 (quote), 131.

11. Adam Smith, *Enquiry into the Nature and Causes of the Wealth of Nations*, ed. W. B. Todd (Oxford, 1976), 418–19, 421.

12. The culminating explication of this contradiction was Thorstein Veblen, *The Theory of the Leisure Class: An Economic Study of Institutions* (New York, 1953 [orig. pub. c. 1912]), although Veblen himself is still enmeshed in middle-class culture; as Norbert Elias noted: "Veblen, as we can see, is hindered in his study of 'conspicuous consumption' by an uncritical use of bourgeois values as criteria for economic behaviour in other societies. He thereby blocks his own way to a sociological analysis of prestige consumption. He has no clear perception of the social compulsions underlying it." *The Court Society*, tr. Edmund Jephcott (New York, 1983), 67. Elias discusses the conflict of noble and bourgeois values in ibid., 66–73.

13. Quoted in Esther B. Aresty, *The Best Behavior: The Course of Good Manners—from Antiquity to the Present—as Seen through Courtesy and Etiquette Books* (New York, 1970), 203. Harriet Beecher Stowe's story "Trials of a Housekeeper" dilated on the embarrassment of being discovered at work in the back of the house. *The Lady's Book* (Godey's), 18 (Jan. 1839), 5.

14. Nicholas B. Wainwright, ed., *A Philadelphia Perspective: The Diary of Sidney George Fisher Covering the Years 1834–1871* (Philadelphia, 1967), 246, 263.

15. Gervase Wheeler, *Homes for the People, in Suburb and Country; the Villa, the Mansion, and the Cottage, Adapted to American Climate and Wants. With Examples Showing How to Alter and Remodel Old Buildings. In a series of One Hundred Original Designs* (New York, 1858), 361.

16. John F. Watson, *Annals of Philadelphia and Pennsylvania, in the Olden Time . . .* ([Philadelphia] 1844 [orig. publ. 1830]), 1:243–44 (quote), 249, 251–52.

17. At the other pole, critics turned on the superfluity of gentility, its pretense and needless extravagance. Gentility had always carried its own critique within itself, skewering the fop and the fashionable lady. The vice of city living was traditionally contrasted with the purity of simple country life. All of these standard criticisms were put to use by middle-class critics resentful of an aristocratic culture that was as repellent as it was fascinating.

18. Much of the language of exaltation was borrowed from religion and was appropriate only in sacred settings.

19. James Fenimore Cooper, *Home As Found* (New York, 1860 [orig. pub. 1838]), 14, 110.

20. Emily Thornwell, *The Lady's Guide to Perfect Gentility, in Manners, Dress, and Conversation . . . also a useful Instructor in Letter Writing* (New York, 1857), 159. A twenty-six-stanza poem entitled "The Wants of Man," attributed to John Quincy Adams, described at great length the life of an English country gentleman as

if that were the highest conceivable ideal. *The Housekeeper's Annual and Ladies' Register for 1844* (Boston, 1843), 76–82.

21. Ralph Ketcham, *Presidents above Party: The First American Presidency, 1789–1829* (Chapel Hill, N.C., 1984).

22. Leon deValinger and Virginia E. Shaw, eds., *A Calendar of Ridgely Family Letters 1742–1899 in the Delaware State Archives,* (Dover, Del., 1951) 2:66.

23. Harriet Beecher Stowe, *Oldtown Folks* (Boston, 1869), 3, 7.

24. Joy Bayless, *Rufus Wilmot: Poe's Literary Executor* (Nashville, Tenn., 1943), 237.

25. Lewis F. Allen, *Rural Architecture. Being a Complete Description of Farm Houses, Cottages, and Out Buildings . . .* (New York, 1852), 166–69.

26. *The Lady's Book* (Godey's), 18 (Jan. 1839): 17.

27. *The Illustrated Manners Book: A Manual of Good Behavior and Polite Accomplishments* (New York, 1855), 98.

28. George Theodore Welch, *Memoirs of Mary Parker Welch, 1818–1912,* ed. Dorothy Welch White (n.p., 1947), 3.

29. Cooper, *Home As Found,* 45, 47, 209, 210.

30. Ibid., 54, 56, 58.

31. Charles Ridgely, Dover, to Charles Inglis, New York, March 17, 1767, folder 100, Ridgely Collection, Hall of Records, Dover, Del.

32. Cooper, *Home As Found,* 62–63.

33. *The Sunday School Magazine,* 1 (New York, 1845): 77.

34. [Catharine Maria Sedgwick] *Home* (Boston, 1835), 35–36, 39–40.

35. Frederick Law Olmsted, Cumberland River, to Charles Loring Brace, New York City, Dec. 1, 1853, Charles Capen McLaughlin, ed., *The Papers of Frederick Law Olmsted.* Vol. 2: *Slavery and the South, 1852–1857,* ed. Charles E. Beveridge, Charles Capen McLaughlin, and David Schuyler (Baltimore, 1981), 234–36.

36. Charles Capen McLaughlin, ed., *The Papers of Frederick Law Olmsted.* Vol. 3: *Creating Central Park, 1857–1861,* ed. Charles E. Beveridge and David Schuyler (Baltimore, 1983), 6; *The Horticulturist* 6 (Aug. 1851): 345–49, reprinted in Andrew Jackson Downing, *Rural Essays* (New York, 1853), 152, discussed in Charles Capen McLaughlin, ed., *The Papers of Frederick Law Olmsted.* Vol. 1: *The Formative Years, 1822–1852,* ed. Charles Capen McLaughlin and Charles E. Beveridge (Baltimore, 1977), 75.

37. McLaughlin, Beveridge, and Schuyler, eds., *Slavery and the South,* 235.

38. Beveridge and Schuyler, eds., *Creating Central Park,* 9.

39. New York *Herald,* Sept. 6, 1857, p. 4, quoted in Beveridge and Schuyler, eds., *Creating Central Park,* 272–73.

40. Quoted in ibid., 272.

41. Olmsted, Central Park, to Parke Godwin, Aug. 1, 1858, in ibid., 201.

42. *Graham's Magazine,* 37 (Sept. 1850): 159.

43. Rev. Francis C. Woodworth, ed., *The Youth's Cabinet: A Book of Gems for the Mind and the Heart, Beautifully Embellished* (New York, 1846), 149. The description of a workman's house caught "Mrs. Hall arranging some light window curtains for the prettily furnished parlor, while a fine curly-haired, blue-eyed little fellow was rolling on the carpet at her feet." *Graham's Magazine,* 37 (Sept. 1850): 161.

44. *Graham's Magazine,* 37 (Sept. 1850): 102.

45. Henry Ward Beecher, "The Advance of a Century," *The Tribune* (New York), July 4, 1876, 37–44, in Alan Trachtenberg, ed., *Democratic Vistas, 1860–1880* (New York, 1970), 71–72.

46. Calvert Vaux, *Villas and Cottages. A Series of Designs Prepared for Execution in the United States,* 2nd ed. (New York, 1864), 157.

47. Lucy Mack Smith, Preliminary Manuscript of *Biographical Sketches of Joseph Smith, the Prophet, and His Progenitors for Many Generations* (London, 1853), typescript, Church Archives, Salt Lake City, p. 39; Richard L. Bushman, *Joseph Smith and the Beginnings of Mormonism* (Urbana, Ill., 1984), 65–68.

48. *Genesee Farmer,* 3 (April 1842): 62.

49. Quoted in Robert Gray Gunderson, *The Log-Cabin Campaign* (n.p., 1957), 72, 74.

50. *Delaware State Journal* (Dover), Dec. 17, 1839.

51. *Delaware State Journal,* July 14, 1840.

52. Ibid.

53. Gunderson, *Log-Cabin Campaign,* 199, 201, 207.

54. *Delaware State Journal,* July 14, 1840.

55. *The Lady's Book* (Godey's), 18 (April 1839): 160.

56. Quoted in Richard D. Brown, *Knowledge Is Power: The Diffusion of Information in Early America, 1700–1865* (New York, 1989), 227.

57. Allen, *Rural Architecture,* xii.

58. Stuart Blumin makes the case for a distinct middle class and thus of a distinct lower class in *The Emergence of the Middle Class: Social Experience in the American City, 1760–1900* (Cambridge, Eng., 1989), but he acknowledges that emblems of middle-class living, like pianos, filtered into the lower classes, suggesting a porous

boundary (see chap. 5). The connection between class, material culture, and democracy absorbed researchers at the time, making censuses of pianos and carpets relevant for determining the health of the polity. For examples, see Edgar W. Martin, *The Standard of Living in 1860: American Consumption Levels on the Eve of the Civil War* (Chicago, 1942), 121–22, reporting on the results of Carroll Wright's 1875 study of Massachusetts.

59. For the black elite, see Gary B. Nash, *Forging Freedom: The Formation of Philadelphia's Black Community, 1720–1840* (Cambridge, Mass., 1988), chap. 7; Emma Jones Lapsansky, "Friends, Wives, and Strivings: Networks and Community Values among Nineteenth-Century Afroamerican Elites," *Pennsylvania Magazine of History and Biography*, 108 (1984): 3–24, and " 'Since They Got Those Separate Churches': Afro-Americans and Racism in Jacksonian Philadelphia," *American Quarterly*, 32 (1980): 54–78; Willard B. Gatewood, *Aristocrats of Color: The Black Elite, 1880–1920* (Bloomington, Ind., 1990).

60. [Joseph Willson] *Sketches of the Higher Classes of Colored Society in Philadelphia* (Philadelphia, 1841), 14–15. For biographical information on Willson, see Gatewood, *Aristocrats of Color*, 3.

61. Lawrence O. Christensen, "Cyprian Clamorgan, The Colored Aristocracy of St. Louis," *Missouri Historical Society Bulletin*, 31 (Oct. 1974): 16, 21, 26, 30. The Christensen article contains the entire text of Cyprian Clamorgan, *The Colored Aristocracy of St. Louis* (St. Louis, 1858).

62. William Ranson Hogan and Edwin Adams Davis, eds., *William Johnson's Natchez: The Ante-bellum Diary of a Free Negro* (Baton Rouge, 1951), 48.

63. Willson, *Sketches of the Higher Classes of Colored Society in Philadelphia*, 56.

64. Ibid., 30, 58.

65. Ibid., 57, 61.

66. Leonard P. Curry, *The Free Black in Urban America, 1800–1850* (Chicago, 1981), 204–7; Dorothy Porter, *Early Negro Writing, 1760–1837* (Boston, 1971), 141.

67. Porter, *Early Negro Writing, 1760–1837*, 164–65.

68. Ibid., 141, 165.

69. Nash, *Forging Freedom*, 254–59.

70. Willson, *Sketches of the Higher Classes of Colored Society in Philadelphia*, 6.

71. Gatewood, *Aristocrats of Color*, 7.

72. Willson, *Sketches of the Higher Classes of Colored Society in Philadelphia*, 64.

73. Mary P. Ryan, *The Cradle of the Middle Class: The Family in Oneida County, New York, 1790–1865* (Cambridge, Eng., 1981), 218–29.

74. [James Forrester] *The Polite Philosopher: or, an Essay on that Art, which Makes a Man happy in Himself, and agreeable to Others* (London, reprinted New York, 1758), 35; Dr. Gregory, *A Father's Legacy To his Daughters* (Portsmouth, N.H., 1786) [bound with Chesterfield, *Principles of Politeness*], 95.

75. *The Housekeeper's Annual and Ladies' Register for 1844* (Boston, 1843), 57.

76. Nicholas Ridgely, Dover, to Mrs. Charles du Pont, Wilmington, May 25, 1841, folder 44, Ridgely Collection, Hall of Records, Dover, Del.

77. Gerda Lerner, "The Lady and the Mill Girl: Changes in the Status of Women in the Age of Jackson," *Mid-Continent American Studies Journal*, 10 (Spring 1969): 5–15; Mary P. Ryan, *Womanhood in America: From Colonial Times to the Present*, 3rd ed. (New York, 1983), 86–94; Barbara Welter, "The Cult of True Womanhood," *American Quarterly*, 18 (Summer 1969): 131–75.

78. Wheeler, *Homes for the People*, 362.

79. Reprinted in *Delaware State Journal*, Dec. 20, 1839.

80. Engraving of the brass works, undated, in Forbes Library Collection, Northampton, Mass.

81. Olivier Zunz, *Making America Corporate, 1870–1920* (Chicago, 1990), chap. 4.

82. *The Manners of the Times; A Satire. In two Parts*. By Philadelphiensis (Philadelphia, 1762).

83. Frances McDougall, *The Housekeepers Book* (1837), quoted in Aresty, *The Best Behavior*, 203.

84. Edward Eggleston, *The Hoosier School-Master: A Novel* (Bloomington, Ind., 1984 [orig. pub. 1871]), 156–57.

85. The caricature of the excessive housekeeper was a commonplace from the mid-nineteenth century on. See Caroline Matilda Kirkland, *A Book for the Home Circle*, (New York, 1853), 130 ff.

86. Catharine E. Beecher and Harriet Beecher Stowe, *The American Woman's Home, or, Principles of Domestic Science; Being a Guide to the Formation and Maintenance of Economic, Healthful, Beautiful and Christian Homes* (Hartford, 1975 [orig. pub. 1869]), 13.

87. Elizabeth Cady Stanton, *Eighty Years and More: Reminiscences 1815–1897* (New York, 1971 [orig. pub. 1898]), 147–48.

88. Ibid., 147.

89. Ibid., 136–37.

90. This issue is discussed from a different perspective in Ryan, *Womanhood in America*, 85–94.

91. Colleen McDannell, *The Christian Home in Victorian America, 1840–1900* (Bloomington, Ind., 1986).

Index

Italicized page numbers indicate illustrations.

List of Illustrations
and Credits

A Note on the Type

This book was set in a digitized version of Janson. The hot-metal version of Janson was a recutting made direct from type cast from matrices long thought to have been made by the Dutchman Anton Janson, who was a practicing type founder in Leipzig during the years 1668–1687. However, it has been conclusively demonstrated that these types are actually the work of Nicholas Kis (1650–1702), a Hungarian, who most probably learned his trade from the master Dutch type founder Dirk Voskens. The type is an excellent example of the influential and sturdy Dutch types that prevailed in England up to the time William Caslon (1692–1766) developed his own incomparable designs from them.

Composed by The Haddon Craftsmen, Inc.,
Scranton, Pennsylvania
Printed and bound by Halliday Lithographers,
West Hanover, Massachusetts
Designed by Margaret M. Wagner